THE **ECON** SOLUTION

Print + Online

ECON Micro⁵ delivers all the key terms and core concepts for the **Principles of Micro Economics** course.

ECON Online provides the complete narrative from the printed text with additional interactive media and the unique functionality of **StudyBits**—all available on nearly any device!

What is a StudyBit™? Created through a deep investigation of students' challenges and workflows, the StudyBit™ functionality of **ECON Online** enables students of different generations and learning styles to study more effectively by allowing them to learn their way. Here's how they work:

COLLECT WHAT'S IMPORTANT
Create StudyBits as you highlight text, images or take notes!

WEAK

FAIR

STRONG

UNASSIGNED

RATE AND ORGANIZE STUDYBITS
Rate your understanding and use the color-coding to quickly organize your study time and personalize your flashcards and quizzes.

StudyBit™

CORRECT

TRACK/MONITOR PROGRESS
Use Concept Tracker to decide how you'll spend study time and study YOUR way!

85%

PERSONALIZE QUIZZES
Filter by your StudyBits to personalize quizzes or just take chapter quizzes off-the-shelf.

CENGAGE
Learning

ECON Microeconomics, 5e
William A. McEachern, University of Connecticut

Contributing Author: Steve Trost, Virginia Tech

Vice President, General Manager, 4LTR Press: Neil Marquardt

Product Director, 4LTR Press: Steven E. Joos

Product Manager: Laura Redden

Content/Media Developer: Sarah Dorger

Product Assistant: Lauren Dame

Marketing Manager, Economics: John Carey

Marketing Manager, 4LTR Press: Christopher Walz

Marketing Coordinator: Casey Binder

Senior Content Project Manager: Colleen A. Farmer

Manufacturing Planner: Ron Montgomery

Production Service: MPS Limited

Sr. Art Director: Bethany Casey

Internal Designer: Lou Ann Thesing

Cover Designer: Curio Press, LLC/Lisa Kuhn

Covers and title page Image: iStockPhoto.com /akindo

Computer and table illustration: iStockPhoto .com/furtaev

Smart Phone illustration: iStockPhoto.com /dashadima

Last ad: Shutterstock.com/Rawpixel.com

Intellectual Property Analyst: Diane Garrity

Intellectual Property Project Manager: Nick Barrows

For product information and technology assistance, contact us at
Cengage Learning Customer & Sales Support, 1-800-354-9706

For permission to use material from this text or product, submit all requests online at **www.cengage.com/permissions**
Further permissions questions can be emailed to
permissionrequest@cengage.com

Unless otherwise noted, all items © Cengage Learning.

Library of Congress Control Number: 2015958165

Student Edition ISBN: 978-1-305-63192-2

Student Edition with Online ISBN: 978-1-305-63194-6

Cengage Learning
20 Channel Center Street
Boston, MA 02210
USA

Cengage Learning is a leading provider of customized learning solutions with employees residing in nearly 40 different countries and sales in more than 125 countries around the world. Find your local representative at **www.cengage.com.**

Cengage Learning products are represented in Canada by Nelson Education, Ltd.

To learn more about Cengage Learning Solutions, visit **www.cengage.com**

Purchase any of our products at your local college store or at our preferred online store **www.cengagebrain.com**

Printed in the United States of America
Print Number: 01   Print Year: 2015

McEACHERN
MICRO ECON⁵

BRIEF CONTENTS

iStockPhoto.com/akindo

CONTENTS

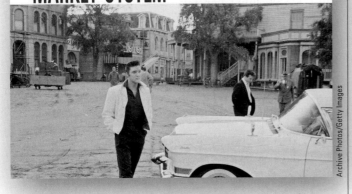

Part 2
INTRODUCTION TO THE MARKET SYSTEM

Archive Photos/Getty Images

Part 3
MARKET STRUCTURE AND PRICING

© iStockphoto.com/alle12

Part 4
RESOURCE MARKETS

© Richard Cavalleri/Shutterstock.com

Part 5
MARKET FAILURE AND PUBLIC POLICY

15 Economic Regulation and Antitrust Policy 252

16 Public Goods and Public Choice 268

17 Externalities and the Environment 284

18 Poverty and Redistribution 304

Part 6
INTERNATIONAL ECONOMICS

Rafael Ramirez/istockphoto

19 International Trade 324

20 International Finance 344

21 Economic Development 360

1 | The Art and Science of Economic Analysis

© Cartoon Network/Everett Collection

LEARNING OUTCOMES

After studying this chapter, you will be able to…

1-1 Explain the economic problem of scarce resources and unlimited wants

1-2 Describe the forces that shape economic choices

1-3 Explain the relationship between economic theory and economic reality

1-4 Identify some pitfalls of economic analysis

1-5 Describe several reasons to study economics

After finishing this chapter go to **PAGE 15** for **STUDY TOOLS**

Topics discussed in Chapter 1 include

- The economic problem
- The scientific method
- Marginal analysis
- Normative versus positive analysis
- Rational self-interest
- Some pitfalls of economic thinking

- Why are comic-strip and TV characters like those in *Adventure Time, The Simpsons,* and *Family Guy* missing a finger on each hand?

- Why do the kids on *South Park* have hands that look like mittens? And where is *Dilbert's* mouth?

- Which college majors pay the most? In what way are people who pound on vending machines relying on theory?

- Why is a good theory like a California Closet?

- What's the big idea with economics?

Finally, how can it be said that in economics "what goes around comes around"? These and other questions are answered in this chapter, which introduces the art and science of economic analysis.

You have been reading and hearing about economic issues for years—unemployment, inflation, poverty, recessions, federal deficits, college tuition, airfares, stock prices, computer prices, smartphone prices, gas prices. When explanations of such issues go into any depth, your eyes may glaze over and you may tune out, the same way you do when a weather forecaster tries to explain high-pressure fronts colliding with moisture carried in from the coast.

> **"Why are comic-strip and TV characters like those in Adventure Time, The Simpsons, and Family Guy missing a finger on each hand?"**

What many people fail to realize is that economics is livelier than the dry accounts offered by the news media. Economics is about making choices, and you make economic choices every day—choices about whether to get a part-time job or focus on your studies, live in a dorm or off campus, take a course in accounting or one in history, get married or stay single, pack a lunch or buy a sandwich. You already know much more about economics than you realize. You bring to the subject a rich personal experience, an experience that will be tapped throughout the book to reinforce your understanding of the basic ideas.

1-1 THE ECONOMIC PROBLEM: SCARCE RESOURCES, UNLIMITED WANTS

Would you like a new car, a nicer home, a smarter phone, tastier meals, more free time, a more interesting social life, more spending money, more leisure, more sleep? Who wouldn't? But even if you can satisfy some of these desires, others keep popping up. *The problem is that although your wants, or desires, are virtually unlimited, the resources available to satisfy these wants are scarce.* A resource is *scarce* when it is not freely available—that is, when its price exceeds zero. Because resources are scarce, you must choose from among your many wants, and whenever you choose, you must forgo satisfying some other wants. The

problem of scarce resources but unlimited wants exists to a greater or lesser extent for each of the 7.4 billion people on earth. Everybody—cab driver, farmer, brain surgeon, dictator, shepherd, student, politician—faces the problem. For example, a cab driver uses time and other scarce resources, such as the taxi, knowledge of the city, driving skills, and gasoline, to earn income. That income, in turn, buys housing, groceries, clothing, trips to Disney World, and thousands of other goods and services that help satisfy some of the driver's unlimited wants. **Economics** examines how people use their scarce resources to satisfy their unlimited wants. Let's pick apart the definition, beginning with resources, then goods and services, and finally focus on the heart of the matter—economic choice, which results from scarcity.

> **economics** The study of how people use their scarce resources to satisfy their unlimited wants

1-1a Resources

Resources are the inputs, or factors of production, used to produce the goods and services that people want. *Goods and services are scarce because resources are scarce.* Resources sort into four broad categories: labor, capital, natural resources, and entrepreneurial ability. **Labor** is human effort, both physical and mental. Labor includes the effort of the cab driver and the brain surgeon. Labor itself comes from a more fundamental resource: *time.* Without time we can accomplish nothing. We allocate our time to alternative uses: We can *sell* our time as labor, or we can *spend* our time doing other things, like sleeping, eating, studying, playing sports, going online, attending class, watching TV, or just relaxing with friends.

Capital includes all human creations used to produce goods and services. Economists often distinguish between physical capital and human capital. *Physical capital* consists of factories, tools, machines, computers, buildings, airports, highways, and other human creations used to produce goods and services. Physical capital includes the cab driver's taxi, the surgeon's scalpel, and the building where your economics class meets (or, if you are taking this course online, your computer and online connectors). *Human capital* consists of the knowledge and skill people acquire to increase their productivity, such as the cab driver's knowledge of city streets, the surgeon's knowledge of human anatomy, and your knowledge of economics.

Natural resources include all *gifts of nature,* such as bodies of water, trees, oil reserves, minerals, even animals. Natural resources can be divided into renewable resources and exhaustible resources. A *renewable resource* can be drawn on indefinitely if used conservatively. Thus, timber is a renewable resource if felled trees are replaced to regrow a steady supply. The air and rivers are renewable resources if they are allowed sufficient time to cleanse themselves of any pollutants. More generally, biological resources like fish, game, livestock, forests, rivers, groundwater, grasslands, and soil are renewable if managed properly. An *exhaustible resource*—such as oil or coal—does not renew itself and so is available in a limited amount. Once burned, each barrel of oil or ton of coal is gone forever. The world's oil and coal deposits are exhaustible.

A special kind of human skill called **entrepreneurial ability** is the talent required to dream up a new product or find a better way to produce an existing one , organize production, and assume the risk of profit or loss. This special skill comes from an entrepreneur. An **entrepreneur** is a profit-seeking decision maker who starts with an idea, organizes an enterprise to bring that idea to life, and then assumes the risk of operation. An entrepreneur pays resource owners for the opportunity to employ their resources in the firm. Every firm in the world today, such as Ford, Microsoft, Google, and Facebook, began as an idea in the mind of an entrepreneur.

Resource owners are paid **wages** for their labor, **interest** for the use of their capital, and **rent** for the use of their natural resources. Entrepreneurial ability is rewarded by **profit**, which equals the *revenue* from items sold minus the *cost* of the resources employed to make those items. Sometimes the entrepreneur suffers a loss. Resource earnings are usually based on the *time* these resources are employed. Resource payments therefore have a time dimension, as in a wage of $10 *per hour,* interest of 6 percent *per year,* rent of $600 *per month,* or profit of $10,000 *per year.*

1-1b Goods and Services

Resources are combined in a variety of ways to produce goods and services. A farmer, a tractor, 50 acres of land, seeds, and fertilizer combine to grow the good: corn. One hundred musicians, musical instruments, chairs, a conductor, a musical score, and a music hall combine to produce the service: Beethoven's *Fifth Symphony.* Corn is a **good** because it is something you can see, feel, and touch; it requires scarce resources to produce; and it satisfies human wants. The book you are now holding, the chair you are sitting in, the clothes you are

---

resources The inputs, or factors of production, used to produce the goods and services that people want; consist of labor, capital, natural resources, and entrepreneurial ability

labor The physical and mental effort used to produce goods and services

capital The buildings, equipment, and human skills used to produce goods and services

natural resources All gifts of nature used to produce goods and services; includes renewable and exhaustible resources

entrepreneurial ability The imagination required to develop a new product or process, the skill needed to organize production, and the willingness to take the risk of profit or loss

entrepreneur A profit-seeking decision maker who starts with an idea, organizes an enterprise to bring that idea to life, and assumes the risk of the operation

wages Payment to resource owners for their labor

interest Payment to resource owners for the use of their capital

rent Payment to resource owners for the use of their natural resources

profit Reward for entrepreneurial ability; sales revenue minus resource cost

good A tangible product used to satisfy human wants

Scarcity means you must choose among options.

services are scarce, not free, and even those that appear to be free come with strings attached. For example, *clean* air and *clean* seawater have become scarce. *Goods and services that are truly free are not the subject of economics. Without scarcity, there would be no economic problem and no need for prices.*

Sometimes we mistakenly think of certain goods as free because they involve no apparent cost to us. Napkins seem to be free at Starbucks. Nobody stops you from taking a fistful. Supplying napkins, however, costs the company millions each year and prices reflect that cost. Some restaurants make special efforts to keep napkin use down— such as packing them tightly into the dispenser or making you ask for them. And Starbucks recently reduced the thickness of its napkins.

You may have heard the expression "There is no such thing as a free lunch." *There is no free lunch because all goods and services involve a cost to someone.* The lunch may seem free to you, but it draws scarce resources away from the production of other goods and services, and whoever provides a free lunch often expects something in return. A Russian proverb makes a similar point but with a bit more bite: "The only place you find free cheese is in a mousetrap." Albert Einstein once observed, "Sometimes one pays the most for things one gets for nothing."

1-1c Economic Decision Makers and Markets

There are four types of decision makers in the economy: households, firms, governments, and the rest of the world. Their interaction determines how an economy's resources are allocated. *Households* play the starring role. As consumers, households demand the goods and services produced. As resource owners, households supply labor, capital, natural resources, and entrepreneurial ability to firms, governments, and the rest of the world. *Firms, governments,* and *the rest of the world* demand the resources that households supply and then use these resources to supply the goods and services that households demand. The rest of the world

wearing, and your next meal are all goods. The performance of the *Fifth Symphony* is a **service** because it is intangible, yet it uses scarce resources to satisfy human wants. Lectures, movies, concerts, phone service, wireless connections, yoga lessons, dry cleaning, and haircuts are all services.

Because goods and services are produced using scarce resources, they are themselves scarce. *A good or service is scarce if the amount people desire exceeds the amount available at a zero price.* Because we cannot have all the goods and services we would like, we must continually choose among them. We must choose among more pleasant living quarters, better meals, nicer clothes, more reliable transportation, faster computers, smarter phones, and so on. Making choices in a world of **scarcity** means we must pass up some goods and services. But not everything is scarce. In fact, some things we would prefer to have less of. For example, we would prefer to have less garbage, less spam e-mail, fewer telemarketing calls, and less pollution. Things we want none of even at a zero price are called *bads*, the opposite of goods.

A few goods and services seem *free* because the amount available at a zero price exceeds the amount people want. For example, air and seawater often seem free because we can breathe all the air we want and have all the seawater we can haul away. Yet, despite the old saying "The best things in life are free," most goods and

> **service** An activity, or intangible product, used to satisfy human wants
>
> **scarcity** Occurs when the amount people desire exceeds the amount available at a zero price

includes foreign households, foreign firms, and foreign governments that supply resources and products to U.S. demanders and demand resources and products from U.S. suppliers.

Markets are the means by which buyers and sellers carry out exchange at mutually agreeable terms. By bringing together the two sides of exchange, markets determine price, quantity, and quality. Markets are often physical places, such as supermarkets, department stores, shopping malls, yard sales, flea markets, and swap meets. But markets also include other mechanisms by which buyers and sellers communicate, such as classified ads, radio and television ads, telephones, bulletin boards, online sites, and face-to-face bargaining. These market mechanisms provide information about the quantity, quality, and price of products offered for sale. Goods and services are bought and sold in **product markets**. Resources are bought and sold in **resource markets**. The most important resource market is the labor, or job, market. Think about your own experience looking for a job, and you'll already have some idea of that market.

1-1d A Simple Circular-Flow Model

Now that you have learned a bit about economic decision makers and markets, consider how all these interact. Such a picture is conveyed by the **circular-flow model**, which describes the flow of resources, products, income, and revenue among economic decision makers. The simple circular-flow model focuses on the primary interaction in a market economy—that between households and firms. Exhibit 1 shows households on the left and firms on the right; please take a look.

Households supply labor, capital, natural resources, and entrepreneurial ability to firms through resource markets, shown in the lower portion of the exhibit. In return, households demand goods and services from firms through product markets, shown on the upper portion of the exhibit. Viewed from the business end, firms demand labor, capital, natural resources, and entrepreneurial ability from households through resource markets, and firms supply goods and services to households through product markets.

The flows of resources and products are supported by the flows of income and expenditure—that is, by the flow of money. So let's add money. The demand and supply of resources come together in resource markets to determine what firms pay for resources. These resource

Exhibit 1

The Simple Circular-Flow Model for Households and Firms

Households earn income by supplying resources to resource markets, as shown in the lower portion of the model. Firms demand these resources to produce goods and services, which they supply to product markets, as shown in the upper portion of the model. Households spend their income to demand these goods and services. This spending flows through product markets as revenue to firms.

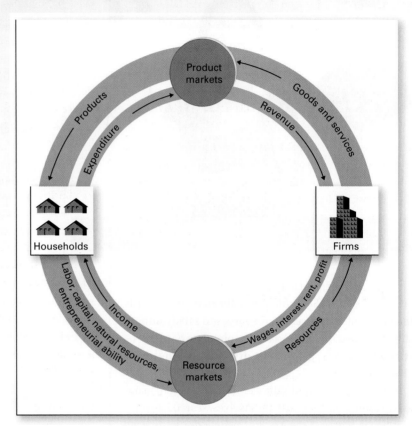

market A set of arrangements by which buyers and sellers carry out exchange at mutually agreeable terms

product market A market in which a good or service is bought and sold

resource market A market in which a resource is bought and sold

circular-flow model A diagram that traces the flow of resources, products, income, and revenue among economic decision makers prices—wages, interest, rent, and profit—flow as *income* to households. The demand and supply of products come together in product markets to determine what households pay for goods and services. These expenditures on goods and services flow as *revenue* to firms. Resources and products flow in one direction—in this case, counterclockwise—and the corresponding payments flow in the other direction—clockwise. What goes around comes around. Take a little time now to trace the logic of the circular flows.

1-2 | THE ART OF ECONOMIC ANALYSIS

An economy results as millions of individuals attempt to satisfy their unlimited wants. Because their choices lie at the heart of the economic problem—coping with scarce resources but unlimited wants—these choices deserve a closer look. Learning about the forces that shape economic choices is the first step toward understanding the art of economic analysis.

1-2a Rational Self-Interest

A key economic assumption is that individuals, in making choices, rationally select what they perceive to be in their best interests. By *rational*, economists mean simply that people try to make the best choices they can, given the available time and information. People may not know with certainty which alternative will turn out to be the best. They simply select the alternatives they *expect* will yield the most satisfaction and happiness. In general, **rational self-interest** means that each individual tries to maximize the expected benefit achieved with a given cost or to minimize the expected cost of achieving a given benefit. Thus, economists begin with the assumption that people look out for their self-interest. For example, a physician who owns a pharmacy prescribes 8 percent more drugs on average than a physician who does not own a pharmacy.[1] A physician who owns a nuclear scanner (used to look inside the human body) is seven times more likely to recommend a scan than a physician who does not own a nuclear scanner.[2] And as one more example of self-interest, the *USA Today* weekly football poll asks coaches to list the top 25 teams in the country. It is no surprise that coaches distort their selections to favor their own teams and their own conferences. And, to make their own records look better, coaches inflate the rankings of teams they have beaten.[3]

Rational self-interest should not necessarily be viewed as blind materialism, pure selfishness, or greed. We all know people who are tuned to radio station WIIFM (What's In It For Me?). For most of us, however, self-interest often includes the welfare of our family, our friends, and perhaps the poor of the world. Even so, our concern for others is influenced by our personal cost of that concern. We may readily volunteer to drive a friend to the airport on Saturday afternoon but are less likely to offer a ride if the flight leaves at 6:00 A.M. When we donate clothes to an organization such as Goodwill Industries, they are more likely to be old and worn than brand new. People tend to give more to charities when their contributions are tax deductible and when contributions garner social approval in the community (as when contributor names are made public or when big donors get buildings named after them).[4] Managers donate more company funds to charitable causes when they own less of the company (and, thus, when their personal cost of contributing is lower).[5] TV stations are more likely to donate airtime for public-service announcements during the dead of night than during prime time (which is why, 80 percent of such announcements air between 11:00 P.M. and 7:00 A.M.). In Asia, some people burn money to soothe the passage of a departed loved one. But they burn fake money, not real money.

The notion of self-interest does not rule out concern for others; it simply means that concern for others is influenced by the same economic forces that affect other economic choices. *The lower the personal cost of helping others, the more help we offer.* We don't like to think that our behavior reflects our self-interest, but it usually does. As Jane Austen wrote in *Pride and Prejudice*, "I have been a selfish being all my life, in practice, though not in principle."

1. Brian Chen, Paul Gertler, and Chuh-Yuh Yang, "Moral Hazard and Economies of Scope in Physician Ownership of Complementary Medical Services," NBER Working Paper 19622 (November 2013).

2. Sandeep Jouhar, *Doctored: The Disillusionment of an American Physician*, (Farrar, Straus, and Giroux, 2014), p. 96.

3. Matthew Kotchen and Matthew Potoski, "Conflicts of Interest Distort Public Evaluations: Evidence from the Top 25 Ballots of NCAA Football Coaches," *Journal of Economic Behavior & Organization*, 107 (November 2014): 51–63.

4. Dean Karlan and Margaret McConnell, "Hey Look at Me: The Effect of Giving Circles on Giving," *Journal of Economic Behavior & Organization* (forthcoming).

5. Ing-Haw Cheng, Harrison Hong, and Kelly Shue, "Do Managers Do Good with Other People's Money?" NBER Working Paper No. 19432 (September 2013).

rational self-interest
Each individual tries to maximize the expected benefit achieved with a given cost or to minimize the expected cost of achieving a given benefit

1-2b Choice Requires Time and Information

Rational choice takes time and requires information, but time and information are themselves scarce and therefore valuable. If you have any doubts about the time and information needed to make choices, talk to someone who recently purchased a home, a car, or a personal computer. Talk to a corporate official trying to decide whether to introduce a new product, sell online, build a new factory, or buy another firm. Or think back to your own experience in choosing a college. You probably talked to friends, relatives, teachers, and guidance counselors. You likely used school catalogs, college guides, and Web sites. You may have even visited some campuses to meet the admissions staff and anyone else willing to talk. The decision took time and money, and it probably involved aggravation and anxiety.

Because information is costly to acquire, we are often willing to pay others to gather and digest it for us. College guidebooks, stock analysts, travel agents, real estate brokers, career counselors, restaurant critics, movie reviewers, specialized Web sites, and *Consumer Reports* magazine attest to our willingness to pay for information that improves our choices. As we'll see next, *rational decision makers continue to acquire information as long as the additional benefit expected from that information exceeds the additional cost of gathering it.*

1-2c Economic Analysis Is Marginal Analysis

Economic choice usually involves some adjustment to the existing situation, or status quo. Amazon.com must decide whether to add a new line of products. The school superintendent must decide whether to hire another teacher. Your favorite jeans are on sale, and you must decide whether to buy another pair. You are wondering whether to carry an extra course next term. You just finished lunch and are deciding whether to order dessert.

Economic choice is based on a comparison of the *expected marginal benefit* and the *expected marginal cost* of the action under consideration. **Marginal** means incremental, additional, or extra. Marginal refers to a change in an economic variable, a change in the status quo. *A rational decision maker changes the status quo if the expected marginal benefit from the change exceeds*

marginal Incremental, additional, or extra; used to describe a change in an economic variable

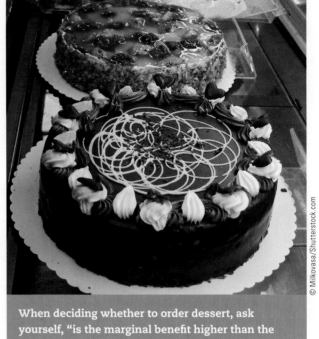

When deciding whether to order dessert, ask yourself, "is the marginal benefit higher than the marginal cost?"

the expected marginal cost. For example, Amazon.com compares the marginal benefit expected from adding a new line of products (the additional sales revenue) with the marginal cost (the additional cost of the resources required). Likewise, you compare the marginal benefit you expect from eating dessert (the additional pleasure or satisfaction) with its marginal cost (the additional money, time, and calories).

Typically, the change under consideration is small, but a marginal choice can involve a major economic adjustment, as in the decision to quit school and find a job. For a firm, a marginal choice might mean building a plant in Mexico or even filing for bankruptcy. By focusing on the effect of a marginal adjustment to the status quo, the economist is able to cut the analysis of economic choice down to a manageable size. Rather than confront a bewildering economic reality head-on, the economist begins with a marginal choice to see how this choice affects a particular market and shapes the economic system as a whole. Incidentally, to the noneconomist, *marginal* usually means relatively inferior, as in "a movie of marginal quality." Forget that meaning for this course and instead think of *marginal* as meaning incremental, additional, or extra.

1-2d Microeconomics and Macroeconomics

Although you have made thousands of economic choices, you probably seldom think about your own economic behavior. For example, why are you reading this book right now rather than doing something else? **Microeconomics** is the study of your economic behavior and the economic behavior of others who make choices about such matters as how much to study and how much to party, how much to borrow and how much to save, what to buy and what to sell. Microeconomics examines individual economic choices and how markets coordinate the choices of various decision makers. Microeconomics explains how price and quantity are determined in individual markets—the market for breakfast cereal, sports equipment, or used cars, for instance.

You have probably given little thought to what influences your own economic choices. You have likely given even less thought to how your choices link up with those made by millions of others in the U.S. economy to determine economy-wide measures such as total production, employment, and economic growth. **Macroeconomics** studies the performance of the economy as a whole. Whereas microeconomics studies the individual pieces of the economic puzzle, as reflected in particular markets, macroeconomics puts all the pieces together to focus on the big picture. Macroeconomics sees the forest, not the trees; the beach, not the grains of sand; and the Rose Bowl parade float, not the individual flowers that shape and color that float.

The national economy usually grows over time, but along the way it sometimes stumbles, experiencing *recessions* in economic activity, as reflected by a decline in production, employment, and other aggregate measures. **Economic fluctuations** are the rise and fall of economic activity relative to the long-term growth trend of the economy. These fluctuations, or *business cycles*, vary in length and intensity, but they usually involve the entire nation and often other nations too. For example, the U.S. economy now produces more than four times as much as it did in 1960, despite experiencing eight recessions since then, including the Great Recession of 2007–2009.

TO REVIEW: The art of economic analysis focuses on how people use their scarce resources in an attempt to satisfy their unlimited wants. Rational self-interest guides individual choice. Choice requires time and information and involves a comparison of the expected marginal benefit and the expected marginal cost of alternative actions. Microeconomics looks at the individual pieces of the economic puzzle; macroeconomics fits the pieces together to form the big picture.

1-3 THE SCIENCE OF ECONOMIC ANALYSIS

Economists use scientific analysis to develop theories, or models, that help explain economic behavior. An **economic theory**, or **economic model**, is a simplification of economic reality that *is used to make predictions about cause and effect in the real world*. A theory, or model, such as the circular-flow model, captures the important elements of the problem under study but need not spell out every detail and interrelation. In fact, adding more details may make a theory more unwieldy and, therefore, less useful. For example, a wristwatch is a model that tells time, but a watch festooned with extra features is harder to read at a glance and is therefore less useful as a time-telling model. The world is so complex that we must simplify it to make sense of things. Store mannequins simplify the human form (some even lack arms and heads). Comic strips and cartoons simplify a character's anatomy—leaving out fingers (in the case of *Adventure Time*, *The Simpsons*, and *Family Guy*) or a mouth (in the case of *Dilbert*), for instance. You might think of economic theory as a stripped-down, or streamlined, version of economic reality.

A good theory helps us understand a messy and confusing world. Lacking a theory of how things work, our thinking can become cluttered with facts, one piled on another, as in a messy closet. You could think of a good theory as a closet organizer for the mind. A good theory offers a helpful guide to sorting, saving, and understanding information.

microeconomics The study of the economic behavior in particular markets, such as that for computers or unskilled labor

macroeconomics The study of the economic behavior of entire economies, as measured, for example, by total production and employment

economic fluctuations The rise and fall of economic activity relative to the long-term growth trend of the economy; also called business cycles

economic theory, or economic model A simplification of reality used to make predictions about cause and effect in the real world

> **"A good theory helps us understand a messy and confusing world."**

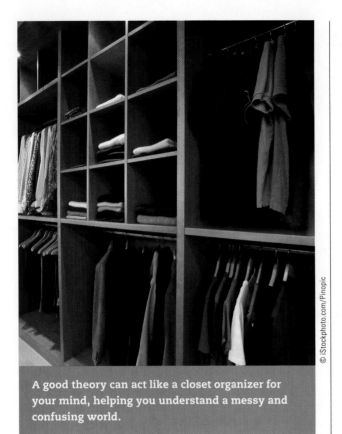

A good theory can act like a closet organizer for your mind, helping you understand a messy and confusing world.

© iStockphoto.com/Pinopic

is widespread enough that people continue to pound on machines that fail to perform (a real problem for the vending machine industry and one reason newer machines are fronted with glass). Yet, if you were to ask these mad pounders to explain their "theory" about how the machine works, they would look at you as if you were crazy.

1-3b The Scientific Method

To study economic problems, economists employ a process called the *scientific method*, which consists of four steps, as outlined in Exhibit 2.

Step One: Identify the Question and Define Relevant Variables

The scientific method begins with curiosity: Someone wants to answer a question. Thus, the first step is to identify the economic question and define the variables relevant to a solution. For example, the question might be, "What is the relationship between the price of Pepsi and the quantity of Pepsi purchased?" In this case, the relevant variables are price and quantity. A **variable** is a measure that can take on different values at different

1-3a The Role of Theory

Most people don't understand the role of theory. Perhaps you have heard, "Oh, that's fine in theory, but in practice it's another matter." The implication is that the theory in question provides little aid in practical matters. People who say this fail to realize that they are merely substituting their own theory for a theory they either do not believe or do not understand. They are really saying, "I have my own theory that works better."

All of us employ theories, however poorly defined or understood. Someone who pounds on the Pepsi machine that just ate a quarter has a crude theory about how that machine works. One version of that theory might be, "The quarter drops through a series of *whatchamacallits*, but sometimes it gets stuck. *If* I pound on the machine, *then* I can free up the quarter and send it on its way." Evidently, this theory

variable A measure, such as price or quantity, that can take on different values at different times

Exhibit 2

The Scientific Method: Step-by-Step

The steps of the scientific method are designed to develop and test hypotheses about how the world works. The objective is a theory that predicts outcomes more accurately than the best alternative theory. A hypothesis is rejected if it does not predict as accurately as the best alternative. A rejected hypothesis can be modified or reworked in light of the test results.

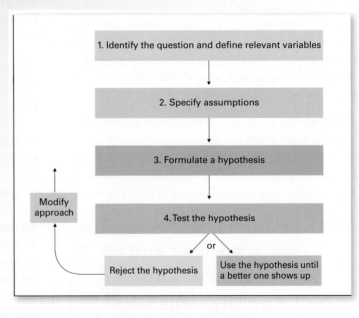

1. Identify the question and define relevant variables

2. Specify assumptions

3. Formulate a hypothesis

4. Test the hypothesis

or

Reject the hypothesis

Use the hypothesis until a better one shows up

Modify approach

times. The variables of concern become the elements of the theory, so they must be selected with care.

Step Two: Specify Assumptions

The second step is to specify the assumptions under which the theory is to apply. One major category of assumptions is the **other-things-constant assumption**—in Latin, the *ceteris paribus* assumption. The idea is to identify the variables of interest and then focus exclusively on the relationships among them, assuming that nothing else important changes—that other things remain constant. Again, suppose we are interested in how the price of Pepsi influences the amount purchased. To isolate the relation between these two variables, we assume that there are no changes in other relevant variables such as consumer income, the average daytime temperature, or the price of Coke.

We also make assumptions about how people behave; these are called **behavioral assumptions**. The primary behavioral assumption is rational self-interest. Earlier we assumed that each decision maker pursues self-interest rationally and makes choices accordingly. Rationality implies that each consumer buys the products expected to maximize his or her level of satisfaction. Rationality also implies that each firm supplies the products expected to maximize the firm's profit. These kinds of assumptions are called behavioral assumptions because they specify how we expect economic decision makers to behave—what makes them tick, so to speak.

Step Three: Formulate a Hypothesis

The third step in the scientific method is to formulate a **hypothesis**, which is a theory about how key variables relate to each other. For example, one hypothesis holds that if the price of Pepsi goes up, other things constant, then the quantity purchased declines. The hypothesis becomes a prediction of what happens to the quantity purchased if the price increases. *The purpose of this hypothesis, like that of any theory, is to help make predictions about cause and effect in the real world.*

If the price of your favorite soft drink rose, would you buy less of it?

© ValeStock/Shutterstock.com

Step Four: Test the Hypothesis

In the fourth step, by comparing its predictions with evidence, we test the validity of a hypothesis. To test a hypothesis, we must focus on the variables in question, while carefully controlling for other effects assumed not to change. The test leads us either to (1) reject the hypothesis, or theory, if it predicts worse than the best alternative theory, or (2) use the hypothesis, or theory, until a better one comes along. If we reject the hypothesis, we can try to go back and modify our approach in light of the results. Please spend a moment now reviewing the steps of the scientific method in Exhibit 2.

1-3c Normative Versus Positive

Economists usually try to explain how the economy works. Sometimes they concern themselves not with how the economy *does* work but how it *should* work. Compare these two statements: "The U.S. unemployment rate is 5.6 percent," and "The U.S. unemployment rate should be lower." The first, called a **positive economic statement**, is an assertion about economic reality that can be supported or rejected by reference to the facts. Positive economics, like physics or biology, attempts to understand the world around us as it is. The second, called a **normative economic statement**, reflects an opinion. And an opinion is merely that—it cannot be shown to be true or false by reference to the facts. Positive statements concern what *is*; normative statements concern what, in someone's opinion, *should be*. Positive statements need not necessarily be true, but they must be subject to verification or refutation by reference to the facts. Theories are expressed as positive statements such as "If the price of Pepsi increases, then the quantity demanded decreases."

Most of the disagreement among economists involves normative debates—such as the appropriate role of government—rather than statements of positive analysis. To be sure, many theoretical issues remain unresolved, but economists generally agree on most fundamental theoretical principles—that is, about positive economic analysis. For example, in a survey of 464 U.S. economists, only 6.5 percent disagreed with the statement "A ceiling on rents reduces the quantity and quality of housing available." This is a positive statement because it can be shown to be consistent or inconsistent with the evidence. In contrast, there was much less agreement on normative statements such as "The distribution of income in the United States should be more equal." Half the economists surveyed "generally agreed," a quarter "generally disagreed," and a quarter "agreed with provisos."[6]

Normative statements, or value judgments, have a place in a policy debate such as the proper role of government, provided that statements of opinion are distinguished from statements of fact. In such policy debates, you are entitled to your own opinion, but you are not entitled to your own facts.

1-3d Economists Tell Stories

Despite economists' reliance on the scientific method for developing and evaluating theories, economic analysis is as much art as science. Formulating a question, isolating the key variables, specifying the assumptions, proposing a theory to answer the question, and devising a way to test the predictions all involve more than simply an understanding of economics and the scientific method. Carrying out these steps requires good intuition and the imagination of a storyteller. Economists explain their theories by telling stories about how they think the economy works. To tell a compelling story, an economist relies on case studies, anecdotes, parables, the personal experience of the listener, and supporting data. Throughout this book, you'll hear stories that bring you closer to the ideas under consideration. These stories, such as the one about the Pepsi machine, breathe life into economic theory and help you personalize abstract ideas.

association-is-causation fallacy The incorrect idea that if two variables are associated in time, one must necessarily cause the other

6. Richard M. Alston et al., "Is There a Consensus among Economists in the 1990s?" *American Economic Review*, 82 (May 1992): 203–209, Table 1.

1-3e Predicting Average Behavior

The goal of economic theory is to predict the impact of economic events on economic choices and, in turn, the effect of these choices on particular markets or on the economy as a whole. Does this mean that economists try to predict the behavior of particular consumers or producers? Not necessarily, because a specific individual may behave in an unpredictable way. But the unpredictable actions of numerous individuals tend to cancel one another out, so the *average behavior* of groups can be predicted more accurately. For example, if the federal government cuts personal income taxes, certain households might save the entire tax cut. On average, however, household spending would increase. Likewise, if Burger King cuts the price of Whoppers, the manager can better predict how much sales will increase than how a specific customer coming through the door will respond. *The random actions of individuals tend to offset one another, so the average behavior of a large group can be predicted more accurately than the behavior of a particular individual.* Consequently, economists tend to focus on the average, or typical, behavior of people in groups—for example, as average taxpayers or average Whopper consumers—rather than on the behavior of a specific individual.

 1-4 # SOME PITFALLS OF FAULTY ECONOMIC ANALYSIS

Economic analysis, like other forms of scientific inquiry, is subject to common mistakes in reasoning that can lead to faulty conclusions. Here are three sources of confusion.

The Fallacy That Association Is Causation

In the past two decades, the number of physicians specializing in cancer treatment increased sharply. At the same time, the incidence of some cancers increased. Can we conclude that physicians cause cancer? No. To assume that event A caused event B simply because the two are associated in time is to commit the **association-is-causation fallacy**, a common error. The fact that one event precedes another or that the two events occur simultaneously does not necessarily mean that one causes the other. Remember: Association is not necessarily causation.

Standing at a concert can help you see better... unless everyone else stands up too! This is an example of the fallacy of composition.

Anna Omelchenko/Fotolia

The Fallacy of Composition

Perhaps you have been to a rock concert where everyone stands to get a better view. At some concerts, most people even stand on their chairs. But even standing on chairs does not improve your view if others do the same, unless you are quite tall. Likewise, arriving early to buy concert tickets does not work if many have the same idea. Earning a college degree to get a better job does not work as well if everyone earns a college degree. These are examples of the **fallacy of composition**, which is an erroneous belief that what is true for the individual, or the part, is also true for the group, or the whole.

The Mistake of Ignoring the Secondary Effects

In many cities, public officials have imposed rent controls on apartments. The primary effect of this policy, the effect that policy makers focus on, is to keep rents from rising. Over time, however, fewer new apartments get built because renting them becomes less profitable. Moreover, existing rental units deteriorate because owners have plenty of customers anyway. Thus, the quantity and quality of housing may decline as a result of what appears to be a reasonable measure to keep rents from rising. The mistake was to ignore the **secondary effects**, or the unintended consequences, of the policy. Economic actions have secondary effects that often turn out to be more important than the primary effects. Secondary effects may develop more slowly and may not be immediately obvious, but good economic analysis tries to anticipate them and take them into account.

1-5 IF ECONOMISTS ARE SO SMART, WHY AREN'T THEY RICH?

Why aren't economists rich? Well, some are, earning over $25,000 per appearance on the lecture circuit. Others top $2 million a year as consultants and expert witnesses.[7] Economists have been appointed to federal cabinet posts, as secretaries of commerce, defense, labor, state, and treasury, for example, and to head the U.S. Federal Reserve System. Economics is the only social science and the only business discipline for which the prestigious Nobel Prize is awarded, and pronouncements by economists are reported in the media daily. A 2015 journal article argued that "the superiority of economists" gives them considerable influence over economic policy.[8] And *The Economist,* a widely respected news weekly from London, has argued that economic ideas have influenced policy "to a degree that would make other social scientists drool."[9]

The economics profession thrives because its models usually do a better job of making economic sense out of a confusing world than do alternative approaches. But not all economists are wealthy, nor is personal wealth the goal of the discipline. In a similar vein, not all doctors are healthy (some even smoke), not all carpenters live in perfectly built homes, not all marriage counselors are happily married, and not all child psychologists have well-adjusted children. Still, those who study economics do reap financial rewards.

Earlier in the chapter, you learned that economic choice involves comparing the expected marginal benefit and the expected marginal cost. Surveys show that students go to college because they believe a college diploma is the ticket to better jobs and higher pay. Put another way, for nearly two-thirds of U.S. high school graduates, the expected marginal benefit of college apparently exceeds the expected marginal cost. The cost of college will be discussed in the next chapter; the focus here is on the benefits of college, particularly expected earnings.

Among college graduates, all kinds of factors affect earnings, such as general

fallacy of composition
The incorrect belief that what is true for the individual, or part, must necessarily be true for the group, or the whole

secondary effects
Unintended consequences of economic actions that may develop slowly over time as people react to events

7. As reported by George Anders, "An Economist's Courtroom Bonanza," *Wall Street Journal*, 19 March 2007.

8. Marion Fourcade, Etienne Ollion, and Yann Algan, "The Superiority of Economists," *Journal of Economic Perspectives*, 29 (Winter 2015): 89–114.

9. "The Puzzling Failure of Economics," *The Economist*, 23 August 1997, p. 11.

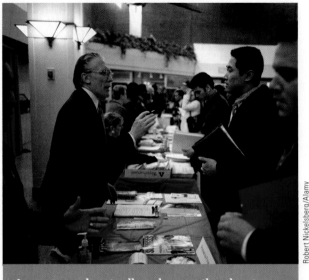

As more people get college degrees, the advantage it gives you in the labor market gets smaller. (Don't worry, it's still worth it.)

Robert Nickelsberg/Alamy

computer majors. Nursing ranked fifth and economics ranked sixth out of the twenty majors listed. Economics had a median pay of $51,400, or 24 percent below the top pay. Elementary education majors held the bottom spot of $33,600, which was only half the top pay.

The dark green bars show the median pay by major for those with 10 to 20 years of job experience. Again, those who had majored in computer engineering led the field with $108,600, an increase of 61 percent over the pay of newer graduates with that degree. Economics majors with 10 to 20 years of job experience saw a 90 percent increase to $97,700. While economics majors with 0 to 5 years experience were paid 25 percent less than the top paying major, among those with at least a decade of job experience, the median pay for economics majors moved up to within 10 percent of the top pay. In fact, economics majors saw their median pay grow more in dollar terms and in percentage terms than did any other major listed. This suggests that those who

ability, effort, occupation, college attended, college major, highest degree earned, appearance, and, yes, luck. PayScale.com collects real-time information on annual pay from its 10 million users. To isolate the effects of a college major on earnings, only workers with a bachelor's as their highest degree are included in the results. Exhibit 3 shows the median earnings in 2015 by major for two groups of college graduates: (1) those with 0 to 5 years of job experience and (2) those with 10 to 20 years of job experience. Majors are listed from the top down by the median annual pay of those with between 0 and 5 years of experience, identified by the light green bars. The top pay of $67,300 went to those who had majored in computer engineering; indeed, the top four slots went to engineering and

Exhibit 3

Median Annual Pay by College Major

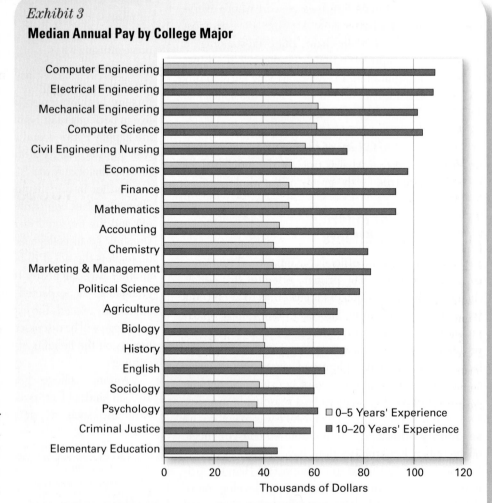

Computer Engineering
Electrical Engineering
Mechanical Engineering
Computer Science
Civil Engineering Nursing
Economics
Finance
Mathematics
Accounting
Chemistry
Marketing & Management
Political Science
Agriculture
Biology
History
English
Sociology
Psychology
Criminal Justice
Elementary Education

□ 0–5 Years' Experience
■ 10–20 Years' Experience

0   20   40   60   80   100   120
Thousands of Dollars

Sources:Median pay data for 2015 were found at http://www.payscale.com/best-colleges/degrees.asp. For a survey of employment opportunities, go to the U.S. Labor Department's Occupational Outlook Handbook at http://www.bls.gov/oco/.

study economics acquire skills that appreciate with experience. The bump in median pay based on experience for the 19 other majors averaged 67 percent. Elementary education remained the lowest paying major among those with 10 to 20 years of experience. Note that the majors ranked toward the top of the list tend to be more quantitative and analytical. The selection of a relatively more challenging major such as engineering or economics may send a favorable signal to future employers. Nursing majors ranked high right out of school, thanks to strong demand for health care. But nurses with 10 to 20 years of experience earned only 29 percent more than those with only 0 to 5 years of experience. This was the slowest growth rate among the 20 majors.

Incidentally, Exhibit 3 ranks only 20 majors, but Payscale.com ranks 207 majors in all. Median pay for economics majors ranked them in the top 10 percent of that larger group of majors.

Remember, the survey was limited to those whose highest degree was the baccalaureate, so it excluded the many economics majors who went on to pursue graduate studies in law, business administration, economics, public administration, journalism, and other fields (a different study found that lawyers with undergraduate degrees in economics earned more on average than lawyers with other majors).

A number of world leaders majored in economics, including three of the last seven U.S. presidents; Prime Minister Stephen Harper of Canada; billionaire and former president of Chile, Sebastian Pinera (who earned a Ph.D. in economics from Harvard); Turkey's first female prime minister, Tansu Ciller (who earned a Ph.D. in economics from the University of Connecticut); Italy's former prime minister, Mario Monti (who earned a Ph.D. in economics from Yale); Greece's former prime minister, Lucas Papademos (who earned a Ph.D. in economics from MIT); U.S. Supreme Court justices Stephen Breyer and Anthony Kennedy; and former justice Sandra Day O'Connor. Other notable economics majors include billionaire Donald Trump, former Hewlett-Packard president (and billionaire) Meg Whitman, former head of Microsoft (and billionaire) Steve Ballmer, CNN founder (and billionaire) Ted Turner, financial guru (and billionaire) Warren Buffett, Walmart founder (and billionaire) Sam Walton, and Scott Adams, creator of *Dilbert*, the mouthless wonder.

1-6 FINAL WORD

This textbook describes how economic factors affect individual choices and how all these choices come together to shape the economic system. Economics is not the whole story, and economic factors are not always the most important. But economic considerations have important and predictable effects on individual choices, and these choices affect the way we live.

Yes, economics is a challenging discipline, but it is also an exciting and rewarding one. The good news is that you already know a lot about economics. To use this knowledge, however, you must cultivate the art and science of economic analysis. You must be able to simplify the world to formulate questions, isolate the relevant variables, and then tell a persuasive story about how these variables relate.

An economic relation can be expressed in words, represented as a table of quantities, described by a mathematical equation, or illustrated as a graph. The appendix to this chapter introduces graphs. You may find a detailed reading of this appendix unnecessary. If you are already familiar with relations among variables, slopes, tangents, and the like, you can probably just browse. But if you have little recent experience with graphs, you might benefit from a more careful reading with pencil and paper in hand.

The next chapter introduces key tools of economic analysis. Subsequent chapters use these tools to explore economic problems and to explain economic behavior that may otherwise seem puzzling. You must walk before you can run, however, and in the next chapter, you will take your first wobbly steps.

STUDY TOOLS 1

READY TO STUDY? IN THE BOOK, YOU CAN:

☐ Work the Problems at the end of the chapter.

☐ Rip out the chapter review card for a handy summary of the chapter and key terms.

ONLINE AT CENGAGEBRAIN.COM YOU CAN:

☐ Collect StudyBits while you read and study the chapter.

☐ Quiz yourself on key concepts.

☐ Prepare for tests with chapter flash cards as well as flash cards that you create.

☐ Watch videos to explore economics further.

CHAPTER 1 PROBLEMS

Your instructor can access the answers to these problems online at http://cengagebrain.com.

1-1 Explain the economic problem of scarce resources and unlimited wants

1. *(Definition of Economics)* What determines whether or not a resource is scarce? Why is the concept of scarcity important to the definition of economics?

1-2 Describe the forces that shape economic choices

2. *(Rational Self-Interest)* Discuss the impact of rational self-interest on each of the following decisions:
   a. Whether to attend college full time or enter the workforce full time
   b. Whether to buy a new textbook or a used one
   c. Whether to attend a local college or an out-of-town college

3. *(Rational Self-Interest)* If behavior is governed by rational self-interest, why do people make charitable contributions of time and money?

4. *(Marginal Analysis)* The owner of a small pizzeria is deciding whether to increase the radius of delivery area by one mile. What considerations must be taken into account if such a decision is to increase profitability?

5. *(Time and Information)* It is often costly to obtain the information necessary to make good decisions. Yet your own interests can be best served by rationally weighing all options available to you. This requires informed decision making. Does this mean that making uninformed decisions is irrational? How do you determine how much information is the right amount?

1-3 Explain the relationship between economic theory and economic reality

6. *(Role of Theory)* What good is economic theory if it can't predict the behavior of a specific individual?

1-4 Identify some pitfalls of economic analysis

7. *(Pitfalls of Economic Analysis)* Review the discussion of pitfalls in economic thinking in this chapter. Then identify the fallacy, or mistake in thinking, in each of the following statements:
   a. Raising taxes always increases government revenues.
   b. Whenever there is a recession, imports decrease. Therefore, to stop a recession, we should increase imports.
   c. Raising the tariff on imported steel helps the U.S. steel industry. Therefore, the entire economy is helped.
   d. Gold sells for about $1,200 per ounce. Therefore, the U.S. government could sell all the gold in Fort Knox at $1,200 per ounce to reduce the national debt.

8. *(Association Versus Causation)* Suppose I observe that communities with lots of doctors tend to have relatively high rates of illness. I conclude that doctors cause illness. What's wrong with this reasoning?

1-5 Describe several reasons to study economics

9. *(Studying Economics)* According to the text, economics majors on average make more money than most other majors and have more job opportunities. Are these the primary motivations one might have for studying economics? What are your motivations for studying economics?

APPENDIX

A1-1 UNDERSTANDING GRAPHS

Take out a pencil and a blank piece of paper. Go ahead. Put a point in the middle of the paper. This is your point of departure, called the **origin**. With your pencil at the origin, draw a straight line off to the right. This line is called the **horizontal axis**. The value of the variable *x* measured along the horizontal axis increases as you move to the right of the origin. Now mark off this line from 0 to 20, in increments of 5 units each. Returning to the origin, draw another line, this one straight north. This line is called the **vertical axis**. The value of the variable *y* measured along the vertical axis increases as you move north of the origin. Mark off this line from 0 to 20, in increments of 5 units each.

Within the space framed by the two axes, you can plot possible combinations of the variables measured along each axis. Each point identifies a value measured along the horizontal, or *x,* axis *and* a value measured along the vertical, or *y,* axis. For example, place point *a* in your graph to reflect the combination where *x* equals 5 units and *y* equals 15 units. Likewise, place point *b* in your graph to reflect 10 units of *x* and 5 units of *y*. Now compare your results with points shown in Exhibit A-1.

A **graph** is a picture showing how variables relate, and a picture can be worth a thousand words. Take a look at Exhibit A-2, which shows the U.S. annual unemployment rate since 1900. The year is measured along the horizontal axis and the unemployment rate is measured as a percentage along the vertical axis. Exhibit A-2 is a *time-series graph,* which shows the value of a variable, in this case the percent of the labor force unemployed, over time. If you had to describe the information presented in Exhibit A-2, the explanation could take many words. The picture shows not only how one year compares to the next but also how one decade compares to another and how the unemployment rate trends over time. The sharply higher unemployment rate during the Great Depression of the 1930s is unmistakable. *Graphs convey information in a compact and efficient way.*

This appendix shows how graphs express a variety of possible relations among variables. Most graphs of interest in this book reflect the relationship between two economic variables, such as the unemployment rate and the year, the price of a product and the quantity demanded, or the price of production and the quantity supplied. Because we focus on just two variables at a time, we usually assume that other relevant variables remain constant.

One variable often depends on another. The time it takes you to drive home depends on your average speed. Your weight depends on how much you eat. The amount of Pepsi you buy depends on the price. A *functional relation* exists between two variables when the value of one variable *depends* on the value of another variable.

Exhibit A-1
Basics of a Graph

Any point on a graph represents a combination of values of two variables. Here point *a* represents the combination of 5 units of variable *x* (measured on the horizontal axis) and 15 units of variable *y* (measured on the vertical axis). Point b represents 10 units of *x* and 5 units of *y*.

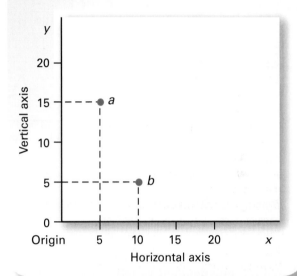

---

origin on a graph depicting two-dimensional space, the zero point

horizontal axis line on a graph that begins at the origin and goes to the right and left; sometimes called the *x* axis

vertical axis line on a graph that begins at the origin and goes up and down; sometimes called the *y* axis

graph a picture showing how variables relate in two-dimensional space; one variable is measured along the horizontal axis and the other along the vertical axis

Exhibit A-2

U.S. Unemployment Rate Since 1900

A time-series graph depicts the behavior of some economic variable over time. Shown here are U.S. unemployment rates since 1900.

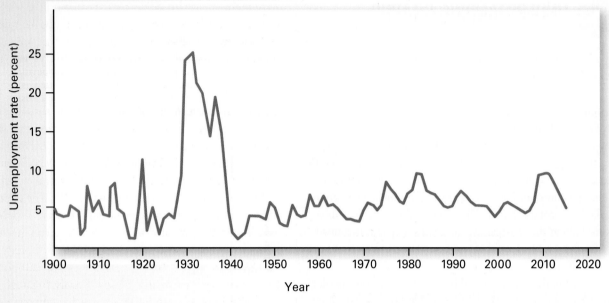

Source: *Historical Statistics of the United States*, 1970; and *Economic Report of the President*, February 2015.

The value of the **dependent variable** depends on the value of the **independent variable**. The task of the economist is to isolate economic relations and determine the direction of causality, if any. Recall that one of the pitfalls of economic thinking is the erroneous belief that association is causation. We cannot conclude that, simply because two events relate in time, one causes the other. There may be no relation between the two events.

A1-1a Drawing Graphs

Let's begin with a simple relation. Suppose you are planning to drive across the country and want to figure out how far you will travel each day. You plan to average 50 miles per hour. Possible combinations of driving time and distance traveled per day appear in Exhibit A-3. One column lists the hours driven per day, and the next column lists the number of miles traveled per day, assuming an average speed of 50 miles per hour. The

dependent variable a variable whose value depends on that of the independent variable

independent variable a variable whose value determines that of the dependent variable

Exhibit A-3

Schedule Relating Distance Traveled to Hours Driven

	Hours Driven per Day	Distance Traveled per Day (miles)
a	1	50
b	2	100
c	3	150
d	4	200
e	5	250

distance traveled, the *dependent* variable, depends on the number of hours driven, the *independent* variable. Combinations of hours driven and distance traveled are shown as *a, b, c, d,* and *e*. Each combination is represented by a point in Exhibit A-4. For example, point *a* shows that if you drive for 1 hour, you travel 50 miles. Point *b* indicates that if you drive for 2 hours, you travel 100 miles. By connecting the points, or possible combinations, we create a line running upward and to the right. This makes sense because, the longer you drive, the farther you travel. Assumed constant along this line is your average speed of 50 miles per hour.

Graph Relating Distance Traveled to Hours Driven

Points a through e depict different combinations of hours driven per day and the corresponding distances traveled. Connecting these points creates a graph.

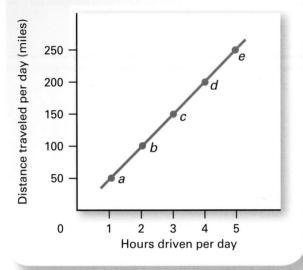

Types of relations between variables include the following:

1. As one variable increases, the other increases—as in Exhibit A-4; this is called a **positive**, or **direct**, **relation** between the variables.

2. As one variable increases, the other decreases; this is called a **negative**, or **inverse**, **relation**.

3. As one variable increases, the other remains unchanged; the two variables are said to be *independent*, or *unrelated*.

One of the advantages of graphs is that they easily convey the relation between variables. We do not need to examine the particular combinations of numbers; we need only focus on the shape of the curve.

A1-1b The Slope of a Straight Line

A more precise way to describe the shape of a curve is to measure its slope. The **slope of a line** indicates how much the vertical variable changes for a given increase in the horizontal variable. Specifically, the slope between any two points along any straight line is the vertical change between these two points divided by the horizontal increase, or

$$\text{Slope} = \frac{\text{Change in the vertical distance}}{\text{Increase in the horizontal distance}}$$

Each of the four panels in Exhibit A-5 indicates a vertical change, given a 10-unit increase in the horizontal variable. In panel (a), the vertical distance increases by 5 units when the horizontal distance increases by 10 units. The slope of the line is therefore 5/10, or 0.5. Notice that the slope in this case is a positive number because the relation between the two variables is positive, or direct. This slope indicates that for every 1-unit increase in the horizontal variable, the vertical variable increases by 0.5 units. The slope, incidentally, does not imply causality; the increase in the horizontal variable does not necessarily *cause* the increase in the vertical variable. The slope simply measures the relation between an increase in the horizontal variable and the associated change in the vertical variable.

In panel (b) of Exhibit A-5, the vertical distance declines by 7 units when the horizontal distance increases by 10 units, so the slope equals −7/10, or −0.7. The slope in this case is a negative number because the two variables have a negative, or inverse, relation. In panel (c), the vertical variable remains unchanged as the horizontal variable increases by 10, so the slope equals 0/10, or 0. These two variables are not related. Finally, in panel (d), the vertical variable can take on any value, although the horizontal variable remains unchanged. Again, the two variables are not related. In this case, any change in the vertical measure, for example a 10-unit change, is divided by 0, because the horizontal value does not change. Any change divided by 0 is mathematically undefined, but as the line tilts toward vertical, its slope gets incredibly large. For practical purposes, we will assume that the slope of this line is not undefined but infinitely large.

A1-1c The Slope, Units of Measurement, and Marginal Analysis

The mathematical value of the slope depends on the units measured on the graph. For example, suppose copper tubing costs $1 a foot. Graphs depicting the relation between total cost and quantity purchased are shown in Exhibit A-6. In panel (a), the total cost increases by $1 for each 1-foot increase in the amount of tubing purchased. Thus, the slope equals 1/1, or 1. If the cost per foot remains the same but units are

positive relation (direct relation) occurs when two variables increase or decrease together; the two variables move in the same direction

negative relation (inverse relation) occurs when two variables move in opposite directions; when one increases, the other decreases

slope of a line a measure of how much the vertical variable changes for a given increase in the horizontal variable; the vertical change between two points divided by the horizontal increase

Exhibit A-5

Alternative Slopes for Straight Lines

The slope of a line indicates how much the vertically measured variable changes for a given increase in the variable measured along the horizontal axis. Panel (a) shows a positive relation between two variables; the slope is 0.5, a positive number. Panel (b) depicts a negative, or inverse, relation. When the x variable increases, the y variable decreases; the slope is 20.7, a negative number. Panels (c) and (d) represent situations in which two variables are unrelated. In panel (c), the y variable always takes on the same value; the slope is 0. In panel (d), the x variable always takes on the same value; the slope is mathematically undefined but we simplify by assuming the slope is infinite.

(a) Positive relation

(b) Negative relation

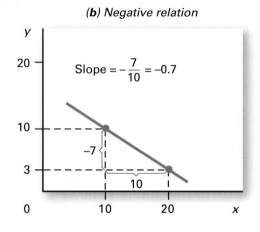

(c) No relation: zero slope

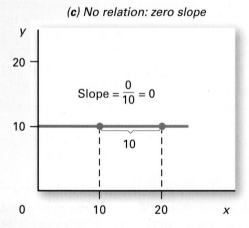

(d) No relation: assumed infinite slope

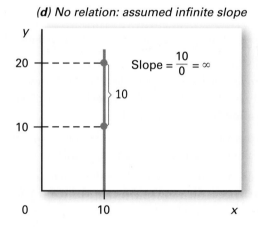

measured not in *feet* but in *yards,* the relation between total cost and quantity purchased is as depicted in panel (b). Now total cost increases by $3 for each 1-*yard* increase in output, so the slope equals 3/1, or 3. Because different units are used to measure the copper tubing, the two panels reflect different slopes, even though the cost is $1 per foot in each panel. Keep in mind that *the slope depends in part on the units of measurement.*

Economic analysis usually involves *marginal analysis,* such as the marginal cost of one more unit of output. The slope is a convenient device for measuring marginal effects because it reflects the change in total cost, measured along the vertical axis, for each 1-unit change in

output, measured along the horizontal axis. For example, in panel (a) of Exhibit A-6, the marginal cost of another *foot* of copper tubing is $1, which also equals the slope of the line. In panel (b), the marginal cost of another *yard* of tubing is $3, which again is the slope of that line. Because of its applicability to marginal analysis, the slope has special relevance in economics.

A1-1d The Slopes of Curved Lines

The slope of a straight line is the same everywhere along the line, but the slope of a curved line differs along the curve, as shown in Exhibit A-7. To find the slope of a

Exhibit A-6

Slope Depends on the Unit of Measure

The value of the slope depends on the units of measure. In panel (a), output is measured in feet of copper tubing; in panel (b), output is measured in yards. Although the cost is $1 per foot in each panel, the slope is different in the two panels because copper tubing is measured using different units.

(a) Measured in feet

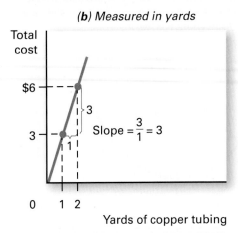

(b) Measured in yards

Exhibit A-7

Slopes at Different Points on a Curved Line

The slope of a curved line varies from point to point. At a given point, such as *a* or *b*, the slope of the curve is equal to the slope of the straight line that is tangent to the curve at the point.

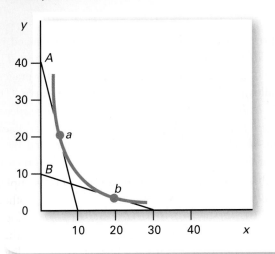

curved line at a particular point, draw a straight line that just touches the curve at that point but does not cut or cross the curve. Such a line is called a tangent to the curve at that point. The slope of the **tangent** gives the slope of the curve at that point. Look at line *A*, which is tangent to the curve at point *a*. As the horizontal value increases

from 0 to 10, the vertical value drops along *A* from 40 to 0. Thus, the vertical change divided by the horizontal change equals −40/10, or −4, which is the slope of the curve at point *a*. This slope is negative because the vertical value decreases as the horizontal value increases. Line *B*, a line tangent to the curve at point *b*, has the slope −10/30, or −0.33. As you can see, the curve depicted in Exhibit A-7 gets flatter as the horizontal variable increases, so the value of its slope approaches zero.

Other curves, of course, will reflect different slopes as well as different changes in the slope along the curve. Downward-sloping curves have negative slopes, and upward-sloping curves, positive slopes. Sometimes curves, such as those in Exhibit A-8, are more complex, having both positive and negative ranges, depending on the horizontal value. In the hill-shaped curve, for small values of *x*, there is a positive relation between *x* and *y*, so the slope is positive. As the value of *x* increases, however, the slope declines and eventually becomes negative. We can divide the curve into two segments: (1) the segment between the origin and point *a*, where the slope is positive; and (2) the segment of the curve to the right of point *a*, where the slope is negative. The slope of the curve at point *a* is 0. The U-shaped curve in Exhibit A-8 represents the opposite relation: *x* and *y* are

> **tangent** a straight line that touches a curve at a point but does not cut or cross the curve; used to measure the slope of a curve at a point

Curves with Both Positive and Negative Slopes

Some curves have both positive and negative slopes. The hill-shaped curve (in red) has a positive slope to the left of point *a*, a slope of 0 at point *a*, and a negative slope to the right of that point. The U-shaped curve (in blue) starts off with a negative slope, has a slope of 0 at point *b*, and has a positive slope to the right of that point.

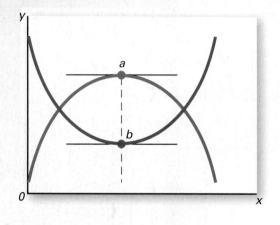

Shift of Line Relating Distance Traveled to Hours Driven

Line *T* appeared originally in Exhibit A-5 to show the relation between hours driven and distance traveled per day, assuming an average speed of 50 miles per hour. If the speed averages only 40 miles per hour, the entire relation shifts to the right to T9, indicating that any given distance traveled requires more driving time. For example, 200 miles traveled takes 4 hours at 50 miles per hour but 5 hours at 40 miles per hour. This figure shows how a change in assumptions, in this case, the average speed, can shift the entire relationship between two variables.

negatively related until point *b* is reached; thereafter, they are positively related. The slope equals 0 at point *b*.

A1-1e Line Shifts

Let's go back to the example of your cross-country trip, where we were trying to determine how many miles you would travel per day. Recall that we measured hours driven per day on the horizontal axis and miles traveled per day on the vertical axis, assuming an average speed of 50 miles per hour. That same relation is shown as line *T* in Exhibit A-8. What happens if the average speed is 40 miles per hour? The entire relation between hours driven and distance traveled would change, as shown by the shift to the right of line *T* to *T'*. With a slower average speed, any distance traveled per day now requires more driving time. For example, 200 miles traveled

requires 4 hours of driving when the average speed is 50 miles per hour (as shown by point *d* on curve *T*), but 200 miles takes 5 hours when your speed averages 40 miles per hour (as shown by point *f* on curve *T'*). Thus, *a change in the assumption about average speed changes the relationship between the two variables observed.* This changed relationship is expressed by a shift of the line that shows how the two variables relate.

That ends our once-over of graphs. Return to this appendix when you need a review.

2 | Economic Tools and Economic Systems

Gary Bryan/Stone+/Getty Images

LEARNING OUTCOMES

After studying this chapter, you will be able to...

2-1 Describe the relationship between choice and opportunity cost

2-2 Explain how comparative advantage, specialization, and exchange affect economic outcomes (output)

2-3 Outline how economies function as production systems

2-4 Describe different economic systems and the decision-making rules that define them

After finishing this chapter go to **PAGE 37** for **STUDY TOOLS**

Topics discussed in Chapter 2 include

- Opportunity cost
- Comparative advantage
- Specialization
- Division of labor
- Production possibilities frontier
- Economic systems
- Three economic questions
- Capitalism, command systems, and in between

▶ Why are you reading this book right now rather than doing something else?

▶ What is college costing you?

▶ Why will you eventually major in one subject rather than continue to take courses in various subjects?

▶ Why is fast food so fast?

▶ Why is there no point crying over spilled milk?

▶ Why does common ownership often lead to common neglect?

These and other questions are addressed in this chapter, which introduces some tools of economic analysis—some tools of the trade.

Chapter 1 introduced the idea that scarcity forces us to make choices, but the chapter said little about how to make economic choices. This chapter develops a framework for evaluating economic alternatives. First, we consider the cost involved in selecting one alternative over others. Next, we develop tools to explore the choices available to individuals and to the economy as a whole. Finally, we examine the questions that different economies must answer—questions about what goods and services to produce, how to produce them, and for whom to produce them.

> **"Why is there no point crying over spilled milk?"**

2-1 CHOICE AND OPPORTUNITY COST

Think about a choice you just made: the decision to begin reading this chapter right now rather than use your time to study for another course, play sports, watch TV, play video games, go online, get some sleep, hang with friends, or do something else. Suppose it's late and your best alternative to reading right now is getting some sleep. The cost of reading is passing up the opportunity of sleep. Because of scarcity, whenever you make a choice, you must pass up another opportunity; you must incur an *opportunity cost*.

2-1a Opportunity Cost

What do we mean when we talk about the cost of something? Isn't it what we must give up—must forgo—to get that thing? The **opportunity cost** of the chosen item or activity is *the value of the best alternative that is forgone.* You can think of opportunity cost as the *opportunity lost.* Sometimes opportunity cost can be measured in terms of money, although, as we shall see, money is usually only part of opportunity cost.

How many times have you heard people say they did something because they "had nothing better to do"? They actually mean they had nothing else going on. Yet, according to the idea of opportunity cost, people *always* do what they do because they have nothing better to do. The choice selected seems, at the time, preferable to any other possible alternative. You are reading this chapter right now because you have nothing better to do. In fact, you are attending college for the same reason: College appears more attractive than your best alternative.

2-1b Opportunity Cost Is Subjective

Like beauty, opportunity cost is in the eye of the beholder. It is subjective. Only the individual making the choice can identify the most attractive alternative. But the chooser seldom knows the actual value of what was passed up because that alternative is "the road not taken." If you give up an evening of pizza and conversation with friends to work on a research paper, you will never know exactly what you gave up. You know only what you

opportunity cost The value of the best alternative forgone when an item or activity is chosen *expected.* Evidently, you expected the benefit of working on that paper to exceed the benefit of the best alternative. (Incidentally, focusing on the best alternative forgone makes all other alternatives irrelevant.)

Calculating Opportunity Cost Requires Time and Information

Economists assume that people rationally choose the most valued alternative. This does not mean you exhaustively assess the value of all possibilities. You assess alternatives as long as the expected marginal benefit of gathering more information about your options exceeds the expected marginal cost (even if you are not aware of making such conscious calculations). In other words, you do the best you can for yourself.

Because learning about alternatives is costly and time consuming, some choices are based on limited or even wrong information. Indeed, some choices may turn out badly (you went for a picnic but it rained; the movie that cost $10 stunk; your new shoes pinched; your new exercise equipment gets no exercise; the stock you bought tanked). Regret about lost opportunities is captured in the common expression "coulda, woulda, shoulda." At the time you made the selection, however, you believed you were making the best use of all your scarce resources, including the time required to gather and evaluate information about your choices.

Time: The Ultimate Constraint

The Sultan of Brunei is among the richest people on Earth, worth billions based on huge oil revenues that flow into his tiny country. He and his royal family (which has ruled since 1405) live in a palace with 1,788 rooms, including 257 bathrooms and a throne room the size of a football field. The family owns hundreds of cars, including dozens of Rolls-Royces; he can drive any of these or pilot one of his seven planes, including the 747 with gold-plated furniture. Supported by such wealth, the Sultan would appear to have overcome the economic problem of scarcity. Yet, though he can buy just about anything he wants, he lacks the time to enjoy all his stuff. If he pursues one activity, he cannot at the same time do something else. Each activity involves an opportunity cost. Consequently, the Sultan must choose from among the competing uses of his scarcest resource, time. Although your alternatives are less exotic, you too face a time constraint, especially as the college term winds down.

sunk cost A cost that has already been incurred, cannot be recovered, and thus is irrelevant for present and future economic decisions

Opportunity Cost Varies With Circumstance

Opportunity cost depends on your alternatives. This is why you are more likely to study on a Tuesday night than on a Saturday night. The opportunity cost of studying is lower on a Tuesday night, because your alternatives are less attractive than on a Saturday night, when more is going on. Suppose you go to a movie on Saturday night. Your opportunity cost is the value of your best alternative forgone, which might be attending a college game. For some of you, studying on Saturday night may rank well down the list of alternatives—perhaps ahead of reorganizing your closet but behind doing your laundry.

Opportunity cost is subjective, but in some cases, money paid for goods and services is a reasonable approximation. For example, the opportunity cost of the new smartphone you bought is the benefit from spending that $300 on the best forgone alternative. The money measure may leave out some important elements, however, particularly the value of the time involved. For example, watching the latest hit movie costs you not only the $10 admission price but also the time needed to get there, watch the movie, and return home.

Even religious practices are subject to opportunity cost. For example, about half the U.S. population attends religious services at least once a month. In some states, so-called blue laws prohibit retail activity on Sunday. Some states have repealed these laws in recent years, thus raising the opportunity cost of church attendance. Researchers have found that when a state repeals its blue laws, religious attendance declines, as do church donations. These results do not seem to be linked to any decline in religiosity before the repeal.[1]

2-1c Sunk Cost and Choice

Suppose you have just finished grocery shopping and are wheeling your cart toward the checkout counters. How do you decide which line to join? Easy. You pick the one with the shortest expected wait. Suppose that line has barely moved for 10 minutes, when you notice that a cashier has opened a new one and invites you to check out. Do you switch to the open cashier, or do you think, "Since I've already spent 10 minutes in this line, I'm staying put"? The 10 minutes you waited represents a **sunk cost**, which is a cost that has already been incurred and cannot be recovered, regardless

1. Jonathan Gruber and Daniel Hungerman, "The Church vs. the Mall: What Happens When Religion Faces Increased Secular Competition?" *Quarterly Journal of Economics*, 123 (May 2008): 831–862.

of what you do next. You should ignore sunk costs in making economic choices. Hence, you should switch lines. *Economic decision makers should consider only those costs that are affected by the choice. Sunk costs have already been incurred and are not affected by the choice, so they are irrelevant.* Likewise, you should walk out on a bad movie, even if you spent $10 to get in. Your $10 is gone, and sitting through that stinker only makes you worse off. The irrelevance of sunk costs is underscored by proverbs such as "Don't throw good money after bad," "Let bygones be bygones," "That's water over the dam," and "There's no point crying over spilled milk." The milk has already spilled, so whatever you do now cannot change that. Or, as Shakespeare's Lady Macbeth put it, "Things without all remedy should be without regard: what's done is done." In other words, forget about it.

Now that you have some idea about opportunity cost, let's see how it helps solve the economic problem.

2-2 COMPARATIVE ADVANTAGE, SPECIALIZATION, AND EXCHANGE

Suppose you live in a dormitory (and also go to college in the 1950s). You and your roommate have such tight schedules that you each can spare only about an hour a week for mundane tasks like ironing shirts and typing papers (granted, in reality you may not iron shirts or

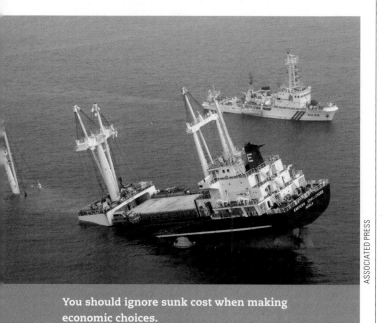

You should ignore sunk cost when making economic choices.

ASSOCIATED PRESS

Does your absolute advantage in both activities mean specialization is no longer a good idea?

Yuritz/Dreamstime.com

type papers, but this example will help you understand some important principles). Each of you must turn in a typed three-page paper every week, and you each prefer ironed shirts when you have the time. Let's say it takes you a half hour to type a handwritten paper. Your roommate is from the hunt-and-peck school and takes about an hour. But your roommate is a talented ironer and can iron a shirt in 5 minutes flat (or should that be, iron it flat in 5 minutes?). You take twice as long, or 10 minutes, to iron a shirt.

During the hour set aside each week for typing and ironing, typing takes priority. If you each do your own typing and ironing, you type your paper in a half hour and iron three shirts in the remaining half hour. Your roommate spends the entire hour typing the paper, leaving no time for ironing. Thus, if you each do your own tasks, the combined output is two typed papers and three ironed shirts.

2-2a The Law of Comparative Advantage

Before long, you each realize that total output would increase if you did all the typing and your roommate did all the ironing. In the hour available for these tasks, you type both papers and your roommate irons 12 shirts. As a result of specialization, total output increases by 9 shirts! You strike a deal to exchange your typing for your roommate's ironing, so you each end up with a typed paper and 6 ironed shirts. Thus, *each of you is better off as a result of specialization and exchange.*

By specializing in the task that you each do better, you rely on the **law of comparative advantage**, which states that the individual with the lower opportunity cost of producing a particular output should

law of comparative advantage The individual, firm, region, or country with the lowest opportunity cost of producing a particular good should specialize in that good specialize in that output. You face a lower opportunity cost of typing than does your roommate, because in the time it takes to type a paper, you could iron 3 shirts whereas your roommate could iron 12 shirts. And if you face a lower opportunity cost of typing, your roommate must face a lower opportunity cost of ironing (try working that out).

2-2b Absolute Advantage Versus Comparative Advantage

The gains from specialization and exchange so far are obvious. A more interesting case arises if you are faster at both tasks. Suppose the example changes only in one respect: Your roommate takes 12 minutes to iron a shirt compared with your 10 minutes. You now have an *absolute advantage* in both tasks, meaning each task takes you less time than it does your roommate. More generally, having an **absolute advantage** means making something using fewer resources than other producers require.

Does your absolute advantage in both activities mean specialization is no longer a good idea? Recall that the law of comparative advantage states that the individual with *the lower opportunity cost* of producing a particular good should specialize in that good. You still take 30 minutes to type a paper and 10 minutes to iron a shirt, so your opportunity cost of typing the paper remains at three ironed shirts. Your roommate takes an hour to type a paper and 12 minutes to iron a shirt, so your roommate could iron five shirts in the time it takes to type a paper. *Because your opportunity cost of typing is lower than your roommate's, you still have a comparative advantage in typing.* Consequently, your roommate must have a comparative advantage in ironing (again, try working this out to your satisfaction). Therefore, you should do all the typing and your roommate, all the ironing. Although you have an absolute advantage in both tasks, your **comparative advantage** calls for specializing in the task for which you have the lower opportunity cost—in this case, typing.

If neither of you specialized, you could type one paper and iron three shirts. Your roommate could still type just the one paper. Your combined output would be two papers and three shirts. If you each specialized according to comparative

absolute advantage The ability to make something using fewer resources than other producers use

comparative advantage The ability to make something at a lower opportunity cost than other producers face

barter The direct exchange of one product for another without using money

advantage, in an hour you could type both papers and your roommate could iron five shirts. Thus, specialization increases total output by two ironed shirts. Even though you are better at both tasks than your roommate, you are comparatively better at typing. Put another way, your roommate, although worse at both tasks, is not quite as bad at ironing as at typing.

Don't think that this is just common sense. Common sense would lead you to do your own ironing and typing because you are better at both. *Absolute advantage focuses on who uses the fewest resources, but comparative advantage focuses on what else those resources could produce—that is, on the opportunity cost of those resources.* Comparative advantage is the better guide to who should do what.

The law of comparative advantage applies not only to individuals but also to firms, regions of a country, and entire nations. Individuals, firms, regions, or countries with the lowest opportunity cost of producing a particular good should specialize in producing that good. Because of such factors as climate, workforce skills, natural resources, and capital stock, certain parts of the country and certain parts of the world have a comparative advantage in producing particular goods. From Washington State apples to Florida oranges, from software in India to hardware in Taiwan—*resources are allocated most efficiently across the country and around the world when production and trade conform to the law of comparative advantage.*

2-2c Specialization and Exchange

In the previous example, you and your roommate specialized and then exchanged output. No money was involved. In other words, you engaged in **barter**, where products are traded directly for other products. Barter works best in simple economies with little specialization and few traded goods. But for economies with greater specialization, *money* facilitates exchange. Money—coins, bills, checks, and debit cards—is a *medium of exchange* because it is the one thing that everyone accepts in return for goods and services.

Because of specialization and comparative advantage, most people consume little of what they produce and produce little of what they consume. Each individual specializes, then exchanges that product for money, which in turn is exchanged for other products. Did you make anything you are wearing? Probably not. Think about the degree of specialization that went into your cotton shirt. A farmer in a warm climate grew the cotton and sold it to someone who spun it into thread, who

Exhibit 1
Specialization in the Production of Cotton Shirts

1. Cotton is grown
2. Spun into thread
3. Woven into fabric
4. Sewn into shirts
5. Shipped to a wholesaler
6. Sold to a retailer
7. Bought by a consumer

sold it to someone who wove it into fabric, who sold it to someone who sewed the shirt, who sold it to a wholesaler, who sold it to a retailer, who sold it to you. Many specialists in the chain of production created that shirt. Exhibit 1 traces these steps. *Specialization and exchange create more interdependence in an economy.*

Evidence of specialization is all around us. Shops at the mall specialize in products ranging from luggage to lingerie. Restaurants range from subs to sushi. Or let your fingers do the walking through the help-wanted ads or Craigslist, where you will find thousands of specializations. Without moving a muscle, you can observe the division of labor within a single industry by watching the credits roll at the end of a movie. The credits list scores of specialists—from gaffer (lighting electrician) to assistant location scout. As an extreme example, more than 3,000 specialists helped create the movie *Avatar*.[2] Even TV dramas, such as *NCIS* or *The Walking Dead*, require hundreds of specialists.

Some specialties may seem odd. For example, professional mourners in Taiwan are hired by grieving families to scream, wail, and otherwise demonstrate the deep grief befitting a proper funeral. The sharp degree of specialization is perhaps most obvious online, where the pool of potential customers is so vast that

> **"The degree of specialization is limited by the extent of market."**

individual sites become finely focused. For example, you can find sites specializing in musical bowls, tongue studs, toe rings, brass knuckles, mouth harps, ferret toys, and cat bandanas—just to name a few of the hundreds of thousands of specialty sites. You won't find such precise specialization at the mall. Adam Smith (1723–1790), who is considered the father of economics, said the degree of specialization is limited by the extent of the market. Online sellers draw on the broadest customer base in the world to find a market niche.

2-2d Division of Labor and Gains From Specialization

Picture a visit to McDonald's: "Let's see, I'll have a Big Mac, an order of fries, and a chocolate shake." In minutes your order is ready. It would take you much longer to make a homemade version of this meal. Why is the McDonald's meal faster, cheaper, and—for some people—tastier than one you could make yourself? Why is fast food so fast? McDonald's takes advantage of the gains resulting from the **division of labor**. Each worker, rather than preparing an entire meal, specializes in separate tasks. This division of labor allows the group to produce much more.

How is this increase in productivity possible? First, the manager can assign tasks according to *individual preferences and abilities*—that is, according to the law of comparative advantage. The worker with the friendly smile and pleasant personality can handle the customers up front; the one with the strong back but few social graces can handle the heavy lifting out back. Second, a worker who performs the same task again and again gets better at it (experience is a good teacher). The worker filling orders at the drive-through, for example, learns to deal with special problems that arise. As another example, consider the experience gained by someone screening bags at airport security. Experience helps the screener distinguish the harmful from the harmless. Third, specialization means

division of labor
Breaking down the production of a good into separate tasks

2. As reported in Hendrik Hertzberg, "And the Oscar Goes To," *The New Yorker*, 15 & 22 February 2010.

no time is lost moving from one task to another. Finally, and perhaps most importantly, the **specialization of labor** allows for the introduction of more sophisticated production techniques—techniques that would not make sense on a smaller scale. For example, McDonald's large shake machine would be impractical in the home. *Specialized machines make each worker more productive.*

To summarize: The specialization of labor (a) takes advantage of individual preferences and natural abilities, (b) allows workers to develop more experience at a particular task, (c) reduces the need to shift among different tasks, and (d) permits the introduction of labor-saving machinery. Specialization and the division of labor occur not only among individuals but also among firms, regions, and, indeed, entire countries. The cotton shirt mentioned earlier might involve growing cotton in one country, turning it into cloth in another, making the shirt in a third, and selling it in a fourth.

We should also acknowledge the downside of specialization. Doing the same thing all day can become tedious. Consider, for example, the assembly line worker whose sole task is to tighten a particular bolt. Such a monotonous job could drive that worker bonkers or lead to repetitive motion injury. Thus, the gains from dividing production into individual tasks must be weighed against any problems caused by assigning workers to repetitive, tedious, and potentially harmful jobs. Fortunately, today many routine tasks, particularly on assembly lines, can be turned over to robots.

© istockphoto.com/EllenMoran

Division of labor puts the "fast" in "fast food."

shaped by the choices of individual decision makers, whether they are consumers, producers, or public officials. Just as resources are scarce for the individual, they are also scarce for the economy as a whole (no fallacy of composition here). An economy has millions of different resources that can be combined in all kinds of ways to produce millions of different goods and services. This section steps back from the immense complexity of the real economy to develop another simple model, which explores the economy's production options.

2-3a Efficiency and the Production Possibilities Frontier or PPF

To get an idea of how well the economy works, you need some perspective; you need a place to stand. Let's develop a model to get some idea of how much an economy can produce with the resources available. What are the economy's production capabilities? Here are the model's assumptions:

1. To simplify matters, output is limited to just two broad classes of products: consumer goods and capital goods.

2. The focus is on production during a given period—in this case, a year.

3. The economy's resources are fixed in both quantity and quality during that period.

4. Society's knowledge about how these resources combine to produce output—that is, the available *technology and know-how*—does not change during the year.

5. Also assumed fixed during the period are the "rules of the game" that facilitate production and exchange. These include such things as the legal system, property rights, tax laws, patent laws, and the manners, customs, and conventions of the market.

The point of these simplifying assumptions is to freeze in time the economy's resources, technology and know-how, and rules of the game so we can focus on the economy's production options. Otherwise, the production possibilities of the economy would be a moving target.

2-3 THE ECONOMY'S PRODUCTION POSSIBILITIES

The focus, up to this point, has been on how individuals choose to use their scarce resources to satisfy their unlimited wants or, more specifically, how they specialize based on comparative advantage. This emphasis on the individual has been appropriate because the economy is

specialization of labor
Focusing work effort on a particular product or a single task

2-3b Inefficient and Unattainable Production

Points inside the PPF, such as *I* in Exhibit 2, identify combinations that do not employ resources efficiently. Note that *C* yields more consumer goods and no fewer capital goods than *I*. And *E* yields more capital goods and no fewer consumer goods than *I*. Indeed, any point along the PPF between *C* and *E*, such as *D*, yields both more consumer goods and more capital goods than *I*. Hence, combination *I* is *inefficient*. By using resources more efficiently, the economy can produce more of at least one good without reducing the production of the other good. Points outside the PPF, such as *U* in Exhibit 2, identify *unattainable* combinations, given the availability of resources, technology and know-how, and rules of the game. Thus, *the PPF not only shows efficient combinations of production but also serves as the boundary between inefficient combinations inside the frontier and unattainable combinations outside the frontier.*

2-3c The Shape of the PPF

Any movement along the PPF involves producing less of one good to produce more of the other. Movements down along the curve indicate that the opportunity cost of more capital goods is fewer consumer goods. For example, moving from point *A* to point *B* *increases* capital production from none to 10 million units but *reduces* consumer units from 50 million to 48 million. Increasing capital goods by 10 million reduces consumer goods only a little. Capital production initially employs resources (such as heavy machinery used to build factories) that produce few consumer goods but are quite productive in making capital.

As shown by the dashed lines in Exhibit 2, each additional 10 million units of capital produced reduce consumer goods by successively

Exhibit 2
The Economy's Production Possibilities Frontier

If the economy uses its available resources and its technology and know-how efficiently to produce consumer goods and capital goods, that economy is on its production possibilities frontier, *AF*. The PPF is bowed out to reflect the law of increasing opportunity cost; the economy must sacrifice more and more units of consumer goods to produce each additional increment of capital goods. Note that more consumer goods must be given up in moving from *E* to *F* than in moving from *A* to *B*, although in each case the gain in capital goods is 10 million units. Points inside the PPF, such as *I*, represent inefficient use of resources. Points outside the PPF, such as *U*, represent unattainable combinations.

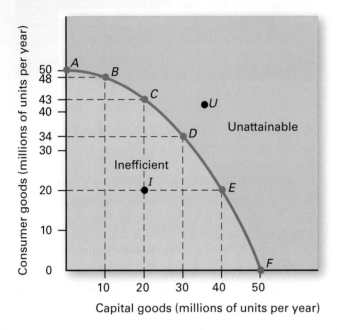

Given the resources, technology and know-how, and rules of the game available in the economy, the **production possibilities frontier**, or **PPF**, identifies possible combinations of the two types of goods that can be produced when available resources are employed efficiently. *Resources are employed efficiently when there is no change that could increase the production of one good without decreasing the production of the other good.* **Efficiency** involves getting the most from available resources.

The economy's PPF for consumer goods and capital goods is shown by the curve *AF* in Exhibit 2. Point *A* identifies the amount produced per year if all the economy's resources are used efficiently to produce consumer goods. Point *F* identifies the amount produced per year if all the economy's resources are used efficiently to produce capital goods. Points along the curve between *A* and *F* identify possible combinations of the two goods that

production possibilities frontier (PPF) A curve showing alternative combinations of goods that can be produced when available resources are used efficiently; a boundary line between inefficient and unattainable combinations

efficiency The condition that exists when there is no way resources can be reallocated to increase the production of one good without decreasing the production of another; getting the most from available resources larger amounts. The resources used to produce more capital are increasingly better suited to producing consumer goods. *The opportunity cost of making more capital goods increases, because not all resources in the economy are perfectly adaptable to the production of both types of goods.* The shape of the production possibilities frontier reflects the **law of increasing opportunity cost**. If the economy uses resources efficiently, the law of increasing opportunity cost states that each additional increment of one good requires the economy to sacrifice successively larger and larger increments of the other good.

The PPF derives its bowed-out shape from the law of increasing opportunity cost. For example, whereas the first 10 million units of capital have an opportunity cost of only 2 million consumer units, the final 10 million units of capital—that is, the increase from E to F—have an opportunity cost of 20 million consumer units. Notice that the slope of the PPF shows the opportunity cost of an increment of capital. As the economy moves down the curve, the curve becomes steeper, reflecting the higher opportunity cost of capital goods in terms of forgone consumer goods. The law of increasing opportunity cost also applies when moving from capital goods to consumer goods. Incidentally, if resources were perfectly adaptable to the production of both consumer goods and capital goods, the PPF would be a straight line, reflecting a constant opportunity cost along the PPF.

2-3d What Can Shift the PPF?

Any production possibilities frontier assumes the economy's resources, technology and know-how, and rules of the game are fixed during the period under consideration. Over time, however, the PPF may shift if resources, technology and know-how, or the rules of the game change. **Economic growth** is an expansion in the economy's production possibilities as reflected by an outward shift of the PPF.

law of increasing opportunity cost To produce more of one good, a successively larger amount of the other good must be sacrificed

economic growth An increase in the economy's ability to produce goods and services; reflected by an outward shift of the economy's production possibilities frontier

Changes in Resource Availability

If people decide to work longer hours, the PPF shifts outward, as shown in panel (a) of Exhibit 3. An increase in the size or health of the labor

Disasters can cause an inward shift or retraction of the PPF.

force, an increase in the skills of the labor force, or an increase in the availability of other resources, such as new oil discoveries, also shifts the PPF outward. In contrast, a decrease of resources shifts the PPF inward, as depicted in panel (b). For example, in 1990 Iraq invaded Kuwait, setting oil fields ablaze and destroying much of Kuwait's physical capital. In West Africa, the encroaching sands of the Sahara destroy thousands of square miles of farmland each year. And in northwest China, a rising tide of wind-blown sand has claimed grasslands, lakes, and forests, and swallowed entire villages, forcing tens of thousands of people to flee.

The new PPFs in panels (a) and (b) appear to be parallel to the original ones, indicating that the resources that changed could produce both capital goods and consumer goods. For example, an increase in electrical power can enhance the production of both, as shown in panel (a). If a resource such as farmland benefits just consumer goods, then increased availability or productivity of that resource shifts the PPF more along the consumer goods axis, as shown in panel (c). Panel (d) shows the effect of an increase in a resource such as construction equipment that is suited only to capital goods.

Increases in the Capital Stock

An economy's PPF depends in part on the stock of human and physical capital. The more capital an economy produces in one period, the more output can be produced in the next period. Thus, producing more capital goods during this period (for example, more machines in the case of physical capital or more education in the case of human capital) shifts the economy's PPF outward in the next period.

Exhibit 3

Shifts of the Economy's Production Possibilities Frontier

When the resources available to an economy change, the PPF shifts. If more resources become available, if technology and know-how improve, or if the rules of the game create greater stability, the PPF shifts outward, as in panel (a), indicating that more output can be produced. A decrease in available resources or an upheaval in the rules causes the PPF to shift inward, as in panel (b). Panel (c) shows a change affecting consumer goods. More consumer goods can now be produced at any given level of capital goods. Panel (d) shows a change affecting capital goods.

(a) Increase in available resources, better technology, more know-how, or improvement in the rules of the game

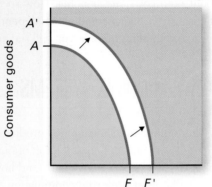

(b) Decrease in available resources or greater uncertainty in the rules of the game

(c) Change in resources, technology, know-how, or rules that benefits consumer goods

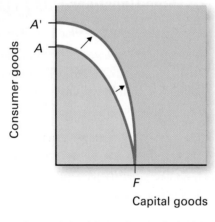

(d) Change in resources, technology, know-how, or rules that benefits capital goods

Technological Change and More Know-how

A technological discovery that employs resources more efficiently could shift the economy's PPF outward. Some discoveries enhance the production of both consumer goods and capital goods, as shown in panel (a) of Exhibit 3. For example, the Internet has increased each firm's ability to find available resources. A technological discovery that benefits consumer goods only, such as more disease-resistant crops, is reflected by a rotation outward of the PPF along the consumer goods axis, as shown in panel (c). Note that point *F* remains unchanged because the breakthrough does not affect the production of capital goods. Panel (d) shows a technological advance in the production of capital goods, such as better software for designing heavy machinery. But even for a given level of technology and a given number of workers, output can increase over time with more know-how. For example, researchers have documented that steel production doubled at a mini-mill even though the technology did not change nor did the number of workers. Through experimentation, workers developed more know-how.[3]

Improvements in the Rules of the Game

The **rules of the game** are the formal and informal institutions that support the economy—the laws, customs, manners, conventions, and other institutional underpinnings that encourage people to pursue productive activity. A more stable political environment and more reliable property rights increase the incentive to work and to invest, and thus help the economy grow. For example, people have more incentive to work if taxes claim less of their paychecks. People have more incentive to invest if they are confident that their investment will not be appropriated by government, stolen by thieves, destroyed by civil unrest, or blown up by terrorists. Greater certainty and stability in the rules of the game shift the economy's PPF outward. On the other hand, greater uncertainty about the rules of the game reduces the economy's productive capacity, as reflected by an inward shift of the PPF. For example, during the Great Recession of 2007–2009, trust in U.S. institutions such as banks, newspapers, Congress, and big corporations declined and this reduced the economy's productive ability.[4]

2-3e What We Learn From the PPF

The PPF demonstrates several ideas introduced so far. The first is *efficiency:* The PPF describes efficient combinations of output, given the economy's resources, technology and know-how, and rules of the game. The second idea is *scarcity:* Given the resources, technology and know-how, and rules of the game, the economy can produce only so much output per period. The PPF slopes downward, because more of one good means less of the other good, thus demonstrating *opportunity cost.* The PPF's bowed-out shape reflects the *law of increasing opportunity cost,* which arises because some resources are not perfectly adaptable to the production of each

type of good. And a shift outward in the PPF reflects *economic growth.*

Finally, because society must somehow select a specific combination of output—a single point—along the PPF, the PPF also underscores the need for *choice.* Selecting a particular combination determines not only the consumer goods available in this period, but also the capital stock available in the next period. One thing the PPF does not tell us is which combination to choose. The PPF tells us only about the costs, not the benefits, of the two goods. To make a selection, we need to know about both costs *and* benefits. How society goes about choosing a particular combination depends on the nature of the economic system, as you will see next.

2-4 ECONOMIC SYSTEMS

Each point along the economy's production possibilities frontier is an efficient combination of outputs. Whether the economy produces efficiently and how the economy selects the most preferred combination depends on the decision-making rules employed. But regardless of how decisions are made, each economy must answer three fundamental questions.

2-4a Three Questions Every Economic System Must Answer

What goods and services are to be produced? How are they to be produced? And for whom are they to be produced? An **economic system** is the set of mechanisms and institutions that resolve the *what, how,* and *for whom* questions. Some criteria used to distinguish among economic systems are (1) who owns the resources, (2) what decision-making process is used to allocate resources and products, and (3) what types of incentives guide economic decision makers.

What Goods and Services Are to Be Produced?

Most of us take for granted the incredible number of choices that go into deciding what gets produced—everything from which new kitchen appliances are introduced and which roads get built, to which of the 10,000 movie scripts purchased by U.S. studios each year get to be among the 650 or so movies made. Although different economies resolve these and millions of other questions using different decision-making rules and mechanisms, all economies must somehow make such choices.

economic system The set of mechanisms and institutions that resolve the what, how, and for whom questions

3. Igal Hendel and Yossi Spiegel, "Small Steps for Workers, a Giant Leap for Productivity." *American Economic Journal: Applied Economics,* 6 February 2014: 73–90.

4. Betsey Stevenson and Justin Wolfers, "Trust in Public Institutions Over the Business Cycle," *American Economic Review,* 101 (May 2011): 281–287.

How Are Goods and Services to Be Produced?

The economic system must determine how output gets produced. Which resources should be used, and how should they be combined to make stuff? How much labor should be used and at what skill levels? What kinds of machines should be used? What new technology should be incorporated into the latest video games? Should the office complex be built in the city or closer to the interstate highway? Millions of individual decisions determine which resources are employed and how these resources are combined.

For Whom Are Goods and Services to Be Produced?

Who will actually consume the goods and services produced? The economic system must determine how to allocate the fruits of production among the population. Should everyone receive equal shares? Should the weak and the sick get more? Should it be "first come, first served," so that those willing to wait in line get more? Should goods be allocated according to height? Weight? Religion? Age? Gender? Race? Looks? Strength? Political connections? Lottery? Majority rule? The value of resources supplied? The question "For whom are goods and services to be produced?" is often referred to as the *distribution question*.

Although the three economic questions were discussed separately, they are closely related. The answer to one depends on the answers to the others. For example, an economy that distributes goods and services uniformly to everyone will, no doubt, answer the what-will-be-produced question differently than an economy that somehow allows more personal choice. As we have seen, laws about resource ownership and the role of government determine the "rules of the game"—the set of conditions that shape individual incentives and constraints. Along a spectrum ranging from the freest to the most regimented types of economic systems, *pure capitalism* would be at one end and the *pure command system* at the other.

2-4b Pure Capitalism

Under **pure capitalism**, there is no government. The rules of the game include the private ownership of resources and the market distribution of products. Owners have *property rights* to the use of their resources and are therefore free to supply those resources to the highest bidder. **Private property rights** allow individual owners to use resources or to charge others for their use. Any income from supplying labor, capital, natural resources, or entrepreneurial ability goes to the individual resource owners. Producers are free to make and sell whatever they think will be profitable. Consumers are free to buy whatever goods they can afford. All this voluntary buying and selling is coordinated by unrestricted markets, where buyers and sellers make their intentions known. Market prices guide resources to their most productive use and channel goods and services to the consumers who value them the most.

Under pure capitalism, markets answer the what, how, and for whom questions. That's why capitalism is also referred to as a *market system*. Markets transmit information about relative scarcity, provide individual incentives, and distribute income among resource suppliers. No individual or small group coordinates these activities. Rather, it is the voluntary choices of many buyers and sellers responding only to their individual incentives and constraints that direct resources and products to those who value them the most.

According to Adam Smith, market forces allocate resources as if by an "invisible hand"—an unseen force that harnesses the pursuit of self-interest to direct resources where they earn the greatest reward. According to Smith, *although each individual pursues his or her self-interest, the "invisible hand" of market forces promotes the general welfare*. Capitalism is sometimes called *laissez-faire;* translated from the French, this phrase means "to let do," or to let people do as they choose without government intervention. Thus, under capitalism, voluntary choices based on rational self-interest are made in unrestricted markets to answer the questions what, how, and for whom.

As we will see in later chapters, pure capitalism has its flaws. The most notable market failures are these:

1. No central authority protects property rights, enforces contracts, and otherwise ensures that the rules of the game are followed.

2. People with no resources to sell could starve.

3. Some producers may try to monopolize markets by eliminating the competition.

4. The production or consumption of some goods involves side effects that can harm or benefit people not involved in the market transaction.

5. Firms have no incentive to produce so-called

pure capitalism An economic system characterized by the private ownership of resources and the use of prices to coordinate economic activity in unregulated markets

private property rights An owner's right to use, rent, or sell resources or property *public goods*, such as national defense, because private firms cannot prevent nonpayers from enjoying the benefits of public goods.

6. Market economies experience *economic fluctuations*, which are alternating periods of expansions and recessions in their level of economic activity, especially in employment and production.

Because of these limitations, countries have modified pure capitalism to allow some role for government. Even Adam Smith believed government should play a role. The United States is among the most market-oriented economies in the world today.

2-4c Pure Command System

In a **pure command system**, resources are directed and production is coordinated not by market forces but by the "command," or central plan, of government. In theory at least, instead of private property, there is public, or *communal*, ownership of property. That's why central planning is sometimes called *communism*. Government planners, as representatives of all the people, answer the three questions through *central plans* spelling out how much steel, how many cars, and how much housing to produce. They also decide how to produce these goods and who gets them.

In theory, the pure command system incorporates individual choices into collective choices, which, in turn, are reflected in the central plans. Command economies often have names that focus on collective choice, such as the People's Republic of China and the Democratic People's Republic of Korea (North Korea). In practice, the pure command system also has flaws, most notably the following:

1. Running an economy is so complicated and requires so much information that some resources are used inefficiently.

2. Because nobody in particular owns resources, each person has less incentive to employ them in their highest-valued use, so some resources are wasted.

3. Central plans may be more reflective of the preferences of central planners, who in many cases are unelected dictators, than the preferences of society.

4. Because government is responsible for all production, the variety of products tends to be more limited than in a capitalist economy.

5. Each individual has less personal freedom in making economic choices.

6. Because profit has no place in a command economy, people have less incentive to invent new and better products or find more efficient ways to make existing products.

Because of these limitations, countries have modified the pure command system to allow a role for markets. North Korea, a country run for decades by three generations of dictators, is perhaps the most centrally planned economy in the world today.

2-4d Mixed and Transitional Economies

No country on earth exemplifies either type of economic system in its pure form. Economic systems have grown more alike over time, with the role of government increasing in capitalist economies and the role of markets increasing in command economies. The United States represents a **mixed system**, with government directly accounting for a little more than one-third of all economic activity. What's more, governments at all levels in the United States regulate the private sector in a variety of ways. For example, local zoning boards determine lot sizes, home sizes, and the types of industries allowed. Federal bodies regulate workplace safety, environmental quality, competitive fairness, food and drug quality, and many other activities.

pure command system
An economic system characterized by the public ownership of resources and centralized planning

mixed system An economic system characterized by the private ownership of some resources and the public ownership of other resources; some markets are regulated by government

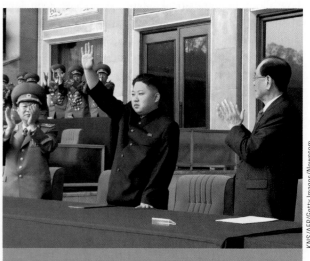

North Korea is as close as there is to a pure command system.

KNS/AFP/Getty Images/Newscom

Although both ends of the spectrum have moved toward the center, capitalism has gained the most converts in recent decades. Perhaps the benefits of markets are no better illustrated than where a country, as a result of war or political upheaval, became divided by ideology into a capitalist economy and a command economy, such as with Taiwan and China or South Korea and North Korea. In each case, the economies began with similar human and physical resources, but once they went their separate ways, economic growth diverged sharply, with the capitalist economies outperforming the command economies. For example, Taiwan's production per capita in 2015 was four times that of China's, and South Korea's production per capita was 18 times that of North Korea.

Consider the experience of the pilgrims in 1620 while establishing Plymouth Colony. They first tried communal ownership of the land. That turned out badly. Crops were neglected and food shortages developed. After three years of near starvation, the system was changed so that each family was assigned a plot of land and granted the fruits of that plot. Yields increased sharply. The pilgrims learned that people take better care of what they own individually; by contrast, common ownership often leads to common neglect.

Recognizing the incentive power of property rights and markets, some of the most die-hard central planners are now allowing a role for markets. For example, about one-fifth of the world's population lives in China, which grows more market oriented each day, even going so far as to give private property constitutional protection on a par with state property. In a poll of Chinese citizens, 74 percent agreed that "the free enterprise system is the best system on which to base the future of the world." Among Americans polled, 71 percent agreed with that statement.[5] A quarter-century ago, the former Soviet Union dissolved into 15 independent republics; most converted state-owned enterprises into private firms. From Moscow to Beijing, from Hungary to Mongolia, the transition to mixed economies now underway in former command economies will shape the world for decades to come.

Note that nations with freer markets tend to rely more on democratic political systems. Recent research finds that democracy increases economic growth by encouraging investment, increasing schooling, promoting economic reforms, and reducing social unrest.[6]

2-4e Economies Based on Custom or Religion

Finally, some economic systems are molded largely by custom or religion. For example, caste systems in India and elsewhere restrict occupational choices. Charging interest is banned under Islamic law. Family relations also play significant roles in organizing and coordinating economic activity. In some countries, businesses are reluctant to hire anyone outside the family because outsiders are less trusted. This limits business growth. Even in the United States, some occupations are still dominated by women, and others by men, largely because of tradition. Your own pattern of consumption and choice of occupation may be influenced by some of these considerations.

2-5 FINAL WORD

Although economies can answer the three economic questions in a variety of ways, this book focuses primarily on the mixed market system, such as exists in the United States. This type of economy blends *private choices*, guided by the price system in competitive markets, with *public choices*, guided by democracy in political markets. The study of mixed market systems grows more relevant as former command economies try to develop markets. The next chapter focuses on the economic actors in a mixed economy and explains why and how government gets into the act.

STUDY TOOLS 2

READY TO STUDY? IN THE BOOK, YOU CAN:

☐ Work the Problems at the end of the chapter.

☐ Rip out the chapter review card for a handy summary of the chapter and key terms.

ONLINE AT CENGAGEBRAIN.COM YOU CAN:

☐ Collect StudyBits while you read and study the chapter.

☐ Quiz yourself on key concepts.

☐ Prepare for tests with chapter flash cards as well as flash cards that you create.

☐ Watch videos to explore economics further.

5. As reported in "Capitalism, Comrade," *Wall Street Journal*, 18 January 2006.

6. Daron Acemoglu, et al., "Democracy Does Cause Growth," American Economic Association annual meetings, 3 January 2015.

CHAPTER 2 PROBLEMS

Your instructor can access the answers to these problems online at http://cengagebrain.com.

2-1 Describe the relationship between choice and opportunity cost

1. *(Sunk Cost and Choice)* Suppose you go to a restaurant and buy an expensive meal. Halfway through, despite feeling quite full, you decide to clean your plate. After all, you think, you paid for the meal, so you are going to eat all of it. What's wrong with this thinking?

2. *(Opportunity Cost)* You can spend spring break either working at home for $80 per day for five days or go to Florida for the week. If you stay home, your expenses will total about $100. If you go to Florida, the airfare, hotel, food, and miscellaneous expenses will total about $700. What's your opportunity cost of going to Florida?

2-2 Explain how comparative advantage, specialization, and exchange affect economic outcomes (output)

3. *(Absolute and Comparative Advantage)* You have the following information concerning the production of wheat and cloth in the United States and the United Kingdom:

Labor Hours Required to Produce One Unit

	The United Kingdom	The United States
Wheat	2	1
Cloth	6	5

   a. What is the opportunity cost of producing a unit of wheat in the United Kingdom? In the United States?
   b. Which country has an absolute advantage in producing wheat? In producing cloth?
   c. Which country has a comparative advantage in producing wheat? In producing cloth?
   d. Which country should specialize in producing wheat? In producing cloth?

4. *(Specialization)* Provide some examples of specialized markets or retail outlets. What makes the Web so conducive to specialization?

2-3 Outline how economies function as production systems

5. *(Shape of the PPF)* Suppose a production possibilities frontier includes the following combinations:

Cars	Washing Machines
0	1,000
100	600
200	0

   a. Graph the PPF, assuming that it has no curved segments.
   b. What is the cost of producing an additional car when 50 cars are being produced?

   c. What is the cost of producing an additional car when 150 cars are being produced?
   d. What is the cost of producing an additional washing machine when 50 cars are being produced? When 150 cars are being produced?
   e. What do your answers tell you about opportunity costs?

6. *(Production Possibilities)* Suppose an economy uses two resources (labor and capital) to produce two goods (wheat and cloth). Capital is relatively more useful in producing cloth, and labor is relatively more useful in producing wheat. If the supply of capital falls by 10 percent and the supply of labor increases by 10 percent, how will the PPF for wheat and cloth change?

7. *(Production Possibilities)* There's no reason why a production possibilities frontier could not be used to represent the situation facing an individual. Imagine your own PPF. Right now—today—you have certain resources—your time, your skills, perhaps some capital. And you can produce various outputs. Suppose you can produce combinations of two outputs, call them studying and partying.
   a. Draw your PPF for studying and partying. Be sure to label the axes of the diagram appropriately. Label the points where the PPF intersects the axes, as well as several other points along the frontier.
   b. Explain what it would mean for you to move upward and to the left along your personal PPF. What kinds of adjustments would you have to make in your life to make such a movement along the frontier?
   c. Under what circumstances would your personal PPF shift outward? Do you think the shift would be a "parallel" one? Why, or why not?

8. *(Shifting Production Possibilities)* Determine whether each of the following would cause the national economy's PPF to shift inward, outward, or not at all:
   a. An increase in average length of annual vacations
   b. An increase in immigration
   c. A decrease in the average retirement age
   d. The migration of skilled workers to other countries

2-4 Describe different economic systems and the decision-making rules that define them

9. *(Economic Systems)* The United States is best described as having a mixed economy. What are some elements of command in the U.S. economy? What are some market elements? What are some traditional elements?

MICRO
ECON
ONLINE

STUDY YOUR WAY
WITH STUDYBITS!

Collect What's Important

WEAK

FAIR

STRONG

UNASSIGNED

Rate and Organize StudyBits

Create Flashcards From Your StudyBits

85%

Track/Monitor Your Progress

CORRECT

INCORRECT

INCORRECT

INCORRECT

Personalize Your Quizzes

4LTR PRESS

3 | Economic Decision Makers

iStockphoto.com/RamonaHumus.com

LEARNING OUTCOMES

After studying this chapter, you will be able to...

3-1 Describe the major sources of income and expenditures for households

3-2 Outline the evolution of production over the centuries from the household to the modern corporation

3-3 Summarize the seven roles of government in an economy

3-4 Explain why countries trade with each other and why they sometimes act to restrict that trade

After finishing this chapter go to **PAGE 54** for **STUDY TOOLS**

Topics discussed in Chapter 3 include

- Evolution of the household
- Evolution of the firm
- Types of firms
- Role of government
- Taxing and public spending
- International trade and finance

- If we live in the age of specialization, then why haven't specialists taken over all production?

- For example, why do most of us still do our own laundry and perform dozens of other tasks for ourselves?

- If the "invisible hand" of competitive markets is so efficient, why does government get into the act?

- And if specialization based on comparative advantage if such a good idea, why do most nations try to restrict imports?

Answers to these and other questions are addressed in this chapter, which discusses the four economic decision makers: households, firms, governments, and the rest of the world.

To develop a better feel for how the economy works, you must become more acquainted with the key players. You already know more about them than you may realize. You grew up in a household. You have dealt with firms all your life, from Sony to Subway. You know much about governments, from taxes to public schools. And you have a growing awareness of the rest of the world, from online sites, to imported goods, to foreign travel. This chapter draws on your abundant personal experience with economic decision makers to consider their makeup and objectives.

> **"If we live in the age of specialization, then why haven't specialists taken over all production?"**

3-1 THE HOUSEHOLD

Households play the starring role in a market economy. Their demand for goods and services determines what gets produced. And their supply of labor, capital, natural resources, and entrepreneurial ability produces that output. As demanders of goods and services and suppliers of resources, households make all kinds of choices, such as what to buy, how much to save, where to live, and where to work. Although a household usually consists of several individuals, we will view each household as a single decision maker.

3-1a The Evolution of the Household

In earlier times, when the economy was primarily agricultural, a farm household was largely self-sufficient. Each family member often specialized in a specific farm task—cooking meals, making clothes, tending livestock, planting crops, mending fences, and so on. These early households produced what they consumed and consumed what they produced. With the introduction of new seed varieties, better fertilizers, and labor-saving machinery, farm productivity increased sharply.

Fewer farmers were needed to grow enough food to feed a nation. At the same time, the growth of urban factories increased the demand for factory labor. As a result, many workers moved from farms to urban factories, where they became more specialized but less self-sufficient.

Households evolved in other ways. For example, in 1950, only about 15 percent of married women with young children were in the labor force. Since then,

Seventy percent of women with children under 18 are in the labor force.

higher levels of education among women and a growing demand for their labor have increased women's earnings, thus raising their opportunity cost of working in the home. This higher opportunity cost contributed to their growing labor force participation. Today, about 70 percent of women with children under 18 are in the labor force.

The rise of two-earner households has reduced specialization in household production—a central feature of the farm family. Households now produce less for themselves and demand more from the market. For example, child-care services and fast-food restaurants have displaced some household production (Americans now consume at least one-third of their calories away from home). Nonetheless, some production still occurs in the home, as we'll explore later.

3-1b Households Maximize Utility

There are about 120 million U.S. households. All those who live together under one roof are considered part of the same household. What exactly do households attempt to accomplish in making decisions? Economists assume that people try to maximize their

utility The satisfaction received from consumption; sense of well-being

level of satisfaction, sense of well-being, happiness, and overall welfare. In short, households attempt to maximize **utility**. Households, like other economic decision makers, are viewed as rational, meaning that they try to act in their best interests and do not deliberately try to make themselves less happy. Utility maximization depends on each household's subjective goals, not on some objective standard. For example, some households maintain neat homes with well-groomed lawns; others pay little attention to their homes and use their lawns as junkyards.

3-1c Households As Resource Suppliers

Households use their limited resources—labor, capital, natural resources, and entrepreneurial ability—in an attempt to satisfy their unlimited wants. They can use these resources to produce goods and services in their homes. For example, they can cook, wash, sew, dust, iron, sweep, vacuum, mop, mow, paint, and fix a leaky faucet. They can also sell these resources in the resource market and use the income to buy goods and services in product markets. The most valuable resource sold by most households is labor.

Panel (a) of Exhibit 1 shows the sources of personal income received by U.S. households in 2014, when personal income totaled $14.9 trillion. As you can

Exhibit 1

Where U.S. Personal Income Comes From and Where It Goes

(a) More than two-thirds of personal income in 2014 was labor income

(b) More than half of U.S. personal income in 2014 was spent on services

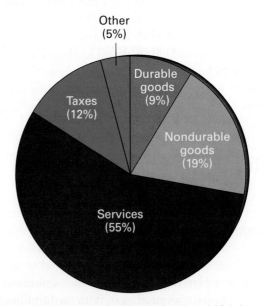

Source: Based on figures from *Survey of Current Business*, Bureau of Economic Analysis, February 2015, Tables 1.5.5 and 2.1. For the latest figures, go to http://www.bea.gov/scb/index.htm.

see, 62 percent of personal income came from wages and salaries. A distant second was transfer payments (to be discussed shortly), at 10 percent of personal income, followed by proprietors' income at 9 percent. *Proprietors* are people who work for themselves rather than for employers; farmers, plumbers, and doctors are often self-employed. Proprietors' income should also be considered a form of labor income. *Thus, more than two-thirds of personal income in the United States comes from labor earnings rather than from the ownership of other resources such as capital or natural resources.*

Because of a limited education, disability, discrimination, poor health, caring for small children, limited job opportunities, or just bad luck, some households have few resources that are valued in the market. Society has made the political decision that individuals in such circumstances should receive short-term public assistance. Consequently, the government gives some households **transfer payments**. *Cash transfers* are monetary payments, such as welfare benefits, Social Security, unemployment compensation, and disability benefits. *In-kind transfers* provide for specific goods and services, such as food, health care, and housing.

3-1d Households As Demanders of Goods and Services

What happens to personal income once it comes into the household? Most goes to personal consumption, which sorts into three broad spending categories: (1) *durable goods*—that is, goods expected to last three or more years—such as an automobile or a refrigerator; (2) *nondurable goods*, such as food, clothing, and gasoline; and (3) *services*, such as haircuts, air travel, and medical care. As you can see from panel (b) of Exhibit 1, spending on durable goods in 2014 claimed 9 percent of U.S. personal income; nondurables, 19 percent; and services, 55 percent. Taxes claimed 12 percent, and all other categories, including saving, claimed just 5 percent. So more than half of all personal income went for services—the fastest growing sector because many services, such as child care, are shifting from do-it-yourself home production to market purchases.

3-2 THE FIRM

Household members once built their own homes, made their own clothes and furniture, grew their own food, and amused themselves with books, games, and hobbies. Over time, however, the efficiency arising from comparative

Specialization and comparative advantage explain why households are no longer self-sufficient.

© Val Thoermer/Shutterstock.com

advantage resulted in a greater specialization among resource suppliers. This section takes a look at firms, beginning with their evolution.

3-2a The Evolution of the Firm

Specialization and comparative advantage explain why households are no longer self-sufficient. But why is a firm the natural result? For example, rather than make a woolen sweater from scratch, couldn't a consumer take advantage of specialization by negotiating with someone who produced the wool, another who spun the wool into yarn, and a third who knit the yarn into a sweater? Here's the problem with that model: If the consumer had to visit each of these specialists and reach an agreement, the resulting *transaction costs* could easily erase the gains from specialization. Instead of visiting and bargaining with each specialist, the consumer can pay someone to do the bargaining—an entrepreneur, who hires all the resources necessary to make the sweater. *An entrepreneur, by contracting for many sweaters rather than just one, is able to reduce the transaction costs per sweater.*

transfer payments
Cash or in-kind benefits given to individuals by the government

For about 200 years, profit-seeking entrepreneurs relied on "putting out" raw material, like wool and cotton, to rural households that turned this into finished products, like woolen goods made from yarn. The system developed in the British Isles, where workers' cottages served as tiny factories, especially during winter months, when farming chores were few (so the opportunity cost was low). This approach, which came to be known as the *cottage industry system*, still exists in some parts of the world today. You might think of this system as partway between household self-sufficiency and the modern firm.

As the British economy expanded in the 18th century, entrepreneurs began organizing the stages of production under one factory roof. Technological developments, such as waterpower and later steam power, increased the productivity of each worker and helped shift employment from rural areas to urban factories. *Work, therefore, became organized in large, centrally powered factories that (1) promoted a more efficient division of labor, (2) allowed for the direct supervision of production, (3) reduced transportation costs, and (4) facilitated the use of machines far bigger than anything used in the home.* The development of large-scale factory production, known as the **Industrial Revolution**, began in Great Britain around 1750 and spread to the rest of Europe, North America, and Australia.

Production, then, evolved from self-sufficient rural households to the cottage industry system, where specialized production occurred in the household, to production in a firm. Today, entrepreneurs combine resources in firms such as factories, mills, offices, stores, and restaurants. **Firms** are economic units formed by profit-seeking entrepreneurs who combine labor, capital, and natural resources to produce goods and services. Just as we assume that households try to maximize utility, we assume that firms try to *maximize profit*. Profit, the entrepreneur's reward, equals sales revenue minus the cost of production, including the opportunity cost of the entrepreneur's time. Thus,

$$\text{Profit} = \text{Revenue} - \text{Cost}$$

Industrial Revolution Development of large-scale factory production that began in Great Britain around 1750 and spread to the rest of Europe, North America, and Australia

firms Economic units formed by profit-seeking entrepreneurs who employ resources to produce goods and services for sale

sole proprietorship A firm with a single owner who has the right to all profits but who also bears unlimited liability for the firm's losses and debts

partnership A firm with multiple owners who share the profits and bear unlimited liability for the firm's losses and debts

3-2b Types of Firms

There are more than 30 million for-profit businesses in the United States. Two-thirds are small retail businesses, small service operations, part-time home-based businesses, and small farms. Each year more than a million new businesses start up and many existing firms fail. A firm is organized in one of three ways: as a sole proprietorship, as a partnership, or as a corporation.

Sole Proprietorships

The simplest form of business organization is the **sole proprietorship**, a single-owner firm. Examples include self-employed plumbers, farmers, and dentists. Most sole proprietorships consist of just the self-employed proprietor—there are no hired employees. To organize a sole proprietorship, the owner simply opens for business by, for example, making a public announcement or taking out a classified ad announcing availability for plumbing services or whatever. The owner is in complete control. But he or she faces unlimited liability and could lose everything, including a home and other personal assets, to settle business debts or other claims against the business. Also, because the sole proprietor has no partners or other investors, raising enough money to get the business up and running and keep it going can be a challenge. One final disadvantage is that a sole proprietorship usually goes out of business when the proprietor dies or leaves the business. Still, a sole proprietorship is the most common type of business, accounting most recently for 71 percent of all U.S. businesses. Nonetheless, because this type of firm is typically small, proprietorships generate just a tiny portion of all U.S. business sales—only 4 percent. But keep in mind that many of the largest businesses in the world today began as an idea of a sole proprietor.

Partnerships

A more complicated form of business is the **partnership**, which involves two or more individuals who agree to combine their funds and efforts in return for a share of any profit or loss. Law, accounting, and medical partnerships typify this business form. Partners have strength in numbers and often find it easier than sole proprietors to raise enough funds to get the business going. But partners may not always agree on what's best for the business. Also, each partner usually faces unlimited liability for any debts or claims against the partnership, so one partner could lose everything because of another partner's mistake. Finally, the death or departure of one partner can disrupt the firm's continuity and require a complete reorganization. The partnership is the least common form of U.S. business, making up only 10 percent of all firms and 15 percent of all business sales.

Corporations

By far the most influential form of business is the corporation. A **corporation** is a legal entity established through articles of incorporation. Shares of stock confer corporate ownership, thereby entitling stockholders to a claim on any profit. A major advantage of the corporate form is that many investors—hundreds, thousands, even millions—can pool their funds, so incorporating represents the easiest way to amass large sums to get a business off the ground. Also, stockholders' liability for any loss is limited to the value of their stock, meaning stockholders enjoy *limited liability*. A final advantage of this form of organization is that the corporation has a life apart from its owners. The corporation survives even if ownership changes hands, and it can be taxed, sued, and even charged with a crime as if it were a person.

The corporate form has some disadvantages as well. A stockholder's ability to influence corporate policy is limited to voting for a board of directors, which oversees the operation of the firm. Each share of stock usually carries with it one vote. The typical stockholder of a large corporation owns only a tiny fraction of the shares and thus has little say. Whereas the income from sole proprietorships and partnerships is taxed only once, corporate income

gets whacked twice—first as corporate profits and second as stockholder income, either as corporate dividends or as realized capital gains. A *realized capital gain* is any increase in the market price of a share that occurs between the time the share is purchased and the time it is sold.

A hybrid type of corporation has evolved to take advantage of the limited liability feature of the corporate structure while reducing the impact of double taxation. The *S corporation* provides owners with limited liability, but profits are taxed only once—as income on each shareholder's personal income tax return. To qualify as an S corporation, a firm must have no more than 100 stockholders and no foreign stockholders.

Corporations make up only 19 percent of all U.S. businesses, but because they tend to be much larger than the other two business forms, corporations account for 81 percent of all business sales. Exhibit 2 shows, by business type, the percentage of U.S. firms and the percentage of U.S. sales. *The sole proprietorship is the most important in sheer numbers, but the corporation is the most important in total sales.*

3-2c Cooperatives

A **cooperative**, or "co-op" for short, is a group of people who cooperate by pooling

> **corporation** A legal entity owned by stockholders whose liability is limited to the value of their stock ownership
>
> **cooperative** An organization consisting of people who pool their resources to buy and sell more efficiently than they could individually

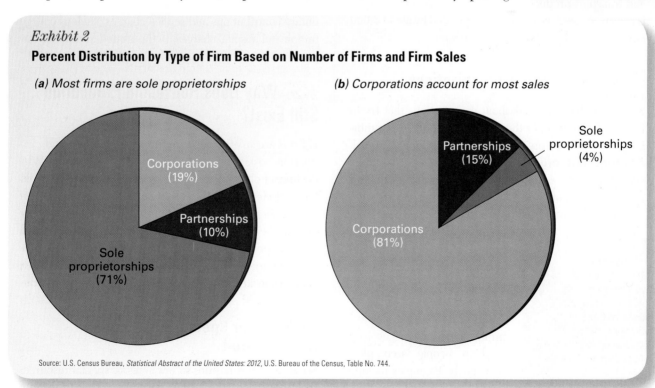

Exhibit 2

Percent Distribution by Type of Firm Based on Number of Firms and Firm Sales

(a) *Most firms are sole proprietorships*

Corporations (19%)
Partnerships (10%)
Sole proprietorships (71%)

(b) *Corporations account for most sales*

Partnerships (15%)
Sole proprietorships (4%)
Corporations (81%)

Source: U.S. Census Bureau, *Statistical Abstract of the United States: 2012*, U.S. Bureau of the Census, Table No. 744.

their resources to buy and sell more efficiently than they could independently. Cooperatives try to minimize costs and operate with limited liability of members. The government grants most cooperatives tax-exempt status. There are two types: consumer cooperatives and producer cooperatives.

Consumer Cooperatives

A *consumer cooperative* is a retail business owned and operated by some or all of its customers in order to reduce costs. Some cooperatives require members to pay an annual fee and others require them to work a certain number of hours each year in the business. Members sometimes pay lower prices than other customers or may share in any revenues that exceed costs. In the United States, consumer cooperatives operate college book stores, credit unions, electric-power facilities, health plans, apartment buildings, and grocery stores.

Producer Cooperatives

In a *producer cooperative*, producers join forces to buy supplies and equipment and to market their output. Each producer's objective is to reduce costs and increase profits. Federal legislation allows farmers to cooperate without violating antitrust laws (to be discussed later in the chapter). Firms in other industries could not do this legally. Farmers pool their funds to purchase machinery and supplies, provide storage and processing facilities, and transport products to market. Sunkist, for example, is a farm cooperative owned and operated by about 6,000 citrus growers in California and Arizona.

3-2d Not-for-Profit Organizations

So far, you have learned about organizations that try to maximize profits or, in the case of cooperatives, to minimize costs. Some organizations have neither as a goal. **Not-for-profit organizations** engage in charitable, educational, humanitarian, cultural, professional, and other activities, often with a social purpose. Any revenue exceeding cost is plowed back into the organization. Government agencies do not have profit as a goal either, but governments are not included in this definition of not-for-profit organizations.

Like businesses, not-for-profit organizations evolved to help people accomplish their goals. Examples include nonprofit hospitals, private

not-for-profit organizations Groups that do not pursue profit as a goal; they engage in charitable, educational, humanitarian, cultural, professional, or other activities, often with a social purpose

Alex Segre/Alamy

Seafood Producers Cooperative (SPC) is a cooperative of over 500 fishermen who harvest their catch in the open ocean at the peak of quality.

schools and colleges, religious organizations, the Red Cross, Greenpeace, charitable foundations, soup kitchens, orchestras, museums, labor unions, and professional organizations. There are about 1.6 million not-for-profit organizations in the United States, and they employ about 12 million workers, or about 8 percent of the U.S. workforce. Not-for-profit hospitals are the largest employers. For example, the Texas Medical Center employs more than 100,000 people, surpassing employment at major corporations such as Apple, Chevron, or Google. But even not-for-profit organizations must somehow pay the bills. Revenue typically includes some combination of voluntary contributions and service charges, such as college tuition and hospital charges. In the United States, not-for-profit organizations are usually exempt from taxes.

3-2e Why Does Household Production Still Exist?

If firms are so efficient at reducing transaction and production costs, why don't they make everything? Why do households still perform some tasks, such as cooking and cleaning? *If a household's opportunity cost of performing a task is below the market price, then the household usually performs that task.* People with a lower opportunity cost of time do more for themselves. For example, janitors are more likely to mow their lawns than are physicians. Let's look at some reasons for household production.

No Skills or Special Resources Are Required

Some activities require so few skills or special resources that householders find it cheaper to do the jobs themselves. Sweeping the kitchen floor requires only a broom and some time, so it's usually performed by household members. Sanding a wooden floor, however, involves special machinery and expertise, so households hire professionals. Similarly, although you wouldn't hire someone to brush your teeth, dental work is not for amateurs. *Households usually perform domestic chores that demand neither expertise nor special machinery.*

Household Production Avoids Taxes

Suppose you are deciding whether to pay someone $3,000 to paint your house or do it yourself. If the income tax rate is one-third, you must earn $4,500 before taxes to have the $3,000 after taxes to pay for the job. And the painter who charges you $3,000 nets only $2,000 after paying $1,000 in taxes. Thus, you must earn $4,500 so that the painter can take home $2,000. If you paint the house yourself, no taxes are involved. The tax-free nature of do-it-yourself activity favors household production over market transactions.

> **"Although you wouldn't hire someone to brush your teeth, dental work is not for amateurs."**

Household Production Reduces Transaction Costs

Getting estimates, hiring a contractor, negotiating terms, and monitoring job performance all take time and require information. Doing the job yourself reduces these transaction costs. Household production also allows for more personal control over the final product than is usually available through the market. For example, some people prefer home cooking because they can prepare home-cooked meals to individual tastes.

Household production often grows during hard times. The economic recession of 2007–2009 prompted some families to shift from market purchases to household production to save money. For example, sales of hair clippers used for home haircuts increased 10 percent in 2008 and 11 percent in 2009.[1]

Technological Advances Increase Household Productivity

Technological breakthroughs are not confined to market production. Vacuum cleaners, washers and dryers, dishwashers, microwave ovens, and other modern appliances reduce the time and often the skill required to perform household tasks. Also, new technologies such as DVRs, HDTVs, broadband downloads, and computer games enhance home entertainment. The **Information Revolution**

Information Revolution
Technological change spawned by the microchip and the Internet that enhanced the acquisition, analysis, and transmission of information

Do it yourself, or pay someone to do it for you?

BuildPix/Construction Photography/Alamy

More advanced technology, such as this robotic lawnmower, can make households more productive.

Macrocosmos/Alamy

1. Mary Pilon, "Per Capita Saving: Home Barbering Grows in Recession," *Wall Street Journal*, 31 August 2009.

spawned by the microchip and the Internet has also enhanced the acquisition, analysis, and transmission of information. Indeed, microchip-based technologies have shifted some production from the firm back to the household. Because of technological change, more people can work from their homes.

3-3 THE GOVERNMENT

You might think that production by households and firms could satisfy all consumer wants. Why must yet another economic decision maker get into the act? After all, governments play some role in every nation on earth.

3-3a The Role of Government

Sometimes the unrestrained operation of markets yields undesirable results. Too many of some goods and too few of other goods get produced. This section discusses the sources of **market failure** and how society's overall welfare may be improved through government intervention in the market.

market failure A condition that arises when the unregulated operation of markets yields socially undesirable results

antitrust laws Prohibitions against price fixing and other anticompetitive practices

monopoly A sole supplier of a product with no close substitutes

natural monopoly One firm that can supply the entire market at a lower per-unit cost than could two or more firms

private good A good, such as pizza, that is both rival in consumption and exclusive

public good A good that, once produced, is available for all to consume, regardless of who pays and who doesn't; such a good is nonrival and nonexclusive, such as a safer community

Establishing and Enforcing the Rules of the Game

Market efficiency depends on people like you using your resources to maximize your utility. But what if you were repeatedly robbed of your paycheck on your way home from work? Or what if, after you worked two weeks in a new job, your boss called you a sucker and said you wouldn't get paid? Why bother working? The market system would break down if you could not safeguard your private property or if you could not enforce contracts. Governments safeguard private property through police protection and enforce contracts through a judicial system. More generally, governments try to make sure that market participants abide by the rules of the game —

that is, play fair. These rules are established through government laws and regulations and also through the customs and conventions of the marketplace. For example, the U.S. Bureau of Weights and Measures regulates the uniformity of measuring devices to promote confidence in market transactions and to ensure fairness between buyers and sellers in the marketplace.

Promoting Competition

Although the "invisible hand" of competition usually promotes an efficient allocation of resources, some firms try to avoid competition through *collusion*, which is an agreement among firms to fix the price and carve up the market. Or an individual firm may try to eliminate the competition by using unfair business practices. For example, to drive out local competitors, a large firm may temporarily sell at a price below cost. Government **antitrust laws** try to promote competition by prohibiting collusion and other anticompetitive practices.

Regulating Natural Monopolies

Competition usually keeps the product price below the price charged by a **monopoly**, a sole supplier to the market. In rare instances, however, a monopoly can produce and sell the product for less than could competing firms. For example, electricity is delivered more efficiently by a single firm that wires the community than by competing firms each stringing its own wires. When it is cheaper for one firm to serve the market than for two or more firms to do so, that one firm is called a **natural monopoly**. Since a natural monopoly faces no competition, it maximizes profit by charging a higher price than would be optimal from society's point of view. A lower price and greater output would improve social welfare. Therefore, the government usually regulates a natural monopoly, forcing it to lower its price and increase output.

Providing Public Goods

So far this book has been talking about private goods, which have two important features. First, private goods are *rival* in consumption, meaning that the amount consumed by one person is unavailable for others to consume. For example, when you and some friends share a pizza, each slice they eat is no longer available for you. Second, the supplier of a private good can easily exclude those who fail to pay. Only paying customers get pizza. Thus, private goods are said to be *exclusive*. So **private goods**, such as pizza, are both rival in consumption and exclusive. In contrast, **public goods** are *nonrival* in consumption. For example, your family's benefit from a safer neighborhood does not reduce your neighbor's benefit. What's more, once produced, public goods are available to all. Suppliers cannot easily prevent consumption by those who fail to pay. For example, reducing terrorism is *nonexclusive*. It benefits all in the community, regardless of who pays to reduce terrorism and who doesn't. Because public goods are *nonrival* and *nonexclusive*, private firms cannot sell them profitably. The government, however, has the authority to enforce tax collections for public goods. Thus, the government provides public goods and funds them with taxes.

Dealing With Externalities

Market prices reflect the private costs and private benefits of producers and consumers. But sometimes production or consumption imposes costs or benefits on third parties—on those who are neither suppliers nor demanders in a market transaction. For example, a paper mill fouls the air breathed by nearby residents, but the price of paper usually fails to reflect such costs. Because these pollution costs are outside, or external to, the market, they are called *externalities*. An **externality** is a cost or a benefit that falls on a third party. A negative externality imposes an external cost, such as factory pollution, auto emissions, or traffic congestion. A positive externality confers an external benefit, such as getting a good education, getting inoculated against a disease (thus reducing the possibility of infecting others), or driving carefully. Because market prices usually do not reflect externalities, governments often use taxes, subsidies, and regulations to discourage negative externalities and encourage positive externalities. For example, a polluting factory may face taxes and regulations aimed at curbing that pollution. And because more educated people can read road signs and have options that pay better than crime, governments try to encourage education with free public schools, subsidized higher education, and by keeping people in school until their 16th birthdays.

A More Equal Distribution of Income

As mentioned earlier, some people, because of poor education, mental or physical disabilities, bad luck, or perhaps the need to care for small children, are unable to support themselves and their families. Because resource markets do not guarantee even a minimum level of

> **"The supplier of a private good can easily exclude those who fail to pay."**

income, transfer payments reflect society's willingness to ensure a basic standard of living to all households. Most Americans agree that government should redistribute income to the poor (note the normative nature of this statement). Opinions differ about who should receive benefits, how much they should get, what form benefits should take, and how long benefits should last.

Full Employment, Price Stability, and Economic Growth

Perhaps the most important responsibility of government is fostering a healthy economy, which benefits just about everyone. The government—through its ability to tax, to spend, and to control the money supply—attempts to promote full employment, price stability, and economic growth. Pursuing these objectives by taxing and spending is called **fiscal policy**. Pursuing them by regulating the money supply is called **monetary policy**. Macroeconomics examines both policies.

3-3b Government's Structure and Objectives

The United States has a *federal system* of government, meaning that responsibilities are shared across levels of government. State governments grant some powers to local governments and surrender some powers to the national, or federal, government. As the system has evolved, the federal government has primary responsibility for national security, economic stability, and promoting market competition. State governments fund public higher education, prisons, and—with aid from the federal government—highways and welfare. Local governments provide primary and secondary education with aid from the state, plus police and fire protection. Here are some distinguishing features of government.

externality A cost or a benefit that affects neither the buyer nor seller, but instead affects people not involved in the market transaction

fiscal policy The use of government purchases, transfer payments, taxes, and borrowing to influence economy-wide variables such as inflation, employment, and economic growth

monetary policy Regulation of the money supply to influence economy-wide variables such as inflation, employment, and economic growth

Difficulty in Defining Government Objectives

We assume that households try to maximize utility and firms try to maximize profit, but what about governments—or, more specifically, what about government decision makers? What do they try to maximize? One problem is that our federal system consists of not one but many governments—approximately 89,150 separate jurisdictions in all, including 1 nation, 50 states, 3,000 counties, 36,000 cities and towns, 12,900 school districts, and 37,200 special districts. What's more, because the federal government relies on offsetting, or countervailing, powers across the executive, legislative, and judicial branches, government does not act as a single, consistent decision maker. Even within the federal executive branch, there are so many agencies and bureaus that at times they seem to work at cross-purposes. For example, at the same time as the U.S. Surgeon General required health warnings on cigarette packages, the U.S. Department of Agriculture pursued policies to benefit tobacco growers. Given this thicket of jurisdictions, branches, and bureaus, one useful theory of government behavior is that elected officials try to maximize the number of votes they get in the next election. So let's assume that elected officials are vote maximizers. In this theory, vote maximization guides the decisions of elected officials who, in turn, oversee government employees.

Voluntary Exchange Versus Coercion

Market exchange relies on the voluntary behavior of buyers and sellers. Don't like tofu? No problem—don't buy any. But in political markets, the situation is different. Any voting rule except unanimous consent must involve some government coercion. Public choices are enforced by the police power of the state. Those who don't pay their taxes could go to prison, even though they may object to some programs those taxes support, such as capital punishment or certain military actions.

No Market Prices

Another distinguishing feature of governments is that public output is usually offered at either a zero price or at some price below the cost of providing it. If you now pay in-state tuition at a public college or university, your tuition probably covers only about half the state's cost of providing your education. Because the revenue side of the government budget is usually separate from the expenditure side, there is no necessary link between the cost of a program and the benefit.

In the private sector, the expected marginal benefit of a product is at least as great as its price; otherwise, nobody would buy it.

3-3c The Size and Growth of Government

One way to track the impact of government over time is by measuring government outlays relative to the U.S. *gross domestic product,* or *GDP,* which is the total value of all final goods and services produced in the United States. In 1929, the year the Great Depression began, all government outlays, mostly by state and local governments, totaled about 10 percent of GDP. At the time, the federal government played a minor role. In fact, during the nation's first 150 years, federal outlays, except during war years, never exceeded 3 percent relative to GDP.

The Great Depression, World War II, a change in macroeconomic thinking, and extraordinary measures following the financial crisis of 2008 boosted the share of government outlays to 38 percent of GDP in 2016, with about two-thirds of that by the federal government. In comparison, government outlays relative to GDP that year were 39 percent in Canada and Japan, 41 percent in the United Kingdom, 44 percent in the Germany, 50 percent in Italy, and 56 percent in France. Government outlays by 31 advanced industrial economies averaged 40 percent of GDP in 2016.[2] Thus, government outlays in the United States relative to GDP are slightly below the average of advanced economies.

Let's look briefly at the composition of federal outlays. Since 1960, defense spending has declined from over half of federal outlays to less than one-fifth by 2016, as shown in Exhibit 3. Redistribution—Social Security, Medicare, and welfare programs—has been the mirror image of defense spending, jumping from only about one-fifth of federal outlays in 1960 more than to half by 2016.

3-3d Sources of Government Revenue

Taxes provide the bulk of revenue at all levels of government. The federal government relies primarily on the individual income tax, state governments rely on income and sales taxes, and local governments rely on the property tax. Other revenue sources include user charges, such as highway tolls and college tuition, and borrowing. For additional revenue, some states also act as monopolies in certain markets, such as selling lottery tickets and liquor.

2. The Organization of Economic Cooperation and Development, *OECD Economic Outlook,* 97 (May 2015), Total Disbursements, General Government, as a Percent of GDP, at http://stats.oecd.org/index.aspx?queryid=51396.

Exhibit 3

Redistribution Has Grown and Defense Has Declined as Share of Federal Outlays: 1960–2016

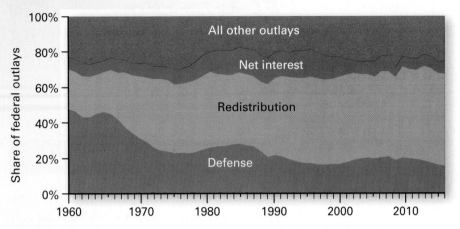

Source: Computed based on figures from the *Economic Report of the President*, February 2015, Table B-80. Figures for 2015 and 2016 are estimates based on the President's budget. For the latest figures, go to http://www.whitehouse.gov/administration/eop/cea/economic-report -of-the-President.

and medical care for the elderly. Corporate taxes and revenue from other sources, such as excise (sales) taxes and user charges, have declined as a share of federal revenue since 1960.

3-3e Tax Principles and Tax Incidence

The structure of a tax is often justified on the basis of one of two general principles. First, a tax could relate to the individual's ability to pay, so those with a greater ability pay more taxes. Income or property taxes often rely on this **ability-to-pay tax principle**. Alternatively, the **benefits-received tax principle** relates taxes to the benefits taxpayers receive from the government activity funded by the tax. For example, the tax on gasoline funds highway construction and maintenance, thereby linking tax payment to road use, since those who drive more pay more gas taxes.

Tax incidence indicates who actually bears the burden of the tax. One way to evaluate tax incidence is by measuring the tax as a percentage of income. Under

Exhibit 4 focuses on the composition of federal revenue since 1960. The share made up by the individual income tax has remained relatively steady, ranging from a low of 42 percent in the mid-1960s to a high of 50 percent in 2001, before averaging about 47 percent from 2011 to 2016. The share from payroll taxes doubled from 16 percent in 1960 to 32 percent in 2016. *Payroll taxes* are deducted from paychecks to support Social Security and Medicare, which fund retirement income

Exhibit 4

Composition of Federal Revenue Between 1960 and 2016

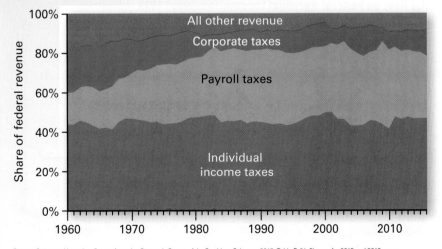

Source: Computed based on figures from the *Economic Report of the President*, February 2015, Table B-21. Figures for 2015 and 2016 are projections based on the President's budget. For the latest figures, go to http://www.whitehouse.gov/administration/eop/cea/economic-report-of -the-President.

ability-to-pay tax principle Those with a greater ability to pay, such as those earning higher incomes or those owning more property, should pay more taxes

benefits-received tax principle Those who get more benefits from the government program should pay more taxes

tax incidence The distribution of tax burden among taxpayers; who ultimately pays the tax

proportional taxation, taxpayers at all income levels pay the same percentage of their income in taxes. A proportional income tax is also called a *flat tax*, since the tax as a percentage of income remains constant, or flat, as income increases. Note that under proportional taxation, although taxes remain constant as a percentage of income, the dollar amount of taxes increases proportionately as income increases.

Under **progressive taxation**, the percentage of income paid in taxes increases as income increases. The **marginal tax rate** indicates the percentage of each additional dollar of income that goes to taxes. Because high marginal rates reduce the after-tax return from working or investing, high marginal rates can reduce people's incentives to work and invest. The seven marginal rates applied to the U.S. personal income tax in 2015 ranged from 10 to 39.6 percent.

The top marginal tax bracket each year during the history of the personal income tax is shown by Exhibit 5. Although the top rate is now lower than it was during most other years, high-income households still pay most of the federal income tax collected. More than 40 percent of U.S. households pay no federal income taxes. According to the U.S. Internal Revenue Service, the top 1 percent of tax filers, based on income, paid 38 percent of all income taxes collected in 2012. Their average tax rate was 23.5 percent. And the top 10 percent of tax filers paid 70 percent of all income taxes collected. Their average tax rate was 18.7 percent. In contrast, the bottom 50 percent of tax filers paid only 2.8 percent of

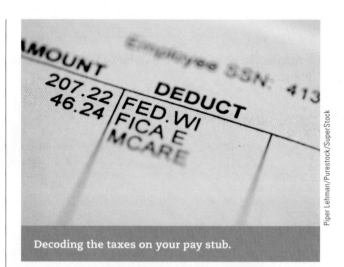

Decoding the taxes on your pay stub.

Piper Lehman/Purestock/SuperStock

all income taxes collected. Their tax rate averaged only 3.0 percent. Whether we look at marginal tax rates or average tax rates, the U.S. income tax is progressive. High-income filers pay the overwhelming share of income taxes.

Finally, under **regressive taxation**, the percentage of income paid in taxes decreases as income increases, so the marginal tax rate declines as income increases. Most U.S. *payroll taxes* are regressive, because they impose a flat rate up to a certain level of income, above which the marginal rate drops to zero. For example, Social Security taxes were levied on the first $118,500 of workers' pay in 2015. Employers pay 6.2 percent and employees pay 6.2 percent (the self-employed pay the entire 12.4 percent).

proportional taxation
The tax as a percentage of income remains constant as income increases; also called a flat tax

progressive taxation
The tax as a percentage of income increases as income increases

marginal tax rate The percentage of each additional dollar of income that goes to the tax

regressive taxation
The tax as a percentage of income decreases as income increases

Exhibit 5

Top Marginal Rate on Federal Personal Income Tax Since 1913

Source: U.S. Internal Revenue Service. For the latest figures on the personal income tax go to http://www.irs.gov/individuals/index.html.

In Egypt, builders often leave the top floor of new construction unfinished to avoid paying property taxes.

Taxes often do more than fund public programs. Some taxes discourage certain activity. For example, a pollution tax can help clean the air. A tax on gasoline can encourage people to work at home, carpool, or use public transportation. Some taxes have unintended consequences. For example, in Egypt a property tax is not imposed until a new building is completed. To avoid such taxes, builders never finish the job; multistory dwellings are usually missing the top floor. As another example of how taxes can distort the allocation of resources, property taxes in Amsterdam and Vietnam were originally based on the width of the building. As a result, buildings there are extremely narrow. As a final example, in 1696 England levied a property tax based on a dwelling's number of windows. As a consequence, property owners boarded up existing windows and new dwellings had fewer widows. These actions cut ventilation and light, creating health hazards, yet the tax persisted for more than 150 years.[3] Such taxes have unintended consequences distort the efficient allocation of resources.

This discussion of revenue sources brings to a close, for now, our examination of the role of government in the U.S. economy. Government has a pervasive influence on the economy, and its role is discussed throughout the book.

3-4 THE REST OF THE WORLD

So far, the focus has been on institutions within the United States—that is, on *domestic* households, firms, and governments. This focus is appropriate because

3. Wallace E. Oates and Robert M. Schwab, "The Window Tax: A Case of Excess Burden," *Journal of Economic Perspectives*, 29 (Winter 2015): 163–180.

our primary objective is to understand the workings of the U.S. economy, still the largest in the world. But the rest of the world affects what U.S. households consume and what U.S. firms produce. For example, Japan and China supply all kinds of manufactured goods to America, thereby affecting U.S. prices, wages, and profits. Likewise, political events in the Middle East can affect what Americans pay for oil. Foreign decision makers, therefore, influence the U.S. economy—what we produce and what we consume. The *rest of the world* consists of the households, firms, and governments in the other 200 or so sovereign nations throughout the world.

3-4a International Trade

In the previous chapter, you learned about comparative advantage and the gains from specialization. These gains explain why householders stopped doing everything for themselves and began to specialize. International trade arises for the same reasons. *International trade occurs because the opportunity cost of producing specific goods differs across countries.* Americans import raw materials like crude oil, bauxite (aluminum ore), and coffee beans and finished goods like cameras, computers, and cut diamonds. U.S. producers export sophisticated products like computer software, aircraft, and movies, as well as agricultural products like wheat, corn, and cotton. Farm exports are why America has long been called the "breadbasket of the world."

Trade between the United States and the rest of the world has increased in recent decades. In 1970, U.S. exports of goods and services amounted to only 6 percent of the gross domestic product. That has increased to about 14 percent today. The top 10 destinations for U.S. exports in order of importance are Canada, Mexico, China, Japan, the United Kingdom, Germany, the Netherlands, South Korea, France, and Brazil.

The **merchandise trade balance** equals the value of exported goods minus the value of imported goods. Goods in this case are distinguished from services, which show up in another trade account. For the last quarter century, the United States has imported more goods than it has exported, resulting in a merchandise trade deficit. Just as a household must pay for its spending, so too must a nation. The merchandise trade deficit must be offset by a surplus in one or more of the other *balance-of-payments* accounts. A nation's

merchandise trade balance The value during a given period of a country's exported goods minus the value of its imported goods

balance of payments is the record of all economic transactions between its residents and residents of the rest of the world.

3-4b Exchange Rates

The lack of a common currency complicates trade between countries. How many U.S. dollars buy a Porsche? An American buyer cares only about the dollar cost; the German carmaker cares only about the *euros* received (the common currency of 19 European countries). To facilitate trade funded by different currencies, a market for foreign exchange has developed. **Foreign exchange** is foreign currency needed to carry out international transactions. The supply and demand for foreign exchange comes together in *foreign exchange markets* to determine the exchange rate. The *exchange rate* measures the price of one currency in terms of another. For example, the exchange rate between the euro and the dollar might indicate that one euro exchanges for $1.10. At that exchange rate, a Porsche selling for €100,000 costs $110,000. The exchange rate affects the prices of imports and exports, and thus helps shape the flow of foreign trade.

3-4c Trade Restrictions

Despite clear gains from international specialization and exchange, nearly all nations restrict trade to some extent. These restrictions can take the form of (1) **tariffs**, which are taxes on imports; (2) **quotas**, which are limits on the quantity of a particular good that can be imported or exported; and (3) other trade restrictions. If specialization according to comparative advantage is so beneficial, why do most countries restrict trade? Restrictions benefit certain domestic producers that lobby governments for these benefits. For example, U.S. growers of sugarcane have benefited from legislation restricting sugar imports, thereby raising U.S. sugar prices. These higher prices hurt domestic consumers, but consumers are usually unaware of this harm. Trade restrictions interfere with the free flow of products across borders and tend to hurt the overall economy.

balance of payments A record of all economic transactions during a given period between residents of one country and residents of the rest of the world

foreign exchange Foreign money needed to carry out international transactions

tariff A tax on imports

quota A legal limit on the quantity of a particular product that can be imported or exported

3-5 FINAL WORD

This chapter examined the four economic decision makers: households, firms, governments, and the rest of the world. Domestic households are by far the most important, for they supply resources and demand goods and services.

If you were to stop reading right now, you would already know more economics than most people. But to understand market economies, you must learn how markets work. The next chapter introduces demand and supply.

STUDY TOOLS 3

READY TO STUDY? IN THE BOOK, YOU CAN:

☐ Work the Problems at the end of the chapter.

☐ Rip out the chapter review card for a handy summary of the chapter and key terms.

ONLINE AT CENGAGEBRAIN.COM YOU CAN:

☐ Collect StudyBits while you read and study the chapter.

☐ Quiz yourself on key concepts.

☐ Prepare for tests with chapter flash cards as well as flash cards that you create.

☐ Watch videos to explore economics further.

CHAPTER 3 PROBLEMS

Your instructor can access the answers to these problems online at http://cengagebrain.com.

3-1 Describe the major sources of income and expenditures for households

1. *(Evolution of the Household)* Determine whether each of the following would increase or decrease the opportunity costs for mothers who decide not to work outside the home. Explain your answers.
    a. Higher levels of education for women
    b. Higher unemployment rates for women
    c. Higher average pay levels for women
    d. Lower demand for labor in industries that traditionally employ women
2. *(Household Production)* Many households supplement their food budget by cultivating small vegetable gardens. Explain how each of the following might influence this kind of household production:
    a. Both husband and wife are professionals who earn high salaries.
    b. The household is located in a city rather than in a rural area.
    c. The household is located in a region where there is a high sales tax on food purchases.
    d. The household is located in a region that has a high property tax rate.
3. *(Household Production)* What factors does a householder consider when deciding whether to produce a good or service at home versus buy it in the marketplace?
4. *(Objectives of the Economic Decision Makers)* In economic analysis, what are the assumed objectives of households, firms, and the government?

3-2 Outline the evolution of production over the centuries from the household to the modern corporation

5. *(Corporations)* How did the institution of the firm get a boost from the advent of the Industrial Revolution? What type of business organization existed before this?
6. *(Sole Proprietorships)* What are the disadvantages of the sole proprietorship form of business?
7. *(Cooperatives)* How do cooperatives differ from typical businesses?
8. *(Evolution of the Firm)* Explain how production after the Industrial Revolution differed from production under the cottage industry system.

3-3 Summarize the seven roles of government in an economy

9. *(Government)* Complete each of the following sentences:
    a. Goods that are nonrival and nonexcludable are known as _____.
    b. _____ are cash or in-kind benefits given to individuals as outright grants from the government.
    c. A(n) _____ confers an external benefit on third parties that are not directly involved in the market transaction.
    d. _____ refers to the government's pursuit of full employment and price stability through variations in taxes and government spending.
10. *(Tax Rates)* Suppose taxes are related to income as follows:

Income	Taxes
$1,000	$200
$2,000	$350
$3,000	$450

    a. What percentage of income is paid in taxes at each level?
    b. Is the tax rate progressive, proportional, or regressive?
    c. What is the marginal tax rate on the first $1,000 of income?
       The second $1,000? The third $1,000?
11. *(Government Revenue)* What are the sources of government revenue in the United States? Which types of taxes are most important at each level of government? Which two taxes provide the most revenue to the federal government?
12. *(Externalities)* Suppose there is an external cost, or negative externality, associated with production of a certain good. What's wrong with letting the market determine how much of this good will be produced?

3-4 Explain why countries trade with each other and why they sometimes act to restrict that trade

13. *(International Trade)* Why does international trade occur? What does it mean to run a deficit in the merchandise trade balance?
14. *(International Trade)* Distinguish between a tariff and a quota. Who benefits from and who is harmed by such restrictions on imports?

4 | Demand, Supply, and Markets

Stockbyte/Getty Images

LEARNING OUTCOMES

After studying this chapter, you will be able to...

4-1 Explain why a demand curve slopes downward

4-2 Identify five things which could shift a demand curve to the right or left

4-3 Explain why a supply curve usually slopes upward

4-4 Identify five things which could shift a supply curve to the right or left

4-5 Explain why surpluses push prices down while shortages drive prices up

4-6 Predict the impact of a change in demand or supply on the equilibrium price and quantity

4-7 Describe the result of a government-set price floor and price ceiling on a market

After finishing this chapter go to **PAGE 72** for **STUDY TOOLS**

Topics discussed in Chapter 4 include

- Demand and quantity demanded
- Movement along a demand curve
- Shift of a demand curve
- Supply and quantity supplied
- Movement along a supply curve
- Shift of a supply curve
- Markets and equilibrium
- Disequilibrium

This chapter introduces demand and supply and shows how they interact in competitive markets. *Demand and supply are the most fundamental and the most powerful of all economic tools*—important enough to warrant a chapter. Indeed, some believe that if you program a computer to answer "demand and supply" to every economic question, you could put many economists out of work. An understanding of the two ideas will take you far in mastering the art and science of economic analysis. Because of the subject matter, this chapter uses more graphs than previous chapters, so you may need to review the Chapter 1 appendix as a refresher.

> **"Why do roses cost more on Valentine's Day than during the rest of the year?"**

4-1 DEMAND

How many six-packs of Pepsi will people buy each month at a price of $4? What if the price is $3? What if it's $5? The answers reveal the relationship between the price of a six-pack and the quantity of Pepsi demanded. Such a relationship is called the *demand* for Pepsi. **Demand** indicates the quantity consumers are both *willing and able* to buy at each price during a given time period, other things constant. Because demand pertains to a specific period—a day, a week, a month—think of demand as the *amounts purchased per period* at each price. Also, notice the emphasis on *willing and able*. You may be *able* to buy a new Harley-Davidson Sportster Forty-Eight that lists for $10,749 because you can afford one, but you may not be *willing* to buy one if motorcycles just don't interest you.

4-1a Law of Demand

In 1962, Sam Walton opened his first store in Rogers, Arkansas, with a sign that read, "Wal-Mart Discount City. We sell for less." Now called Walmart, this store chain sells more than any other retailer in the world because prices there are among the lowest around. As a consumer, you understand why people buy more at a lower price. Sell for less, and the world will beat a path to your door. Walmart, for example, sells on average over 20,000 pairs of shoes *an hour*. This relation between the price and the quantity demanded is an economic law. The **law of demand** says that the quantity of a good that consumers are willing and able to buy per period varies inversely, or negatively, with the price, other things equal. Thus, the higher the price, the smaller the quantity demanded; the lower the price, the greater the quantity demanded.

Demand, Wants, and Needs

Consumer demand and consumer wants are not the same. As we have seen, wants are unlimited. You may want a new Mercedes-Benz SL65 Roadster convertible, but the $215,250 price tag is likely beyond your budget (that is, the quantity you demand at that price is zero). Nor is

> **demand** A relation between the price of a good and the quantity that consumers are willing and able to buy per period, other things constant

> **law of demand** The quantity of a good that consumers are willing and able to buy per period relates inversely, or negatively, to the price, other things constant

demand the same as need. You may need a new muffler for your car, but a price of $300 is just too high for you right now. If, however, the price drops enough—say, to $200—then you may be both willing and able to buy one.

Substitution Effect of a Price Change

What explains the law of demand? Why, for example, does the quantity demanded increase as the price declines? The explanation begins with unlimited wants confronting scarce resources. Many goods and services can help satisfy particular wants. For example, you can satisfy your hunger with pizza, tacos, burgers, chicken, or hundreds of other foods. Similarly, you can satisfy your desire for warmth in the winter with warm clothing, a home heating system, a trip to Hawaii, or in many other ways. Clearly, some alternatives are more appealing than others (a trip to Hawaii is more fun than warm clothing). In a world without scarcity, everything would be free, so you would always choose the most attractive alternative. Scarcity, however, is the reality, and the degree of scarcity of one good relative to another helps determine each good's relative price.

Notice that the definition of *demand* includes the other-things-constant assumption. Among the "other things" assumed to remain constant are the prices of other goods. For example, if the price of pizza declines while other prices remain constant, pizza becomes relatively cheaper. Consumers are more *willing* to purchase pizza when its relative price falls; they substitute pizza for other goods. This idea is called the **substitution effect of a price change**. On the other hand, an increase in the price of pizza, other things constant, increases the opportunity cost of pizza—that is, the amount of other goods you must give up to buy pizza. This higher opportunity cost causes some consumers to substitute

> **❝Sell for less, and the world will beat a path to your door.❞**

other goods for the now higher-priced pizza, thus reducing their quantity of pizza demanded. Remember that *it is the change in the relative price—the price of one good relative to the prices of other goods—that causes the substitution effect*. If all prices changed by the same percentage, there would be no change in relative prices and no substitution effect.

Income Effect of a Price Change

A fall in the price of a good increases the quantity demanded for a second reason. Suppose you earn $30 a week from a part-time job, so $30 is your money income. **Money income** is simply the number of dollars received per period, in this case, $30 per week. Suppose you spend all that on pizza, buying three a week at $10 each. What if the price drops to $6? At that lower price, you can now afford five pizzas a week. Your money income remains at $30 per week, but the price drop increases your **real income**—that is, your income measured by what it can buy. The price reduction, other things constant, increases the purchasing power of your income, thereby increasing your *ability* to buy pizza. The quantity you demand will likely increase because of the **income effect of a price change**. You may not increase your quantity demanded to five pizzas, but you could. If you decide to purchase four pizzas a week when the price drops to $6, you would still have $6 remaining to buy other stuff. Thus, the income effect of a lower price increases your real income and thereby increases your ability to buy pizza and other goods, making you better off. The income effect is reflected in Walmart's slogan, which trumpets low prices: "Save money. Live better." Because of the income effect, consumers typically increase their quantity demanded when the price declines.

Conversely, an increase in the price of pizza, other things constant, reduces real income, thereby reducing your ability to buy pizza and other goods. Because of the income effect, consumers typically reduce their quantity demanded when the price increases. The more important the item is as a share of your budget, the bigger the income effect. That's why, for example, consumers cut back on a variety of purchases when the price of gasoline spikes, as it did in 2012. And why those same consumers increase spending on a variety of goods when the price of gasoline falls, as it did in late 2014 and early 2015. Again, note that money income, not real income, is assumed

substitution effect of a price change When the price of a good falls, that good becomes cheaper compared to other goods so consumers tend to substitute that good for other goods

money income The number of dollars a person receives per period, such as $400 per week

real income Income measured by the goods and services it can buy; real income changes when the price changes

income effect of a price change A fall in the price of a good increases consumers' real income, making consumers more able to purchase goods; for a normal good, the quantity demanded increases to remain constant along a demand curve. Because a change in price changes your real income, real income varies along a demand curve. The lower the price, the greater your real income.

4-1b Demand Schedule and Demand Curve

Demand can be expressed as a *demand schedule* or as a *demand curve*. Panel (a) of Exhibit 1 shows a hypothetical demand schedule for pizza. In describing demand, we must specify the units measured and the period considered. In our example, the unit is a 12-inch regular pizza and the period is a week. The schedule lists possible prices, along with the quantity demanded at each price. At a price of $15, for example, consumers demand 8 million pizzas per week. As you can see, the lower the price, other things constant, the greater the quantity demanded. Consumers substitute pizza for other foods. And as the price falls, real income increases, causing consumers to increase the quantity of pizza they demand. If the price drops as low as $3, consumers demand 32 million per week.

The demand schedule in panel (a) appears as a **demand curve** in panel (b), with price measured on the vertical axis and the quantity demanded per week on the horizontal axis. Each price-quantity combination listed in the demand schedule in the left panel becomes a point in the right panel. Point *a*, for example, indicates that if the price is $15, consumers demand 8 million pizzas per week. Connecting points forms the demand curve for pizza, labeled *D*. (By the way, some demand curves are straight lines, some are curved lines, and some are even crooked lines, but for simplicity they all are called demand *curves*.)

A demand curve slopes downward, reflecting the *law of demand*: Price and quantity demanded are inversely related, other things constant. Besides money income, also assumed constant along the demand curve are the prices of other goods. Thus, along the demand curve, the price of pizza changes *relative to the prices of other goods*. The demand curve therefore shows the effect of a change in the *relative price* of pizza—that is, relative to other prices, which do not change.

Take care to distinguish between *demand* and *quantity demanded*. The *demand* for pizza is not a specific amount, but rather the *entire relationship* between price and quantity demanded—represented by the demand schedule or the demand curve. An individual point on the demand curve indicates the **quantity demanded** at a particular price. For example, at a price of $12, the quantity demanded is 14 million pizzas per week. If the price drops from $12 to, say, $9, this is shown in Exhibit 1 by *a movement along the demand curve*—in this case from point *b* to point *c*. Any movement along a demand curve reflects a *change in quantity demanded*, not a change in demand. Got that?

The law of demand applies to the millions of products sold by grocery stores, department stores, clothing stores, shoe stores, drugstores, music stores, bookstores, hardware stores, other retailers,

Exhibit 1

Market Demand Schedule and Market Demand Curve for Pizza

The market demand curve D shows the quantity of pizza demanded, at various prices, by all consumers. Price and quantity demanded are inversely related to other things constant, reflecting the law of demand.

(a) Demand schedule

	Price per Pizza	Quantity Demanded per Week (millions)
a	$15	8
b	12	14
c	9	20
d	6	26
e	3	32

(b) Demand curve

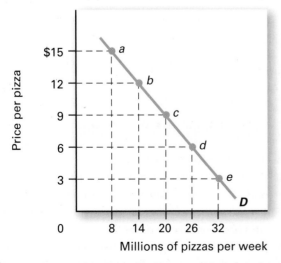

Millions of pizzas per week

demand curve A curve showing the relation between the price of a good and the quantity consumers are willing and able to buy per period, other things constant

quantity demanded The amount of a good consumers are willing and able to buy per period at a particular price, as reflected by a point on a demand curve travel agencies, and restaurants, as well as through mail-order catalogs, Craigslist, classified ads, online sites, stock markets, real estate markets, job markets, flea markets, yard sales, and all other markets. The law of demand applies even to choices that seem more personal than economic, such as whether or not to own a pet. For example, after New York City passed an anti-dog-litter law, law-abiding owners had to follow their dogs around the city with scoopers, plastic bags—whatever would do the job. Because the law in effect raised the personal cost of owning a dog, the quantity of dogs demanded decreased. Some dogs were abandoned, increasing strays in the city. The number of dogs left at animal shelters doubled. The law of demand predicts this inverse relation between cost, or price, and quantity demanded.

It is useful to distinguish between **individual demand**, which is the demand of an individual consumer such as you, and **market demand**, which is the sum of the individual demands of all consumers in the market. In most markets, there are many consumers, sometimes millions. *The market demand curve shows the quantities demanded per period by all consumers at various prices.* Unless otherwise noted, when we talk about demand, we are referring to market demand, as shown in Exhibit 1.

Tough anti-poop laws increase the cost of owning a dog thereby, reducing the quantity of dogs demanded.

individual demand The relation between the price of a good and the quantity purchased per period by an individual consumer, other things constant

market demand The relation between the price of a good and the quantity purchased per period by all consumers in the market, other things constant; sum of the individual demands in the market

normal good A good, such as new clothes, for which demand increases, or shifts rightward, as consumer income rises

inferior good A good, such as used clothes, for which demand decreases, or shifts leftward, as consumer income rises

4-2 WHAT SHIFTS A DEMAND CURVE?

A demand curve isolates the relation between the price of a good and quantity demanded when other factors that could affect demand remain unchanged. What are those other factors?

Variables that can affect market demand are (1) the money income of consumers, (2) the prices of other goods, (3) consumer expectations, (4) the number or composition of consumers in the market, and (5) consumer tastes. How could changes in each affect demand?

Kevin Giszewski/Shutterstock.com

4-2a Consumer Income

Exhibit 2 shows the market demand curve D for pizza. This demand curve assumes a given money income. Suppose consumer income increases. Some consumers are then willing and able to buy more pizza at each price, so market demand increases. The demand curve shifts to the right from D to D'. For example, at a price of $12, the amount of pizza demanded increases from 14 million to 20 million per week, as indicated by the movement from point b on demand curve D to point f on demand curve D'. In short, *an increase in demand—that is, a rightward shift of the demand curve—means that consumers are willing and able to buy more pizza at each price.*

Goods are classified into two broad categories, depending on how consumers respond to changes in money income. The demand for a **normal good** increases as money income increases. Because pizza is a normal good, its demand curve shifts rightward when money income increases. Most goods are normal. In contrast, demand for an **inferior good** actually decreases as money income increases, so the demand curve shifts leftward. Examples of inferior goods include bologna sandwiches, used furniture, and used clothes. As money income increases, consumers tend to switch from these inferior goods to normal goods (such as roast beef sandwiches, new furniture, and new clothes).

4-2b The Prices of Other Goods

Again, the prices of other goods are assumed to remain constant along a given demand curve. Now let's bring these other prices into play. Consumers have various ways of trying to satisfy any particular want. Consumers choose among substitutes based on relative prices. For example, pizza and tacos are substitutes, though not perfect ones. An increase in the price of tacos, other things constant, reduces the quantity of tacos demanded along a given taco demand

Exhibit 2

An Increase in the Market Demand for Pizza

An increase of the market demand for pizza is shown by a rightward shift of the curve, indicating that the quantity demanded increases at each price. For example, at a price of $12, quantity demanded increases from 14 million (point *b*) to 20 million (point *f*).

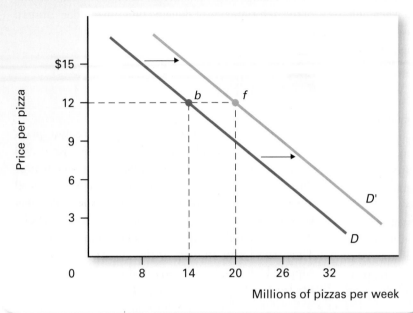

income expectations can shift the demand curve. For example, a consumer who learns about a pay raise might increase demand well before the raise takes effect. A college senior who lands that first full-time job may buy a new car even before graduation. Likewise, a change in consumers' *price expectations* can shift the demand curve. For example, if you expect the price of pizza to jump next week, you may buy an extra one today for the freezer, shifting this week's demand for pizza rightward. Or if people come to believe that home prices will climb next year, some will increase their demand for housing now, shifting this year's demand for housing rightward. The expectation of lower prices has the opposite effect. For example, during the recession of 2007–2009, people expected home prices to continue falling, so they put off buying homes, shifting the demand for housing leftward. Such expectations can often be self-fulfilling.

curve. An increase in the price of tacos also increases the demand for pizza, shifting the demand curve for pizza to the right. Two goods are considered **substitutes** if an increase in the price of one shifts the demand for the other rightward.

Goods used in combination are called **complements.** Examples include Pepsi and pizza, milk and cookies, hot dogs and hot-dog buns, cars and gasoline, computer software and hardware, and airline tickets and rental cars. Two goods are considered **complements** if an increase in the price of one decreases the demand for the other, shifting that demand curve leftward. For example, an increase in the price of Pepsi shifts the demand curve for pizza leftward. But most pairs of goods selected at random are *unrelated*—for example, pizza and housing, or milk and gasoline. Still, an increase in the price of an unrelated good reduces the consumers' real income and can thereby reduce the demand for pizza and other goods. For example, a sharp increase in housing prices reduces the income left over for other goods, such as pizza.

4-2c Consumer Expectations

Another factor assumed constant along a given demand curve is consumer expectations about factors that influence demand, such as incomes or prices. A change in consumers'

4-2d Number or Composition of Consumers

As mentioned earlier, the market demand curve is the sum of the individual demand curves of all consumers in the market. If the number of consumers changes, the demand curve will shift. For example, if the population grows, the demand curve for pizza will shift rightward. Even if total population remains unchanged, demand could shift with a change in the composition of the population. For example, an increase over time in teenagers as a share of the population could shift pizza demand rightward. A baby boom would shift rightward the demand for car seats and baby food. A growing Latino population would affect the demand for Latino foods.

> **substitutes** Goods, such as tacos and pizza, that relate in such a way that an increase in the price of one shifts the demand for the other rightward
>
> **complements** Goods, such as Pepsi and pizza, that relate in such a way that an increase in the price of one shifts the demand for the other leftward

4-2e Consumer Tastes

Do you like anchovies on your pizza? How about sauerkraut on your hot dogs? Are you into tattoos and body piercings?

Is music to your ears more likely to be rock, country, hip-hop, reggae, R&B, jazz, funk, Latin, gospel, new age, or classical? Choices in food, body art, music, sports, clothing, books, movies, TV shows—indeed, all consumer choices—are influenced by consumer tastes. **Tastes** are nothing more than your likes and dislikes as a consumer. What determines tastes? Your desires for food when hungry and drink when thirsty are largely biological. So too is your desire for comfort, rest, shelter, friendship, love, status, personal safety, and a pleasant environment. Your family background affects some of your tastes—your taste in food, for example, has been shaped by years of home cooking. Other influences include the surrounding culture, peer pressure, and religious convictions. So economists can say a little about the origin of tastes, but they claim no special expertise in understanding how tastes develop and change over time. Economists recognize, however, that tastes have an important impact on demand. For example, although pizza is popular, some people just don't like it and those who are lactose intolerant can't stomach the cheese topping. Thus, most people like pizza but some don't.

In our analysis of consumer demand, *we will assume that tastes are given and are relatively stable.* Tastes are assumed to remain constant along a given demand curve. A change in the tastes for a particular good would shift that good's demand curve. For example, a discovery that the tomato sauce and cheese combination on pizza promotes overall health could change consumer tastes, shifting the demand curve for pizza to the right. But because a change in tastes is so difficult to isolate from changes in other determinants of demand, we should be reluctant to attribute a shift of the demand curve to a change in tastes. We therefore try to rule out other possible reasons for a shift of the demand curve before accepting a change in tastes as the explanation.

That wraps up our look at changes in demand. Before we turn to supply, you should remember the distinction between a **movement along a given demand curve** and a **shift of a demand curve**. A change in *price*, other things constant, causes a *movement along a demand curve*, changing the quantity demanded. A change in one of the determinants of demand other than price causes a *shift of a demand curve*, changing demand.

4-3 SUPPLY

Just as demand is a relation between price and quantity demanded, supply is a relation between price and quantity supplied. **Supply** indicates how much producers are *willing and able* to offer for sale per period at each possible price, other things constant. The **law of supply** states that the quantity supplied is usually directly related to its price, other things constant. Thus, the lower the price, the smaller the quantity supplied; the higher the price, the greater the quantity supplied.

4-3a Supply Schedule and Supply Curve

Exhibit 3 presents the market *supply schedule* and the market **supply curve** S for pizza. Both show the quantities supplied per week at various possible prices by the thousands of pizza makers in the economy. As you can see, price and quantity supplied are directly, or positively, related. Producers have a profit incentive to offer more at a higher price than at a lower price, so the supply curve slopes upward.

Here are two reasons why producers offer more for sale when the price rises. First, as the price increases, other things constant, a producer becomes more *willing* to supply the good. Prices act as signals to existing and potential suppliers about the rewards for producing various goods. A higher pizza price attracts resources from lower-valued uses. *A higher price makes producers more willing to increase quantity supplied.*

Second, higher prices also increase the producer's *ability* to supply the good. The law of increasing opportunity cost, as noted in Chapter 2, states that the opportunity cost of producing more of a particular good rises as output increases—that is, the *marginal cost* of production increases as output increases. Because producers face a higher marginal cost for additional output, they need to get a higher price for that output to be *able* to increase the quantity supplied. *A higher*

tastes Consumer preferences; likes and dislikes in consumption; assumed to remain constant along a given demand curve

movement along a demand curve A change in quantity demanded resulting from a change in the price of the good, other things constant

shift of a demand curve Movement of a demand curve right or left resulting from a change in one of the determinants of demand other than the price of the good

supply A relation between the price of a good and the quantity that producers are willing and able to sell per period, other things constant

law of supply The amount of a good that producers are willing and able to sell per period is usually directly related to its price, other things constant

supply curve A curve showing the relation between price of a good and the quantity producers are willing and able to sell per period, other things constant

Exhibit 3

The Market Supply Schedule and Market Supply Curve for Pizza

The market supply curve *S* shows the quantities of pizza supplied, at various prices, by all pizza makers. Price and quantity supplied are directly related.

(a) Supply schedule

Price per Pizza	Quantity Supplied per Week (millions)
$15	28
12	24
9	20
6	16
3	12

(b) Supply curve

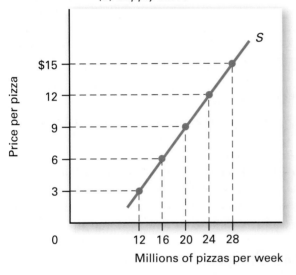

On the other hand, a lower price makes production less attractive, so suppliers are less willing and less able to offer the good. For example, a mining company "reacted quickly to steep copper price declines in 2008 by curbing production at its North American sites and implementing layoffs at its mines and corporate headquarters."[1]

As with demand, we distinguish between *supply* and *quantity supplied*. *Supply* is the entire relationship between prices and quantities supplied, as reflected by the supply schedule or supply curve. **Quantity supplied** refers to a particular amount offered for sale at a particular price, as reflected by a point on a supply curve. We also distinguish between **individual supply**, which is the supply of an individual producer, and **market supply**, which is the sum of individual supplies of all producers in the market. Unless otherwise noted, the term *supply* refers to market supply.

4-4 WHAT SHIFTS A SUPPLY CURVE?

The supply curve isolates the relation between the price of a good and the quantity supplied, other things constant. Assumed constant along a supply curve are the determinants of supply other than the price of the good, including (1) the state of technology and know-how, (2) the prices of resources, (3) the prices of other goods, (4) producer expectations, and (5) the number of producers in the market. Let's see how a change in each affects the supply curve.

4-4a State of Technology and Know How

Recall from Chapter 2 that the state of technology and know-how represents the economy's knowledge about how to combine resources efficiently. Along a given supply curve, technology and know-how are assumed to remain unchanged. If a better technology or a better production process is discovered, production costs will fall, so suppliers will be more willing and able to supply the good at each price.

1. Andrew Johnson, "Freeport Outsourcing Will Cut 60 Valley Jobs," *Arizona Republic*, 23 February 2010.

price makes producers more able to increase quantity supplied. As a case in point, a higher price for gasoline increases a producer's ability to extract oil from tar sands, to drill deeper, and to explore in less accessible areas, such as the remote jungles of the Amazon, the stormy waters of the North Sea, or the frozen tundra above the Arctic Circle. For example, at a market price of $45 per barrel, extracting oil from tar sands is unprofitable, but at a price of $50 per barrel, such production is profitable.

Thus, a higher price makes producers more *willing* and more *able* to increase quantity supplied. Producers are more *willing* because production becomes more attractive than other uses of the resources involved. Producers are more *able* because they can afford to cover the higher marginal cost that typically results from increasing output.

quantity supplied The amount offered for sale per period at a particular price, as reflected by a point on a supply curve

individual supply The relation between the price of a good and the quantity an individual producer is willing and able to sell per period, other things constant

market supply The relation between the price of a good and the quantity all producers are willing and able to sell per period, other things constant

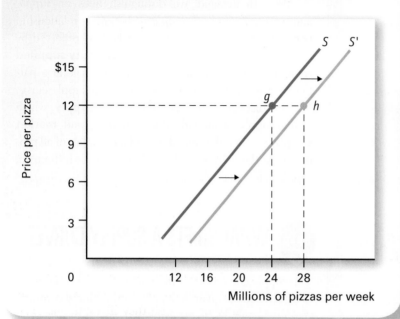
For example, new techniques helped Marathon Oil cut drilling time for a new well from 56 days in 2006 to only 24 days in 2009.[2] Consequently, supply will increase, as reflected by a rightward shift of the supply curve. In our pizza example, suppose a new, high-tech oven that costs the same as existing ovens can bake pizza in half the time. Such a breakthrough would shift the market supply curve rightward, as from S to S' in Exhibit 4, indicating that more is supplied at each possible price. For example, at a price of $12, the amount supplied increases from 24 million to 28 million pizzas per week, as shown in Exhibit 4 by the movement from point g to point h. In short, *an increase in supply—that is, a rightward shift of the supply curve—means that producers are willing and able to sell more pizza at each price.*

4-4b Resource Prices

The prices of resources employed to make the good affect the cost of production and therefore the supply of the good. For example, suppose the price of mozzarella cheese falls. This reduces the cost of making pizza, so producers are more willing and better able to supply

2. Ben Casselman, "Oil Industry Boom—in North Dakota," *Wall Street Journal*, 26 February 2010.

pizza. The supply curve for pizza shifts rightward, as shown in Exhibit 4. On the other hand, an increase in the price of a resource reduces supply, meaning a shift of the supply curve leftward. For example, a higher price of mozzarella increases the cost of making pizza. Higher production costs decrease supply, as reflected by a leftward shift of the supply curve.

4-4c Prices of Other Goods

Nearly all resources have alternative uses. The labor, building, machinery, ingredients, and knowledge needed to run a pizza business could produce other goods instead. A drop in the price of one of these other goods, with the price of pizza unchanged, makes pizza production more attractive. For example, if the price of Italian bread declines, some bread makers become pizza makers so the supply of pizza increases, shifting the supply curve of pizza rightward as in Exhibit 4. On the other hand, if the price of Italian bread increases, supplying pizza becomes relatively less attractive compared to supplying Italian bread. The opportunity cost of supplying pizza increases. As resources shift from pizza to bread, the supply of pizza decreases, or shifts to the left.

4-4d Producer Expectations

Changes in producer expectations can shift the supply curve. For example, if pizza makers expect higher pizza prices in the future, some will expand operations now, thereby shifting the supply curve rightward. If, however, a good can be easily stored (crude oil, for example, can be left in the ground), expecting higher prices in the future might prompt some producers to *reduce* their current supply while awaiting the higher price. Thus, an expectation of higher prices in the future could either increase or decrease current supply, depending on the good. More generally, any change affecting future profitability, such as a change in business taxes, could shift the supply curve now.

4-4e Number of Producers in the Market

Because market supply sums the amounts supplied at each price by all producers in that market, market supply depends on the number of producers in that market. If that number increases, supply will increase, shifting the supply curve to the right. If the number of producers decreases, supply will decrease, shifting the supply curve to the left. As an example of increased supply, the number of gourmet coffee bars has more than quadrupled in the United States since 1990 (think Starbucks), shifting the supply curve of gourmet coffee to the right.

Finally, note again the distinction between a **movement along a supply curve** and a **shift of a supply curve**. A change in *price*, other things constant, causes *a movement along a supply curve,* changing the quantity supplied. A change in one of the determinants of supply other than price causes a *shift of a supply curve,* changing supply.

You are now ready to bring demand and supply together.

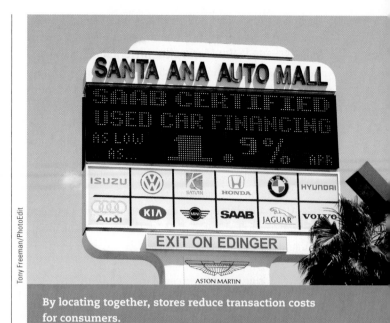

By locating together, stores reduce transaction costs for consumers.

4-5 DEMAND AND SUPPLY CREATE A MARKET

Demanders and suppliers have different views of price. Demanders pay the price and suppliers receive it. Thus, a higher price is bad news for consumers but good news for producers. As the price rises, consumers reduce their quantity demanded along the demand curve and producers increase their quantity supplied along the supply curve. How is this conflict between producers and consumers resolved?

4-5a Markets

Markets sort out differences between demanders and suppliers. A *market,* as you know from Chapter 1, includes all the arrangements used to buy and sell a particular good or service. Markets reduce **transaction costs**—the costs of time and information required for exchange. For example, suppose you are looking for a summer job. One approach might be to go from employer to employer looking for openings. But this could have you running around for days or weeks. A more efficient strategy would be to pick up a copy of the local newspaper or go online and look for job openings. Classified ads and Web sites, which are elements of the job market, reduce the transaction costs of bringing workers and employers together.

The coordination that occurs through markets takes place not because of some central plan but because of Adam Smith's "invisible hand." For example,

auto dealers in your community tend to locate together, usually on the outskirts of town, where land is cheaper. The dealers congregate not because they all took an economics course or because they like one another's company but because grouped together they become a more attractive destination for car buyers. A dealer who makes the mistake of locating away from the others misses out on a lot of business. Similarly, stores locate together so that more shoppers will be attracted by the call of the mall. From Orlando theme parks to Broadway theaters to Las Vegas casinos, suppliers in a particular market tend to congregate to attract demanders. Some groupings can be quite specialized. For example, shops in Hong Kong that sell dress mannequins cluster along Austin Road. And diamond merchants in New York City congregate within the same few blocks.

4-5b Market Equilibrium

To see how a market works, let's bring together market demand and market supply. Exhibit 5 shows the market for pizza, using schedules in panel (a) and curves in panel (b). Please take a look now. Suppose the price initially is $12. At that price,

movement along a supply curve Change in quantity supplied resulting from a change in the price of the good, other things constant

shift of a supply curve Movement of a supply curve left or right resulting from a change in one of the determinants of supply other than the price of the good

transaction costs The costs of time and information required to carry out market exchange producers supply 24 million pizzas per week, but consumers demand only 14 million, resulting in an *excess quantity supplied*, or a **surplus**, of 10 million pizzas per week. Producers compete by dropping the price. Suppliers don't like getting stuck with unsold pizzas. Competition among producers puts downward pressure on the price, as shown by the arrow pointing down in the graph. As the price falls, producers reduce their quantity supplied and consumers increase their quantity demanded. The price continues to fall as long as quantity supplied exceeds quantity demanded.

Alternatively, suppose the price initially is $6. You can see from Exhibit 5 that at that price consumers demand 26 million pizzas but producers supply only 16 million, resulting in an *excess quantity demanded*, or a **shortage**, of 10 million pizzas per week. Consumers compete to buy pizza, which is in short supply. Consumer competition forces the price higher. Profit-maximizing producers and eager consumers create market pressure for a higher price, as shown by the arrow pointing up in the graph. As the price rises, producers increase their quantity supplied and consumers reduce their quantity demanded. The price continues to rise as long as quantity demanded exceeds quantity supplied.

Thus, *a surplus creates downward pressure on the price, and a shortage creates upward pressure.* As long as quantity demanded differs from quantity supplied, this

> **"A surplus creates downward pressure on the price, and a shortage creates upward pressure."**

difference forces a price change. Note that a shortage or a surplus depends on the price. There is no such thing as a general shortage or a general surplus, only a

surplus At a given price, the amount by which quantity supplied exceeds quantity demanded; a surplus usually forces the price down

shortage At a given price, the amount by which quantity demanded exceeds quantity supplied; a shortage usually forces the price up

Exhibit 5

Equilibrium in the Pizza Market

Market equilibrium occurs at the price where quantity demanded equals quantity supplied. This is shown at point *c*, where the price is $9 and the quantity is 20 million pizzas per week . Above the equilibrium price, quantity supplied exceeds quantity demanded. This creates a surplus,which puts downward pressure on the price. Below the equilibrium price, quantity demanded exceeds quantity supplied. The resulting shortage puts upward pressure on the price.

(a) Market schedules

Millions of Pizzas per Week

Price per Pizza	Quantity Demanded	Quantity Supplied	Surplus or Shortage	Effect on Price
$15	8	28	Surplus of 20	Falls
12	14	24	Surplus of 10	Falls
9	20	20	Equilibrium	Remains the same
6	26	16	Shortage of 10	Rises
3	32	12	Shortage of 20	Rises

(b) Market curves

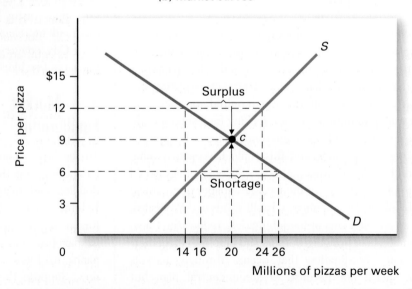

shortage or a surplus at a particular price.

To repeat, buyers prefer a lower price and sellers prefer a higher price. A market reaches equilibrium when the quantity demanded equals quantity supplied. In **equilibrium**, the independent plans of buyers and sellers exactly match, so market forces exert no pressure for change. In Exhibit 5, the demand and supply curves intersect at the *equilibrium point*, identified as point *c*. The *equilibrium price* is $9 per pizza, and the *equilibrium quantity* is 20 million per week. At that price and quantity, the market *clears*. Because there is no shortage or surplus, there is no pressure for the price to change. The demand and supply curves form an "x" at the intersection. You could say that the equilibrium point is found where "x" marks the spot.

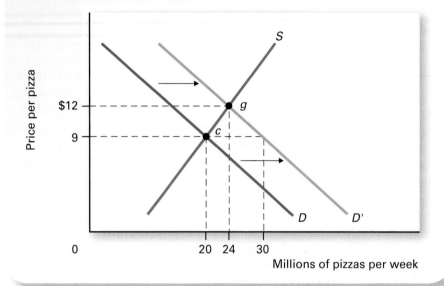

Markets indicate the price, quantity, and variety of goods available to you—from the latest social network to the smartest phone. You should be interested in equilibrium prices because they are what you usually pay for the thousands of goods and services you consume.

A market finds equilibrium through the independent actions of thousands, or even millions, of buyers and sellers. In one sense, the market is personal because each consumer and each producer makes a personal decision about how much to buy or sell at a given price. In another sense, the market is impersonal because it requires no conscious communication or coordination among consumers or producers. The price does all the talking. *Impersonal market forces synchronize the personal and independent decisions of many individual buyers and sellers to achieve equilibrium price and quantity.* Prices reflect relative scarcity. For example, to rent a 26-foot truck one way from San Francisco to Austin, U-Haul recently charged $3,236. Its one-way charge for that same truck from Austin to San Francisco was just $399. Why the difference? Far more people wanted to move from San Francisco to Austin than vice versa, so U-Haul had to pay its own employees to drive the empty trucks back from Texas. Rental rates reflected that extra cost.

4-6 CHANGES IN EQUILIBRIUM PRICE AND QUANTITY

Equilibrium occurs when the plans of demanders and suppliers exactly match. Once a market reaches equilibrium, that price and quantity remain stable until something affects demand or supply. A change in any non-price determinant of demand or supply usually changes equilibrium price and quantity in a predictable way, as you'll see.

4-6a Shifts of the Demand Curve

In Exhibit 6, demand curve *D* and supply curve *S* intersect at point *c* to yield the initial equilibrium price of $9 and the initial equilibrium quantity of 20 million 12-inch regular pizzas per week. Now suppose that one of the determinants of demand changes in a way that increases demand, shifting the demand curve to the right

equilibrium The condition that exists in a market when the plans of buyers match those of sellers, so quantity demanded equals quantity supplied and the market clears from *D* to *D′*. Any of the following could shift the demand for pizza rightward: (1) an increase in the money income of consumers (because pizza is a normal good); (2) an increase in the price of a substitute, such as tacos, or a decrease in the price of a complement, such as Pepsi; (3) a change in consumer expectations that causes people to demand more pizzas now; (4) a growth in the number of pizza consumers; or (5) a change in consumer tastes—based, for example, on a discovery that the tomato sauce on pizza has antioxidant properties that improve overall health.

After the demand curve shifts rightward to *D′* in Exhibit 6, the amount demanded at the initial price of $9 is 30 million pizzas, which exceeds the amount supplied of 20 million by 10 million pizzas. Competition among consumers for the limited quantity supplied puts upward pressure on the price. As the price increases, the quantity demanded decreases along the new demand curve *D′*, and the quantity supplied increases along the existing supply curve *S* until the two quantities are equal once again at equilibrium point *g*. The new equilibrium price is $12, and the new equilibrium quantity is 24 million pizzas per week. Thus, given an upward-sloping supply curve, an increase in demand increases both equilibrium price and quantity. For example, an increase in demand explains why roses cost more on Valentine's Day, why TV ads cost more on the Super Bowl broadcast, and why hotel rooms cost more in the host city during Super Bowl weekend.

A decrease in demand would initially create a surplus. Competition among producers to sell pizzas would lower both equilibrium price and quantity. These results can be summarized as follows: *Given an upward-sloping supply curve, a rightward shift of the demand curve increases both equilibrium price and quantity and a leftward shift decreases both equilibrium price and quantity.*

4-6b Shifts of the Supply Curve

Let's now consider shifts of the supply curve. In Exhibit 7, as before, we begin with demand curve *D* and supply curve *S* intersecting at point *c* to yield an equilibrium price of $9 and an equilibrium quantity of 20 million pizzas per week. Suppose one of the determinants of supply changes, increasing supply from *S* to *S′*. Changes that could shift the supply curve rightward include (1) a technological breakthrough in pizza ovens; (2) a reduction in the price of a resource such as mozzarella cheese; (3) a decline in the price of another good such as Italian bread; (4) a change in expectations that encourages pizza makers to expand production now; or (5) an increase in the number of pizzerias.

After the supply curve shifts rightward in Exhibit 7, the amount supplied at the initial price of $9 increases from 20 million to 30 million, so producers now supply 10 million more pizzas than consumers demand. Pizza makers compete to sell the surplus by lowering the price. As the price falls, the quantity supplied declines along the new

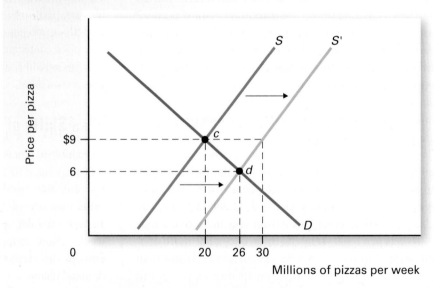

Exhibit 7

Effects of an Increase in Market Supply

An increase in supply is shown by a shift of the supply curve rightward, from *S* to *S′*. Quantity supplied exceeds quantity demanded at the original price of $9 per pizza, putting downward pressure on the price. As the price falls, quantity supplied decreases along supply curve *S′*, and quantity demanded increases along demand curve *D*. The new equilibrium price of $6 is reached at point *d*, where quantity demanded once again equals quantity supplied.

Exhibit 8

Effects of an Increase in Both Demand and Supply

When both demand and supply increase, the equilibrium quantity also increases. The effect on price depends on which curve shifts more. In panel (a), the demand curve shifts more, so the price rises. In panel (b), the supply curve shifts more, so the price falls.

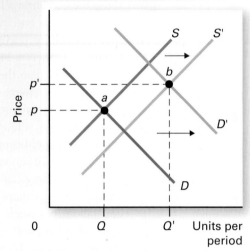

(a) Shift of demand dominates

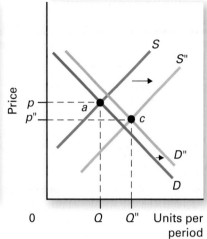

(b) Shift of supply dominates

supply curve and the quantity demanded increases along the existing demand curve until a new equilibrium point d is established. The new equilibrium price is $6, and the new equilibrium quantity is 26 million pizzas per week. In short, an increase in supply reduces the price and increases the quantity. This recent *Wall Street Journal* headline captures the idea: "Global Oil Glut Sends Prices Plunging."[3] On the other hand, a decrease in supply increases the price but decreases the quantity. As a case in point, a recent worldwide shortage af baby eels, an Asian delicacy, rocketed the price to more than $2,000 per pound.[4] Thus, *given a downward-sloping demand curve, a rightward shift of the supply curve decreases price but increases quantity, and a leftward shift increases price but decreases quantity.*

4-6c Simultaneous Shifts of Demand and Supply Curves

As long as only one curve shifts, we can say how equilibrium price and quantity will change. If both curves shift, however, the outcome is less obvious. For example, suppose both demand and supply increase, or shift rightward, as in Exhibit 8. Note that in panel (a),

demand shifts more than supply, and in panel (b), supply shifts more than demand. In both panels, equilibrium quantity increases. The change in equilibrium price, however, depends on which curve shifts more. If demand shifts more, as in panel (a), equilibrium price increases. For example, between 1995 and 2005, the demand for housing increased more than the supply, so both price and quantity increased. But if supply shifts more, as in panel (b), equilibrium price decreases. For example, in the last decade, the supply of personal computers has increased more than the demand, so price has decreased and quantity has increased.

Conversely, if both demand and supply decrease, or shift leftward, equilibrium quantity decreases. But, again, we cannot say what will happen to equilibrium price unless we examine relative shifts. (You can use Exhibit 8 to consider decreases in demand and supply by viewing D' and S' as the initial curves.) If demand shifts more, the price will fall. If supply shifts more, the price will rise.

If demand and supply shift in opposite directions, we can say what will happen to equilibrium price. Equilibrium price will increase if demand increases and supply decreases. Equilibrium price will decrease if demand decreases and supply increases. Without reference to particular shifts, however, we cannot say what will happen to equilibrium quantity.

3. Written by Russell Gold, this story appeared in October 14, 2014.

4. Clark Canfield, "Candia Man Cited for 41 Pounds of Illegal Eels in Maine," *Concord Monitor*, 9 April 2013.

Exhibit 9

Effects of Shifts of Both Demand and Supply

When the demand and supply curves shift in the same direction, equilibrium quantity also shifts in that direction. The effect on equilibrium price depends on which curve shifts more. If the curves shift in opposite directions, equilibrium price will move in the same direction as demand. The effect on equilibrium quantity depends on which curve shifts more.

	Shift of demand	
	Demand increases	**Demand decreases**
Supply increases	Equilibrium price change is indeterminate. Equilibrium quantity increases.	Equilibrium price falls. Equilibrium quantity change is indeterminate.
Supply decreases	Equilibrium price rises. Equilibrium quantity change is indeterminate.	Equilibrium price change is indeterminate. Equilibrium quantity decreases.

Shift of supply

These results are no doubt confusing, but Exhibit 9 summarizes the four possible combinations of changes. Using Exhibit 9 as a reference, please take the time right now to work through some changes in demand and supply to develop a feel for the results.

4-7 DISEQUILIBRIUM

disequilibrium The condition that exists in a market when the plans of buyers do not match those of sellers; a temporary mismatch between quantity supplied and quantity demanded as the market seeks equilibrium

price floor A minimum legal price below which a product cannot be sold; to have an impact, a price floor must be set above the equilibrium price

A surplus exerts downward pressure on the price, and a shortage exerts upward pressure. Markets, however, don't always reach equilibrium quickly. During the time required to adjust, the market is said to be in disequilibrium. **Disequilibrium** is usually temporary as market forces push toward equilibrium. But sometimes, often as a result of government intervention, when market forces are suppressed, disequilibrium can last a while, perhaps decades, as we will see next.

4-7a Price Floors

Sometimes public officials force a price above the equilibrium level. For example, the federal government regulates some agriculture prices in an attempt to ensure farmers a higher and more stable income than they would otherwise earn. To achieve a higher price, the government imposes a **price floor**, or a *minimum* selling price that is above the equilibrium price. Panel (a) of Exhibit 10 shows the effect of a $2.50 per gallon price floor for milk. At that price, farmers supply 24 million gallons per week, but consumers demand only 14 million gallons, yielding a surplus of 10 million gallons. This surplus milk will pile up on store shelves, eventually souring. To take it off the market, the government usually agrees to buy the surplus milk. The federal government, in fact, has spent billions buying and storing surplus agricultural products over the years. Note, to have an impact, a price floor must be set *above* the equilibrium price. A price floor set at or below the equilibrium price wouldn't matter (how come?). Price floors distort markets and reduce economic welfare.

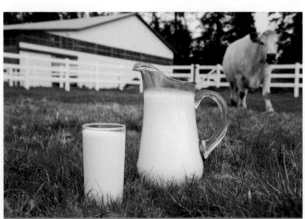

The U.S. government often buys surplus milk that results from a price floor imposed above the equilibrium market price.

Stephanie Horrocks/Istockphoto

Exhibit 10

Effects of Price Floors and Price Ceilings

A price floor set above the equilibrium price results in a surplus, as shown in panel (a). A price floor set at or below the equilibrium price has no effect. A price ceiling set below the equilibrium price results in a shortage, as shown in panel (b). A price ceiling set at or above the equilibrium price has no effect.

(a) Price floor for milk

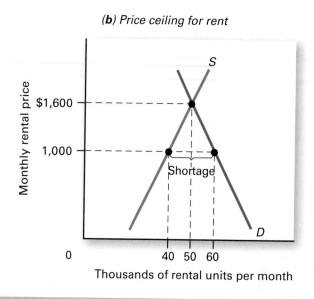

(b) Price ceiling for rent

4-7b Price Ceilings

Sometimes public officials try to keep a price below the equilibrium level by setting a **price ceiling**, or a *maximum* selling price. Concern about the rising cost of rental housing in some cities prompted city officials to impose rent ceilings. Panel (b) of Exhibit 10 depicts the demand and supply of rental housing. The vertical axis shows monthly rent, and the horizontal axis shows the quantity of rental units. The equilibrium, or market-clearing, rent is $1,600 per month, and the equilibrium quantity is 50,000 housing units. Suppose city officials set a maximum rent of $1,000 per month. At that ceiling price, 60,000 rental units are demanded, but only 40,000 supplied, resulting in a housing shortage of 20,000 units. Because of the price ceiling, the rental price no longer rations housing to those who value it the most. Other devices emerge to ration housing, such as long waiting lists, personal connections, and the willingness to make under-the-table payments, such as "key fees," "finder's fees," high security deposits, and the like. To have an impact, a price ceiling must be set *below* the equilibrium price. A price ceiling set at or above equilibrium wouldn't matter. (Again, why not?) Price floors and ceilings distort markets and reduce economic welfare.

Government intervention is not the only source of market disequilibrium. Sometimes, when new products are introduced or when demand

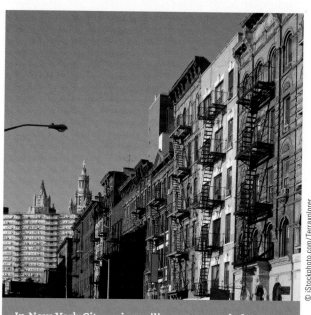

In New York City, price ceilings commonly known as "rent control" help contribute to acute housing shortages.

price ceiling A maximum legal price above which a product cannot be sold; to have an impact, a price ceiling must be set below the equilibrium price suddenly changes, it takes a while to reach equilibrium. For example, popular toys and best-selling books sometimes sell out. On the other hand, some products attract few customers and pile up unsold on store shelves, awaiting a "clearance sale."

4-8 FINAL WORD

Demand and supply are the building blocks of a market economy. Although a market usually involves the interaction of many buyers and sellers, few markets are consciously designed. Just as the law of gravity works whether or not we understand Newton's principles, market forces operate whether or not participants understand demand and supply. These forces arise naturally, much the way car dealers cluster on the outskirts of town to attract more customers.

Markets have their critics. Some observers may be troubled, for example, that Boston Patriots quarterback Tom Brady earns a salary that could pay 675 new schoolteachers $40,000 a year; or that corporate head Ralph Lauren earned enough in a recent year to pay for 1,600 new schoolteachers; or that U.S. consumers spend more than $60 billion a year on their pets.[5] On your next trip to the supermarket, notice how much shelf space goes to pet products—often an entire aisle. PetSmart, a chain store, sells over 12,000 different pet items. Veterinarians offer cancer treatment, cataract removal, root canals,

kidney transplants, even acupuncture. Kidney dialysis for a pet can cost over $75,000 per year.

In a market economy, consumers are kings and queens. Consumer sovereignty rules, deciding what gets produced. Those who don't like the market outcome usually look to government for a solution through price ceilings and price floors, regulations, income redistribution, and public finance more generally.

5. Arlene Weintraub, "The Rising Cost of Health Care—for Cats and Dogs," *Bloomberg Business*, 17 February 2015 at http://www.bloomberg.com/news/articles/2015-02-17/the-rising-costs-of-health-care-for-cats-and-dogs.

STUDY TOOLS 4

READY TO STUDY? IN THE BOOK, YOU CAN:

☐ Work the Problems at the end of the chapter.

☐ Rip out the chapter review card for a handy summary of the chapter and key terms.

ONLINE AT CENGAGEBRAIN.COM YOU CAN:

☐ Collect StudyBits while you read and study the chapter.

☐ Quiz yourself on key concepts.

☐ Prepare for tests with chapter flash cards as well as flash cards that you create.

☐ Watch videos to explore economics further.

CHAPTER 4 PROBLEMS

Your instructor can access the answers to these problems online at http://cengagebrain.com.

4-1 Explain why a demand curve slopes downward

1. *(Shifting Demand)* Using demand and supply curves, show the effect of each of the following on the market for cigarettes:
   a. A cure for lung cancer is found.
   b. The price of cigars increases.
   c. Wages increase substantially in states that grow tobacco.
   d. A fertilizer that increases the yield per acre of tobacco is discovered.
   e. There is a sharp increase in the price of matches, lighters, and lighter fluid.
   f. More states pass laws restricting smoking in restaurants and public places.

2. *(Substitutes and Complements)* For each of the following pair of goods, determine whether the goods are substitutes, complements, or unrelated:
   a. Peanut butter and jelly
   b. Private and public transportation
   c. Coke and Pepsi
   d. Alarm clocks and automobiles
   e. Golf clubs and golf balls

4-2 Identify five things which could shift a demand curve to the right or left

3. *(Demand Shifters)* List five things that are held constant along a market demand curve, and identify the change in each that would shift that demand curve to the right—that is, that would increase demand.

4-3 Explain why a supply curve usually slopes upward

4. *(Supply)* Why is a firm willing and able to increase the quantity supplied as the product price increases?

5. *(Supply)* What is the law of supply? Give an example of how you have observed the law of supply at work. What is the relationship between the law of supply and the supply curve?

4-4 Identify five things which could shift a supply curve to the right or left

6. *(Supply Shifters)* List the five things that are held constant along a market supply curve, and identify the change in each that would shift that supply curve to the right—that is, that would increase supply.

7. *(Demand and Supply)* How do you think each of the following affected the world price of oil? (Use demand and supply analysis.)
   a. Tax credits were offered for expenditures on home insulation.
   b. The Alaskan oil pipeline was completed.
   c. The ceiling on the price of oil was removed.
   d. Oil was discovered in the North Sea.
   e. Sport utility vehicles and minivans became popular.
   f. The use of nuclear power declined.

8. *(Demand and Supply)* What happens to the equilibrium price and quantity of ice cream in response to each of the following? Explain your answers.
   a. The price of dairy cow fodder increases.
   b. The price of beef decreases.
   c. Concerns arise about the high fat content of ice cream. Simultaneously, the price of sugar (used to produce ice cream) increases.

4-5 Explain why surpluses push prices down while shortages drive prices up

9. *(Market Surplus)* Why would firms accept a lower price if there is a market surplus?

10. *(Market Shortage)* Why would firms raise the price if there is a market shortage, and why would some consumers pay that higher price. At what point would firms stop raising the price?

4-6 Predict the impact of a change in demand or supply on the equilibrium price and quantity

11. *(Equilibrium)* "If a price is not an equilibrium price, there is a tendency for it to move to its equilibrium level. Regardless of whether the price is too high or too low to begin with, the adjustment process will increase the quantity of the good purchased." Explain, using a demand and supply diagram.

12. *(Equilibrium)* Assume the market for corn is depicted as in the table that appears below.
   a. Complete the table below.
   b. What market pressure occurs when quantity demanded exceeds quantity supplied? Explain.
   c. What market pressure occurs when quantity supplied exceeds quantity demanded? Explain.
   d. What is the equilibrium price?
   e. What could change the equilibrium price?
   f. At each price in the first column of the table below, how much is sold?

Price per Bushel	Quantity Demanded (millions of bushels)	Quantity Supplied (millions of bushels)	Surplus/ Shortage	Will Price Rise or Fall?
$1.80	320	200	_____	_____
2.00	300	230	_____	_____
2.20	270	270	_____	_____
2.40	230	300	_____	_____
2.60	200	330	_____	_____
2.80	180	350	_____	_____

13. *(Market Equilibrium)* Determine whether each of the following statements is true, false, or uncertain. Then briefly explain each answer.
   a. In equilibrium, all sellers can find buyers.
   b. In equilibrium, there is no pressure on the market to produce or consume more than is being sold.
   c. At prices above equilibrium, the quantity exchanged exceeds the quantity demanded.
   d. At prices below equilibrium, the quantity exchanged is equal to the quantity supplied

14. *(Changes in Equilibrium)* What are the effects on the equilibrium price and quantity of steel if the wages of steelworkers rise and, simultaneously, the price of aluminum rises?

4-7 Describe the result of a government-set price floor or price ceiling on a market

15. *(Price Floor)* There is considerable interest in whether the minimum wage rate contributes to teenage unemployment. Draw a demand and supply diagram for the unskilled labor market, and discuss the effects of a minimum wage. Who is helped and who is hurt by the minimum wage law?

5 | Elasticity of Demand and Supply

Archive Photos/Getty Images

LEARNING OUTCOMES

After studying this chapter, you will be able to…

5-1 Define and graph the price elasticity of demand

5-2 Identify the determinants of the price elasticity of demand

5-3 Define and graph the price elasticity of supply

5-4 Describe other measures of elasticity

After finishing this chapter go to **PAGE 88** for **STUDY TOOLS**

Topics discussed in Chapter 5 include:

- Price elasticity of demand
- Determinants of price elasticity
- Price elasticity and total revenue
- Price elasticity of supply
- Income elasticity of demand
- Cross-price elasticity of demand

A s you learned in Chapter 1, macroeconomics concentrates on aggregate markets—on the big picture. But the big picture is a mosaic pieced together from individual decisions made by households, firms, governments, and the rest of the world. To understand how a market economy works, you must take a closer look at these individual choices, especially at the role of prices. In a market economy, prices tell producers and consumers about the relative scarcity of resources and products.

> **"What does the supply curve look like for Cadillacs once owned by Elvis Presley?"**

A downward-sloping demand curve and an upward-sloping supply curve form a powerful analytical tool. To use this tool wisely, you must learn more about these curves. The more you know, the better you can predict the effects of a change in the price on quantity. Decision makers are willing to pay dearly for such knowledge. For example, Taco Bell would like to know what happens to sales if taco prices change. Governments would like to know how a hike in cigarette taxes affects teenage smoking. Colleges would like to know how tuition increases affect enrollments. And subway officials would like to know how fare changes affect ridership. To answer such questions, you must learn how responsive consumers and producers are to price changes. This chapter introduces the idea of *elasticity*, a measure of *responsiveness*.

5-1   PRICE ELASTICITY OF DEMAND

Just before a recent Thanksgiving, Delta Airlines cut fares for some seats on more than 10,000 domestic flights. Was that a good idea? A firm's success or failure often depends on how much it knows about the demand for its product. For Delta's total revenue to increase, the gain in tickets sold would have to more than make up for the decline in ticket prices. Likewise, the operators of Taco Bell would like to know what happens to sales if the price drops from, say, $1.10 to $0.90 per taco. The law of demand tells us that a lower price increases quantity demanded, but by how much? How sensitive is quantity demanded to a change in price? After all, if quantity

demanded increases enough, a price cut could be a profitable move for Taco Bell.

5-1a   Calculating Price Elasticity of Demand

Let's get more specific about how sensitive changes in quantity demanded are to changes in price. Take a look at the demand curve in Exhibit 1. At the initial price of $1.10 per taco, consumers demand 95,000 a day. If the price drops to $0.90, quantity demanded increases to 105,000. Is such a response a little or a lot? The *price elasticity of demand* measures, in a standardized way, how responsive consumers are to a change in price. *Elasticity* is another word for *responsiveness*. In simplest terms, the

Exhibit 1

Demand Curve for Tacos

If the price of tacos drops from $1.10 to $0.90, the quantity demanded increases from 95,000 to 105,000.

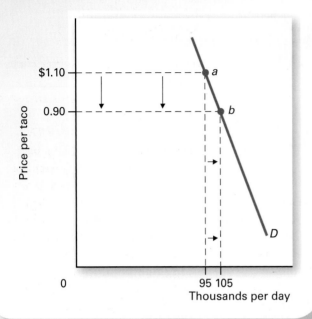

price elasticity of demand measures the percentage change in quantity demanded divided by the percentage change in price, or

$$\text{Price elasticity of demand} = \frac{\text{Percentage change in quantity demanded}}{\text{Percentage change in price}}$$

So what's the price elasticity of demand when the price of tacos falls from $1.10 to $0.90—that is, what's the price elasticity of demand between points *a* and *b* in Exhibit 1? For price elasticity to be a clear and reliable measure, we should get the same result between points *a* and *b* as we get between points *b* and *a*. To ensure that consistency, we must take the average of the initial price and the new price and use that as the base for computing the percentage change in price. For example, in Exhibit 1,

the base used to calculate the percentage change in price is the average of $1.10 and $0.90, which is $1.00. The percentage change in price is therefore the change in price, −$0.20, divided by $1.00, which works out to be −20 percent.

The same holds for changes in quantity demanded. In Exhibit 1, the base used for computing the percentage change in quantity demanded is the average of 95,000 and 105,000, which is 100,000. So the percentage increase in quantity demanded is the change in quantity demanded, 10,000, divided by 100,000, which works out to be 10 percent. So the resulting price elasticity of demand between points *a* and *b* (and between points *b* and *a*) is the percentage change in quantity demanded, 10 percent, divided by the percentage change in price, −20 percent, which is −0.5 (=10%/−20%).

Let's generalize the **price elasticity formula**. If the price changes from p to p', other things constant, the quantity demanded changes from q to q'. The change in price can be represented as Δp and the change in quantity as Δq. The formula for calculating the price elasticity of demand E_D between the two points is the percentage change in quantity demanded divided by the percentage change in price, or

$$E_D = \frac{\Delta q}{(q + q')/2} \div \frac{\Delta p}{(p + p')/2}$$

Again, because the average quantity and average price are used as the bases for computing percentage change, the same elasticity results whether going from the higher price to the lower price or the other way around.

Elasticity expresses a relationship between two amounts: the percentage change in quantity demanded and the percentage change in price. Because the focus is on the *percentage change*, we don't need to be concerned with how output or price is measured. For example, suppose the good in question is apples. It makes no difference in the elasticity formula whether we measure apples in pounds, bushels, or even tons. All that matters is the percentage change in quantity demanded. Nor does it matter whether we measure price in U.S. dollars, Mexican pesos, Zambian kwacha, or Vietnamese dong. All that matters is the percentage change in price.

price elasticity of demand Measures how responsive quantity demanded is to a price change; the percentage change in quantity demanded divided by the percentage change in price

price elasticity formula Percentage change in quantity demanded divided by the percentage change in price; the average quantity and the average price are used as bases for computing percentage changes in quantity and in price

Finally, the law of demand states that price and quantity demanded are inversely related, so the change in price and the change in quantity demanded move in opposite directions. In the elasticity formula, the numerator and the denominator have opposite signs, leaving the price elasticity of demand with a negative sign. Because constantly referring to elasticity as a negative number gets old fast, from here onward we treat the price elasticity of demand as an absolute value, or as a positive number. For example, the absolute value of the elasticity measured in Exhibit 1 is 0.5. Still, from time to time, you will be reminded that we are discussing price elasticity as absolute values.

5-1b Categories of Price Elasticity of Demand

As you'll see, the price elasticity of demand usually varies along a demand curve. Ranges of elasticity can be divided into three categories, depending on how responsive quantity demanded is to a change in price. If the percentage change in quantity demanded is less than the percentage change in price, the resulting elasticity has an absolute value between 0 and 1.0. That portion of the demand curve is said to be **inelastic**, meaning that quantity demanded is relatively unresponsive to a change in price. For example, the elasticity derived in Exhibit 1 between points a and b was 0.5, so that portion of the demand curve is inelastic. If the percentage change in quantity demanded just equals the percentage change in price, the resulting elasticity has an absolute value of 1.0, and that portion of a demand curve is **unit elastic**. Finally, if the percentage change in quantity demanded exceeds the percentage change in price, the resulting elasticity has an absolute value exceeding 1.0, and that portion of a demand curve is said to be **elastic**. In this case, the change in price has a relatively large effect on quantity demanded. For example, Amazon.com experimented with the price of e-books and found, using the midpoint formula, that a price decline of 40 percent increased the quantity demanded by 54 percent, yielding a price elasticity of 1.35.[1] In summary, *the price elasticity of demand is*

inelastic *if its absolute value is between 0 and 1.0, unit elastic if equal to 1.0, and elastic if greater than 1.0.*

5-1c Elasticity and Total Revenue

Knowledge of price elasticity of demand is especially valuable to producers, because it indicates how a price change affects total revenue. **Total revenue** (TR) is price (p) multiplied by quantity demanded (q) at that price, or $TR = p \times q$. What happens to total revenue when price decreases? Well, according to the law of demand, a lower price increases quantity demanded, which tends to increase total revenue. But, a lower price means producers get less revenue from each unit sold, which tends to decrease total revenue. The overall impact of a lower price on total revenue therefore depends on the net result of these opposite effects. *If the positive effect of a greater quantity demanded more than offsets the negative effect of a lower price, then total revenue rises.* More specifically, if demand is elastic, the percentage increase in quantity demanded exceeds the percentage decrease in price, so total revenue increases. If demand is unit elastic, the percentage increase in quantity demanded just equals the percentage decrease in price, so total revenue remains unchanged. Finally, if demand is inelastic, the positive impact of an increase in quantity demanded on total revenue is more than offset by the negative impact of a decrease in price, so total revenue falls.

5-1d Price Elasticity and the Linear Demand Curve

A look at elasticity along a particular type of demand curve, the linear demand curve, ties together the ideas

inelastic demand A change in price has relatively little effect on quantity demanded; the percentage change in quantity demanded is less than the percentage change in price; the resulting price elasticity has an absolute value less than 1.0

unit-elastic demand The percentage change in quantity demanded equals the percentage change in price; the resulting price elasticity has an absolute value of 1.0

elastic demand A change in price has a relatively large effect on quantity demanded; the percentage change in quantity demanded exceeds the percentage change in price; the resulting price elasticity has an absolute value exceeding 1.0

total revenue Price multiplied by quantity demanded at that price

1. Calculated based on data appearing in Steven Cohen, "I'm Backing Amazon and Authors Should Too," *Wall Street Journal*, 24 October 2014.

Exhibit 2

Demand, Price Elasticity, and Total Revenue

Where the demand curve is elastic, a lower price increases total revenue. Total revenue reaches a maximum at the rate of output where demand curve is unit elastic. Where the demand curve is inelastic, further decreases in price reduce total revenue.

(a) Demand and price elasticity

(b) Total revenue

Exhibit 2, a $10 drop in price always increases quantity demanded by 100 units. But the price elasticity of demand is larger on the higher-price end of the demand curve than on the lower-price end. Here's why. Consider a movement from point a to point b on the upper end of the demand curve in Exhibit 2. The $10 price drop is a percentage change of 10/85, or 12 percent, using the midpoint formula in all these computations. The 100-unit increase in quantity demanded is a percentage change of 100/150, or 67 percent. Therefore, the price elasticity of demand between points a and b is 67%/12%, which equals 5.6. Between points d and e on the lower end, however, the $10 price decrease is a percentage change of 10/15, or 67 percent, and the 100-unit quantity increase is a percentage change of 100/850, or only 12 percent. The price elasticity of demand is 12%/67%, or 0.2. In other words, *if the demand curve is linear, consumers are more responsive to a given price change when the initial price is high than when it's low.*

Demand becomes less elastic as we move down the curve. At a point halfway down the linear demand curve in Exhibit 2, the elasticity is 1.0. *This halfway point divides a linear demand curve into an elastic upper half and an inelastic lower half.* You can observe a clear relationship between the elasticity of demand in panel (a) and total revenue in panel (b). Notice that where demand is elastic, a decrease in price increases total revenue because the gain in revenue from selling more units (represented by the large blue rectangle) exceeds the loss in revenue from selling all units at the lower price (the small pink rectangle). But where demand is inelastic, a price decrease reduces total revenue because the gain in revenue from selling more units (the small blue

discussed so far. A **linear demand curve** is simply a straight-line demand curve, as in panel (a) of Exhibit 2. Panel (b) shows the total revenue generated by each price-quantity combination along the demand curve in panel (a). Recall that total revenue equals price times quantity. Please take a moment now to see how the demand curve and total revenue curve relate.

Because the demand curve is linear, its slope is constant, so a given decrease in price always causes the same unit increase in quantity demanded. For example, along the demand curve in

linear demand curve
A straight-line demand curve; such a demand curve has a constant slope but usually has a varying price elasticity

rectangle) is less than the loss in revenue from selling all units at the lower price (the large pink rectangle). And where demand is unit elastic, the gain and loss of revenue exactly cancel each other out, so total revenue at that point remains constant (thus, total revenue peaks in the lower panel).

Knowing a product's elasticity can help a supplier with its pricing decisions. If demand is inelastic, a producer would never willingly cut the price because doing so would reduce total revenue. The percentage increase in quantity demanded would be less than the percentage decrease in price. Why cut the price if selling more cuts total revenue?

To review, total revenue increases as the price declines until the midpoint of the linear demand curve is reached, where total revenue peaks. In Exhibit 2, total revenue peaks at $25,000 per period, where quantity demanded equals 500 units. To the right of the midpoint of the demand curve, total revenue declines as the price falls. More generally, regardless of whether demand is straight or curved, there is a consistent relationship between the price elasticity of demand and total revenue: *A price decline increases total revenue if demand is elastic, has no effect on total revenue if demand is unit elastic, and decreases total revenue if demand is inelastic.* Finally, note that a downward-sloping linear demand curve has a constant slope but a varying elasticity, so *the slope of a demand curve is not the same as the price elasticity of demand.*

> ❝The slope of a demand curve is not the same as the price elasticity of demand.❞

5-1e Constant-Elasticity Demand Curves

Again, price elasticity measures the responsiveness of consumers to a change in price. The shape of the demand curve for a firm's product is key in the pricing and output decision. This responsiveness varies along a linear demand curve unless the demand curve is horizontal or vertical, as in panels (a) and (b) of Exhibit 3. These two demand curves, along with the special demand curve in panel (c), are all called *constant-elasticity demand curves* because the elasticity does not change along the curves.

Perfectly Elastic Demand Curve

The horizontal demand curve in panel (a) indicates that consumers demand all that is offered for sale at the given price p (the quantity actually demanded depends on the amount supplied at that price). If the price rises above p, however, quantity demanded drops to zero. This is a **perfectly elastic demand curve**, and its elasticity value is infinity, a number too large to be defined. You may think this an odd sort of demand curve: Consumers, as a result of a small increase in price, go from demanding as much as is supplied to demanding none of the good. Consumers are so sensitive to price changes that they tolerate no price increase. As you will see in a later chapter, this behavior reflects the demand for the output of any individual producer when many producers supply identical products at the market price of p.

Perfectly Inelastic Demand Curve

Along the vertical demand curve in panel (b) of Exhibit 3, quantity demanded does not vary when the price changes. This demand curve expresses consumer sentiment when "price is no object." For example, if you are extremely rich and need insulin to survive, price would be no object. No matter how high the price, you would continue to demand whatever it takes. And if the price of insulin should drop, you would not increase your quantity demanded. Another example of perfectly inelastic demand comes from Shakespeare's play *Richard III*. After his horse is slain in battle, the king, at the mercy of the enemy, cries out, "A horse! A horse! My kingdom for a horse!" The king is willing to pay a high price indeed—his kingdom—for a horse. On a less lofty level, Ben Franklin expressed a similar sentiment when he observed, "Necessity never made a good bargain." Because the percentage

perfectly elastic demand curve A horizontal line, which means that any price increase would reduce quantity demanded to zero; the elasticity has an absolute value of infinity

Exhibit 3

Constant-Elasticity Demand Curves

The three panels show constant-elasticity demand curves, so named because the elasticity value does not change along the demand curve. Along the perfectly elastic, or horizontal, demand curve of panel (a), consumers demand all that is offered for sale at price *p*, but demand nothing at a price above *p*. Along the perfectly inelastic, or vertical, demand curve of panel (b), consumers demand amount *Q* regardless of price. Along the unit-elastic demand curve of panel (c), total revenue is the same for each price-quantity combination.

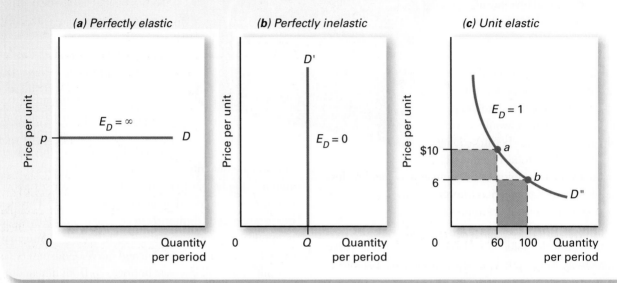

change in quantity demanded is zero for any given percentage change in price, the numerical value of the price elasticity is zero. A vertical demand curve is called a **perfectly inelastic demand curve**.

Unit-Elastic Demand Curve

Panel (c) in Exhibit 3 presents a demand curve that is unit elastic everywhere. Along a **unit-elastic demand curve**, any percentage change in price causes the exact opposite percentage change in quantity demanded. Because changes in price and in quantity demanded are offsetting, total revenue remains constant for every price-quantity combination along the curve. For example, when the price falls from $10 to $6, the quantity demanded increases from 60 to 100 units. The price drops by $4/$8, or 50 percent, and the quantity increases by 40/80, or 50 percent. The

pink shaded rectangle shows the loss in total revenue from cutting the price; the blue shaded rectangle shows the gain in total revenue from selling more at the lower price. Because the demand curve is unit elastic, the revenue gained from selling more just offsets the revenue lost from lowering the price, so total revenue remains unchanged at $600.

Each demand curve in Exhibit 3 is called a **constant-elasticity demand curve** because the elasticity is the same all along the curve. In contrast, the downward-sloping linear demand curve examined earlier had a different elasticity value at each point along the curve. Exhibit 4 lists the absolute values for the five categories of price elasticity we have discussed, summarizing the effects of a 10 percent price increase on quantity demanded and on total revenue. Give this exhibit some thought now, and see if you can draw a demand curve for each category of elasticity.

5-2 DETERMINANTS OF THE PRICE ELASTICITY OF DEMAND

So far we have explored the technical properties of demand elasticity and discussed why it varies along a downward-sloping demand curve. But we have yet to consider why

perfectly inelastic demand curve A vertical line, which means that any price change has no effect on the quantity demanded; the elasticity value is zero

unit-elastic demand curve Everywhere along the demand curve, the percentage change in price causes an equal but offsetting percentage change in quantity demanded, so total revenue is unchanged; the elasticity has an absolute value of 1.0

constant-elasticity demand curve The type of demand that exists when price elasticity is the same everywhere along the curve; the elasticity value is unchanged

Exhibit 4

Summary of Price Elasticity of Demand: Effects of a 10 Percent Increase in Price

Absolute Value of Price Elasticity	Type of Demand	What Happens to Quantity Demanded	What Happens to Total Revenue
$E_D = 0$	Perfectly inelastic	No change	Increases by 10 percent
$0 < E_D < 1$	Inelastic	Drops by less than 10 percent	Increases by less than 10 percent
$E_D = 1$	Unit elastic	Drops by 10 percent	No change
$1 < E_D < \infty$	Elastic	Drops by more than 10 percent	Decreases
$E_D = \infty$	Perfectly elastic	Drops to 0	Drops to 0

elasticity is different for different goods. Several factors influence the price elasticity of demand.

5-2a Availability of Substitutes

As we saw in Chapter 4, your particular wants can be satisfied in a variety of ways. A rise in the price of pizza makes other food relatively cheaper. If close substitutes are available, an increase in the price of pizza prompts some consumers to buy substitutes. But if nothing else satisfies quite like pizza, the quantity of pizza demanded does not decline as much. *The greater the availability of substitutes and the more similar these substitutes are to the good in question, the greater that good's price elasticity of demand.*

The number and similarity of substitutes depend on how the good is defined. *The more narrow the definition, the more substitutes and, thus, the more elastic the demand.* For example, the demand for Post Raisin Bran is more elastic than the demand for raisin bran in general because there are more substitutes for Post Raisin Bran, including Kellogg's Raisin Bran and Total Raisin Bran, than for raisin bran generally. The demand for raisin bran, however, is more elastic than the demand for breakfast cereals more generally because the consumer has many substitutes for raisin bran, such as cereals made from corn, rice, wheat, or oats, and processed with or without honey, nuts, fruit, or chocolate. To give you some idea of the range of elasticities, the price elasticity of demand for Post Raisin Bran has been estimated to be -2.5 versus -0.9 for all breakfast cereals.[2]

Apple iTunes music downloads fell by 14 percent in 2014, because the company faced stiff competition from free online music videos and music streaming services, such as Spotify. To compete better in the market, Apple bought the subscription streaming service Beats Music for $3 billion.[3] Pro team owners worry that live TV broadcasts cut game attendance, especially now that more households enjoy large-screen HDTVs plus DVRs with playback capabilities. A study of attendance at Scottish Premier League soccer matches found that TV broadcasts cut pay-at-the-gate attendance by 30 percent.[4] This is why home teams black out TV coverage if a game is not sold out before a certain date.

Because the Internet has made price comparisons across sellers much easier, consumers of those goods have become more price-sensitive. Amazon.com, for example, lists sellers of a particular product from lowest to highest price. Thus, the demand for each seller's product has become more elastic.[5]

Certain goods—some prescription drugs, for instance—have no close substitutes. The demand for such goods tends to be less elastic than for goods with close substitutes, such as Bayer aspirin. Knowledgeable shoppers tend to buy the generic brand, which costs less than the name brand. For example, when pharmacists shop for headache medicine for their families, they buy generic brands more than do other shoppers. And when chefs buy kitchen staples, such as flour and sugar, they buy generic brands more than do regular shoppers.[6] Much advertising is aimed at establishing in the consumer's mind the uniqueness of a particular product—an effort to convince consumers "to accept no substitutes." Why might a firm want to make the demand for its product less elastic?

5-2b Share of the Consumer's Budget Spent on the Good

Recall that a higher price reduces quantity demanded in part because a higher price reduces the real spending power of consumer income. Because spending on some goods claims a large share of the consumer's

2. See Jerry A. Hausman, "The Price Elasticity of Demand for Breakfast Cereal," in *The Economics of New Goods*, T. F. Bresnahan and J. J. Gordon, eds. (University of Chicago Press, 1997).

3. Hannah Karp, "Apple iTunes Sees Big Drop in Music Sales," *Wall Street Journal*, 24 October 2014.

4. Grant Allan and Graeme Roy, "Does Television Crowd Out Spectators?," *Journal of Sports Economics*, 5 (December 2008): 592–605.

5. For evidence of how the Internet has made consumers more price sensitive, see Glenn Ellison and Sara Ellison, "Search, Obfuscation, and Price Elasticities on the Internet," *Econometrica*, 77 (March 2009): 427–452.

6. Bart Bronnenberg et al. "Do Pharmacists Buy Bayer? Informed Shoppers and the Brand Premium," NBER Working Paper No. 20295 (July 2014).

The price elasticity of demand for one brand of pain-killer is higher than for all brands combined. If the price of only one brand rises, you can switch to another brand. But if the price of all brands increases, you are less likely to change your purchasing habits.

Richard Levine/Alamy

budget, a change in the price of such a good has a substantial impact on the consumer's *ability* to buy it. An increase in the price of housing, for example, reduces the ability to buy housing. The income effect of a higher price reduces the quantity demanded. In contrast, the income effect of an increase in the price of, say, paper towels is trivial because paper towels represent such a tiny share of any budget. *The more important the item is as a share of the consumer's budget, other things constant, the greater is the income effect of a change in price, so the more elastic is the demand for the item.* Hence, the quantity of housing demanded is more responsive to a given percentage change in price than is the quantity of paper towels demanded.

5-2c Duration of Adjustment Period

Consumers can substitute lower-priced goods for higher-priced goods, but finding substitutes usually takes time. Suppose your college announces a sharp increase in room and board fees, effective next term. Some students will move off campus before that term begins; others may wait until the next academic year. Over time, the college may get fewer applicants and more incoming students will choose off-campus housing. The longer the adjustment period, the greater the consumers' ability to substitute away from relatively higher-priced products toward lower-priced substitutes. Thus, *the longer the period of adjustment, the more responsive the change in quantity demanded is to a given change in price.* Here's another example: Between 1973 and 1974, OPEC (Organization of the Petroleum Exporting Countries) raised gasoline prices 45 percent, but the quantity demanded initially decreased just 8 percent. As more time passed, however, people bought smaller cars and relied more on public transportation. They also bought more energy-efficient appliances and insulated their homes better. Thus, the percentage change in quantity demanded was greater the longer consumers adjusted to the price hike.

Exhibit 5 shows how demand becomes more elastic over time. Given an initial price of $1.00 at point *e*, let D_w be the demand curve one week after a price change; D_m, one month after; and D_y, one year after. Suppose the price increases to $1.25. The more time consumers have to respond to the price increase, the greater the reduction in quantity demanded. The demand curve D_w shows that

Exhibit 5

Demand Becomes More Elastic Over Time

D_w is the demand curve one week after a price increase from $1.00 to $1.25. Along this curve, quantity demanded per day falls from 100 to 95. One month after the price increase, quantity demanded has fallen to 75 along D_m. One year after the price increase, quantity demanded has fallen to 50 along D_y. At any given price, D_y is more elastic than D_m, which is more elastic than D_w.

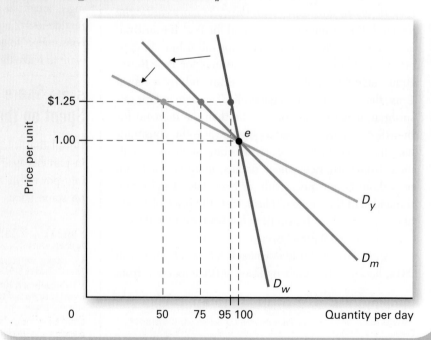

one week after the price increase, the quantity demanded has not declined much—in this case, from 100 to 95 per day. The demand curve D_m indicates a reduction to 75 per day after one month, and demand curve D_y shows a reduction to 50 per day after one year. Notice that among these demand curves and over the range starting from point e, the flatter the demand curve, the more price elastic the demand. Here, elasticity seems linked to the slope because we begin from a common point—the price-quantity combination at point e.

5-2d Elasticity Estimates

Let's look at some estimates of the price elasticity of demand for particular goods and services. Remember, finding alternatives when the price increases takes time. Thus, when estimating price elasticity, economists often distinguish between a period during which consumers have little time to adjust—let's call it the *short run*—and a period during which consumers can more fully adjust to a price change—let's call it the *long run*. Exhibit 6

Exhibit 6

Selected Price Elasticities of Demand (Absolute Values)

Product	Short Run	Long Run
Cigarettes (among adults)	—	0.4
Electricity (residential)	0.1	1.9
Air travel	0.1	2.4
Beer	0.3	—
Medical care and hospitalization	0.3	0.9
Gasoline	0.4	1.5
Milk	0.4	—
Fish (cod)	0.5	—
Wine	0.7	1.2
Movies	0.9	3.7
Natural gas (residential)	1.4	2.1
Automobiles	1.9	2.2
Chevrolets	—	4.0

Sources: F. Chaloupka, "Rational Addictive Behavior and Cigarette Smoking," *Journal of Political Economy*, (August 1991); Hsaing-tai Cheng and Oral Capps, Jr., "Demand for Fish," *American Journal of Agricultural Economics*, (August 1998); Shanjun Li, Joshua Linn, and Erich Muehlegger, "Gasoline Taxes and Consumer Behavior," *American Economic Journal: Economic Policy*, 6 (November 2014): 302–342; Douglas Young et al., "Alcohol Consumption, Measurement Error, and Beverage Prices," *Journal of Studies on Alcohol* (March 2003); Christopher Ruhm et al., "What U.S. Data Should Be Used to Measure the Price Elasticity of Demand for Alcohol?" *Journal of Health Economics*, 31 (December 2012): 851–862; and H. Houthakker and L. Taylor, *Consumer Demand in the United States: Analysis and Projections*, 2nd ed. (Harvard University Press, 1970).

> **"Consumers can substitute lower-priced goods for higher-priced goods, but finding substitutes usually takes time."**

provides short-run and long-run price elasticity estimates for selected products.

The price elasticity of demand is greater in the long run because consumers have more time to adjust. For example, if the price of electricity rose today, consumers in the short run might cut back a bit in their use of electrical appliances, and those in homes with electric heat might lower the thermostat in winter. Over time, however, consumers would switch to more energy-efficient appliances, insulate their homes better, and perhaps switch from electric heat. So the demand for electricity is more elastic in the long run than in the short run, as shown in Exhibit 6. In fact, in every instance where estimates for both the short run and the long run are available, demand is more elastic in the long run than the short run. Notice also that the demand for Chevrolets is more elastic than the demand for automobiles more generally. Chevrolets have many more substitutes than do automobiles in general. There are no close substitutes for cigarettes, even in the long run, so the demand for cigarettes among adults is price inelastic.

5-3 PRICE ELASTICITY OF SUPPLY

Prices signal both sides of the market about the relative scarcity of products. Higher prices discourage consumption but encourage production. Lower prices encourage consumption but discourage production. The price elasticity of demand measures how responsive consumers are to a price change. Likewise, the **price elasticity of supply** measures how responsive producers are to a price change. Supply elasticity is calculated in the same way as demand elasticity. In simplest terms, the price elasticity of supply equals the percentage change in quantity supplied divided by the percentage change in price. Because a higher price usually increases quantity supplied, the percentage change in price and the percentage change in quantity

price elasticity of supply Measures the responsiveness of quantity supplied to a price change; the percentage change in quantity supplied divided by the percentage change in price supplied move in the same direction, so the price elasticity of supply is usually a positive number.

Exhibit 7 depicts a typical upward-sloping supply curve. As you can see, if price increases from p to p', quantity supplied increases from q to q'. Price and quantity supplied move in the same direction. Let's look at the elasticity formula for the supply curve. The price elasticity of supply is

$$E_s = \frac{\Delta q}{(q + q')/2} \div \frac{\Delta p}{(p + p')/2}$$

where Δq is the change in quantity supplied and Δp is the change in price. This is the same formula used to compute price elasticity of demand except that q here is quantity supplied, not quantity demanded. The terminology for supply elasticity is the same as for demand elasticity: If supply elasticity is less than 1.0, supply is **inelastic**; if it equals 1.0, supply is **unit elastic**; and if it exceeds 1.0, supply is **elastic**.

inelastic supply A price change has relatively little effect on quantity supplied; the percentage change in quantity supplied is less than the percentage change in price; the price elasticity of supply is less than 1.0

unit-elastic supply The percentage change in quantity supplied equals the percentage change in price; the price elasticity of supply equals 1.0

elastic supply A price change has a relatively large effect on quantity supplied; the percentage change in quantity supplied exceeds the percentage change in price; the price elasticity of supply exceeds 1.0

perfectly elastic supply curve A horizontal line, which means that any price decrease drops the quantity supplied to zero; the elasticity value is infinity

perfectly inelastic supply curve A vertical line, which means that a price change has no effect on the quantity supplied; the elasticity value is zero

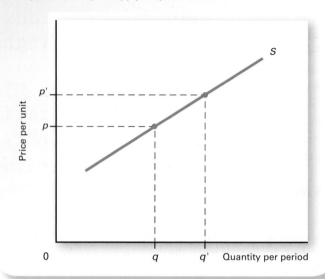

Exhibit 7

Price Elasticity of Supply

If price increases from p to p', quantity supplied increases from q to q'. Price and quantity supplied move in the same direction, so price elasticity of supply is a positive number.

5-3a Constant Elasticity Supply Curves

Again, price elasticity of supply measures how responsive producers are to a change in price. This responsiveness varies along a linear supply curve unless the curve is horizontal or vertical, as in panels (a) and (b) of Exhibit 8, or passes through the origin, as in panel (c). These three supply curves are called *constant-elasticity supply curves* because the elasticity value does not change along the curves.

Perfectly Elastic Supply Curve

At one extreme is a horizontal supply curve, such as supply curve S in panel (a) of Exhibit 8. In this case, producers supply none of the good at a price below p but supply any amount at price p (the quantity actually supplied at price p depends on the quantity demanded at that price). Because a tiny increase from a price just below p to a price of p results in an unlimited quantity supplied, this is called a **perfectly elastic supply curve**, which has a numerical value of infinity. As individual consumers, we typically face perfectly elastic supply curves. When we go to the supermarket, we can usually buy as much as we want at the posted price but none at a lower price. Obviously all consumers together cannot buy an unlimited amount at the prevailing price (recall the fallacy of composition from Chapter 1).

Perfectly Inelastic Supply Curve

The least responsive relationship is where there is no change in the quantity supplied regardless of price, as shown by the vertical supply curve S' in panel (b) of Exhibit 8. Because the percentage change in quantity supplied is zero, regardless of the change in price, the price elasticity of supply is zero. This is a **perfectly inelastic supply curve**. Any good in fixed supply, such as Picasso paintings, 1995 Dom Perignon champagne, or Cadillacs once owned by Elvis Presley, has a perfectly inelastic supply curve. The actual price will depend on the demand curve.

Exhibit 8

Constant-Elasticity Supply Curves

In each of the three panels is a constant-elasticity supply curve, so named because the elasticity value does not change along the curve. Supply curve *S* in panel (a) is perfectly elastic, or horizontal. Along *S*, firms supply any amount of output demanded at price *p*, but supply none at prices below *p*. Supply curve *S'* is perfectly inelastic, or vertical. *S'* shows that quantity supplied is independent of price. In panel (c), *S''*, a straight line from the origin, is a unit-elastic supply curve. Any percentage change in price results in the same percentage change in quantity supplied.

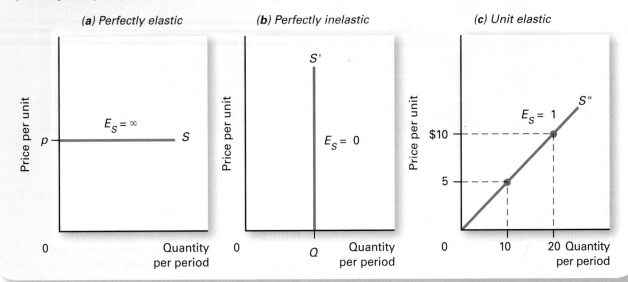

Unit-Elastic Supply Curve

Any supply curve that is a straight line from the origin—such as *S''* in panel (c) of Exhibit 8—is a **unit-elastic supply curve**. This means a percentage change in price always generates an identical percentage change in quantity supplied. For example, along *S''* a doubling of the price results in a doubling of quantity supplied. Note that unit elasticity is based not on the slope of the line but on the fact that the linear supply curve is a ray from the origin.

5-3b Determinants of Supply Elasticity

The elasticity of supply indicates how responsive producers are to a change in price. Their response depends on how easy it is to alter quantity supplied if the price changes. If the cost of supplying additional units rises sharply as output expands, then a higher price causes little increase in quantity supplied, so supply tends to be inelastic. But if the marginal cost rises slowly as output expands, the lure of a higher price prompts a large increase in quantity supplied. In this case, supply is more elastic.

One determinant of supply elasticity is the length of the adjustment period under consideration. Just as demand becomes more elastic over time as consumers adjust to price changes, supply also becomes more elastic over time as producers adjust to price changes. The longer the adjustment period under consideration, the more able producers are to adapt to a price change. Exhibit 9 presents different supply curves for each of three periods. S_w is the supply curve when the period of adjustment is a week. As you can see, a higher price generates little response in quantity supplied because firms have little time to adjust. This supply curve is inelastic between $1.00 and $1.25.

S_m is the supply curve when the adjustment period under consideration is a month. Firms have more time to vary output. Thus, supply is more elastic when the adjustment period is a month than when it's a week. Supply is yet more elastic when the adjustment period is a year, as is shown by S_y. As the adjustment period lengthens, the supply response increases.

unit-elastic supply curve A percentage change in price causes an identical percentage change in quantity supplied; depicted by a supply curve that is a straight line from the origin; the elasticity value equals 1.0

The supply of window-washing services has a much higher price elasticity of supply than does oil production. Can you think of a few reasons why?

For example, if the price of oil increases, oil producers in the short run can try to pump more from existing wells, but in the long run, a higher price stimulates more exploration. Research confirms the positive link between the price elasticity of supply and the length of the adjustment period. *The elasticity of supply is typically greater the longer the period of adjustment.*

The ability to increase quantity supplied in response to a higher price differs across industries. For example, the time lag between and oil discovery and production averages four to six years, but can take longer.[7] Oil discovered on Alaska's north slope in 1967 did not begin to flow south until a decade later. More generally, the response time is slower for suppliers of oil, electricity, and timber (where expansion may take years) than for suppliers of window-washing services, lawn maintenance, and hot-dog vending (where expansion may take only days).

5-4 OTHER ELASTICITY MEASURES

Price elasticities of demand and supply are frequently used in economic analysis, but two other elasticity measures also provide valuable information.

5-4a Income Elasticity of Demand

What happens to the demand for new cars, fresh vegetables, or computer software if consumer income increases by, say, 10 percent? The answer is of great interest to producers because it helps them predict the effect of changing

Exhibit 9

Supply Becomes More Elastic Over Time

The supply curve one week after a price increase, S_w, is less elastic, at a given price, than the supply curve one month later, S_m, which is less elastic than the supply curve one year later, S_y. Given a price increase from \$1.00 to \$1.25, quantity supplied per day increases to 110 units after one week, to 140 units after one month, and to 200 units after one year.

7. Rabah Areski, Valerie A. Ramey, and Liugang Sheng, "News Shocks in Open Economies: Evidence from Giant Oil Discoveries," NBER Working Paper No. 20857 (January 2015).

consumer income on quantity sold and on total revenue. The **income elasticity of demand** measures how responsive demand is to a change in consumer income. Specifically, *the income elasticity of demand measures the percentage change in demand divided by the percentage change in income that caused it.*

As noted in Chapter 4, the demand for some products, such as used furniture and used clothing, actually declines, or shifts leftward, as income increases. Thus, the income elasticity of demand for such goods is negative. Goods with income elasticities less than zero are called *inferior goods*. But the demand for most goods increases, or shifts rightward, as income increases. These are called *normal goods* and have income elasticities greater than zero.

Let's take a closer look at normal goods. Suppose demand increases as income increases but by a smaller percentage than income increases. In such cases, the income elasticity is greater than 0 but less than 1. For example, people buy more food as their incomes rise, but the percentage

Inferior or normal good?

increase in demand is less than the percentage increase in income. Normal goods with income elasticities less than 1 are called *income inelastic*. *Necessities* such as food, rental housing, and clothing often have income elasticities less than 1. Goods with income elasticity greater than 1 are called *income elastic*. *Luxuries* such as high-end cars, vintage wines, and meals at upscale restaurants have income elasticities greater than 1. By the way, the terms *inferior goods, necessities,* and *luxuries* are not value judgments about the merits of particular goods; these terms are simply convenient ways of classifying economic behavior.

Exhibit 10 presents income elasticity estimates for some goods and services. The figures indicate, for example, that as income increases, consumers spend proportionately more on wine, restaurant meals, and owner-occupied housing. Spending on food and rental housing also increases as income increases, but less than proportionately. Spending on beer declines as income increases. So as income rises, the demand for restaurant meals increases more in percentage terms than does the demand for food, and the demand for owner-occupied housing increases more in percentage terms than does the demand for rental housing. The demand for wine increases sharply, while the demand for beer declines. Flour also has negative income elasticity. According to these estimates, beer and flour are inferior goods.

5-4b Cross-Price Elasticity of Demand

A firm that produces an entire line of products has a special interest in how a change in the price of one item affects the demand for another. For example, the Coca-Cola Company needs to know how changing the price of Cherry Coke affects sales of Classic Coke. The company also needs to know the relationship between the price of Coke and the demand for Pepsi and vice

Exhibit 10
Selected Income Elasticities of Demand

Product	Income Elasticity	Product	Income Elasticity
Wine	5.03	Health Care	1.00
Private education	2.46	Clothing	0.92
Automobiles	2.45	Coca-Cola	0.68
Cigarettes	2.0	Beef	0.62
Owner-occupied housing	1.49	Food	0.51
Furniture	1.48	Coffee	0.51
Dental service	1.42	Gasoline and oil	0.48
Restaurant meals	1.40	Rental housing	0.43
Spirits ("hard" liquor)	1.21	Pork	0.18
Shoes	1.10	Beer	−0.09
Chicken	1.06	Flour	−0.36

Sources: Ivan Bloor, "Food for Thought," *Economic Review,* (September 1999); F. Gasmi et al., "Econometric Analysis of Collusive Behavior in a Soft-Drink Market," *Journal of Economics and Management Strategy,* (Summer 1992); X. M. Gao et al., "A Microeconomic Model Analysis of U.S. Consumer Demand for Alcoholic Beverages," *Applied Economics,* (January 1995); H. Houthakker and L. Taylor, *Consumer Demand in the United States: Analyses and Projections,* 2nd ed. (Harvard University Press, 1970); C. Huang et al., "The Demand for Coffee in the United States, 1963–77," *Quarterly Review of Economics and Business,* (Summer 1980); G. Brester and M. Wohlgenant, "Estimating Interrelated Demands for Meats Using New Measures for Ground and Table Cut Beef," *American Journal of Agricultural Economics,* (November 1991); and Donald Kenkel, Maximilian Schmeiser, and Carly Urban, "Is Smoking Inferior? Evidence from Variation in the Earned Income Tax Credit," NBER Working Paper No. 20097 (May 2014). Note the income elasticity for cigarettes is for lower income smokers only.

income elasticity of demand The percentage change in demand divided by the percentage change in consumer income; the value is positive for normal goods and negative for inferior goods versa. Likewise, Apple needs to know how changing the price of one iPhone model affects the demand for other iPhone models. The responsiveness of the demand for one good to changes in the price of another good is called the **cross-price elasticity of demand**. This is defined as the percentage change in the demand of one good divided by the percentage change in the price of another good. Its numerical value can be positive, negative, or zero, depending on whether the two goods in question are substitutes, complements, or unrelated, respectively.

Substitutes

If an increase in the price of one good leads to an increase in the demand for another good, their cross-price elasticity is positive and the two goods are *substitutes*. For example, an increase in the price of Coke, other things constant, shifts the demand for Pepsi rightward, so the two are substitutes. The cross-price elasticity between Coke and Pepsi has been estimated at about 0.7, indicating that a 10 percent increase in the price of one increases the demand for the other by 7 percent.[8]

Complements

If an increase in the price of one good leads to a decrease in the demand for another, their cross-price elasticity is negative and the goods are *complements*. For example, an increase in the price of gasoline, other things

> **cross-price elasticity of demand** The percentage change in the demand of one good divided by the percentage change in the price of another good; it's positive for substitutes, negative for complements, and zero for unrelated goods

8. F. Gasmi, J. J. Laffont, and Q. Vuong, "Econometric Analysis of Collusive Behavior in a Soft-Drink Market," *Journal of Economics and Management Strategy*, 1 (June 1992): 277–311.

constant, shifts the demand for tires leftward because people drive less and replace their tires less frequently. Gasoline and tires have a negative cross-price elasticity and are complements.

To Review: The cross-price elasticity of demand is positive for substitutes and negative for complements. Most pairs of goods selected at random are unrelated, so their cross-price elasticity is zero, such as socks and sushi.

5-5 FINAL WORD

Because this chapter has been more quantitative than earlier ones, the mechanics may have overshadowed the intuitive appeal and neat simplicity of elasticity. *Elasticity measures the willingness and ability of buyers and sellers to alter their behavior in response to changes in their economic circumstances.* Firms try to estimate the price elasticity of demand for their products. Governments also have an ongoing interest in various elasticities. For example, state governments want to know the effect of an increase in the sales tax on total tax receipts, and local governments want to know how an increase in income affects the demand for real estate and thus the revenue generated by a given property tax rate. International groups are interested in elasticities; for example, OPEC is concerned about the price elasticity of demand for oil—in the short run and in the long run. Because a corporation often produces an entire line of products, it also has a special interest in cross-price elasticities. Some corporate economists estimate elasticities for a living. The online appendix to this chapter shows how price elasticities of demand and supply shed light on who ultimately pays a tax.

STUDY TOOLS 5

READY TO STUDY? IN THE BOOK, YOU CAN:

☐ Work the Problems at the end of the chapter.

☐ Rip out the chapter review card for a handy summary of the chapter and key terms.

ONLINE AT CENGAGEBRAIN.COM YOU CAN:

☐ Collect StudyBits while you read and study the chapter.

☐ Quiz yourself on key concepts.

☐ Prepare for tests with chapter flash cards as well as flash cards that you create.

☐ Watch videos to explore economics further.

CHAPTER 5 PROBLEMS

Your instructor can access the answers to these problems online at http://cengagebrain.com.

5-1 Define and graph the price elasticity of demand

1. *(Calculating Price Elasticity of Demand)* Suppose that 50 units of a good are demanded at a price of $1 per unit. A reduction in price to $0.20 results in an increase in quantity demanded to 70 units. Using the midpoint formula, show that these data yield a price elasticity of 0.25. By what percentage would a 10 percent rise in the price reduce the quantity demanded, assuming price elasticity remains constant along the demand curve?

2. *(Price Elasticity and Total Revenue)* Fill in the blanks for each price-quantity combination listed in the following table. Now graph this relationship, making sure to label each axis. What relationship have you depicted?

P	Q	Price Elasticity	Total Revenue
$9	1	_____	_____
$8	2	_____	_____
$7	3	_____	_____
$6	4	_____	_____
$5	5	_____	_____
$4	6	_____	_____
$3	7	_____	_____
$2	8	_____	_____

3. *(Categories of Price Elasticity of Demand)* For each of the following absolute values of price elasticity of demand, indicate whether demand is elastic, inelastic, perfectly elastic, perfectly inelastic, or unit elastic. In addition, determine what would happen to total revenue if a firm raised its price in each elasticity range identified.

	Absolut Value	Elasticity	Effect of Price Increase
a	$E_D = 2.5$		
b	$E_D = 1.0$		
c	$E_D = \infty$		
d	$E_D = 0.8$		

5-2 Identify the determinants of the price elasticity of demand

4. *(Determinants of Price Elasticity)* Why is the price elasticity of demand for Coca-Cola greater than the price elasticity of demand for soft drinks generally?

5. *(Determinants of Price Elasticity)* Would the price elasticity of demand for electricity be more elastic over a shorter or a longer period of time?

5-3 Define and graph the price elasticity of supply

6. *(Price Elasticity of Supply)* Calculate the price elasticity of supply for each of the following combinations of price and quantity supplied. In each case, determine whether supply is elastic, inelastic, perfectly elastic, perfectly inelastic, or unit elastic.
   a. Price falls from $2.25 to $1.75; quantity supplied falls from 600 units to 400 units.
   b. Price falls from $2.25 to $1.75; quantity supplied falls from 600 units to 500 units.
   c. Price falls from $2.25 to $1.75; quantity supplied remains at 600 units.
   d. Price increases from $1.75 to $2.25; quantity supplied increases from 466.67 units to 600 units.

5-4 Describe other measures of elasticity

7. *(Cross-Price Elasticity)* Rank the following in order of increasing (from negative to positive) cross-price elasticity of demand with coffee. Explain your reasoning.

   Bleach _____ Tea _____ Cream _____ Cola _____

8. *(Income Elasticity of Demand)* Calculate the income elasticity of demand for each of the following goods:

	Quantity Demanded When Income Is $10,000	Quantity Demanded When Income Is $20,000
Good 1	10	25
Good 2	4	5
Good 3	3	2

9. *(Other Elasticity Measures)* Complete each of the following sentences:
   a. The income elasticity of demand measures, for a given price, the _____ in quantity demanded divided by the _____ income from which it resulted.
   b. If a decrease in the price of one good causes a decrease in demand for another good, the two goods are _____.
   c. If the value of the cross-price elasticity of demand between two goods is approximately zero, they are considered _____.

APPENDIX
PRICE ELASTICITY AND TAX INCIDENCE

A contributing factor to the Revolutionary War was a British tax on tea imported by the American Colonies. The tea tax led to the Boston Tea Party, during which colonists dumped tea leaves into Boston Harbor. There was confusion about who would ultimately pay such a tax: Would it be paid by suppliers, demanders, or both? As you will see, tax incidence—that is, who pays a tax—depends on the price elasticities of demand and supply.

DEMAND ELASTICITY AND TAX INCIDENCE

Panel (a) of Exhibit A-1 depicts the market for tea leaves, with demand D and supply S. Before the tax is imposed, the intersection of demand and supply yields a market price of $1.00 per ounce and a market quantity of 10 million ounces per day. Now suppose a tax of $0.20 is imposed on

each ounce sold. Recall that the supply curve represents the amount that producers are willing and able to supply at each price. Because the government now collects $0.20 in tax for each ounce sold, that amount must be added to the original supply curve to get a supply curve that includes the tax. Thus, the shift of the supply curve from S to S_t reflects the decrease in supply resulting from the tax. *The effect of a tax on tea is to decrease the supply by the amount of the tax.* The demand curve remains the same because nothing happened to demand; only the quantity demanded changes.

The result of the tax in panel (a) is to raise the equilibrium price from $1.00 to $1.15 and to decrease the equilibrium quantity from 10 million to 9 million ounces. As a result of the tax, consumers pay $1.15, or $0.15 more per ounce, and producers receive $0.95 after the tax, or $0.05 less per ounce. Thus, consumers pay $0.15 of the $0.20 tax as a higher price, and producers pay $0.05 as a lower receipt.

The shaded rectangle of panel (a) shows the total tax collected, which equals the tax per ounce of $0.20 times

---

Exhibit A-1

Effects of Price Elasticity of Demand on Tax Incidence

The imposition of a $0.20-per-ounce tax on tea shifts the supply curve leftward from S to S_t. In panel (a), which has a less elastic demand curve, the market price rises from $1.00 to $1.15 per ounce and the market quantity falls from 10 million to 9 million ounces per day. In panel (b), which has a more elastic demand curve, the same tax leads to an increase in price from $1.00 to $1.05; market quantity falls from 10 million to 7 million ounces per day. The more elastic the demand curve, the more the tax is paid by producers in the form of a lower net-of-tax receipt.

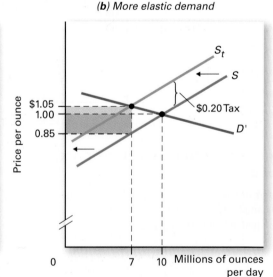

(a) Less elastic demand   (b) More elastic demand

the 9 million ounces sold, for a total of $1.8 million in tax revenue per day. You can see that the original price line at $1 divides the shaded rectangle into two portions—an upper portion (light pink) showing the share of the tax paid by consumers through a higher price and a lower portion (dark pink) showing the tax paid by producers through a lower net-of-tax receipt.

The same situation is depicted in panel (b) of Exhibit A-2, except that demand is more elastic than in the left panel. Consumers in panel (b) cut their quantity demanded more sharply as the price increases, so producers cannot as easily pass the tax along as a higher price. The tax increases the price by $0.05, to $1.05, and the net-of tax receipt to suppliers declines by $0.15 to $0.85. Total tax revenue equals $0.20 per ounce times 7 million ouncess old, or $1.4 million per day. Again, the upper portion of the shaded rectangle shows the share of the tax paid by consumers through a higher price, and the lower portion shows the share paid by producers through a lower net-of-tax receipt. The tax is the difference between the amount consumers pay and the amount producers receive.

More generally, as long as the supply curve slopes upward, the more price elastic the demand, the more tax producers pay as a lower net-of-tax receipt and the less consumers bear as a higher price. Also notice that the amount sold decreases more in panel (b) than in panel (a): Other things constant, total tax revenue declines more when demand is more elastic. Because tax revenue falls as the price elasticity of demand increases, governments around the world tend to tax products with inelastic demand, such as cigarettes, liquor, beer, gasoline, gambling, salt, coffee, and, yes, tea.

SUPPLY ELASTICITY AND TAX INCIDENCE

The effect of the elasticity of supply on tax incidence is shown in Exhibit A-2. The same demand curve appears in both panels, but the supply curve is more elastic in panel (a). Again we begin with an equilibrium price of $1.00 per ounce and an equilibrium quantity of 10 million ounces of tea leaves per day. Once the sales tax of $0.20 per ounce is imposed, supply decreases in both panels to reflect the tax. Notice that in panel (a),the price rises to $1.15, or $0.15 above the pretax price of $1.00, while in panel (b), the price increases by only $0.05. Thus, where supply is more elastic, more of the tax is passed on to consumers in panel (a). The more easily suppliers can cut production in response to a newly imposed tax, the more of the tax consumers pay. More generally, as long as the demand curve slopes downward, *the more elastic the supply, the less tax producers pay and the more tax consumers pay*.

We conclude that *the less elastic the demand and the more elastic the supply, the greater the share of the tax paid by consumers*. The side of the market that's more nimble (that is, more price elastic) in adjusting to a price increase is more able to stick the other side of the market with more of the tax.

Exhibit A-2

Effects of Price Elasticity of Supply on Tax Incidence

The imposition of a $0.20-per-ounce tax on tea shifts leftward both the more elastic supply curve in panel (a) and the less elastic supply curve of panel (b). In panel (a) the market price rises from $1.00 to $1.15 per ounce. In panel (b), the price rises only to $1.05 per ounce. Thus, the more elastic the supply curve, the more the tax is paid by consumers as a higher price.

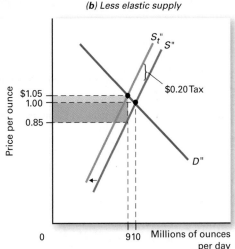

6 | Consumer Choice and Demand

UpperCut Images/Getty Images

LEARNING OUTCOMES

After studying this chapter, you will be able to...

6-1 Explain why marginal utility decreases as more of a good or service is consumed

6-2 Given tastes, the prices for two different goods, and a budget constraint, describe the utility-maximizing condition in your own words

6-3 Explain how can you get a consumer surplus from consuming a particular good if, in equilibrium, your marginal valuation of the good just equals the price you pay

After finishing this chapter go to **PAGE 102** for **STUDY TOOLS**

Topics discussed in Chapter 6 include:

- Total and marginal utility
- Law of diminishing marginal utility
- Utility-maximizing condition
- Consumer surplus
- Role of time in demand
- Time price of goods

You have already learned two reasons why demand curves slope downward. The first is the *substitution effect* of a price change. When the price of a good falls, consumers substitute that now-cheaper good for other goods. The second is the *income effect* of a price change. When the price of a good falls, real incomes increase, boosting consumers' ability to buy more.

> **"How much do you eat when you can eat all you want?"**

Demand is so important that it needs more attention. This chapter develops the law of demand based on the utility, or satisfaction, of consumption. As usual, the assumption is that you and other consumers try to maximize utility, or satisfaction. The point of this chapter is not to teach you how to maximize utility—that comes naturally. But learning the economic principles behind your behavior will help you understand the implications of that behavior, making predictions more accurate.

6-1 UTILITY ANALYSIS

Suppose you and a friend are dining out. After dinner, your friend asks how you liked your meal. You wouldn't say, "I liked mine twice as much as you liked yours." Nor would you say, "It deserves a rating of 86 on the Consumer Satisfaction Index." The utility, or satisfaction, you derive from that meal cannot be compared with another person's experience, nor can your utility be measured based on some objective standard. But you might say something such as, "I liked it better than my last meal here" or "I liked it better than campus food." More generally, you can say whether one of your experiences is more satisfying than another. Even if you say nothing about your likes and dislikes, we can draw conclusions about your preferences by observing your behavior. For example, we can conclude that you prefer apples to oranges if, when the two are priced the same, you buy apples every time.

6-1a Tastes and Preferences

As introduced in Chapter 3, *utility* is the sense of pleasure, or satisfaction, that comes from consumption. Utility is subjective. The utility you derive from a particular good, service, or activity depends on your *tastes and preferences*—your likes and dislikes in consumption. Some things are extremely appealing to you and others are not. You may not understand, for example, why someone would pay good money for sharks' fin soup, calves' brains, polka music, or martial arts movies. Few Americans like bugs, but 80 percent of the world's population eat them with pleasure.[1]

As noted in Chapter 4, your desires for food and drink are largely biological, as are your desires for comfort, rest, shelter, friendship, love, status, personal safety, amusement, and a pleasant environment. Your family background shapes some of your tastes, such as food preferences. Other influences include the culture, peer pressure, religious convictions, and prevailing technology. As an example of how a change in technology can affect tastes, more Americans now track calories and nutrients using smartphone apps, so meals on average are becoming more nutritious per calorie.[2] So economists can say something about the origin of tastes, but

1. Dana Goodyear, "Grubs: Eating Bugs to Save the Planet," *The New Yorker*, 15 and 22 August 2011.

2. Melinda Beck and Amy Schatz, "Americans' Eating Habits Take a Healthier Turn, Study Finds," *Wall Street Journal*, 16 January 2014.

they claim no particular expertise. *Economists assume simply that tastes are given and are relatively stable—that is, different people may have different tastes, but an individual's tastes are not constantly in flux.*

To be sure, tastes for some products do change over time. Here are six examples: (1) over the last three decades, hiking boots, work boots, and duck boots replaced running shoes as everyday footwear among many college students; (2) Americans began consuming leaner cuts of beef after a report linked the fat in red meat to a greater risk of cancer; (3) because of the decline in the popularity of baseball cards, the number of shops that sell and trade these cards fell from about 10,000 in the early 1990s to fewer than 1,500 by 2015; (4) the increased appeal of locally grown produce has more than tripled the number of farmers' markets in the United States since 1995; (5) because of research supporting the health benefits of almonds, Americans now consume ten times more than in 1965; and (6) in the 1970s, professional bowlers were celebrities, earning more on average than pro football players, but due to a decline in bowling's popularity, most pro bowlers now must hold second jobs to make ends meet.

Although some tastes do change over time, economists believe they are stable enough to allow us to examine relationships such as that between price and quantity demanded. If tastes were not stable enough, then we could not reasonably make the other-things-constant assumption required for demand analysis. We could not even draw a demand curve.

> **"**The utility you derive from a particular good, service, or activity depends on your *tastes and preferences.***"**

6-1b Law of Diminishing Marginal Utility

Suppose it's a hot summer day and you are extremely thirsty after running four miles. You pour yourself an 8-ounce glass of ice water. That first glass is wonderful, and it puts a serious dent in your thirst. The next glass is not quite as wonderful, but it is still pretty good. The third one is just fair; and the fourth glass you barely finish.

What can we say about the *utility*, or satisfaction, you get from water? Let's first distinguish between *total utility* and *marginal utility*. **Total utility** is the total satisfaction you derive from consumption. In this example, total utility is the total satisfaction you get from four glasses of water. **Marginal utility** is the change in total utility resulting from a one-unit change in consumption. For example, the marginal utility of a third glass of water is the change in total utility resulting from drinking that third glass.

Your experience with water reflects an economic law—the **law of diminishing marginal utility**. This law states that the more of a good you consume per period, other things constant, the smaller the increase in your total utility from additional consumption—that is, the smaller the marginal utility of each additional unit consumed. The marginal utility you derive from each additional glass of water declines as you drink more. You enjoy the first glass a lot, but each additional glass provides less and less marginal utility. If forced to drink a fifth glass, you wouldn't like it; your marginal utility would be negative—you would experience *disutility*.

Diminishing marginal utility is a feature of all consumption. A second foot-long sub sandwich at one meal, for most people, would provide little or no marginal utility. You might still enjoy a second movie on Friday night, but a third would probably be too much to take. In fact, almost anything repeated enough could become torture, such as being forced to watch the same movie or listen to the same song over and over and over. Yes, variety is the spice of life.

A long, cold winter spent cooped up inside can cause "cabin fever." Each additional cold day adds disutility. But the fever breaks with the arrival of the first warm day of spring, which is something special. That first warm, glorious day causes such delirious joy that this jump in marginal utility has its own fevered name—"spring fever." Spring fever is eventually "cured" by many warm days like the first. By the time August rolls around, you attach much less marginal utility to yet another warm day.

For some goods, the drop in marginal utility with additional consumption is greater. A second copy of the

total utility The total satisfaction you derive from consumption; this could refer to either your total utility of consuming a particular good or your total utility from all consumption

marginal utility The change in your total utility from a one-unit change in your consumption of a good

law of diminishing marginal utility The more of a good a person consumes per period, the smaller the increase in total utility from consuming one more unit, other things constant same daily newspaper would likely provide you no marginal utility (in fact, the design of newspaper vending machines relies on the fact that a buyer takes no more than one).[3] Likewise, a second viewing of the same movie at one sitting usually yields no additional utility. More generally, expressions such as "Been there, done that" and "Same old, same old" convey the idea that, for many activities, things start to get old fast. Restaurants depend on the law of diminishing marginal utility when they offer all-you-can-eat specials—and no doggie bags allowed, because the deal is all you can eat now, not now and over the next few days. Incidentally, if you ordered the all-you-can-eat special, you continue to eat as long as your expected marginal utility from another bite is positive.

> "Each person has a uniquely subjective utility scale."

6-2 MEASURING UTILITY

So far, the description of utility has used such words as *wonderful, good,* and *fair.* The analysis can't be pushed very far with such subjective language. To predict consumer behavior, we need to develop a consistent way of viewing utility.

6-2a Units of Utility

Let's go back to the water example. Although there really is no objective way of measuring utility, if

As we consume more of anything, the marginal utility of each additional unit falls.

3. This example appears in Marshall Jevons, *The Fatal Equilibrium* (Cambridge, Mass.: MIT Press, 1985).

pressed, you could be more specific about how much you enjoyed each glass of water. For example, you might say the second glass was half as good as the first, the third was half as good as the second, the fourth was half as good as the third, and you passed up a fifth glass because you expected no positive utility. To get a handle on this, let's assign arbitrary numbers to the utility you get from water, so the pattern reflects your expressed level of satisfaction. Let's say the first glass provides you with 40 units of utility, the second with 20, the third with 10, and the fourth with 5. A fifth glass, if you were forced to drink it, would cause negative utility, or disutility—in this case, say, −2 units. *Developing numerical values for utility allows us to be more specific about the utility of consumption.* If it would help, you could think of these units more playfully as thrills, kicks, or jollies—as in, getting your kicks from consumption.

By attaching a numerical measure to utility, we can compare the total utility a particular consumer gets from different goods as well as the marginal utility that the consumer gets from additional consumption. Thus, we can employ units of utility to evaluate a consumer's preferences. Note, however, that we cannot compare utility levels across consumers. *Each person has a uniquely subjective utility scale.*

The first column of Exhibit 1 lists possible quantities of water you might consume after running four miles on a hot day. The second column presents the total utility derived from that consumption, and the third column shows the marginal utility of each additional glass of water. Recall that marginal utility is the change in total utility from consuming an additional unit of the good. You can see from the second column that total utility increases with each of the first four glasses

Exhibit 1

Utility Derived From Water Consumption After Running Four Miles

Amount Consumed (8-ounce glasses)	Total Utility	Marginal Utility
0	0	—
1	40	40
2	60	20
3	70	10
4	75	5
5	73	−2

Exhibit 2

Utility Derived From Water Consumption After Running Four Miles

Total utility, shown in panel (a), increases with each of the first four glasses of water consumed but by smaller and smaller amounts. The fifth glass causes total utility to fall, implying that marginal utility is negative, as shown in panel (b).

(a) Total utility

(b) Marginal utility

but by smaller and smaller amounts. The third column shows that the first glass of water yields 40 units of utility, the second glass yields an additional 20 units, and so on. Marginal utility declines after the first glass of water, becoming negative with the fifth glass. *At any level of consumption, marginal utilities sum to yield the total utility of that amount.* Total utility is graphed in panel (a) of Exhibit 2. Again, because of diminishing marginal utility, each additional glass of water adds less to total utility, so total utility increases for the first four glasses but at a decreasing rate. Panel (b) shows the law of diminishing marginal utility.

6-2b Utility Maximization in a World Without Scarcity

Economists assume that your purpose for drinking water, as with all your consumption, is to *maximize your total utility*. So how much water do you consume? If the

price of water is zero, you drink water as long as doing so increases total utility. Each of the first four glasses of water adds to your total utility. *If a good is free, you increase consumption as long as marginal utility is positive.* Let's broaden the analysis to a world of two goods—pizza and movie rentals. We continue to translate the satisfaction you receive from consumption into units of utility. Based on your tastes and preferences, suppose your total utility and marginal utility from consumption are as presented in Exhibit 3. The first four columns apply to pizza and the second four to movie rentals. Please spend a little time right now with each column.

Notice from columns (3) and (7) that each good shows diminishing marginal utility. Given this set of preferences,

Exhibit 3

Total and Marginal Utilities From Pizza and Movies

Pizza

(1) Consumed per Week	(2) Total Utility	(3) Marginal Utility	(4) Marginal Utility per Dollar if $p = \$8$
0	0	—	—
1	56	56	7
2	88	32	4
3	112	24	3
4	130	18	2¼
5	142	12	1½
6	150	8	1

Movie Rentals

(5) Viewed per Week	(6) Total Utility	(7) Marginal Utility	(8) Marginal Utility per Dollar if $p = \$4$
0	0	—	—
1	40	40	10
2	68	28	7
3	88	20	5
4	100	12	3
5	108	8	2
6	114	6	1½

how much of each good would you consume per week? At a zero price, you would increase consumption as long as marginal utility is positive. Thus, you would consume at least the first six pizzas and first six movies because the sixth unit of each good yields positive marginal utility. Did you ever go to a party where the food and drinks were free to you? How much did you eat and drink? You ate and drank until you didn't want any more—that is, until the marginal utility of another bite and another sip fell to zero. Your consumption was determined not by prices or your income but simply by your tastes.

6-2c Utility Maximization in a World of Scarcity

Alas, goods are usually scarce, not free. Suppose the price of a pizza is $8, the rental price of a movie is $4, and your part-time job pays $40 per week after taxes. Your utility is still based on your tastes, but your income is now limited. How do you allocate your income between the two goods to maximize utility? To get the ball rolling, suppose you start off spending your entire $40 budget on pizza, purchasing five a week, which yields a total of 142 units of utility. You quickly realize that if you buy one less pizza, you free up enough income in your budget to rent two movies. Would total utility increase? Sure. You give up 12 units of utility, the marginal utility of the fifth pizza, to get 68 units of utility from the first two movies. Total utility zooms from 142 to 198. Then you notice that if you cut back to three pizzas, you give up 18 units of utility from the fourth pizza but gain a total of 32 units of utility from the third and fourth movies. This is another utility-increasing move.

Further reductions in pizza consumption, however, would reduce your total utility because you would give up 24 units of utility from the third pizza but gain only 14 units from the fifth and sixth movies. Thus, you quickly find that the utility-maximizing combination is three pizzas and four movies per week, for a total utility of 212. This means spending $24 on pizza and $16 on movies. *You are in equilibrium when consuming this combination because any affordable change would reduce your utility.*

6-2d Utility-Maximizing Conditions

Once a consumer is in equilibrium, there is no way to increase utility by reallocating the budget. Any change decreases utility. But,

wait, there's more: In equilibrium, the last dollar spent on each good yields the same marginal utility. Let's see how this works. Column (4) in Exhibit 3 shows the marginal utility of pizza divided by a price of $8. Column (8) shows the marginal utility of movies divided by a price of $4. The equilibrium combination of three pizzas and four movies exhausts the $40 budget and adds 3 units of utility for the last dollar spent on each good. **Consumer equilibrium** is achieved when the budget is exhausted and the last dollar spent on each good yields the same marginal utility. In equilibrium, the marginal utility of a pizza divided by its price equals the marginal utility of a movie divided by its price. In short, the consumer gets the same bang from the last buck spent on each good. This equality can be expressed as:

$$\frac{MU_p}{p_p} = \frac{MU_m}{p_p}$$

where MU_p is the marginal utility of pizza, p_p is the price of pizza, MU_m is the marginal utility of movies, and p_m is the rental price. The consumer reallocates spending until the last dollar spent on each product yields the same marginal utility. Although this example considers only two goods, the logic of utility maximization applies to any number of goods.

In equilibrium, higher-priced goods must yield more marginal utility than lower-priced goods—enough additional utility to compensate for their higher price. Because a pizza costs twice as much as a movies rental, the marginal utility of the final pizza purchased must, in equilibrium, be twice that of the final movie rented.

consumer equilibrium
The condition in which an individual consumer's budget is exhausted and the last dollar spent on each good yields the same marginal utility; therefore, utility is maximized

Indeed, the marginal utility of the third pizza, 24, is twice that of the fourth movie, 12. Economists do not claim that you consciously equate the ratios of marginal utility to price, but they do claim that you act as if you made such calculations.

Thus, you decide how much of each good to purchase by considering your tastes, market prices, and your income. Consumers maximize utility by equalizing the marginal utility from the last dollar spent on each good. Research suggests that people act as if they try to maximize utility. Evidence of rational decision-making is strongest for those with more wealth, more income, and more education.[4]

6-2e Marginal Utility and the Law of Demand

How does utility analysis relate to your demand for pizza? The discussion so far yields a single point on your demand curve for pizza: At a price of $8, you demand three pizzas per week. This is based on income of $40 per week, a price of $4 per movie rental, and your tastes reflected by the utility tables in Exhibit 3. Knowing that three pizzas are demanded when the price is $8 offers no clue about the shape of your demand curve for pizza. To generate another point, let's see what happens to quantity demanded if the price of pizza changes, while keeping other things constant (such as tastes, income, and the price of movie rentals). Suppose the price of a pizza drops from $8 to $6.

Exhibit 4 is the same as Exhibit 3, except the price per pizza is $6. Your original choice was three pizzas and four movie rentals. At that combination and with the price of pizza now $6, the marginal utility per dollar spent on the third pizza is 4, while the marginal utility per dollar spent on the fourth movie remains at 3. The marginal utilities of the last dollar spent on each good are no longer equal. What's more, the original combination of three pizzas and four movies now leaves $6 unspent. So you could still buy your original combination but have $6 left to spend (this, incidentally, shows the income effect of the lower price). You can increase utility by adjusting your consumption.

In light of your utility schedules in Exhibit 4, you would increase your consumption to four pizzas per week. This strategy exhausts your budget and equates the marginal utilities of the last dollar expended on each good. Your movie rentals remain unchanged. The marginal utility of the fourth pizza, 18, divided by the price

4. Syngjoo Choi et al., "Who Is (More) Rational?" *American Economic Review*, 104 (June 2014): 1518–1550.

Exhibit 4

Total and Marginal Utilities From Pizza and Movies After the Price of Pizza Decreases From $8 to $6

Pizza

(1) Consumed per Week	(2) Total Utility	(3) Marginal Utility	(4) Marginal Utility per Dollar if $p = \$6$
0	0	—	—
1	56	56	$9\frac{1}{3}$
2	88	32	$5\frac{1}{3}$
3	112	24	4
4	130	18	3
5	142	12	2
6	150	8	$1\frac{1}{3}$

Movie Rentals

(5) Viewed per Week	(6) Total Utility	(7) Marginal Utility	(8) Marginal Utility per Dollar if $p = \$4$
0	0	—	—
1	40	40	10
2	68	28	7
3	88	20	5
4	100	12	3
5	108	8	2
6	114	6	$1\frac{1}{2}$

of $6 yields 3 units of utility per dollar of expenditure, the same as you get from the fourth movie. You are in equilibrium once again. Total utility increases by the 18 units you derive from the fourth pizza. Thus, you are clearly better off as a result of the lower price.

We now have a second point on your demand curve for pizza—if the price is $6, you demand four pizzas. The two points are presented as *a* and *b* in Exhibit 5. We could continue to change the price of pizza and thereby generate additional points on the demand curve, but you can get some idea of the demand curve's downward slope from these two points. The shape of the demand curve for pizza matches our expectations based on the law of demand: Price and quantity demanded are inversely related. (Try estimating your price elasticity of

Exhibit 5

Your Demand Curve for Pizza Generated From Marginal Utility

At a price of $8 per pizza, the consumer is in equilibrium when consuming three pizzas per week (point *a*).If the price falls to $6, quantity demanded increases to four pizzas (point *b*). Points a and b are two points on this consumer's demand curve for pizza.

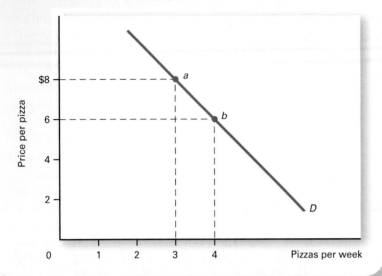

demand between points *a* and *b*. Hint: What does your total spending on pizza tell you?)

We have gone to some lengths to see how you (or any consumer) maximize utility. Given prices and your income, your tastes and preferences naturally guide you to the best bundle. You are not even conscious of your behavior. The urge to maximize utility is like the force of gravity—both work whether or not you understand them. Even animal behavior seems consistent with the law of demand. Wolves, for example, exhibit no territorial concerns when

Both wolves and people obey the law of demand by placing more value on things when faced with increased scarcity.

game is plentiful. But when game becomes scarce, wolves carefully mark their territory and defend it against intruders. Thus, wolves appear to value game more when it is scarce.

6-3 APPLICATIONS OF UTILITY ANALYSIS

Now that you have some understanding of utility, consider a few applications of utility analysis. The first section looks at the bonus, or surplus, that you get from consuming goods. The second section adds up the consumer surplus of all buyers in the market. And the final section focuses on the role of time in consumption.

6-3a YOUR Consumer Surplus

In our earlier example, utility increased when the price of pizza fell from $8 to $6. In this section, we take a closer look at how consumers benefit from a lower price. Suppose your demand for foot-long sub sandwiches is as shown in Exhibit 6. Recall that in constructing an individual's demand curve, we hold tastes, income, and the prices of other goods constant. Only the price of the good in question varies. At a price of $8 or above, you find that the marginal utility of other goods that you could buy for $8 is higher than the marginal utility of a sub sandwich. Consequently, you demand no subs. At a price of $7, you are willing and able to buy one per month, so the marginal utility of that first sub exceeds the marginal utility you expected from spending that $7 on your best alternative—say, a movie ticket. A price of $6 prompts you to buy two subs a month. The second sub is worth at least $6 to you. At a price of $5, you buy three subs, and at $4, you buy four. *The value of that fourth sub must at least equal the price; otherwise, you wouldn't buy it.* Along the demand curve, therefore, the price reflects your **marginal valuation** of the good, or the dollar value to you of the marginal utility derived from consuming each additional unit.

Notice that if the price is $4, you can purchase four subs for $4 each, even though you would have been willing to pay more for each of the first three subs. The first sandwich provides marginal

marginal valuation
The dollar value of the marginal utility derived from consuming each additional unit of a good

Exhibit 6

Your Consumer Surplus From Sub Sandwiches Increases as the Price Declines

At a given quantity of sub sandwiches, the height of the demand curve shows the value of the last one purchased. The area under the demand curve for a specific quantity shows the total value a consumer attaches to that quantity. At a price of $4, the consumer purchases four subs. The first one is valued at $7, the second at $6, the third at $5, and the fourth at $4. The consumer values four at $22. Because the consumer pays $4 per sub, all four can be purchased for $16. The difference between what the consumer would have been willing to pay ($22) and what the consumer actually pays ($16) is called consumer surplus. When the price is $4, the consumer surplus is $6, as represented by the dark shaded area under the demand curve above $4. When the price of subs falls to $3, consumer surplus increases by $4, as reflected by the lighter shaded area, to a total of $10.

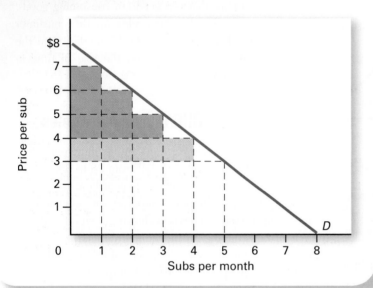

is $22 − $16 = $6, as approximated by the six darker shaded blocks in Exhibit 6. Consumer surplus equals the value of the total utility you receive from consuming the sandwiches minus your total spending on them. *Consumer surplus is reflected by the area under the demand curve but above the price.*

If the price falls to $3, you buy five subs a month. Apparently, you feel that the marginal utility from the fifth one is worth at least $3. The lower price means that you get all five for $3 each, even though each except the fifth one is worth more to you than $3. Your consumer surplus when the price is $3 is the value of the total utility from the first five, which is $7 + $6 + $5 + $4 + $3 = $25, minus your cost, which is $3 × 5 = $15. Thus, your consumer surplus is $25 − $15 = $10, as indicated by both the dark and the light shaded blocks in Exhibit 6. So if the price declines to $3, your consumer surplus increases by $4, as reflected by the four lighter-shaded blocks in Exhibit 6. You can see how consumers benefit from lower prices.

Incidentally, in some cases your consumer surplus is huge, such as from a bottle of water if you are dying of thirst, a winter coat if you are at risk of freezing, or a pair of glasses if you can't see without them.

utility that you valued at $7; the second you valued at $6; and the third you valued at $5. In fact, if you had to, rather than go without subs, you would have been willing to pay $7 for the first, $6 for the second, and $5 for the third. The dollar value of the total utility of the first four sandwiches is $7 + $6 + $5 + $4 = $22 per month. But when the price is $4, you get all four for a total of $16. Thus, a price of $4 confers a **consumer surplus**, or a consumer bonus, equal to the difference between the maximum amount you would have been willing to pay ($22) rather than go without subs altogether and what you actually pay ($16). When the price is $4, your consumer surplus

consumer surplus The difference between the most a consumer would pay for a given quantity of a good and what the consumer actually pays

6-3b Market Demand and Consumer Surplus

Let's talk now about the market demand for a good, assuming the market consists of you and two other consumers. *The market demand curve is simply the horizontal sum of the individual demand curves for all consumers in the market.* Exhibit 7 shows how the demand curves for three consumers in the market for sub sandwiches sum horizontally to yield the market demand. At a price of $4, for example, you demand four subs per month, Brittany demands two, and Chris demands none. The market demand at a price of $4 is therefore six sandwiches. At a price of $2, you demand six per month, Brittany four, and Chris two, for a market demand of 12. *The market demand curve shows the total quantity demanded per period by all consumers at various prices.* Consumer

Ciaran Griffin/Stockbyte/Getty Images

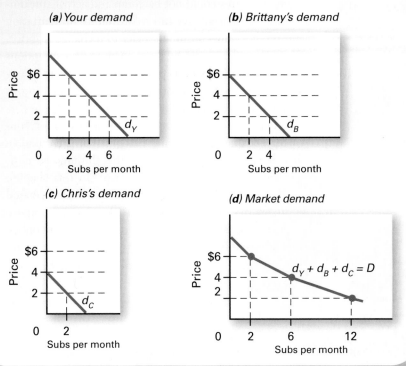

Exhibit 7

Sum Individual Demand Curves Horizontally to Derive the Market Demand for Sub Sandwiches

At a price of $4 per sub, you demand 4 per month, Brittany demands 2, and Chris demands 0. Quantity demanded at a price of $4 is $4 + 2 + 0 = 6$ subs per month. At a lower price of $2, you demand 6, Brittany demands 4, and Chris demands 2. Quantity demanded at a price of $2 is 12 subs. The market demand curve D is the horizontal sum of individual demand curves d_Y, d_B, and d_C.

(a) Your demand

(b) Brittany's demand

(c) Chris's demand

(d) Market demand

hypertension medicine.[5] Consumer surplus can be used to measure economic welfare and to compare the effects of different market structures, different tax structures, and different public programs, such as for medical care.

6-3c The Role of Time in Demand

Because consumption does not occur instantly, time plays a role in demand analysis. Consumption takes time and, as Ben Franklin said, time is money—time has a positive value for most people. Consequently, consumption has a *money price* and a *time price*. Goods are demanded because of the benefits they offer. It is not the microwave oven, personal computer, airline trip, or headache medicine that you value but the services they provide. Other things constant, you would gladly pay more to get the same benefit in less time, as with faster ovens, computers, airline trips, and headache relief. Likewise, you are willing to pay more for food that is easier to eat such as

surplus can be used to examine market demand as well as individual demand. *At a given price, consumer surplus for the market is the difference between the most consumers would pay for that quantity and the amount they do pay.*

Instead of just three consumers in the market, suppose there are many. Exhibit 8 presents market demand for a good with millions of consumers. If the price is $2 per unit, each person adjusts his or her quantity demanded until the marginal valuation of the final unit purchased equals $2. But each consumer also gets to buy all other units for $2 each. In Exhibit 8, the dark shading, bounded above by the demand curve and below by the price line at $2, depicts the consumer surplus. The light shading shows the gain in consumer surplus if the price drops to $1. Notice that if this good were given away, the consumer surplus would increase to include the white area below the demand curve.

Consumer surplus is the net benefit consumers get from market exchange. Again, consumer surplus can be substantial. For example, a recent study estimated that U.S. consumers enjoy a surplus of $23 billion a year from

Exhibit 8

Market Demand and Consumer Surplus

5. Lee Branstetter, Chirantan Chatterjee, and Matthew Higgins, "Regulation and Welfare:
Evidence from Paragraph IV
Generic Entry in the Pharmaceutical Industry," *RAND Journal of Economics*, forthcoming.

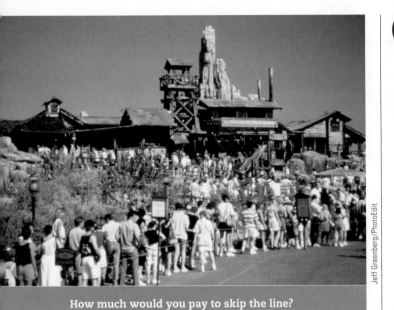

How much would you pay to skip the line?

Jeff Greenberg/PhotoEdit

This chapter has analyzed consumer choice by focusing on utility, or satisfaction, people derive from consumption. We assumed that utility could be measured in some systematic way for a particular consumer, even though utility measures could not be compared across consumers. The goal has been to explore utility maximization and predict how consumers react to a change in price. We judge a theory not by the realism of its assumptions but by the accuracy of its predictions. Based on this criterion, the theory of consumer choice presented in this chapter has proven to be quite useful.

Again, to maximize utility, you or any other consumer need not understand the material presented in this chapter. Economists assume that the urge to maximize utility is natural and instinctive. In this chapter, we simply tried to analyze that process. A more general approach to consumer choice, one that does not require a specific measure of utility, is developed in the online appendix to this chapter.

seedless grapes, seedless oranges, and KFC's "boneless" chicken wings.

Your willingness to pay more for time-saving goods and services depends on the opportunity cost of your time. Differences in the value of time among consumers help explain differences in the consumption patterns observed in the economy. For example, a retired couple has more leisure time than a working couple and may clip discount coupons and search newspaper ads for bargains, sometimes even going from store to store for particular grocery items on sale that week. The working couple tends to ignore the coupons and sales, eats out more often, and shops more at convenience stores, where they pay extra for the "convenience." The retired couple is more inclined to drive to a vacation destination, whereas the working couple flies.

Just inside the gates at Disneyland, Disney World, and Universal Studios are boards listing the waiting times of each attraction and ride. At that point, the dollar cost of admission has already been paid, so the marginal dollar cost of each ride and attraction is zero. The waiting times offer a menu of the marginal *time costs* of each ride or attraction. Incidentally, people willing to pay up to $55 an hour at Disney World and $60 an hour at Disneyland (plus the price of admission), until recently, could take VIP tours that bypass the lines. And at Universal Studios, you can still pay extra for a pass to the front of the line. How much would you pay to avoid the lines for the day?

Differences in the opportunity cost of time among consumers shape consumption patterns and add another dimension to our analysis of demand.

STUDY TOOLS 6

READY TO STUDY? IN THE BOOK, YOU CAN:

- ☐ Work the Problems at the end of the chapter.
- ☐ Rip out the chapter review card for a handy summary of the chapter and key terms.

ONLINE AT CENGAGEBRAIN.COM YOU CAN:

- ☐ Collect StudyBits while you read and study the chapter.
- ☐ Quiz yourself on key concepts.
- ☐ Prepare for tests with chapter flash cards as well as flash cards that you create.
- ☐ Watch videos to explore economics further.

CHAPTER 6 PROBLEMS

Your instructor can access the answers to these problems online at http://cengagebrain.com.

6-1 Explain why marginal utility decreases as more of a good or service is consumed

1. *(Law of Diminishing Marginal Utility)* Some restaurants offer "all you can eat" meals. How is this practice related to diminishing marginal utility? What restrictions must the restaurant impose on the customer to make a profit?

2. *(Law of Diminishing Marginal Utility)* Complete each of the following sentences:
   a. Your tastes determine the _____ you derive from consuming a particular good.
   b. _____ utility is the change in _____ utility resulting from a(n) _____ change in the consumption of a good.
   c. As long as marginal utility is positive, total utility is _____.
   d. The law of diminishing marginal utility states that as an individual consumes more of a good during a given time period, other things constant, total utility _____.

3. *(Marginal Utility)* Is it possible for marginal utility to be negative while total utility is positive? If yes, under what circumstances is it possible?

6-2 Given tastes, the prices for two different goods, and a budget constraint, describe the utility-maximizing condition in your own words

4. *(Utility Maximization)* The following tables illustrate Eileen's utilities from watching first-run movies in a theater and from renting movies online. Suppose that she has a monthly movie budget of $36, each movie ticket costs $6, and each video rental costs $3.

Movies in a Theater

Q	TU	MU	MU/P
0	0	____	____
1	200	____	____
2	290	____	____
3	370	____	____
4	440	____	____
5	500	____	____
6	550	____	____
7	590	____	____

Online Movies

Q	TU	MU	MU/P
0	0	____	____
1	250	____	____
2	295	____	____
3	335	____	____
4	370	____	____
5	400	____	____
6	425	____	____

   a. Complete the tables.
   b. Do these tables show that Eileen's preferences obey the law of diminishing marginal utility? Explain your answer.
   c. How much of each good does Eileen consume in equilibrium?
   d. Suppose the prices of both types of movies drop to $1 while Eileen's movie budget shrinks to $10. How much of each good does she consume in equilibrium?

5. *(Utility Maximization)* Suppose that a consumer has a choice between two goods, X and Y. If the price of X is $2 and the price of Y is $3, how much of X and Y does the consumer purchase per period, given an income of $17 per period? Use this information about marginal utility:

Units	MU_X	MU_Y
1	10	5
2	8	4
3	2	3
4	2	2
5	1	2

6. *(The Law of Demand and Marginal Utility)* Daniel allocates his budget of $24 per week among three goods. Use the following table of marginal utilities for good A, good B, and good C to answer the questions below:

Q_A	MU_A	Q_B	MU_B	Q_C	MU_C
1	50	1	75	1	25
2	40	2	60	2	20
3	30	3	40	3	15
4	20	4	30	4	10
5	15	5	20	5	7.5

   a. If the price of A is $2, the price of B is $3, and the price of C is $1, how much of each does Daniel purchase in equilibrium?
   b. If the price of A rises to $4 while other prices and Daniel's budget remain unchanged, how much of each does he purchase in equilibrium?
   c. Using the information from parts (a) and (b), draw the demand curve for good A. Be sure to indicate the price and quantity demanded for each point on the curve.

6-3 Explain how can you get a consumer surplus from consuming a particular good if, in equilibrium, your marginal valuation of the good just equals the price you pay

7. *(Consumer Surplus)* Suppose the linear demand curve for shirts slopes downward and that consumers buy 500 shirts per year when the price is $30 and 1,000 shirts per year when the price is $25.
   a. Compared to the prices of $30 and $25, what can you say about the marginal valuation that consumers place on the 300th shirt, the 700th shirt, and the 1,200th shirt they might buy each year?
   b. With diminishing marginal utility, are consumers deriving any consumer surplus if the price is $25 per shirt? Explain.
   c. Use a market demand curve to illustrate the change in consumer surplus if the price drops from $30 to $25.

8. *(Consumer Surplus)* Suppose supply of a good is perfectly elastic at a price of $5. The market demand curve for this good is linear, with zero quantity demanded at a price of $25. Given that the slope of this linear demand curve is −0.25, draw a supply and demand graph to illustrate the consumer surplus that occurs when the market is in equilibrium.

9. *(Role of Time in Demand)* In many amusement parks, you pay an admission fee to the park but you do not need to pay for individual rides. How do people choose which rides to go on?

10. *(Consumer Surplus)* If, toward the end of the day, some people become indifferent whether or not they go on another ride, how can we say that they derived consumer surplus from their visit to the amusement park that day?

7 | Production and Cost in the Firm

LEARNING OUTCOMES

After studying this chapter, you will be able to...

7-1 Distinguish the three types of profit and explain what each reflects

7-2 Describe the most important feature of production in the short run and what causes it

7-3 Explain why average cost is at a minimum when marginal cost equals average cost

7-4 Explain the sources of economies of scale and diseconomies of scale

After finishing this chapter go to **PAGE 117** for **STUDY TOOLS**

Topics discussed in Chapter 7 include:

• Explicit cost and implicit costs
• Economic profit and normal profit
• Increasing returns and diminishing returns
• Total product and marginal product
• Fixed cost and variable cost
• Short run and long run
• Economies and diseconomies of scale
• Minimum efficient scale

Chapter 6 explored the consumer behavior shaping the demand curve. You were asked to think like a consumer, or demander. This chapter considers the producer behavior shaping the supply curve. You must now think like a producer, or supplier. You

> **"Why do too many cooks spoil the broth?"**

may feel more natural as a consumer (after all, you are one), but you already know a lot more about producers than you may realize. You have been around them all your life—Walmart, Starbucks, Google, Exxon, Amazon.com, Apple, Home Depot, McDonald's, Twitter, Facebook, Pizza Hut, Ford, Gap, supermarkets, department stores, drugstores, convenience stores, shoe stores, dry cleaners, and hundreds more. So you already have some idea how businesses operate. They all have the same goal— they try to maximize profit, which is revenue minus cost. This chapter introduces the cost side of the profit equation.

7-1 COST AND PROFIT

With demand, we assume that consumers try to maximize utility, a goal that motivates their behavior. With supply, we assume that producers try to maximize *profit,* and this goal motivates their behavior. *Firms try to earn a profit by transforming resources into salable products.* Over time, firms that survive and thrive are those that are more profitable. Unprofitable firms eventually fail. Each year, millions of new firms enter the marketplace and many existing firms leave. Each firm's decision makers must choose what goods and services to produce and what resources to employ. They must make plans while confronting uncertainty about consumer demand, resource availability, and the intentions of other firms in the market. *The lure of profit is so strong, however, that eager entrepreneurs are always ready to pursue their dreams.*

7-1a Explicit and Implicit Costs

To hire a resource, a firm must pay at least the resource's *opportunity cost*—that is, at least what the resource could earn in its best alternative use. For most resources, a cash payment approximates the opportunity cost. For example, the $3 per pound that Domino's Pizza pays for cheese must at least equal the cheese producer's opportunity cost of supplying it.

Firms do not make direct cash payments for resources they own. For example, a firm pays no rent to operate in a company-owned building. Similarly, small-business owners usually don't pay themselves an hourly wage. Yet these resources are not free. *Whether hired in resource markets or owned by the firm, all resources have an opportunity cost.* Company-owned buildings can be rented or sold; small-business owners can find other work.

A firm's **explicit costs** are its actual cash payments for resources: wages, rent, interest, insurance, taxes, and the like. In addition to these direct cash outlays, or explicit costs, the firm also incurs **implicit costs**, which are the opportunity costs of using resources owned by the firm or provided by the firm's owners. Examples include the use of a company-owned building,

> **explicit cost** Opportunity cost of resources employed by a firm that takes the form of cash payments
>
> **implicit cost** A firm's opportunity cost of using its own resources or those provided by its owners without a corresponding cash payment

use of company funds, and the time of the firm's owners. Like explicit costs, implicit costs are opportunity costs. But unlike explicit costs, implicit costs require no cash payment and no entry in the firm's *accounting statement*, which records its revenues, explicit costs, and accounting profit.

7-1b Alternative Measures of Profit

An example may help clarify the distinction between explicit and implicit costs. Wanda Wheeler earns $50,000 a year as an aeronautical engineer with the Sky-high Aircraft Corporation. On her way home from work one day, she gets an idea for a rounder, more friction-resistant airplane wheel. She decides to quit her job and start a business, which she calls Wheeler Dealer. To buy the necessary machines and equipment, she withdraws $20,000 from a savings account earning interest of $1,000 a year. She hires an assistant and starts producing the wheel using the spare bay in her condominium's parking garage, which she had been renting to a neighbor for $100 a month.

Sales are slow at first—people keep telling her she is just trying to reinvent the wheel—but her wheel eventually gets rolling. When Wanda reviews the firm's performance after the first year, she is pleased. As you can see in the upper portion of Exhibit 1, company revenue in 2015 totaled $105,000. After paying her assistant and for materials and equipment, the firm shows an accounting profit of $64,000. **Accounting profit** equals total revenue minus explicit costs. Accountants use this profit to determine a firm's taxable income.

But accounting profit ignores the opportunity cost of Wanda's own resources used in the firm. First is the opportunity cost of her time. Remember, she quit a $50,000-a-year job to work full time on her business, thereby forgoing that salary. Second is the $1,000 in annual interest she passes up by funding the operation from her own savings. And third, by using the spare bay in the garage for the business,

accounting profit A firm's total revenue minus its explicit costs

economic profit A firm's total revenue minus its explicit and implicit costs

normal profit A firm's accounting profit when all resources earn their opportunity cost; equal to implicit cost

Exhibit 1

Wheeler Dealer Accounts, 2015

Total revenue		$105,000
Less explicit costs:		
Assistant's salary	−$21,000	
Material and equipment	−$20,000	
Equals accounting profit		$64,000
Less implicit costs:		
Wanda's forgone salary	−$50,000	
Forgone interest on savings	−$1,000	
Forgone garage rental	−$1,200	
Equals economic profit		$11,800

she forgoes $1,200 per year in rental income. The forgone salary, interest, and rental income are implicit costs because she no longer earns income from the best alternative uses of these resources.

Economic profit equals total revenue minus all costs, both implicit and explicit; *economic profit takes into account the opportunity cost of all resources used in production.* In Exhibit 1, accounting profit of $64,000 less implicit costs of $52,200 yields an economic profit of $11,800. Economic profit is what Wanda Wheeler earns as an entrepreneur—an amount over and above what all her resources could earn in their best alternative use. What would happen to the accounting statement if Wanda decided to pay herself a salary of $50,000 per year? Explicit costs would increase by $50,000, and implicit costs would decrease by $50,000. Thus, accounting profit would decrease by $50,000, but economic profit would not change because it already reflects both implicit and explicit costs.

There is one other profit measure to consider. The accounting profit just sufficient to ensure that *all* resources used by the firm earn their opportunity cost is called a **normal profit**. Wheeler Dealer earns a normal profit when accounting profit equals implicit costs—the sum of the salary Wanda gave up at her regular job ($50,000), the interest she gave up by using her own savings ($1,000), and the rent she gave up on her garage ($1,200). Thus, if the accounting profit is $52,200 per year—the opportunity cost of resources Wanda supplies to the firm—the company earns a normal profit. *Any accounting profit in excess of a normal profit is economic profit.*

If accounting profit is large enough, it can be divided into normal profit and economic profit. The $64,000 in accounting profit earned by Wanda's firm consists of (1) a normal profit of $52,200, which covers her implicit costs—the opportunity cost of resources she supplies the firm, and (2) an economic profit of $11,800, which is over and above what these resources, including Wanda's time, could earn in their best alternative use.

As long as economic profit is positive, Wanda is better off running her own firm than working for Skyhigh Aircraft. If total revenue had been only $50,000, an accounting profit of only $9,000 would have covered less than one-fifth of her salary, to say nothing of her forgone rent and interest. Because Wanda would not have covered her implicit costs, she would be facing an *economic loss*. She would be better off back in her old job.

To understand profit maximization, you must develop a feel for both revenue and cost. In this chapter, you begin learning about the cost of production, starting with the relationship between inputs and outputs.

> **"Economic profit equals total revenue minus *all* costs, both implicit and explicit; economic profit takes into account the opportunity cost of resources used in production."**

7-2 PRODUCTION IN THE SHORT RUN

We shift now from a discussion of profit, which is why firms exist, to a discussion of how firms operate. Suppose a new McDonald's just opened in your neighborhood and business is booming far beyond expectations. The manager responds to the unexpected demand by quickly hiring more workers. But cars are still backed up into the street waiting for a parking space. The solution is to add a drive-through window, but such an expansion takes time.

7-2a Fixed and Variable Resources

Some resources, such as labor, are called **variable resources** because they can be varied quickly to change the output rate. But adjustments in other resources take more time. Resources that cannot be altered easily—the size of the building, for example—are called **fixed resources**. When considering the time required

to change the quantity of resources employed, economists distinguish between the short run and the long run. In the **short run**, at least one resource is fixed. In the **long run**, no resource is fixed.

Output can be changed in the short run by adjusting variable resources, but the size, or *scale,* of the firm is fixed in the short run. In the long run, all resources can be varied. The length of the long run differs from industry to industry because the nature of production differs. For example, the size of a McDonald's outlet can be increased more quickly than can the size of an auto plant. Thus, the long run for that McDonald's is shorter than the long run for an automaker.

7-2b Law of Diminishing Marginal Returns

Let's focus on the short-run link between resource use and the rate of output by considering a hypothetical moving company called Smoother Mover. Suppose the company's fixed resources, such as a warehouse, are already in place and labor is the only variable resource. Exhibit 2 relates the amount of labor employed to the amount of output produced. Labor is measured by worker-days, which is one worker for one day, and output is measured by tons of furniture moved per day. The first column shows the amount of labor employed, which ranges from 0 to 8 worker-days. The second column shows the tons of furniture moved per day, or the **total product**, at each level of employment. The relationship between the amount of resources employed and total product is called the firm's **production function**. The third column

variable resource Any resource that can be varied in the short run to increase or decrease production

fixed resource Any resource that cannot be varied in the short run

short run A period during which at least one of a firm's resources is fixed

long run A period during which all resources under the firm's control are variable

total product A firm's total output

production function The relationship between resources employed and a firm's total product

Exhibit 2

Short-Run Relationship Between Units of Labor and Tons of Furniture Moved

Units of the Variable Resource (worker-days)	Total Product (tons moved per day)	Marginal Product (tons moved per day)
0	0	—
1	2	2
2	5	3
3	9	4
4	12	3
5	14	2
6	15	1
7	15	0
8	14	−1

While a second mover makes moving a sofa a lot easier, adding a third will not make much difference. Thus marginal returns are diminishing.

shows the **marginal product** of each worker—that is, the change in total product resulting from an additional unit of labor, assuming other resources remain unchanged. Spend a little time now getting acquainted with the three columns.

Increasing Marginal Returns

Without labor, nothing gets moved, so total product is zero. If one worker is hired, that worker must do all the driving, packing, crating, and moving. Some of the larger items, such as couches and major appliances, cannot easily be moved by a single worker. Still, in our example one worker moves 2 tons of furniture per day. When a second worker is hired, some division of labor occurs, and two together can move the big stuff more easily, so production more than doubles to 5 tons per day. The marginal product of the second worker is 3 tons per day. Adding a third worker allows for a finer division of labor. For example, one can pack fragile items while the other two do the heavy lifting. Total product is 9 tons per day, 4 tons more than with two workers. Because the marginal product increases, the firm experiences **increasing marginal returns** from labor as each of the first three workers is hired.

marginal product The change in total product when a particular resource increases by one unit, all other resources constant

increasing marginal returns The marginal product of a variable resource increases as each additional unit of that resource is employed

law of diminishing marginal returns As more of a variable resource is added to a given amount of other resources, marginal product eventually declines and could become negative

Diminishing Marginal Returns

A fourth worker's marginal product is less than that of a third worker. Hiring still more workers increases total product by successively smaller amounts, so the marginal product declines after three workers. With that fourth worker, the **law of diminishing marginal returns** takes hold. This law states that as more of a variable resource is combined with a given amount of other resources, marginal product eventually declines. *The law of diminishing marginal returns is the most important feature of production in the short run.* As more and more labor is hired, marginal product could even turn negative, so total product would decline. For example, when Smoother Mover hires an eighth worker, workers start getting in each other's way, and they take up valuable space in the moving van. As a result, an eighth worker actually subtracts from total output, yielding a negative

> **"The law of diminishing marginal returns is the most important feature of production in the short run."**

marginal product. Likewise, a McDonald's outlet can hire only so many workers before congestion and confusion in the work area cut total product ("too many cooks spoil the broth").

7-2c Total and Marginal Product Curves

Exhibit 3 illustrates the relationship between total product and marginal product, using data from Exhibit 2. Note that because of increasing marginal returns, marginal product in panel (b) increases with each of the first three workers. With marginal product increasing, total product in panel (a) increases at an increasing rate (although this is hard to see in Exhibit 3). But once decreasing marginal returns set in, which begins with the fourth worker, marginal product declines. Total product continues to increase but at a decreasing rate. As long as marginal product is positive, total product increases. Once marginal product turns negative, total product starts to fall. Exhibit 3 summarizes all this by sorting production into three ranges: increasing marginal returns, diminishing but positive marginal returns, and negative marginal returns. These ranges for marginal product correspond with total product that increases at an increasing rate, increases at a decreasing rate, and declines.

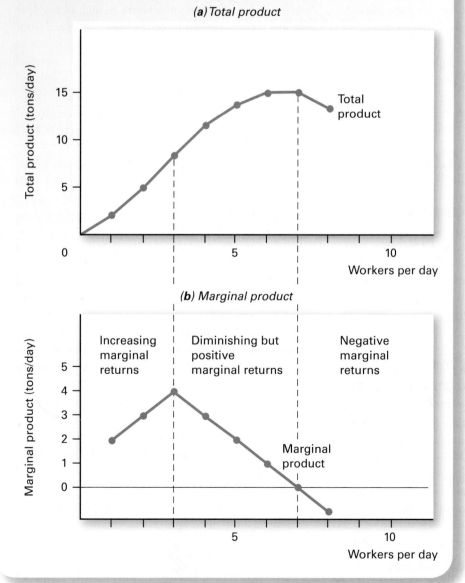

Exhibit 3

Total and Marginal Product of Labor

When marginal product is rising, total product increases by increasing amounts. When marginal product is falling but still positive, total product increases by decreasing amounts. When marginal product equals 0, total product is at a maximum. When marginal product is negative, total product is falling.

(a) Total product

(b) Marginal product

7-3 COSTS IN THE SHORT RUN

Now that we have explored the relationship between the amount of resources employed and the rate of output, let's consider how the cost of production varies as output varies. There are two kinds of costs in the short run: fixed and variable. Fixed cost pays for fixed resources and variable cost pays for variable resources. A firm incurs a **fixed cost** in the short run, even if no output is produced. For example, in the steel industry, giant ovens must remain hot even when the plant isn't making steel. Otherwise, bricks inside would disintegrate. And a huge vacuum that sucks out pollutants

fixed cost Any production cost that is independent of the firm's rate of output must run continuously because turning its motors off and on can damage them.[1] In the mining industry, even if no production is underway, operations must still be put on "care and maintenance" if mining is to continue at some point in the future.[2] Similarly, even if Smoother Mover hires no labor and moves no furniture, it must pay property taxes, insurance, vehicle registration, plus any opportunity cost for warehouse and equipment. By definition, fixed cost is just that: fixed—it does not vary with output in the short run. Suppose the *fixed cost* for Smoother Mover is $200 per day.

Variable cost, as the name implies, is the cost of variable resources—in this case, labor. When no labor is employed, output is zero, as is variable cost. As workers are hired, output increases, as does variable cost. Variable cost depends on the amount of labor employed and on the wage. At a wage of $100 per day, *variable cost* equals the number of workers employed times $100.

7-3a Total Cost and Marginal Cost in the Short Run

Exhibit 4 offers cost data for Smoother Mover. The table lists the cost of production associated with alternative rates of output. Column (1) shows possible rates of output in the short run, measured in tons of furniture moved per day.

Total Cost

Column (2) shows the fixed cost (FC) at each rate of output. Note that fixed cost, by definition, remains constant at $200 per day regardless of output. Column (3) shows the labor needed to produce each rate of output based on

---

variable cost Any production cost that changes as the rate of output changes

total cost The sum of fixed cost and variable cost, or $TC = FC + VC$

marginal cost The change in total cost resulting from a one-unit change in output; the change in total cost divided by the change in output, or $MC = \Delta TC/\Delta q$

---

1. Robert Guy Matthews, "Fixed Costs Chafe Steel Mills," *Wall Street Journal*, 10 June 2009.

2. Ryan Randazzo, "Miami Mine to Restart; Hiring 650," *Arizona Republic*, 11 March 2012.

Exhibit 4

Short-Run Total and Marginal Cost Data for Smoother Mover

(1) Tons Moved per Day (q)	(2) Fixed Cost (FC)	(3) Workers per Day	(4) Variable Cost (VC)	(5) Total Cost (TC = FC + VC)	(6) Marginal Cost $MC = \Delta TC/\Delta q$
0	$200	0	$ 0	$200	—
2	200	1	100	300	$50.00
5	200	2	200	400	33.33
9	200	3	300	500	25.00
12	200	4	400	600	33.33
14	200	5	500	700	50.00
15	200	6	600	800	100.00

the productivity figures reported in the previous two exhibits. For example, moving 2 tons a day requires one worker, 5 tons requires two workers, and so on. Only the first six workers are listed, because additional workers would add nothing to output and so would not be hired. Column (4) lists variable cost (VC) per day, which equals $100 times the number of workers employed. For example, the variable cost of moving 9 tons of furniture per day is $300 because this output rate requires three workers. Column (5) lists the **total cost** (TC), the sum of fixed cost and variable cost: $TC = FC + VC$. As you can see, when output is zero, variable cost is zero, so total cost consists entirely of the fixed cost of $200. Incidentally, because total cost is the opportunity cost of all resources used by the firm, total cost includes a normal profit but not an economic profit. Think about that.

Marginal Cost

Of special interest to the firm is how total cost changes as output changes. In particular, what is the marginal cost of producing another unit? The **marginal cost** (MC) of production listed in column (6) of Exhibit 4 is simply the change in total cost divided by the change in output, or $MC = \Delta TC/\Delta q$, where Δ means "change in." For example, increasing output from 0 to 2 tons increases total cost by $100 (= $300 − $200). The marginal cost of each of the first 2 tons is the change in total cost, $100, divided by the change in output, 2 tons, or $100/2, which equals $50. The marginal cost of each of the next 3 tons is $100/3, or $33.33.

Notice in column (6) that marginal cost first decreases, then increases. *Changes in marginal cost reflect changes in the marginal productivity of the variable resource.* Because of increasing marginal returns, the second worker produces more than the first and the third worker produces more than the second. This greater productivity results in a falling marginal cost for the first 9 tons moved. Beginning with the fourth worker, the firm experiences diminishing marginal returns from labor, so the marginal cost of output increases. *When the firm experiences increasing marginal returns, the marginal cost of output falls; when the firm experiences diminishing marginal returns, the marginal cost of output increases.* Thus, marginal cost in Exhibit 4 first falls and then rises, because marginal returns from labor first increase and then diminish.

Total and Marginal Cost Curves

Exhibit 5 shows cost curves for the data in Exhibit 4. Because fixed cost does not vary with output, the fixed cost curve is a horizontal line at the $200 level in panel (a). Variable cost is zero when output is zero, so the *variable cost curve* starts from the origin. The *total cost curve* sums the fixed cost curve and the variable cost curve. The total cost curve is simply the variable cost curve shifted vertically by the fixed cost.

In panel (b) of Exhibit 5, marginal cost declines until the ninth unit of output and then increases, reflecting labor's increasing and then diminishing marginal returns. With each successive unit of output, total cost increases by the marginal cost of that unit. Thus, *the slope of the total cost curve at each rate of output equals the marginal cost at that rate of output.* Based on what happens to marginal cost, the total cost curve can be divided into two sections:

1. Because of increasing marginal returns from labor, marginal cost at first declines, so total cost initially increases by successively smaller amounts and the total cost curve becomes less steep.

2. Because of diminishing marginal returns from labor, marginal cost starts increasing after the ninth unit

> **"Changes in marginal cost reflect changes in the marginal productivity of the variable resource."**

of output, so total cost increases by successively larger amounts and the total cost curve becomes steeper.

Keep in mind that economic analysis is marginal analysis. Marginal cost is the

Exhibit 5

Total and Marginal Cost Curves for Smoother Mover

In panel (a), fixed cost is $200 at all levels of output. Variable cost starts from the origin and increases slowly at first as output increases. As the variable resource generates diminishing marginal returns, variable cost begins to increase more rapidly. Total cost is the vertical sum of fixed cost and variable cost. In panel (b), marginal cost first declines, reflecting increasing marginal returns from the variable resource (labor in this example) and then increases, reflecting diminishing marginal returns.

key to economic decisions. Marginal cost indicates how much total cost increases if one more unit is produced or how much total cost drops if production declines by one unit.

7-3b Average Cost in the Short Run

Although marginal cost is of most interest, the average cost per unit of output is also useful. We can distinguish between average variable cost and average total cost. These measures appear in columns (5) and (6) of Exhibit 6. Column (5) lists **average variable cost**, or *AVC*, which equals variable cost divided by output, or $AVC = VC/q$. The final column lists **average total cost**, or *ATC*, which equals total cost divided by output, or $ATC = TC/q$. Each measure of average cost first declines as output expands and then increases.

7-3c Relationship Between Marginal Cost and Average Cost

To understand the relationship between marginal cost and average cost, let's begin with an example of college grades. Think about how your grades each

term affect your grade point average (GPA). Suppose you do well your first term, starting your college career with a 3.4 (out of 4.0). Your grades for the second term drop to 2.8, reducing your GPA to 3.1. You slip again in the third term to a 2.2, lowering your GPA to 2.8. Your fourth-term grades improve a bit to 2.4, but your GPA continues to slide to 2.7. In the fifth term, your grades improve to 2.7, leaving your GPA unchanged at 2.7. And in the sixth term, you get 3.3, pulling your GPA up to 2.8. Notice that when your term grades are below your GPA, your GPA falls. Even when your term performance improves, your GPA continues to fall until your term grades at least equal your GPA. Your term grades first pull down your GPA and then eventually pull it up.

Let's now take a look at the relationship between marginal cost and average cost. In Exhibit 6, marginal cost has the same relationship to average cost as your term grades have to your GPA. You can observe this marginal-average relationship in columns (4) and (5).

> **"Marginal cost indicates how much total cost increases if one more unit is produced or how much total cost drops if production declines by one unit."**

average variable cost Variable cost divided by output, or $AVC = VC/q$

average total cost Total cost divided by output, or $ATC = TC/q$; the sum of average fixed cost and average variable cost, or $ATC = AFC + AVC$

Exhibit 6

Short-Run Total, Marginal, and Average Cost Data for Smoother Mover

(1) Tons Moved per Day (q)	(2) Variable Cost (VC)	(3) Total Cost (TC = FC + VC)	(4) Marginal Cost (MC = ΔTC/Δq)	(5) Average Variable Cost (AVC = VC/q)	(5) Average Total Cost (ATC = TC/q)
0	$0	$200	0	—	∞
2	100	300	$50.00	$50.00	$150.00
5	200	400	33.33	40.00	80.00
9	300	500	25.00	33.33	55.55
12	400	600	33.33	33.33	50.00
14	500	700	50.00	35.71	50.00
15	600	800	100.00	40.00	53.33

Because of increasing marginal returns from the first three workers, marginal cost falls for the first 9 tons of furniture moved. Because marginal cost is below average cost, marginal cost pulls down average cost. Marginal cost equals average variable cost when output is 12 tons, and marginal cost exceeds average variable cost when output exceeds 12 tons, so marginal cost pulls up average variable cost.

Exhibit 7 shows the same marginal cost curve first presented in Exhibit 5, along with average cost curves based on data in Exhibit 6. At low rates of output, marginal cost declines as output expands because of increasing marginal returns from labor. As long as marginal cost is below average cost, marginal cost pulls down average cost as output expands. At higher rates of output,

> "When marginal cost is less than average cost, average cost declines. When marginal cost is above average cost, average cost increases."

marginal cost increases because of diminishing marginal returns from labor. Once marginal cost exceeds average cost, marginal cost pulls up average cost. The fact that marginal cost first pulls average cost down and then pulls it up explains why the average cost curves have U shapes. The shapes of the average variable cost curve and the average total cost curve are determined by the shape of the marginal cost curve, so each is shaped by increasing, then diminishing, marginal returns.

Notice also that the rising marginal cost curve intersects both the average variable cost curve and the average total cost curve where these average curves reach their minimum. This occurs because the marginal pulls down the average where the marginal is below the average and pulls up the average where the marginal is above the average. One more thing: The distance between the average variable cost curve and the average total cost curve is *average fixed cost*, or *AFC*, which gets smaller as the rate of output increases. (Why does average fixed cost get smaller?)

The law of diminishing marginal returns determines the shapes of short-run cost curves. When the marginal product of labor increases, the marginal cost of output falls. Once diminishing marginal returns take hold, the marginal cost of output rises. Thus, marginal cost first falls and then rises. And the marginal cost curve dictates the shapes of the average cost curves. When marginal cost is less than average cost, average cost declines. When marginal cost is above average cost, average cost increases. Got it? If not, please reread this paragraph.

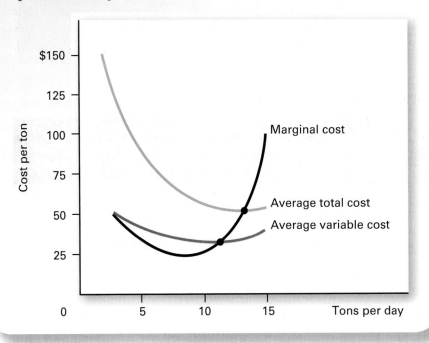

Exhibit 7

Average and Marginal Cost Curves for Smoother Mover

Average variable cost and average total cost curves first decline, reach low points, and then rise. Overall, they have U shapes. When marginal cost is below average variable cost, average variable cost is falling. When marginal cost equals average variable cost, average variable cost is at its minimum. When marginal cost is above average variable cost, average variable cost is increasing. The same relationship holds between marginal cost and average total cost.

7-4 COSTS IN THE LONG RUN

So far, the analysis has focused on how costs vary as the rate of output increases in the short run for a firm of a given size. In the long run, all inputs that are under the firm's control can be varied, so there is no fixed cost. The long run is not just a succession of short runs. The long run is best thought of as a *planning horizon*. In the long run, the choice of input combinations is flexible. But once the size of the plant has been selected and the concrete has been poured, the firm has fixed costs and is operating in the short run. Firms plan for the long run, but they produce in the short run. We turn now to long-run costs.

7-4a Economies of Scale

Recall that the shape of the short-run average total cost curve is determined primarily by increasing and diminishing marginal returns from the variable resource. A different principle shapes the long-run cost curve. If a firm experiences **economies of scale**, long-run average cost falls as the scale of the firm expands. Consider some sources of economies of scale. *A larger firm size often allows for larger, more specialized machines and greater specialization of labor.* For example, compare the household-size kitchen of a small restaurant with the kitchen at a McDonald's. At low rates of output, the smaller kitchen produces meals at a lower average cost than does McDonald's. But if production in the smaller kitchen increases beyond, say, 100 meals per day, a kitchen on the scale of McDonald's would make meals at a lower average cost. Thus, because of economies of scale, the long-run average cost for a restaurant may fall as size increases. As a case in point, the idea for McDonald's snack wrap started when a franchisee suggested that the company find more uses for the strips of chicken served with dipping sauce. Selling more chicken allowed each restaurant to cook new batches more frequently, which meant customers got a fresher product.[3]

A larger scale of operation allows a firm to use larger, more efficient machines and to assign workers to more specialized tasks. Production techniques such as the assembly line can be introduced only if the rate of output is sufficiently large. For example, as the iPhone 6 was introduced, assembly lines in Zhengzhou, China, were producing 7,500 an hour.[4] More generally, *as the scale of a firm increases, capital substitutes for labor and complex machines substitute for simpler machines.*

7-4b Diseconomies of Scale

Often another force, called **diseconomies of scale**, may eventually take over as a firm expands its plant size, increasing long-run average cost as output expands. For example, Oasis of the Seas, the world's largest cruise liner, can accommodate 6,300 guests, but the ship is too large to

Ruth Peterkin/Alamy

visit some of the world's most popular destinations, such as Venice and Bermuda.[5] More generally in a firm, as the amount and variety of resources employed increase, so does the *task of coordinating all these inputs.* As the workforce grows, additional layers of management are needed to monitor production. And management becomes more critical as the firm gets bigger.[6] In the thicket of bureaucracy that develops, communications may get mangled. Top executives have more difficulty keeping in touch with the

---

economies of scale
Forces that reduce a firm's average cost as the scale of operation expands in the long run

diseconomies of scale
Forces that may eventually increase a firm's average cost as the scale of operation expands in the long run

---

3. As reported by Janet Adamy, "For McDonald's It's a Wrap," *Wall Street Journal,* 30 January 2007.

4. Ian Parker, "The Shape of Things To Come," *The New Yorker,* 2 March 2015, p. 120.

5. Sarah Nassauer, "What It Takes to Keep a City Afloat," *Wall Street Journal,* 3 March 2010.

6. Nicholas Bloom, et al. "The New Empirical Economics of Management," NBER Working Paper No. 20102 (May 2014).

factory floor because information is distorted as it moves up and down the chain of command. Indeed, in large organizations, rumors may become a primary source of information, reducing efficiency and increasing average cost.

The financial crisis of 2008 resulted in part because some financial institutions had grown so large and complex that top executives couldn't accurately assess the risks of the financial products their companies were buying and selling. One could argue that such firms were experiencing diseconomies of scale. For example, "Former Citigroup CEO Charles Prince apologized for his firm's role in the financial crisis, suggesting bank executives were wholly unaware of the risks posed by collateralized debt securities on the firm's books."[7]

Note that *diseconomies of scale result from a larger firm size, whereas diminishing marginal returns result from using more variable resources in a firm of a given size.*

7-4c Long-Run Average Cost Curve

Because of the special nature of technology in its industry, suppose a firm must choose from among three possible plant sizes: small, medium, and large. Exhibit 8 presents this simple case. The average total cost curves for the three sizes are SS', MM', and LL'. Which size should the firm build to minimize average cost? The appropriate size, or *scale*, for the firm depends on how much output the firm wants to produce per period. For example, if q is the desired output rate, average cost is lowest with a small plant size. If the desired output rate is q', the medium plant size offers the lowest average cost. With the medium plant, the firm experiences economies of scale. With the large plant, the firm experiences diseconomies of scale.

More generally in Exhibit 8, for output less than q_a, average cost is lowest when the plant is small. For output

7. As reported by Michael Crittenden, "Citi's Prince: I'm Sorry," *Wall Street Journal*, 8 April 2010. For more evidence, see David Wessel, *In Fed We Trust*, (Crown Business, 2009); Michael Lewis, *The Big Short*, (Norton, 2010); and Roger Lowenstein, *The End of Wall Street*, (Penguin Press, 2010).

Exhibit 8

Short-Run Average Total Cost Curves Form the Long-Run Average Cost Curve, or Planning Curve

Curves *SS9*, *MM9*, and *LL9* show short-run average total costs for small, medium, and large plants, respectively. For output less than q_a, average cost is lowest when the plant is small. Between q_a and q_b, average cost is lowest with a medium-size plant. If output exceeds q_b, the large plant offers the lowest average cost. The long-run average-cost curve connects these low-cost segments of each curve and is identified as *SabL9*.

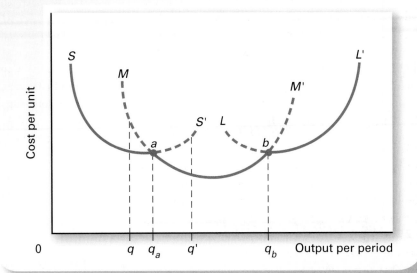

between q_a and q_b, average cost is lowest for the medium plant. And for output that exceeds q_b, average cost is lowest when the plant is large. The **long-run average cost curve**, or *LRAC* curve, sometimes called the firm's *planning curve*, connects portions of the three short-run average cost curves that are lowest for each output rate. In Exhibit 8, that curve consists of the line segments connecting S, a, b, and L'. So even though the firm experiences diseconomies of scale with the largest plant size, the large firm is the one to build if the firm must produce more than q_b.

Now suppose there are many possible plant sizes. Exhibit 9 presents a sample of short-run cost curves shown in pink. The long-run average cost curve, shown in red, is formed by connecting the points on the various short-run average cost curves that represent the lowest per-unit cost for each rate of output. Each of the short-run average cost curves is tangent to the long-run average cost curve, or *planning curve*. If we could display enough short-run cost curves, we would have a different plant size for each rate of output. *These points of tangency represent the least-cost way of producing each particular rate of output,*

long-run average cost curve A curve that indicates the lowest average cost of production at each rate of output when the size, or scale, of the firm varies; also called the planning curve

Exhibit 9

Many Short-Run Average Total Cost Curves Form a Firm's Long-Run Average Cost Curve, or Planning Curve

With many possible plant sizes, the long-run average cost curve is the envelope of portions of the short-run average cost curves. Each short-run curve is tangent to the long-run average cost curve. Each point of tangency represents the least-cost way of producing that rate of output.

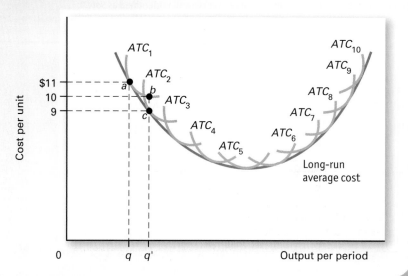

average cost along ATC_1. But average cost is lower with a larger plant. With the plant size associated with ATC_2, the average cost of producing q' would be minimized at \$9 per unit at point c. *Each point of tangency between a short-run average cost curve and the long-run average cost curve represents the least-cost way of producing that particular rate of output.*

In the long run, a firm can vary all the inputs under its control. Some resources, however, are not under the firm's control, and the inability to vary them may contribute to diseconomies of scale.

It is possible for average cost to neither increase nor decrease with changes in firm size. If neither economies of scale nor diseconomies of scale are apparent over some range of output, a firm experiences **constant long-run average cost**.

Perhaps economies and diseconomies of scale exist simultaneously in the firm but have offsetting effects. Exhibit 10 presents a firm's long-run average cost curve, or *LRAC* curve, which is divided into output rates reflecting economies of scale, constant long-run average costs, and diseconomies of scale. The output rate must reach quantity A for the firm to achieve the

given resource prices and the technology. For example, the short-run average total cost curve ATC_1 is tangent to the long-run average cost curve at point a, where \$11 is the lowest average cost of producing output q. Note, however, that other output rates along ATC_1 have a lower average cost. For example, the average cost of producing q' is only \$10, as identified at point b. Point b depicts the lowest average cost along ATC_1. So, while the point of tangency reflects the least-cost way of producing a particular rate of output, that tangency point does not reflect the minimum average cost for this particular plant size.

If the firm decides to produce q', which size plant should it choose to minimize the average cost of production? Output rate q' could be produced at point b, which represents the minimum

> **"In the long run, a firm can vary all the inputs under its control."**

constant long-run average cost A condition that occurs if, over some range of output, long-run average cost neither increases nor decreases with changes in firm size

minimum efficient scale The lowest rate of output at which a firm takes full advantage of economies of scale

minimum efficient scale, which is the lowest rate of output at which long-run average cost is at a minimum.

7-4d Economies and Diseconomies of Scale at the Firm Level

Our discussion so far has referred to a particular plant—a movie theater or a restaurant, for example. But a firm could also be a collection of plants, such as the hundreds of movie theaters in a chain or the thousands of McDonald's restaurants. More generally, we can distinguish between economies and diseconomies of scale at the *plant level*—that is, at a particular location—and at the *firm level*, where the firm is a collection of plants.

Exhibit 10

A Firm's Long-Run Average Cost Curve

Up to output level *A*, long-run average cost falls as the firm experiences economies of scale. Output level *A* is the minimum effi- cient scale—the lowest rate of output at which the firm takes full advantage of economies of scale. Between *A* and *B*, the average cost is constant. Beyond output level *B*, long-run average cost increases as the firm experiences diseconomies of scale.

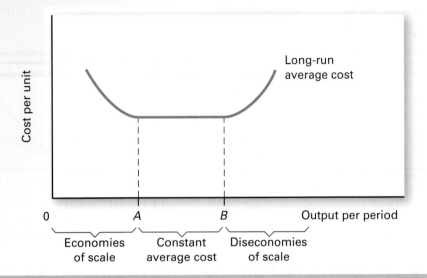

Large firms do what they can to reduce diseconomies of scale. For example, IBM undertook a massive restruc- turing program to decentralize into six smaller decision- making groups. Some big corporations have even spun off parts of their operations to form new corporations. For example, from Hewlett-Packard came Agilent Tech- nologies, AT&T created Lucent Technologies, and drug maker Abbot Laboratories spun off AbbVie.

7-5 FINAL WORD

By considering the relationship between production and cost, we have developed the foundation for a theory of firm behavior. Despite what may appear to be a tangle of short-run and long-run cost curves, *only two relationships between resources and output underlie all the curves. In the short run, it's increasing and diminishing returns from the variable resource. In the long run, it's economies and dis- economies of scale.* If you understand the sources of these two phenomena, you grasp the central points of the chap- ter. Our examination of production and cost in the short run and long run lays the groundwork for a firm's supply curve, to be developed in the next chapter.

STUDY TOOLS 7

READY TO STUDY? IN THE BOOK, YOU CAN:

☐ Work the Problems at the end of the chapter.

☐ Rip out the chapter review card for a handy summary of the chapter and key terms.

ONLINE AT CENGAGEBRAIN.COM YOU CAN:

☐ Collect StudyBits while you read and study the chapter.

☐ Quiz yourself on key concepts.

☐ Prepare for tests with chapter flash cards as well as flash cards that you create.

☐ Watch videos to explore economics further.

CHAPTER 7 PROBLEMS

Your instructor can access the answers to these problems online at http://cengagebrain.com.

7-1 Distinguish the three types of profit and explain what each reflects

1. *(Explicit and Implicit Costs)* Amos McCoy is currently raising corn on his 100-acre farm and earning an accounting profit of $100 per acre. However, if he raised soybeans, he could earn accounting profit of $200 per acre. Is he currently earning an economic profit? Why or why not?

2. *(Explicit and Implicit Costs)* Determine whether each of the following is an explicit cost or an implicit cost:
   a. Payments for labor purchased in the labor market
   b. A firm's use of a warehouse that it owns and could rent to another firm
   c. Rent paid for the use of a warehouse not owned by the firm
   d. The wages that firm owners could earn if they did not work for themselves

3. *(Alternative Measures of Profit)* Calculate the accounting profit or loss as well as the economic profit or loss in each of the following situations:
   a. A firm with total revenues of $150 million, explicit costs of $90 million, and implicit costs of $40 million
   b. A firm with total revenues of $125 million, explicit costs of $100 million, and implicit costs of $30 million
   c. A firm with total revenues of $100 million, explicit costs of $90 million, and implicit costs of $20 million
   d. A firm with total revenues of $250,000, explicit costs of $275,000, and implicit costs of $50,000

4. *(Alternative Measures of Profit)* Why is it reasonable to think of normal profit as a type of cost to the firm?

7-2 Describe the most important feature of production in the short run and what causes it

5. *(Production in the Short Run)* Complete the following table. At what point does diminishing marginal returns set in?

Units of the Variable Resource	Total Product	Marginal Product
0	0	—
1	10	___
2	22	___
3	___	9
4	___	4
5	34	___

6. *(Costs in the Short Run)* Identify each of the curves in the following graph:

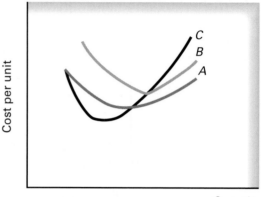

7-3 Explain why average cost is at a minimum when marginal cost equals average cost

7. *(Total Cost and Marginal Cost)* Complete the following table, assuming that each unit of labor costs $75 per day.

Quantity of Labor per Day	Output per Day	Fixed Cost	Variable Cost	Total Cost	Marginal Cost
0	___	$300	$___	$___	$___
1	5	___	75	___	15
2	11	___	150	450	12.5
3	15	___	___	525	___
4	18	___	300	600	25
5	20	___	___	___	37.5

a. Graph the fixed cost, variable cost, and total cost curves for these data.
b. What is the marginal product of the third unit of labor?
c. What is average total cost when output is 18 units per day?

8. *(Total Cost and Marginal Cost)* Complete the following table, where *L* is units of labor, *Q* is units of output, and *MPL* is the marginal product of labor.

L	Q	MPL	VC	TC	MC	ATC
0	0	___	$0	$12	___	___
1	6	___	$3	15	___	___
2	15	___	$6	___	___	___
3	21	___	$9	___	___	___
5	26	___	$15	___	___	___

a. At what quantity of labor do the marginal returns to labor begin to diminish?

b. What is the average variable cost when $Q = 24$?

c. What is this firm's fixed cost?

d. What is the wage rate per day?

9. *(Relationship Between Marginal Cost and Average Cost)* Assume that labor and capital are the only inputs used by a firm. Capital is fixed at 5 units, which cost $100 each. Each worker can be hired for $200 per day. Complete the following table to show average variable cost *(AVC)*, average total cost *(ATC)*, and marginal cost *(MC)*.

Quantity of Labor	Total Output	AVC	ATC	MC
0	0	___	___	___
1	100	___	___	___
2	250	___	___	___
3	350	___	___	___
4	400	___	___	___
5	425	___	___	___

7-4 Explain the sources of economies of scale and diseconomies of scale

10. *(Long-Run Costs)* Suppose the firm has only three possible scales of production as shown below:

a. Which scale of production is most efficient when $Q = 65$?

b. Which scale of production is most efficient when $Q = 75$?

c. Trace out the long-run average cost curve on the diagram.

11. *(Scale Economies)* Identify sources of economies of scale and diseconomies of scale.

8 | Perfect Competition

© iStockphoto.com/alle12

LEARNING OUTCOMES

After studying this chapter, you will be able to…

8-1 Describe the market structure of perfect competition

8-2 Determine the perfectly competitive firm's profit-maximizing output in the short run

8-3 Outline the conditions under which a firm should produce in the short run rather than shut down, even though it incurs an economic loss

8-4 Describe a perfectly competitive firm's short-run supply curve

8-5 Explain why in perfect competition, there are no economic profits or losses in the long run

8-6 Explain why, in some perfectly competitive industries, market supply curves slope upward in the long run

8-7 Summarize how market equilibrium in perfect competition results in productive efficiency and allocative efficiency

After finishing this chapter go to **PAGE 139** for **STUDY TOOLS**

Topics discussed in Chapter 8 include:

- Market structure
- Price takers
- Marginal revenue
- Golden rule of profit maximization
- Loss minimization
- Short-run supply curve
- Long-run supply curve
- Competition and efficiency
- Producer surplus
- Gains from exchange

- What do wheat and gold have in common?
- Why might a firm continue to operate even though it's losing money?
- Why do many firms fail to earn an economic profit?
- How can it be said that the more competitive the industry, the less individual firms compete with each other?
- What's the difference between making stuff right and making the right stuff?
- And what's so perfect about perfect competition?

Answers to these and other questions are provided in this chapter, which examines the first of four market structures—perfect competition.

The previous chapter developed cost curves for an individual firm in the short run and in the long run. In light of these costs, how much should a profit-maximizing firm produce and what price should it charge? To discover the firm's profit-maximizing output and price, we revisit an old friend—demand. Demand and supply, together, guide the firm to maximize any profit or minimize any loss. In the next few chapters, we examine how firms respond to their market environments in deciding what to supply, in what quantities, and at what price. We continue to assume that firms try to maximize profit or minimize any loss.

> **"What's so perfect about perfect competition?"**

8-1 AN INTRODUCTION TO PERFECT COMPETITION

Market structure describes the important features of a market, such as the number of suppliers (are there many or few?), the product's degree of uniformity (do firms in the market supply identical products, or are there differences across firms?), the ease of entry into and exit from the market (can firms come and go easily or are entry and exit blocked?), and the forms of competition among firms (do firms compete based on price alone or do they also compete through advertising and product differences?). The various features will become clearer as we examine each of the four market structures in the next few chapters. *A firm's decisions about how much to produce or what price to charge depend on the structure of the market.*

Before we get started, a few words about terminology. An *industry* consists of all firms that supply output to a particular *market*, such as the auto market, the shoe market, or the wheat market. The terms *industry* and *market* are used interchangeably throughout this chapter.

8-1a Perfectly Competitive Market Structure

We begin with **perfect competition**, in some ways the most basic of market structures. A *perfectly competitive* market is characterized by (1) many buyers and sellers—so many that each buys or sells only a tiny fraction of the total amount in the market; (2) firms sell a **commodity**, which is a standardized product, such as a bushel of wheat, a gallon of milk, a

market structure
Important features of a market, such as the number of firms, product uniformity across firms, firm's ease of entry and exit, and forms of competition

perfect competition
A market structure with many fully informed buyers and sellers of a standardized product and with no obstacles to entry or exit of firms in the long run

commodity
A standardized product; a product that does not differ across producers, such as a bushel of wheat or an ounce of gold

© iStockPhoto.com/Jan Gottwald

dozen eggs, an ounce of gold, or a share of Google stock; such a product does not differ across suppliers; (3) market participants are fully informed about all prices and production processes; and (4) firms and resources are freely mobile—that is, over time they can easily enter or leave the industry without facing obstacles like patents, licenses, and high capital costs.

If these conditions exist in a market, an individual buyer or seller has no control over the price. Price is determined by market demand and supply. Once the market establishes the price, any firm is free to supply whatever quantity maximizes its profit. *A perfectly competitive firm is so small relative to the market that the firm's supply decision does not affect the market price.* Examples of perfectly competitive markets include those for most agricultural products, such as wheat, corn, cotton, and livestock; markets for basic metals, such as gold, silver, tin, and copper; markets for widely traded stock, such as Google, Apple, Bank of America, and General Electric; markets for foreign exchange, such as yen, euros, pounds, and pesos; and markets for some of the million plus smartphone apps now available. Again, there are so many buyers and sellers that the actions of any one cannot influence the market price. For example, about 68,000 farmers in the United States raise hogs, and tens of millions of U.S. households buy pork products. The model of perfect competition allows us to make a number of predictions that hold up pretty well when compared to the real world. Perfect competition is also an important benchmark for evaluating the efficiency of other types of markets. Let's look at demand under perfect competition.

8-1b Demand Under Perfect Competition

Suppose the market in question is the world market for wheat and the firm in question is a typical wheat farm in Kansas. In the world market for wheat, there are hundreds of thousands of farms, so any one supplies only a tiny fraction of market output. For example, the thousands of wheat farmers in Kansas together produce less than 3 percent of the world's supply of wheat. In Exhibit 1, the market price of wheat of $5 per bushel is determined in panel (a) by the intersection of the market demand curve D and the market supply curve S. Once the market determines the price, any farmer can sell all he or she wants to at that market price.

Each farm is so small relative to the market that each has no impact on the market price. Because all farmers produce an identical product—bushels of wheat, in this case—anyone who charges more than the market price sells no wheat. For example, a farmer charging $5.05 per bushel would find no buyers. Of course, any farmer is free to charge less than

Exhibit 1

Market Equilibrium and a Firm's Demand Curve in Perfect Competition

In panel (a), the market price of $5 is determined by the intersection of the market demand and market supply curves. A perfectly competitive firm can sell any amount at that price. The demand curve facing the perfectly competitive firm is horizontal at the market price, as shown by demand curve *d* in panel (b).

the market price, but why do that when all wheat can be sold at the market price? Farmers aren't stupid (if they are, they don't last long). *The demand curve facing an individual farmer is, therefore, a horizontal line drawn at the market price.* In our example, the demand curve facing an individual farmer, identified as *d* in panel (b), is drawn at the market price of $5 per bushel. Thus, each farmer faces a horizontal, or a *perfectly elastic,* demand curve for wheat. A perfectly competitive firm is called a **price taker** because that firm must "take," or accept, the market price—as in "take it or leave it."

It has been said, "In perfect competition there is no competition." Ironically, two neighboring wheat farmers in perfect competition are not really rivals. They both can sell all they want at the market price. The amount one sells has no effect on the market price or on the amount the other can sell.

8-2 SHORT-RUN PROFIT MAXIMIZATION

Each firm tries to maximize economic profit. Firms that ignore this strategy don't survive for long. Economic profit equals total revenue minus total cost, including both explicit and implicit costs. Implicit cost, remember, is the opportunity cost of resources owned by the firm and includes a normal profit. Economic profit is any profit above normal profit. How do firms maximize profit? You have already learned that a perfectly competitive firm has no control over price. What that firm does control is its rate of output—its quantity supplied. The question each wheat farmer asks is this: *How much should I supply to earn the most profit?*

8-2a Total Revenue Minus Total Cost

The firm maximizes economic profit by finding the quantity at which total revenue exceeds total cost by the greatest amount. The firm's total revenue is simply its output times the price. Column (1) in Exhibit 2 shows the farmer's output possibilities measured in bushels of wheat per day. Column (2) shows the market price of $5 per bushel, a price that does not vary with the farmer's output. Column (3) shows the farmer's total revenue, which is price times quantity, or column (2) times column (1). And column (4) shows the

price taker A firm that faces a given market price and whose quantity supplied has no effect on that price; a perfectly competitive firm that decides to produce must accept, or "take," the market price

Exhibit 2

Maximizing Short-Run Profit for a Perfectly Competitive Firm

(1) Bushels of Wheat per Day (q)	(2) Marginal Revenue (Price) (p)	(3) Total Revenue (TR = p × q)	(4) Total Cost (TC)	(5) Marginal Cost (MC = ΔTC/Δq)	(6) Average Total Cost (ATC = TC/q)	(7) Economic Profit or Loss = TR − TC
0	—	$ 0	$15.00	—	—	$−15.00
1	$5	5	19.75	$ 4.75	$19.75	−14.75
2	5	10	23.50	3.75	11.75	−13.50
3	5	15	26.50	3.00	8.83	−11.50
4	5	20	29.00	2.50	7.25	−9.00
5	5	25	31.00	2.00	6.20	−6.00
6	5	30	32.50	1.50	5.42	−2.50
7	5	35	33.75	1.25	4.82	1.25
8	5	40	35.25	1.50	4.41	4.75
9	5	45	37.25	2.00	4.14	7.75
10	5	50	40.00	2.75	4.00	10.00
11	5	55	43.25	3.25	3.93	11.75
12	5	60	48.00	4.75	4.00	12.00
13	5	65	54.50	6.50	4.19	10.50
14	5	70	64.00	9.50	4.57	6.00
15	5	75	77.50	13.50	5.17	−2.50
16	5	80	96.00	18.50	6.00	−16.00

farmer's total cost of supplying each quantity shown. Total cost already includes a normal profit, so total cost includes all opportunity costs. Although the table does not distinguish between fixed and variable costs, fixed cost must equal $15 per day because total cost is $15 when output is zero. The presence of fixed cost tells us that at least one resource is fixed, so the farm must be operating in the short run.

At each output rate, total revenue in column (3) minus total cost in column (4) yields the farmer's economic profit or economic loss in column (7). As you can see, total revenue exceeds total cost at rates of output between 7 and 14 bushels, so the farm earns an *economic profit* at those output rates. Economic profit is maximized at $12 per day when the farm produces 12 bushels of wheat per day (the $12 and 12 bushels combination here is just a coincidence).

These hypothetical data are graphed in panel (a) of Exhibit 3, which shows the total revenue and total cost curves. As output increases by 1 bushel, total revenue increases by $5, so the farm's total revenue curve is a straight line emanating from the origin, with a slope of 5. The short-run total cost curve has the backward S shape introduced in Chapter 7, showing increasing and then diminishing marginal returns from the variable resource. Total cost always increases as more output is produced.

Subtracting total cost from total revenue is one way to find the profit-maximizing output. For output less than 7 bushels and greater than 14 bushels, total cost exceeds total revenue. The economic loss is measured by the vertical distance between the two curves. Between 7 and 14 bushels per day, total revenue exceeds total cost. The economic profit, again, is measured by the vertical distance between the two curves. *Profit is maximized at the rate of output where total revenue exceeds total cost by the greatest amount.* Profit is greatest when 12 bushels are produced per day.

> **"**It has been said, 'In perfect competition there is no competition.'**"**

8-2b Marginal Revenue Equals Marginal Cost

Another way to find the profit-maximizing rate of output is to focus on marginal revenue and marginal cost. **Marginal revenue**, or **MR**, is the change in total revenue from selling another unit of output. In perfect competition, each firm is a price taker, so selling one more unit increases total revenue by the market price. Thus, *in perfect competition, marginal revenue is the market price*—in this example, $5. Column (2) of Exhibit 2 presents the farm's marginal revenue from each bushel of wheat.

In the previous chapter, you learned that *marginal cost* is the change in total cost from producing another unit of output. Column (5) of Exhibit 2 shows the farm's marginal cost for each bushel of wheat. Marginal cost first declines, reflecting increasing marginal returns in the short run as more of the variable resource is employed. Marginal cost then increases, reflecting diminishing marginal returns from adding more of the variable resource.

The firm increases production as long as each additional unit of output adds more to total revenue than to total cost— that is, as long as marginal revenue exceeds marginal cost. Comparing columns (2) and (5) in Exhibit 2, we see that marginal revenue exceeds marginal cost for each of the first 12 bushels of wheat. The marginal cost of bushel 13, however, is $6.50, compared with its marginal revenue of $5. Therefore, producing bushel 13 would reduce economic profit by $1.50. The farmer, as a profit maximizer, limits output to 12 bushels per day. More generally, a firm expands output as long as marginal revenue exceeds marginal cost and stops expanding before marginal cost exceeds marginal revenue. A shorth and expression for this approach is the **golden rule of profit maximization**, which says that a profit-maximizing firm produces where marginal revenue equals marginal cost.

8-2c Economic Profit in the Short Run

Per-unit revenue and cost data from Exhibit 2 are graphed in panel (b) of Exhibit 3. Because marginal revenue in perfect competition equals the market price, the marginal revenue curve is a horizontal line at the market price of $5, which is also the perfectly competitive firm's demand curve. At any quantity measured along the demand curve, marginal revenue is the price. Because

Exhibit 3

Short-Run Profit Maximization for a Perfectly Competitive Firm

In panel (a), the total revenue curve for a perfectly competitive firm is a straight line with a slope of 5, the market price. Total cost increases with output, first at a decreasing rate and then at an increasing rate. Economic profit is maximized where total revenue exceeds total cost by the greatest amount, which occurs at 12 bushels of wheat per day. In panel (b), marginal revenue is a horizontal line at the market price of $5. Economic profit is maximized at 12 bushels of wheat per day, where marginal revenue equals marginal cost (point *e*). That profit equals 12 bushels multiplied by the amount by which the market price of $5 exceeds the average total cost of $4. Economic profit is identified by the shaded rectangle in panel (b).

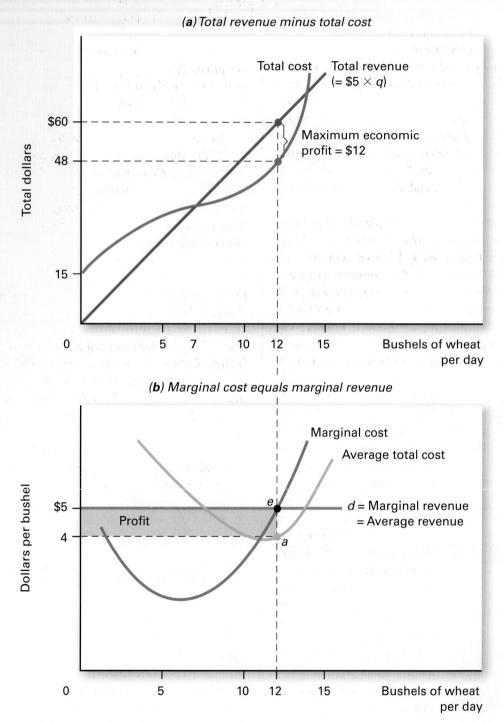

(a) Total revenue minus total cost

(b) Marginal cost equals marginal revenue

the perfectly competitive firm can sell any quantity for the same price per unit, marginal revenue is also **average revenue**, or **AR**. Average revenue equals total revenue divided by quantity, or $AR = TR/q$. Regardless of the output rate, therefore, the following equality holds along a perfectly competitive firm's demand curve:

> Market price = Marginal revenue = Average revenue

The marginal cost curve intersects the marginal revenue curve at point *e*, where output is about 12 bushels per day. At lower rates of output, marginal revenue exceeds marginal cost, so the farm could increase profit by expanding output. At greater rates of output, marginal cost exceeds marginal revenue, so the farm could increase profit by reducing output. Profit itself appears as the shaded rectangle in panel (b) of Exhibit 3. The height of that rectangle, *ae*, equals the price (or average revenue) of $5 minus the average total cost of $4. Price minus average total cost yields an average profit of $1 per bushel. Profit per day, $12, equals the average profit per bushel, $1 (denoted by *ae*), times the 12 bushels produced.

Note that with the total cost and total revenue curves, we measure economic profit by the vertical *distance* between the two curves, as shown in panel (a). But with the per-unit curves of panel (b), we measure economic profit by an *area*—that is, by multiplying the average profit of $1 per bushel times the 12 bushels sold.

8-3 SHORT-RUN LOSS MINIMIZATION

A firm in perfect competition has no control over the market price. Sometimes that price is so low that a firm loses money no matter how much it produces. Such a firm can either continue to produce at a loss or temporarily shut down. But even if the firm shuts down, it cannot, *in the short run*, go out of business or produce

> **"A profit-maximizing firm produces where marginal revenue equals marginal cost."**

something else. The short run is by definition a period too short to allow existing firms to leave the industry. In a sense, firms are stuck in their industry in the short run.

8-3a Fixed Cost and Minimizing Losses

When facing a loss, should a firm temporarily shut down? Intuition suggests the firm should. But keep in mind that the firm faces two types of costs in the short run: fixed cost, such as property taxes and fire insurance, which must be paid even if the firm produces nothing, and variable cost, such as labor, which depends on the amount produced. A firm that shuts down in the short run must still pay its fixed cost. But, by selling some output, the revenue generated may cover all the firm's variable cost and a portion of its fixed cost. *A firm produces rather than shuts down if total revenue exceeds the variable cost of production.* After all, if total revenue exceeds variable cost, that excess covers at least a portion of fixed cost.

Let's look at the same cost data presented in Exhibit 2, but now suppose the market price of wheat is only $3 a bushel, not $5. This new situation is presented in Exhibit 4. Because of the lower price, total cost in column (4) exceeds total revenue in column (3) at all output rates. Each quantity results in a loss, as indicated by column (8). If the firm produces nothing, it loses the fixed cost of $15 per day. But, by producing anywhere from 6 to 12 bushels, the firm can cut that loss. From column (8), you can see that the loss is minimized at $10 per day where 10 bushels are produced. Compared to losing $15 a day by shutting down, producing 10 bushels adds $5 more to total revenue than to total cost. That additional $5 pays some of the firm's fixed cost, thus reducing the economic loss to $10 per day.

Panel (a) of Exhibit 5 presents the firm's total cost and total revenue curves for data in Exhibit 4. The total cost curve remains as in Exhibit 3. Because the price

© Piotr Malczyk/Shutterstock.com

Exhibit 4
Minimizing Short-Run Losses for a Perfectly Competitive Firm

(1) Bushels of Wheat per Day (q)	(2) Marginal Revenue (Price) (p)	(3) Total Revenue (TR = p × q)	(4) Total Cost (TC)	(5) Marginal Cost (MC = ΔTC/Δq)	(6) Average Total Cost (ATC = TC/q)	(7) Average Variable Cost (AVC = VC/q)	(8) Economic Profit or Loss = TR − TC
0	—	$ 0	$15.00	—	—	—	$−15.00
1	$3	3	19.75	$ 4.75	$19.75	$4.75	−16.75
2	3	6	23.50	3.75	11.75	4.25	−17.50
3	3	9	26.50	3.00	8.83	3.83	−17.50
4	3	12	29.00	2.50	7.25	3.50	−17.00
5	3	15	31.00	2.00	6.20	3.20	−16.00
6	3	18	32.50	1.50	5.42	2.92	−14.50
7	3	21	33.75	1.25	4.82	2.68	−12.75
8	3	24	35.25	1.50	4.41	2.53	−11.25
9	3	27	37.25	2.00	4.14	2.47	−10.25
10	3	30	40.00	2.75	4.00	2.50	−10.00
11	3	33	43.25	3.25	3.93	2.57	−10.25
12	3	36	48.00	4.75	4.00	2.75	−12.00
13	3	39	54.50	6.50	4.19	3.04	−15.50
14	3	42	64.00	9.50	4.57	3.50	−22.00
15	3	45	77.50	13.50	5.17	4.17	−32.50
16	3	48	96.00	18.50	6.00	5.06	−48.00

is $3, the total revenue curve now has a slope of 3, so it's flatter than at a price of $5. The total revenue curve now lies below the total cost curve for all output rates. The vertical distance between the two curves measures the economic loss at each output rate. If the farmer produces nothing, the loss is the fixed cost of $15 per day. The vertical distance between the two curves is minimized at an output rate of 10 bushels per day, where the loss is $10 per day.

8-3b Marginal Revenue Equals Marginal Cost

We get the same result using marginal analysis. The per-unit data from Exhibit 4 are graphed in panel (b) of Exhibit 5. First we find the rate of output where marginal revenue equals marginal cost. Marginal revenue equals marginal cost at an output of 10 bushels per day. At that output, the market price of $3 exceeds the average variable cost of $2.50. Because price exceeds average variable cost, total revenue covers variable cost plus a portion of fixed cost. Specifically, $2.50 of the price pays the average variable cost, and the remaining $0.50 helps pay some of average fixed cost (average fixed cost equals average total cost of $4.00 minus average variable cost of $2.50). This still leaves a loss of $1 per bushel, which when multiplied by 10 bushels yields an economic loss

of $10 per day, identified in panel (b) by the pink-shaded rectangle. *The bottom line is that the firm produces rather than shuts down if there is some rate of output where the price at least covers average variable cost.* (Why is the farmer better off in the short run operating at a loss rather than shutting down?)

8-3c Shutting Down in the Short Run

If total revenue exceeds variable costs, the farmer produces in the short run. You may have read or heard of firms reporting a loss; most continue to operate. In fact, many new firms lose money during the first few years of operations. Still, they hang on because they hope to be profitable eventually (for example, the TV network UPN lost more than $1 billion during its first 11 years before merging with the WB network to form the CW network). But *if average variable cost exceeds the price at all rates of output, the firm shuts down.* After all, why produce if doing so only adds to the loss? For example, a wheat price of $2 would fall below the average variable cost at all rates of output. Faced with such a low price, a farmer would shut down and lose just fixed cost, rather than produce and lose both fixed cost plus some variable cost.

From column (7) of Exhibit 4, you can also see that the lowest price at which the farmer would just cover average variable cost is $2.47 per bushel, when output

Exhibit 5

Short-Run Loss Minimization for a Perfectly Competitive Firm

Because total cost everywhere exceeds total revenue in panel (a), the firm suffers a loss no matter how much is produced. The loss is minimized where output is 10 bushels per day. Panel (b) shows that marginal revenue equals marginal cost at point e. The loss is equal to output of 10 multiplied by the difference between average total cost ($4) and price ($3). Because price exceeds average variable cost ($2.50), the firm is better off continuing to produce in the short run, since revenue covers some fixed cost.

(a) Total cost and total revenue

(b) Marginal cost equals marginal revenue

is 9 bushels per day. At this price, the farmer is indifferent between producing and shutting down, because either way the loss is the $15 per day in fixed cost. Any price above $2.47 allows the farmer, by producing, to also cover some fixed cost.

Shutting down is not the same as going out of business. In the short run, even a firm that shuts down keeps productive capacity intact—paying rent, insurance, and property taxes, keeping water pipes from freezing in the winter, and so on. For example, some ice cream shops shut down for the winter in cooler climates, a business serving a college community may close during term breaks, an auto plant responds to slack sales by temporarily halting production, and Yahoo! recently shut down for a week to save money. A firm that shuts down does not escape fixed cost. When demand picks up again, production resumes. If the market outlook remains grim, the firm may decide to leave the market, but that's a long-run decision. The short run is defined as a period during which some costs remain fixed, so a firm cannot escape those costs in the short run, no matter what it

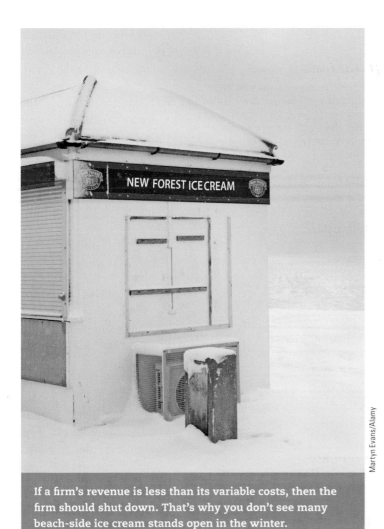

If a firm's revenue is less than its variable costs, then the firm should shut down. That's why you don't see many beach-side ice cream stands open in the winter.

Martyn Evans/Alamy

does. *Fixed cost is sunk cost in the short run, unavoidable whether the firm produces or shuts down.*

Likewise, a concert promoter may cancel an event because of poor ticket sales even though the hall has already been rented and the talent hired. And a movie producer may pull the plug on a nearly completed film that looks like a turkey to avoid sinking millions more into advertising and distribution. Concert promoters and movie producers want to cut their losses. They don't want to throw more good money after bad.

8-4 SHORT-RUN SUPPLY CURVES

If average variable cost exceeds price at all output rates, the firm shuts down in the short run. But if price exceeds average variable cost, the firm produces the quantity at which marginal revenue equals marginal cost. As we'll see, a firm changes the rate of output if the market price changes.

8-4a Short-Run Firm Supply Curve

For a firm in perfect competition in the short run, the relationship between price and quantity is summarized in Exhibit 6. Points 1, 2, 3, 4, and 5 identify where the marginal cost curve intersects alternative marginal revenue, or demand, curves. At a market price as low as p_1, the firm shuts down rather than produce at point 1 because that price is below average variable cost. So the loss-minimizing output rate at price p_1 is zero, as identified by q_1. At price p_2, the price just equals average variable cost, so the firm is indifferent between producing q_2 and shutting down; either way the firm loses what it must pay to cover fixed cost. Point 2 is called the *shutdown point*. If the price is p_3, the firm produces q_3 to minimize its short-run loss (see if you can identify that loss in the diagram). At p_4, the firm produces q_4 to earn a normal profit, because price equals average total cost. Point 4 is called the *break-even point*. If the price rises to p_5, the firm earns short-run economic profit by producing q_5 (see if you can identify that economic profit in the diagram).

At prices below p_2, the firm shuts down in the short run. The quantity supplied when the price is p_2 or higher is determined by the intersection of the firm's marginal cost curve and its demand, or marginal revenue, curve. As long as the price covers average variable cost, the firm supplies the quantity at which the upward-sloping marginal cost curve intersects the marginal revenue, or demand, curve. Thus, *that portion of the firm's marginal cost curve that intersects and rises above the lowest point on its average variable cost curve becomes the **short-run firm supply curve**.* In Exhibit 6, the short-run supply curve is the upward-sloping portion of the marginal cost curve, beginning at point 2, the shutdown point. The solid portion of the short-run supply curve indicates the quantity the firm offers for sale at each price.

8-4b The Short-Run Industry Supply Curve

Exhibit 7 presents examples of how supply curves for three firms with identical marginal cost curves can be summed *horizontally* to form the short-run industry supply curve (in perfect competition, there are many more

short-run firm supply curve A curve that shows how much a firm supplies at each price in the short run; in perfect competition, that portion of a firm's marginal cost curve that intersects and rises above the low point on its average variable cost curve

Exhibit 6

Summary of a Perfectly Competitive Firm's Short-Run Output Decisions

At price p_1, the firm produces nothing because p_1 is less than the firm's average variable cost. At price p_2, the firm is indifferent between shutting down or producing q_2 units of output, because in either case, the firm suffers a loss equal to its fixed cost. At p_3, it produces q_3 units and suffers a loss that is less than its fixed cost. At p_4, the firm produces q_4 and just breaks even, earning a normal profit, because p_4 equals average total cost. Finally, at p_5, the firm produces q_5 and earns an economic profit. The firm's short-run supply curve is that portion of its marginal cost curve at and rising above the minimum point of average variable cost (point 2).

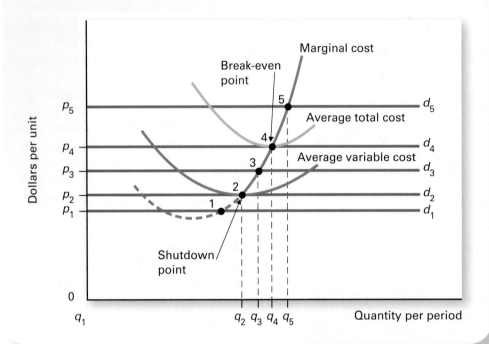

firms). The **short-run industry supply curve** is the horizontal sum of all firms' short-run supply curves. At a price below p, no output is supplied. At price p, each of the three firms supplies 10 units, so the market supplies 30 units per period. At p', which is above p, each firm supplies 20 units per period, so the market supplies 60 units.

8-4c Firm Supply and Market Equilibrium

Exhibit 8 shows the relationship between the short-run profit-maximizing output of the individual firm and market equilibrium price and quantity. Suppose there are 100,000 identical wheat farmers in this market. Their individual supply curves (represented by the portions of the marginal cost curve at and rising above the average variable cost) are summed horizontally

short-run industry supply curve A curve that indicates the quantity supplied by the industry at each price in the short run; in perfect competition, the horizontal sum of each firm's short-run supply curve

to yield the market, or industry, supply curve. The market supply curve appears in panel (b), where it intersects the market demand curve to determine the market price of $5 per bushel. At that price, each farmer supplies 12 bushels per day, as shown in panel (a), which sums to 1,200,000 bushels for the market, as shown in panel (b). Each farmer in the short run earns an economic profit of $12 per day, represented by the shaded rectangle in panel (a).

TO REVIEW: A perfectly competitive firm supplies the short-run quantity that maximizes profit or minimizes loss. When confronting a loss, a firm either produces an output that minimizes that loss or shuts down temporarily.

In open markets like the fish market shown here, the prices may change from day to day and are a function not only of the day's supply of and demand for fish, but also of local customs related to haggling.

© iStockphoto.com/aluxum

Exhibit 7

Firm Supply Curves Sum Horizontally to Form the Market Supply Curve

At price p, each firm supplies 10 units of output and the market supplies 30 units per period. At price p', each firm supplies 20 units and the market supplies 60 units per period. The, market supply curve in panel (d) is the horizontal sum of the individual firm supply curves s_A, s_B, and s_C.

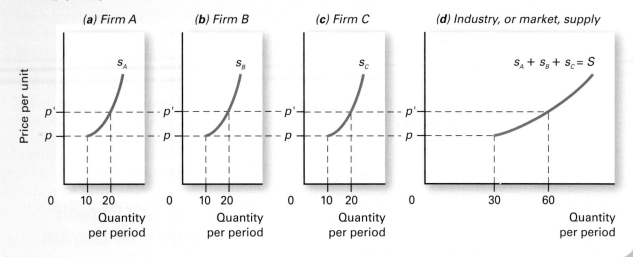

Given the conditions for perfect competition, the market converges toward the equilibrium price and quantity. But how is that equilibrium actually reached? In the real world, markets operate based on customs and conventions, which vary across markets. For example, the rules acceptable on the New York Stock Exchange are not the same as those followed in the market for fresh fish.

Exhibit 8

Short-Run Profit Maximization and Market Equilibrium in Perfect Competition

The market supply curve S in panel (b) is the horizontal sum of the supply curves of all 100,000 identical firms in this perfectly competitive industry. The intersection of S with the market demand curve D determines the market price of $5. That price, in turn, determines the height of the perfectly elastic demand curve facing the representative firm in panel (a). That firm produces 12 bushels per day (where marginal cost equals marginal revenue of $5) and earns economic profit in the short run of $1 per bushel, or $12 in total per day.

8-5 PERFECT COMPETITION IN THE LONG RUN

In the short run, the quantity of variable resources can change, but other resources, which mostly determine firm size, are fixed. In the long run, however, a firm has time to enter and leave and to adjust its size—that is, to adjust its *scale* of operations. In the long run, there is no distinction between fixed and variable cost because all resources under the firm's control are variable.

Short-run economic profit encourages new firms to enter the market in the long run and may prompt existing firms to get bigger. Economic profit attracts resources from industries where firms are losing money or earning only a normal profit. This expansion in the number and size of firms shifts the industry supply curve rightward in the long run, driving down the price. New firms continue to enter a profitable industry and existing firms continue to expand as long as economic profit is greater than zero. Entry and expansion stop only when the resulting increase in supply drives down the price enough to erase economic profit. In the case of

> **"** Short-run economic profit attracts new entrants in the long run and may cause existing firms to expand. **"**

wheat farming, economic profit attracts new wheat farmers and may encourage existing wheat farmers to expand. *Short-run economic profit attracts new entrants in the long run and may cause existing firms to expand. Market supply thereby increases, driving down the market price until economic profit disappears.*

On the other hand, a short-run loss forces some firms to leave the industry in the long run or to reduce their scale of operation. In the long run, departures and reductions in scale shift the market supply curve to the left, thereby increasing the market price until remaining firms just break even—that is, earn a normal profit.

8-5a Zero Economic Profit in the Long Run

In the long run, firms in perfect competition earn just a normal profit, which means zero economic profit. Exhibit 9 shows a representative firm and the market in long-run equilibrium. Market supply adjusts as firms enter or leave or change their size. *This long-run adjustment continues until the market supply curve intersects the market*

Exhibit 9

Long-Run Equilibrium for a Firm and Industry in Perfect Competition

In long-run equilibrium, the firm produces *q* units of output per period and earns a normal profit. At point *e*, price, marginal cost, marginal revenue, short-run average total cost, and long-run average cost are all equal. There is no reason for new firms to enter the market or for existing firms to leave. As long as the market demand and supply curves remain unchanged, the industry will continue to produce a total of *Q* units of output at price *p*.

(a) Firm

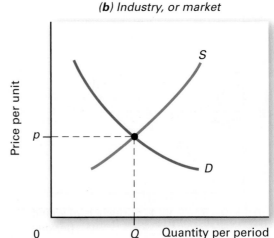

(b) Industry, or market

demand curve at a price that corresponds to the lowest point on each firm's long-run average cost curve, or LRAC curve. Because the long run is a period during which all resources under a firm's control are variable, *a firm in the long run is forced by competition to adjust its scale until average cost is minimized.* A firm that fails to minimize average cost will not survive in the long run. At point *e* in panel (a) of Exhibit 9, the firm is in equilibrium, producing *q* units per period and earning just a normal profit. At point *e*, price, marginal cost, short-run average total cost, and long-run average cost are all equal. No firm in the market has any reason to change its output, and no outside firm has any incentive to enter this industry, because firms in this market are earning normal, but not economic, profit. In other words, all resources employed in this industry earn their opportunity costs. No resource employed in this industry can earn more elsewhere.

8-5b Long-Run Adjustment to a Change of Demand

To explore the long-run adjustment process, let's consider how a firm and an industry respond to an increase in market demand. Suppose that the costs facing each firm do not depend on the number of firms in the industry (an assumption explained soon).

Increase of Demand

Exhibit 10 shows a perfectly competitive firm and industry in long-run equilibrium, with the market supply curve intersecting the market demand curve at point *a* in panel (b). The market-clearing price is *p*, and the market quantity is Q_a. The firm, shown in panel (a), supplies *q* units at that market price, earning a normal profit. This representative firm produces where price, or marginal revenue, equals marginal cost, short-run average total cost, and long-run average cost. (Remember, a normal profit is included in the firm's average cost curves.)

Now suppose market demand increases, as reflected by a rightward shift of the market demand curve, from *D* to *D′* in panel (b), causing the market price to increase in the short run to *p′*. For example, as consumers in China and South Korea shift from tea to coffee, this has increased the world demand for coffee.[1] Each firm responds to the higher price by expanding output along its short-run supply, or marginal cost, curve until its quantity

1. Leslie Josephs, "Coffee Prices Soar at Online Auctions," *Wall Street Journal*, 27 October 2014.

Exhibit 10

Long-Run Adjustment in Perfect Competition to an Increase of Demand

An increase of market demand from *D* to *D′* in panel (b) moves the short-run market equilibrium point from *a* to *b*. Output in the short run increases to Q_b, and the market price rises to *p′*. The price rise shifts up the individual firm's demand curve from *d* to *d′* in panel (a). The firm responds to the higher price by increasing output to *q′* and earns economic profit identified by the shaded rectangle. Economic profit attracts new firms to the industry in the long run. Market supply shifts right to *S′* in panel (b), pushing the market price back down to *p*. In panel (a), the firm's demand curve shifts back down to *d*, erasing economic profit. The short-run adjustment for the industry is from point *a* to point *b* in panel (b), but the long-run adjustment is from point *a* to point *c*.

(a) Firm

(b) Industry, or market

supplied increases to q', shown in panel (a) of Exhibit 10. At that output, the firm's marginal cost curve intersects the new marginal revenue curve, which is also the firm's new demand curve, d'. Note that in the short run, each firm now earns an economic profit, shown by the shaded rectangle. Because all firms increase their quantity supplied, industry quantity supplied increases to Q_b in panel (b).

Short-run economic profit attracts new firms in the long run. Their entry shifts the market supply curve to the right, which forces the price down. Firms continue to enter as long as they can earn economic profit. The market supply curve eventually shifts out to S', where it intersects D' at point c, returning the price to its initial equilibrium level, p. The firm's demand curve drops from d' back down to d. As a result, each firm reduces output from q' back to q, and, once again, each earns just a normal profit. Notice that although industry output increases from Q_a to Q_c, each firm's output returns to q. In this example, the additional output comes entirely from new firms drawn to the industry rather than from more output by existing firms (existing firms don't expand in this example because an increase in scale would increase average cost).

Short-run economic profit attracts new firms to the industry in the long run. But new entry shifts out market supply, forcing the market price down until economic profit disappears. In panel (b) of Exhibit 10, the short-run adjustment to increased demand is from point a to point b; the long-run adjustment moves to point c.

Decrease of Demand

Next, let's trace the effects of a decrease of demand on the long-run market adjustment. The initial long-run equilibrium in Exhibit 11 is the same as in Exhibit 10. Market demand and supply curves intersect at point a in panel (b), yielding an equilibrium price p and an equilibrium quantity Q_a. As shown in panel (a), each firm earns a normal profit in the long run by producing output rate q, where price, or marginal revenue, equals marginal cost, short-run average total cost, and long-run average cost.

Now suppose that market demand declines, as reflected in panel (b) by a leftward shift of the market demand curve, from D back to D''. For example, the growth of online shopping means fewer customer visits to brick-and-mortar stores chains such as Macy's, Target, and Best Buy.[2] In the short run, this forces the market price down to p''. With the market price lower, the demand curve facing each individual firm drops from d to d''. Each firm responds in the short run by reducing

2. Shelly Banjo and Drew FitzGerald, "Macy's Adjusts to Less Foot Traffic," *Wall Street Journal*," 16.

Exhibit 11

Long-Run Adjustment in Perfect Competition to a Decrease of Demand

A decrease of demand to D'' in panel (b) disturbs the long-run equilibrium at point a. The price drops to p'' in the short run; output falls to Q_f. In panel (a), the firm's demand curve shifts down to d''. Each firm cuts output to q'' and suffers a loss. As some firms leave the industry in the long run, the market supply curve shifts left to S''. Market price rises to p as output falls further to Q_g. At price p, the remaining firms once again earn a normal profit. Thus, the short-run adjustment is from point a to point f in panel (b); the long-run adjustment is from point a to point g.

(a) *Firm*

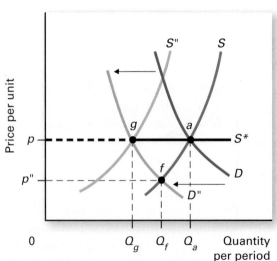

(b) *Industry, or market*

quantity supplied to q'' where the firm's marginal cost equals its now-lower marginal revenue, or price. Market output falls to Q_f. Because the lower market price is below average total cost, each firm operates at a loss. This loss is shown by the shaded rectangle in Exhibit 11. Note, the price must still be above the average variable cost, because the firm's short-run supply curve, MC, is defined as that portion of the firm's marginal cost curve at and above its average variable cost curve.

A short-run loss forces some firms out of business in the long run. As firms exit, market supply decreases, or shifts leftward, so the price increases along market demand curve D''. Firms continue to leave until the market supply curve decreases to S'', where it intersects D'' at point g. Market output has fallen to Q_g, and price has returned to p. With the price back up to p, remaining firms once again earn a normal profit. When the dust settles, each remaining firm produces q, the initial equilibrium quantity. But, because some firms have left the industry, market output has fallen from Q_a to Q_g. Again, note that the adjustment involves the departure of firms from the industry rather than a reduction in the scale of remaining firms, as a reduction in scale would increase each firm's long-run average cost.

8-6 LONG-RUN INDUSTRY SUPPLY CURVE

Thus far, we have looked at a perfectly competitive firm's and industry's response to changes in demand, distinguishing between a short-run adjustment and a long-run adjustment. In the short run, a firm alters quantity supplied by moving up or down its marginal cost curve (that portion at and above average variable cost) until marginal cost equals marginal revenue, or price. If the price is too low to cover minimum average variable cost, a firm shuts down in the short run. Short-run economic profit (or loss) prompts some firms in the long run to enter (or leave) the industry or to adjust firm size until firms still in the industry earn just a normal profit.

In Exhibits 10 and 11, we began with an initial long-run equilibrium point; then, in response to a shift of the demand curve, we found a new long-run equilibrium

point. In each case, the price changed in the short run but not in the long run. Market output increased in Exhibit 10 and decreased in Exhibit 11. Connecting these long-run equilibrium points yields the *long-run industry supply curve,* labeled S^* in Exhibits 10 and 11. The **long-run industry supply curve** shows the relationship between price and quantity supplied once firms fully adjust to any short-term economic profit or loss resulting from a change in demand.

iStockphoto.com//DNY59

Since the pencil industry does not significantly affect demand for the materials required (wood, rubber, and metal), it is likely a constant-cost industry.

8-6a Constant-Cost Industries

The industry we have examined thus far is called a **constant-cost industry** because each firm's long-run average cost curve does not shift up or down as industry output changes. In a **constant-cost industry**, each firm's per-unit costs are independent of the number of firms in the industry. *The long-run supply curve for a constant-cost industry is horizontal,* as is depicted by S^* in Exhibits 10 and 11. A constant-cost industry uses such a small portion of the resources available that expanding industry output does not bid up resource prices. For example, output in the pencil industry can expand without bidding up the prices of wood, graphite, and rubber, because the pencil industry uses such a tiny share of the market supply of these resources.

8-6b Increasing-Cost Industries

The firms in some industries encounter higher average costs as industry output expands in the long run. Firms in these **increasing-cost industries** find that expanding output bids up the prices of some resources

long-run industry supply curve A curve that shows the relationship between price and quantity supplied by the industry once firms adjust in the long run to any change in market demand

constant-cost industry An industry that can expand or contract without affecting the long-run per-unit cost of production; the long-run industry supply curve is horizontal

increasing-cost industry An industry that faces higher per-unit production costs as industry output expands in the long run; the long-run industry supply curve slopes upward or otherwise increases per-unit production costs, and these higher costs shift up each firm's cost curves. For example, a market expansion of oil production could bid up the prices of drilling rigs and the wages of petroleum engineers and geologists, raising per-unit production costs for each oil producer. Likewise, more housing construction could bid up what developers must pay for land, carpenters, lumber, and other building materials.

To illustrate the equilibrium adjustment process for an increasing-cost industry, we begin again in long-run equilibrium in Exhibit 12, with the firm shown in panel (a) and the industry in panel (b). Market demand curve D in panel (b) intersects short-run market supply curve S at equilibrium point a to yield market price p_a and market quantity Q_a. When the price is p_a, the demand (and marginal revenue) curve facing each firm is d_a as shown in panel (a). The firm supplies quantity q, where the price, or marginal revenue, equals marginal cost. At that output, average total cost equals the price,

so the firm earns no economic profit in this long-run equilibrium.

Suppose the market demand curve in panel (b) shifts to the right from D to D'. The new demand curve intersects the short-run market supply curve S at point b, yielding the market price p_b and market quantity Q_b. With this price increase, each firm's demand curve shifts from da up to d_b. The firm's new short-run equilibrium occurs at point b in panel (a), where the marginal cost curve intersects the new demand curve, which is also the marginal revenue curve. Each firm produces output q_b. In the short run, each firm earns an economic profit equal to q_b times the difference between price p_b and the average total cost at that rate of output. So far, the sequence of events is the same as for a constant-cost industry.

Economic profit attracts new firms. Because this is an increasing-cost industry, new entrants drive up the cost of production, raising each firm's marginal and average cost curves. In panel (a) of Exhibit 12, MC and ATC shift up to

Exhibit 12

Long-Run Adjustment for an Increasing-Cost Industry in Perfect Competition

An increase of demand to D' in panel (b) disturbs the initial equilibrium at point a. Short-run equilibrium is established at point b, where D' intersects the short-run market supply curve S. At the higher price p_b, the firm's demand curve shifts up in panel (a) to d_b, and its output increases to q_b. At point b, the firm is now earning economic profit, which attracts new firms. As new firms enter this market, input prices get bid up, so each firm's marginal and average cost curves rise. New firms increase the short-run market supply curve from S to S'. The intersection of the new market supply curve, S', with D' determines the market price, p_c. At pc, individual firms are earning a normal profit. Point c shows the long-run equilibrium combination of price and quantity. By connecting long-run equilibrium points a and c in panel (b), we obtain the upward-sloping long-run market supply curve S^* for this increasing-cost industry.

(a) Firm

(b) Industry, or market

MC' and ATC'. (We assume for simplicity that new average cost curves are vertical shifts of the initial ones, so the minimum efficient plant size remains the same.)

The entry of new firms also shifts the short-run industry supply curve to the right in panel (b), thus reducing the market price along D'. *New firms enter the industry until the combination of a higher production cost and a lower price squeezes economic profit to zero.* This long-run equilibrium occurs when the entry of new firms has shifted the short-run industry supply curve out to S', which lowers the price until it equals the minimum on each firm's new average total cost curve. The market price does not fall back to the initial equilibrium level because each firm's average total cost curve has increased, or shifted up, with the expansion of industry output. The intersection of the new short-run market supply curve, S', and the new market demand curve, D', determines the new long-run market equilibrium point, c. Points a and c in panel (b) are both on the *upward-sloping* long-run supply curve $S*$ for this increasing-cost industry.

In constant-cost industries, each firm's costs depend simply on the scale of its plant and its rate of output. For increasing-cost industries, each firm's costs depend also on the number of firms in the market. By bidding up the price of resources, long-run expansion in an increasing-cost industry increases each firm's marginal and average costs. The long-run supply curve slopes upward, like $S*$ in Exhibit 12.

TO REVIEW: In the short run, firms in perfect competition can earn an economic profit, a normal profit, or an economic loss in the short run. But in the long run, the entry or exit of firms and adjustments in each firm's size squeeze economic profit to zero. Firms in a perfectly competitive industry earn only a normal profit in the long run. This is true whether the industry in question experiences constant costs or increasing costs in the long run. Notice that, regardless of the nature of costs in the industry, the market supply curve is more elastic in the long run than in the short run. In the long run, firms can adjust all their resources, so they are better able to respond to changes in price. One final point: Firms in an industry could theoretically experience a lower average cost as industry output expands in the long run, resulting in a downward-sloping long-run industry supply curve. But such an outcome is considered so rare that we do not examine it.

As mentioned at the outset, perfect competition provides a useful benchmark for evaluating the efficiency of markets. Let's examine the qualities of perfect competition that make it so useful.

PERFECT COMPETITION AND EFFICIENCY

How does perfect competition stack up as an efficient user of resources? Two concepts of efficiency are used to judge market performance. The first, called *productive efficiency*, refers to producing output at the least possible cost. The second, called *allocative efficiency*, refers to producing the output that consumers value the most. *Perfect competition guarantees both productive efficiency and allocative efficiency in the long run.*

8-7a Productive Efficiency: Making Stuff Right

Productive efficiency occurs when each firm produces at the minimum point on its long-run average cost curve, so the market price equals the minimum average cost. The entry and exit of firms and any adjustment in the scale of each firm ensure that each firm produces at the minimum of its long-run average cost curve. Firms that do not reach minimum long-run average cost must, to avoid continued losses, either adjust their scale or leave the industry. Thus, *perfect competition produces output at minimum average cost in the long run.*

8-7b Allocative Efficiency: Making the Right Stuff

Just because *production* occurs at the least possible cost does not mean that the *allocation* of resources is the most efficient one possible. The products may not be the ones consumers want. This situation is akin to that of the airline pilot who informs passengers that there's good news and bad news: "The good news is that we're making record time. The bad news is that we're lost!" Likewise, firms may be producing goods efficiently but producing the wrong goods—that is, making stuff right but making the wrong stuff.

Allocative efficiency occurs when each firm produces the output that consumers value most. How do we know that perfect competition guarantees allocative efficiency? The answer lies with the market demand

> **productive efficiency**
> Each firm employs the least-cost combination of inputs; minimum average cost in the long run
>
> **allocative efficiency**
> Each firm produces the output most preferred by consumers; marginal benefit equals marginal cost

and supply curves. Recall that the demand curve reflects the marginal value that consumers attach to each unit of the good, so the market price is the amount people are willing and able to pay for the final unit they consume. We also know that, in both the short run and the long run, the equilibrium price in perfect competition equals the marginal cost of supplying the last unit sold. Marginal cost measures the opportunity cost of resources employed to produce that last unit sold. Thus, the demand and supply curves intersect at the combination of price and quantity at which *the marginal value, or the marginal benefit, that consumers attach to the final unit purchased, just equals the opportunity cost of the resources employed to produce that unit.*

As long as marginal benefit equals marginal cost, the last unit produced is valued by consumers as much as, or more than, any other good those resources could have produced. There is no way to reallocate resources to increase the total value of all output in the economy. Thus, there is no way to reallocate resources to increase the total utility or total benefit consumers reap from production. *When the marginal benefit that consumers derive from a good equals the marginal cost of producing that good, that market is said to be allocatively efficient.*

$$\text{Marginal benefit} = \text{Marginal cost}$$

Firms not only are making stuff right, but they are also making the right stuff.

8-7c What's so Perfect About Perfect Competition?

If the marginal cost of supplying a good just equals the marginal benefit to consumers, does this mean that market exchange confers no net benefits to participants? No. Market exchange usually benefits both consumers and

Exhibit 13

Consumer Surplus and Producer Surplus for a Perfectly Competitive Market

Consumer surplus is represented by the area above the market-clearing price of $10 per unit and below the demand curve; it appears as the blue triangle. Producer surplus is represented by the area above the short-run market supply curve and below the market-clearing price of $10 per unit; it appears as the gold area. At a price of $5 per unit, there would be no producer surplus. At a price of $6 per unit, producer surplus would be the gold shaded area between $5 and $6. A price of $5 just covers each firm's average variable cost.

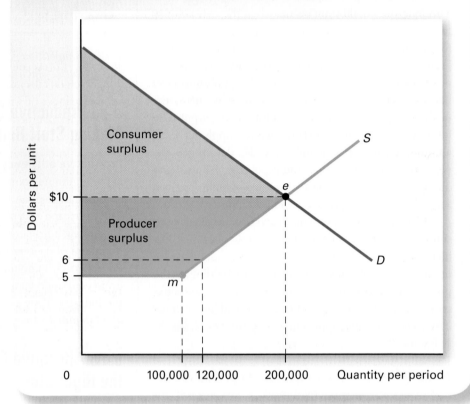

producers. Recall that consumers enjoy a surplus from market exchange because the most they would be willing and able to pay for each unit of the good usually exceeds what they actually do pay. Exhibit 13 depicts a market in short-run equilibrium. The *consumer surplus* in this exhibit is represented by blue shading, which is the area below the demand curve but above the market-clearing price of $10.

Producers in the short run also usually derive a net benefit, or a surplus, from market exchange, because the price they receive exceeds the least they would accept to supply that quantity in the short run. Recall that the short-run market supply curve is the sum of each firm's marginal cost curve at and above its minimum average variable cost. Point *m* in Exhibit 13 is the minimum point on the market supply curve; it indicates that at a price of $5, quantity supplied is 100,000 units. At prices below $5, quantity supplied would be zero because firms could not cover average variable cost. A price of $5 just covers average variable cost.

If the market price rises to $6, quantity supplied increases until marginal cost equals $6. Market output increases from 100,000 to 120,000 units. Total revenue in this market increases from $500,000 to $720,000. Part of the higher revenue covers the higher marginal cost of production. But the rest provides a bonus to producers. After all, suppliers would have offered the first 100,000 units for only $5 each. If the price is $6, firms get to supply these 100,000 units for $6 each. Producer surplus at a price of $6 is the gold-shaded area between the prices of $5 and $6.

In the short run, **producer surplus** equals the total revenue producers are paid minus their variable cost of production. In Exhibit 13, the market-clearing price is $10 per unit, and producer surplus is depicted by the gold-shaded area between a price of $5 and the market price of $10. If the market price is less than $5, firms will shut down, so they garner no producer surplus. Any price that exceeds average variable cost, which is $5 in this example, generates a producer surplus. A high enough price could yield economic profit.

The combination of consumer surplus and producer surplus shows the gains from voluntary exchange. Productive and allocative efficiency in the short run occurs at equilibrium point *e*, which also is the combination of price and quantity that maximizes the sum of consumer surplus and producer surplus, thus maximizing social welfare. **Social welfare** is the overall well-being of people in the economy. Even though marginal cost equals marginal benefit for the final unit produced and consumed, both producers and consumers usually derive a surplus, or a bonus, from market exchange. Voluntary exchange typically makes both sides of the market better off (win-win). And competition usually improves product quality as well. For example, one study found that the entry of one more hospital to a local market increased the heart attack survival rate by about 10 percent.[3]

8-8 FINAL WORD

Let's review the assumptions of a perfectly competitive market and see how each relates to ideas developed in this chapter. *First,* there are many buyers and many sellers. This assumption ensures that no individual buyer or seller can influence the price (although recent experiments show that competition occurs even with few buyers and sellers). *Second,* firms produce a commodity, or a uniform product. If consumers could distinguish among the products of different suppliers, they might prefer one firm's product even at a higher price, so different producers could sell at different prices. In that case, not every firm would be a price taker—that is, each firm's demand curve would no longer

be horizontal. *Third,* market participants have full information about all prices and all production processes. Otherwise, some producers could charge more than the market price, and some uninformed consumers would pay that higher price. Also, through ignorance, some firms might select outdated technology or fail to recognize opportunities for short-run economic profits. *Fourth,* in the long run, all resources are mobile, with nothing preventing firms from entering profitable markets or leaving losing markets. If firms couldn't enter profitable markets, then some firms already in those markets could earn economic profit in the long run. If firms couldn't exit losing markets, then market supply couldn't decline enough in the long run to erase the economic losses of remaining firms.

Perfect competition is not the most common market structure observed in the real world. The markets for agricultural products, metals such as gold and silver, widely traded stocks, and foreign exchange come close to being perfect. But even if not a single example could be found, the model would still be useful for analyzing market behavior. As you will see in the next two chapters, perfect competition provides a valuable benchmark for evaluating the efficiency of other market structures.

producer surplus A bonus for producers in the short run; the amount by which total revenue from production exceeds variable cost

social welfare The overall well-being of people in the economy; maximized when the marginal cost of production equals the marginal benefit to consumers

STUDY TOOLS 8

READY TO STUDY? IN THE BOOK, YOU CAN:

☐ Work the Problems at the end of the chapter.

☐ Rip out the chapter review card for a handy summary of the chapter and key terms.

ONLINE AT CENGAGEBRAIN.COM YOU CAN:

☐ Collect StudyBits while you read and study the chapter.

☐ Quiz yourself on key concepts.

☐ Prepare for tests with chapter flash cards as well as flash cards that you create.

☐ Watch videos to explore economics further.

3. Nicholas Bloom et al., "The Impact of Competition on Management Quality: Evidence from Public Hospitals," *Journal of Economic Studies*, (forthcoming).

CHAPTER 8 PROBLEMS

Your instructor can access the answers to these problems online at http://cengagebrain.com.

8-1 Describe the market structure of perfect competition

1. *(Market Structure)* Define market structure. What factors are considered in determining the market structure of a particular industry?
2. *(Perfect Competition Characteristics)* Describe the characteristics of perfect competition.
3. *(Demand Under Perfect Competition)* What type of demand curve does a perfectly competitive firm face? Why?

8-2 Determine the perfectly competitive firm's profit-maximizing output in the short run

4. *(Short-Run Profit Maximization)* A perfectly competitive firm has the following fixed and variable costs in the short run. The market price for the firm's product is $150.

Output	FC	VC	TC	TR	Profit/Loss
0	$100	$ 0	___	___	___
1	$100	$100	___	___	___
2	$100	$180	___	___	___
3	$100	$300	___	___	___
4	$100	$440	___	___	___
5	$100	$600	___	___	___
6	$100	$780	___	___	___

   a. Complete the table.
   b. At what output rate does the firm maximize profit or minimize loss?
   c. What is the firm's marginal revenue at each positive level of output? Its average revenue?
   d. What can you say about the relationship between marginal revenue and marginal cost for output rates below the profit-maximizing (or loss-minimizing) rate? For output rates above the profit-maximizing (or loss-minimizing) rate?

8-3 Outline the conditions under which a firm should produce in the short run rather than shut down, even though it incurs an economic loss

5. *(Minimizing Loss in the Short Run)* Explain the different options a firm has for minimizing losses in the short run.
6. *(Short-Run Loss)* Suppose a firm decides to shut down in the short run. What is the resulting loss?

8-4 Describe a perfectly competitive firm's short-run supply curve

7. *(The Short-Run Firm Supply Curve)* Use the following data to answer the questions below:

Q	VC	MC	AVC
1	$10	___	___
2	$16	___	___
3	$20	___	___
4	$25	___	___
5	$31	___	___
6	$38	___	___
7	$46	___	___
8	$55	___	___
9	$65	___	___

   a. Calculate the marginal cost and average variable cost for each level of production.
   b. How much would the firm produce if it could sell its product for $5? For $7? For $10?
   c. Explain your answers.
   d. Assuming that its fixed cost is $3, calculate the firm's profit at each of the production levels determined in part (b).

8. *(The Short-Run Firm Supply Curve)* Each of the following situations could exist for a perfectly competitive firm in the short run. In each case, indicate whether the firm should produce in the short run or shut down in the short run, or whether additional information is needed to determine what it should do in the short run.
   a. Total cost exceeds total revenue at all output levels.
   b. Variable cost exceeds total revenue at all output levels.
   c. Total revenue exceeds fixed cost at all output levels.
   d. Marginal revenue exceeds marginal cost at the current output level.
   e. Price exceeds average total cost at all output levels.
   f. Average variable cost exceeds price at all output levels.
   g. Average total cost exceeds price at all output levels.

8-5 Explain why in perfect competition, there are no economic profits or losses in the long run

9. *(Zero Economic Profits in Long Run)* Why would firms choose to operate in a perfectly competitive market even though they earn no economic profit in the long run?
10. *(Zero Economic Profits in Long Run)* Why is there no economic profit for perfectly competitive firms in the long run? Why is there no economic loss?

8-6 Explain why, in some perfectly competitive industries, market supply curves slope upward in the long run

11. *(The Long-Run Industry Supply Curve)* A normal good is being produced in a constant-cost, perfectly competitive industry. Initially, each firm is in long-run equilibrium.
    a. Graphically illustrate and explain the short-run adjustments for the market and the firm to a decrease in consumer incomes. Be sure to discuss any changes in output levels, prices, profits, and the number of firms.
    b. Next, show on your graph and explain the long-run adjustment to the drop in income. Be sure to discuss any changes in output levels, prices, profits, and the number of firms.

12. *(Long-Run Industry Supply)* Why does the long-run industry supply curve for an increasing-cost industry slope upward? What causes the increasing costs in an increasing-cost industry?

13. *(Perfect Competition in the Long Run)* Draw the short- and long-run cost curves for a competitive firm in long-run equilibrium. Indicate the long-run equilibrium price and quantity.
    a. Discuss the firm's short-run response to a reduction in the price of a variable resource.
    b. Assuming that this is a constant-cost industry, describe the process by which the industry returns to long-run equilibrium following a change in market demand.

14. *(The Long-Run Industry Supply Curve)* The following graph shows possible long-run market supply curves for a perfectly competitive industry. Determine which supply curve indicates a constant-cost industry and which an increasing-cost industry.

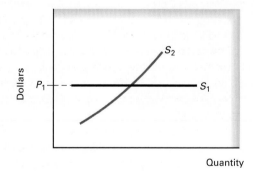

a. Explain the difference between a constant-cost industry and an increasing-cost industry.
b. Distinguish between the long-run impact of an increase in market demand in a constant-cost industry and the impact in an increasing-cost industry.

8-7 Summarize how market equilibrium in perfect competition results in productive efficiency and allocative efficiency

15. *(What's So Perfect About Perfect Competition)* Use the following data to answer the questions.

Quantity	Marginal Cost	Marginal Benefit
0	—	—
1	$2	$10
2	$3	$9
3	$4	$8
4	$5	$7
5	$6	$6
6	$8	$5
7	$10	$4
8	$12	$3

a. For the product shown, assume that the minimum point of each firm's average variable cost curve is at $2. Construct a demand and supply diagram for the product and indicate the equilibrium price and quantity.
b. On the graph, label the area of consumer surplus as *f*. Label the area of producer surplus as *g*.
c. If the equilibrium price were $2, what would be the amount of producer surplus?

9 | Monopoly

LEARNING OUTCOMES

After studying this chapter, you will be able to…

9-1 List three barriers to entry and explain how each can help create market power

9-2 Distinguish marginal revenue and average revenue for a monopolist, and explain why marginal revenue is less than average revenue

9-3 Determine the profit-maximizing or loss-minimizing production level for a monopolist

9-4 Summarize what causes the deadweight loss of monopoly

9-5 Outline the factors that could cause the deadweight loss of monopoly to be lower or higher than expected

9-6 Explain why a firm with market power might decide to charge different groups different prices

After finishing this chapter go to **PAGE 158** for **STUDY TOOLS**

Topics discussed in Chapter 9 include:

- Barriers to entry
- Price elasticity and marginal revenue
- Profit maximization and loss minimization
- Welfare cost of monopoly
- Price discrimination
- Perfect price discrimination

© Hung Chung Chih/Shutterstock.com

- How can a firm monopolize a market?
- Why aren't most markets monopolized?
- Why don't most monopolies last?
- Why don't monopolies charge the highest possible price?
- How has China monopolized the world market for pandas?
- Why was the head of Starbucks worried about his coffee becoming a commodity?
- Do student and senior discount stem from corporate generosity?
- Why are there so many airfares for the same flight?

These and other questions are answered in this chapter, which looks at our second market structure—monopoly.

A t this point you already know something about how competitive markets work, but there are other types of markets. *Monopoly* is from the Greek, meaning "one seller." Monopolists sell electricity, postage stamps, hot dogs at sports arenas, some patented products, some prescription drugs, and other goods and services with no close substitutes. You have probably heard about the evils of monopoly. You may have even played the board game *Monopoly* on a rainy day. Now we sort out fact from fiction.

> ❝Why was the head of Starbucks worried about his coffee becoming a commodity?❞

Like perfect competition, pure monopoly is not as common as other market structures. But by understanding monopoly better, you become more familiar with market structures that lie between the extremes of perfect competition and pure monopoly. This chapter examines the sources of monopoly power, how a monopolist maximizes profit, differences between monopoly and perfect competition, and why a monopolist sometimes charges different prices for the same product.

9-1 BARRIERS TO ENTRY

As noted in Chapter 3, a *monopoly* is the sole supplier of a product with no close substitutes. There is only one supplier in the market but there are many demanders, so many that no buyer has any control over the price. Why do some markets come to be dominated by a single supplier? A monopolized market is characterized by **barriers to entry**, which are restrictions on the entry of new firms into an industry. Because of barriers, new firms cannot profitably enter that market. Let's examine three types of entry barriers: legal restrictions, economies of scale, and control of an essential resource.

9-1a Legal Restrictions

One way to prevent new firms from entering a market is to make entry illegal. Patents, licenses, and other legal restrictions imposed by the government provide some producers with legal protection against competition.

Patents and Invention Incentives

In the United States, a **patent** awards an inventor the exclusive right to sell a good or service for 20 years from the date the patent is filed with the patent office. Originally enacted in 1790, patent laws encourage inventors to invest the time and money required to discover and develop new products and processes. If others could simply copy successful products, inventors would have less incentive to incur the up-front costs of invention. Abraham Lincoln said that "the patent system added the fuel of interest to the fire of genius." The 20-year clock starts ticking as soon as the application is filed, thus providing a stimulus to turn inventions into marketable products, a process called **innovation**.

barrier to entry Any impediment that prevents new firms from entering an industry and competing on an equal basis with existing firms

patent A legal barrier to entry that grants the holder the exclusive right to sell a product for 20 years from the date the patent application is filed

innovation The process of turning an invention into a marketable product

Research shows that stronger patent protection accelerates the introduction of new drugs.[1] A small firm without the resources to market and legally defend a promising patent usually sells that patent to a larger firm, one better positioned to make the most of it.[2] The point is that a promising patent, like any valuable resource, usually ends up where it will create the most value. For example, small drug companies often sell patents with the most potential to larger drug companies, or, more directly, the larger company buys the smaller company.

Licenses and Other Entry Restrictions

Governments often confer monopoly status by awarding an individual firm the exclusive right to supply a particular good or service. Federal licenses give certain firms the right to broadcast radio and TV signals. State licenses authorize suppliers of medical care, haircuts, legal advice, and many other products. A license may not grant a monopoly, but it does block entry and often gives firms *market power,* which is the power to charge prices above the competitive level without losing all their customers. Thus, a license can serve as an effective barrier against new competitors. Governments also grant monopoly rights to sell hot dogs at civic auditoriums, collect garbage, provide bus and taxi service, and supply other services ranging from electricity to cable TV. Sometimes the government itself may claim that right by outlawing competitors. For example, many state governments sell liquor and lottery tickets, and the U.S. Postal Service has the exclusive right to deliver first-class mail to your mailbox.

9-1b Economies of Scale

A monopoly sometimes occurs naturally if a firm experiences *economies of scale,* as reflected by the downward-sloping, long-run average cost curve shown in Exhibit 1. In such instances, a single firm can supply market demand at a lower average cost per unit than could two or more firms, each producing less. Put another way, market demand is not great enough to allow more than one firm to achieve sufficient economies of scale. Thus, a single firm emerges from the competitive process as the only low-cost supplier in the market. For example, even though electricity *production* has become more competitive, electricity *transmission* still exhibits economies of scale. Once wires

Having more than one company run power lines would be more costly than having a single firm do it.

are strung throughout a community, the cost of linking an additional household to the power grid is relatively low. Consequently, the average cost of delivering electricity declines as more households are wired into an existing system.

A monopoly that emerges from economies of scale is called a *natural monopoly,* to distinguish it from the artificial monopolies created by government patents, licenses, and other legal barriers to entry. A new entrant cannot sell enough to experience the economies of scale achieved by an established natural monopolist. Therefore, market

Exhibit 1

Economies of Scale as a Barrier to Entry

A monopoly sometimes emerges naturally if a firm experiences economies of scale as reflected by a downward-sloping, long-run average cost curve. One firm can satisfy market demand at a lower average cost per unit than could two or more firms each operating at smaller rates of output.

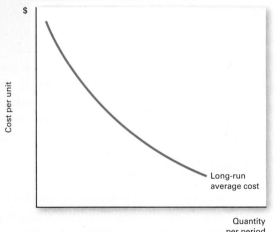

1. Eli Cockburn, Jean Lanjouw, and Mark Schankerman, "Patents and the Global Diffusion of New Drugs," NBER Working Paper No. 20492 (September 2014).

2. Alberto Galasso, Mark Schankerman, and Carlos Serrano, "Trading and Enforcing Patent Rights," *RAND Journal of Economics,* 44 (Summer 2013): 275–312.

entry is naturally blocked. A later chapter gets into the regulation of natural monopolies.

9-1c Control of Essential Resources

Sometimes the source of monopoly power is a firm's control over some resource critical to production. Here are four examples. (1) Alcoa was the sole U.S. maker of aluminum from the late 19th century until World War II. Its monopoly power initially stemmed from production patents that expired in 1909, but for the next three decades Alcoa controlled the supply of bauxite, the key raw material in making aluminum. (2) Professional sports leagues try to block the formation of competing leagues by signing the best athletes to long-term contracts and by seeking the exclusive use of sports stadiums and arenas. (3) China is a monopoly supplier of pandas to the world's zoos. The National Zoo in Washington, D.C., for example, rents its pair of pandas from China for $1 million a year. To limit the supply, China stipulates that any offspring becomes China's property.[3] For example, in 2010 an offspring of the Washington pair was shipped back to China. Other zoos around the world have similar arrangements with China. (4) Finally, for decades, the world's diamond trade was controlled primarily by De Beers Consolidated Mines, which mined diamonds and also bought most of the world's supply of rough diamonds.

Monopoly profits often spring from supplying something that other producers can't match. For example, Starbucks over the years has built up a unique "experience" for the customer, including baristas who know customer orders by heart and a comfortable atmosphere that encourages patrons to relax and linger. That uniqueness has given Starbucks the market power to grow and to charge a premium price that has rocketed the company's stock price more than 60-fold between 1992 and 2015. But a memo from the company chairman to employees warned that the pressure to grow could "commoditize" Starbucks, making it more vulnerable to competition from other coffee shops and even from fast-food chains. Once a product loses its uniqueness—in this case, by going from a special experience to just another cup of coffee—the supplier loses market power and profitability.[4]

Local monopolies are more common than national or international monopolies. In rural areas, monopolies may include the only grocery store, movie theater, restaurant, or gas station for miles around. These are natural monopolies for products sold in local markets. But long-lasting monopolies are rare because economic profit attracts competitors. Also, over time, technological change tends to break down barriers to entry. For example, the development of wireless transmission of long-distance calls created competitors to AT&T. Wireless transmission is also erasing the monopoly held by local cable TV providers and even local phone service. Likewise, text messaging, email, the Internet, and firms such as FedEx and UPS now compete with the U.S. Postal Service's monopoly.

9-2 REVENUE FOR A MONOPOLIST

Because a monopoly, by definition, supplies the entire market, the demand curve for a monopolist's output is also the market demand curve. The monopolist's demand curve therefore slopes downward, reflecting the law of demand—price and quantity demanded are inversely related. Let's look at demand, average revenue, and marginal revenue for a monopolist.

9-2a Demand, Average Revenue, and Marginal Revenue

Suppose De Beers still controlled the diamond market. Exhibit 2 shows the demand curve for high-quality 1-carat diamonds. De Beers, for example, can sell three diamonds a day at $7,000 each. That price-quantity combination yields total revenue of $21,000 (=$7,000 × 3). Total revenue divided by quantity is the *average revenue per diamond*, which also is $7,000. Thus, the monopolist's price equals the average revenue per unit. To sell a fourth diamond, De Beers must lower the price to $6,750. Total revenue from selling four diamonds is $27,000 (=$6,750 × 4), and average revenue is $6,750. All along the demand curve, price equals average revenue. Therefore, *the demand curve is also the monopolist's average revenue curve*, just as the perfectly competitive firm's demand curve is that firm's average revenue curve.

What's the marginal revenue from selling a fourth diamond? When De Beers drops the price from $7,000 to $6,750, total revenue increases from $21,000 to $27,000. Thus, *marginal revenue*—the change in total revenue from selling one more diamond—is $6,000, which is less than the price, or average revenue, of $6,750. *For a monopolist, marginal revenue is less than*

3. Sophia Yan, "How China's Booming Panda Business Works," *CNN Money*, 15 October 2013, at http://money.cnn.com/gallery/news/economy/2013/10/14/china-panda-business/index.html.
4. The company memo is discussed in Janet Adamy, "Starbucks Chairman Says Trouble May Be Brewing," *Wall Street Journal*, 24 February 2007.

Exhibit 2

A Monopolist's Gain and Loss in Total Revenue from Selling a Fourth Unit

If De Beers increases quantity supplied from 3 to 4 diamonds per day, the gain in revenue from the fourth diamond is $6,750. But the monopolist loses $750 from selling the first 3 diamonds for $6,750 each instead of $7,000 each. Marginal revenue from the fourth diamond equals the gain minus the loss, or $6,750 − $750 = $6,000. Thus, the marginal revenue of $6,000 is less than the price of $6,750.

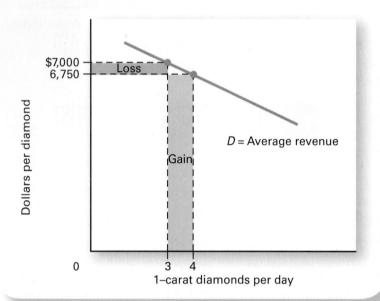

the price, or average revenue. Recall that for a perfectly competitive firm, marginal revenue equals the price, or average revenue, because that firm can sell all it supplies at the market price.

9-2b The Gain and Loss From Selling One More Unit

A closer look at Exhibit 2 reveals why a monopolist's marginal revenue is less than the price. By selling another diamond, De Beers gains the revenue from that sale. For example, De Beers gets $6,750 from the fourth diamond, as shown by the blue-shaded vertical rectangle marked "Gain." But to sell that fourth unit, De Beers must sell all four diamonds for $6,750 each. Thus, to sell a fourth diamond, De Beers must sacrifice $250 on each of the first three diamonds, which could have been sold for $7,000 each. This loss in revenue from the first three units totals $750 (=$250 × 3) and is identified in Exhibit 2 by the pink-shaded horizontal rectangle marked "Loss." The net change in total revenue from selling the fourth diamond—that is, the marginal revenue from the fourth diamond—equals the *gain* minus the *loss*, which equals

$6,750 minus $750, or $6,000. So marginal revenue equals the gain minus the loss, or the price minus the revenue forgone by selling all units for a lower price. Because a monopolist's marginal revenue equals the price minus the loss, you can see why the marginal revenue is less than the price.

Incidentally, this analysis assumes that all units are sold at the market price; for example, the four diamonds are sold for $6,750 each. Although this is usually true, later in the chapter you will learn how some monopolists try to increase profit by charging different customers different prices.

9-2c Revenue Schedules

Let's flesh out more fully the revenue schedules behind the demand curve of Exhibit 2. Column (1) of Exhibit 3 lists the quantity of diamonds demanded per day, and column (2) lists the corresponding price, or average revenue. Together, the two columns are the demand schedule for 1-carat diamonds. The price in column (2) times the quantity in column (1) yields the monopolist's *total revenue* schedule in column (3). So $TR = p \times Q$. As De Beers sells more, total revenue increases until quantity reaches 15 diamonds.

Marginal revenue, the change in total revenue from selling one more diamond, appears in column (4). In shorthand, $MR = \Delta TR / \Delta Q$, or the change in total revenue divided by the change in quantity. Note in Exhibit 3 that after the first unit, marginal revenue is less than price. As the price declines, the gap between price and marginal revenue widens. As the price declines, the *loss* from selling all diamonds for less increases (because quantity increases) and the *gain* from selling another diamond decreases (because the price falls).

9-2d Revenue Curves

The schedules in Exhibit 3 are graphed in Exhibit 4, which shows the demand and marginal revenue curves in panel (a) and the total revenue curve in panel (b). Recall that total revenue equals price times quantity. Note that *the marginal revenue curve is below the demand curve and that total revenue reaches a maximum where marginal revenue is zero*. Please take a minute now to study these relationships—they are important.

Again, along the demand curve, price equals average revenue, so the demand curve is also the monopolist's

Exhibit 3

Revenue for De Beers, a Monopolist

To sell more, the monopolist must lower the price on all units sold. Because the revenue lost from selling all units at a lower price must be subtracted from the revenue gained from selling another unit, marginal revenue is less than the price. At some point, marginal revenue turns negative, as shown here when the price is reduced to $3,500.

(1) 1-Carat Diamonds per Day (Q)	(2) Price (average revenue) (p)	(3) Total Revenue (TR = p × Q)	(4) Marginal Revenue (MR = ΔTR/ΔQ)
0	$7,750	0	—
1	7,500	$ 7,500	$7,500
2	7,250	14,500	7,000
3	7,000	21,000	6,500
4	6,750	27,000	6,000
5	6,500	32,500	5,500
6	6,250	37,500	5,000
7	6,000	42,000	4,500
8	5,750	46,000	4,000
9	5,500	49,500	3,500
10	5,250	52,500	3,000
11	5,000	55,000	2,500
12	4,750	57,000	2,000
13	4,500	58,500	1,500
14	4,250	59,500	1,000
15	4,000	60,000	500
16	3,750	60,000	0
17	3,500	59,500	−500

average revenue curve. In Chapter 5, you learned that the price elasticity for a straight-line demand curve declines as the price falls. When demand is elastic—that is, when the percentage increase in quantity demanded more than offsets the percentage decrease in price—a decrease in price increases total revenue. Therefore, *where demand is elastic, marginal revenue is positive, and total revenue increases as the price falls.* On the other hand, where demand is inelastic—that is, where the percentage increase in quantity demanded is less than the percentage decrease in price—a decrease in price reduces total revenue. In other words, the loss in revenue from selling all diamonds for the lower price overwhelms the gain in revenue from selling more diamonds. Therefore, *where demand is inelastic, marginal revenue is negative, and total revenue decreases as the price falls.*

From Exhibit 4, you can see that marginal revenue turns negative if the price drops below $3,750, indicating

inelastic demand below that price. *A profit-maximizing monopolist would never expand output to the inelastic range of demand because doing so would reduce total revenue.* It would make no sense to sell more if total revenue drops in the process. Also note that demand is unit elastic at the price of $3,750. At that price, marginal revenue is zero and total revenue reaches a maximum.

9-3 PROFIT MAXIMIZATION AND COST MINIMIZATION FOR A MONOPOLIST

In perfect competition, each firm's choice is confined to *quantity* because the market has already determined the price. The perfect competitor is a *price taker. The monopolist, however, can choose either the price or the quantity, but choosing one determines the other—they come in pairs.* For example, if De Beers decides to sell 10 diamonds a day, consumers would demand that many only at a price of $5,250 per diamond. Alternatively, if De Beers decides to sell diamonds for $6,000 each, consumers would demand 7 a day. Because the monopolist can choose any price-quantity combination on the demand curve, we say the monopolist is a *price maker.* More generally, any firm that has some control over what price to charge is a **price maker**.

9-3a Profit Maximization

Exhibit 5 repeats revenue schedules from Exhibits 3 and 4 and also includes a short-run cost schedule similar to those already introduced in the two previous chapters. Please take a little time now to become familiar with this table. Then ask yourself this question: Which price-quantity combination should De Beers select to maximize profit? As was the case with perfect competition, the monopolist can approach profit maximization in two ways—the total approach and the marginal approach.

> **price maker** A firm with some power to set the price because the demand curve for its output slopes downward; a firm with market power

Exhibit 4

Monopoly Demand, Marginal Revenue, and Total Revenue

Where demand is price elastic, marginal revenue is positive, so total revenue increases as the price falls. Where demand is price inelastic, marginal revenue is negative, so total revenue decreases as the price falls. Where demand is unit elastic, marginal revenue is zero, so total revenue is at a maximum, neither increasing nor decreasing.

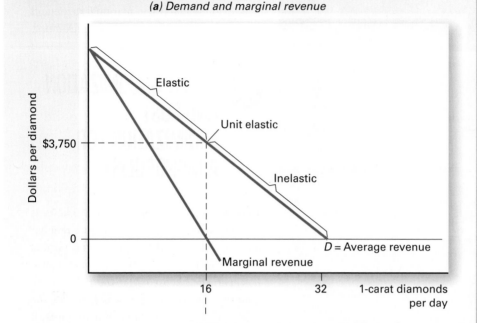

(a) Demand and marginal revenue

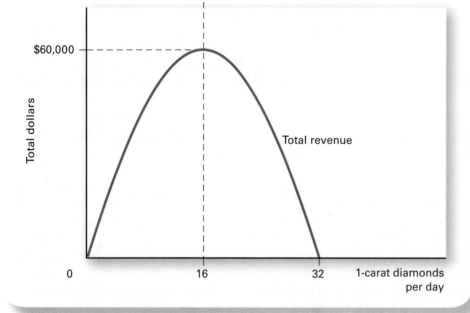

(b) Total revenue

column (8) of Exhibit 5. As you can see, maximum profit is $12,500 per day, which occurs at 10 diamonds per day. At that quantity, total revenue is $52,500 and total cost is $40,000.

Marginal Revenue Equals Marginal Cost

De Beers, as a profit-maximizing monopolist, increases output if doing so adds more to total revenue than to total cost. So De Beers expands output as long as marginal revenue, shown in column (4) of Exhibit 5, exceeds marginal cost, shown in column (6). But De Beers stops short of producing where marginal cost exceeds marginal revenue. Again, profit is maximized at $12,500 when 10 diamonds per day are sold. For the 10th diamond, marginal revenue is $3,000 and marginal cost is $2,750. As you can see, if output exceeds 10 diamonds per day, marginal cost exceeds marginal revenue. An 11th diamond's marginal cost of $3,250 exceeds its marginal revenue of $2,500. For simplicity, we say that *the profit-maximizing output occurs where marginal revenue equals marginal cost,* which, you will recall, is the golden rule of profit maximization.

Total Revenue Minus Total Cost

The profit-maximizing monopolist employs the same decision rule as the competitive firm. *The monopolist supplies the quantity at which total revenue exceeds total cost by the greatest amount.* Economic profit appears in

Graphical Solution

The revenue and cost schedules in Exhibit 5 are graphed in Exhibit 6, with per-unit cost and revenue curves in panel (a) and total cost and revenue curves in panel (b). The intersection of the two marginal curves

Exhibit 5

Short-Run Costs and Revenue for a Monopolist

(1) Diamonds per Day (Q)	(2) Price (p)	(3) Total Revenue (TR = p × Q)	(4) Marginal Revenue (MR = ΔTR/ΔQ)	(5) Total Cost (TC)	(6) Marginal Cost (MC = ΔTC/ΔQ)	(7) Average Total Cost (ATC = TC/Q)	(8) Total Profit or Loss (= TR − TC)
0	$7,750	0	—	$15,000	—	—	$−15,000
1	7,500	$ 7,500	$7,500	19,750	$ 4,750	$19,750	−12,250
2	7,250	14,500	7,000	23,500	3,750	11,750	−9,000
3	7,000	21,000	6,500	26,500	3,000	8,833	−5,500
4	6,750	27,000	6,000	29,000	2,500	7,250	−2,000
5	6,500	32,500	5,500	31,000	2,000	6,200	1,500
6	6,250	37,500	5,000	32,500	1,500	5,417	5,000
7	6,000	42,000	4,500	33,750	1,250	4,821	8,250
8	5,750	46,000	4,000	35,250	1,500	4,406	10,750
9	5,500	49,500	3,500	37,250	2,000	4,139	12,250
10	5,250	52,500	3,000	40,000	2,750	4,000	12,500
11	5,000	55,000	2,500	43,250	3,250	3,932	11,750
12	4,750	57,000	2,000	48,000	4,750	4,000	9,000
13	4,500	58,500	1,500	54,500	6,500	4,192	4,000
14	4,250	59,500	1,000	64,000	9,500	4,571	−4,500
15	4,000	60,000	500	77,500	13,500	5,167	−17,500
16	3,750	60,000	0	96,000	18,500	6,000	−36,000
17	3,500	59,500	−500	121,000	25,000	7,118	−61,500

> **"The monopolist can choose either the price or the quantity, but choosing one determines the other—they come in pairs."**

De Beers sells more diamonds as long as the marginal revenue of increasing quantity outweighs the marginal cost.

at point *e* in panel (a) indicates that profit is maximized when 10 diamonds are sold. At that quantity, we move up to the demand curve to find the profit-maximizing price of $5,250. Average total cost of $4,000 is identified by point *b*. The average profit per diamond equals the price of $5,250 minus the average total cost of $4,000. Economic profit is the average profit per unit of $1,250 multiplied by the 10 diamonds sold, for a total profit of $12,500 per day, as identified by the blue-shaded rectangle. *So the profit-maximizing rate of output is found where the marginal cost curve intersects the marginal revenue curve.*

Exhibit 6

Monopoly Costs and Revenue

Profit is maximized by producing where marginal cost equals marginal revenue, which is point *e* in panel (a). A profit-maximizing monopolist supplies 10 diamonds per day and charges $5,250 per diamond. Total profit, shown by the blue rectangle in panel (a), is $12,500, the profit per unit multiplied by the number of units sold. In panel (b), profit is maximized by producing where total revenue exceeds total cost by the greatest amount, which occurs at an output rate of 10 diamonds per day. Maximum profit is total revenue ($52,500) minus total cost ($40,000), or $12,500. In panel (a) profit is measured by an area and in panel (b) by a vertical distance. That's because panel (a) measures cost, revenue, and profit per unit of output while panel (b) measures them as totals at each level of output.

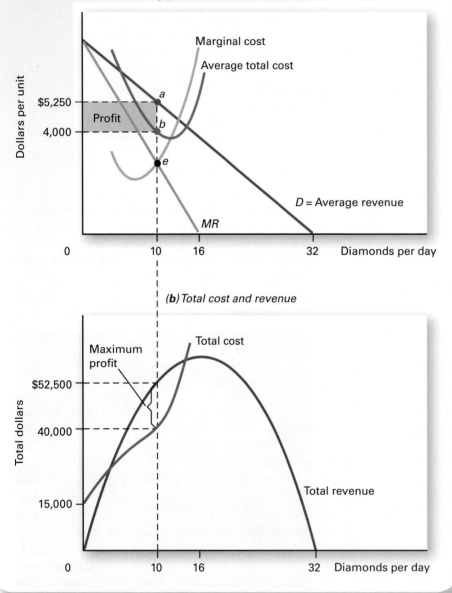

(a) *Per-unit cost and revenue*

(b) *Total cost and revenue*

where total revenue exceeds total cost by the greatest amount. Again, profit is maximized where De Beers sells 10 diamonds per day. Total profit in panel (b) is measured by the *vertical distance* between the two total curves; in panel (a), total profit is measured by the shaded *area* formed by multiplying average profit per unit by the number of units sold.

One common myth about monopolies is that they charge the highest price possible. But the monopolist is interested in maximizing profit, not price. What the monopolist can charge is limited by consumer demand. De Beers, for example, could charge $7,500, but selling only one diamond a day would result in a big loss. Indeed, De Beers could charge $7,750 or more but would sell no diamonds. So charging the highest possible price is not consistent with maximizing profit. A monopolist may be able to set the price, but the quantity demanded at that price is determined by consumers. *Even the most powerful monopolist must obey the law of demand.*

9-3b Short-Run Losses and the Shutdown Decision

A monopolist is not assured an economic profit. Although a monopolist is the sole supplier of a good with no close substitutes, the demand for that good may not generate economic profit in either the short run or the long run. After all, many new products are protected from direct competition by patents, yet most of the 300,000 or so U.S. patents issued each year never turn into profitable

In panel (b), the firm's profit or loss is measured by the vertical distance between the total revenue and total cost curves. De Beers expands output if the increase in total revenue from selling another diamond exceeds the increase in total cost. *The profit-maximizing firm produces* products. And even a monopolist that is initially profitable may eventually suffer losses because of rising costs, falling demand, or market entry of similar products. For example, Coleco, the original mass producer of Cabbage Patch dolls, went bankrupt after that craze died down. And Cuisinart, the company that introduced the food processor, soon faced many imitators and filed for bankruptcy (though the name lives on). In the short run, the loss-minimizing monopolist, like the loss-minimizing perfect competitor, must decide whether to produce or to shut down. *If the price covers average variable cost, the monopolist produces, at least*

Jacques Chenet/Woodfin Camp/Getty Images

Being a monopoly does not always guarantee long-run success. Just ask Coleco, the maker of the wildly popular Cabbage Patch dolls, who went bankrupt after the craze died down.

in the short run. If not, the monopolist shuts down, at least in the short run.

Exhibit 7 brings average variable cost back into the picture. Recall from Chapter 7 that average variable cost and average fixed cost sum to average total cost. Loss minimization occurs in Exhibit 7 at point e, where the marginal revenue curve intersects the marginal cost curve. At the equilibrium rate of output, Q, price p is found on the demand curve at point b. That price exceeds average variable cost, at point c, but is below average total cost, at point a. Because price covers average variable cost and a portion of average fixed cost, this monopolist loses less by producing Q than by shutting down. The loss, identified by the shaded rectangle, equals the average loss per unit, ab, times the quantity sold, Q. The firm shuts down in the short run if the average variable cost curve is above the demand curve, or average revenue curve, at all output rates.

Recall that a perfectly competitive firm's supply curve is that portion of the marginal cost curve at or above the average variable cost curve. The intersection of a monopolist's marginal revenue and marginal cost curves identifies the profit-maximizing (or loss-minimizing) quantity, but the price is found up on the demand curve. Because the equilibrium quantity can be found along a monopolist's marginal cost curve, but the equilibrium price appears on the demand curve, no single curve traces points showing unique combinations of both the price and quantity supplied. Because no curve reflects combinations of price and quantity supplied, *there is no monopolist supply curve.*

9-3c Long-Run Profit Maximization

For perfectly competitive firms, the distinction between the short run and the long run is important because entry and exit of firms can occur in the long run, erasing any economic profit or loss. For the monopolist, the distinction between the short run and long run is less relevant. *If a monopoly is insulated from competition by high barriers that block new entry, economic profit can persist into the long run.* Yet short-run profit is no guarantee of long-run profit. For example, suppose the monopoly relies on a patent. Patents last only so long and even while a product is under patent, the monopolist often must defend it in court (patent litigation has nearly doubled in the last decade). On the other hand, a monopolist may be able to erase a loss (most firms lose money initially) or increase profit in the long run by adjusting the scale of the firm or by advertising to increase demand. A monopolist unable to erase a loss will, in the long run, leave the market.

Exhibit 7

The Monopolist Minimizes Losses in the Short Run

Marginal revenue equals marginal cost at point *e*. At quantity *Q*, price *p* (at point *b*) is less than average total cost (at point *a*), so the monopolist suffers a loss, identified by the pink rectangle. But the monopolist continues to produce rather than shut down in the short run because price exceeds average variable cost (at point *c*). Here the price covers all variable cost and a portion of fixed cost.

9-3d Available for a Limited Time Only

Given the law of diminishing marginal utility, some firms selling a unique product may limit availability to increase its marginal value to the consumer. For example, McDonald's makes its McRib sandwich "available for a limited time only," usually in the fall. The same holds for KFC's Double Down sandwich. And Disney has movies in its vault (such as *Cinderella*, *Dumbo*, and *Peter Pan*) that appear in theaters from time to time for limited periods. Thus, suppliers sometimes limit availability to enhance product appeal.

9-4 PERFECT COMPETITION AND MONOPOLY COMPARED

If monopolists are no greedier than perfect competitors (because both maximize profit), if monopolists do not charge the highest possible price (because the highest price would reduce quantity demanded to zero), and if

monopolists are not guaranteed a profit (because demand for the product may be weak), then what's the problem with monopoly? To get a handle on the problem, let's compare monopoly with the benchmark established in the previous chapter—perfect competition.

9-4a Price and Output Under Perfect Competition

Let's begin with the long-run equilibrium price and output in a perfectly competitive market. Suppose the long-run market supply curve in perfect competition is horizontal, as shown by S_c in Exhibit 8. Because this is a constant-cost industry, the horizontal long-run supply curve also shows marginal cost and average total cost at each quantity. Equilibrium in perfect competition occurs at point *c*, where the market demand and market supply curves intersect to yield price p_c and quantity Q_c. Remember, the demand curve reflects the marginal benefit of each unit purchased. In competitive equilibrium, the marginal benefit of the final unit sold equals the marginal cost to society of producing that final unit. As noted in the previous chapter, when the marginal benefit that consumers derive from a good equals the marginal cost of producing that good, that market is said to be efficient and to maximize social welfare. There is no way of reallocating resources to increase the total value of output or to increase social welfare. Because consumers are able to purchase Q_c units at price p_c, they enjoy a net benefit from consumption, or a consumer surplus, measured by the entire shaded triangle, acp_c.

9-4b Price and Output Under Monopoly

Now suppose that instead of perfect competition, the entire output is supplied by a single firm—that is, by a monopolist. With only one firm in the industry, the industry demand curve *D* in Exhibit 8 becomes the monopolist's demand curve, so the price the monopolist charges determines the market quantity. Because

Exhibit 8

Perfect Competition and Monopoly Compared

A perfectly competitive industry would produce output Q_c, determined by the intersection of the market demand curve D and the market supply curve S_c. The price would be p_c. A monopoly that could produce output at the same minimum average cost as a perfectly competitive industry would produce output Q_m, determined at point b, where the marginal cost curve intersects the monopolist's marginal revenue curve. The monopolist would charge price p_m. Thus, given the same costs, output is lower and price is higher under monopoly than under perfect competition. Consumer surplus is greater with perfect competition.

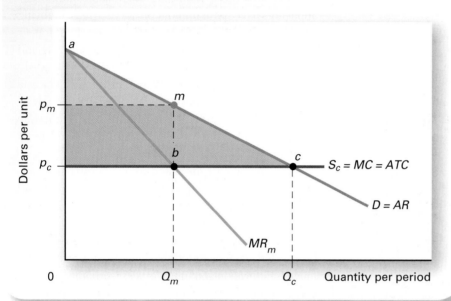

the monopolist's demand curve slopes downward, the marginal revenue curve also slopes downward and is beneath the demand curve, as is indicated by MR_m in Exhibit 8. Suppose the monopolist can produce at the same constant cost in the long run as can firms in the perfectly competitive industry. The monopolist maximizes profit by equating marginal revenue with marginal cost, which occurs at point b, yielding equilibrium price p_m and market output Q_m. Again, the price shows the consumers' marginal benefit for unit Q_m. This marginal benefit, identified at point m, exceeds the monopolist's marginal cost, identified at point b. Because marginal benefit exceeds marginal cost, society would be better off if output expanded beyond Q_m. *The monopolist restricts quantity below what would maximize social welfare.* Even though the monopolist restricts output, consumers still derive some benefit, just not as much as with perfect competition. Consumer surplus is shown by the smaller triangle, amp_m.

> **"The monopolist restricts quantity below what would maximize social welfare."**

9-4c Allocative and Distributive Effects

Consider the allocative and distributive effects of monopoly versus perfect competition. In Exhibit 8, consumer surplus under perfect competition is the large triangle, acp_c. Under monopoly, consumer surplus shrinks to the smaller triangle amp_m, which in this example is only one-fourth as large (how do we know that?). The monopolist earns economic profit equal to the shaded rectangle. By comparing the situation under perfect competition with that under monopoly, you can see that the monopolist's economic profit comes entirely from what was consumer surplus under perfect competition. Because the profit rectangle reflects a transfer from consumer surplus to monopoly profit, this amount is not lost to society and so is not considered a welfare loss.

Notice, however, that consumer surplus resulting from monopoly is reduced by more than the profit rectangle. Consumers under monopoly also lose the triangle mcb. The mcb triangle is called the **deadweight loss of monopoly** because it is a loss to consumers but a gain to nobody. This loss results from *the allocative inefficiency arising from the higher price and reduced output of a monopoly.*

Again, society would be better off if output exceeded the monopolist's profit-maximizing quantity, because the marginal benefit of more output exceeds its marginal cost. Under monopoly, the price, or marginal benefit, always exceeds marginal cost. Empirical estimates of the annual deadweight loss of monopoly in the United States have ranged from about 1 percent to about

deadweight loss of monopoly Net loss to society when a firm with market power restricts output and increases the price

5 percent of national income. Applied to national income data for 2015, these estimates imply a deadweight loss of monopoly that year ranging from about $580 to $2,900 per capita—not a trivial amount.

9-5 · PROBLEMS WITH DEADWEIGHT LOSS ESTIMATES

The actual cost of monopoly could differ from the deadweight loss described so far. These costs could be lower or higher. Here's the reasoning.

9-5a Why the Deadweight Loss Might Be Lower

If economies of scale are substantial enough, a monopolist might be able to produce output at a lower cost per unit than could competitive firms. Therefore, the price, or at least the cost of production, could be lower under monopoly than under competition. The deadweight loss shown in Exhibit 8 may also overstate the true cost of monopoly because monopolists might, in response to public scrutiny and political pressure, keep prices below the profit-maximizing level. Although monopolists would like to earn as much profit as possible, they realize that if the public outcry over high prices and high profit grows loud enough, some sort of government intervention could reduce or even erase that profit. For example, the prices and profit of drug companies, which individually are monopoly suppliers of medicines still under patent, come under scrutiny from time to time by elected officials who propose regulating drug prices or taxing "windfall profits." Drug firms might try to avoid such treatment by keeping prices below the level that would maximize profit. Finally, a monopolist might keep the price below the profit-maximizing level to avoid attracting competitors to the market. For example, some observers claim that Alcoa, when it was the only U.S. producer of aluminum, kept prices low enough to discourage entry by potential rivals.

9-5b Why the Deadweight Loss Might Be Higher

Another line of reasoning suggests that the deadweight loss of monopoly might be greater than shown in our simple diagram. *If resources must be devoted to securing and maintaining a monopoly position, monopolies may impose a greater welfare loss than simple models suggest.* For example, radio and TV broadcasting rights confer on the recipient the use of a particular band of the scarce broadcast spectrum. In the past, these rights have been given away by government agencies to the applicants deemed most deserving. Because these rights are so valuable, numerous applicants have spent millions on lawyers' fees, lobbying expenses, and other costs to make themselves appear the most deserving. The efforts devoted to securing and maintaining a monopoly right are largely a social waste because they use up scarce resources but add not one unit to output. Activities undertaken by individuals or firms to influence public policy to directly or indirectly redistribute income to themselves are referred to as **rent seeking**.

The monopolist, insulated from the rigors of competition in the marketplace, might also grow fat and lazy—and become inefficient. Because some monopolies could still earn an economic profit even if the firm is inefficient, corporate executives might waste resources by creating a more comfortable life for themselves. Long lunches, afternoon golf, plush offices, corporate jets, and excessive employee benefits might make company life more pleasant, but they increase production costs and raise prices.

Economists have also noted that a firm with monopoly power in the product market may be able to leverage that power in the resource market as well, driving down resource earnings, particularly for resources specialized to that industry. Thus, resource earnings would decline, but this would not necessarily translate into a lower price to consumers. It could simply mean higher profit for the monopolist. In this case, monopoly not only harms consumers, but harms resource suppliers as well.[5]

Monopolists have also been criticized for being slow to adopt the latest production techniques, being reluctant to develop new products, and generally lacking innovation. Because monopolists are largely insulated from the rigors of competition, they might take it easy. It's been said that "The best of all monopoly profits is a quiet life."

Not all economists believe that monopolies manage their resources with any less vigilance than perfect competitors do. Some argue that because monopolists are protected from rivals, they are in a good position to capture the fruits of any innovation and therefore are more innovative than competitive firms are. For example,

rent seeking Activities undertaken by individuals or firms to influence public policy in a way that increases their incomes

5. Dwight Lee and Robert Tollison, "The Welfare Costs of Monopoly Are Larger Than You Think," *Managerial and Decision Sciences,* 32 (March 2011): 85–89.

two researchers recently concluded that if chipmaker Intel were a monopoly and thus did not have to devote resources to compete with its only real rival, Advanced Micro Devices, the company would be more innovative.[6] Others believe that if a monopolist strays from the path of profit maximization, its share price will drop enough to attract someone who will buy a controlling interest and shape up the company. This market for corporate control is said to keep monopolists on their toes.

9-6 PRICE DISCRIMINATION

In the model developed so far, to sell more output, a monopolist must lower the price. In reality, a monopolist can sometimes increase profit by charging higher prices to those who value the product more. This practice of charging different prices to different groups of consumers is called **price discrimination**. For example, children, students, and senior citizens often pay lower admission prices to ball games, movies, amusement parks, and other events. You may believe that firms do this out of some sense of fairness to certain groups, but the primary goal is to boost profits. Let's see how and why.

9-6a Conditions for Price Discrimination

To be a candidate for price discrimination, a firm's product must meet certain conditions. First, the demand curve for the firm's product must slope downward, indicating that the firm is a price maker—that is the producer has some market power, some ability to set the price. Second, there must be at least two groups of consumers for the product, each with a different price elasticity of demand. Third, the firm must be able, at little cost, to charge each group a different price for essentially the same product. Finally, the firm must be able to prevent those who pay the lower price from reselling the product to those paying the higher price. Sometimes customers can be sorted by age, such as children under 12 and senior citizens. Sometimes customers are separated in time, such as afternoon versus evening moviegoers, or lunch versus dinner patrons at restaurants. Such intertemporal price discrimination works because the product cannot be resold by one patron to another. For example, a customer who buys lunch cannot resell that meal to a dinner customer.[7]

6. Ronald Goettler and Brett Gordon, "Does AMD Spur Intel to Innovate More?" *Journal of Political Economy*, 119 (December 2011): 1141–1200.

7. Ralph Bayer, "Intertemporal Price Discrimination and Competition," *Journal of Economic Behavior & Organization*, 73 (February 2010): 273–293.

9-6b A Model of Price Discrimination

Exhibit 9 shows the effects of price discrimination. Consumers are sorted into two groups with different demand elasticities. For simplicity, let's assume that the firm produces at a constant long-run average and marginal cost of $1.00. *At a given price*, the price elasticity of demand in panel (b) is greater than that in panel (a). Think of panel (b) as reflecting the demand by college students, senior citizens, or some other group more sensitive to the price. *This firm maximizes profit by finding the price in each market that equates marginal revenue with marginal cost.* For example, consumers with a lower price elasticity pay $3.00, and those with a higher price elasticity pay $1.50. Profit maximization means charging a lower price to the group with the more elastic demand—that is, charging less to the group more sensitive to the price. Despite the price difference, the firm gets the same marginal revenue of $1.00 from the last unit sold to each group. Note that charging both groups $3.00 would erase any profit from that right-hand group of consumers, who would be priced out of the market. Charging both groups $1.50 would lead to negative marginal revenue from the left-hand group, which would reduce total profit. No single price could generate the profit achieved through price discrimination.

9-6c Examples of Price Discrimination

Let's look at some examples of price discrimination. Because businesspeople face unpredictable yet urgent demands for travel, and because their employers pay such expenses, businesspeople tend to be less sensitive to price than are householders. In other words, businesspeople have a less elastic demand for travel costs than do householders, so airlines try to maximize profits by charging businesses more than households. Business-class tickets cost much more than coach-class tickets. Business seats offer more room than coach seats, and the food is a little better, but the difference in ticket prices far exceeds any difference in the airline's cost of providing such service. Even within a class of tickets, airlines charge different rates based on how far in advance tickets are purchased. Householders usually plan their trips well in advance and often spend the weekend. But business travel is more unpredictable, more urgent, and seldom involves a weekend stay. The airlines sort out the two groups by offering discount fares only

price discrimination
Increasing profit by charging different groups of consumers different prices for the same product

Exhibit 9

Price Discrimination with Two Groups of Consumers

A monopolist facing two groups of consumers with different demand elasticities may be able to practice price discrimination to increase profit or reduce any loss. With marginal cost the same in both markets, the firm charges a higher price to the group in panel (a), which has less elastic demand than the group in panel (b).

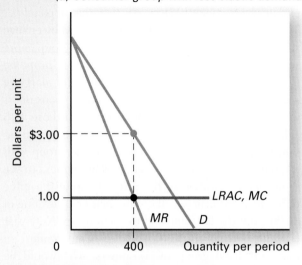

(a) Consumer group with less elastic demand

(b) Consumer group with more elastic demand

to travelers who buy tickets well in advance or who fly standby. More generally, airlines use computer models to price discriminate depending on the circumstances. Still, an airline's ability to charge a higher price for a particular seat is limited by competition from other airlines.

Ticket pricing at concerts or sporting events is another example. Research indicates that price discrimination at concerts yields more revenue than single-price ticketing. The yield is higher in markets with greater variation in demand across consumer groups.[8]

Here are other examples of price discrimination: IBM wanted to charge business users of its laser printer more than home users. To distinguish between the two groups, IBM decided to slow down the home printer to 5 pages a minute (versus 10 for the

business model). To do this, they added an extra chip that inserted pauses between pages.[9] Thus, IBM could sell the home model for less than the business model without cutting into sales of its business model. Intel offered two versions of the same computer chip; the cheaper version was the expensive version with some extra work done to reduce its speed. Apple uses differences in gigabytes of memory to price discriminate across iPad customers. Again, the differences in price are greater than the differences in Apple's costs for the memory. And Adobe stripped some features from its Photoshop CD to offer a cheaper version, Photoshop Elements.

As mentioned earlier, because lunch patrons are typically more sensitive to prices than dinner patrons, restaurants price lunch items lower than similar items on the dinner menu. Restaurants

In a classic example of price discrimination, IBM intentionally slowed down their printers made for personal use so they could charge their business customers a higher price.

8. Pascal Courty and Mario Pagliero, "The Impact of Price Discrimination on Revenue: Evidence from the Concert Industry," *Review of Economics and Statistics*, 94 (February 2012): 359–369.

9. Carl Shapiro and Hal Varian, *Information Rules: A Strategic Guide to the Network Economy* (Harvard Business School Press, 1999), p. 59.

© Tomislav Pinter/Shutterstock.com

also feature lower "happy-hour" prices for a limited food and drink menu. Major amusement parks, such as Disney World and Universal Studios, distinguish between local residents and out-of-towners when it comes to the price of admission. Out-of-towners typically spend substantial amounts on airlines and lodging just to be there, so they are less sensitive to the admission price than are local residents. The problem is how to charge a lower price to locals. The parks do this by making discount coupons available at local businesses, such as dry cleaners, which vacationers are less likely to visit. The Las Vegas monorail sorts out the locals from the visitors by charging only $1 for those presenting a Nevada driver's license and $5 for those without one.

Exhibit 10

Perfect Price Discrimination

If a monopolist can charge a different price for each unit sold, it may be able to practice perfect price discrimination. By setting the price of each unit equal to the maximum amount consumers are willing to pay for that unit (shown by the height of the demand curve), the monopolist can reap an economic profit equal to the area of the shaded triangle. Consumer surplus is zero. Ironically, this outcome is efficient because the monopolist has no incentive to restrict output, so there is no deadweight loss.

9-6d Perfect Price Discrimination

The demand curve shows the marginal value of each unit consumed, which is also the maximum amount consumers would pay for each unit. If the monopolist could charge a different price for each unit sold—a price reflected by the height of the demand curve—the firm's marginal revenue from selling one more unit would equal the price of that unit. Thus, the demand curve would become the firm's marginal revenue curve. **Perfect price discrimination** is charging a different price for each unit sold.

In Exhibit 10, again for simplicity, the monopolist is assumed to produce at a constant average and marginal cost in the long run. A perfectly discriminating monopolist, like any producer, would maximize profit by producing the quantity at which marginal revenue equals marginal cost. Because the demand curve is now the marginal revenue curve, the profit-maximizing quantity occurs where the demand, or marginal revenue, curve intersects the marginal cost curve, identified at point *e* in Exhibit 10. Price discrimination is a way of increasing profit. The area of the shaded triangle *aec* shows the perfectly discriminating monopolist's economic profit.

By charging a different price for each unit sold, the perfectly discriminating monopolist is able to convert every dollar of consumer surplus into economic profit. Although this practice seems unfair to consumers, perfect price discrimination gets high marks based on allocative efficiency. Because such a monopolist does not have to lower the price to all customers to sell more, there is no reason to restrict output. In fact, because this is a constant-cost industry, Q is the same quantity produced in perfect competition (though in perfect competition, the triangle *aec* would be consumer surplus, not economic profit). As with the perfectly competitive outcome, the marginal benefit of the final unit produced and consumed just equals its marginal cost. And although perfect price discrimination yields no consumer surplus, the total benefit consumers derive from consuming this good just equals their total cost. Note also that because the monopolist does not restrict output, *there is no deadweight loss.* Thus, perfect price discrimination enhances social welfare when compared with monopoly output in the

perfect price discrimination
Charging a different price for each unit sold

absence of price discrimination. But the monopolist reaps all net gains from production, while consumers just break even on the deal because their total benefit equals their total cost.

The pricing of cell phone service reflects a firm's effort to capture more consumer surplus as profit. Pricing alternatives include (1) a per-minute price with no basic fee, (2) a flat rate for the month plus a price per minute, and (3) a flat rate for unlimited calls. These alternatives allow the company to charge those who use fewer minutes more per minute than those who call more. Such suppliers are trying to convert some consumer surplus into profit.

9-7 FINAL WORD

Pure monopoly, like perfect competition, is not that common. Perhaps the best examples are firms producing patented items that provide unique benefits, such as certain prescription drugs, but patents eventually expire so generic substitutes become available. Some firms may enjoy monopoly power in the short run, but the lure of economic profit encourages rivals to hurdle seemingly high entry barriers in the long run. Changing technology also works against monopoly in the long run. For example, the railroad monopoly was erased by the interstate highway system. AT&T's monopoly on long-distance phone service crumbled as wireless technology replaced copper wire. The U.S. Postal Service's monopoly on first-class mail is being eroded by text messaging, emailing, online banking, e-commerce, social networking outlets such as Twitter, Facebook, Instagram, and Tumblr, and by private firms offering overnight delivery. To attract more business, the U.S. Postal Service has lowered rates for Internet sellers, such as Amazon.com, and offers these sellers Sunday delivery.[10] De Beers has lost its grip on the diamond market. And cable TV is losing its local monopoly to technological breakthroughs in fiber-optics technology, wireless broadband, and Internet streaming.

Although perfect competition and pure monopoly are rare, our examination of them yields a framework to help understand market structures that lie between the two extremes. Many firms have some degree of monopoly power—that is, they face downward-sloping demand curves. The next chapter discusses the two market structures that lie in the gray region between perfect competition and monopoly.

10. Laura Stevens, "U.S. Mail Cuts Prices, Chafing UPS and FedEx," *Wall Street Journal*, 4 September 2014.

STUDY TOOLS 9

READY TO STUDY? IN THE BOOK, YOU CAN:

☐ Work the Problems at the end of the chapter.

☐ Rip out the chapter review card for a handy summary of the chapter and key terms.

ONLINE AT CENGAGEBRAIN.COM YOU CAN:

☐ Collect StudyBits while you read and study the chapter.

☐ Quiz yourself on key concepts.

☐ Prepare for tests with chapter flash cards as well as flash cards that you create.

☐ Watch videos to explore economics further.

CHAPTER 9 PROBLEMS

Your instructor can access the answers to these problems online at http://cengagebrain.com.

9-1 List three barriers to entry and explain how each can help create market power

1. *(Barriers to Entry)* Explain how economies of scale can be a barrier to entry.
2. *(Barriers to Entry)* Identify the other two barriers to entry and explain how they block new firms from this market.

9-2 Distinguish marginal revenue and average revenue for a monopolist, and explain why marginal revenue is less than average revenue

3. *(Monopoly)* Suppose that a certain manufacturer has a monopoly on the sorority and fraternity ring business (a constant-cost industry) because it has persuaded the "Greeks" to give it exclusive rights to their insignia.
   a. Using demand and cost curves, draw a diagram depicting the firm's profit-maximizing price and output level.
   b. Why is marginal revenue less than price for this firm?
   c. On your diagram, show the deadweight loss that occurs because the output level is determined by a monopoly rather than by a competitive market.
   d. What would happen to price and output if the Greeks decided to charge the manufacturer a royalty fee of $3 per ring?

9-3 Determine the profit-maximizing or loss-minimizing production level for a monopolist

4. *(Short-Run Profit Maximization)* Answer the following questions on the basis of the monopolist's situation illustrated in the following graph.
   a. At what output rate and price does the monopolist operate?
   b. In equilibrium, approximately what is the firm's total cost and total revenue?
   c. What is the firm's economic profit or loss in equilibrium?

9-4 Summarize what causes the deadweight loss of monopoly

5. *(Monopoly and the Allocation of Resources)* What is the problem with monopoly? Compare monopoly to the benchmark of perfect competition established in the previous chapter. Use the exhibit below for reference. Identify the deadweight loss.

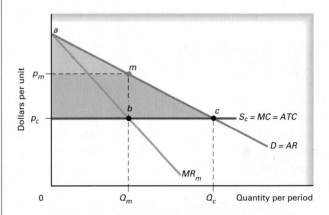

9-5 Outline the factors that could cause the deadweight loss of monopoly to be lower or higher than expected

6. *(Allocative and Distributive Effects)* Why is society worse off under monopoly than under perfect competition, even if both market structures face the same constant long-run average cost curve?
7. *(Welfare Cost of Monopoly)* Explain why the welfare loss of a monopoly may be smaller or larger than the loss shown in the exhibit above.

9-6 Explain why a firm with market power might decide to charge different groups different prices

8. *(Conditions for Price Discrimination)* List three conditions that must be met for a monopolist to price discriminate successfully.
9. *(Price Discrimination)* Explain how it may be profitable for South Korean manufacturers to sell new autos at a lower price in the United States than in South Korea, even with transportation costs included.
10. *(Perfect Price Discrimination)* Why is the perfectly discriminating monopolist's marginal revenue curve identical to the demand curve it faces?

10 | Monopolistic Competition and Oligopoly

David Young-Wolf/PhotoEdit

LEARNING OUTCOMES

After studying this chapter, you will be able to...

10-1 Outline the monopolistic and competitive elements of monopolistic competition

10-2 Describe the sources of oligopoly and explain why some industries become oligopolies

10-3 Explain why predicting oligopoly behavior is so difficult

10-4 Summarize the similarities and differences between an oligopoly and perfect competition in terms of price, output, and long-run profitability

After finishing this chapter go to **PAGE 177** for **STUDY TOOLS**

Topics discussed in Chapter 10 include:

- Monopolistic competition
- Product differentiation
- Excess capacity
- Oligopoly
- Collusion and cartels
- Price leadership
- Prisoner's dilemma
- Game theory

- Why is Perrier water sold in green, tear-shaped bottles?
- Why are some shampoos sold only in salons?
- Why do some pizza makers deliver?
- Which market structure is like a golf tournament and which is more like a tennis match?
- Why do airlines sometimes engage in airfare warfare?

- Why was the OPEC oil cartel created, and why has it met with only spotty success?
- Why is there a witness protection program?

To answer these and other questions, we turn in this chapter to the vast gray area that lies between perfect competition and monopoly.

Perfect competition and monopoly are extreme market structures. Under perfect competition, many suppliers offer an identical product and, in the long run, entry and exit erase economic profit. A monopolist supplies a product with no close substitutes in a market where natural or artificial barriers keep out would-be competitors, so a monopolist can earn economic profit in the long run. These polar market structures are logically appealing and offer a useful description of some industries observed in the economy.

> **"Why was the OPEC oil cartel created, and why has it met with only spotty success?"**

But most firms fit into neither market structure. Some markets have many sellers producing goods that vary slightly, such as the convenience stores that abound. Other markets consist of just a few sellers that in some industries produce essentially identical products, or commodities (such as oil or steel), and in other industries produce differentiated goods (such as automobiles or breakfast cereal). This chapter examines the two remaining market structures that together account for most firms in the economy.

10-1 MONOPOLISTIC COMPETITION

As the expression *monopolistic competition* suggests, this market structure is something of a mashup of monopoly and competition. **Monopolistic competition** describes a market in which many producers offer products that are substitutes but are not viewed as identical by consumers. Because the products of different suppliers differ slightly—for example, some convenience stores are closer to you than others—the demand curve for each is not horizontal but instead slopes downward. Each supplier has some power over the price it can charge. But there are so many buyers that no buyer can influence the price. Thus, the firms that populate this market are not *price takers*, as they would be under perfect competition, but, rather, are *price makers*. Because barriers to entry are low, firms in monopolistic competition can, in the long run, enter or leave the market with ease. Consequently, there are enough sellers that they behave competitively. There are also enough sellers that each tends to get lost in the crowd. For example, in a large metropolitan area, an individual restaurant, gas station, drugstore, dry cleaner, or convenience store tends to act *independently*. Or consider the market for mobile apps. Apple's App Store opened in 2008 with 500 apps. At that time there were probably only one or a few apps for a particular purpose. But the Apple Store now offers more than a million apps, and chances are there are enough apps for some uses that each app supplier acts independently. In other market structures, there may be only two or three sellers in each market, so they keep an eye on one another; they act

monopolistic competition A market structure with many firms selling products that are substitutes but different enough that each firm's demand curve slopes downward; firm entry is relatively easy *interdependently.* You will see the relevance of this distinction later in the chapter.

10-1a Product Differentiation

In perfect competition, the product is a commodity, meaning it's identical across producers, such as a bushel of wheat or an ounce of gold. In monopolistic competition, the product differs somewhat among sellers, as with the difference between one rock radio station and another, or one convenience store and another. Sellers can differentiate their products in four basic ways.

Physical Differences

The most obvious way products differ is in their physical appearance and their qualities. Packaging is also designed to make a product stand out in a crowded field, such as a distinctive bottle of water (Perrier) and instant soup in a cup (Lipton's Cup-a-Soup). Physical differences are seemingly endless: size, weight, color, taste, texture, and so on. Shampoos, for example, differ in color, scent, thickness, lathering ability, and bottle design. Particular brands aim at consumers with dandruff and those with normal, dry, or oily hair.

Location

The number and variety of locations where a product is available is another type of differentiation—*spatial differentiation.* Some products seem to be available everywhere, including online; finding other products requires some search and travel. If you live in a metropolitan area, you are no doubt accustomed to the many convenience stores that populate the region. Each wants to be closest to you when you need milk, bread, or nachos—thus, the proliferation of stores. As the name says, these mini-grocery stores are selling *convenience.* Their prices are higher and selections more limited than at regular grocery stores, but they are usually closer to customers, don't have long lines, and in some cases are open 24/7.

Services

Products also differ in terms of their accompanying services. For example, some products are delivered to your door, such as Domino's pizza and Amazon books; some products are delivered to your smartphone, TV, or computer, such as software, e-books, video games, and movies; other products are cash and carry. Some products are demonstrated by a well-trained sales staff; others are mostly self-service. Some products include online support and toll-free help lines; others come with no help at all. Some sellers provide money-back guarantees; others say "no refunds." The quality and range of accompanying services often differentiate otherwise close substitutes.

Product Image

A final way products differ is in the image the producer tries to foster in the customer's mind. Producers try to create and maintain brand loyalty through product promotion and advertising. For example, suppliers of sportswear, clothing, watches, and cosmetics often pay for

"The Champagne of Table Wars."

"A Whisky and Perrier—a Perfect Entente.

Perrier's distinctive bottle makes it stand out on the shelf—an effective form of product differentiation.

endorsements from athletes, fashion models, and other celebrities. Some producers emphasize the care and attention to detail in each item. For example, Hastens, a small, family-owned Swedish bedding company, underscores the months of labor required to hand-craft each bed—as a way to justify the $70,000 price tag. Some producers try to demonstrate high quality based on where products are sold, such as shampoo sold only in salons. Some products tout their all-natural ingredients, such as Ben & Jerry's ice cream, Tom's of Maine toothpaste, and Nantucket Nectars beverages, or appeal to environmental concerns by focusing on recycled packaging, such as the Starbucks "85% post-consumer-fiber" cup sleeve. More generally, firms advertise to increase sales and profits. Two Yahoo! researchers claim that each dollar of online advertising increased a typical firm's sales more than tenfold.[1]

10-1b Short-Run Profit Maximization or Loss Minimization

Because each monopolistic competitor offers a product that differs somewhat from what others supply, each has some control over the price charged. This *market power* means that each firm's demand curve slopes downward. Because many firms offer close but not identical products, any firm that raises its price can expect to lose some customers to rivals. By way of comparison, a price hike by an individual firm would cost a monopolist fewer customers but would cost a perfect competitor *all* customers. Therefore, a monopolistic competitor faces a demand curve that tends to be more elastic than a monopolist's but less elastic than a perfect competitor's. Please take a moment to think about that.

> **"A firm's demand curve is more elastic the more substitutes there are and the less differentiated its product is."**

1. Randall Lewis and David Reiley, "Does Retail Advertising Work? Measuring the Effects of Advertising on Sales via a Controlled Experiment on Yahoo!" American Economics Association annual meetings, 3 January 2010.

Recall that the availability of substitutes for a given product affects its price elasticity of demand. The price elasticity of the monopolistic competitor's demand depends on (1) the number of rival firms that produce similar products and (2) the firm's ability to differentiate its product from those of its rivals. *A firm's demand curve is more elastic the more substitutes there are and the less differentiated its product is.*

Marginal Revenue Equals Marginal Cost

From our study of monopoly, we know that a downward-sloping demand curve means the marginal revenue curve also slopes downward and lies below the demand curve. Exhibit 1 depicts demand and marginal revenue curves for a monopolistic competitor. The exhibit also presents average and marginal cost curves. Remember that the forces that determine the cost of production are largely independent of the forces that shape demand, so there is nothing special about a monopolistic competitor's cost curves. In the short run, a firm that can at least cover its variable cost increases output as long as marginal revenue exceeds marginal cost. A monopolistic competitor maximizes profit just as a monopolist does: *the profit-maximizing quantity occurs where marginal revenue equals marginal cost; the profit-maximizing price for that quantity is found up on the demand curve.* Exhibit 1 shows the price and quantity combinations that maximize short-run profit in panel (a), and minimize short-run loss in panel (b). In each panel, the marginal cost and marginal revenue curves intersect at point e, yielding equilibrium output q, equilibrium price p, and average total cost c.

Maximizing Profit or Minimizing Loss in the Short Run

Recall that the short run is a period too brief to allow firms to enter or leave the market. The demand and cost conditions shown in panel (a) of Exhibit 1 indicate that this firm earns economic profit in the short run. At the firm's profit-maximizing quantity, average total cost, c, is below the price, p. Price minus average total cost is the firm's profit per unit, which, when multiplied by the quantity, yields economic profit, shown by the blue rectangle. Again, the profit-maximizing quantity is found where marginal revenue equals marginal cost; price is found up on the demand curve at that quantity. Thus, a monopolistic competitor, like a monopolist, has no supply curve—that is, *there is no curve that uniquely relates prices and corresponding quantities supplied.*

The monopolistic competitor, like monopolists and perfect competitors, is not guaranteed an economic

Exhibit 1

Monopolistic Competitor in the Short Run

The monopolistically competitive firm produces the level of output at which marginal revenue equals marginal cost (point *e*) and charges the price indicated by point *b* on the downward-sloping demand curve. In panel (a), the firm produces *q* units, sells them at price *p*, and earns a short-run economic profit equal to $(p - c)$ multiplied by *q*, shown by the blue rectangle. In panel (b), the average total cost exceeds the price at the output where marginal revenue equals marginal cost. Thus, the firm suffers a short-run loss equal to $(c - p)$ multiplied by *q*, shown by the pink rectangle.

(a) Maximizing short-run profit

(b) Minimizing short-run loss

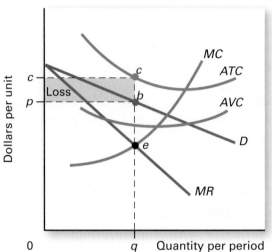

profit or even a normal profit. The firm's demand and cost curves could be as shown in panel (b), where the average total cost curve lies entirely above the demand curve, so no quantity allows the firm to escape a loss. In such a situation, the firm must decide whether to produce at a loss or to shut down in the short run. The rule here is the same as with perfect competition and monopoly: as long as price exceeds average variable cost, the firm in the short run loses less by producing than by shutting down. If no price covers average variable cost, the firm shuts down. Recall that the halt in production may be only temporary; shutting down is not the same as going out of business. Firms that expect economic losses to persist may, in the long run, leave the industry.

Short-run profit maximization in monopolistic competition is quite similar to that under

> **"The profit-maximizing quantity occurs where marginal revenue equals marginal cost; the profit-maximizing price for that quantity is found up on the demand curve."**

monopoly. But the stories differ in the long run, as we'll see next.

10-1c Zero Economic Profit in the Long Run

Low barriers to entry in monopolistic competition mean that short-run economic profit attracts new entrants in the long run. Because new entrants offer similar products, they draw customers away from other firms in the market, thereby reducing the demand facing other firms. Entry continues in the long run until economic profit disappears. *Because market entry is easy, monopolistically competitive firms earn zero economic profit in the long run.*

On the other side of the ledger, economic losses drive some firms out of business in the long run. As firms leave the industry, their customers switch to the remaining firms, increasing the demand for those products.

Exhibit 2

Long-Run Equilibrium in Monopolistic Competition

With monopolistic competition, if existing firms earn economic profit in the short run, new firms will enter the industry in the long run. This entry reduces the demand facing each firm. In the long run, each firm's demand curve shifts leftward until marginal revenue equals marginal cost (point *a*) and the demand curve is tangent to the average total cost curve (point *b*). Economic profit is zero at output *q*. With zero economic profit, no more firms will enter, so the industry is in long-run equilibrium. The same long-run adjustment occurs if firms suffer a short-run loss. In the long-run firms leave until remaining firms earn just a normal profit.

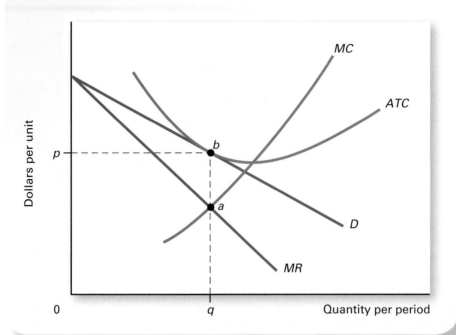

Firms continue to leave in the long run until the remaining firms have enough customers to earn normal profit, but not economic profit.

Exhibit 2 shows long-run equilibrium for a typical monopolistic competitor. In the long run, entry and exit shifts each firm's demand curve until economic profit disappears—that is, until the price, or average revenue, equals average total cost. In Exhibit 2, the marginal revenue curve intersects the marginal cost curve at point *a*. At the equilibrium quantity, *q*, the average total cost curve is tangent to the demand curve at point *b*. Because average total cost equals the price, the firm earns no economic profit but does earn a normal profit (how do we know this?). At all other quantities, the firm's average total cost curve lies above the demand curve, so the firm would lose money by reducing or expanding production.

Thus, because entry is easy in monopolistic competition, short-run economic profit attracts new entrants in the long run. The demand curve facing each monopolistic competitor shifts left until economic profit disappears. A short-run economic loss prompts some firms to leave

the industry in the long run until remaining firms earn just a normal profit. In summary: *Monopolistic competition is like monopoly in the sense that firms in each of the two markets face demand curves that slope downward. Monopolistic competition is like perfect competition in the sense that easy entry and exit eliminate economic profit or economic loss in the long run.*

10-1d Monopolistic Competition and Perfect Competition Compared

How does monopolistic competition compare with perfect competition in terms of efficiency? In the long run, neither earns economic profit, so what's the difference? The difference traces to the demand curves facing individual firms in each of the two market structures. Exhibit 3 presents the long-run equilibrium price and quantity for a typical firm in each market structure, assuming each firm has identical cost curves. In each case, the marginal cost curve intersects the marginal revenue curve at the quantity where the average total cost curve is tangent to the firm's demand curve.

A perfect competitor's demand curve is a horizontal line drawn at the market price, as shown in panel (a). This demand curve is tangent to the lowest point of the firm's long-run average total cost curve. Thus, a perfect competitor in the long run produces at the lowest possible average cost. In panel (b), a monopolistic competitor faces a downward-sloping demand curve because its product differs somewhat from those of other suppliers. In the long run, the monopolistic competitor produces less than required to achieve the lowest possible average cost. Thus, the price and average cost in monopolistic competition, identified as *p'* in panel (b), exceed the price and average cost in perfect competition, identified as *p* in panel (a). *If firms have the same cost curves, the monopolistic competitor produces less and charges more than the perfect competitor does in the long run, though neither earns economic profit.*

Exhibit 3

Perfect Competition Versus Monopolistic Competition in Long-Run Equilibrium

Cost curves are assumed to be the same in each panel. The perfectly competitive firm of panel (a) faces a demand curve that is horizontal at market price *p*. Long-run equilibrium occurs at output *q*, where the demand curve is tangent to the average total cost curve at its lowest point. The monopolistically competitive firm of panel (b) is in long-run equilibrium at output *q'*, where demand is tangent to the average total cost curve. Because the demand curve slopes downward in panel (b), however, the tangency does not occur at the minimum point of average total cost. Thus, the monopolistically competitive firm produces less output and charges a higher price than does a perfectly competitive firm with the same cost curves. Neither firm earns economic profit in the long run. Each earns normal profit. The firm in monopolistic competition has excess capacity, meaning that it could reduce average cost by increasing its rate of output.

(a) Perfect competition

(b) Monopolistic competition

Firms in monopolistic com-petition are not producing at minimum average cost. They are said to have **excess capacity**, because production falls short of the quantity that would achieve the lowest average cost. Excess capacity means that each producer could easily serve more customers and, in the process, lower average cost. *The marginal value of increased output would exceed its marginal cost, so greater output would increase social welfare.* Such excess capacity exists with gas stations, drugstores, convenience stores, restaurants, motels, bookstores, flower shops, and firms in other monopolistic competitive industries. A specific example is the funeral business. Industry analysts argue that the nation's 19,000 funeral directors could efficiently handle 4 million funerals a year, but only about 2.4 million people die each year. So the industry operates at only 60 percent of capacity, resulting in a higher average cost per funeral because valuable resources remain idle much of the time.

Many small colleges also operate with excess capacity. Most could easily educate more students, but to attract them, a college would have to cut tuition to the point where it could not survive. Thus, many small colleges continue to operate with much excess capacity.[2]

One other difference between perfect competition and monopolistic competition does not show up in Exhibit 3. Although the cost curves drawn in each panel of the exhibit are identical, firms in monopolistic competition spend more to differentiate their products than do firms in perfect competition, where products are identical. This higher cost of product differentiation shifts the average cost curve upward.

Some economists have argued that monopolistic competition results in too many suppliers and in artificial product differentiation. The counterargument is that consumers are willing to pay a higher price for a wider selection. According to this latter view, consumers benefit from more choice among gas stations, restaurants, convenience stores, clothing stores, funeral homes, drugstores, textbooks, and many other goods and services. For example, what if half of the restaurants in your area were to close just so the remaining ones could reduce their excess capacity? Some consumers, including you, might be disappointed if

excess capacity The difference between a firm's profit-maximizing quantity and the quantity that minimizes average cost; firms with excess capacity could reduce average cost by increasing quantity

2. This example is from Sandy Baum and Michael McPherson, "Monopolistic Competition and the Very Small College," *Chronicle of Higher Education,* 8 January 2012.

a local favorite closed. Recent research suggests that differences in consumer tastes help explain the existence of monopolistic competition.[3] Not only do tastes differ a lot across consumers, but individual consumers also prefer variety and are willing to pay extra for it.[4]

Perfect competitors and monopolistic competitors are so numerous in their respective markets that an action by any one of them has little or no effect on the behavior of others in the market. Another important market structure on the continuum between perfect competition and monopoly has just a few firms. We explore this market structure in the balance of the chapter.

10-2 OLIGOPOLY

The final market structure we examine is *oligopoly*, a Greek word meaning "few sellers." When you think of "big business," you are thinking of **oligopoly**, an industry dominated by just a few firms. Perhaps three or four account for more than half the industry supply. Many industries, including steel, automobiles, oil, breakfast cereals, cigarettes, personal computers, and operating systems software, are *oligopolistic*. Because an oligopoly has only a few firms, each one must consider the effect of its own actions on competitors' behavior in the market. Oligopolists are therefore said to be *interdependent*. There may be few suppliers but there are many demanders, so many that no buyer has any control over the price.

10-2a Varieties of Oligopoly

In some oligopolies, such as steel or oil, the product is identical, or undifferentiated, across producers. Thus, an **undifferentiated oligopoly** sells a commodity, such as an ingot of steel or a barrel of oil. But in other oligopolies, such as automobiles or breakfast cereals, the product is differentiated across producers. A **differentiated oligopoly** sells products that differ across producers, such as a Toyota Camry versus a Honda Accord.

The more similar the products, the greater the interdependence among firms in the industry. For example, because steel ingots are essentially identical, steel producers are quite sensitive to each other's pricing. Even a small rise in one producer's price sends customers to rivals. But with differentiated oligopoly, such as the auto industry, producers are not quite as sensitive about each other's prices. As with monopolistic competitors,

oligopolists differentiate their products through (1) physical qualities, (2) sales locations, (3) services offered with the product, and (4) the image of the product established in the consumer's mind.

Because of interdependence, the behavior of any particular firm is difficult to predict. *Each firm knows that any changes in its product's quality, price, output, or advertising policy may prompt a reaction from its rivals. And each firm may react if another firm alters any of these features.* Monopolistic competition is like a professional golf tournament, where each player strives for a personal best. Oligopoly is more like a tennis match, where each player's actions depend on how and where the rival hits the ball. Here's another analogy to help you understand the effects of interdependence: Did you ever find yourself in an awkward effort to get around someone coming toward you on a sidewalk? You each end up turning this way and that in a brief, clumsy encounter. You each are trying to figure out which way the other will turn. But since neither can read the other's mind, neither can work out the problem independently. The solution is for one of you to put your head down and just walk. The other can then easily adjust.

Why have some industries evolved into oligopolies, dominated by only a few firms? Although the reasons are not always clear, *an oligopoly can often be traced to some form of barrier to entry, such as economies of scale, legal restrictions, brand names built up by years of advertising, or control over an essential resource.* In the previous chapter, we examined barriers to entry as they applied to monopoly. Those same principles apply to oligopoly.

10-2b Economies of Scale

Perhaps the most important barrier to entry is economies of scale. Recall that the minimum efficient scale is the lowest output at which the firm takes full advantage of economies of scale. If a firm's minimum efficient scale is relatively large compared to industry output, then only a few firms are needed to satisfy industry demand. For example, an automobile plant of minimum efficient scale could make enough cars to supply nearly 5 percent of the U.S. market. If there were 100 auto plants, each would supply such a tiny portion of the market that the average cost per car would be higher than if only 20 plants manufacture

oligopoly A market structure characterized by so few firms that each behaves interdependently

undifferentiated oligopoly An oligopoly that sells a commodity, or a product that does not differ across suppliers, such as an ingot of steel or a barrel of oil

differentiated oligopoly An oligopoly that sells products that differ across suppliers, such as automobiles or breakfast cereal

3. Francesco Di Comite, Jacques-Francois Thisse, and Hylke Vandebussche, "Verti-zontal Differentiation in Monopolistic Competition," *Journal of International Economics*, 93 (May 2014): 50–66.

4. Shon Ferguson, "Endogenous Product Differentiation, Market Size and Prices," *Review of International Economics*, 23 (February 2015): 45–61.

Exhibit 4
Economies of Scale as a Barrier to Entry

At point *b*, an existing firm can produce *M* or more automobiles at an average cost of c_b. A new entrant able to sell only *S* automobiles would incur a much higher average cost of c_a at point *a*. If automobile prices are below c_a, a new entrant would suffer a loss. In this case, economies of scale serve as a barrier to entry, insulating firms that have achieved minimum efficient scale from new competitors.

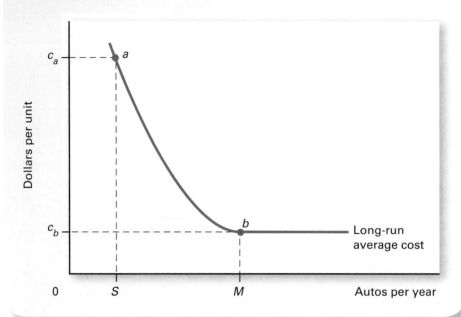

autos. In the automobile industry, economies of scale create a barrier to entry. To compete with existing producers, a new entrant must sell enough automobiles to reach a competitive scale of operation.

Exhibit 4 presents the long-run average cost curve for a typical firm in the industry. If a new entrant can sell only *S* cars, the average cost per unit, c_a, far exceeds the average cost, c_b, of a manufacturer that sells enough cars to reach the minimum efficient size, *M*. If autos sell for less than c_a, a potential entrant can expect to lose money, and this prospect discourages entry. For example, John DeLorean tried to break into the auto industry in the early 1980s with a modern design featured in the *Back to the Future* movies. But his company managed to build and sell only 8,583 DeLoreans before going bankrupt. If an auto plant costs $1 billion to build, just paying for the plant would have cost over $100,000 per DeLorean sold.

10-2c The High Cost of Entry

Potential entrants into oligopolistic industries could face another problem. The total investment needed to reach the minimum efficient size is often gigantic. For example, about 100 hours of video is uploaded to YouTube every minute. To make sure that no copyright laws are violated, YouTube spent hundreds of millions of dollars on a system to vet videos as they are uploaded. Any potential rival for YouTube would have to develop its own verification system or risk being sued for copyright infringement. That outlay creates a barrier to entry. Likewise, a new auto plant or new semiconductor plant can cost over $3 billion. The average cost of developing and testing a new drug exceeds $800 million (only 1 in 25 drug candidates identified by the industry ever makes it to market).[5]

Advertising a new product enough to compete with established brands may also require enormous outlays. Established brands have a tremendous advantage in the market, and that edge is usually durable.[6] Some brand loyalties even pass across generations, as in a family's preferences for automobiles.[7]

High start-up costs and well-established brand names create huge barriers to entry, especially because the market for new products is so uncertain (four out of five new consumer products don't survive). An unsuccessful product could cripple a start-up firm. The prospect of such a loss discourages many potential entrants. That's why most new products come from large, well-established firms. For example, Colgate-Palmolive spent $100 million introducing Total toothpaste, as did McDonald's in its failed attempt to sell the Arch Deluxe as an upscale burger. Unilever lost $160 million when its new detergent, Power, washed out. And thousands of employees worked four years developing the Amazon Fire Phone, but it had few buyers, even after the price dropped to 99 cents (plus a two-year phone contract).[8]

Firms often spend millions and sometimes billions trying to differentiate their products. Some of these outlays

5. As reported in "Little Big Pharma," *Wall Street Journal*, 6 December 2006.

6. Bart Bronnenberg, Jean-Pierre Dube, and Matthew Gentzkow, "The Evolution of Brand Preference: Evidence from Consumer Migration," *American Economic Review*, 102 (October 2012): 2472–2508.

7. Soren Anderson et al., "The Intergenerational Transmission of Automobile Brand Preference," NBER Working Paper No.19535 (October 2013).

8. David Streitfeld, "Amazon Drops Price of Its Struggling Fire Phone to 99 Cents," *New York Times*, 8 September 2014.

While there are hundreds of types of cereals, there are only a handful of companies that make the large majority of them.

Richard Levine/Alamy

offer consumers useful information and wider choice. But some spending seems to offer neither. For example, Pepsi and Coke spend billions on messages such as "Live for Now" or "Open Happiness." Regardless, *product differentiation expenditures create barriers to entry.*

10-2d Crowding Out the Competition

Oligopolies compete with existing rivals and try to block new entry by offering a variety of products. Entrenched producers may flood the market with new products in part to crowd out other new entries. For example, a few cereal makers offer more than a dozen products each. Many of these variations offer little that is new. One study of 25,500 new products introduced during one year found only 7 percent offered new or added benefits.[9] *Multiple products from the same brand dominate shelf space and attempt to crowd out new entrants.*

This does not mean that small producers can't survive. Brenda Jensen, for example, handcrafts two-pound wheels of cheese in her small business, Hidden Springs Creamery of Wesby, Wisconsin. She produces only about 12,000 pounds a year. But she survives because her award-winning cheese sells for $20 to $40 a pound at boutique retailers.

9. The study was carried out by Market Intelligence Service and was reported in "Market Makers," *The Economist,* 14 March 1998.

> **"Colluding firms, compared with competing firms, usually produce less, charge more, block new firms, and earn more economic profit."**

10-3 THREE APPROACHES TO OLIGOPOLY

Because oligopolists are interdependent, analyzing their behavior is complicated. No single model or single approach explains oligopoly behavior completely. At one extreme, oligopolists may try to coordinate their behavior so they act collectively as a single monopolist, forming a cartel, such as OPEC. At the other extreme, oligopolists may compete so fiercely that price wars erupt, such as those that break out among airlines, tobacco companies, computer chipmakers, and wireless service providers.

Several theories have been developed to explain oligopoly behavior. We will study three of the better-known approaches: collusion, price leadership, and game theory. As you will see, each has some relevance in explaining observed behavior, although none is entirely satisfactory as a general theory of oligopoly. Thus, *there is no general theory of oligopoly but rather a set of theories, each based on the diversity of observed behavior in an interdependent market.*

10-3a Collusion and Cartels

In an oligopolistic market, there are just a few firms so, to decrease competition and increase profit, these firms may try to *collude,* or conspire to rig the market. **Collusion** is an agreement among firms in the industry to divide the market and fix the price. A **cartel** is a group of firms that agree to collude so they can act as a monopoly to increase economic profit. Cartels are more likely among sellers of a commodity, like oil or steel. *Colluding firms, compared with competing firms, usually produce less, charge more, block new firms, and earn more economic profit. Consumers pay higher prices, and potential entrants are denied the opportunity to compete.*

Collusion and cartels are illegal in the United States. And more nations around the world, particularly those in Europe,

collusion An agreement among firms to increase economic profit by dividing the market and fixing the price

cartel A group of firms that agree to coordinate their production and pricing decisions to reap monopoly profit are cracking down on collusion and cartels.[10] Still, monopoly profit can be so tempting that some firms break the law. For example, top executives at Archer Daniels Midland were convicted of conspiring with four Asian competitors to rig the $650 million world market for lysine, an amino acid used in animal feed. And French authorities fined Procter & Gamble $234 million and Colgate $35 million for attempting to fix the price of laundry detergent.[11] Some other countries are more tolerant of cartels and a few even promote them, as with the 12 member-nations of OPEC. If OPEC ever met in the United States, its representatives could be arrested for price fixing. Cartels can operate worldwide because there are no international laws against them.

Suppose all firms in an industry formed a cartel. The market demand curve, *D*, appears in Exhibit 5. What price maximizes the cartel's profit, and how is output allocated among participating firms? The first task of the cartel is to determine its marginal cost of production. Because a cartel acts like a monopoly that runs many plants, the marginal cost curve for the cartel in Exhibit 5 is the horizontal sum of each firm's marginal cost curve. The cartel's marginal cost curve intersects the market's marginal revenue curve to determine the output that maximizes the cartel's profit. This intersection yields quantity *Q*. The cartel's price, *p*, is read off the demand curve at that quantity.

So far, so good. To maximize cartel profit, output *Q* must be allocated among cartel members so that each member's marginal cost equals *c*. Any other allocation would lower cartel profit. Thus, *for cartel profit to be maximized, output must be allocated so that the marginal cost for the final unit produced by each firm is identical.* Let's look at why this is easier said than done.

Differences in Average Cost

If all firms had identical average cost curves, output and profit would be easily allocated across firms (each firm would produce the same amount), but if costs differ, as they usually do, problems arise. The greater the difference in average costs across firms, the greater the differences

10. See, for example, Cento Veljanovski, "Punishing European Cartels," *World Economic Journal*, 12 (January 2011): 163–176.

11. "France Fines P&G and Colgate for Laundry Prices," Associated Press, 8 December 2011.

Exhibit 5

Cartel as a Monopolist

A cartel acts like a monopolist. Here, *D* is the market demand curve, *MR* the associated marginal revenue curve, and *MC* the horizontal sum of the marginal cost curves of cartel members (assuming all firms in the market join the cartel). Cartel profits are maximized when the industry produces quantity *Q* and charges price *p*.

in economic profit among them. If cartel members try to equalize each firm's economic profit, a high-cost firm would need to sell more than would a low-cost firm. But this allocation scheme would violate the cartel's profit-maximizing condition. Thus, *if average costs differ across firms, the output allocation that maximizes cartel profit yields unequal profit across cartel members.* Firms earning less profit could drop out of the cartel. A dropout could attract customers and increase economic profits by charging a little less than the cartel price. Such dropouts undermine the cartel.

Usually, the allocation of output is the result of haggling among cartel members. Firms that are more influential or more adept at bargaining get a larger share of output and profit. Allocation schemes are sometimes based on geography or on the historical division of output among firms. OPEC, for example, allocates output in proportion to each member country's share of estimated oil reserves. Cartel members of Norway's cement market base output on each firm's share of industry capacity.[12]

Number of Firms in the Cartel

The more firms in an industry, the more difficult it is to negotiate an acceptable allocation of output among

12. Lars-Hendrik Roller and Frode Steen, "On the Workings of a Cartel: Evidence from the Norwegian Cement Industry," *American Economic Review*, 96 (March 2006): p. 322.

them. *Consensus becomes harder to achieve as the number of firms grows.* And the more firms in the industry, the more likely that some will become dissatisfied and bolt from the cartel.

New Entry

If a cartel can't prevent new entry or can't force new entrants to join the cartel, new firms could increase industry output, force prices down, squeeze economic profit, and disrupt the cartel. A cartel's success therefore depends on barriers that block the entry of new firms or at least require new entrants to join the cartel.

Cheating

Perhaps the biggest problem in keeping a cartel together is the powerful temptation to cheat on the agreement. Because oligopolists usually operate with excess capacity, some cheat on the price. By offering a price slightly below the cartel price, any cartel member can usually increase sales and profit. Even if cartel members keep an eagle eye on each firm's price, one firm can increase sales by offering extra services, secret rebates, or other concessions. Research suggests that cheating increases as the number of firms in the cartel grows.[13] Cartels collapse once cheating becomes widespread.

OPEC's Spotty History

The problems of establishing and maintaining a cartel are reflected in the spotty history of OPEC. Many members are poor countries that rely on oil as their major source of revenue, so they argue over the price and their market share. OPEC members also cheat on the cartel. In 1980, the price of oil exceeded $90 a barrel (measured in 2015 dollars). During the 1990s, the price averaged around $36 a barrel and dipped under $20 a barrel. Prices topped $150 in 2008, but fell under $50 by the end of that year. And between early 2014 and early 2015 the price per barrel dropped from over $110 to under $50. Like other cartels, OPEC has difficulty with new entry. The high prices resulting from OPEC's early success attracted new oil supplies from non-OPEC members operating in the North Sea, Mexico, Siberia, and the United States. The high price also made extraction from oil sands more economical. As a result of new exploration and other oil sources,

> **"A cartel's success depends on barriers that block the entry of new firms or at least require new entrants to join the cartel."**

such as shale, more than 60 percent of the world's oil now comes from non-OPEC sources. A *New York Times* headline captured the cartel's problem: "OPEC Split as Oil Prices Fall Sharply."[14]

Technological Change

Any effort to cartelize, or monopolize, a market is vulnerable to technological change, which can introduce new and cheaper supply sources. In the case of crude oil, for example, bigger and better oil rigs opened up exploration in previously inaccessible sources of crude oil, such as the North Sea. Extracting crude oil from tar sands also brought to the market another production method. Yet another source has been from the combination of horizontal drilling and hydraulic fracturing, which allowed the United States to double oil production between 2008 and 2014, to become one of the world's leading producer of oil and natural gas. To repeat, technological change represents a challenge to any cartel.

International Crackdowns on Cartels

Finally, as noted earlier, although there are no worldwide laws against international cartels, in the mid-1990s regulators began making it more difficult to operate cartels. More generally, there is now more international cooperation in identifying and prosecuting collusive behavior.[15]

TO REVIEW: In those countries where cartels are legal, establishing and maintaining an effective cartel is more difficult if (1) the product is differentiated among firms, (2) average costs differ among firms, (3) there are many firms in the industry, (4) entry barriers are low, (5) cheating on the cartel agreement becomes widespread, or (6) the industry is undergoing technological change. Efforts to cartelize the world supply of a number of products, including bauxite, copper, tin, and coffee, have failed so far. Russia, Iran, and Qatar have formed a natural gas cartel, but so far there has been no attempt to limit production or fix the price.[16]

13. John A. List, "The Economics of Open Air Markets," NBER Working Paper 15420 (October 2009).

14. This article, by Clifford Krauss appeared 13 October 2014.

15. Margaret Levenstein and Valerie Suslow, "Breaking Up Is Hard to Do: Determinants of Cartel Duration," *Journal of Law and Economics,* 54 (May, 2011): 455–492.

16. Eldar O. Kasayev, "The Myth of the Natural Gas OPEC," *The National Interest,* 11 February 2013, at http://nationalinterest.org/commentary/the-myth-natural-gas-opec-8082.

10-3b Price Leadership

An informal, or *tacit*, form of collusion occurs if there is a **price leader** who sets the price for the rest of the industry. Typically, a dominant firm sets the market price, and other firms follow that lead, thereby avoiding price competition. The price leader also initiates any price changes, and, again, others follow. The steel industry was an example of the price-leadership form of oligopoly. Typically, U.S. Steel, the largest firm in the industry, would set the price for various products. Public pressure on U.S. Steel not to raise prices eventually shifted the price-leadership role onto less prominent producers, resulting in a rotation of leadership among firms. Although the rotating price leadership reduced price conformity, price leadership kept prices high.

Like other forms of collusion, price leadership faces obstacles. Most importantly, the practice violates U.S. antitrust laws. Second, the greater the product differentiation among sellers, the less effective price leadership is as a means of collusion. Third, there is no guarantee that other firms will follow the leader. Firms that fail to follow a price increase take business away from firms that do. Fourth, unless there are barriers to entry, a profitable price attracts new entrants, which could destabilize the price-leadership agreement. And finally, as with formal cartels, firms are tempted to cheat on the agreement to boost sales and profit.

10-3c Game Theory

How do firms act when they recognize their interdependence but either cannot or do not collude? Because oligopoly involves interdependence among a few firms, we can think of interacting firms as players in a game. **Game theory** examines oligopolistic behavior as a series of strategic moves and countermoves among rival firms. This approach analyzes the behavior of decision makers, or players, whose choices affect one another. Game theory is not really a separate model of oligopoly but a general approach, an approach that focuses on each player's incentives to cooperate—say, through cartels or price leaders—or to compete, in ways to be discussed now.

To get some feel for game theory, let's work through the **prisoner's dilemma**, the most widely examined game. The game originally considered a situation in which two thieves, let's call them Ben and Jerry, are caught near the crime scene and brought to police headquarters, where they are interrogated in separate rooms. The police know the two guys did it but can't prove it, so they need a confession. Each thief faces a choice of confessing, thereby "squealing" on the other, or "clamming up," thereby denying any knowledge of the crime. If one confesses, turning state's evidence, he is granted immunity from prosecution and goes free, while the other guy gets 10 years. If both clam up, each gets only a 1-year sentence on a technicality. If both confess, each gets 5 years.

What will Ben and Jerry do? The answer depends on the assumptions about their behavior—that is, what *strategy* each pursues. A **strategy** reflects a player's game plan. In this game, suppose each player tries to save his own skin—each tries to minimize his time in jail, regardless of what happens to the other (after all, there is no honor among

Rubberball/Jupiter Images

Rubberball/Jupiterimages

What will Ben and Jerry do? The answer depends on the assumptions about their behavior—that is, what strategy each pursues.

Exhibit 6

The Prisoner's Dilemma Payoff Matrix (years in jail)

This matrix shows the years each thief can expect to spend in jail based on his actions and the actions of the other prisoner. Ben's payoff is in red and Jerry's in blue.

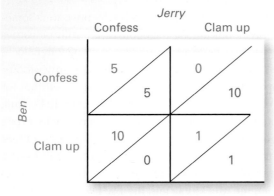

thieves). Exhibit 6 shows the *payoff matrix* for the prisoner's dilemma. A **payoff matrix** is a table listing the rewards (or, in this case, the penalties) that Ben and Jerry can expect based on the strategy each pursues.

Ben's choices are shown down the left margin and Jerry's across the top. Each prisoner can either confess or clam up. The numbers in the matrix indicate the prison time in years each can expect based on the corresponding strategies. Ben's numbers are in red and Jerry's in blue. Take a moment now to see how the matrix works. Notice that the punishment each player receives depends on the strategy he chooses *and* on the strategy the other player chooses.

What strategies are rational, assuming that each player tries to minimize jail time? For example, put yourself in Ben's shoes. You know that Jerry, who is being questioned in another room, will either confess or clam up. If Jerry confesses, the left column of Exhibit 6 shows the penalties. If you confess too, you both get 5 years in jail, but if you clam up, you get 10 years and Jerry "walks." So, if you think Jerry will confess, you should too.

What if you believe Jerry will clam up? The right-hand column shows the two possible outcomes. If you confess, you do no time, but if you clam up too, you each get 1 year in jail. Thus, if you think Jerry will clam up, you're better off confessing. In short, whatever Jerry does, Ben is better off confessing. The same holds for Jerry. He's better off confessing, regardless of what Ben does. So each has an incentive to confess and each gets 5 years in jail. This is called the **dominant-strategy equilibrium** of the game because each player's action does not depend on what he thinks the other player will do.

But notice that if each crook could just hang tough and clam up, both would be better off. After all, if both confess, each gets 5 years, but if both clam up, the police can't prove otherwise, so each gets only 1 year in jail on a technicality. If each could trust the other to clam up, they both would be better off. But there is no way for the two to communicate or to coordinate their actions. That's why police investigators keep suspects apart, that's why organized crime threatens "squealers" with death, and that's why the witness protection program tries to shield "squealers."

Price-Setting Game

The prisoner's dilemma applies to a broad range of economic phenomena including pricing policy and advertising strategy. For example, consider the market for gasoline in a rural community with only two gas stations, Texaco and Exxon. Here the oligopoly consists of two sellers, or a **duopoly**. Suppose customers are indifferent between the brands and focus only on the price. Each station posts its daily price early in the morning before learning about the other station's price. To keep things simple, suppose only two prices are possible—a low price or a high price. If both charge the low price, they split the market and each earns a profit of $500 per day. If both charge the high price, they also split the market, but profit jumps to $700 each. If one charges the high price but the other the low one, the low-price station gets most of the business, earning a profit of $1,000, leaving the high-price station with only $200.

Exhibit 7 shows the payoff matrix, with Texaco's strategy down the left margin and Exxon's across the top. Texaco's profit appears in red, and Exxon's in blue. Suppose you own the Texaco station and are trying to decide what to charge. If Exxon charges the low price, you earn $500 charging the low price but only $200 charging the high price. So you earn more charging the low price. If, instead, Exxon charges the high price, you earn $1,000 charging the low price and $700 charging the high price. Again, you earn more charging the low price. Exxon faces the same incentives. Thus, each charges the low price, regardless of what the other does.

The prisoner's dilemma outcome is an equilibrium

> **payoff matrix** In game theory, a table listing the payoffs that each player can expect from each move based on the actions of the other player
>
> **dominant-strategy equilibrium** In game theory, the outcome achieved when each player's choice does not depend on what the other player does
>
> **duopoly** A market with only two suppliers; a special type of oligopoly market structure

CHAPTER 10: Monopolistic Competition and Oligopoly   **173**

Exhibit 7

Price-Setting Payoff Matrix (profit per day)

This matrix shows the daily profit each gas station can expect to earn based on the price each charges. Texaco's price is in red and Exxon's is in blue.

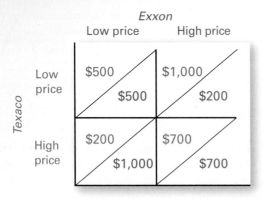

because each player maximizes profit, given the price chosen by the other. Neither gas station can increase profit by changing its price, given the price chosen by the other firm. A situation in which a player chooses its best strategy given the strategies chosen by other firms is called a **Nash equilibrium**, named after Nobel Prize winner and former Princeton professor John Nash. (He inspired the award-winning movie *A Beautiful Mind* starring Russell Crowe as Nash.)

In this prisoner's dilemma, each charges the low price, earning $500 a day, although each would earn $700 charging the high price. Think of yourself as a member of the oil cartel discussed earlier, where the cartel determines the price and sets production quotas for each member. If you think other firms in the cartel will stick with their quotas, you can increase your profit by cutting your price and thereby increasing quantity sold. If you think the other firms will cheat on the cartel by cutting the price, then you should too—otherwise, you will get your clock cleaned by those cheaters. Either way,

Nash equilibrium A situation in which a firm, or a player in game theory, chooses the best strategy given the strategies chosen by others; no participant can improve his or her outcome by changing strategies even after learning of the strategies selected by other participants

your incentive as a cartel member is to cheat on your quota. All members have an incentive to cheat, although all would earn more by sticking to the agreement that maximizes joint profit. Cheating is a Nash equilibrium, unless the cartel has real teeth to keep members in line—that is, unless cartel members have the strategy imposed on them.

This incentive to cut prices is why price wars sometimes break out among oligopolists. Even in industries with just two or three firms, competition often locks these rivals in a steel-cage death match for survival. For example, the recent headline "Price War Intensifies for Top Wireless Providers" reflects how AT&T, Verizon, Sprint, and T-Mobile are scrapping every day to attract new customers.[17] Likewise, McDonald's and Burger King at one point were each selling two beef patties with one slice of cheese on a bun for $1—a dollar-menu duel between the McDouble and the BK Dollar Double.[18] A bitter price war with Dell cut Hewlett-Packard's earnings on each $500 personal computer sold to a razor-thin $1.75.[19] Early profits in the animated movie business attracted entry, which over time cut profit and led to some bankruptcies. And just before a recent Thanksgiving weekend, a price war erupted in airfares. American Airlines first announced holiday discounts. Delta responded with cuts of up to 50 percent. Within hours, American, United, and other major carriers said they would match Delta's reductions. All these airlines were losing money at the time, and all three sought bankruptcy protection. So go the price wars.

In the traditional advertising game, there are no winners as both brands choose a big advertising budget in equilibrium that results in lower profits.

Lux Igitur/Alamy

Cola War Game

As a final example of a prisoner's dilemma, consider the marketing strategies of Coke and Pepsi. Suppose each is putting together a promotional budget for the coming year, not knowing the other's plans. The choice boils down to adopting either a moderate budget or a big budget—one that involves multiple Super Bowl ads, showy in-store displays, and other marketing efforts aimed mostly at attracting customers from each

17. This headline topped a news account by Thomas Gryta, *Wall Street Journal*, 9 December 2014.

18. See http://www.mcdonalds.com

19. David Bank, "H-P Posts 10% Increase in Revenue," *Wall Street Journal*, 20 November 2003.

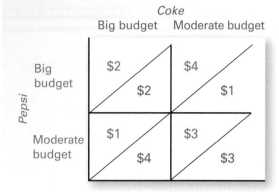

other. If each adopts a big budget, their costly efforts will, for the most part, cancel each other out and limit each company's profit to $2 billion a year. If each adopts a moderate promotional budget, the money saved boosts profit for each to $3 billion a year. And if one adopts a big budget but the other does not, the heavy promoter captures a bigger market share and earns $4 billion, while the other loses market share and earns only $1 billion. What to do, what to do?

Exhibit 8 shows the payoff matrix for the two strategies, with Pepsi's choices listed down the left margin and Coke's across the top. In each cell of the matrix, Pepsi's profit appears in red, and Coke's in blue. Let's look at Pepsi's decision. If Coke adopts a big promotional budget, Pepsi earns $2 billion by doing the same but only $1 billion by adopting a moderate budget. Thus, if Coke adopts a big budget, so should Pepsi. If Coke adopts a moderate budget, Pepsi earns $4 billion with a big budget and $3 billion with a moderate one. Again, Pepsi earns more with a big budget. Coke faces the same incentives, so both adopt big budgets, earning $2 billion each in profit, even though each would have earned $3 billion with a moderate budget.

The prisoner's dilemma can be used to analyze other business decisions, such as how much to invest in research and development (R&D). Because of the prisoner's dilemma, a firm often ends up investing more in R&D than is optimal for that firm.[20]

20. Rabar Amir et al., "R&D as a Prisoner's Dilemma and R&D-Avoiding Cartels," *The Manchester School,* 79 (January 2011): 81–99.

One-Shot Versus Repeated Games

The outcome of a game often depends on whether it is a *one-shot game* or a *repeated game*. The classic prisoner's dilemma is a one-shot game. If the game is to be played just once, the strategy of confessing makes you better off regardless of what the other player does. Your choice won't influence the other player's behavior. But if the same players repeat the prisoner's dilemma, as would likely occur with the price-setting game, the cola war game, and the OPEC cartel, other possibilities unfold. In a repeated-game setting, each player has a chance to establish a reputation for cooperation and thereby may be able to encourage other players to do the same. After all, the cooperative solution—whether that involves clamming up, maintaining a high price, or adopting a moderate marketing budget—makes both sides better off than if both fail to cooperate.

Experiments have shown that the strategy with the highest payoff in repeated games turns out to be the simplest—**tit-for-tat**. You begin by cooperating in the first round. On every round thereafter, you cooperate if the other player cooperated in the previous round, and you cheat if your opponent cheated in the previous round. In short, in any given round, you do whatever your opponent did in the previous round. The tit-for-tat strategy offers the other player immediate rewards for cooperation and immediate punishment for cheating. Some cartels seem to exhibit tit-for-tat strategies.

Coordination Game

In the **coordination game**, a Nash equilibrium occurs when each player chooses the same strategy. For example, you are driving on a country road and have to decide whether to drive on the right or the left side. Suppose you decide to drive on your left. If the driver coming from the opposite direction also drives on his or her left, you pass each other without incident, so the cost to each of you is zero. But if the other player drives on the right-hand side, the probability of a crash increases. If, instead, you choose to drive on the right-hand side, you encounter no problems if the oncoming driver does the same, but face a greater likelihood of crashing if the other driver chooses the left-hand side. In this game, cost is minimized when both players choose the same strategy. And

tit-for-tat In game theory, a strategy in repeated games when a player in one round of the game mimics the other player's behavior in the previous round; an optimal strategy for getting the other player to cooperate

coordination game A type of game in which a Nash equilibrium occurs when each player chooses the same strategy; neither player can do better than matching the other player's strategy

> **"The prisoner's dilemma shows how difficult a cooperative solution might be even though cooperation benefits all players."**

each strategy is a Nash equilibrium because no player can improve on that outcome, given the other player's choice. So if you choose the left-hand side and the other player chooses his or her left-hand side, then you can do no better and would do worse choosing the right-hand side.

TO REVIEW: Our discussion has given you some idea of game theory by focusing mostly on the prisoner's dilemma. Other games can be more complicated and involve more strategic interaction. Because firms are interdependent, oligopoly gives rise to all kinds of behavior and many approaches. Each approach helps explain certain behavior observed in oligopolistic markets. The *cartel,* or *collusion,* model shows why oligopolists might want to cooperate in fixing the market price; but that model also explains why a cartel is hard to establish and maintain. The *price-leadership* model explains why and how firms may charge the same price without explicitly establishing a formal cartel. Finally, *game theory,* expressed here mostly by the prisoner's dilemma, shows how difficult a cooperative solution might be even though cooperation benefits all players. Game theory is more of an approach to oligopoly than a distinct model. Some sellers are now using online experiments to learn more about market behavior. This could lead to more reliable models of oligopoly.[21]

10-4 COMPARISON OF OLIGOPOLY AND PERFECT COMPETITION

As we have seen, each approach explains a piece of the oligopoly puzzle. But each has limitations, and none provides a complete picture of oligopoly behavior. Because there is no typical, or representative, model of oligopoly, "the" oligopoly model cannot be compared with the competitive model. We might, however, imagine an experiment in which we took the many firms that populate a competitive industry and, through a series of giant mergers, combined them to form, say, four firms. We would thereby transform the industry from perfect competition to oligopoly. How would firms in this industry behave before and after the massive merger?

10-4a Oligopoly Price Is Usually Higher

With fewer competitors after the merger, remaining firms would become more interdependent. Oligopoly models presented in this chapter suggest why firms may try to coordinate their pricing policies. *If oligopolists engaged in some sort of implicit or explicit collusion, industry output would be smaller and the price would be higher than under perfect competition.* Even if oligopolists did not collude but simply operated with excess capacity, the price would be higher and the quantity lower with oligopoly than with perfect competition. The price could become lower temporarily under oligopoly compared with perfect competition if a price war broke out among oligopolists. Two rivals, Intel and Advanced Micro Devices, together account for the entire market for a specific type of computer chip, yet these two are always at each other's throat, thereby keeping prices and profits down. In fact, competition between the two yields an estimated $12 billion a year in consumer surplus.[22] Behavior also depends on whether there are barriers to entry. The lower the barriers to entry into the oligopoly, the more oligopolists act like perfect competitors.

10-4b Oligopoly Profit Is Usually Higher

In the long run, easy entry prevents perfect competitors from earning more than a normal profit. With oligopoly, however, there may be barriers to entry, such as economies of scale or a way to differentiate a product such as with brand names, which allow firms to earn long-run economic profit. *With barriers to entry, we should expect profit in the long run to be higher under oligopoly than under perfect competition.*

© aarrows/Shutterstock.com

21. Liran Einav et al., "Assessing Sales Strategies in Online Markets Using Matched Listings, *American Economic Journal: Microeconomics,* (forthcoming).

22. Ronald Goettler and Brett Gordon, "Does AMD Spur Intel to Innovate More?" *Journal of Political Economy,* 119 (December, 2011): 1141–1200.

Profit rates do in fact appear to be higher in industries where a few firms account for a high proportion of industry sales. Some economists view these higher profit rates as troubling evidence of market power. But not all economists share this view. Some note that the largest firms in oligopolistic industries tend to earn the highest rate of profit. Thus, the higher profit rates observed in oligopolistic industries do not necessarily stem from market power per se. Rather, these higher profit rates stem from the greater efficiency arising from economies of scale in these large firms. An individual firm can also achieve greater market power and higher profit by differentiating its product. For example, hospitals that are more effective at treating heart attacks have higher market shares and are more likely to expand over time.[23]

Exhibit 9

Comparison of Market Structures

	Perfect Competition	Monopoly	Monopolistic Competition	Oligopoly
Number of firms	Most	One	Many	Few
Control over price	None	Complete	Limited	Some
Product differences	None	Only one supplier	Some	None or some
Barriers to entry	None	Insurmountable	Low	Substantial
Number of buyers	Many	Many	Many	Many
Examples	Wheat	Local electricity	Convenience stores	Automobiles

10-5 FINAL WORD

Firms in monopolistic competition and in oligopoly face a downward-sloping demand curve for their products. With monopolistic competition, there are so many firms in the market that each tends to get lost in the crowd. Each behaves independently. But with oligopoly, there are so few firms in the market that each must consider the impact that its quality pricing, output, and marketing decisions will have on other firms. Each oligopolist behaves interdependently, and this makes oligopoly difficult to analyze. As a result, there are different models and approaches to oligopoly, three of which were discussed in this chapter.

The analytical results derived in this chapter are not as clear-cut as for the polar cases of perfect competition and monopoly. Still, we can draw some general conclusions using perfect competition as a guide. In the long run, perfect competitors operate at minimum average cost, while other types of firms (including monopolies) usually operate with excess capacity. Therefore, given identical cost curves, monopolists, monopolistic competitors, and oligopolists tend to charge higher prices than perfect competitors do, especially in the long run. In the long run, monopolistic competitors, like perfect competitors, earn only a normal profit because entry barriers are low. Monopolists and oligopolists can earn economic profit in the long run if new entry is restricted. In a later chapter, we examine government policies aimed at increasing competition. *Regardless of the market structure, however, profit maximization prompts firms to produce where marginal revenue equals marginal cost.*

This chapter has moved us from the extremes of perfect competition and monopoly to the gray area inhabited by most firms. Exhibit 9 compares features and examples of the four market structures. Please take a moment now to review these key distinctions. Some of these issues are revisited later when we explore the government's role in promoting market competition.

STUDY TOOLS 10

READY TO STUDY? IN THE BOOK, YOU CAN:

☐ Work the Problems at the end of the chapter.

☐ Rip out the chapter review card for a handy summary of the chapter and key terms.

ONLINE AT CENGAGEBRAIN.COM YOU CAN:

☐ Collect StudyBits while you read and study the chapter.

☐ Quiz yourself on key concepts.

☐ Prepare for tests with chapter flash cards as well as flash cards that you create.

☐ Watch videos to explore economics further.

23. Amitabh Chandra et al. "Healthcare Exceptionalism? Productivity and Allocation in the U.S. Healthcare Sector," NBER Working Paper No. 19200 (July 2013).

CHAPTER 10 PROBLEMS

Your instructor can access the answers to these problems online at http://cengagebrain.com.

10-1 Outline the monopolistic and competitive elements of monopolistic competition

1. *(Short-Run Profit Maximization)* A monopolistically competitive firm faces the following demand and cost structure in the short run:

Output	Price	FC	VC	TC	TR	Profit/ Loss
0	$100	$100	$0	—	—	—
1	90	—	50	—	—	—
2	80	—	90	—	—	—
3	70	—	150	—	—	—
4	60	—	230	—	—	—
5	50	—	330	—	—	—
6	40	—	450	—	—	—
7	30	—	590	—	—	—

   a. Complete the table.
   b. What is the highest profit or lowest loss available to this firm?
   c. Should this firm operate or shut down in the short run? Why?
   d. What is the relationship between marginal revenue and marginal cost as the firm increases output?

2. *(Monopolistic Competition and Perfect Competition Compared)* Illustrated below are the marginal cost and average total cost curves for a small firm that is in long-run equilibrium.
   a. Locate the long-run equilibrium price and quantity if the firm is perfectly competitive.
   b. Label the price and quantity p_1 and q_1.
   c. Draw in a demand and marginal revenue curve to illustrate long-run equilibrium if the firm is monopolistically competitive. Label the price and quantity p_2 and q_2.
   d. How do the monopolistically competitive firm's price and output compare to those of the perfectly competitive firm?
   e. How do long-run profits compare for the two types of firms?

3. *(Characteristics of Monopolistic Competition)* Why is a firm in monopolistic competition said to be competitive? In what sense is that firm monopolistic?

10-2 Describe the sources of oligopoly and explain why some industries become oligopolies

4. *(Oligopoly Power)* What are three sources of oligopolies?
5. *(Varieties of Oligopolies)* Do the firms in an oligopoly act independently or interdependently? Explain your answer.

10-3 Explain why predicting oligopoly behavior is so difficult

6. *(Price Leadership)* Why might a price-leadership model of oligopoly not be an effective means of collusion in an oligopoly?
7. *(Collusion and Cartels)* Why would each of the following induce some members of OPEC to cheat on their cartel agreement?
   a. Newly joined cartel members are less-developed countries.
   b. The number of cartel members doubles from 12 to 24.
   c. International debts of some members grow.
   d. Expectations grow that some members will cheat.
8. *(Collusion and Cartels)* Use revenue and cost curves to illustrate and explain the sense in which a cartel behaves like a monopolist.
9. *(Game Theory)* Suppose there are only two automobile companies, Ford and Chevrolet. Ford believes that Chevrolet will match any price it sets, but Chevrolet too is interested in maximizing profit. Use the following price and profit data to answer the following questions.

Ford's Selling Price	Chevrolet's Selling Price	Ford's Profits (millions)	Chevrolet's Profits (millions)
$ 4,000	$ 4,000	$ 8	$ 8
4,000	8,000	12	6
4,000	12,000	14	2
8,000	4,000	6	12
8,000	8,000	10	10
8,000	12,000	12	6
12,000	4,000	2	14
12,000	8,000	6	12
12,000	12,000	7	7

   a. What price will Ford charge?
   b. What price will Chevrolet charge once Ford has set its price?
   c. What is Ford's profit after Chevrolet's response?
   d. If the two firms collaborated to maximize joint profits, what prices would they set?

e. Given your answer to part (d), how could undetected cheating on price cause the cheating firm's profit to rise?

10. *(Game Theory)* While grading a final exam, an economics professor discovers that two students have virtually identical answers. She is convinced the two cheated but cannot prove it. The professor speaks with each student separately and offers the following deal: Sign a statement admitting to cheating. If both students sign the statement, each will receive an "F" for the course. If only one signs, he is allowed to withdraw from the course while the other student is expelled. If neither signs, both receive a "C" because the professor does not have sufficient evidence to prove cheating.
   a. Draw the payoff matrix.
   b. Which outcome do you expect? Why?

11. *(Oligopoly Behavior)* Why is firm behavior under oligopoly so difficult to predict?

10-4 Summarize the similarities and differences between an oligopoly and perfect competition in terms of price, output, and long-run profitability

12. *(Market Structures)* Determine whether each of the following is a characteristic of perfect competition, monopolistic competition, oligopoly, and/or monopoly:
    a. A large number of sellers
    b. Product is a commodity
    c. Advertising by firms
    d. Barriers to entry
    e. Firms are price makers

11 | Resource Markets

© Richard Cavalleri/Shutterstock.com

LEARNING OUTCOMES

After studying this chapter, you will be able to…

11-1 Determine the profit-maximizing number of workers for a firm to hire

11-2 Explain why resource owners are more willing and more able to increase the quantity supplied of the resources they own as resource prices increase

11-3 Explain why some resource price differences are temporary while others are permanent

11-4 Clarify the distinction between a resource's opportunity cost and its economic rent

11-5 Describe the economic logic of optimal resource use

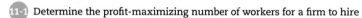

After finishing this chapter go to **PAGE 193** for **STUDY TOOLS**

Topics discussed in Chapter 11 include:

- Demand and supply of resources
- Opportunity cost and economic rent
- Marginal revenue product
- Marginal resource cost
- Changes in resource demand
- Optimal resource use

- Why do truck drivers in the United States earn at least 20 times more than bicycle-rickshaw drivers in India?

- Why do surgeons earn twice as much as general practitioners?

- Why does prime Iowa corn acreage cost more than scrubland in the high plains of Montana?

- Why might a broadband Internet connection boost some wages and depress others?

- Why are buildings in downtown Chicago taller than those in the suburbs and taller than those in downtown Phoenix?

- How might higher gas prices reduce obesity?

To answer these and other questions, we turn to the demand and supply of resources.

You say you've been through this demand-and-supply drill already? True. But the earlier focus was on product markets—that is, on markets for final goods and services. Goods and services are produced by resources—labor, capital, natural resources, and entrepreneurial ability. Demand and supply in resource markets determine the price and quantity of resources. And the ownership of resources determines the distribution of earnings throughout the economy.

> **"Why are buildings in downtown Chicago taller than those in the suburbs?"**

Because your earnings depend on the market value of your resources, you should find this chapter on resource markets particularly relevant to your future. Certainly, one consideration in your career choice is the expected earnings associated with alternative careers. The next three chapters examine how demand and supply interact to establish market prices for various resources.

11-1 THE ONCE-OVER

Just to prove you already know more about resource markets than you may think, try answering the questions that arise in the following examples of resource demand and supply.

11-1a Resource Demand

Let's begin with the demand for labor. The manager of Target estimates that hiring another sales clerk would increase total revenue by $500 per week but increase total cost by $400 per week. Should Target hire another sales clerk? Sure, because profit would increase by $100 per week. *As long as the additional revenue from employing another worker exceeds the additional cost, the firm should hire that worker.*

What about capital? Suppose that you run a lawn service during the summer, getting an average of $50 per lawn. You have all the business you can handle. You mow about 15 lawns a week, for total revenue of $750 a week. You are thinking of upgrading to a larger, faster mower

> **"A producer demands another unit of a resource as long as its marginal revenue exceeds its marginal cost."**

called the Lawn Monster, but it would cost you an extra $500 per week. The bigger mower would cut your time per lawn in half, enabling you to mow 30 lawns per week, so your total revenue would double to $1,500. Should you make the switch? Because the additional revenue of $750 exceeds the additional cost of $500, you should move up to the Monster.

What about natural resources? A neighbor offers Farmer Jones the chance to lease 100 acres of farmland. Jones figures that farming the extra land would cost $70 per acre but would yield $60 per acre in additional revenue. Should Jones lease the extra land?

What do you think? Because the additional cost of farming that land would exceed the additional revenue, the answer is no.

These examples show that a *producer demands another unit of a resource as long as its marginal revenue exceeds its marginal cost.*

11-1b Resource Supply

You likely also understand the logic behind resource supply. Suppose you are trying to decide between two jobs that are identical in all ways except that one pays more than the other. Is there any question which one you'll take? If the working conditions are equally attractive, you would choose the higher-paying job. Now let's say your choice is between two jobs that pay the same. One has normal 9-to-5 hours, but the other starts at 5 a.m., an hour when your body tends to reject conscious activity. Which would you choose? You would pick the one that suited your tastes.

> **❝People supply their resources to the highest-paying alternative, other things constant.❞**

People supply their resources to the highest-paying alternative, other things constant. Because other things are not always constant, people must be paid more for jobs less suited to their tastes. Your utility depends on both monetary and nonmonetary aspects of the job. Most people must be paid more for jobs that are dirty, dangerous, dull, exhausting, illegal, low status, have no future, have no benefits, or involve inconvenient hours than for jobs that are clean, safe, interesting, energizing, legal, high status, have bright prospects, have good benefits, or involve convenient hours.

11-2 DEMAND AND SUPPLY OF RESOURCES

In markets for goods and services—that is, in product markets—households are the demanders and firms are the suppliers. Households demand the goods and services that maximize utility, and firms supply the goods and services that maximize profit. In resource markets, roles are reversed: Firms are demanders and households are suppliers. Firms demand the resources that maximize profit, and households supply the resources that maximize utility. *Any differences between the profit-maximizing goals of firms and the utility-maximizing goals of households are sorted out through voluntary exchange in resource markets.*

Exhibit 1 presents the market for a particular resource—in this case, carpenters. As you can see, the demand curve slopes downward and the supply curve slopes upward. *Like the demand and supply for final goods and services, the demand and supply for resources depend*

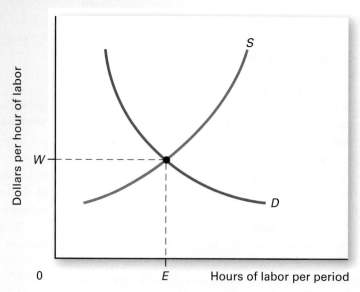

Exhibit 1

Resource Market for Carpenters

The intersection of the upward-sloping supply curve of carpenters with the downward-sloping demand curve for carpenters determines their equilibrium wage, *W*, and their level of employment, *E*.

on the willingness and ability of buyers and sellers to engage in market exchange. This market converges to the equilibrium wage, or the market price, for this type of labor.

11-2a Market Demand for Resources

Why do firms employ resources? Resources produce goods and services, which firms try to sell for a profit. A firm values not the resource itself but the resource's ability to produce goods and services. Because the value of any resource depends on the value of what it produces, the demand for a resource is said to be a **derived demand**—arising from the demand for the final product. For example, a carpenter's pay derives from the demand for the carpenter's output, such as a kitchen cabinet or a new deck. A professional baseball player's pay derives from the public's demand for ballgames. A truck driver's pay derives from the demand for transporting goods. A teacher's pay derives from the marginal value of student learning. The derived nature of resource demand helps explain why professional baseball players usually earn more than professional hockey players, why surgeons earn more than general practitioners, and why drivers of big rigs earn more than drivers. Derived demand also explains why, in the face of an industry-wide slump in box-office sales, Hollywood stars like Tom Cruise, Brad Pitt, and Cameron Diaz accepted pay cuts.

The market demand curve for a particular resource is the sums horizontally the demand curves for that resource in all its different uses. For example, the market demand for carpenters adds together the demands for carpenters in residential and commercial construction, remodeling, cabinetmaking, and so on. Similarly, the market demand for timber sums the demand for this resource as lumber, railway ties, furniture, pencils, toothpicks, paper products, firewood, and so on. The demand curve for a resource, like the demand for the goods produced by that resource, slopes downward, as depicted in Exhibit 1.

As the price of a resource falls, producers are more willing and able to employ that resource. Consider first the producer's greater *willingness* to hire resources as the resource price falls. In developing the demand curve for a particular resource, we assume the prices of other resources remain constant. So if the price of a particular resource falls, it becomes cheaper compared with other resources that could produce the same output. Firms therefore are more willing to hire this resource rather than hire other, now relatively more costly, resources. Thus, we observe *substitution in production*—carpenters for masons, coal for oil, security alarms for security guards, and backhoes for grave diggers, as the relative prices of carpenters, coal, security alarms, and backhoes fall.

A lower price for a resource also increases a producer's *ability* to hire that resource. For example, if the wage of carpenters falls, home builders can hire more carpenters for the same total cost. The lower resource price means the firm is *more able* to employ the resource.

11-2b Market Supply of Resources

The market supply curve for a resource sums horizontally all the individual supply curves for that resource. Resource suppliers are more *willing* and more *able* to increase quantity supplied as the resource price increases, so the market supply curve slopes upward, as in Exhibit 1. Resource suppliers are more *willing* because a higher resource price, other things constant, means more goods and services can be purchased with the earnings from each unit of the resource supplied. Resource prices are signals about the rewards for supplying resources. A high resource price tells the resource owner, "The market will reward you more for what you supply." Higher prices draw resources from lower-valued uses, including leisure. For example, as the wage for carpenters increases, other things constant, the quantity of labor supplied increases. Some carpenters give up leisure to work more.

The second reason a resource supply curve slopes upward is that resource owners are more *able* to increase the quantity supplied as the resource price increases. For example, a higher carpenter's wage means more apprentices can afford to undergo the extensive training to become carpenters. A higher wage *enables* resource suppliers to increase their quantity supplied. Similarly, a higher timber price enables loggers to harvest trees in less accessible forests, a higher gold price enables miners to extract the metal from lower-grade ore or from mines three miles above sea level in the Peruvian Andes[1], and a higher oil price enables producers to drill deeper, to explore more remote parts of the world, and to squeeze oil from tar sands that contain less oil.

11-3 TEMPORARY AND PERMANENT RESOURCE PRICE DIFFERENCES

People have a strong interest in selling their resources to the highest bidder, other things constant. *Resources tend to flow to their highest-valued use.* If, for example, carpenters can earn more building

1. William Finnegan, "Tears of the Sun: The Gold Rush at the Top of the World," *The New Yorker*, 20 April 2015, p. 56.

derived demand
Resource demand that arises from the demand for the product the resource produces

The demand for carpenters is derived from the demand for new houses.

homes than making furniture, and if the two activities are otherwise equally attractive (or unattractive) to carpenters, they will move out of furniture making and into home building until wages in the two uses are equal. Because resource owners seek the highest pay, *other things constant*, earnings should tend toward equality for different uses of the same type of resource. For example, suppose carpenters who build homes earn $25 per hour, which is $5 more than carpenters who make furniture. This difference is shown in Exhibit 2 by an initial wage of $25 per hour in panel (a) and an initial wage of $20 per hour in panel (b). This gap encourages some carpenters to move from furniture making into home building, pulling up the wage in furniture making and driving down the wage in home building. Carpenters migrate into home building until wages equalize. In Exhibit 2, labor supply shifts leftward for furniture making and rightward for home building until the wage reaches $24 in both markets. Note that 2,000 hours of labor per day shift from furniture making to home building. *As long as the nonmonetary aspects of supplying resources to alternative uses are identical and as long as resources are freely mobile, resources adjust across uses until they earn the same in different uses.*

Sometimes earnings appear to differ for seemingly similar resources. For example, corporate economists on average earn more than academic economists, and land in the city goes for more than land in the country. As you

will now see, these pay differences also reflect the workings of demand and supply.

11-3a Temporary Differences

Resource prices might differ temporarily across markets because adjustment takes time. As you have seen, however, a difference between the prices of similar resources prompts resource owners and firms to make adjustments that drive resource prices toward equality, as with the carpenters in Exhibit 2. The process may take years, but when resource markets are free to adjust, price differences trigger the reallocation of resources, which equalizes earnings for similar resources.

11-3b Permanent Differences

Not all resource price differences cause reallocation. For example, for the price of a square yard of land along New York's Fifth Avenue you could buy several acres of land in Upstate New York. Yet such a difference does not prompt upstaters to supply their land to New York City—obviously that's impossible. Likewise, the price of farmland varies widely, reflecting differences in the land's fertility and location. Such differences do not trigger shifts of resource supply. Similarly, certain wage differentials stem in part from the different costs of acquiring the education and training needed to perform particular tasks. This difference explains why brain surgeons earn more than general practitioners, why ophthalmologists earn more than optometrists, and why airline pilots earn more than truck drivers.

Differences in the nonmonetary aspects of similar jobs also lead to pay differences. For example, other things constant, most people would require higher pay to work in a noisy, grimy factory than in a pleasant office. Similarly, academic economists earn less than corporate economists, in part because academic economists typically have more freedom in their daily schedules, their attire, their choices of research topics, and even in their public statements.

Some price differences are temporary because they spark shifts of resource supply away from lower-paid uses and toward higher-paid uses. Other price differences cause no such shifts and are permanent. Permanent price differences are explained by *a lack of resource mobility* (urban land vs. rural land), *differences in the inherent quality of the resource* (fertile land vs. scrubland), *differences in the time and money involved in developing the necessary skills* (certified public accountant vs. file clerk), or *differences in nonmonetary aspects of the job* (lifeguard at Malibu Beach vs. prison guard at San Quentin).

Exhibit 2

Market for Carpenters in Alternative Uses

Suppose initially the hourly wage of carpenters is $25 in the home-building market but only $20 in the furniture-making market, and suppose also that carpenters view the jobs as equally attractive (or unattractive), aside from the wage. This wage differential prompts some carpenters to shift from furniture making to home building until the wage is identical in the two markets. In panel (b), the reduction of labor supplied to furniture making increases the market wage from $20 to $24. In panel (a), the increase of labor supplied to home building reduces the market wage from $25 to $24. Note that 2,000 carpenter-hours per day shift from furniture making to home building.

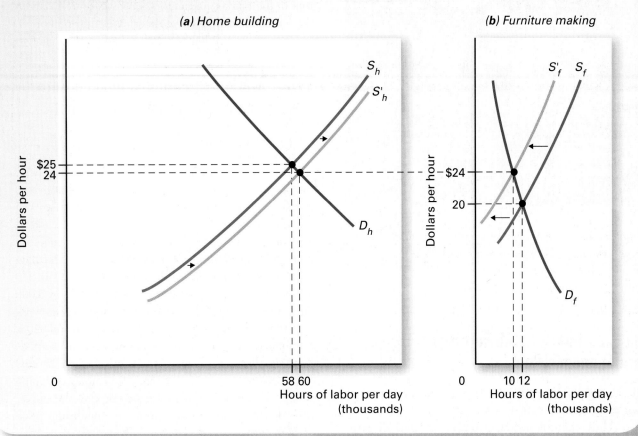

(a) Home building   *(b)* Furniture making

11-4 OPPORTUNITY COST AND ECONOMIC RENT

LeBron James earned about $21 million during the season ending in 2015 playing professional basketball plus an estimated $44 million that year from product endorsements around the world.[2] But he would probably have been willing to play basketball and endorse products for less. The question is, how much less? What was his best alternative? Suppose his best alternative was to sell Rolls-Royces in Beverly Hills, where he could expect to earn $500,000 a year in commissions. And suppose, aside from the pay gap, he was indifferent between car sales and continuing to play basketball and endorse products, so the nonmonetary aspects of the jobs evened out. Thus, he had to be paid at least $500,000 a year to play basketball and endorse products and this represents his opportunity cost. *Opportunity cost is what that resource could earn in its best alternative use.*

The amount James earned in excess of his opportunity cost is called *economic rent*. **Economic rent** is that portion of a resource's earnings that exceeds the amount needed to keep the resource in its present use. Economic rent is, as the saying goes, "pure gravy." In LeBron's case, economic rent was $64.5 million in 2015. Economic rent is producer surplus earned by resource suppliers. The *division* of earnings between opportunity cost and economic rent depends on the

> **economic rent** Portion of a resource's earnings that exceeds its opportunity cost

2. Kurt Badenhausen, "LeBron James Leads the NBA's Endorsement All-Stars 2015," *Forbes*, 13 February 2015, at http://www.forbes.com/sites/kurtbadenhausen/2015/02/13/lebron-james-leads-the-nbas-endorsement-all-stars-2015/.

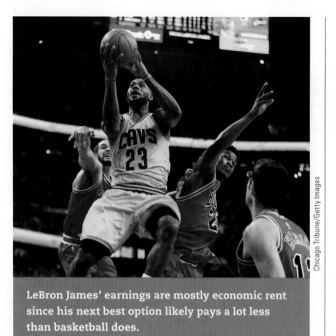

Chicago Tribune/Getty Images

LeBron James' earnings are mostly economic rent since his next best option likely pays a lot less than basketball does.

resource owner's elasticity of supply. *In general, the less elastic the resource supply, the greater the economic rent as a proportion of total earnings.* To develop a feel for the difference between opportunity cost and economic rent, let's consider three resource markets.

11-4a Market A: All Earnings are Economic Rent

If the supply of a resource to a particular market is perfectly inelastic, that resource has no alternative use. Thus, there is no opportunity cost, and all earnings are economic rent. For example, scrubland in the high plains of Montana has no use other than for grazing cattle. The supply of this land is depicted by the red vertical line in panel (a) of Exhibit 3, which indicates that the 10 million acres have no alternative use. Because supply is fixed, the rent paid to graze cattle on this land has no effect on the quantity of land supplied for cattle grazing. *The land's opportunity cost is zero, so all earnings are economic rent, shown by the blue-shaded area.* Here, fixed supply determines the equilibrium quantity of the resource, but demand determines the equilibrium price.

11-4b Market B: All Earnings are Opportunity Cost

At the other extreme is the market in which a resource can earn as much in its best alternative use as in its present use. This situation is illustrated by the perfectly

elastic supply curve in panel (b) of Exhibit 3, which shows the market for janitors in the local school system. Here, janitors earn \$15 an hour and supply 1,000 hours of labor per day. If the school system paid less than \$15 per hour, janitors could find jobs elsewhere, perhaps in nearby factories, where the wage is \$15 per hour. *All earnings reflect opportunity cost.* There is no economic rent in the market for janitors. In this resource market, the horizontal supply curve determines the equilibrium wage, but demand determines the equilibrium quantity.

11-4c Market C: Earnings Include Both Economic Rent and Opportunity Cost

If the supply curve slopes upward, most resource suppliers earn economic rent in addition to their opportunity cost. For example, if the market wage for unskilled work in your college community increases from \$10 to \$20 per hour, the quantity of labor supplied would increase, as would the economic rent earned by these workers. This market occurs in panel (c) of Exhibit 3, where the pink shading identifies opportunity cost and the blue shading, economic rent. If the wage increases from \$10 to \$20 per hour, the quantity supplied increases by 5,000 hours per day. For those who had been willing to work for \$10 per hour, the difference between \$10 and \$20 is economic rent. *When resource supply slopes upward, as it usually does, earnings consist of both opportunity cost and economic rent.* In the case of an upward-sloping supply curve and a downward-sloping demand curve, both demand and supply determine equilibrium price and quantity.

Note that specialized resources tend to earn a higher proportion of economic rent than do resources with alternative uses. Thus, LeBron James earned a greater *proportion* of his income as economic rent than did the janitor who cleaned the team's locker room. James would have taken a huge pay cut if he didn't play professional basketball and endorse products, but the janitor could probably have found another job that paid nearly the same.

TO REVIEW: Given a resource demand curve that slopes downward, when the resource supply curve is vertical (perfectly inelastic), all earnings are economic rent; when that supply curve is horizontal (perfectly elastic), all earnings are opportunity cost; and when that supply curve slopes upward (an elasticity greater than zero but less than infinity), earnings divide between economic rent and opportunity cost. Remember, *the opportunity cost of a resource is what that resource could earn in its best alternative use. Economic rent is earnings in excess*

Exhibit 3
Opportunity Cost and Economic Rent

In panel (a), the resource supply curve is vertical, indicating that the resource has no alternative use. The price is demand-determined, and all earnings are economic rent (blue-shaded area). In panel (b), the resource supply curve is horizontal at $15 per hour, indicating that the resource can also earn that much in its best alternative use. Employment is demand-determined, and all earnings are opportunity cost (pink-shaded area). Panel (c) shows an upward-sloping resource supply curve. Earnings are partly opportunity cost and partly economic rent (blue-shaded area). Both demand and supply determine the equilibrium price and quantity.

(a) All earnings are economic rent

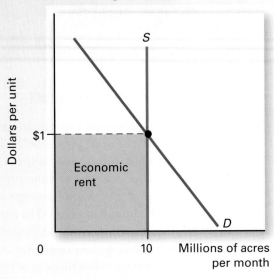

(b) All earnings are opportunity cost

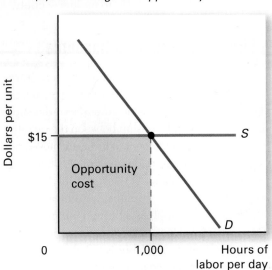

(c) Earnings divide between economic rent and opportunity cost

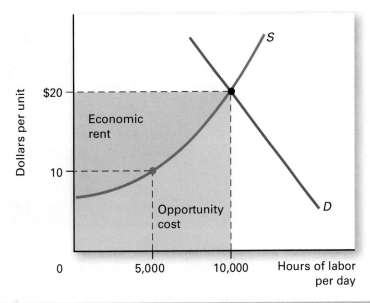

of opportunity cost. Economic rent to a resource holder is like economic profit to the firm.

This completes our introduction to resource demand and supply. In the balance of the chapter, we take a closer look at resource demand. The determinants of resource demand are largely the same whether we are talking about labor, capital, or natural resources. The supply of different resources, however, has certain peculiarities depending on the resource, so the supply of resources is taken up in the next chapter.

11-5 A CLOSER LOOK AT RESOURCE DEMAND

Although production usually involves many resources, we cut the analysis down to size by focusing on a single resource, assuming that employment of other resources remains constant. As usual, we assume that firms try to maximize profit and households try to maximize utility.

11-5a Firm's Demand for a Resource

You may recall that when production costs were introduced in Chapter 7, we considered a moving company, where labor was the only variable resource in the short run. We examined the relationship between the quantity of labor employed and the amount of furniture moved per day. The same approach is used in Exhibit 4, where only one resource varies. Column (1) lists possible employment levels of the variable resource, here measured as workers per day. Column (2) lists the amount produced, or total product, and column (3) lists the marginal product. The *marginal product* of labor is the change in total product from employing one more unit of labor.

With only one worker, total product is 10 units as is the marginal product. The marginal product of a second worker is 9 units. Notice in this example that diminishing marginal returns set in immediately—that is, right after the first worker.

Although labor is the variable resource here, we could examine the marginal product of any resource. For example, we could consider the number of lawns cut per week by varying the quantity of capital. We might start off with very little capital—imagine cutting grass with scissors—and then move up to a push mower, a power mower, and the Lawn Monster. By holding labor constant and varying the quantity of capital employed, we could compute the marginal product of capital. Likewise, we could compute the marginal product of natural resources by examining crop production for varying amounts of farmland, holding other inputs constant.

marginal revenue product The change in total revenue when an additional unit of a resource is employed, other things constant

Simon Potter/Image Source

11-5b Marginal Revenue Product

The important question is: what happens to the firm's *revenue* when additional workers are hired? The first three columns of Exhibit 4 show how output changes with more workers. The *marginal revenue product* of labor indicates how much total revenue changes as more labor is employed, other things constant. The **marginal revenue product** of any resource is the change in the firm's total revenue resulting from employing an additional unit of the resource, other things constant. You could think of the marginal revenue product as the firm's "marginal benefit" from hiring one more unit of

Exhibit 4

Marginal Revenue Product When a Firm Sells in a Competitive Market

Because of diminishing marginal returns, the marginal product of labor declines as more is employed, as shown in column (3). Because this firm sells its product in a competitive market, it can sell all it wants at the market price of $20 per unit, as shown in column (4). The marginal product of labor in column (3) times the product price of $20 in column (4) yields the marginal revenue product of labor in column (6). Labor's marginal revenue product is the change in total revenue as a result of hiring another unit of labor.

(1) Workers per Day	(2) Total Product	(3) Marginal Product	(4) Product Price	(5) Total Revenue (5) = (2) × (4)	(6) Marginal Revenue Product (6) = (3) × (4)
0	0	—	$20	$ 0	—
1	10	10	20	200	$200
2	19	9	20	380	180
3	27	8	20	540	160
4	34	7	20	680	140
5	40	6	20	800	120
6	45	5	20	900	100
7	49	4	20	980	80
8	52	3	20	1040	60

the resource. *Marginal revenue product depends on how much additional output the resource produces and at what price that output is sold.*

Selling Output in Competitive Markets

The calculation of marginal revenue product is simplest when the firm sells in a perfectly competitive market, which is the assumption underlying Exhibit 4. An individual firm in perfect competition can sell as much as it wants at the market price. The marginal revenue product, listed in column (6) of Exhibit 4, is the change in total revenue from hiring an additional unit of the resource. For the perfectly competitive firm, the marginal revenue product is simply the marginal product of the resource multiplied by the product price of $20. Notice that because of diminishing returns, the marginal revenue product falls steadily as the firm employs more of the resource.

Selling Output With Some Market Power

If the firm has some power in the product market—that is, some ability to set the price—the demand curve for that firm's output slopes downward. To sell more, the firm must lower its price. Exhibit 5 reproduces the first two columns of Exhibit 4. But column (3) now shows the

Exhibit 5

The Marginal Revenue Product When a Firm Sells with Market Power

To sell more, a firm with market power must lower the price, as indicated in column (3). Total revenue in column (4) equals total product in column (2) times the product price in column (3). Labor's marginal revenue product in column (5) equals the change in total revenue from hiring another worker. The marginal revenue product declines both because of diminishing marginal returns from labor and because the product price must fall to sell more.

(1) Workers per Day	(2) Total Product	(3) Product Price	(4) Total Revenue (4) = (2) × (3)	(5) Marginal Revenue Product
0	0	—	—	—
1	10	$40	$400	$400
2	19	35	665	265
3	27	31	837	172
4	34	28	952	115
5	40	25	1000	48
6	45	23	1035	35
7	49	21	1029	−6
8	52	19	988	−41

price at which that output can be sold. Total output multiplied by the price yields the firm's total revenue, which appears in column (4).

The marginal revenue product of labor, which is the change in total revenue from adding another worker, appears in column (5). For example, the first worker produced 10 units per day, which sell for $40 each, yielding total revenue and marginal revenue of $400. Hiring the second worker adds 9 more units to total product, but to sell 9 more units, the firm must lower the price from $40 to $35. Total revenue increases to $665, which means the marginal revenue product from hiring a second worker is $265. *For firms selling with some market power, the marginal revenue product curve slopes downward both because of diminishing marginal returns and because additional output can be sold only if the price falls.* A profit-maximizing firm is willing and able to pay as much as the marginal revenue product for an additional unit of the resource. Thus, *the marginal revenue product curve can be thought of as the firm's demand curve for that resource.* You could think of the marginal revenue product curve as the marginal benefit to the firm of hiring each additional unit of the resource. As one example, the marginal revenue product of a top college football player, each of whom would later be drafted into the National Football League, has been estimated to exceed $1 million a year in football revenue for his college.[3]

TO REVIEW: Whether a firm sells its product in a competitive market or sells with some market power, the marginal revenue product of a resource is the change in total revenue resulting from a 1-unit change in that resource, other things constant. The marginal revenue product curve of a resource is also the demand curve for that resource—it shows the most a firm would be willing and able to pay for each additional unit of the resource. For firms selling in competitive markets, the marginal revenue product curve slopes downward only because of diminishing marginal returns to the resource. For firms selling with some market power, the marginal revenue product curve slopes downward both because of diminishing marginal returns and because additional output can be sold only if the price falls. *For all types of firms, the marginal revenue product is the change in total revenue resulting from hiring an additional unit of the resource.*

11-5c Marginal Resource Cost

If we know a firm's marginal revenue product, can we determine how much labor that firm should employ to maximize profit? Not yet, because we also need to know

3. Robert Brown, "Research Note: Estimates of College Football Player Rents," *Journal of Sports Economics*, 12 (April 2011): 200–212.

Exhibit 6

Market Equilibrium for a Resource and the Firm's Employment Decision

Market demand and supply of a resource, in panel (a), determine that resource's market wage and quantity. In panel (b), an individual firm can employ as much as it wants at the market wage, so that wage becomes the firm's marginal resource cost curve. The marginal resource cost curve also is the supply curve of that resource to the firm. In panel (b), a resource's marginal revenue product is the firm's demand curve for that resource. The firm maximizes any profit (or minimizes any loss) by hiring a resource up to the point where the resource's marginal revenue product equals its marginal resource cost, which is six workers per day in this example.

(a) Market

(b) Firm

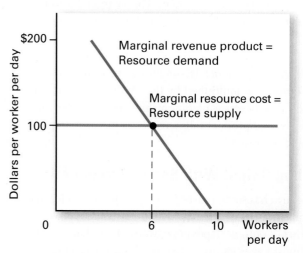

how much labor costs the firm. Specifically, what is the **marginal resource cost**—what does another unit of labor cost the firm? The typical firm hires such a tiny fraction of the market supply that the firm's hiring decision has no effect on the market price of the resource. Thus, each firm usually faces a given market price for the resource and decides only on how much to hire at that price.

For example, panel (a) of Exhibit 6 shows the market for factory workers, measured as workers per day. The intersection of market demand and market supply determines the market wage of $100 per day. Panel (b) shows the situation for the firm. The market wage becomes the firm's marginal resource cost of labor. The *marginal resource cost* curve is the horizontal line drawn at the $100 level in panel (b); this is the labor supply curve to the firm. Panel (b) also shows the marginal revenue product curve, or resource demand curve, based on the schedule presented in Exhibit 4. The marginal revenue product curve indicates the additional revenue the firm gets from adding another worker.

marginal resource cost
The change in total cost when an additional unit of a resource is hired, other things constant

11-5d Maximizing Profit or Minimizing Loss

Given a marginal resource cost of $100 per worker per day, how much labor should the firm employ to maximize profit? *The firm hires more labor as long as doing so adds more to revenue than to cost—that is, as long as labor's marginal revenue product exceeds its marginal resource cost. The firm stops adding labor once the two are equal.* If marginal resource cost is a constant $100 per worker, the firm hires six workers per day because the marginal revenue product from hiring a sixth worker equals $100. Thus, the firm hires additional workers until

Marginal revenue product = Marginal resource cost

This equality holds for all types of resources employed, whether the firm sells in perfectly competitive markets or sells with some market power. Profit maximization occurs where labor's marginal revenue product equals the market wage. Based on data presented so far, we can't yet determine the firm's actual profit because we don't yet know about the firm's other costs. We do know, however, that in Exhibit 6, a seventh worker would add

$100 to cost but would add less than that to revenue, so hiring a seventh worker would reduce the firm's profit (or increase any loss).

Whether a firm sells in competitive markets or with some market power, the profit-maximizing level of employment occurs where the marginal revenue product of labor equals its marginal resource cost. Similarly, profit-maximizing employment of other resources, such as natural resources or capital, occurs where their respective marginal revenue products equal their marginal resource costs. Each unit of a resource must "pull its own weight"—that is, each unit must bring in additional revenue that at least covers its additional cost.

> **"The profit-maximizing level of employment occurs where the marginal revenue product of labor equals its marginal resource cost."**

11-5e Optimal Input and Optimal Output Decisions

In earlier chapters, you learned how to find the profit-maximizing level of output. Maximum profit (or minimum loss) occurs where the marginal revenue from

output equals its marginal cost. Likewise, maximum profit (or minimum loss) occurs where the marginal revenue from an *input* equals its marginal cost. The two approaches are equivalent ways of deriving the same principle of profit maximization. For example, in Exhibit 6, the firm maximizes profit by hiring six workers when the market wage is $100 per day. Exhibit 4 indicates that a sixth worker adds 5 units to output, which sell for $20 each, yielding labor's marginal revenue product of $100. The *marginal revenue* of that output is the change in total revenue from selling another unit of output, which is $20. The *marginal cost* of that output is the change in total cost, $100, divided by the change in output, 5 units; so the marginal cost of output is $100/5, or $20. Thus, *in equilibrium, the marginal revenue of output equals its marginal cost.* Now that you have some idea of how to derive the demand for a resource, let's discuss what could shift the resource demand curve.

11-5f Changes in Resource Demand

As we have seen, a resource's marginal revenue product depends on the resource's marginal product and the price at which that product is sold. Two things can change a resource's marginal product: (1) a change in the amount of other resources employed and (2) a change in technology. Only one thing can change the price of the product: a change in demand for the product. Let's consider first changes that could affect marginal product, then changes that could affect demand for the product.

Change in Other Resources Employed

Although our focus so far has been on a single input, in reality the marginal product of any resource depends on the quantity and quality of other resources used in production. Sometimes resources are *substitutes*. For example, coal substitutes for oil in generating electricity. And ATMs substitute for tellers in handling bank transactions. If two resources are **substitutes**, an increase in the price of one increases the demand for the other. An increase in the price of oil increases the demand for coal, and an increase in the market wage of tellers increases the demand for ATMs.

Sometimes resources are *complements*—trucks and truck drivers, for example. If two resources are **complements**, a decrease in the price of one leads to an increase in the demand for the other. If the price of tractor-trailers decreases, the quantity demanded increases, which increases the demand for truck drivers. More generally, any increase in the quantity and quality of a complementary resource, such as trucks, raises the marginal productivity of the resource in question, such as truck drivers, and so increases the demand for that resource. A bigger and better truck makes the driver more productive. One big reason a truck driver in the United States earns much more than a bicycle-rickshaw driver in India is the truck. And sometimes the same resource can complement or substitute for another resource, depending on resource quality. For example, recent research suggests that a broadband Internet connection complement skilled labor but substitutes for unskilled labor. A broadband connection helps skilled workers execute non-routine abstract reasoning, but substitutes for the routine tasks of unskilled workers.[4]

Changes in Technology

Technological improvements can boost the productivity of some resources but make other resources obsolete.

The introduction of computer-controlled machines increased the demand for computer-trained machinists but reduced the demand for machinists without computer skills. The development of synthetic fibers, such as rayon and Orlon, increased

resource substitutes
Resources that substitute in production; an increase in the price of one resource increases the demand for the other

resource complements
Resources that enhance one another's productivity; a decrease in the price of one resource increases the demand for the other

the demand for acrylics and polyesters but reduced the demand for natural fibers, such as cotton and wool. Breakthroughs in fiber-optic and satellite telecommunications increased the demand for fiberglass and satellites and reduced the demand for copper wire. Widespread adoption of HDTV increased the demand for broadcasters with clear complexions and reduced the demand for other broadcasters.

Computer programs are changing job prospects in fields such as law, medicine, accounting, and architecture. For example, Quicken's WillMaker software has written more wills than any lawyer alive. In medicine, software such as 5-Minute Clinical Consult is available on smartphones to help doctors diagnose more than a thousand medical and surgical conditions. In accounting, software such as TurboTax completes tax forms with ease. And in architecture, three-dimensional modeling programs such as Home Designer help configure all aspects of a structure. As software and hardware get cheaper, better, and easier to use, the demand for some professional services declines. Incidentally, when technology erodes the value of human capital, older workers are more likely to retire than to retrain.[5]

Changes in the Demand for the Final Product

Because the demand for a resource is *derived* from the demand for the final output, any change in the demand for output affects resource demand. For example, the growing popularity of cable news networks and online news sites has reduced the demand for newsprint, which has fallen 60 percent since 2001. And an increase in the price of gasoline reduced the demand for activities that usually require transportation, such as restaurant visits. (Incidentally, and somewhat off the point, one recent study found that higher gas prices reduced the incidence of obesity, apparently because of fewer restaurant trips and more walking instead of driving.)[6]

TO REVIEW: The demand for a resource depends on its marginal revenue product, which is the change in total revenue resulting from employing one more unit of the resource. Any change that increases a resource's marginal revenue product increases that resource's demand.

4. Anders Akerman, Ingvil Gaarder, and Magne Mogstad, "The Skill Complementarity of Broadband Internet," *Quarterly Journal of Economics* (forthcoming).

5. Avner Ahituv and Joseph Zeira, "Technical Progress and Early Retirement," *Economic Journal*, 121 (March 2011): 171–193.

6. Charles Courtemanche, "A Silver Lining? The Connection between Gasoline Prices and Obesity," *Economic Inquiry*, 49 (July 2011): 935–957.

11-5g Optimal Use of More Than One Resource

As long as marginal revenue product exceeds marginal resource cost, a firm can increase any profit or reduce any loss by employing more of that resource. Again, the firm hires more of a resource until the marginal revenue product just equals the marginal resource cost. This principle holds for each resource employed. One of the questions at the beginning of this chapter asked why buildings in downtown Chicago are taller than those in the suburbs. Land and capital, to a large extent, substitute in the production of building space. Because land is more expensive downtown than in the suburbs, builders downtown substitute capital for land, building *up* instead of *out*. Hence, buildings are taller closer to the center of the city and are tallest in cities where land is most expensive. Buildings in Chicago and New York City, for example, are taller than those in Salt Lake City and Phoenix.

The high price of land in metropolitan areas has other implications for the efficient use of resources. For example, in New York City, as in many large cities, food carts seem to be on every corner. New York City has more than 5,000 of them. Why are they so common? Consider the resources needed to supply sidewalk food: land, labor, capital, food, and perhaps a tiny morsel of entrepreneurial ability. Which of these do you suppose is most expensive in New York City? Retail space along Madison Avenue's Golden Mile can rent for an average of $1,000 a year per square foot (even after the drop that followed the financial crisis of 2008). Because operating a food cart is restricted to 50 square feet, renting that space could cost as much as $50,000 a year. Aside from the necessary public permits, however, space on the public sidewalk is free to vendors. Profit-maximizing street vendors substitute public sidewalks for costly commercial space. (Incidentally, does free public space mean sidewalk vendors earn long-run economic profit? Why or why not?)

11-6 FINAL WORD

A firm hires more of a resource until the marginal revenue product of that resource equals its marginal cost. The objective of profit maximization ensures that to produce any given level of output, firms employ the least-cost combination of resources and thereby use the economy's resources most efficiently. Although our focus has been on the marginal productivity of each resource, we should keep in mind that an orchestra of resources combines to produce output, so the marginal productivity of a particular resource depends in part on the amount and quality of other resources employed.

STUDY TOOLS 11

CHAPTER 11 PROBLEMS

Your instructor can access the answers to these problems online at http://cengagebrain.com.

11-1 Determine the profit-maximizing number of workers for a firm to hire

1. *(Resource Demand)* How do firms and individuals determine if it's worth it to (a) invest in capital improvements, (b) hire additional workers, or (c) decide where to work?
2. *(Profit Maximization)* What is a firm's profit maximizing rule in deciding how many workers to hire?

11-2 Explain why resource owners are more willing and more able to increase the quantity supplied of the resources they own as resource prices increase

3. *(Market Supply for Resources)* Explain why the market supply curve of a resource slopes upward.
4. *(Resource Demand and Supply)* Answer each of the following questions about the labor market:
   a. Which economic decision makers determine the demand for labor? What is their goal, and what decision criteria do they use in trying to reach that goal?
   b. Which economic decision makers determine the supply of labor? What is their goal and what decision criteria do they use in trying to reach that goal?
   c. In what sense is the demand for labor a derived demand?

11-3 Explain why some resource price differences are temporary while others are permanent

5. *(Resource Price Differences)* Distinguish between how the market reacts to a temporary difference in prices for the same resource and how the market reacts to a permanent difference for similar resources. Why do the reactions differ?

11-4 Clarify the distinction between a resource's opportunity cost and its economic rent

6. *(Opportunity Cost and Economic Rent)* Define economic rent. In the graph below, assume that the market demand curve for labor is initially D_1.

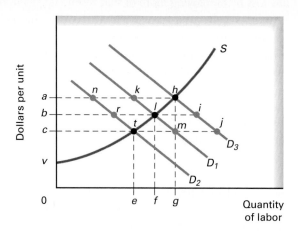

a. What are the equilibrium wage rate and employment level? What is the economic rent? What is the opportunity cost?
b. Next, assume that the price of a substitute resource increases, other things constant. What happens to demand for labor? What are the new equilibrium wage rate and employment level? What happens to economic rent? What is the opportunity cost?
c. Suppose instead that demand for the final product drops, other things constant. Using labor demand curve D_1 as your starting point, what happens to the demand for labor? What are the new equilibrium wage rate and employment level? Does the amount of economic rent change? Does opportunity cost change?

11-5 Describe the economic logic of optimal resource use

7. *(Firm's Demand for a Resource)* Use the following data to answer the questions that follow. Assume a perfectly competitive product market.

Units of Labor	Units of Output
0	0
1	7
2	13
3	18
4	22
5	25

a. Calculate the marginal revenue product for each additional unit of labor if output sells for $3 per unit.
b. Draw the demand curve for labor based on the above data and the $3-per-unit product price.
c. If the wage rate is $15 per hour, how much labor will be hired?

d. Using your answer to part (c), compare the firm's total revenue to the total amount paid for labor. Who gets the difference?

e. What would happen to your answers to parts (b) and (c) if the price of output increased to $5 per unit, other things constant?

8. *(Shifts of Resource Demand)* A local pizzeria hires college students to make pizza, wait on tables, take phone orders, and deliver pizzas. For each situation described, determine whether the demand for student employees by the restaurant would increase, decrease, or remain unchanged. Explain each answer.

a. The demand for pizza increases.

b. Another pizzeria opens up next door.

c. An increase in the minimum wage raises the cost of hiring student employees.

d. The restaurant buys a computer system for taking phone orders.

e. The restaurant develops a Web site so customers can order online.

9. *(Selling Output as a Price Taker)* If a competitive firm hires another full-time worker, total output increases from 100 units to 110 units per week. Suppose that labor is the only resource and that the market price of output is $25 per unit. What is the maximum weekly wage at which the firm would hire that additional worker?

12 | Labor Markets and Labor Unions

Mathew Hayward/Alamy

LEARNING OUTCOMES

After studying this chapter, you will be able to...

12-1 Explain why the quantity of labor supplied increases with the wage, other things remain constant

12-2 Describe why some workers earn higher wages than other workers

12-3 Summarize the objectives of labor unions and outline strategies used to achieve these objectives

12-4 Give reasons why unionization rates have declined in recent decades

After finishing this chapter go to **PAGE 213** for **STUDY TOOLS**

Topics discussed in Chapter 12 include:

- Theory of time allocation
- Backward-bending labor supply curve
- Nonwage determinants of labor supply
- Why wages differ
- Winner-take-all labor markets
- Unions and collective bargaining
- Union wages and employment
- Trends in union membership

- How do you divide your time between work and leisure?
- Why do some people work less if the wage increases enough?
- For example, why do unknown rock bands play hours for peanuts, while famous bands play much less for much more?
- Why are butchers more likely than surgeons to mow their own lawns?

- What determines the wage structure in the economy?
- What else besides the wage affects your labor supply?
- In what sense have labor unions become the victims of their own success?

This chapter digs deeper into labor markets and wage determination.

Because of the division of labor and comparative advantage, the U.S. workforce is becoming more specialized. For example, the U.S. Census of 1850 identified 324 job titles. The 2010 Census identified about 100 times more. Differences in pay across job specialties can be huge. These differences should interest anyone deciding on a career.

> **"Why do unknown rock bands play hours for peanuts while famous bands play much less for much more?"**

You can be sure of one thing: demand and supply play a central role in all this. You have already considered the demand for resources. Demand depends on a resource's marginal revenue product. The first half of this chapter focuses on the supply of labor, then brings demand and supply together to arrive at the market wage. The second half considers the role of labor unions. We examine the economic impact of unions and review recent trends in union membership.

12-1 LABOR SUPPLY

As a resource supplier, you have a labor supply curve for each of the many possible uses of your labor. To some markets, your quantity supplied is zero over the realistic range of wages. The qualifier "over the realistic range" is added because, for a high enough wage (say, $1 million per hour), you might supply labor to just about *any* activity. In most labor markets, your quantity supplied may be zero either because you are *willing* but *unable* to perform the job (professional golfer, airline pilot, novelist) or because you are *able* but *unwilling* to do so (soldier of fortune, prison guard, taxi driver). You have as many individual supply curves as there are labor markets, just as you have as many individual demand curves as there are markets for goods and services. Your labor supply to each market depends, among other things, on your abilities,

your taste for the job, and the opportunity cost of your time. Your supply to a particular labor market assumes that wages in other markets are constant, just as your demand for a particular product assumes that other prices are constant.

12-1a Labor Supply and Utility Maximization

Recall the definition of economics: *the study of how people use their scarce resources in an attempt to satisfy their unlimited wants*—that is, how people use their scarce resources to maximize their utility. Two sources of utility are of special interest in this chapter: the consumption of goods and services and the enjoyment of leisure. The utility derived from consumption serves as the foundation of demand. Another valuable source of utility is leisure—time spent relaxing with friends, sleeping, eating, watching TV, gaming, reading for pleasure, and in other recreation. Leisure is a normal good that, like other goods, is subject to the law of diminishing marginal utility. Thus, the more leisure time you have, the less you value an additional hour of it. Sometimes you may have so much leisure that you "have time on your hands" and are "just killing time." As that sage of the comic page Garfield the cat once lamented, "Spare time would be more fun if I had less to spare." Or as Shakespeare wrote, "If all the year were playing holidays, to sport would be as tedious as to work." Leisure's diminishing marginal utility explains why some of the "idle rich" grow bored of their idleness.

Three Uses of Time

Some of you are at a point in your careers when you have few resources other than your time. Time is the raw material of life. You can use your time in three ways. First, you can undertake **market work**—selling your time in the labor market. In return for a wage, you surrender control of your time to the employer. Second, you can undertake **nonmarket work**—using time to produce your own goods and services. Nonmarket work includes the time you spend doing laundry, making a sandwich, or cleaning up after yourself. Nonmarket work also includes the time spent acquiring skills and education that enhance your productivity. Although studying and attending class may provide little immediate utility, you expect that the knowledge and perspective so gained will enrich your future. Third, you can spend time in **leisure**—using your time in nonwork pursuits. You may know people who appear to specialize in leisure. After all, hard work pays off in the future, but laziness pays off right now.

market work Time sold as labor

nonmarket work Time spent getting an education or on do-it-yourself production for personal consumption

leisure Time spent on nonwork activities

Work and Utility

Unless you are among the fortunate few, work is not a pure source of utility, as it's often boring, uncomfortable, and aggravating. In short, time spent working can be "a real pain," a source of *disutility*—the opposite of utility. And work is subject *to increasing marginal disutility*—the more you work, the greater the marginal disutility of working another hour. In the extreme, you can get burned out from overwork. You may work nonetheless, because your earnings buy goods and services. You expect the utility from these products to more than offset the disutility of work. Thus, the *net utility of work*—the utility of the additional consumption possibilities from earnings minus the disutility of the work itself—usually makes some amount of work an attractive use of your time. In the case of market work, your income buys goods and services. In the case of nonmarket work, either you produce goods and services directly, as in making yourself a sandwich, or you invest your time in education with an expectation of higher future earnings and higher future consumption possibilities.

Utility Maximization

Within the limits of a 24-hour day, seven days a week, you balance your time among market work, nonmarket work, and leisure to maximize utility. As a rational consumer, *you attempt to maximize utility by allocating your time so that the expected marginal utility of the last unit of time spent in each activity is identical.* Thus, in the course of a week or a month, the expected marginal utility of the last hour of leisure equals the expected net marginal utility of the last hour of market work, which equals the expected net marginal utility of the last hour of nonmarket work. In the case of time devoted to acquiring more human capital, you must consider the marginal utility expected from the future increase in earnings that result from your enhanced productivity.

Maybe at this point you are saying, "Wait a minute. I don't know what you're talking about. I don't allocate my time like that. I just sort of bump along, doing what feels good." Economists do not claim that you are even aware of making these marginal calculations. But as a rational decision maker, you allocate your scarce time trying to satisfy your unlimited wants, or trying to maximize utility. And utility maximization, or "doing what feels good," implies that you act *as if* you allocated your time to derive the same expected net marginal utility from the many possible uses of your time.

You probably have settled into a rough plan for meals, work, entertainment, study, sleep, and so on—a plan that fits your immediate goals. This plan is probably in constant flux as you make expected and unexpected adjustments in your use of time. For example, last weekend you may have failed to crack a book, despite good intentions. This morning you may have overslept because you were up late. Over a week, a month, or a year, however, your use of time is roughly in line with an allocation that maximizes utility as you perceive it at the time. Put another way, if you could alter your use of time to increase your utility, you would do so. Nobody's stopping you! You may emphasize immediate gratification over long-term goals, but, hey, that's your choice and you bear the consequences. *This time-allocation process ensures that at the margin, the expected net utilities from the last unit of time spent in each activity are equal.*

Because information is costly and because the future is uncertain, you sometimes make mistakes. You don't always get what you expect. Some mistakes are minor, such as going to a movie that turns out to be a waste of time. But other mistakes can be costly. For example, some people are now studying for a field that will grow crowded by the time they graduate, while other people may be acquiring skills that new technology could soon make obsolete.

Implications

The theory of time allocation described thus far has several implications for individual choice. First, consider the choices among market work, nonmarket work, and leisure. The higher your market wage, other things constant, the higher your opportunity cost of leisure and nonmarket work. For example, those who earn a high wage spend less time in nonmarket work, other things constant. Surgeons are less likely to mow their lawns than are butchers. And among those earning the same wage, those more productive in nonmarket work—handy around the house, good cooks—do more for themselves. Conversely, those who are all thumbs around the house and have trouble boiling water hire more household services and eat out more.

By the same logic, the higher the expected earnings right out of high school, other things constant, the higher the opportunity cost of attending college. Most young, successful movie stars do not go to college, and many even drop out of high school, as noted in an earlier chapter. Promising athletes often turn professional as soon as they can. But the vast majority of people, including female basketball stars, do not face such a high opportunity cost of higher education. As one poor soul lamented, "Since my wife left me, my kids joined a cult, my job is history, and my dog died, I think now might be a good time to go back for an MBA."

12-1b Wages and Individual Labor Supply

To breathe life into the time-allocation problem, consider your choices for the summer. If you can afford to, you can take the summer off, spending it entirely on leisure, perhaps as a fitting reward for a rough academic year. Or you can get a job. Or you can undertake nonmarket work, such as cleaning the garage, painting the house, or attending summer school. As a rational decision maker, you select the mix of leisure, market work, and nonmarket work that you expect will maximize your utility. And the optimal combination is likely to involve spending some time on each activity. For example, even if you work, you might still squeeze in one or two summer courses.

Suppose the only summer job available is some form of unskilled labor, such as working in a fast-food restaurant or for the municipal parks department. For simplicity, let's assume that you view all these as equally attractive (or unattractive) in terms of their nonmonetary aspects, such as working conditions, working hours, job prospects, and so on. (These nonmonetary aspects are discussed in the next section.) If there is no difference among these unskilled jobs, the most important question for you in deciding how much market labor to supply is this one: What's the market wage?

Suppose the wage is $7 per hour, not even the legal minimum. Rather than working for a wage that low, you might decide to work around the house, attend summer school, take a really long nap, travel across the country to find yourself, or perhaps pursue some combination of these. In any case, you supply no market labor at such a low wage. The market wage must rise to $8 before you supply any market labor. Suppose at a wage of $8, you supply 20 hours per week, perhaps taking fewer summer courses and shorter naps.

As the wage increases, your opportunity cost of time spent in other activities rises, so you substitute market work for other uses of your time. You decide to work 30 hours per week at a wage of $9 per hour, 40 hours at $10, 48 hours at $11, and 55 hours at $12. At a wage of $13 you go to 60 hours per week; you are starting to earn serious money—$780 a week. If the wage hits $14 per hour, you decide to cut back a little to 58 hours per week. Despite the cutback, your weekly pay rises to $812. Finally, if the wage hits $15, you cut back to 55 per week, earning $825. To explain why you may eventually reduce the quantity of labor supplied, let's consider the impact of wage increases on your time allocation.

Substitution and Income Effects

A higher wage has two effects on your use of time. First, because each hour of work now buys more goods and services, a higher wage increases the opportunity cost of leisure and nonmarket work. Thus, as the wage increases, you substitute market work for other activities. This is the **substitution effect of a wage increase**. Second, a higher wage means a higher income for a given number of hours. This higher income increases your demand for all normal goods. Because leisure is a normal good, a higher income increases your demand for leisure, thereby reducing your allocation of time to market work. The **income effect of a wage increase** tends to reduce the quantity of labor supplied to market work. As the Greek philosopher Aristotle observed, "The end of labor is to gain leisure."

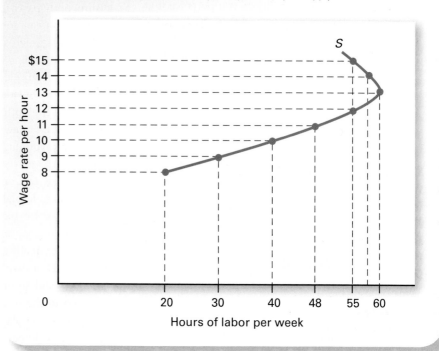

Exhibit 1

Your Labor Supply Curve During the Summer

When the substitution effect of a wage increase outweighs the income effect, the quantity of labor you supply increases with the wage. Above some wage, shown here at $13 per hour, the income effect dominates. Above that wage, your supply curve bends backward. Further increases in the wage reduce the quantity of labor you supply.

As your wage increases, the substitution effect causes you to work more, but the income effect causes you to work less and demand more leisure. In our example, the substitution effect exceeds the income effect for wages up to $13 per hour, resulting in more labor supplied as the wage increases. When the wage reaches $14, however, the income effect exceeds the substitution effect, causing you to reduce the quantity of labor supplied.

Backward-Bending Labor Supply Curve

The labor supply curve just described appears in Exhibit 1. As you can see, this slopes upward until the wage reaches $13 per hour; then the curve bends backward. The **backward-bending supply curve** gets its shape if the income effect of a higher wage eventually dominates the substitution effect, reducing the quantity of labor supplied as the wage increases. We see evidence of a backward-bending supply curve particularly among high-wage individuals, who reduce their work hours and consume more leisure as their wage increases. For example, entertainers typically perform less as they become more successful. Unknown musicians play for hours for hardly any money; famous musicians play much less for much more. But the backward-bending supply curve may also apply to ordinary workers, such as you during the summer or to New York City taxi drivers, who reduced their hours after an increase in taxi fares.[1] The income effect of rising real wages helps explain the decline in the U.S. workweek from an average of 60 hours in 1900 to about 40 hours in 1960 to about 34 hours today.

1. Orley Ashenfelter, Kirk Doran, and Bruce Schaller, "A Shred of Credible Evidence on the Long-Run Elasticity of Labor Supply," *Economica*, 77 (October 2010): 637–650.

substitution effect of a wage increase A higher wage encourages more work because other activities now have a higher opportunity cost

income effect of a wage increase A higher wage raises a worker's income, increasing the demand for all normal goods, including leisure, so the quantity of labor supplied to market work decreases

backward-bending supply curve of labor As the wage rises, the quantity of labor supplied may eventually decline; the income effect of a higher wage increases the demand for leisure, which reduces the quantity of labor supplied enough to more than offset the substitution effect of a higher wage

> **"As your wage increases, the substitution effect causes you to work more, but the income effect causes you to work less and demand more leisure."**

Flexibility of Hours Worked

The model we have been discussing assumes that workers have some control over how much they work. Opportunities for part-time work and overtime allow workers to put together their preferred quantity of hours. Workers also have some control over the timing and length of their vacations. More generally, individuals usually have some control over how long to stay in school, when to enter or leave the workforce, and when to retire. Thus, most people actually have more control over the number of hours worked than you might think.

12-1c Nonwage Determinants of Labor Supply

The supply of labor to a particular market depends on a variety of factors other than the wage, just as the demand for a particular good depends on factors other than the price. As we have already seen, the supply of labor to a particular market depends on wages in other labor markets. What nonwage factors shape a college student's labor supply for the summer?

Other Sources of Income

Although some jobs are rewarding in a variety of nonmonetary ways, the main reason people work is to earn money. Thus, your willingness to supply labor depends on income from other sources, including from family, savings, student loans, and scholarships. A student who receives a generous scholarship, for example, faces less pressure to work in the summer or during the college term. More generally, wealthy people have less incentive to work. For example, multimillion-dollar lottery winners often quit their jobs. And those who inherit a large sum are more likely to retire early.[2]

2. As found in research by Jeffrey Brown, Courtney Coile, and Scott Weisbenner, "The Effect of Inheritance Receipt on Retirement," *Review of Economics and Statistics*, 92 (August 2010): 425–434.

On the other hand, a decrease in wealth would prompt some people to work more, thus increasing their supply of labor. For example, the stock market decline between 2008 and 2009 reduced the wealth that people planned to draw on during retirement. As a result, many had to put retirement plans on hold and instead worked more to rebuild their retirement nest eggs. This increased supply of labor is shown by the rightward shift of the labor supply curve.

Nonmonetary Factors

Labor is a special kind of resource. Unlike capital or natural resources, which can be supplied regardless of the whereabouts of the resource owner, the supplier of labor must be where the work is performed. Because individuals must usually be physically present to supply labor, such *nonmonetary factors* as the difficulty of the job, the quality of the work environment, and the status of the position become important to labor suppliers. For example, deckhands on crab boats in the icy waters off Alaska can earn over $10,000 for five days of work, but the job is dangerous, winter temperatures seldom exceed zero, and daily shifts allow only three hours of sleep.

Consider the different working conditions you might encounter. A campus job that lets you study on the job is more attractive than one with no study time. Some jobs offer flexible hours; other work schedules are rigid. Is the workplace air-conditioned, or do you have to sweat it out? The more attractive the working conditions, the more labor you supply to that market, other things constant. Finally, some jobs convey more status than others. For example, the president of the United States earns less than one-tenth that of corporate heads, but there is no shortage of applicants for the job. Similarly, U.S. Supreme Court justices typically take a huge pay cut to accept the job.

The Value of Job Experience

All else equal, you are more inclined to take a position that provides valuable job experience. Serving as the assistant treasurer for a local business during the summer provides better job experience and looks better on a résumé than serving mystery meat at the college cafeteria. Some people are willing to accept relatively low wages now for the promise of higher wages in the future. For example, new lawyers are eager to fill clerkships for judges, though the pay is low and the hours long, because these positions offer experience and contacts future employers value. Likewise, athletes who play in the minor leagues for little pay believe that experience will give them a shot at the major leagues. Thus, *the more a job enhances future earning possibilities, the greater the supply of labor, other things constant.* Consequently, the pay in such jobs is usually lower than for jobs that impart less valuable experience. Sometimes the pay is zero, as with some internships.

Taste for Work

Just as the taste for goods and services differs among consumers, the taste for work also differs among labor suppliers. Some people prefer physical labor and hate office work. Some become surgeons; others can't stand the sight of blood. Some become airline pilots; others are afraid to fly. Teenagers prefer jobs at Starbucks and Gap to those at McDonald's and Burger King. Many struggling writers, artists, actors, and dancers could earn more elsewhere, but prefer the creative process and the chance, albeit slim, of becoming rich and famous in the arts. For example, the 120,000 members of the Screen Actors Guild earn a median pay from acting of less than $10,000 a year, and among recent fine-arts graduates, two of the top three occupations are waiters and retail sales.

Some people have such strong preferences for certain jobs that they expect no pay, such as auxiliary police officers or volunteer firefighters. Likewise, most computer hackers earn nothing beyond the twisted satisfaction they get from making other people suffer. And graffiti artists spend hours defacing property while risking arrest for whatever kicks they get from leaving their marks.

As with the taste for goods and services, economists do not try to explain how work preferences develop. They simply argue that your preferences are relatively stable and, at a given wage, you supply more labor to jobs you like. Based on taste, workers seek jobs in a way that tends to minimize the disutility of work. This is not to say that everyone ends up in his or her most preferred position. The transaction costs of job information and of changing jobs may prevent some matchups that might otherwise seem desirable. But in the long run, people tend to find jobs that suit them. We are not likely to find tour guides who hate to travel, zookeepers who are allergic to animals, or garage mechanics who hate getting their hands dirty.

12-1d Market Supply of Labor

In the previous section, we considered those factors, both monetary and nonmonetary, that influence individual labor supply. *The supply of labor to a particular market is the horizontal sum of all the individual supply curves.* The horizontal sum at each particular wage is found by adding the quantities supplied by each worker. If an individual supply curve of labor bends backward, does this mean that the market supply curve for labor also bends backward? Not necessarily. Because different individuals have different opportunity costs and different tastes for work, the bend in the supply curve occurs at different wages for different individuals. And, for some individuals, the labor supply curve may not bend backward over the realistic range of wages. Exhibit 2 shows how just three individual labor supply curves sum to yield a market supply curve that slopes upward.

How responsive is the quantity of labor supplied to changes in the wage? In other words, what is labor's elasticity of supply with respect to the wage? Although that is a complicated question, an average of many studies suggests an elasticity of about 0.3, meaning that a 10 percent increase in the wage, other things constant, would increase the quantity of labor supplied by 3 percent.[3]

12-2 WHY WAGES DIFFER

Just as both blades of scissors contribute equally to cutting paper, both labor demand and labor supply determine the market wage. Exhibit 3 shows average hourly wages for 135.1 million U.S. workers. Workers are sorted into 22 general occupations from the highest to the lowest wage as of May 2014. Management earned the highest average wage, at $54.08 an hour. The lowest is the $10.57 an hour averaged by workers preparing and serving food. Wage differences across labor markets trace to differences in labor demand and in labor

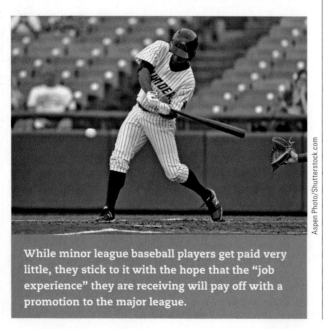

While minor league baseball players get paid very little, they stick to it with the hope that the "job experience" they are receiving will pay off with a promotion to the major league.

Aspen Photo/Shutterstock.com

3. Michael Keane, "Labor Supply and Taxes: A Survey," *Journal of Economic Literature,* 49 (December 2011): 961–1075.

Exhibit 2

Deriving the Market Labor Supply Curve From Individual Labor Supply Curves

The individual labor supply curve in panel (a) bends backward. The market supply curve, however, may still slope upward over the relevant range of wages.

(a) Worker A **(b)** Worker B **(c)** Worker C **(d)** Market supply

supply, as you will see. The previous chapter discussed the elements that influence the demand for resources and examined labor in particular. In brief, *a profit-maximizing firm hires labor up to the point where labor's* *marginal revenue product equals its marginal resource cost*—that is, where the last unit employed increases total revenue enough to cover the added cost. Because we have already discussed what affects the demand for

Exhibit 3

Average Hourly Wage by Occupation in the United States

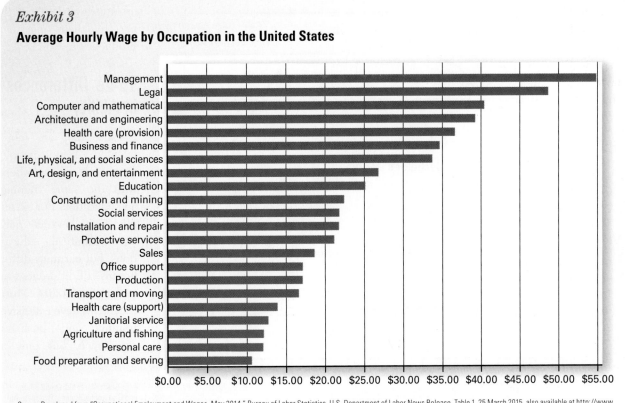

Source: Developed from "Occupational Employment and Wages, May 2014," Bureau of Labor Statistics, U.S. Department of Labor News Release, Table 1, 25 March 2015, also available at http://www.bls.gov/news.release/pdf/ocwage.pdf.

labor—namely, labor's marginal revenue product—let's focus more on labor supply.

12-2a Differences in Training, Education, Age, and Experience

Some jobs pay more because they require a long and expensive training period, which reduces market supply because few are willing to incur the time and expense required. But such training increases labor productivity, thereby increasing demand for the skills. Reduced supply and increased demand both raise the market wage. For example, certified public accountants (CPAs) earn more than file clerks because the extensive training of CPAs limits the supply to this field and because this training increases the productivity of CPAs compared to file clerks.

Exhibit 4 shows how education and experience affect earnings. Age groups are indicated on the horizontal axis and average annual earnings on the vertical axis. To standardize things, pay is for the highest level of education achieved. The relationship between income and education is clear. At every age, those with more education earn more. For example, workers with professional degrees earned at least twice as much as those with bachelor's degrees and at least five times those without high school diplomas.

Age itself also has an important effect on income. Earnings tend to increase as workers acquire job experience and get promoted. Among more educated workers, experience pays more. For example, among those with professional degrees, workers in the 55–64 age group earned on average 73 percent more than those in the 25–34 age group. But among those without high school diplomas, workers in the 55–64 age group earned on average only 26 percent more than those in the 25–34 age group. Research suggests that, because of the greater physical demands of their jobs, blue-collar workers tend to wear out faster with age than do white-collar workers.[4] Differences in earnings in Exhibit 4 reflect the normal workings of resource markets, whereby workers are rewarded according to their marginal productivity.

12-2b Differences in Ability

Because they are more talented, some people earn more than others with the same training and education. For example, two lawyers may have identical educations, but earnings differ because of differences in underlying ability. Most executives have extensive training and business experience, but only a

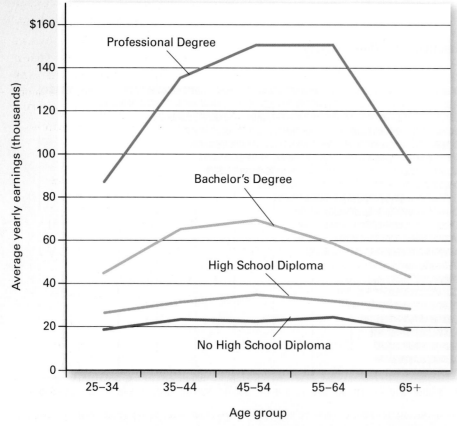

Exhibit 4

Age, Education, and Pay

For every age group, workers with more education earn more. The premium paid for years of experience also increases more for those with more education.

Source: Drawn from figures appearing in U.S. Bureau of the Census, *Statistical Abstract of the United States: 2012* (U.S. Bureau of the Census, 2012), Table 232.

4. G. Brant Morefield, David Ribar, and Christopher Ruhm, "Occupational Status and Health Transitions," *The B.E. Journal of Economic Analysis & Policy*, Berkeley Electronic Press, 11 (3), pages 8.

Crab fishermen in the Bering Sea off the coast of Alaska get paid quite well to accept the risk that the job entails.

few get to head large corporations. In professional basketball, some players earn up to 50 times more than others even on the same team. From lawyers to executives to professional athletes, pay differences reflect differing abilities as expressed in different marginal productivities. Sometimes the wage for certain abilities gets bid up because of sharp increases in demand. For example, software coders have been much in demand lately, fueled by the information revolution.[5] There is also evidence that taller and better looking people earn more. Finally, it turns out that students who are more popular in high school, as reflected by their number of friends, other things equal, earned more later in life.[6]

12-2c Differences in Risk

Research indicates that jobs with a higher probability of injury or death, such as coal mining, usually pay more than other jobs, other things constant. Russians working at the partially disabled Chernobyl nuclear power plant earned 10 times the national average, but workers there face continued health risk from radiation exposure. Sex workers in Mexico earn 23 percent more for unprotected sex.[7] Truck drivers for American contractors in Iraq earned over $100,000 a year, but the job was dangerous. Workers also earn more, other things constant, in seasonal jobs such as construction, where the risk of unemployment is greater.

5. Andy Kessler, "Mothers, Tell Your Children to Be Software Coders," *Wall Street Journal*, 26 September 2014.
6. Gabriella Conti et al., "Popularity," *Journal of Human Resources*, 48 (Fall 2013): 1072–1094.
7. See Paul Gertler et al., "Risky Business: The Market for Unprotected Commercial Sex," *Journal of Political Economy*, 113 (June 2005): 518–550.

12-2d Geographic Differences

People have a strong incentive to sell their resources in the market where they can earn the most. For example, the National Basketball Association attracts talent from around the world. About 20 percent of NBA players come from abroad. Likewise, thousands of foreign-trained physicians migrate to the United States each year for the high pay. The same goes for nurses (a nurse from the Philippines can earn six times more in the United States). The flow of labor is not all one way: Some Americans seek their fortune abroad, with baseball players going to Japan and basketball players going to Europe and China (incidentally, China limits each basketball team to no more than two foreign players). Workers often face migration hurdles. Any reduction in these hurdles would reduce wage differentials across countries.

12-2e Discrimination

Sometimes wage differences stem from racial or gender discrimination in the job market. Although such discrimination is illegal, history shows that certain groups—including African Americans, Hispanics, and women—have systematically earned less than others of equal ability. For example, among all full-time, year-round U.S. workers, females in 1980 earned only 60 percent of what males earned. By 2015, females earned 80 percent of male pay. Because some women do more housework and childcare than men do, they may have less job experience and tend to seek more flexible positions, both of which reduce their pay. Discrimination is discussed more fully in a later chapter.

> **"Wage differences trace to training, education, age, experience, ability, risk of injury, risk of job loss, geography, and racial and gender discrimination."**

TO REVIEW: Wage differences trace to training, education, age, experience, ability, risk of injury, risk of job loss, geography, and racial and gender discrimination.

Other things equal, members of organized labor earn more than other workers. The balance of this chapter discusses the effects of labor unions on labor markets.

12-3 UNIONS AND COLLECTIVE BARGAINING

Few aspects of labor markets make news more than labor unions. Labor negotiations, strikes, picket lines, confrontations between workers and employers—all fit TV's "action news" format. Despite media attention, only about one in nine U.S. workers is a union member and nearly all union agreements are reached without a strike. But labor unions are more important than their current membership indicates. Let's examine the types of unions and the tools they use to seek higher pay and better benefits for their members.

labor union A group of workers who organize to improve their terms of employment

craft union A union whose members have a particular skill or work at a particular craft, such as plumbers or carpenters

industrial union A union consisting of both skilled and unskilled workers from a particular industry, such as all autoworkers or all steelworkers

collective bargaining The process by which union and management negotiate a labor agreement

mediator An impartial observer who helps resolve differences between union and management

binding arbitration Negotiation in which union and management must accept an impartial observer's resolution of a dispute

strike A union's attempt to withhold labor from a firm to halt production

12-3a Types of Unions

A **labor union** is a group of workers who join together to improve their terms of employment. Labor unions in the United States date back to the early days of national independence, when workers in a particular craft—such as carpenters, shoemakers, or printers—formed a local group to seek higher wages and better working conditions. A **craft union** is limited to workers with a particular skill, or craft. Each craft union kept its individual identity but combined forces with other craft unions to form a national organization in 1886, the *American Federation of Labor* (AFL). The Clayton Act of 1914 exempted labor unions from antitrust laws, meaning that *unions at competing companies could legally join forces.* Unions were also tax exempt. Membership jumped during World War I but fell by half between 1920 and 1933, as the government retreated from its support of union efforts.

The *Congress of Industrial Organizations* (CIO) was formed in 1935 to serve as a national organization of unions in mass-production industries, such as autos or steel. Although the AFL organized workers in particular crafts, such as plumbers or carpenters, the CIO consisted of unions whose membership embraced all workers in a particular industry. These **industrial unions** included unskilled, semiskilled, and skilled workers in an industry, such as all autoworkers or all steelworkers.

12-3b Collective Bargaining, Mediation, and Arbitration

Collective bargaining is the process by which representatives of union and management negotiate a mutually agreeable contract specifying wages, employee benefits, and working conditions. A tentative agreement, once reached, goes to the membership for a vote. If accepted, the agreement holds for the years of the contract. If the agreement is rejected, the union can return to the bargaining table to continue negotiations. If negotiations reach an impasse and the public interest is involved, government officials may ask an independent mediator to step in. A **mediator** is an impartial observer who listens to each side separately and then suggests a resolution. If each side still remains open to a settlement, the mediator brings them together to work out a contract, but the mediator has no power to impose a settlement. In certain critical sectors, such as police and fire protection, where a strike could harm the public interest, differences are sometimes settled through **binding arbitration**. A neutral third party evaluates each position and issues a ruling that both sides must accept. Some disputes skip the mediation and arbitration steps and go directly from impasse to strike.

12-3c The Strike

A major source of union power is a **strike**, which is a union's attempt to withhold labor to stop production, thereby hoping to force the firm into accepting the union's position. But strikes are also risky for workers, who earn no company pay or benefits during the strike and could lose their jobs permanently. Union funds and, in certain states, unemployment benefits, may aid strikers some, but incomes still fall substantially during a strike. *Although neither party usually wants a strike, both sides, rather than concede on key points, usually*

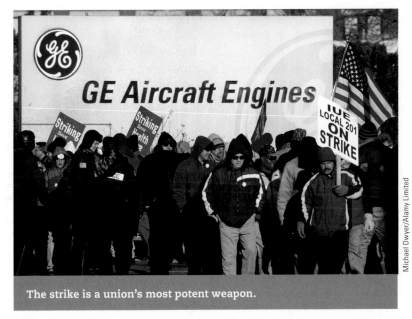

The strike is a union's most potent weapon.

act as if they could endure one. Unions usually picket the employer to prevent or discourage so-called strikebreakers, or "scabs," from crossing the picket lines to work. But the targeted firm, by hiring temporary workers and nonstriking union workers, can sometimes continue production.

Some industries are more vulnerable to strikes—industries that deal in perishable goods, such as strawberries, and industries where picket lines can turn away lots of customers, such as Broadway theaters or hotels. But in other industries, advances in technology have reduced the effectiveness of strikes, as petroleum and chemical workers learned when strikers found that skeleton crews of supervisors could run computer-controlled refineries for a long time.

12-4 UNION WAGES AND EMPLOYMENT

Samuel Gompers, the AFL's founder and long-time head, was once asked what unions want. "More!" he roared. Union members, like everyone else, have unlimited wants. But because resources are scarce, choices must be made. A menu of union desires includes higher wages, more benefits, greater job security, better working conditions, and so on. To keep the analysis manageable, let's focus on a single objective,

> **"A menu of union desires includes higher wages, more benefits, greater job security, better working conditions, and so on."**

higher wages, and consider three ways unions might increase wages: (1) by forming an inclusive, or industrial, union; (2) by forming an exclusive, or craft, union; and (3) by increasing the demand for union labor.

12-4a Inclusive, or Industrial, Unions: Negotiating a Higher Industry Wage

The market demand and supply curves for a particular type of labor are labeled D and S in panel (a) of Exhibit 5. In the absence of a union, the market wage is W and industry employment is E. At the market wage, each firm faces a horizontal, or perfectly elastic, supply of labor curve, as depicted by s in panel (b) of Exhibit 5. Thus, each firm can hire as much labor as it wants at the market wage of W. The firm hires workers up to the point where labor's marginal revenue product equals its marginal resource cost, resulting in e units of labor in panel (b). As we saw earlier, in equilibrium, labor is paid a wage just equal to its marginal revenue product.

With the *inclusive, or industrial,* approach, the union tries to negotiate industry-wide wages for each class of labor. Suppose the union negotiates a wage above the market-clearing level. Specifically, suppose the negotiated wage is W' in panel (a), meaning that no labor is supplied at a lower wage. In effect, the market supply of labor is perfectly elastic at the union wage out to point a. To the right of point a, however, the wage floor no longer applies; aS becomes the relevant portion of the labor supply curve. For an industry facing a wage floor of W', the entire labor supply curve becomes $W'aS$, which has a kink where the wage floor joins the upward-sloping portion of the original labor supply curve.

Once this wage floor is negotiated for the industry, each firm faces a horizontal supply curve of labor at the collectively bargained wage, W'. Because the union wage is higher than the market-clearing wage, each firm hires less labor. Consequently, the higher wage reduces employment; the quantity

Exhibit 5

Effects of Labor Union's Wage Floor

Without a labor union, the market wage is *W* in panel (a). At that wage, each firm can hire as much labor as it wants. The individual firm in panel (b) hires more labor until the marginal revenue product equals the market wage, *W*. Each firm hires *e* units of labor, and industry employment is *E*. If a union negotiates a wage *W'*, which is above the market wage *W*, the supply curve facing the firm shifts up from *s* to *s'*. Each firm hires less labor, *e'*, so industry employment falls to *E'*. At the union wage there is now an excess quantity of labor supplied equal to *E"* 2*E'*.

(a) Industry

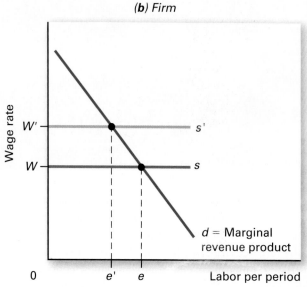

(b) Firm

of labor demanded by the industry drops from *E* to *E'* in panel (a). At wage *W'* workers in the industry would like to supply *E"*, which exceeds the quantity of labor demanded, *E'*. Ordinarily this excess quantity supplied would force the wage down. But because union members agree *collectively* to the union wage, individual workers can't work for less, nor can employers hire them for less. *With the inclusive, or industrial, union, which negotiates with the entire industry, the wage is higher and employment lower than they would be in the absence of a union.*

The union must somehow ration the limited jobs available, such as by awarding them based on worker seniority, personal connections within the union, or lottery. Those who can't find union jobs must turn to the nonunion sector. *This increases the supply of labor in the nonunion sector, which drives down the nonunion wage.* So wages are relatively higher in the union sector, first, because unions bargain for a wage that exceeds the market-clearing wage, and, second, because

those unable to find union jobs crowd into the nonunion sector. Studies show that union wages average about 15 percent above the wages of similarly qualified nonunion workers. Union members also earn higher nonwage compensation, such as pensions, health insurance, and paid leave.[8]

Exhibit 6 compares median weekly earnings of union and nonunion workers. Note that unions are less successful at raising wages in more competitive sectors. For example, unions have less impact on food-and-drink service, manufacturing, and wholesale, and retail trade, where product markets tend to be more competitive. Unions have greater success boosting wages in government, transportation, construction, and utilities—sectors that tend to be less competitive. When there is more competition in the product market, employers cannot easily pass along higher union wages as higher product prices. New

> **"Union wages average about 15 percent above the wages of similarly qualified nonunion workers."**

8. George I. Long, "Differences Between Union and Nonunion Compensation," *Monthly Labor Review*, (April 2013): 16–23.

Exhibit 6

Median Weekly Full-Time Earnings Are Higher for Union Workers

Unions are more successful at raising wages in less competitive markets, such as government, transportation, and construction, and utilities. In more competitive markets, such as food and drink service, manufacturing, and wholesale and retail trade, employers cannot easily pass along higher union wages as higher product prices. Nonunion firms can enter the industry, pay workers market wages, which are below union wages, and attract customers by selling the product for less.

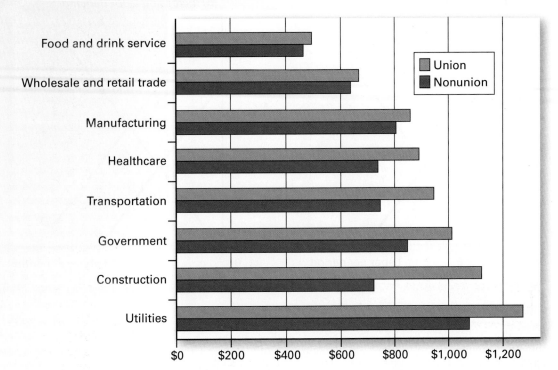

Source: U.S. Bureau of Labor Statistics, "Union Members Summary," 23 January 2015, Table 4, at http://www.bls.gov/news.release/union2.t04.htm. Figures are for full-time workers in 2014.

nonunion firms can enter the industry, pay market wages, and sell the product for less.

12-4b Exclusive, or Craft, Unions: Reducing Labor Supply

One way to increase wages while avoiding an excess quantity of labor supplied is to somehow reduce the supply of labor, shown in Exhibit 7 as a leftward shift of the labor supply curve in panel (a). This supply reduction increases the wage and reduces employment. Successful supply restrictions of this type require that the union first limit its membership, and, second, force all employers in the industry to hire only union members. The union can restrict membership with higher initiation fees, longer apprenticeship periods, tougher qualification exams, more restrictive licensing requirements, and so on. But even if unions restrict membership, they still have difficulty unionizing all firms in the industry.

Although wage setting is more typical of industrial unions, such as autos or steel, restricting supply is more typical of craft unions, such as unions of carpenters, plumbers, or bricklayers. Nonunion professional occupations—doctors, lawyers, and accountants, for instance—also impose entry restrictions through education, examination, and licensing requirements. These restrictions, usually defended as protecting the public, are often little more than self-serving attempts to increase wages by restricting labor supply.

12-4c Increasing Demand for Union Labor

A third way to increase wages is to increase the demand for union labor by somehow shifting the labor demand curve outward as from *D* to *D″* in panel (b) of Exhibit 7. This is an attractive alternative *because it increases both the wage and employment,* so there is no need to restrict labor supply or to ration jobs among union members.

Exhibit 7

Effect of Reducing Labor Supply or Increasing Labor Demand

If a union can successfully restrict labor supply in an industry, the supply curve shifts to the left from S to S', as in panel (a). The wage increases from W to W', but at the cost of reducing employment from E to E'. If a union can increase the demand for union labor, as in panel (b), the demand curve shifts right from D to D", raising the wage and increasing employment.

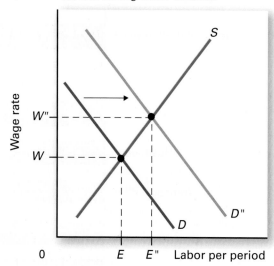

Here are some ways unions try to increase the demand for union labor.

Increase Demand for Union-Made Goods

The demand for union labor may be increased through a direct appeal to consumers to buy only union-made products. Because the demand for labor is a derived demand, increasing the demand for union-made products increases the demand for union labor.

Restrict Supply of Nonunion-Made Goods

Another way to increase the demand for union labor is to restrict the supply of products that compete with union-made products. This approach also relies on the derived nature of labor demand. The United Auto Workers, for example, has supported restrictions on imported cars. Fewer imported cars means greater demand for cars produced by U.S. workers, who are mostly union members. This strategy became less effective when foreign automakers, such as Toyota, established nonunion plants in the United States. But unions still try to restrict imports. In early 2015, for example, the AFL-CIO threatened to withhold campaign contributions from any member of Congress who supported the Trans-Pacific Partnership, a free-trade agreement with 11 Asian nations.[9]

Increase Productivity of Union Labor

Some observers claim union representation improves labor-management relations. According to this theory, unions increase worker productivity by minimizing conflicts, resolving differences, and at times even straightening out workers who goof off. In the absence of a union, a dissatisfied worker may simply quit, increasing job turnover. Turnover is costly to the firm because the departing worker leaves with company-specific, on-the-job training that increases productivity. With a union, however, workers can resolve problems through union channels. For example, one study found that workers in unionized nursing homes were more productive than workers in other nursing homes.[10] Quit rates are in fact significantly lower among union workers (although this could also be due to the higher pay and better benefits). If unions increase the productivity of workers, the demand for union labor increases.

9. Melanie Trottman, "Unions to Fight Trade Pact by Freezing Political Donations," *Wall Street Journal*, 10 March 2015.

10. Aaron Sojourner et al., "Impacts of Unionization on Employment, Product Quality and Productivity: Regression Discontinuity Evidence for Nursing Homes," *Industrial & Labor Relations Review*, (forthcoming).

Featherbedding

Yet another way unions try to increase jobs for union members is by **featherbedding**, which makes employers hire more labor than they demand. For example, union rules require that each Broadway theater have a permanent "house" carpenter, electrician, and property manager. Once the play opens, these workers show up only on payday. The union may also require that the box office be staffed by at least three people. More generally, featherbedding often blocks the adoption of new technologies that would make more efficient use of labor. This reduces a firm's competitiveness, which is one reason why unions try to organize all firms in an industry, such as all auto plants or all construction firms.

Featherbedding does not create an increase in demand, in the sense of shifting the demand curve to the right. Instead, it forces an employer to a point to the right of the labor demand curve. The union tries to limit a firm to an all-or-none choice: Either hire so many workers for the job, or we'll strike. Thus, with featherbedding, *the union attempts to dictate not only the wage but also the quantity that must be hired at that wage, thereby moving employers to the right of their labor demand curve.*

TO REVIEW: We have examined three ways that unions try to raise members' wages: (1) by negotiating a wage floor above the equilibrium wage for the industry then somehow rationing the limited jobs among union members; (2) by restricting the supply of labor; and (3) by increasing the demand for union labor. Unions try to increase the demand for union labor in four ways: (a) through a direct public appeal to buy only union-made products; (b) by restricting the supply of products made by nonunion labor; (c) by reducing labor turnover and otherwise increasing labor's marginal productivity; and (d) through featherbedding, which forces employers to hire more union workers than they want or need.

12-4d Trends in Union Membership

In 1955, about 35 percent of U.S. workers belonged to unions. Since then, union membership as a fraction of the workforce has declined steadily. By 2014, only 11.1 percent of U.S. workers belonged to unions, about the same rate as in 1900. Government workers are much more unionized than other workers—35.7 percent of government workers are belong to unions versus just 6.6 percent of private-sector workers; about half of all union members are now government workers. A typical union member is a schoolteacher. Compared with other industrialized countries, the United States ranks relatively low in the extent of unionization, though rates abroad have been declining as well. For example among 33 advanced economies, on average, 17 percent of workers were unionized in 2014, down from 20 percent in 2000. Iceland had the highest unionization rate recently, at 83 percent; Turkey had the lowest, at 5 percent.

> **"In 1955, about 35 percent of U.S. workers belonged to unions. By 2014, only 11.1 percent of U.S. workers belonged to unions, about the same rate as in 1900."**

The bar graph in Exhibit 8 indicates U.S. union membership rates by age and gender in 2014. The rates for men, shown by the blue bars, are higher than the rates for women, in part because women work more in the service sector, where union membership is lower. The highest membership rates are for middle-aged males. Although the exhibit does not show it, black workers have a higher union membership rate than white workers (13.2 percent vs. 10.8 percent), in part because African Americans are employed more by government and by heavy industries such as autos and steel, where union representation is higher. Union membership is below average among Asians (10.1 percent) and those of Hispanic origin (9.7 percent).

Union membership rates also vary across states. New York had the highest unionization rate, at 24 percent, and North Carolina the lowest, at 3 percent. Unionization rates in right-to-work states average only half the rates in other states. In **right-to-work states**, workers in unionized companies do not have to join the union or pay union dues. Over the years, the number of right-to-work states has increased to nearly half of all states, and this has hurt the union movement. Exhibit 9 shows right-to-work states in blue and other states in white as of December 2013. The map also shows unionization rates by state. What's the rate in your state?

featherbedding Union efforts to force employers to hire more workers than demanded at a particular wage

right-to-work states States where workers in unionized companies do not have to join the union or pay union dues

Exhibit 8

Unionization Rates by Age and Gender

Unionization rates for men, shown by the blue bars, are higher than the rates for women, in part because men work more in manufacturing and women work more in the service sector, where union membership is lower. The highest membership rates are for middle-aged men.

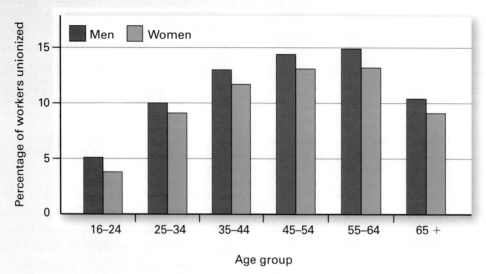

Source: U.S. Bureau of Labor Statistics, "Union Members Summary," 23 January 2015, Table 1, at http://www.bls.gov/news.release/union2.t01.htm. Figures show union membership in 2014 as a percentage of all U.S. wage and salary workers.

Exhibit 9

Right-to-Work States and Unionization Percentage by State

Shaded areas show right-to-work states, where workers in unionized companies do not have to join the union or pay union dues. Numbers indicate union membership as a percentage of all wage and salary workers in each state. States with right-to-work laws average only about half the percent of workers who belong to unions as other states.

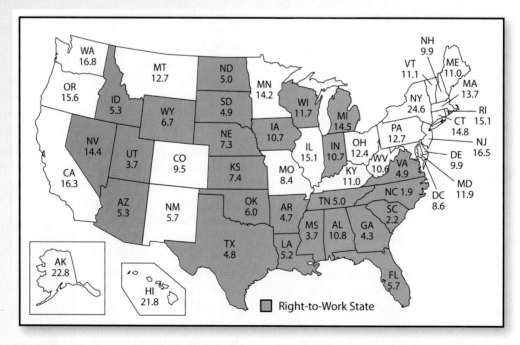

Source: U.S. Bureau of Labor Statistics, "Union Members Summary," 23 January 2015, Table 5, at http://www.bls.gov/news.release/unions2.t05.htm; and the National Right to Work Committee at www.nrtwc.org. Unionization rates are for 2014 and right-to-work states are as of 2015.

The decline in union membership rates is also due to structural changes in the U.S. economy. Unions have long been more important in the industrial sector than in the service sector. But employment in the industrial sector, which includes manufacturing, mining, and construction, has declined in recent decades as a share of all jobs. What's more, union jobs are a dwindling share of jobs in the industrial sector. For example, in the last three decades, U.S. manufacturing jobs have declined from 20 million to 16 million. But the union share of those jobs dropped from 8 million to only 2 million. Nonunion jobs in manufacturing increased.

Another factor in the decline of the union movement is a growth in market competition, particularly from imports. Increased competition from nonunion employers, both foreign and domestic, has reduced the ability of unionized firms to pass on higher labor costs as higher prices. And fewer union members mean fewer voters who belong to unions, so unions have lost political clout.

The near disappearance of the strike has cut union power. During the 1970s, an average of about 300 strikes a year in the United States involved 1,000 or more workers. In the past decade, there have been only about 15 such strikes a year on average. Worse still for organized labor, many recent strikes have ended badly for union workers; companies such as Caterpillar, Continental Airlines, Hormel Foods, International Paper, and Phelps Dodge Copper hired replacement workers. Union members are now less inclined to strike because of the increased willingness of employers to hire strikebreakers and the increased willingness of workers—both union and nonunion—to work during a strike. Strikes also cut company profits, which hurts workers whose pay is tied to profits, thus dampening the incentive to strike.

Finally, when unions first appeared in the United States, working conditions were dreadful. Hours were long, pay was low, and the workplace was often dangerous. Unions helped deliver higher pay, reduced work hours, and created a safer workplace. What's more, with the support of unions, the federal government broadened worker protections against unfair dismissal, plant closings, worker injuries, and unemployment. Social Security, Medicare, and other transfer programs also buffer workers from the ravages of poor health and old age. Because of all these improvements, the average worker feels less compelled to rely on unions for protection. In this sense, unions have become victims of their own success.

12-5 FINAL WORD

The first half of this chapter focused on labor supply and explained why wages differ across occupations and among individuals within an occupation. The interaction of labor demand and supply determines wages and employment. The second half of the chapter explored the effect of unions on the labor market. At one time, unions dominated some key industries. But as global competition intensifies, employers have a harder time passing higher union labor costs along to consumers. Both in the United States and in other industrial economies, union members represent a dwindling segment of the labor force. Now only 6.6 percent of private-sector workers in the United States are union members. Half of all union members in the United States are government workers.

STUDY TOOLS 12

READY TO STUDY? IN THE BOOK, YOU CAN:

☐ Work the Problems at the end of the chapter.

☐ Rip out the chapter review card for a handy summary of the chapter and key terms.

ONLINE AT CENGAGEBRAIN.COM YOU CAN:

☐ Collect StudyBits while you read and study the chapter.

☐ Quiz yourself on key concepts.

☐ Prepare for tests with chapter flash cards as well as flash cards that you create.

☐ Watch videos to explore economics further.

CHAPTER 12 PROBLEMS

Your instructor can access the answers to these problems online at http://cengagebrain.com.

12-1 Explain why the quantity of labor supplied increases with the wage, other things remain constant

1. *(Market Supply of Labor)* The following table shows the hours per week supplied to a particular market by three individuals at various wage rates. Calculate the total hours per week (Q_T) supplied to the market.

Hourly Wage	Hours per Week			
	Q_1	Q_2	Q_3	Q_T
$ 15	20	0	0	___
16	25	0	0	___
17	35	10	0	___
18	45	25	10	___
19	42	40	30	___
20	38	37	45	___

Why does the quantity supplied tend to increase with the hourly wage? Which individuals, if any, have backward-bending supply curves in the wage range shown? Does the market supply curve bend backward in the wage range shown in the table?

2. *(Substitution and Income Effects)* Suppose that the cost of living increases, thereby reducing the purchasing power of your income. If your money wage doesn't increase, you may work *more* hours because of this cost-of-living increase. Is this response predominantly an income effect or a substitution effect? Explain.

3. *(Nonwage Determinants of Labor Supply)* Suppose that two jobs are exactly the same except that one is performed in an air-conditioned workplace. How could you measure the value workers attach to such a job amenity?

12-2 Describe why some workers earn higher wages than other workers

4. *(Why Wages Differ)* Why might permanent wage differences occur between different markets for labor or within the same labor market?

12-3 Summarize the objectives of labor unions and outline strategies used to achieve these objectives

5. *(Craft and Industrial Unions)* Both industrial unions and craft unions attempt to raise their members' wages, but each goes about it differently. Explain the difference in approaches and describe the impact these differences have on excess quantity of labor supplied.

6. *(Union Objectives)* What other objectives besides higher wages do unions pursue?

7. *(Union Strategies)* What strategies do unions employ to achieve their wage objectives?

12-4 Offer reasons why unionization rates have declined in recent decades

8. *(Unionization Rates)* What trends have worked against the union movement during the last half century? What has happened to the effectiveness of strikes and why?

9. *(Industrial Unions)* Review the logic underlying the exhibit below. Then determine the effect, on the industry and a typical firm, of an increase in the demand for industry output. Show your conclusions on a graph. Does the magnitude of the increase in demand make a difference?

Effects of Labor Union's Wage Floor

10. *(The Strike)* Why might firms in industries with high fixed costs be inclined to prevent strikes or end strikes quickly?

11. *(Industrial Unions)* Why are unions more effective at raising wages in oligopolistic industries than in competitive industries?

ECON ONLINE

PREPARE FOR TESTS ON THE STUDYBOARD!

◯ CORRECT

◯ INCORRECT

◯ INCORRECT

◯ INCORRECT

Personalize Quizzes from Your StudyBits

Take Practice Quizzes by Chapter

CHAPTER QUIZZES

▶ Chapter 1

Chapter 2

Chapter 3

Chapter 4

4LTR PRESS

13 | Capital, Interest, Entrepreneurship, and Corporate Finance

Raymond McCrea Jones/Redux

LEARNING OUTCOMES

After studying this chapter, you will be able to...

13-1 Derive a firm's demand curve for investment, and determine its marginal cost of investing

13-2 Explain what determines the interest rate for loanable funds

13-3 Describe four reasons why interest rates differ across markets

13-4 Demonstrate how to convert future dollars into their present value

13-5 Summarize how entrepreneurs drive the economy forward

13-6 Distinguish between stocks and bonds, and explain which involves more risk and why

After finishing this chapter go to **PAGE 232** for **STUDY TOOLS**

Topics discussed in Chapter 13 include:

- Production, saving, and time
- Consumption, saving, and time
- Optimal investment
- Loanable funds market
- Present value and discounting
- Role of the entrepreneur
- Corporate finance
- Stocks, bonds, and securities exchanges

- Why is a movie download only half the price of a movie ticket?
- Why do you burn your mouth eating pizza?
- What's seed money, and why can't Farmer Jones grow much without it?
- What's the harm in pirated software, music, and DVDs?
- Why are state lottery jackpots worth much less than the advertised millions?

- Who is and is not an entrepreneur?
- Which U.S. corporation is the most valuable in the world?

These and other questions are answered in this chapter, which examines how businesses get started and how they are financed.

So far, our discussion of resources has focused primarily on labor markets. This emphasis is appropriate because labor generates most income—more than two-thirds of the total. The rewards of labor, however, depend in part on the amount and quality of the other resources employed, particularly capital. A farmer plowing a field with a tractor is more productive than one scraping the soil with a stick. This chapter first looks at the role of capital in production—its cost and its expected return. Second, we consider the role the entrepreneur plays in driving the economy forward. Finally, we explore the sources and uses of corporate finance.

> **"Who is and is not an entrepreneur?"**

13-1 THE ROLE OF TIME IN PRODUCTION AND CONSUMPTION

Time is important in both production and consumption. In this section, we first consider the role of time in the production decision, then show why firms borrow household savings. Next, we consider the role of time in the consumption decision and show why households are rewarded to save, or to defer consumption. By bringing together borrowers and savers, we find the market interest rate.

13-1a Production, Saving, and Time

Suppose Jones is a primitive farmer in a simple economy. Isolated from any neighbors or markets, he literally scratches out a living on a plot of land, using only some crude sticks. While his crop is growing, none of it is available for current consumption. Because production takes time, Jones must rely on food saved from prior harvests. The longer the growing season, the more he must save. Thus, even in this simple example, it is clear that *production cannot occur without savings.*

With his current resources, consisting of land, labor, seed corn, fertilizer, and some crude sticks, Jones grows about 100 bushels of corn a year. He soon realizes that if he had a plow—a type of investment good, or capital—his productivity would increase. Making a plow in such a primitive setting, however, is time consuming and would keep him away from his fields for a year. Thus, the plow has an opportunity cost of 100 bushels of corn. He could not survive this drop in production without enough corn saved from previous harvests.

The question is: Should he invest his time in the plow? The answer depends on the cost and benefit of the plow. We already know that the plow's opportunity cost is 100 bushels—the forgone output. The benefit depends on how much the plow increases crop production and how long it lasts. Jones figures that the plow would boost annual yield by 50 bushels and would last his lifetime. In making the investment decision, he compares the current cost to the future benefit. Suppose he decides that adding 50 bushels a year outweighs the one-time cost of 100 bushels to make the plow.

In making the plow, Jones produces capital to increase his productivity. More capital in an economy means more goods can be produced in the future.

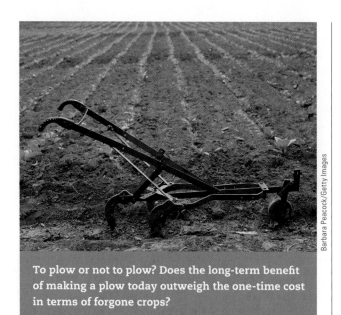

To plow or not to plow? Does the long-term benefit of making a plow today outweigh the one-time cost in terms of forgone crops?

Advanced industrial economies are characterized by abundant capital accumulation.

You can see why production cannot occur without savings. *Production requires savings because production take time—time during which goods and services are not available from current production.* Now let's modernize the example by introducing the ability to borrow. Many farmers visit the bank each spring to borrow enough "seed money" to get by until the harvest. Likewise, other businesses often borrow at least a portion of the start-up funds needed to get going. Thus, in a modern economy, producers need not rely just on their own savings. Banks and other financial institutions serve as *intermediaries* between savers and borrowers. Financial markets for stocks and bonds also help channel savings to producers.

Let's take a look at the incentive to save.

13-1b Consumption, Saving, and Time

Did you ever burn the roof of your mouth eating a slice of pizza? Have you done this more than once? Why do you persist in such self-mutilation? You persist because that bite of pizza is worth more to you now than the same bite a minute from now. In fact, you are willing to risk burning your mouth rather than wait just a minute until the pizza has lost its destructive properties. In a small way, this reflects the fact that you and other consumers value

positive rate of time preference Consumers value present consumption more than future consumption

interest rate Interest per year as a percentage of the amount saved or borrowed

present consumption more than *future* consumption. Not pie in the sky; pie now. You and other consumers are said to have a **positive rate of time preference**.

Because you value present consumption more than future consumption, you are willing to pay more to consume now rather than wait. And prices often reflect this greater willingness to pay. Consider the movies. You pay about twice as much for a movie ticket than to download the movie three months later. The same is true for books. By waiting for the paperback edition, you can usually save more than half the hardback price. And once a new iPad comes out, buyers willing to wait six months can usually get that model for hundreds less. Photo developers, dry cleaners, fast-food restaurants, furniture stores promising same-day delivery, cable news networks, and other suppliers tout the speed of their services, knowing that consumers prefer earlier availability. Thus, *impatience* is one explanation for a positive rate of time preference. Another is *uncertainty*. If you wait, something might prevent you from consuming the good. A T-shirt slogan captures this point best: "Life is uncertain. Eat dessert first."

> **"Because people value present consumption more than future consumption, they must be rewarded to postpone consumption—to delay gratification."**

Because people value present consumption more than future consumption, they must be rewarded to postpone consumption—to delay gratification. By saving a portion of their incomes in financial institutions such as banks, people forgo present consumption for a greater ability to consume in the future. Interest is the reward for postponing consumption. The **interest rate** is the annual reward for saving as a percentage of the amount saved. For example, if the interest rate is 5 percent, the reward, or interest, is $5 per year for each $100 saved. The higher the interest rate, other things constant, the more consumers are rewarded for saving, so the more they save, other things constant. You will learn more about this later in the chapter.

13-1c Optimal Investment

In a market economy characterized by specialization and exchange, Farmer Jones no longer needs to produce his own capital, nor need he rely on his own savings. He can purchase capital with borrowed funds. More generally, firms invest now in the expectation of a future return. Because the return is in the future, a would-be investor must estimate how much a particular investment will yield this year, next year, the year after, and in all years during the productive life of the investment. *Firms buy new capital goods only if they expect this investment to yield a higher return than other possible uses of their funds.*

To understand the investment decision in a modern economy, let's switch from the farm to a golf course to consider another simple example. The operators of the Hacker Haven Golf Course are thinking about buying some solar-powered golf carts. The model under consideration, called the Weekend Warrior, sells for $5,000, requires no maintenance or operating expenses, and is expected to last indefinitely. *The expected rate of return of each cart equals the expected annual earnings divided by the cart's purchase price.* More generally, the **expected rate of return on capital** is the expected annual earnings divided by capital's purchase price. The first cart is expected to generate rental income of $1,000 per year. This income, divided by the cost of the cart, yields an expected rate of return on the investment of $1,000/$5,000, or 20 percent per year. Additional carts will be used less. A second is expected to generate $750 per year in rental income, yielding a rate of return of $750/$5,000, or 15 percent; a third cart, $500 per year, or 10 percent; and a fourth cart, $250 per year, or 5 percent. They don't expect a fifth cart to get rented at all, so it has a zero expected rate of return.

Should the operators of Hacker Haven invest in golf carts, and if so, how many? Suppose they plan to borrow the money to buy the carts. The number of carts they purchase depends on the interest rate they must pay for

> **❝Firms buy new capital goods only if they expect this investment to yield a higher return than other possible uses of their funds.❞**

borrowing. If the market interest rate exceeds 20 percent, the cost of borrowing would exceed the expected rate of return for even the first cart, so the club would buy no carts. What if the operators have enough cash on hand to buy the carts? Suppose the market interest rate also reflects what club owners could earn on savings. If the interest rate earned on savings exceeded 20 percent, course owners would earn more saving their money than buying golf carts. *The market interest rate is the opportunity cost, and hence the marginal cost, of investing in capital.*

> **❝The market interest rate is the opportunity cost, and hence the marginal cost, of investing in capital.❞**

What if the market rate is 8 percent per year? At that rate, the first three carts, all with expected returns exceeding 8 percent, would each yield more than the market rate. A fourth cart would lose money, because its expected rate of return is only 5 percent. Exhibit 1 measures the interest rate along the vertical axis and the amount invested in golf carts along the horizontal axis. The step-like relationship shows the expected rate of return earned on additional dollars invested in golf carts. This relationship also indicates the amount invested in golf carts at each interest rate, so you can view this step-like relationship as Hacker Haven's demand curve for this type of investment. For example, the first cart costs $5,000 and earns a rate of return of 20 percent. A firm should reject any investment with an expected rate of return that falls below the market rate of interest.

The horizontal line at 8 percent indicates the market interest rate, which is Hacker Haven's opportunity cost and marginal cost of investing. You could view this line as the supply curve of investment faced by Hacker Haven. The course operators' objective is to choose an investment strategy that maximizes profit. Profit is maximized when $15,000 is invested in the carts—that is, when three carts are purchased. The expected return from a fourth cart is 5 percent, which is below the opportunity cost of funds. Therefore, investing in four or more carts would reduce total profit.

expected rate of return on capital The expected annual earnings divided by capital's purchase price

Exhibit 1

Exhibit 1

Expected Rate of Return on Golf Carts and the Opportunity Cost of Funds

An individual firm invests in any project with an expected rate of return that exceeds the market interest rate. At an interest rate of 8 percent, Hacker Haven invests $15,000 in three golf carts.

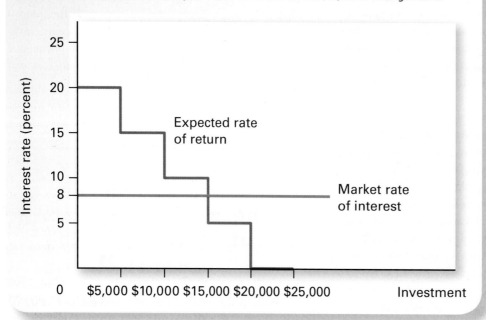

Intellectual Property

One potentially valuable capital resource is information, or so-called **intellectual property**, which is any intangible asset created by human knowledge and ideas. Intellectual property is costly to create, but, once created, it can be reproduced at low cost. For example, the first copy of a Windows 7 took about 2,500 Microsoft programmers, developers, and testers years to develop at a cost of billions. But each additional copy can be streamed over the Internet for virtually nothing. As soon as Microsoft sells a copy, that first customer could become a potential supplier of that product.

Because of this special supply characteristic, the original producer often has difficulty controlling the distribution and may have trouble getting paid. To help with these problems, the U.S. Constitution granted Congress the power "to promote the Progress of Science and useful Arts, by securing for limited Times to Authors and Inventors the exclusive Right to use their respective Writings and Discoveries." This was the only "Right"

So far, we have looked at the investment decision for a single golf course, but there are over 14,000 golf courses in the United States. The industry demand for golf carts shows the relationship between the amount all courses invest and the expected rate of return. Like the step-like relationship in Exhibit 1, the investment demand curve for the golf industry slopes downward. The lower the market rate of interest, the more invested in golf carts.

Let's move beyond golf carts and consider the investment decisions of all industries: publishing, software, farming, fast food, sporting goods, and thousands more. Individual industries have downward-sloping demand curves for investment. More is invested when the opportunity cost of borrowing is lower, other things constant. A downward-sloping investment demand curve for the entire economy can be derived, with some qualifications, from a horizontal summation of all industries' downward-sloping investment demand curves.

We have now discussed investing in physical capital. Whether the firm borrows money or draws on savings, the market interest rate represents the opportunity cost of investment. Let's shift gears and turn to a less tangible form of capital—intellectual property.

intellectual property
An intangible asset created by human knowledge and ideas

Pirated movies are sold all over the world and represent one of the largest examples of property rights violations.

grgreg/iStockphoto.com

spelled out in the U.S. Constitution as initially ratified by the states (the Bill of Rights, the first 10 amendments to the Constitution, was ratified later). Originators are thereby better able to benefit from their creations. A *patent* establishes property rights to an invention or other technical advances. A *copyright* confers property rights to an original expression of an author, artist, composer, or computer programmer (e.g., this textbook is copyrighted). And a *trademark* establishes property rights in unique commercial marks and symbols, such as McDonald's golden arches, Nike's swoosh, or Apple's iconic apple with a bite out of it.

Granting property rights is one thing; enforcing them is another. (Do you have any pirated software, music, or movies?) Much of the software, music, and movies sold around the world, particularly in Indonesia, Zimbabwe, Vietnam, China, India, and Russia, are pirated editions of products developed in the United States. For example, Windows 7, which retailed for about $320 in the United States, was available in China in pirated form for as little as $3 even before its U.S. release date. Websites around the world offered step-by-step instructions on how to find and install prerelease, pirated versions. Worldwide more than 40 percent of all software in use is pirated. The ready availability of pirated software stunts development of a homegrown software industry in countries where piracy thrives. And some movies are available on the black market as DVDs even before they open in U.S. theaters.

Enforcing property rights is costly, and this diminishes the incentive to create new products and new ideas. Pirated videos, music, computer games, and software bring no royalties to the artists, no wages to industry workers, no income to the producers or programmers, and no taxes to the government. Even within the United States, the music industry has been devastated by the ease with which music can be shared online. Between 2000 and 2014, music-industry revenue dropped 50 percent. Sharing music files is not a victimless crime: Since 2000, for example, more than one-fourth of music industry workers lost their jobs as sales declined. Most musicians now earn more from touring than from recordings.

Intellectual property is an intangible asset that fuels the digital economy. How society nurtures incentives to create new ideas, inventions, and artistic creations affects economic development around the globe.[1]

1. Susan Athey and Scott Stern, "The Nature and Incidence of Software Piracy: Evidence from Windows," Chapter 15 in *Economic Analysis of the Digital Economy*, Avi Goldfarb et al., eds. (University of Chicago Press, 2015); Michael Driscoll, "Selling Songs for a Song? Scrutinizing the Streaming Model," *Wall Street Journal*, 27 March 2015; Joel Mokyr, "Intellectual Property Rights, the Industrial Revolution, and the Beginning of Modern Economic Growth," *American Economic Review*, 99 (May 2009): 349–355; "Software Pirates in China Beat Microsoft to the Punch," Reuters, 18 October 2009; and World Intellectual Property Organization at http://www.wipo.int.

13-2 THE MARKET FOR LOANABLE FUNDS

You earlier learned why producers are willing to pay interest to borrow money: *Money provides a command over resources, making production possible.* The simple principles developed for Farmer Jones and Hacker Haven can be generalized to other producers. The major demanders of loans are entrepreneurs who typically borrow to start firms and to invest in physical capital, such as machines, trucks, and buildings, and in intellectual property, such as patents, copyrights, and trademarks. At any time, a firm has a variety of investment opportunities. The firm ranks these from highest to lowest, based on the expected rates of return. *The firm increases investment until the expected rate of return on that marginal investment just equals the market interest rate.* With other inputs held constant, the demand curve for investment slopes downward.

But entrepreneurs are not the only demanders of loans. As we have seen, households value present consumption more than future consumption; they are willing to pay extra to consume now rather than later. One way to ensure that goods and services are available now is to borrow for present consumption, as reflected by home mortgages, car loans, and credit card purchases. Some people also borrow to invest in their human capital, as reflected by college loans; Americans owed more than $1 trillion in student loans as of 2015. The household's demand curve for loans, like the firm's demand for loans, slopes downward, indicating that consumers are more willing and able to borrow at lower interest rates, other things constant. The government and the rest of the world are also demanders of loans.

13-2a Demand for Loanable Funds

The **demand for loanable funds** curve shows the negative relationship between the market interest rate and the quantity of loans demanded, other things constant. This curve is based on the expected rate of return these borrowed funds yield when invested in capital. Each firm has a downward-sloping demand curve for loanable funds, reflecting a declining rate of return on investment. With some qualifications, the

demand for loanable funds The negative relationship between the market interest rate and the quantity of loanable funds demanded, other things constant

Exhibit 2

Market for Loanable Funds

Because of the declining expected rate of return on capital, the quantity of loanable funds demanded is inversely related to the interest rate. The market rate of interest, 8 percent, is found where the demand curve for loanable funds intersects the supply curve of loanable funds. An increase in the demand for loanable funds from *D* to *D′* raises the market interest rate from 8 percent to 9 percent and increases the equilibrium quantity of loanable funds from $1.0 trillion to $1.1 trillion.

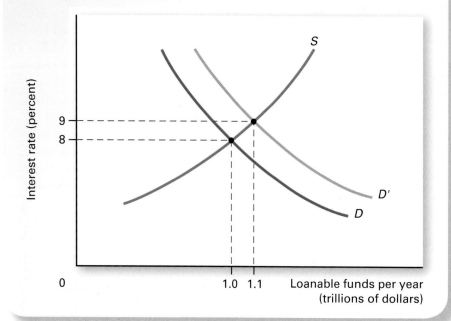

institutions play the role of *financial intermediaries* in what is known as the market for loanable funds. The higher the interest rate, other things constant, the greater the reward for saving. As people save more, the quantity of loanable funds increases. The **supply of loanable funds** curve shows the positive relationship between the market interest rate and the quantity of savings supplied, other things constant, as reflected by the usual upward-sloping supply curve shown as S in Exhibit 2. In recent years, a lot of savings have come from abroad, especially China. Factors assumed constant along this supply curve include the expected rate of inflation and people's retirement plans.

13-2c Market Interest Rate

The **loanable funds market** brings together borrowers, or demanders of loanable funds, and savers, or suppliers of loanable funds, to determine the market interest rate. The demand curve and supply curve of loanable funds come together, as in Exhibit 2, to determine the market interest rate. In this case, the equilibrium interest rate of 8 percent is the only one that exactly matches the wishes of borrowers and savers. The equilibrium quantity of loanable funds is $1.0 trillion per year. Any change in the demand or supply of loanable funds changes the market interest rate. For example, a major technological breakthrough that increases the productivity of capital increases its expected rate of return, shifting the demand curve

demand for loanable funds of each firm can be summed horizontally to yield the market demand for loanable funds, shown as *D* in Exhibit 2. Factors assumed constant along this demand curve include the expected rate of inflation, the prices of other resources, the level of technology, the customs and conventions of the market, and the tax laws.

13-2b Supply of Loanable Funds

Banks are willing to pay interest on savings because they can, in turn, lend these savings to those who need credit, such as farmers, golf courses, construction companies, home buyers, college students, and entrepreneurs looking to start a new business or buy capital goods. Banks and other financial

supply of loanable funds The positive relationship between the market interest rate and the quantity of loanable funds supplied, other things constant

loanable funds market The market in which savers (suppliers of loanable funds) and borrowers (demanders of loanable funds) come together to determine the market interest rate and the quantity of loanable funds exchanged

> **"The demand curve and supply curve of loanable funds come together to determine the market interest rate."**

for loanable funds rightward, as shown in the movement from D to D'. Such an increase in the demand for loanable funds would raise the equilibrium interest rate to 9 percent and increase the market quantity of loanable funds to $1.1 trillion per year.

13-3 WHY INTEREST RATES DIFFER

So far, we have been talking about *the* market interest rate, implying that only one rate prevails in the loanable funds market. At any particular time, however, a range of interest rates coexist depending on the circumstances of the borrower. Exhibit 3 shows interest rates for loans in various markets. The interest rate for home mortgages is relatively low because this loan is backed up by the home itself. The so-called **prime rate** is the interest rate lenders charge their most trustworthy business borrowers. The highest is the rate charged on credit card balances. Let's see why interest rates differ.

13-3a Risk

Some borrowers are more likely than others to *default* on their loans—that is, not to pay them back. Before a bank lends money, it usually requires a borrower to put up **collateral**, which is an asset pledged by the borrower that can be sold to pay off the loan in the event of a default. With business loans, any valuable asset—land, buildings, machinery, or intellectual property—the firm owns can serve as collateral. With a home mortgage, the home itself becomes collateral. And with a car loan, the car becomes collateral. The more valuable the collateral backing up the loan, other things constant, the lower the interest rate charged on that loan. For example, the interest rate charged on car loans is usually higher than on home loans. A car loses

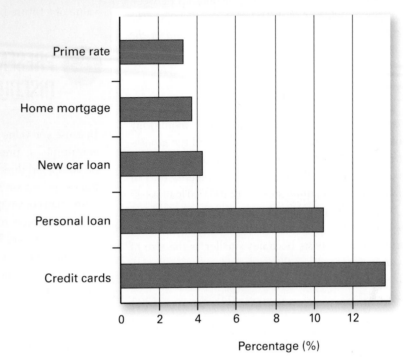

Exhibit 3

Interest Rates Charged for Different Types of Loans

Interest rates are higher for riskier loans. Rates for home mortgages and new cars are relatively low because these loans are backed up by the home or car as collateral. Personal loans and credit card balances face the highest rates, because these loans are riskier—that is, the likelihood borrowers fail to repay the loans is greater and the borrower offers no collateral.

Sources: Federal Reserve Board; Bankrate.com; and Money.msn.com. Rates are as of August 2015. The home mortgage figure is for a 30-year fixed rate, new car loans are for 48 months, and personal loans are for two years.

its value more quickly than a home does, and a car can be driven away by a defaulting borrower, whereas a home usually increases in value and stays put (home prices declined leading up to the Great Recession, creating trouble for both borrowers and banks, but that was unusual). So a car typically offers worse collateral than a home—hence, the interest charged on a car loan is usually higher. Interest rates are higher still for personal loans and credit cards, because such borrowers usually offer no collateral.

Within types of loans, borrowers with a bad credit history are charged higher interest, assuming they can borrow at all. For example, borrowers considered poor credit risks are charged more than twice as much interest on personal loans than borrowers considered good credit risks.

prime rate The interest rate lenders charge their most trustworthy business borrowers

collateral An asset pledged by the borrower that can be sold to pay off the loan in the event the borrower defaults

13-3b Duration of the Loan

The future is uncertain, and the further into the future a loan is to be repaid, the more uncertain that repayment becomes. Bad things can happen over time. Thus, as the duration of a loan increases, lenders require a higher interest rate to compensate for the greater risk. The **term structure of interest rates** is the relationship between the duration of a loan and the interest rate charged. *The interest rate usually increases with the duration of the loan, other things constant.*

13-3c Administration Costs

The costs of executing the loan agreement, monitoring the loan, and collecting payments are called the *administration costs* of the loan. These costs, as a proportion of the loan, decrease as the size of the loan increases. For example, the cost of administering a $100,000 loan is less than 10 times the cost of administering a $10,000 loan. Consequently, that portion of the interest charge reflecting administration costs becomes smaller as the size of the loan increases, other things constant, thus reducing the interest rate for larger loans.

> **❝**At any given time, interest rates may differ across borrowers because of differences in risk, maturity, administrative costs, and tax treatment.**❞**

13-3d Tax Treatment

Differences in the tax treatment of different types of loans also affects the interest rate charged. For example, the interest earned on loans to state and local governments is not subject to federal income taxes. Because lenders focus on their after-tax rate of interest, state and local governments pay a lower interest rate than otherwise similar borrowers pay.

TO REVIEW: The demand and supply of loanable funds determine the market interest rate. At any given time, interest rates may differ across borrowers because of differences in risk, maturity, administrative costs, and tax treatment. Now we move on to consider the present value of a future benefit.

13-4 PRESENT VALUE AND DISCOUNTING

Because you value present consumption more than future consumption, present and future consumption cannot be compared directly. Someone who "eats like there's no tomorrow" apparently values present consumption much more than consumption tomorrow. A way of standardizing the discussion is to measure all consumption in terms of its present value. **Present value** is the current value of a payment or payments to be received in the future. For example, how much would you pay now to receive $100 one year from now? Put another way, what is the *present value* to you of receiving $100 one year from now?

13-4a Present Value of Payment One Year Hence

Suppose the market interest rate is 8 percent and you can either lend or borrow at that rate. One way to determine how much you would pay for the opportunity to receive $100 one year from now is to ask how much you would have to save now, at the market interest rate, to end up with $100 one year from now. Here's the problem we are trying to solve: What amount of money, if saved at an interest rate of, say, 8 percent, would accumulate to $100 one year from now? We can calculate the answer with a simple formula:

$$\text{Present value} \times 1.08 = \$100$$

or:

$$\text{Present value} = \frac{\$100}{1.08} = \$92.59$$

Thus, if the interest rate is 8 percent, $92.59 is the present value of receiving $100 one year from now; it is the most you would pay today to receive $100 one year from now. Rather than pay more than $92.59, you could simply deposit your $92.59, earn the market interest rate of 8 percent, and end up with $100 a year from now

term structure of interest rates The relationship between the duration of a loan and the interest rate charged; typically interest rates increase with the duration of the loan, because longer loans are considered more risky

present value The value today of income to be received in the future (ignoring taxes). Dividing the future payment by 1 plus the prevailing interest rate to express it in today's dollars is called **discounting**.

The present value of $100 to be received one year from now depends on the interest rate. The more that present consumption is preferred to future consumption, the more must be offered savers to defer consumption. *The higher the interest rate, the more any future payment is discounted and the lower its present value.* Put another way, the higher the interest rate, the less you need to save now to yield a given amount in the future. For example, if the interest rate is 10 percent, the present value of receiving $100 one year from now is $100/1.10, which equals $90.91.

> **"The higher the interest rate, the more any future payment is discounted and the lower its present value."**

On the other hand, the less present consumption is preferred to future consumption, the less savers need to be paid to defer consumption, so the lower the interest rate. The lower the interest rate, the less the future income is discounted and the greater its present value. A lower interest rate means that you must save more now to yield a given amount in the future. As a general rule, the present value of receiving an amount one year from now is

$$\text{Present value} = \frac{\text{Amount received one year from now}}{1 + \text{interest rate}}$$

For example, when the interest rate is 5 percent, the present value of receiving $100 one year from now is

$$\text{Present value} = \frac{\$100}{1 + 0.05} = \frac{\$100}{1.05} = \$95.24$$

13-4b Present Value for Payments in Later Years

Now consider the present value of receiving $100 two years from now. What amount of money, if deposited at the market interest rate of 5 percent, would total

> **"The present value of a given payment is smaller the further into the future that payment is to be received."**

$100 after two years? After one year, the value would be the present value times 1.05, which would then earn the market interest rate during the second year. After two years, the deposit would have accumulated to the present value times 1.05 times 1.05. Thus, we have the equation:

$$\text{Present value} \times 1.05 \times 1.05$$
$$= \text{Present value} \times (1.05)^2 = \$100$$

Solving for the present value yields

$$\text{Present value} = \frac{\$100}{(1.05)^2} = \frac{\$100}{1.1025} = \$90.70$$

If the $100 were to be received three years from now, we would discount the payment over three years:

$$\text{Present value} = \frac{\$100}{(1.05)^3} = \$86.38$$

If the interest rate is i, the present value of M dollars received t years from now is

$$\text{Present value} = \frac{M}{(1 + i)^t}$$

Because $(1 + i)$ is greater than 1, the more times it is multiplied by itself (as determined by t), the larger the denominator and the smaller the present value. Thus, *the present value of a given payment is smaller the further into the future that payment is to be received.*

13-4c Present Value of an Income Stream

So far, we have figured out the present value of a single sum to be received in the future. Most investments, however, yield a stream of income over time. In cases where the income is received for a period of years, the present value of each receipt can be computed individually and the results summed to yield the present value of the entire income stream.

discounting Converting future dollar amounts into present value

For example, the present value of receiving $100 next year and $150 the year after is simply the present value of the first year's receipt plus the present value of the second year's receipt. If the interest rate is 5 percent,

$$\text{Present value} = \frac{\$100}{1.05} + \frac{\$150}{(1.05)^2} = \$231.29$$

13-4d Present Value of an Annuity

A given sum of money received each year for a specified number of years is called an **annuity**. Such an income stream is called a *perpetuity* if it continues indefinitely. The present value of receiving a certain amount forever seems like it should be a very large sum indeed. But because future income is valued less the more distant into the future it is to be received, the present value of receiving a particular amount forever is not much more than that of receiving it for, say, 20 years.

To determine the present value of receiving $100 a year forever, we need only ask how much money must be deposited in a savings account to yield $100 in interest each year. If the interest rate is 1 percent, a deposit of $10,000 will earn $100 per year. Thus, the present value of receiving $100 a year indefinitely when the interest rate is 1 percent is $10,000. More generally, the present value of receiving a sum each year forever equals the amount received each year divided by the interest rate.

Present value of receiving M dollars

$$\text{each year forever} = \frac{M}{i}$$

The concept of present value is useful for investment decisions. What about your decision to invest in human capital—to go to college? A chart in the previous chapter showed that those with at least a college degree earned nearly twice as much as those with just a high school diploma. We could compute the present value of an education by discounting earnings based on that level of education, then summing total earnings over your working life. Even without doing the calculations, we can say with reasonable certainty that the present value of at least a college education will be nearly twice that of just a high school education. To develop an appreciation for present value and discounting, consider this: after discounting and taxes, the present value of a recent $258 million Powerball lottery prize paid out over 30 years was less than one-third that amount.

annuity A given sum of money received each year for a specified number of years

This discussion of present value and discounting concludes our treatment of capital and interest. We now turn to a special factor of production: entrepreneurial ability, or entrepreneurship.

13-5 ENTREPRENEURSHIP

In a market economy, people are free to risk their time and savings to start a business. If the business succeeds, they are rewarded with profit. If it fails, they could lose their life's savings plus all the time they put into their enterprise. Chances of success are not great—only about one-third of new businesses in the United States last at least five years.[2] But many survive, some thrive, and a few make their founders rich. Despite the high failure rate, the profit motive and the drive to create something of lasting value, to make a mark in the world, attract many would-be entrepreneurs.

13-5a Role of the Entrepreneur

An entrepreneur comes up with an idea, turns that idea into a marketable product, accepts the risk of success or failure, and claims any resulting profit or loss. That idea might be a new product, a better version of an existing product, or a more efficient way of making something already available. Because each of those activities often involves long and costly development, such ventures are risky. Entrepreneurs must have the confidence to accept that risk and must inspire confidence in others needed to succeed, such as resource suppliers, lenders, investors, and consumers. But a good idea, in itself, does not guarantee profit. To succeed, an entrepreneur must figure out how best to transform that idea into reality. An entrepreneur must obtain the *financial capital* needed to start or expand the business. An entrepreneur must then bring together the necessary resources to produce and market the product.

Because there is no formal market for entrepreneurship, entrepreneurs become their own bosses—that is, they hire themselves. In addition to entrepreneurship, or entrepreneurial ability, some supply other resources to the firm. Imagine an entrepreneur who comes up with a good idea, borrows start-up money from a bank, and hires a manager to line up all the other resources required to bring that idea to life. The entrepreneur promises to pay resource suppliers at least their opportunity cost; otherwise, they would go elsewhere. This entrepreneur, by hiring a manager and by agreeing to pay all resources, supplies nothing other than entrepreneurship. Yet the entrepreneur has acquired

2. Daniel Kahneman, *Thinking, Fast and Slow* (Farrar, Straus and Giroux, 2011), p. 256.

the right to control these resources in return for the promise to pay at least the market rate. Despite what may seem like limited involvement, this entrepreneur owns the firm, and the firm consists of a bundle of contracts or agreements between the entrepreneur and resource suppliers. At the end of the week or month or year, the entrepreneur can claim as profit whatever is left after paying all other resources. The entrepreneur is the *residual claimant*, the one who gets to keep what's left over and who is responsible for covering any loss.

What distinguishes the role of the entrepreneur is not the management of resources in the firm but the power to decide who manages those resources. An entrepreneur who decides to manage the firm, and many do, would still delegate some decisions to employees. Therefore, don't think that an entrepreneur must manage the firm. *An entrepreneur must simply have the authority to hire and fire the manager.*

In reality, an entrepreneur seldom has the limited role described above. An entrepreneur often manages the business, at least in the beginning, and usually supplies at least some of the financial capital required to get the business off the ground, because banks may be reluctant to lend to a risky startup. And, in reality, entrepreneurship is quite risky. One survey of about 22,000 new U.S. enterprises between 1987 and 2008 found that while a few entrepreneurs earned over a billion dollars when they sold their firms, most came away with nothing.[3]

> **"What distinguishes the role of the entrepreneur is not the management of resources in the firm but the power to decide who manages those resources."**

3. Robert Hall and Susan Woodward, "The Burden of Nondiversifiable Risk of Entrepreneurship," *American Economic Review*, 100 (June 2010): 1163–1194.

AP Images/Paul Sakuma

Steve Jobs: an entrepreneur with many good ideas.

Though the rewards from innovation are often meager for individual entrepreneurs, society as a whole benefits greatly,[4] as we'll see next.

13-5b Entrepreneurs Drive the Economy Forward

Entrepreneurs create new or better products, new production methods, or new ways of doing business. These are sources of technological progress and economic growth in the economy. Successful entrepreneurs initiate creative change, thereby driving the economy forward.

New Products

Some entrepreneurs come up with new products, opening up markets that had not before existed. For example, Levi Strauss and his partner Jacob Davis in 1873 won a patent for fastening blue denim with small metal studs to create the most popular clothing in the world, now called Levi's jeans. As another example, as a Harvard undergraduate, Mark Zuckerberg was the primary creator of the social-networking site Facebook. By 2015, Facebook had more than 1.4 billion active users. Zuckerberg, the chief executive officer, had an estimated net worth of $35 billion.

Improve Existing Products

Some entrepreneurs begin with an existing product and make it better. For example, Howard Schultz took the simple cup of coffee and turned it into a $70 billion corporation by offering higher quality and greater variety in a more inviting setting. Founded by Schultz in 1985, Starbucks now employs more than 190,000 people at more than 20,000 locations around the world. Guy Laliberte founded Cirque du Soleil in 1984 as a modern update on the circus. By 2015 he had created more than 21 different shows, some staying put and some touring. For his creative efforts, he had accumulated a personal net worth of $1.9 billion as of 2015.

New Production Methods

Some entrepreneurs combine resources more efficiently to reduce costs. They use less costly materials,

4. William Baumol, "Innovation: Meager Private Gains, Enormous Social Gains," *Entrepreneurship Research Journal*, 1 (Issue 4, 2011), Berkeley Electronic Press, at http://www.bepress.com/erj/.

Mark Zuckerberg's idea earned him billions of dollars.

Corporate Inventors

Inventors are considered entrepreneurs if they bear the risk of success or failure. But most inventors are hired hands. Corporations such as Pfizer, Intel, and Apple employ thousands of scientists and engineers to improve existing products, develop new ones, and devise more efficient ways to make things. These corporate inventors still get paid even in years when their creative juices slow to a trickle. Because these hired inventors take no more risk than most other employees, they are not considered entrepreneurs.

Exhibit 4 shows the sources of invention since 1990 as measured by the number of U.S. patents awarded. Patents increased 235 percent between 1990 and 2014. IBM led all organizations, with 2.5 percent of all patents in 2014. Samsung was second, with 1.6 percent. But the share of patents awarded to individual inventors fell from 19 percent in 1990 to only 6 percent in 2014. Individual inventors usually are considered entrepreneurs, even those who sell their patents to those better able to turn them into a marketable product and defend against copy-cats.[5] These inventors take on risks in a way that inventors who work for corporations do not. So self-employed inventors usually are considered entrepreneurs.

Managers

Most entrepreneurs do more than simply sell their good ideas for others to run with. They try to bring their ideas to the market by going into business. But, as already noted, founding a business does not necessarily mean the entrepreneur must manage it. For example, Dean Kamen, inventor of the Segway Human Transporter, created a company to make and market his invention. He hired a manager to run the company because Kamen was too busy inventing other things (besides the Segway, he holds patents for a water purifier, a mobile dialysis system, the first insulin pump, and an all-terrain electric wheelchair, among other things). Even though he didn't manage the business himself, he was still an entrepreneur because he had the power to hire and fire the manager (he eventually sold the company). The manager was a well-paid and important employee but not an entrepreneur.

Stockholders

More than half of all households in the United States own corporate stock, either directly or indirectly, and thus take on the risk of a corporation's success or failure. Does this risk-bearing make the stockholder an entrepreneur? No. Entrepreneurs do more than assume the risk of success or failure. They begin with a bright idea and usually

employ newer technologies, and generally make better use of resources. Henry Ford, for example, introduced the assembly line, where automobiles move along a conveyer and the workers stay put. Ford didn't invent the automobile, but his assembly line made owning one affordable for millions of Americans. Similarly, Ray Croc didn't invent the hamburger or the hamburger stand, but he applied the principles of mass production to make McDonald's hamburgers quickly and cheaply, first across the nation and then around the world. The company he founded was valued at about $100 billion in 2015.

New Ways of Doing Business

Some entrepreneurs step outside existing business models to create new ways of doing business. For example, Michael Dell began in 1984 with $1,000 and an idea to sell personal computers directly to customers rather than through retailers. His made-to-order computers sold by phone and now over the Internet make Dell one of the world's largest computer sellers, with sales exceeding $155 million *a day*. Mary Kay Ash did the same for skin care products and cosmetics. By selling directly to consumers around the world through independent Mary Kay consultants, she created Mary Kay, Inc., a company with annual sales exceeding $4 billion.

13-5c Who Are Not Entrepreneurs?

Some people may carry out a particular function of an entrepreneur. For example, they may dream up a new product or process, they may manage resources, or they may assume the risk of success or failure. But carrying out just one of these roles does not usually make for an entrepreneur. One way of appreciating the role of an entrepreneur is to identify those who are not serving that role.

5. Alberto Galasso, Mark Schankerman, and Carlos Serrano, "Trading and Enforcing Patent Rights," *RAND Journal of Economics*, 44 (Summer 2013): 275–312.

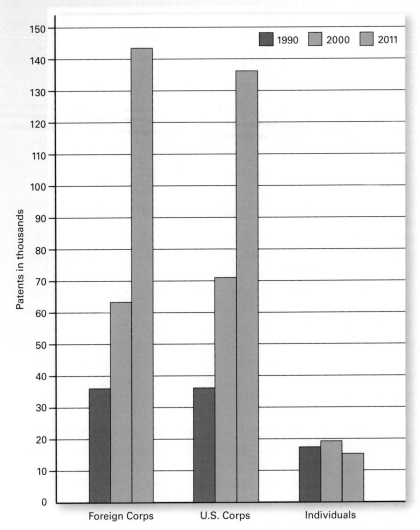

Exhibit 4

Source of U.S. Patents

Patents in thousands

Legend: 1990, 2000, 2011

Categories: Foreign Corps, U.S. Corps, Individuals

Sources: Sources: U.S. Bureau of the Census, *Statistical Abstract of the United States: 2012* (Washington, DC: U.S. Bureau of the Census, 2012), Table 778; and U.S. Patent and Trademark Office, "Patenting by Organization: 2014," at http://www.uspto.gov/web/offices/ac/ido/oeip/taf/topo_14.pdf, p. A1–1.

During the Industrial Revolution, labor-saving machinery and improved transportation and communication networks made large-scale production more profitable, but building huge factories filled with heavy machinery required substantial investments. The corporate structure became the easiest way to finance such outlays, and by 1920, corporations accounted for most employment and output in the U.S. economy. Back in Chapter 3, you learned about the pros and cons of the corporate form of business. Thus far, however, little has been said about corporate finance. As noted in Chapter 3, a corporation is a legal entity, distinct from its shareholders. The corporation may own property, earn a profit, sue or be sued, incur debt, even be found guilty of a crime. Stockholders, the owners of the corporation, are liable only to the extent of their investment in the firm. Use of the abbreviation Inc. or Corp. in the company name serves as a warning to potential creditors that stockholders will not accept personal liability for debts of the company.

13-6a Corporate Stock and Retained Earnings

figure out how to profit from that idea. An individual stockholder, on the other hand, typically has little say in a firm's operation (and most stockholders like it that way).

TO REVIEW: The entrepreneur is a prime mover in a market economy—a visionary, someone who can see what others can't. By coming up with new products, making existing products better, finding better ways to make things, of finding new ways of doing business, the entrepreneur drives the economy forward. This concludes our discussion of entrepreneurs. You now have sufficient background to consider how firms, especially corporations, are financed.

Corporations fund investment in three ways: by issuing stock, by retaining some of their profits, and by borrowing. Corporations issue and sell stock to raise money for operations and for new plants and equipment. Suppose the founder of a new firm has met with early success, but finds that to remain competitive, the firm needs to achieve economies of scale, which means the firm must grow fast. To fund that growth, the entrepreneur decides to incorporate. The newly incorporated company issues 1,000,000 shares of stock. The entrepreneur takes 100,000 shares as *owner's equity* in the corporation. The rest are sold to the public for $50 per share, which raises $45 million for the company. The

> **❝Corporations fund investment in three ways: by issuing stock, by retaining some of their profits, and by borrowing.❞**

entrepreneur, in effect, has already paid for his or her shares with the "sweat equity" required to come up with the idea, found the company, and get it rolling. The initial sale of stock to the public is called an **initial public offering**, or **IPO**. A *share* of **corporate stock** is a claim on the net income and assets of a corporation, as well as the right to vote on corporate directors and on other important matters. A person who buys 1 percent of the 1,000,000 shares issued thereby owns 1 percent of the corporation, is entitled to 1 percent of any profit, and gets to cast 1 percent of the votes on important corporate decisions.

Corporations must pay corporate income taxes on any profit. After-tax profit is either paid as **dividends** to shareholders or reinvested in the corporation. Reinvested profit, or **retained earnings,** helps the firm grow. Stockholders usually expect dividends, but the corporation is not required to pay dividends, and most new firms don't. Once shares

are issued, their price tends to fluctuate directly with the firm's profit prospects. People buy stock because the firm is expected to eventually pay dividends and because they hope the share price will appreciate, or increase, over time. Of course, stock prices can also fall. For example, between the end of 2007 and 2008, the market value of corporate stocks owned by U.S. residents fell from $19,108 billion to $13,845 billion, for a drop of 28 percent and one of the largest annual declines in decades. Exhibit 5 shows that decline. Fortunately, stock prices also rise, as they did during five of six years following 2008. By 2014, stock holdings of U.S. residents were priced 28 percent above their 2007 level and 77 percent above their 2008 level.

13-6b Corporate Bonds

Again, a corporation can acquire funds by issuing stock, by retaining earnings, or by borrowing. To borrow money, the corporation can go to a bank for a loan or it can issue and sell bonds. A **bond** is the corporation's promise to pay back the lender a fixed sum of money on the designated *maturity date* plus make interest payments until that date. For example, a corporation might sell for $1,000 a bond that promises to make an annual interest payment of, say, $80 for 20 years and to repay the $1,000 at the end of 20 years.

The payment stream from bonds is more predictable than that from stocks. Unless this corporation goes bankrupt, it must pay bondholders as promised. In contrast, stockholders are last in line when resource suppliers get paid, so bondholders get paid before stockholders. Investors usually consider bonds less risky than stocks, although bonds involve risks too. Risks include corporate

initial public offering
The initial sale of corporate stock to the public

corporate stock
Certificate reflecting part ownership of a corporation

dividends After-tax corporate profit paid to stockholders rather than retained by the firm and reinvested

retained earnings
After-tax corporate profit reinvested in the firm rather than paid to stockholders as dividends

bond Certificate reflecting a firm's promise to pay the lender periodic interest and to repay the borrowed sum of money on the designated maturity date

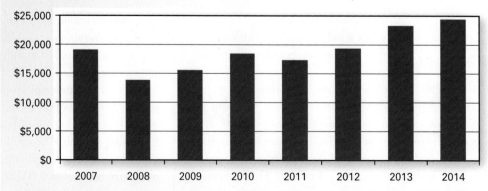

Exhibit 5

Market Value of Stocks Held by U.S. Residents at Year-End in Billions.

Source: Board of Governors of the Federal Reserve System, "Flow of Funds Guide," Table L.10, "Assets and Liabilities of the Personal Sector 1," 12 March 2015, at http://www.federalreserve.gov/releases/z1/current/accessible/l10.htm.

bankruptcy and higher market interest rates. For example, suppose you buy a bond that pays 8 percent interest. Soon after that purchase, the market interest rate increases, so newly issued bonds pay 10 percent interest. Your 8 percent bond is less attractive to lenders than the new bonds, so the market value of your bond declines. The value of your bond drops until bond buyers are indifferent between buying your 8 percent bond and buying a 10 percent bond.

Other things equal, corporations issue more bonds when interest rates are low, because their interest payments on those bonds will be lower. For example, during the low-interest years of 2012 through 2014, corporations issued record amounts of bonds—well over $1 trillion was sold to U.S. investors in 2014 alone.[6]

13-6c Securities Exchanges

Once stocks and bonds have been issued and sold, owners of these securities are free to resell them on *securities exchanges*. In the United States, the *Securities and Exchange Commission (SEC)* is the federal body that regulates securities markets. The largest securities market is the New York Stock Exchange (now *NYSE Euronext*), which trades the securities of about 2,800 major corporations, including about 500 non-U.S. companies. Altogether, more than 5,000 corporations trade on major U.S. exchanges. Another 10,000 or so, mostly smaller corporations, are traded through a network of brokers in what is known as the *over-the-counter market*. Corporations traded on major exchanges and over the counter are called publicly traded companies. There are also about 6 million much smaller corporations that are not publicly traded; shares of these nontraded corporations are individually owned by families or just a few stockholders. Plus there are about 21 million sole proprietorships and about 3 million partnerships. The 15,000 or so publicly traded corporations, though they are just a fraction of 1 percent of all businesses, account for the overwhelming share of employment and sales in the United States.

Nearly all the securities traded each business day are *secondhand securities* in the sense that they have already been issued by the corporation. So the bulk of daily transactions do not finance firms in need of investment funds. Most money from daily trading goes from a securities buyer to a securities seller. *Institutional investors*, such as banks, insurance companies, and mutual funds, account for most of the trading volume on major exchanges. By providing a *secondary market* for securities, exchanges enhance the *liquidity* of securities—that is, the exchanges make the securities more readily sold for cash and thus more attractive to own. Of growing importance in securities exchanges are *hedge funds*, which often follow complex strategies to invest for institutions and for wealthy clients.

The secondary markets for stocks also determine the current market value of the corporation. The market value of a firm at any given time can be found by multiplying the share price by the number of shares issued. Because the share price fluctuates throughout the trading day, so does the value of the corporation. In theory, the share price reflects the present value of the discounted stream of expected profit. Just to give you some idea, Apple, the top-valued U.S. corporation, had a market value of $742 billion at the close of the trading day on April 6, 2015. The 50 most valuable U.S. corporations that day had a combined market value of more than $9 trillion. Companies on U.S. stock exchanges accounted for about half of the world's stock market value.[7]

Securities prices give corporate management some indication of the wisdom of raising investment funds through retained earnings, new stock issues, or new bond issues. The greater a corporation's expected profit, other things constant, the higher the value of shares on the stock market and the lower the interest rate that would have to be paid on new bond issues. Securities markets usually promote the survival of the fittest by allocating investment funds to those firms able to make the most profitable use of them. *Thus, securities markets allocate funds more readily to successful firms than to firms in financial difficulty.* Some firms may be in such poor shape that they can't issue new securities.

The New York Stock Exchange is the largest stock exchange on the planet.

6. Mike Cherney, "Companies Take Advantage of Low Interest Rates to Issue Bonds," *Wall Street Journal*, 21 August 2014.

7. Jonathan Clements, "Four Reasons to Boost Your Foreign Stock Exposure," *Wall Street Journal*, 20 February 2015.

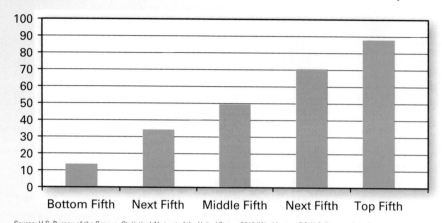

Exhibit 6

Percentage of U.S. Families Owning Corporate Stock by Income Group

Source: U.S. Bureau of the Census, *Statistical Abstract of the United States*: 2012 (Washington, DC: U.S. Bureau of the Census, 2012), 750.

Consider Exhibit 6, which lists, according to family income, the percentage of U.S. residents who own corporate stock. Note that among the poorest fifth of families, only 14 percent own stocks. Among the richest fifth, 88 percent own stocks.

A new source of finance is **crowdfunding**, which is raising money from many people through online platforms, such as Kickstarter. For example, the developer of an interactive watch needed $100,000 to fund production so he promised everyone who contributed $120 one of these watches. He was able to raise the $100,000 in just two hours.[8] After 37 days, he raised $10 million from about 69,000 people. Federal legislation has eased restrictions on the sale of securities to facilitate crowdfunding.

One final point: When economists talk about investing, they have in mind purchases of new capital, such as new machines and new buildings. When the media talk about investing, they usually mean buying stocks and bonds. To an economist, Farmer Jones is investing only when he buys new farm equipment, not when he buys stocks. As noted already, the overwhelming share of stock transactions are in secondary markets, so the money goes from buyers to sellers, and does not go toward new capital purchases. Regardless, secondary markets make shares more readily convertible into cash, more liquid, and thus more attractive to own.

crowdfunding Raising money from many people through an online platform

8. This section draws on material in Ajay Agrawal, Avi Goldfarb, and Christian Catalini, "Some Simple Economics of Crowdfunding," in *Innovation Policy and the Economy*, Josh Learner and Scott Stern, eds. (University of Chicago Press, 2014): 63–97.

This chapter introduced you to capital, interest, entrepreneurship, and corporate finance. Capital is a more complicated resource than this chapter has conveyed. For example, the demand curve for investment is a moving target, not the stable relationship drawn in Exhibit 1. An accurate depiction of the investment demand curve calls for knowledge of the marginal product of capital and the price of output in the future. But capital's productivity changes with breakthroughs in technology and with changes in the employment of other resources. The future price of the product can also vary widely. Consider, for example, the dilemma of a firm contemplating an investment in oil-drilling rigs, when the price of crude oil fluctuated between $10 and $145 per barrel, as it has over the last two decades.

STUDY TOOLS 13

READY TO STUDY? IN THE BOOK, YOU CAN:

☐ Work the Problems at the end of the chapter.

☐ Rip out the chapter review card for a handy summary of the chapter and key terms.

ONLINE AT CENGAGEBRAIN.COM YOU CAN:

☐ Collect StudyBits while you read and study the chapter.

☐ Quiz yourself on key concepts.

☐ Prepare for tests with chapter flash cards as well as flash cards that you create.

☐ Watch videos to explore economics further.

CHAPTER 13 PROBLEMS

Your instructor can access the answers to these problems online at http://cengagebrain.com.

13-1 Derive a firm's demand curve for investment, and determine its marginal cost of investing

1. *(Role of Time)* Complete the following sentences with a word or a phrase:

   a. If Bryan values current consumption more than future consumption, he has a(n) _____.

   b. The reward to households for forgoing current consumption is _____.

2. *(Investment)* What is the firm's marginal cost of investing?

Expected Rate of Return on Golf Carts and the Opportunity Cost of Funds

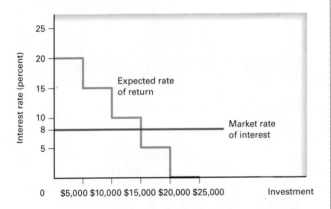

3. *(Optimal Investment)* Look at the exhibit above. If the operators of the golf course revised their revenue estimates so that each cart is expected to earn 5 percent less, how much would they invest in carts if the market interest rate is 8 percent? How much would they invest if the interest rate is 3 percent?

13-2 Explain what determines the interest rate for loanable funds

4. *(Supply of Loanable Funds)* Explain why the supply of loanable funds curve slopes upward to the right.

5. *(Demand for Loanable Funds)* Explain why the demand for loanable funds curve slopes downward to the right.

6. *(Market for Loanable Funds)* Using the demand-supply for loanable funds diagram, show the effect on the market interest rate of each of the following:

   a. An increase in the purchase price of capital

   b. An increase in the productivity of capital

   c. A shift in preferences toward present consumption and away from future consumption

13-3 Describe four reasons why interest rates differ across markets

7. *(Why Interest Rates Differ)* At any given time, a range of interest rates prevails in the economy. What four factors contribute to differences in interest rates across consumers?

13-4 Demonstrate how to convert future dollars into their present value

8. *(Present Value)* Calculate the present value of each of the following future payments. (For some of these problems you may wish to use the online calculator available at http://www.moneychimp.com/articles/finworks /fmpresval.htm.)

   a. A $10,000 lump sum received 1 year from now if the market interest rate is 8 percent

   b. A $10,000 lump sum received 2 years from now if the market interest rate is 10 percent

   c. A $1,000 lump sum received 3 years from now if the market interest rate is 5 percent

   d. A $25,000 lump sum received 1 year from now if the market interest rate is 12 percent

   e. A $25,000 lump sum received 1 year from now if the market interest rate is 10 percent

   f. A perpetuity of $500 per year if the market interest rate is 6 percent

9. *(Present Value of an Income Stream)* Suppose the market interest rate is 10 percent. Would you be willing to lend $10,000 if you were guaranteed to receive $1,000 at the end of each of the next 12 years plus a $5,000 payment 15 years from now? Why or why not?

13-5 Summarize how entrepreneurs drive the economy forward

10. *(Role of Entrepreneurs)* Describe four ways that entrepreneurs affect the economy.

11. *(Entrepreneurship)* What entrepreneurial idea do you have? How would your idea contribute to the economy?

13-6 Distinguish between stocks and bonds, and explain which involves more risk and why

12. *(Corporate Finance)* Describe three ways in which corporations acquire funds for investment.

13. *(Stocks and Bonds)* What's the difference between stocks and bonds. Which is more risky to own and why?

14. *(Securities Exchanges)* What role do securities exchanges play in financing corporations?

14 Transaction Costs, Asymmetric Information, and Behavioral Economics

B Christopher/Alamy

LEARNING OUTCOMES

After studying this chapter, you will be able to…

14-1 Describe the criteria a firm should apply when deciding whether to produce a component part or to purchase that part in the market

14-2 Explain the optimal amount of search for information when shopping for a product

14-3 Define asymmetric information, and explain why it may pose a problem for market operations

14-4 Summarize how labor markets try to cope with the problem of asymmetric information

14-5 Identify two types of limitations that can undermine rational decisions

After finishing this chapter go to **PAGE 250** for **STUDY TOOLS**

Topics discussed in Chapter 14 include:

- Transaction costs
- Vertical integration
- Bounded rationality
- Economies of scope
- Optimal search
- Winner's curse
- Asymmetric information
- Adverse selection
- Principal-agent problem
- Moral hazard
- Signaling and screening
- Behavioral economics

In the first third of this chapter, we step inside the firm to reconsider some simplifying assumptions about how firms work. We ask: Why do firms exist? How do they decide what to make themselves and what to buy from other firms? These steps

"Why is buying a used car such a gamble?"

toward realism move us beyond the simple depiction of the firm offered to this point. In the second third of this chapter, we challenge some simplifying assumptions about the information available to market participants. We ask: How does the lack of certain information affect behavior and shape market outcomes? And in the final third of the chapter, we consider why some economists are drawing on findings from psychology to enrich models of economic behavior. Specifically, we consider why many people eat too much, drink too much, smoke too much, and do other things that appear to be at odds with their rational self-interest. Overall, this chapter should help you develop a more realistic view of how the economy works.

14-1 THE FIRM'S RATIONALE AND SCOPE OF OPERATION

The competitive model assumes that all participants in the market know everything they need to about the price and availability of all inputs, outputs, and production processes. The firm is assumed to be headed by a brilliant decision maker with a computer-like ability to calculate all the relevant marginal products. This individual knows everything necessary to solve complex production and pricing problems. The irony is that if the marginal products of all inputs could be measured easily and if prices for all inputs could be easily determined, there would be little reason for production to take place in firms. In a world characterized by perfect competition, perfect information, constant returns to scale, and costless exchange, the consumer could bypass the firm to deal directly with resource suppliers, purchasing inputs in the appropriate amounts. Someone who wanted a table

could buy timber, have it milled, hire a carpenter, hire a painter, and end up with a finished product. The consumer could carry out transactions directly with each resource supplier.

14-1a The Firm Reduces Transaction Costs

So why is production carried out within firms? About 80 years ago, in a classic article, Nobel Prize winner Ronald Coase asked the question, "Why do firms exist?"[1] Why do people organize in the hierarchical structure of the firm and coordinate their decisions through a manager rather than simply relying on market exchange? His answer would not surprise today's students of economics: *Organizing activities through the hierarchy of the firm is usually more efficient than market exchange because production requires the coordination of many transactions*

---

1. "The Nature of the Firm," *Economica*, 4 (November 1937): 386–405.

among many resource suppliers. In short, firms are superior to markets when production is complicated.

Consider again the example of purchasing a table by contracting directly with all the different resource suppliers—from the logger to the painter who applied the finishing varnish. Using resource markets directly involves (1) the cost of determining what inputs are needed and how they should be combined, and (2) the cost of reaching an agreement with each resource supplier *over and above* the direct costs of the timber, nails, machinery, paint, and labor required to make the table. Where inputs are easily identified, measured, priced, and hired, production can be carried out through a price-guided "do-it-yourself" approach using the market. For example, getting your house painted is a relatively simple task: You can buy the paint and brushes and hire painters by the hour. You become your own painting contractor, hiring inputs in the market and combining them to do the job. Likewise consider different approaches to a European vacation. One traveler plans every aspect of a trip—booking flights, reserving hotel rooms, planning excursions, transportation, meals, and so on. A second traveler buys a packaged tour that includes everything. And a third traveler books all the flights but buys a land package covering hotels and excursions.

Where the costs of identifying the appropriate inputs and negotiating for each specific contribution are high, consumers minimize transaction costs by purchasing the finished product from a firm. For example, although some people serve as their own contractor when painting a house, fewer do so when building a house; most buy a home already built or hire a building contractor. *The more complicated the task, the greater the ability to economize on transaction costs through specialization and centralized control.* For example, attempting to buy a new car by contracting with the thousands of suppliers required to assemble one would be time consuming, costly, and impossible for almost anyone. What type of skilled labor should be hired and at what wages? How much steel, aluminum, plastic, glass, paint, and other materials should be purchased? How should resources be combined and in what proportions? Anyone without a detailed knowledge of auto production couldn't do it. (General Motors and Ford, for example, each deal with more than 20,000 suppliers.) That's why consumers buy assembled cars rather than contract separately with each resource supplier.

vertical integration
The expansion of a firm into stages of production earlier or later than those in which it specializes, such as a steel maker that also mines iron ore

Joy Brown/Shutterstock.com

At the margin, some activities could go either way, with some consumers using firms and some hiring resources directly in markets. The choice depends on each consumer's skill and opportunity cost of time. For example, some people may not want to be troubled with hiring all the inputs to get their house painted. Instead, they simply hire a firm for an agreed-on price—they hire a painting contractor. As you will see later in the chapter, however, hiring a contractor may give rise to other problems of quality control.

14-1b The Boundaries of the Firm

So far, the chapter has explained why firms exist: *Firms minimize the transaction costs and the production costs of economic activity.* The next question is: What are the efficient boundaries of the firm? The theory of the firm described in earlier chapters is largely silent on the boundaries of the firm—that is, on the appropriate degree of vertical integration. **Vertical integration** is the expansion of a firm into stages of production earlier or later than those in which it specializes. For example, a steel company may decide (1) to integrate backward to mine iron ore and even mine the coal used to smelt iron ore and/or (2) to integrate forward to fashion raw steel into various components. A large manufacturer employs an amazing variety of production processes, but on average about half of the cost of production goes to purchase inputs from other firms. For example, General Motors and Ford each spends over $50 billion a year on parts, materials, and services. The amount exceeds the annual output of some countries.

Outsourcing occurs when a firm buys products, such as auto parts, or services, such as data processing, from outside suppliers. How does the firm determine which activities to undertake and which to purchase from other firms? A firm relies on the division of labor and the law of comparative advantage to focus on what it does best, what it considers its **core competency**. Should Dell manufacture its own computer chips or buy them from another firm? The answer depends on the benefits and costs of internal production versus market purchases. The point bears repeating: *Internal production and market purchases are alternative ways of organizing transactions.* The choice depends on which is a more efficient way of carrying out the transaction in question. Keep in mind that market prices coordinate transactions *between* firms, whereas managers coordinate activities *within* firms. The market coordinates resources by meshing the independent plans of separate decision makers, but a firm coordinates resources through the conscious direction of the manager.

The usual assumption is that transactions are organized by market exchange unless markets pose problems. Market exchange allows each firm to benefit from specialization and comparative advantage. For example, Apple specializes in creating iPhones and buys phone chips from Taiwan Semiconductor, a specialist. At this point, it might be useful to discuss some criteria firms consider when deciding whether to purchase a particular input from the market.

Bounded Rationality of the Manager

To direct and coordinate activity in a conscious way in the firm, a manager must understand how all the pieces of the puzzle fit together. As the firm takes on more and more activities, however, the manager may start losing track of details, so the quality of managerial decisions suffers. The more tasks the firm takes on, the longer the lines of communication between the manager and production workers who must implement the decision. One constraint on vertical integration is the manager's **bounded rationality**, which limits the amount of information a manager can comprehend about the firm's operation. As the firm takes on more and more functions, coordination and communication become more difficult. Distance can also stretch management's ability. For example. the farther a business entity is from company headquarters, the

poorer the performance of that entity.[2] And a firm performing more tasks can experience diseconomies similar to those it experiences when it expands output beyond the efficient scale of production. The solution is for the firm to reduce its functions to those where it has a comparative advantage—its core competency.

Incidentally, outsourcing is growing on college campuses. The number of college bookstores run by outside companies has more than doubled in the last two decades. Barnes & Noble, for example, runs over 650 of them. But college outsourcing has moved beyond bookstores to dozens of activities including food service, custodial service, real estate management, laundry, parking, printing, and security. The growing consensus is that colleges should focus on their core competency, teaching and research, while outsourcing other functions to specialists.

Minimum Efficient Scale

As noted when firm costs were introduced in Chapter 7, the *minimum efficient scale* is the minimum rate of output at which economies of scale are fully exploited. For example, suppose that minimum efficient scale in the production of personal computers is 1 million per month, as shown by the firm's long-run average cost curve in panel (a) of Exhibit 1. Suppose this also turns out to be the amount that maximizes profit. Because the computer chip is an important component in a personal computer, should the PC maker integrate backward into chip production? What if the minimum efficient scale in chip production is 5 million per month? As you can see in panel (b) of Exhibit 1, the average cost of producing 1 million chips is much higher than the average cost at the minimum efficient scale of chip production. The PC manufacturer therefore minimizes costs by buying chips from a chipmaker of optimal size. More generally, *other things constant, a firm should buy an input if the market price is below what it would cost the firm to make.*

Easily Observable Quality

If an input is well defined and its quality is easily determined

2. Arturs Kalnins and Francine Lafontaine, "Too Far Away? The Effects of Distance to Headquarters on Business Establishment Performance," *American Economic Journal: Microeconomics*, 5 (August 2013): 157–179.

outsourcing A firm buys inputs from outside suppliers

core competency Area of specialty; the product or phase of production a firm supplies with greatest efficiency

bounded rationality The notion that there is a limit to the information that a firm's manager can comprehend and act on

Exhibit 1

Minimum Efficient Scale and Vertical Integration

The manufacturer in panel (a) is producing at the minimum efficient scale of 1,000,000 computers per month. That output requires 1,000,000 computer chips. If the computer manufacturer produced its own chips, the cost would be much higher than if it buys them from a chipmaker operating on a much larger scale. As panel (b) shows, economies of scale in chip production are far from exhausted when 1,000,000 chips a month are produced.

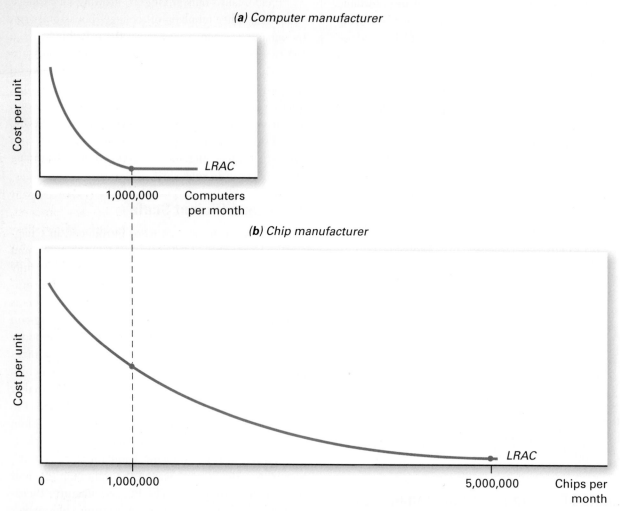

(a) Computer manufacturer

(b) Chip manufacturer

at the time of purchase, that input is more likely to be purchased in the market than produced internally, other things constant. For example, a flour mill typically buys wheat in the market rather than growing its own, as the quality of the wheat can be easily assessed upon inspection. In contrast, the quality of certain inputs can be determined only during production. Firms whose reputations depend on the operation of a key component are likely

> **"Other things constant, a firm should buy an input if the market price is below what it would cost the firm to make."**

to produce the component, especially if the quality varies widely across producers over time and can't be easily observed by inspection. For example, suppose that the manufacturer of a sensitive measuring instrument requires a crucial gauge, the quality of which can be observed only as the gauge is assembled. If the firm produces the gauge itself, it can closely monitor quality. Incidentally, firms that are more vertically integrated are also in a better position to capture the returns from research and development, so they do more of it.[3]

Producers sometimes integrate backward so they can offer consumers a guarantee about the quality of the components or ingredients in a product. For example, some chicken suppliers, such as Tyson and Perdue, can advertise the upbringing of their chickens because they raise their own. KFC, however, omits this family background because the company makes no claim about raising them, focusing instead on how well the company cooks chicken.

Many Suppliers

A firm wants an uninterrupted supply of components. If there are many suppliers of a component, a firm is more likely to buy it than make it, other things constant. Not only do abundant suppliers ensure a dependable source of components, but competition keeps the price down and quality up. On the other hand, a firm that cannot rely on a consistent supply of components may make its own to ensure a reliable source.

TO REVIEW: If a firm relies on market purchases of inputs rather than on vertical integration, it can benefit from the specialization and comparative advantage of individual suppliers. Other things constant, the firm is more likely to buy a component rather than produce it if (1) buying the component is cheaper than making it, (2) the component is well defined and its quality easily observable, and (3) there are many suppliers of the component.

14-1c Economies of Scope

So far we have considered issues affecting the optimal degree of vertical integration in producing a particular product. Even with outsourcing, the focus is on how best to produce a particular product, such as an automobile or a computer. But some firms branch into product lines that do not have a vertical relationship. **Economies of scope** exist when it's cheaper to produce two or more different items in one firm than to produce them in separate firms. For example, General Electric produces thousands of different products ranging from light bulbs to jet engines. By spreading outlays for research and development and marketing (the

company's motto is "Imagination at work") over many different products, GE can reduce those costs per unit. Or consider economies of scope on the farm. A farm family often grows a variety of crops and raises different farm animals—animals that recycle damaged crops and food scraps into meat and fertilizer. With economies of *scale*, the average cost per unit of output falls as the *scale* of the firm increases; *with economies of scope, average costs per unit fall as the firm supplies more types of products—that is, as the scope of the firm increases.* The cost of some outlays, such as for research and development, can be spread across product lines. For example, the 3M Company sells more than 55,000 different products, from street lights to little yellow sticky pads. Because it produces such an array of products, the company spends a sizable share of its revenue, 8 percent, on research and development.[4]

> **"With *economies of scale*, the average cost per unit of output falls as the scale of the firm increases; with *economies of scope*, average costs per unit fall as the firm supplies more types of products—that is, as the scope of the firm increases."**

Our focus has been on why firms exist, why they often integrate vertically, why they outsource, and why they

economies of scope
Average costs decline as a firm makes a range of different products rather than specializing in just one product

---

3. Daron Acemoglu et al., "Vertical Integration and Technology: Theory and Evidence," *Journal of the European Economic Association*, 8 (September 2010): 989–1033.

4. "The Roots of Creativity: Throwing Muses," *The Economist*, 17 March 2012, p. 93.

sometimes produce a range of products. These steps toward realism move us beyond the simple picture of the firm created earlier. The next section challenges some simplifying assumptions about the amount of information available to market participants.

14-2 MARKET BEHAVIOR WITH IMPERFECT INFORMATION

For the most part, our analysis of market behavior has assumed that market participants have full information about products and resources. For consumers, full information involves knowledge about a product's price, quality, and availability. For firms, full information includes knowledge about the marginal productivity of various resources, about the appropriate technology for combining them, about the competition, and about the demand for the firm's product. In reality, *reliable information is often costly for both consumers and producers.* This section examines the impact of less-than-perfect information on market behavior.

14-2a Optimal Search With Imperfect Information

Suppose you want to buy a new computer. You need information about the quality and features of each model and the prices at various retail outlets and online sites. To learn more about your choices, you may talk with friends and experts, read promotional brochures and computer publications, and visit online sites. Once you narrow your choice to one or two models, you may visit the mall, or let your fingers do the walking through the *Yellow Pages,* computer catalogs, online search engines, newspaper ads, Craigslist and the like. Searching for the lowest price for a particular model involves a cost, primarily the opportunity cost of your time. This cost obviously varies from individual to individual and from item to item. Some people actually enjoy shopping, but this

"shop 'til you drop" attitude does not necessarily carry over to all types of purchases. *For most of us, the process of gathering consumer information can be considered nonmarket work.*

Marginal Cost of Search

In your quest for product information, you gather the easy and obvious information first. You may check on the price and availability online and at the few electronics stores at the mall. But as your search widens, the *marginal cost* of information increases, both because you may have to travel greater distances to check prices and services and because the opportunity cost of your time increases as you spend more time acquiring information. Consequently, the marginal cost curve for information slopes upward, as is shown in Exhibit 2. Note that a certain amount of information, I_f, is common knowledge and is freely available, so its marginal cost is zero.

Marginal Benefit of Search

The *marginal benefit* of acquiring additional information is a higher quality for a given price or a lower price for a given quality. The marginal benefit is relatively large at first, but as you gather more information and grow more acquainted with the market, additional information yields less and less marginal benefit. For example, the likelihood of uncovering valuable

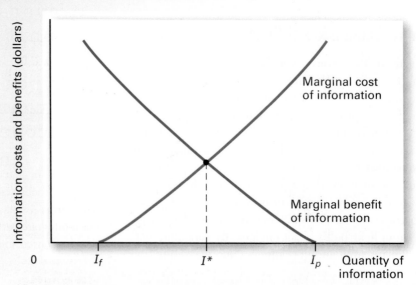

Exhibit 2

Optimal Search With Imperfect Information

When information is not free, additional information is acquired as long as its marginal benefit exceeds its marginal cost. Equilibrium, or optimal search, occurs where marginal benefit equals marginal cost. *I** is the optimal quantity of information.

information, such as an added feature or a lower price, at the second store or Website visited is greater than the likelihood of finding this information at the twentieth store or Website visited. Thus, the marginal benefit curve for additional information slopes downward, as is shown in Exhibit 2.

Optimal Search

Market participants continue to gather information as long as the marginal benefit of additional information exceeds its marginal cost. *Optimal search occurs where the marginal benefit just equals the marginal cost,* which in Exhibit 2 is where the two marginal curves intersect. Notice that at search levels exceeding the equilibrium amount, the marginal benefit of additional information is still positive but below the marginal cost. Notice also that at some point the value of additional information reaches zero, as identified by I_p on the horizontal axis. This level of information could be identified as *full information.* The high marginal cost of acquiring I_p, however, makes it impractical to become fully informed. Thus, firms and consumers, by gathering the optimal amount of information, I°, have less-than-full information about the price, availability, and quality of products and resources.

> **"Optimal search occurs where the marginal benefit just equals the marginal cost."**

Implications

This search model was developed by Nobel laureate George Stigler, who showed that the price of a product can differ among sellers because some consumers are unaware of lower prices elsewhere.[5] Thus, *search costs result in price dispersion, or different prices for the same product.* Some sellers call attention to price dispersions by claiming to have the lowest prices around and by promising to match any competitor's price—for example, Walmart makes such a promise. *Search costs also lead to quality differences across sellers, even for identically priced products, because enough consumers find the expected marginal cost of finding a higher-quality product outweighs the expected marginal benefit.*

There are other implications of Stigler's search model. The more expensive the item, the greater the price dispersion in dollar terms, so the greater the expected marginal benefit from shopping around. You are more likely to shop around for a new car than for a new toothbrush. Also, as earnings increase in an economy, so does the opportunity cost of time, resulting in less searching and more price dispersion. On the other hand, any technological change that reduces the marginal cost of information lowers the marginal cost curve in Exhibit 2, increasing the optimal amount of information and reducing price dispersion. For example, some online sites, like mySimon.com, identify the lowest prices for books, airfares, automobiles, computers, and dozens of other products. And Amazon.com usually lists availability from lowest to highest price. As a result of more readily available price information, consumers have become much more price sensitive.[6] Researchers who investigated the relationship between gas prices and consumer searches found that as gas prices increase, so does Web traffic on sites that report prices at individual gas stations.[7] Thus, by reducing search costs, the Internet reduces the average price and also reduces price dispersion. For example, travelers who purchase airline tickets online pay 11 percent less for a given seat than those who purchase offline.[8]

Here's another example of how information technology can improve market performance and enhance social welfare. Between 1997 and 2001, mobile phone service was introduced throughout one state in India with a large fishing industry. Researchers found that the adoption of mobile phones by fishermen and wholesalers sharply reduced price dispersions, in the process increasing both consumer and producer welfare.[9]

14-2b The Winner's Curse

In 1996, the federal government auctioned off leases to valuable space on the scarce radio spectrum. The space was to be used for cell phones and wireless networks. The bidding was carried out in the face of great uncertainty about what were then new markets. Bidders had little experience

5. George Stigler, "The Economics of Information," *Journal of Political Economy,* 69 (June 1961): 213–225.

6. Glenn Ellison and Sara Fisher Ellison, "Search, Obfuscation, and Price Elasticities on the Internet," *Econometrica,* 77 (March 2009): 427–452.

7. Matthew Lewis and Howard Marvel, "When Do Consumers Search?" *Journal of Industrial Economics,* 59 (Issue 3, 2011): 457–483.

8. Anirban Sengupta and Steven Wiggins, "Airline Pricing, Price Dispersion, and Ticket Characteristics On and Off the Internet," *American Economic Journal: Economic Policy,* 6 (February 2014): 272–307.

9. Robert Jensen, "The Digital Provide: Information (Technology), Market Performance, and Welfare in the South Indian Fisheries Sector," *Quarterly Journal of Economics,* 122 (August 2007): 879–924.

with the potential value of such leases. At the time, 89 companies made winning bids for 493 licenses totaling $10.2 billion. But by 1998, it became clear that many of the winning bidders couldn't pay, and many went bankrupt.[10] The auction eventually collected only half the winning bids. In auctions for products of uncertain value, such as wireless communications licenses, why do so many "winners" end up losers?

When bids were submitted, the true value of space on the radio spectrum could only be estimated. Suppose the average bid for a license was $10 million, with some higher and others lower. Suppose also that the winning bid was $20 million. The winning bid was not the average bid, which may have been the most reliable estimate of the true value, but the highest bid, which was the most optimistic estimate. Winners of such bids are said to experience the **winner's curse** because they often lose money after winning the bid, paying the price of being overly optimistic. In a 2008 auction of the radio spectrum, some winning bidders also defaulted. And in a 2014 auction, airwave rights sold for $34 billion, or more than three times what the government set as minimum acceptable bids. How many winning bidders will default remain to be seen.[11]

The winner's curse applies to all cases of bidding in which the true value is unknown at the outset. For example, online auctions, such as eBay, often sell items of unknown value. Movie companies often bid up the price of screenplays to what some argue are unrealistic levels (only about 5 percent of screenplays studios purchase ever become movies). Likewise, publishers

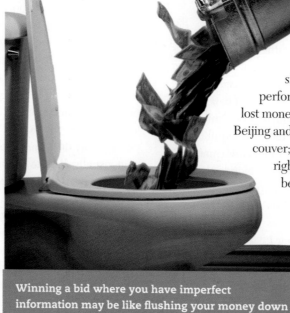

Winning a bid where you have imperfect information may be like flushing your money down the toilet if you fall prey to the "winner's curse."

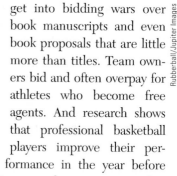

get into bidding wars over book manuscripts and even book proposals that are little more than titles. Team owners bid and often overpay for athletes who become free agents. And research shows that professional basketball players improve their performance in the year before signing a multiyear contract, but performance declines after that.[12] NBC lost money on the 2008 Summer Olympics in Beijing and the 2010 Winter Olympics in Vancouver; at the time of the bid for broadcast rights, the Olympic cities had not even been selected.

With perfect information about market value, potential buyers would never bid more than that market value. But *when competitive bidding is coupled with imperfect information, the winning bidder often ends up an overly optimistic loser.*

> ❝When competitive bidding is coupled with imperfect information, the winning bidder often ends up an overly optimistic loser.❞

14-3 ASYMMETRIC INFORMATION IN PRODUCT MARKETS

We have considered the effects of costly information and limited information on market behavior. But the issue becomes more complicated if one side of the market knows more than the other side does, a problem of **asymmetric information**. There are two types of

winner's curse The plight of the winning bidder who overestimates an asset's true value

asymmetric information One side of the market has better information about the product than does the other side

10. Scott Ritter, "FCC Says Several Bidders to Return Wireless Licenses," *Wall Street Journal*, 18 June 1998.

11. Edward Wyatt, "Bidding in U.S. Auction of Airwaves Reaches $34 Billion," *New York Times*, 24 November, 2014.

12. Kevin Stiroh, "Playing for Keeps: Pay and Performance in the NBA," *Economic Inquiry*, 45 (January 2007): 145–161.

Rubberball/Jupiter Images

information that a market participant may want but lack: information about a product's *characteristics* and information about *actions* taken by the other party to the transaction. This section examines several examples of asymmetric information in the product market and the effects on market efficiency.

14-3a Hidden Characteristics: Adverse Selection

When one side of the market knows more than the other side about important product characteristics, the asymmetric information problem involves **hidden characteristics**. For example, the seller of a used car normally has abundant personal experience with important *characteristics* of that vehicle, such as any accidents, breakdowns, gas mileage, maintenance record, performance in bad weather, overall dependability and so on. A prospective buyer can only guess at these characteristics based on the car's appearance, ratings in *Consumer Reports*, and perhaps a test drive. The buyer cannot really know how well that car performs without driving it under varying traffic, weather, and road conditions.

To simplify the analysis, suppose there are only two types of used cars for sale: good ones and bad ones, or "lemons." A buyer who is certain about a car's type would be willing to pay $10,000 for a good used car but only $4,000 for a lemon. Again, only the seller knows which type is for sale. Prospective buyers believe that half the used cars on the market are good ones and half are lemons and are willing to pay, say, $7,000 for a car of unknown quality (the average expected value of cars on the market). Would $7,000 become the market price of used cars?

So far, the analysis has ignored the actions of potential sellers, who know which type of car they have. Because sellers of good cars can get only $7,000 for cars they know to be worth $10,000 on average, many will keep their cars in the family or will sell them only to

"When sellers have better information about a product's quality than buyers do, lower-quality products dominate the market."

friends or relatives. But sellers of lemons will find $7,000 an attractive price for a car they know to be worth only $4,000. As a result, the proportion of good cars for sale on the market will fall and the proportion of lemons will rise, reducing the average value of used cars on the market. As buyers come to realize that the mix has shifted toward lemons, they will reduce what they are willing to pay for cars of unknown quality. As the market price of used cars falls, potential sellers of good cars become even more reluctant to sell at such a low price, so the proportion of lemons increases, leading to still lower prices. The process could continue until few good cars were for sale on the open market. More generally, *when sellers have better information about a product's quality than buyers do, lower-quality products dominate the market.*

When those on the informed side of the market self-select in a way that harms the uninformed side of the market, the problem is one of **adverse selection**. In our example, car sellers, the informed side, self-select—that is, they decide whether or not to offer their cars for sale—in a way that increases the proportion of lemons for sale.

Because of adverse selection, those still willing to buy on the open market often get stuck with lemons. There is empirical support for adverse selection in used car markets. For example, owners of lemons try to sell them to ill-informed buyers, while owners of good cars either keep them or sell them to friends and relatives.[13]

13. George Sheldon and Winand Emons, "The Market for Used Cars: New Evidence of the Lemons Phenomenon," *Applied Economics*, 41 (Issue 22, 2009): 2867–2885; and Alessandro Gavazza, Alessandro Lizzeri, and Nikita Roketskiy, "A Quantitative Analysis of the Used-Car Market," *American Economic Review*, 104 (November 2014): 3668–3700.

hidden characteristics
One side of the market knows more than the other side about product characteristics that are important to the other side

adverse selection
Those on the informed side of the market self-select in a way that harms those on the uninformed side of the market

Some services, such as haircuts, do not suffer from the "principal-agent problem" since the consumer can directly observe what the barber or stylist is doing. Only when actions are hidden does the problem arise.

Brenda Bullock/Alamy

14-3b Hidden Actions: The Principal-Agent Problem

A second type of problem occurs when one side of a transaction can pursue an unobservable *action* that affects the other side. Whenever one side of an economic relationship can take a relevant action that the other side cannot observe, the situation is described as one of **hidden actions**. In this age of specialization, there are many tasks we do not perform for ourselves because others do them better and because others have a lower opportunity cost of time. Suppose your car isn't working and you have no clue what's wrong. The mechanic you hire may have other objectives in mind, such as minimizing on-the-job effort or maximizing the amount you're charged. But the mechanic's actions are hidden from you. Although your car's problem may be only a loose connection, the mechanic could inflate the bill by charging you for work not needed or not performed.

hidden actions One side of an economic relationship can do something that the other side cannot observe

principal-agent problem The agent's objectives differ from those of the principal, and one side can pursue hidden actions

principal A person or firm who hires an agent to act on behalf of that person or firm

agent A person or firm who is supposed to act on behalf of the principal

> **"The *principal-agent problem* arises when the goals of the agent are incompatible with those of the principal and when the agent can pursue hidden actions."**

(Such problems have been documented on TV by shows like *60 Minutes*, where hidden cameras expose this behavior.) This asymmetric information problem occurs because one side of a transaction can pursue *hidden actions* that affect the other side. When buyers have difficulty monitoring and evaluating the quality of goods or services purchased, some suppliers may substitute poor-quality resources, exercise less diligence in providing the service, or simply charge too much.

The problem that arises from hidden actions is called the **principal-agent problem**, which describes a relationship in which one party, known as the **principal**, contracts with another party, known as the **agent**, in the expectation that the agent will act on behalf of the principal. *The problem arises when the goals of the agent are incompatible with those of the principal and when the agent can pursue hidden actions.* For example, you are the *principal* and the garage mechanic is your *agent*. You could also confront a principal-agent problem when you deal with a doctor, lawyer, stockbroker, plumber, building contractor, or real estate agent, to name a few. For example, real estate agents are usually better informed than their clients about the housing market. Research suggests that agents exploit this asymmetry by encouraging their clients to sell their homes too cheaply and too quickly.[14]

Any employer-employee relationship could become a principal-agent problem, with the employer as the principal and the employee as the agent. Again, the problem arises because the agent's objectives are not the same as the principal's *and* because the agent's actions are hidden. Not all principal-agent relationships pose a problem. For example, when you hire someone to cut your hair or your lawn, there are no hidden actions so you can judge the results for yourself.

14. Steven Levitt and Chad Syverson, "Market Distortions When Agents Are Better Informed: The Value of Information in Real Estate Transactions," *Review of Economics and Statistics*, 90 (November 2008): 599–611.

14-3c Asymmetric Information in Insurance Markets

Asymmetric information also creates problems in insurance markets. For example, from an insurer's point of view, the ideal candidate for health insurance is someone who leads a long, healthy life, then dies peacefully while sleeping. But many people are poor risks for health insurers because of hidden characteristics (unhealthy genes) or hidden actions (smoking and drinking excessively, getting exercise only on trips to the refrigerator, and thinking a balanced meal consists of some beef jerky and a six-pack of beer). In the insurance market, it is the buyers, not the sellers, who have more information about the characteristics and actions that predict their likely need for insurance in the future.

If the insurance company has no way of distinguishing among applicants, it must charge those who are good health risks the same price as those who are poor ones. This price is attractive to poor risks but not to good ones, some of whom will not buy insurance. The insured group becomes less healthy on average, so rates must rise, making insurance even less attractive to healthy people. *Because of adverse selection, insurance buyers tend to be less healthy than the population as a whole.* Adverse selection was used as an argument for the health care reform measure in 2010. If only the less healthy buy insurance, then premiums must increase, making coverage less attractive to healthy people. If this process continues, at some point it becomes a "death spiral," where no insurance is available. In general, adverse selection reduces the range of policies that insurance companies offer.[15]

The insurance problem is compounded by the fact that once people buy insurance, their behavior may change in a way that increases the probability that a claim will be made. For example, those with health insurance may take less care of their health, and those with theft insurance may take less care of their valuables. This incentive problem is referred to as *moral hazard*. **Moral hazard** occurs when an individual's behavior changes in a way that increases the likelihood of an unfavorable outcome. More generally, *moral hazard is a principal-agent problem because it occurs when those on one side of a transaction have an incentive to shirk responsibilities because the other side is unable to observe them.* The responsibility could be to repair a car, maintain one's health, or safeguard one's valuables. Both the mechanic and the insurance buyer may take advantage of the ignorant party. In the car-repair example, the mechanic is the agent; in the insurance example, the policy buyer is the principal. Thus, moral hazard arises when someone can undertake hidden action; this could be either the agent or the principal, depending on the situation.

Because of moral hazard, the more attractive are disability benefits, the more likely workers will try to claim disability. For example, the shorter the wait time before receiving disability benefits and the higher the disability payments, the greater the share of workers who become long-term disability beneficiaries.[16] Moral hazard was also a frequent topic of debate each time the federal government decided to bail out or not bail out a company or industry during the 2008 global financial crisis. For example, if an investment bank was rescued after its past risky behavior, would such a bank be more inclined to take similar risks in the future? Some observers believe the answer is yes.

14-3d Coping With Asymmetric Information

There are ways of reducing the consequences of asymmetric information. An incentive structure or an information-revealing system can be developed to reduce the problems associated with the lopsided availability of information. For example, all states now have "lemon laws" that offer compensation to buyers of new or used cars that turn out to be lemons. Used-car dealers may also offer warranties to reduce the buyer's risk of getting stuck with a lemon. For example, some sellers offer money-back guarantees, though consumers are usually wary of such offers.[17] Most auto-repair garages provide written estimates before a job is done, and many return the defective parts to the customer as evidence that the repair was necessary and was carried out. People often get multiple estimates for major repairs.

Insurance companies deal with adverse selection and moral hazard in a variety of ways. Prior to recent federal legislation, most required applicants to undergo a physical exam and to answer questions about their medical history and lifestyle (false information could block benefits). Preexisting medical conditions were not usually covered. To avoid adverse selection, an insurer often covers all those in a group, such as all company employees, not just those who would

> **moral hazard** A situation in which one party, as a result of a contract, has an incentive to shirk responsibilities in a way that harms the other party to the contract

16. David Autor, Mark Duggan, and Jonathan Gruber, "Moral Hazard and Claims Deterrence in Private Disability Insurance," *American Economic Journal: Applied Economics*, 6 (October 2014): 110–141.

17. James Roberts, "Can Warranties Substitute for Reputation?" *American Economic Journal: Microeconomics*, 3 (August 2011): 69–85.

15. Liran Einav and Amy Finkelstein, "Selection in Insurance Markets: Theory and Empirics in Pictures," *Journal of Economic Perspectives*, 25 (Winter 2011): 115–138.

otherwise self-select. Insurers reduce moral hazard by making the policyholder pay, say, the first $250 of a claim as a "deductible" and by requiring the policyholder to copay a percentage of a claim. There is evidence that higher deductibles reduce health-care use without reducing the level of health.[18] Also, as more claims are filed, insurance premiums go up and the policy could be canceled. Property insurers reduce premiums for those who install security systems, smoke alarms, or sprinkler systems, and who take other safety precautions. And sometimes health-insurance providers can market their products in a way that attracts healthier customers, such as by offering a free gym membership with each policy.

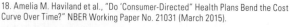

If you go to an exclusive club, the doorman plays the role of the screener and looks for signals such as nice clothes or cool friends.

 ## 14-4 ASYMMETRIC INFORMATION IN LABOR MARKETS

Our market analysis for particular kinds of labor typically assumes that workers are more or less interchangeable. In equilibrium, each worker in a particular labor market is assumed to be paid the same wage, a wage equal to the marginal revenue product of the last unit of labor hired. But what if ability differs across workers? Differences in ability present no particular problem as long as these differences can be readily observed by the employer. If the productivity of each worker is easily quantified through measures such as crates of oranges picked, quantity of garments sewn, or number of cars sold, these can and do serve as the basis for pay. And such incentives seem to affect behavior. For example, when the British National Health Service changed the pay basis of dentists from "contact hours" with patients to the number of cavities filled, dentists found more cavities and filled them in only a third of the time they took under the contact-hour pay scheme.[19] When teachers in India were rewarded for test results, students performed better.[20] And when the U.S. government reduced what it paid for office visits, physicians spent less time with each patient.[21]

Because production often requires a team effort, the employer may not be able to attribute specific outputs to particular workers. When information about each worker's marginal productivity is hard to come by, employers usually pay all workers by the hour. Sometimes the pay combines an hourly rate with incentive pay linked to a measure of productivity. For example, a sales representative typically earns a base salary plus a commission tied to sales. At times, the task of evaluating performance is left to customers. Workers who provide personal services, such as waiters, barbers, beauticians, pizza deliverers, and bellhops, rely partly or mostly on tips. These services are "personal" and visible, so customers are usually in the best position to judge the quality and timeliness of service and to tip accordingly.

14-4a Adverse Selection in Labor Markets

A job applicant's true abilities—motivation, work habits, skills, ability to get along with others, and the like—are, to a large extent, *hidden characteristics*. In a labor market with hidden characteristics, employers might be better off offering a higher wage. The higher the wage, the more attractive the job is to more-qualified workers. Research finds that higher wages attract more qualified applicants as measured by IQ, personality, and aptitude for the type of work in question.[22] Paying a higher wage also encourages those who are hired not to goof off or otherwise jeopardize an attractive job. Paying above-market wages to attract and retain more-productive

18. Amelia M. Haviland et al., "Do 'Consumer-Directed' Health Plans Bend the Cost Curve Over Time?" NBER Working Paper No. 21031 (March 2015).

19. John Pencavel, "Piecework and On-the-Job Screening," Working Paper, Stanford University, (June 1975).

20. Karthik Muralidharan and Venkatesh Sundararaman, "Teacher Performance Pay: Experimental Evidence from India," *Journal of Political Economy*, 119 (February 2011): 39–77.

21. Graig Garthwaite, "The Doctor Might See You Now: The Supply Effects of Public Health Insurance Expansion," *American Economic Journal: Economic Policy*, 4 (August 2012): 190–215.

22. Ernesto Dal Bo, Frederico Finan, and Martin Rossi, "Strengthening State Capabilities: The Role of Financial Incentives in the Call to Public Service," *Quarterly Journal of Economics*, 128 (August 2013): 1169–1218.

workers is called paying **efficiency wages**, something that Henry Ford did.

14-4b Signaling and Screening

The person on the side of the market with hidden characteristics and hidden actions has an incentive to say the right thing. For example, a job applicant might say, "Hire me because I am hardworking, reliable, prompt, highly motivated, and just an all-around great employee." Or an insurer might say, "You're in good hands with Allstate." But such claims appear self-serving and thus are not necessarily believable. To cut through this fog, both sides of the market try to develop credible ways of communicating reliable information about qualifications.

Signaling is the attempt by the informed side of the market to communicate information that the other side would find valuable. Consider signaling in the job market. Because some jobs require abilities that are unobservable on a résumé or in an interview, job applicants offer proxy measures, such as years of education, college grades, and letters of recommendation. A proxy measure is called a *signal*, which is an observable indicator of some hidden characteristic. A signal is sent by the informed side of the market to the uninformed side and is useful as long as less-qualified applicants face more difficulty sending the same signal.

To identify the best workers, employers try to *screen* applicants. **Screening** is the attempt by the uninformed side of the market to uncover the relevant but hidden characteristics of the informed party. An initial screen might check each résumé for spelling and typographical errors. Although not important in themselves, such errors suggest a lack of attention to detail—which could reduce labor productivity. The uninformed party must identify signals that less-productive individuals have more difficulty sending. A signal that can be sent with equal ease by all workers, regardless of their productivity, does not provide a useful way of screening applicants. But if, for example, more-productive workers find it easier to graduate from college than do less-productive workers, a college degree is a measure worth using to screen workers. In this case, education may be valuable, not necessarily

> **"Successful screening helps labor markets operate more efficiently, and benefits more productive workers."**

because of its direct effect on a worker's productivity, but simply because it enables employers to distinguish among types of workers. In fact, the actual pay increase from a fourth year of college that results in graduation is several times the pay increase from just a third year of college. This finding is consistent with the screening theory of education. Other research suggests that the ability to graduate from college seems to be a good signal about market productivity and is usually reflected by pay right out of college. On the other hand, a high school diploma conveys such limited information about worker productivity that high school graduates usually have to work years before their pay reflects their producitvity.[23]

More generally, when employers have a successful screening device, they can offer workers what would be considered "good jobs"—that is, higher wages with more discretion on the job.[24] Thus, successful screening helps labor markets operate more efficiently, and benefits more productive workers. Some companies spend a great deal recruiting the right worker. As an extreme example, "Apple employs three recruiters whose sole task is to identify designers to join the group; together they find perhaps one a year."[25] And Google reportedly hires only 1 out of every 400 of its job applicants.

TO REVIEW: Because the potential productivity of job applicants cannot be measured directly, an employer must rely on proxy measures to screen applicants. *The most valuable proxy is a signal that can be sent more easily by more productive workers and also is a good predictor of future productivity.*

23. Peter Arcidiacono, Patrick Bayer, and Aurel Hizmo, "Beyond Signaling and Human Capital: Education and the Revelation of Ability," *American Economic Journal: Applied Economics*, 2 (October 2010): 76–104.

24. Bjorn Bartling, Ernst Fehr, and Klaus Schmidt, "Screening, Competition, and Job Design: Economic Origins of Good Jobs," *American Economic Review*, 102 (April 2012): 834–864.

25. Ian Parker, "The Shape of Things to Come: How an Industrial Designer Became Apple's Greatest Product," *The New Yorker*, 23 February 2015, p. 123.

efficiency wage theory The idea that offering high wages attracts a more talented labor pool and encourages those hired to perform well to keep their jobs

signaling Using a proxy measure to communicate information about unobservable characteristics; the signal is more effective if more-productive workers find it easier to send than do less-productive workers

screening The process used by employers to select the most qualified workers based on observable characteristics, such as a job applicant's level of education and course grades

14-5 BEHAVIORAL ECONOMICS

Traditional economics assumes that people act rationally to maximize their overall well-being. People know what they want, they try to make the most of what they have, they make choices that are fairly consistent given the circumstances, and they follow through with those choices. In short, *the traditional economic approach assumes that people pursue their rational self-interest*. And according to Adam Smith, the pursuit of self-interest promotes the general good, so the market system works in a reinforcing and beneficial cycle. In the extreme, this standard approach views the economy as populated by calculating, unemotional maximizers who pursue their rational self-interest.

Viewing people as robot-like maximizers is a simplification that can be defended on the grounds that this approach is easy to spell out in a theoretical model and it yields clear, testable implications about how people behave. Much empirical work backs up this version of human nature. And even if people don't actually make such complex calculations, they act as if they do. For example, they act as if they can maximize utility by equating the relevant marginal utilities.

On the other hand, psychologists have come to believe that people are prone to mistakes, are fickle and inconsistent, and often do not get the best deal when making choices. Psychologists investigate the biases, faulty assumptions, and errors that affect how people make decisions in all aspects of life. In recent decades, some economists have begun to rely on findings from psychology to look at instances where people do not act according to traditional economic theory. The convergence of economics and psychology eventually created a new field of study referred to as behavioral economics, a field pursued by a small but growing band of economists. **Behavioral economics** borrows insights from psychology to help explain some economic decisions. This approach questions some assumptions of traditional economics, particularly the assumptions of (1) unbounded rationality and (2) unbounded willpower.

> **"Because we have only so much brainpower and only so much time, we cannot be expected to solve complex production or consumption problems optimally."**

Patrik Giardino/AGE Fotostock

14-5a Unbounded Rationality

Nobel Prize winner Herbert Simon was an early critic of the idea that people have unlimited information-processing capabilities. He introduced the term "bounded rationality" to describe a more realistic conception of human problem-solving ability, a term used earlier in this chapter to help explain optimal firm size. Because we have only so much brainpower and only so much time, we cannot be expected to solve complex production or consumption problems optimally. When faced with lots of information that we aren't sure how to process, most of us rely on simple rules of thumb for guidance. The simplest rule of thumb in the face of a difficult decision is to do nothing. For example, when faced with better options after electricity deregulation, many consumers failed to explore their new choices and, instead, simply stayed with their existing supplier.[26]

Psychologists find that people are prone to inertia, even when doing nothing may cost them money. In the face of uncertainty, doing nothing or doing little also means that people are inclined to accept default rules. For example, employees have a strong tendency to stick to whatever savings option an employer presented to them as the default option, even when they could choose better options. Many accept the default option even when that option is not to save at all, and thereby miss out on any free money

behavioral economics
An approach that borrows insights from psychology to help explain economic choices

26. Ali Hortacsu, Seyed Ali Madanizadeh, and Steven L. Puller, "Power to Choose? An Analysis of Consumer Inertia in the Residential Electricity Market," NBER Working Paper No. 20988 (February 2015).

> **"We humans, even when we know what's best for us, often lack the discipline to follow through."**

available through a company-match program. Inertia is also why, once a decision is made, or made for him or her, the chooser tends to stick with that option even when circumstances change. One researcher found that insurance companies exploit customer inertia by raising premiums on existing policies even as they make alternative policies more attractive to new buyers.[27] In short, we humans try to avoid making some decisions even when the consequences of no decision are costly. In that regard, we do not seem to be pursuing our self-interest.

14-5b Unbounded Willpower

A second assumption of traditional economics is that people, once they make a decision, have unbounded willpower—that is, they have complete self-control. But we humans, even when we know what's best for us, often lack the discipline to follow through. Most of us have, despite our best intentions, ended up eating, drinking, or spending too much, and exercising, saving, or studying too little.

14-5c Neuroeconomics

Traditional economics looks at how people react to a change in their incomes, in prices, or in some other factor affecting their choices. Thus, the traditional approach is based on what people do in response to a change in their economic circumstances. Some behavioral economists are now digging deeper into economic choices by drawing on advances in brain-imaging technology. This new sub-field of behavioral economics, called **neuroeconomics**, examines how economic decision making affects areas of the brain.

For example, in a typical experiment, a test subject is asked to make an economic decision. The experimenter, using magnetic resonance imaging (or MRI), then measures activity in the parts of the brain associated with that choice. By mapping brain activity, these researchers

hope to develop more realistic models of economic decision making.

Here are three types of choices that test subjects have been asked to make:

1. Choices involving uncertainty and risk (for example, would you prefer having $100 for certain or, instead, having a 50 percent chance of $300 and a 50 percent chance of zero?)

2. Choices involving present versus future outcomes (for example, would you prefer receiving $100 today or $125 one year from today?)

3. Social choices involving strategic interactions with other people (for example, how much of a $100 reward would you be willing to share with someone you didn't know?)

The findings of neuroeconomists have challenged the traditional view that economic choices boil down to a simple process of utility maximization. Their laboratory results suggest a more complex interaction among competing objectives. For example, your rational self-interest is sometimes in conflict with your ethical sense of fairness. You often feel concern for others and may try to help them even when that's at odds with your rational self-interest. But, as noted in Chapter 1, even your concern for others is shaped by the cost of your concern. For example, people are more apt to contribute your old clothes, not their new ones, to charity, and they donate more to charities if their contributions are tax deductible.

Although neuroeconomists use different methods than traditional economics, both groups have the same goal: Developing better economic models to explain and predict economic choices.[28]

14-6 FINAL WORD

The firm has evolved through a natural selection process as the form of organization that minimizes both transaction and production costs. Ways of organizing production that are more efficient will be selected by the competitive system for survival. Attributes that yield an economic profit will thrive, and those that do not will fall away. The form of organization selected may not be optimal in the sense that it cannot be improved upon,

neuroeconomics
Mapping brain activity while subjects make economic choices; the goal is to develop better models of economic decision making

27. Keith Marzilli Ericson, "Consumer Inertia and Firm Pricing in the Medicare Part D Prescription Drug Insurance Exchange," *American Economic Journal: Economic Policy*, 6 (February 2014): 38–64.

28. Colin Camerer, "A Review Essay About Foundations of Neuroeconomic Analysis by Paul Glimcher," *Journal of Economic Literature*, 51 (December 2014): 1155–1182.

but it is the most efficient of those that have been tried. If there is a way to organize production that is more efficient, some entrepreneur will stumble on it one day and will be rewarded with greater profit. The improvement may not always be the result of conscious design. Once a more efficient way of organizing production is uncovered, others will imitate it.

In conventional demand-and-supply analysis, trades occur in impersonal markets, and the buyer has no special concern about who is on the sell side. But with asymmetric information, the mix and characteristics of the other side of the market become important. When the problem of adverse selection is severe enough, some markets may cease to function. Market participants try to overcome the limitations of asymmetric information by signaling, screening, and trying to be quite explicit and transparent about the terms of the transaction.

Behavioral economists have borrowed insights from psychology to help explain some economic choices that seem inconsistent with rational self-interest. Psychologists argue that because people have trouble with complex choices, they tend to do nothing or settle for whatever default option is presented. And people often lack the self-control to put up with near-term costs for long-term benefits.

STUDY TOOLS 14

READY TO STUDY? IN THE BOOK, YOU CAN:

☐ Work the Problems at the end of the chapter.

☐ Rip out the chapter review card for a handy summary of the chapter and key terms.

ONLINE AT CENGAGEBRAIN.COM YOU CAN:

☐ Collect StudyBits while you read and study the chapter.

☐ Quiz yourself on key concepts.

☐ Prepare for tests with chapter flash cards as well as flash cards that you create.

☐ Watch videos to explore economics further.

CHAPTER 14 PROBLEMS

Your instructor can access the answers to these problems online at http://cengagebrain.com.

14-1 Describe the criteria a firm should apply when deciding whether to produce a component part or to purchase that part in the market

1. *(Make or Buy)* List the criteria a firm applies in deciding whether to produce a component part or purchase it in the market.
2. *(Boundaries of the Firm)* Ashland Oil buys its crude oil in the market. Larger oil refiners, such as Texaco, drill for their own crude oil. Why do some oil companies drill for their own crude oil and others buy crude oil in the market?
3. *(Economies of Scope)* Distinguish between economies of scale and economies of scope. Why do some firms produce multiple product lines, while others produce only one?

14-2 Explain the optimal amount of search for information when shopping for a product

4. *(Search with Imperfect Information)* The following questions concern the accompanying graph.
   a. Identify the two curves shown on the graph, and explain their upward or downward slopes.
   b. Why does curve *A* intersect the horizontal axis?
   c. What is the significance of quantity *d*?
   d. What does *e* represent?
   e. How would the optimal quantity of information change if the marginal benefit of information increased—that is, if the marginal benefit curve shifted upward?

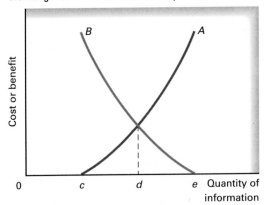

5. *(Search with Imperfect Information)* Determine the effect of each of the following on the optimal level of search.
   a. The consumer's wage increases, other things constant.
   b. One seller guarantees to offer the lowest price on the market.
   c. The technology of gathering and transmitting market information improves.

14-3 Define asymmetric information, and explain why it may pose a problem for market operations

6. *(Asymmetric Information)* Define asymmetric information. Distinguish between hidden characteristics and hidden actions. Which type of asymmetric information contributes to the principal-agent problem?
7. *(The Principal-Agent Problem)* Discuss the nature of the principal-agent problem. Determine which is the principal and which is the agent in each of the following relationships:
   a. A firm that produces export goods and the export management company that helps market its goods overseas
   b. The management of a firm and its stockholders
   c. A homeowner and the plumber hired to make repairs
   d. A dentist and a patient
   e. An employee-pension management firm and the company using its services
8. *(Adverse Selection and Moral Hazard)* Describe the problems faced by health insurance companies as a result of adverse selection and moral hazard. How do insurance companies try to reduce these problems?

14-4 Summarize how labor markets try to cope with the problem of asymmetric information

9. *(Signaling and Screening)* Describe the functions of signaling and of screening in labor markets.
10. *(Signaling)* Give an example of signaling in each of the following situations:
    a. Choosing a doctor
    b. Applying to graduate school
    c. Filling out a form for a dating service

14-5 Identify two types of limitations that can undermine rational decisions

11. *(Behavioral Economics)* A management consultant advised a small business owner to fully analyze all transaction costs, delineate the boundaries of the business, and develop an equation to calculate exactly economies of scope. The owner replied that there were not enough hours in the day to gather all this information and so the owner would just keep running the business in the same way as usual. What assumption from traditional economics is in dispute here?
12. *(Limitations of Rationality)* Describe two limitations that make rational economic decisions more challenging.

15 | Economic Regulation and Antitrust Policy

LEARNING OUTCOMES

After studying this chapter, you will be able to...

15-1 Describe three types of government regulation of business

15-2 Evaluate alternative ways government can regulate a natural monopoly

15-3 Describe two alternative theories of economic regulation

15-4 Summarize the driving causes behind each of the four U.S. merger waves

15-5 Evaluate whether the U.S. economy has become more competitive or less competitive since 1958, and explain why

After finishing this chapter go to **PAGE 266** for **STUDY TOOLS**

Topics discussed in Chapter 15 include:

- Regulating natural monopolies
- Theories of economic regulation
- Antitrust policy
- Per se illegality
- Rule of reason
- Merger waves
- Competitive trends
- Problems with antitrust policy

- If the "invisible hand" of competition yields such desirable results for the economy, why does the government need to regulate business?

- Is monopoly ever better than competition?

- Who benefits most when government regulates monopoly?

- What has been the experience of government enforcement of antitrust and why are regulators currently interested in Apple and Google?

- Is the U.S. economy becoming more competitive or less competitive?

Answers to these and other questions are addressed in this chapter, which discusses government regulation of business.

Businesspeople praise competition but they love monopoly. They praise competition because it harnesses the diverse and often conflicting objectives of various market participants and channels them into the efficient production of goods and services. And competition does this as if by "an invisible hand." Businesspeople love monopoly because it provides the surest path to economic profit in the long run—and, after all, profit is the name of the game for any business. The fruits of monopoly are so tempting that a firm might try to eliminate competitors or conspire with them to raise prices. As Adam Smith observed nearly two and a half centuries ago, "People of the same trade seldom meet together, even for merriment or diversion, but the conversation ends in a conspiracy against the public, or in some contrivance to raise prices."

The tendency of firms to seek monopolistic advantage is understandable, but monopoly usually harms consumers as well as other producers. Public policy can play a role by promoting competition in those markets where competition seems desirable and by reducing the harmful effects of monopoly in those markets where the output can be most efficiently supplied by one or just a few firms.

> **"Why are federal antitrust regulators currently interested in Apple and Google?"**

15-1 TYPES OF GOVERNMENT REGULATION

You'll recall that a monopolist supplies a product with no close substitutes, so a monopolist can usually charge a higher price than would prevail with competition. When only a few firms serve a market, they are sometimes able to coordinate their actions, either explicitly or implicitly, to act like a monopolist. The ability of a firm to raise the price without losing all its sales to rivals is called **market power**. Any firm facing a downward-sloping demand curve has some control over the price and thus some market power. The presumption is that a monopoly, or a group of firms acting as a monopoly, restricts output to charge a higher price than competing firms would charge. With output restricted, the marginal benefit of the final unit sold exceeds its marginal cost, so expanding output would increase social welfare. *By failing to expand output to the point where marginal benefit equals marginal cost, firms with market power produce less of the good and charge a higher price than would be socially optimal.*

Other distortions have also been associated with monopolies. For example, some critics argue that because a monopoly is insulated from competition, it is not as innovative as aggressive competitors would be. Worse still, because of their size and economic importance, monopolies may influence government to protect and enhance their monopoly power.

Three kinds of government policies are designed to alter or control firm behavior: social regulation, economic

market power The ability of a firm to raise its price without losing all its customers to rival firms

> **"By failing to expand output to the point where marginal benefit equals marginal cost, firms with market power produce less of the good and charge a higher price than would be socially optimal."**

regulation, and antitrust policy. **Social regulation** tries to improve health and safety, such as by control of unsafe working conditions and dangerous products. For example, in 1972, Congress created the Consumer Product Safety Commission with a mission to keep unsafe products off the market. The Commission forces the recall of about 400 different products each year. State and local governments also regulate a variety of safety issues such as helmet use for riders of bicycles and motorcycles. Health care reform is another example of social regulation; the 2010 health care act was the broadest social legislation since the Great Depression. Social regulation can have far-reaching economic consequences, but such regulation is not the focus of this chapter.

social regulation
Government regulation aimed at improving health and safety

economic regulation
Government regulation of natural monopoly, where, because of economies of scale, average production cost is lowest when a single firm supplies the market

antitrust policy
Government regulation aimed at preventing monopoly and fostering competition in markets where competition is desirable

Economic regulation aims to control the price, output, the entry of new firms, and the quality of service *in industries in which monopoly appears inevitable or even desirable*. Government oversight of a *natural monopoly*, such as local electricity transmission or a subway system, is an example of economic regulation. Several other industries, such as land and air transportation, have also been regulated in the past. Federal, state, and local governments carry out economic regulation. **Antitrust policy** outlaws attempts to monopolize, or cartelize, markets in which competition is desirable. Antitrust policy is pursued in the courts by government attorneys and by individual firms that charge other firms with violating antitrust laws. Economic regulation and antitrust policy are examined in this chapter. Let's turn first to economic regulation—specifically, the regulation of natural monopolies.

15-2 REGULATING A NATURAL MONOPOLY

Because of economies of scale, a natural monopoly has a long-run average cost curve that slopes downward over the range of market demand. This means that the lowest average cost is achieved when one firm serves the entire market. For example, a subway system is a natural monopoly. If two competing systems tunnel parallel routes throughout a city, the average cost per trip would be higher than if a single system provided this service.

15-2a Unregulated Profit Maximization

Exhibit 1 shows the demand and cost conditions for a natural monopoly, in this case a metropolitan subway system. A natural monopoly usually faces huge initial capital costs, such as those associated with digging a subway system, building a natural gas pipeline, launching a communications satellite, or wiring a city for electricity or cable TV. Once capital is in place, average cost falls as output increases, so the average cost curve slopes downward over a broad range of output. In this situation, average cost is lowest when a single firm supplies the market.

An unregulated monopolist, like any other firm, chooses the price-quantity combination that maximizes profit. In Exhibit 1, the monopolist—in this case, the operator of a subway system—maximizes profit by producing where marginal revenue equals marginal cost—that is, where 50 million riders per month pay $4 per trip. The monopolist reaps the profit identified by the blue-shaded rectangle. The *abc* triangle, which is the area below the demand curve and above the $4 price, measures the consumer surplus—consumers' net gain from riding the subway. The problem with letting the monopolist maximize profit is that the resulting price-output combination is inefficient in terms of social welfare. Consumers pay a price that far exceeds the marginal cost of providing the service. *The marginal value of additional output exceeds its marginal cost, so social welfare would increase if output expanded.*

Exhibit 1

Regulating a Natural Monopoly

With a natural monopoly, the long-run average cost curve slopes downward where it intersects the market demand curve. The unregulated firm maximizes profit by producing where marginal revenue equals marginal cost, in this case, 50 million trips per month at a price of $4.00 per trip. This outcome is inefficient because price, or marginal benefit, exceeds marginal cost. To achieve the efficient output rate, regulators could set the price at $0.50 per trip. The subway would sell 105 million trips per month, which would be the efficient quantity. But at $0.50 per trip, the subway would lose money and would require a subsidy to keep going. As an alternative, regulators could set the price at $1.50 per trip. The subway would sell 90 million trips per month and would just break even (because price equals average cost).

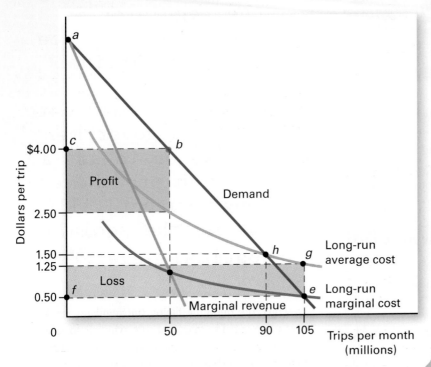

Government can increase social welfare by forcing the monopolist to lower the price and expand output. To accomplish this, government can either operate the monopoly itself, as it does with most urban transit systems, or *regulate* a privately owned monopoly, as government does with some urban transit systems, local phone services, cable TV service, and electricity transmission. Government-owned or government-regulated monopolies are called **public utilities**. Here we focus on government regulation, though the issues discussed are similar if the government owns and operates the monopoly.

15-2b Setting Price Equal to Marginal Cost

Many facets of a natural monopoly have been regulated, but the price-output combination gets the most attention. Suppose government regulators require the monopolist to produce the level of output that is efficient—that is, where the price, which also measures the marginal benefit to consumers, equals the marginal cost of the good. This price-output combination is depicted in Exhibit 1 as point *e*, where the demand curve, or the marginal benefit curve, intersects the marginal cost curve, yielding a price of $0.50 per trip and quantity of 105 million trips per month. Consumers clearly prefer this price to the $4 charged by the unregulated monopolist. The consumer surplus from riding the subway jumps from triangle *abc* without regulation to triangle *aef* with regulation.

Notice, however, that the monopolist now has a problem. The average cost of supplying each of the 105 million trips per month is $1.25, identified by point *g* on the average cost curve. This is more than double the regulated price of $0.50. Rather than earning a profit, the monopolist suffers a loss—in this case, $0.75 per trip, for a total loss of $79 million a month, identified by the pink-shaded rectangle. *Forcing a natural monopolist to produce where price, or marginal benefit, equals marginal cost results in an economic loss to this monopolist.* In the long run, the monopolist would go out of business rather than endure such a loss.

15-2c Subsidizing the Natural Monopolist

How can regulators encourage the monopolist to stay in business yet still produce where price equals marginal cost? The government can cover the loss—*subsidize* the firm so it earns a normal profit. Bus and subway fares are typically set below the average cost of providing the service, with the difference made up by government subsidies. For example, government subsidies pay more than 40 percent of the Washington, D.C. Metro subway system. Amtrak gets a federal subsidy covering about a third

public utilities
Government-owned or government-regulated monopolies

CHAPTER 15: Economic Regulation and Antitrust Policy 255

Government subsidies cover more than 40 percent of the cost of the Washington, D.C. Metro.

Kumar Sriskandan/Alamy

of its operating budget. One drawback with the subsidy solution is that, to provide the subsidy, the government must raise taxes or forgo public spending in some other area. Thus, the subsidy has an opportunity cost and could easily result in inefficiencies and distortions elsewhere in the economy.

15-2d Setting Price Equal to Average Cost

Although some public utilities are subsidized, most are not. Instead, regulators try to establish a price that provides the monopolist with a "fair return." Recall that the average cost curve includes a normal profit. Thus, *setting price equal to average cost* provides a normal, or "fair," profit for the monopolist. In Exhibit 1, the demand curve intersects the average cost curve at point *h*, yielding a price of $1.50 per trip and a quantity of 90 million trips a month. This price-output combination allows the monopolist to stay in business without a subsidy.

Setting price equal to average total cost enhances social welfare compared to the unregulated situation. The monopolist would prefer an economic profit but accepts a normal profit to stay in business. After all, a normal profit is the most this firm could expect if resources were redirected to their best alternative uses. But note that the marginal benefit of the 90 millionth trip exceeds its marginal cost. Therefore, expanding output beyond 90 million trips per month would increase social welfare.

15-2e The Regulatory Dilemma

Setting price equal to marginal cost yields the *socially optimal* allocation of resources because *the consumers' marginal benefit from the last unit sold equals the marginal cost of producing that last unit*. In our example,

setting the price at $0.50 equates marginal benefit and marginal cost, but the monopolist faces losses unless government provides a subsidy. These losses disappear if price equals average cost, which in our example is $1.50. The higher price ensures a normal profit, but output still falls 15 million trips short of the socially optimal level.

> **"The dilemma facing the regulator is whether to set price equal to marginal cost, which is socially optimal but requires a government subsidy, or to set a breakeven price even though output falls short of the socially optimal level."**

Thus, the dilemma facing the regulator is whether to set price equal to marginal cost, which is socially optimal but requires a government subsidy, or to set a breakeven price even though output falls short of the socially optimal level. There is no right answer. Compared with the unregulated profit-maximizing price of $4, both reduce the price, increase output, erase economic profit, increase consumer surplus, and increase social welfare. Although Exhibit 1 lays out the options neatly, regulators usually face a cloudier picture. Demand and cost curves can only be estimated, and the regulated firm may withhold or distort information. For example, a natural monopoly may overstate costs so it can charge more.

15-3 ALTERNATIVE THEORIES OF ECONOMIC REGULATION

Why do governments regulate certain industries? Why not let market forces allocate resources? There are two views of government regulation. The first has been implicit in the discussion so far—namely, that economic regulation is in the *public interest*. Economic regulation promotes social welfare by keeping prices down when one or just a few firms serve a market. A second, darker, view is that economic regulation is not in the public interest but is in the *special interest* of producers. According to this view, *well-organized producer groups expect to profit from economic regulation and persuade public officials to impose restrictions that existing producers find attractive, such as limiting entry into the industry or preventing competition among existing firms.* Individual producers have more to gain or to lose from regulation than do individual consumers. Producers typically are also better organized and more focused than consumers and are therefore better able to bring about regulations that favor producers.

15-3a Special Interests, Economic Regulation, and Deregulation

To understand how and why producer interests could influence public regulation, think back to the last time you got a haircut. Most states regulate the training and licensing of barbers and beauticians. If any new regulation affecting the profession is proposed, who do you suppose has more interest in that legislation, you or someone who cuts hair for a living? *Producers have an intense interest in matters that affect their livelihood, so they try to shape such legislation.* Those who cut hair for a living often try to restrict entry by requiring thousands of hours of instruction. At any public hearings on haircut regulations, industry officials provide self-serving testimony, while consumers largely ignore the whole thing.

As a consumer, you do not specialize in getting haircuts. You purchase haircuts, cold cuts, hardware, software, underwear, and thousands of other goods and services. You have no *special interest* in haircuts.

> **"Producers have an intense interest in matters that affect their livelihood, so they try to shape such legislation."**

Some economists argue that because consumers ignore such matters, regulators often favor producer interests. Well-organized producer groups, as squeaky wheels in the legislative machinery, get the most grease in the form of favorable regulations. Such regulations are usually introduced under the guise of advancing consumer interests or protecting the public. Producer groups may argue that unbridled competition in their industry would hurt consumers. More than 100 trades and occupations now face licensing requirements by state or local governments.[1] For example, the alleged problem of "cutthroat" competition among taxi drivers led to regulations that eliminated price competition and restricted the number of taxis in most large metropolitan areas. New York City has 10,000 fewer taxis now than it did 70 years ago (Mexico City has many more taxis per 100,000 residents). As a result, taxis in New York City are harder to find and fares are higher. To operate a cab in New York City, someone must purchase a "medallion." The purchase price reflects the market value to a taxi owner of regulations that restrict entry and set fares above the competitive level. The average price of a taxi medallion increased from $27,000 in 1968 to more than $1,000,000 in 2013. Regulation gives medallion owners an abiding interest in blocking entry. If market entry and taxi fares were deregulated, cabs would become more plentiful, fares would fall to competitive levels, and medallions would become worthless. Some other U.S. cities, such as Milwaukee, have similar taxi regulations. Given the value of regulations as a barrier to entry in this market, you can understand the threat posed by Uber, the mobile-app based transportation system that operates without medallions. Uber's app allows you to get a ride in minutes for less than the cost of regulated taxis. Though the regulatory standing of Uber in New York City remains a question, just the threat of this rival cut the value of medallions in 2014 by 16 percent to about $840,000.

Moving companies in many states are insulated by similar regulations. For example, in 2012, a freshly formed company, Wildcat Moving of Lexington, Kentucky, wanted to open for business in that state. Kentucky regulations required that the applicant show (1) it was "fit, willing, and able to perform" moving services, and (2) that existing moving services were "inadequate" to serve this

Michal Besser/Alamy

---

1. Dick Carpenter et al., *License to Work: A National Study of Burdens from Occupational Licensing* (Institute of Justice, 2012) at https://www.ij.org /licensetowork.

market. This turns out to be an insurmountable barrier to entry, as existing movers challenge the application. In fact, of the 39 new applicants in Kentucky between 2005 and 2012, none was able to get its application approved.

Regulation may be introduced under the guise of quality control, such as keeping "quacks" out of certain professions. But entry restrictions usually reduce competition and increase prices. The special-interest theory may be valid even when the initial intent of the legislation was in the consumer interest. Over time, the regulatory machinery may shift toward the special interests of producers, who, in effect, "capture" the regulating agency. This **capture theory of regulation** was discussed by George Stigler, the Nobel laureate mentioned in the previous chapter. He argued that "as a general rule, regulation is acquired by the industry and is designed and operated for its benefit."[2]

Critics charge that the Securities and Exchange Commission (SEC) failed to uncover the massive fraud by Bernie Madoff, despite numerous complaints to the agency, because the SEC was captured by the industry it was supposed to regulate. For example, some SEC lawyers didn't want to ruffle feathers because they hoped to land high-paying jobs in the securities industry after building contacts and experience in Washington.[3]

It was in response to this capture theory of regulation that government began deregulating some industries, starting with the airline industry in the late 1970s. Regulation offered an anticompetitive environment for firms and labor unions in airlines, trucking, electricity, telecommunications, and other industries. Deregulation opened up these industries to new entry and new ways of doing business, and consumers have been the primary beneficiaries. Thus, deregulation for the most part has been in the public interest.

TO REVIEW: Economic regulation tries to reduce the harmful consequences of monopolistic behavior in those markets where the output can be most efficiently supplied by one or a few firms. But over time regulations may come to serve producer interests more than than the public interest. We now turn to antitrust policy, which tries to promote competition in those markets where competition seems desirable.

capture theory of regulation Producers' political power and strong stake in the regulatory outcome lead them, in effect, to "capture" the regulating agency and prevail on it to serve producer interests

2. George Stigler, "The Theory of Economic Regulation," *Bell Journal of Economics and Management Science*, 3 (Spring 1971) p. 3.

3. See Erin Arvedlund, *Too Good to Be True: The Rise and Fall of Bernie Madoff* (Penguin Group, 2009) p. 199.

15-4 ANTITRUST LAW AND ENFORCEMENT

Although competition typically ensures the most efficient use of the nation's resources, an individual competitor would rather be a monopolist. If left alone, a firm might try to create a monopoly by driving competitors out of business, by merging with competitors, or by colluding with competitors. *Antitrust policy* reflects government attempts to reduce anticompetitive behavior and promote a market structure that leads to greater competition. *Antitrust policy attempts to promote socially desirable market performance.*

> **"Antitrust policy attempts to promote socially desirable market performance."**

15-4a Origins of Antitrust Policy

Economic developments in the last half of the 19th century created bigger firms serving wider markets. Perhaps the two most important developments were (1) technological breakthroughs that led to a larger optimal plant size in manufacturing and (2) the rise of the railroad from 9,000 miles of track in 1850 to 167,000 miles by 1890, which reduced transport costs. *Economies of scale and cheaper transport costs extended the geographical size of markets,* so firms grew larger to serve these larger markets.

Sharp declines in the national economy in 1873 and 1883, however, panicked large manufacturers. Because their heavy fixed costs required large-scale production, they cut prices in an attempt to stimulate sales. Price wars erupted, creating economic turmoil. Firms desperately sought ways to stabilize their markets. One solution was for competing firms to form a *trust* by transferring their voting stock to a single board of trustees, which would vote in the interest of the industry. Early trusts were formed in the sugar, tobacco, and oil industries. Although the impact of these early trusts is still debated today, they allegedly pursued anticompetitive practices to develop and maintain a monopoly advantage. Gradually the word trust came to mean any firm or group of firms that tried to monopolize a market.

Sherman Antitrust Act of 1890

In the presidential election of 1888, the major political parties put antitrust planks in their platforms. This consensus culminated in the **Sherman Antitrust Act of 1890**, the first national legislation in the world against monopoly. The law prohibited trusts, restraint of trade, and monopolization, but the law's vague language allowed room for much anticompetitive activity.

Clayton Act of 1914

The **Clayton Act of 1914** was passed to outlaw certain practices not prohibited by the Sherman Act and to stop a monopoly before it developed. For example, the Clayton Act outlaws price discrimination when it creates a monopoly. You'll recall that *price discrimination* charges different customers different prices for the same good. The act also prohibits *tying contracts* and *exclusive dealing* if they substantially lessen competition. **Tying contracts** require the buyer of one good to purchase another good as part of the deal. For example, a seller of a patented machine might require customers to buy other supplies. **Exclusive dealing** means a customer must agree not to buy any of the product from other suppliers. For example, a manufacturer might sell computer chips to a computer maker only if the computer maker agrees not to buy chips from other manufacturers. Another prohibition of the act is **interlocking directorates**, whereby the same individual serves on the boards of directors of competing firms. For example, two individuals serving on the boards of both Apple and Google were forced to resign from one.[4] Finally, acquiring the corporate stock of a competing firm is outlawed if this would substantially lessen competition.

Federal Trade Commission Act of 1914

The **Federal Trade Commission (FTC) Act of 1914** established a federal body to help enforce antitrust laws. The president appoints the five commissioners, who are assisted by a staff of economists and lawyers. The Sherman, Clayton, and FTC acts together provide the framework for U.S. antitrust laws. Subsequent amendments and court decisions have clarified and embellished these laws. A loophole in the Clayton Act was closed in 1950 with the passage of the *Celler-Kefauver Anti-Merger Act,* which prevents one firm from buying the *physical assets* of another firm if the effect is to reduce competition. This law can block both **horizontal mergers**, or the merging of

4. Miguel Helft, "Google and Apple Eliminate Another Tie," *New York Times*, 13 October 2009.

firms that produce the same type of product, such as Coke and Pepsi, and **vertical mergers**, or the merging of firms where one supplies inputs to the other or demands output from the other, such as Microsoft software going into Dell hardware.

15-4b Antitrust Enforcement

Any law's effectiveness depends on the vigor and vigilance of enforcement. The pattern of antitrust enforcement goes something like this: Either the Antitrust Division of the U.S. Justice Department or the FTC charges a firm or group of firms with breaking the law. Federal agencies are usually acting on a complaint by a customer or a competitor. At that point, those charged with wrongdoing may be able, without admitting guilt, to sign a **consent decree**, whereby they agree not to do whatever they had been charged with. If the accused contests the charges, evidence from both sides is presented in a court trial, and a judge or jury decides. Some decisions may be appealed all the way to the Supreme Court, and in such cases the courts may render new interpretations of existing laws.

For example, in April 2012 the Antitrust Division of the Justice Department filed suit against Apple and five of the nation's largest publishers, alleging that they conspired to limit competition in the pricing of e-books. According to the charges, Apple and the publishers agreed to stop competing on price and, instead, to

trust Any firm or group of firms that tries to monopolize a market

Sherman Antitrust Act of 1890 First national legislation in the world against monopolies; prohibited trusts, restraint of trade, and monopolization, but the law was vague and, by itself, ineffective

Clayton Act of 1914 Outlawed certain anticompetitive practices not prohibited by the Sherman Act, including price discrimination, tying contracts, exclusive dealing, interlocking directorates, and buying the corporate stock of a competitor

tying contract A seller of one good requires a buyer to purchase other goods as part of the deal

exclusive dealing A supplier prohibits its customers from buying from other suppliers of the product

interlocking directorate A person serves on the boards of directors of two or more competing firms

Federal Trade Commission (FTC) Act of 1914 Established a federal body to help enforce antitrust laws; run by commissioners assisted by economists and lawyers

horizontal merger A merger in which one firm combines with another that produces the same type of product

vertical merger A merger in which one firm combines with another from which it had purchased inputs or to which it had sold output

consent decree The accused party, without admitting guilt, agrees not to do whatever it was charged with if the government drops the charges increase prices enough to guarantee Apple a 30 percent "commission" on each e-book sold. According to the charges, Apple and the book publishers wanted to thwart Amazon.com from pricing new e-books at only $9.99. Apple was found guilty, but that decision was appealed in 2014.[5]

15-4c Per Se Illegality and the Rule of Reason

The courts have interpreted antitrust laws in essentially two different ways. One set of practices has been declared **per se illegal**—that is, illegal regardless of the economic rationale or consequences. For example, under the Sherman Act, all agreements among competing firms to fix prices, restrict output, or otherwise restrain competition are viewed as per se illegal. To prove guilt under a per se rule, the government need only show that the offending practice took place. Thus, the government need only examine each firm's *behavior*.

Another set of practices falls under the **rule of reason**. Here the courts also take into account the facts surrounding the particular offense—namely, the reasons why the offending practice was adopted and its effect on competition. The rule of reason was first set forth in 1911, when the Supreme Court held that Standard Oil had illegally monopolized the petroleum refining industry. Standard Oil had allegedly come to dominate 90 percent of the market by acquiring more than 120 competitors and by practicing **predatory pricing** to drive remaining rivals out of business—for example, by temporarily selling below marginal cost or dropping the price only in certain markets. In finding Standard

> **"Any law's effectiveness depends on the vigor and vigilance of enforcement."**

Oil guilty, the Court focused on both the company's *behavior* and the *market structure* that resulted from that behavior. Based on this approach, the Court found that the company had behaved *unreasonably* and ruled that the monopoly should be broken up.

But in 1920, the rule of reason led the Supreme Court to find U.S. Steel not guilty of monopolization. In that case, the Court ruled that not every contract or combination in restraint of trade is illegal—only those that "unreasonably" restrained trade violated antitrust laws. The Court said that *mere size is not an offense*. Although U.S. Steel clearly possessed market power, the company, in the Court's view, had not violated antitrust laws because it had not unreasonably used that power. The Court switched positions in 1945, ruling that although Alcoa's conduct might be reasonable and legal, its mere possession of market power—Alcoa controlled 90 percent of the aluminum ingot market—violated antitrust laws per se. Here the Court was using *market structure* rather than firm *behavior* as the test of legality.

15-4d Mergers and Public Policy

Some firms have pursued rapid growth by merging with other firms or by acquiring other firms. Much of what the Antitrust Division in the U.S. Justice Department and the FTC's Bureau of Competition do is approve or reject proposed mergers and acquisitions. As a guiding rule, regulators challenge any merger that would "create, enhance, or entrench market power." In determining possible harmful effects that a merger might have on competition, regulators sometimes consider its impact on the share of sales accounted for by the largest firms in the industry. If a few firms account for a relatively large share of sales, the industry is said to be *concentrated*. As a measure of sales concentration, the Justice Department and FTC often use the **Herfindahl-Hirschman Index, or HHI**, which is found by squaring the percentage of market share of each firm in the market and then summing these squares. For example, if the industry consists of 100 firms of equal size, the HHI is $100 [= 100 \times (1)^2]$. If the industry is a pure monopoly, its index is $10,000 [= (100)^2]$, the largest possible value. *The more firms in the industry and the more equal their size, the smaller the HHI.* Because market shares are squared, this index gives greater weight to firms with

per se illegal In antitrust law, business practices deemed illegal regardless of their economic rationale or their consequences

rule of reason Before ruling on the legality of a business practice, a court examines why it was undertaken and what effect it has on competition

predatory pricing Pricing tactics employed by a dominant firm to drive competitors out of business, such as temporarily selling below marginal cost or dropping the price only in certain markets

Herfindahl-Hirschman Index, or HHI A measure of market concentration that squares each firm's percentage share of the market, then sums these squares

5. Brian X. Chen and Nicole Perlroth, "Settlement in Apple Case Over E-Books Is Approved," *New York Times*, 21 November 2014.

Transtock Inc/Alamy

Exhibit 2

Herfindahl-Hirschman Index (HHI) Based on Market Shares in Three Industries

Each of the three industries shown has 44 firms. The HHI is found by squaring each firm's market share then summing the squares. Under each industry, each firm's market share is shown in the left column and the square of the market share is shown in the right column. For ease of exposition, only the market shares of the top four firms differ across industries. The remaining 40 firms have 1 percent market share each. The HHI for Industry III is nearly triple that for each of the other two industries.

Firm	Industry I		Industry II		Industry III	
	Market Share (percent)	Market Share Squared	Market Share (percent)	Market Share Squared	Market Share (percent)	Market Share Squared
A	23	529	15	225	57	3,249
B	18	324	15	225	1	1
C	13	169	15	225	1	1
D	6	36	15	225	1	1
Remaining 40 firms	1 each	40	1 each	40	1 each	40
HHI		**1,098**		**940**		**3,292**

larger market shares, as can be seen in Exhibit 2. Each industry has 44 firms, but, for ease of exposition, only the market share of the top 4 firms differs across industries. Note that the index for Industry III is nearly triple that for each of the two other industries. Please take a minute now to work through the logic of the exhibit.

> **"Regulators challenge any merger that would 'create, enhance, or entrench market power.'"**

The Justice Department and FTC guidelines sort all mergers into one of two categories: *horizontal mergers,* which involve firms in the same market, and *nonhorizontal mergers,* which include all other types of mergers. Of greatest interest for antitrust purposes are horizontal mergers, such as a merger between competing oil companies like Shell and Chevron. The government challenges any merger in an industry that meets two conditions: (1) the HHI exceeds 2,500 and (2) the merger increases the index by more than 200 points.

Mergers in an industry with an index of less than 1,500 are seldom challenged.[6] Other factors, such as the ease of entry into the market, the stability of market shares, and gains in efficiency, are considered for indexes between 1,500 and 2,500. For example, regulators are less likely to challenge a merger in an industry where market share fluctuates a lot.

15-4e Four Merger Waves

There have been four merger waves in this country over the last 125 years, as outlined in Exhibit 3. Between 1887 and 1904 some of the twentieth century's largest firms, including U.S. Steel and Standard Oil, were formed. Mergers during this first wave tended to be horizontal. For example, the firm that is today the United States Steel Corporation was created in 1901 through a billion-dollar merger that involved dozens of individual steel producers and two-thirds of the industry's production capacity. This merger wave was a reaction to technological progress in transportation, communication, and manufacturing. Simply put, it became easier and cheaper to run a corporation that stretched across the nation, so firms merged to reach national markets and to achieve economies of scale. During this first wave, similar merger activity occurred in Canada, Great Britain, and elsewhere, creating dominant firms, some of which still exist. The U.S. merger wave cooled with the severe national recession of 1904 and with the first stirrings of antitrust laws with real bite.

6. Merger guidelines were revised in 2010. See the guidelines at http://www.justice.gov/atr/public/guidelines/hmg-2010.html.

Exhibit 3

Four U.S. Merger Waves Since 1887

Wave	Years	Dominant Type of Merger	Examples	Stimulus
First	1887–1904	Horizontal	U.S. Steel, Standard Oil	Span national markets
Second	1916–1929	Vertical	Copper refiner with copper fabricator	Stock market boom
Third	1948–1969	Conglomerate	Litton Industries	Diversification
Fourth	1982–present	Horizontal and vertical	Banking, telecommunications, health services, insurance	Span national and global markets, stock market boom

Because antitrust laws began to restrain *horizontal* mergers, *vertical* mergers became more common during the second merger wave between 1916 and 1929. A vertical merger is one between a firm that either supplies the other firm inputs or demands the other firm's outputs—the merger of firms at different stages of the production process. For example, a copper refiner merges with a fabricator of copper piping. The stock market boom of the 1920s fueled this second wave, and the stock market crash of 1929 stopped it cold.

The Great Depression and World War II cooled mergers for two decades, but the third merger wave got under way after the war. More than 200 of the 1,000 largest firms in 1950 disappeared by the early 1960s as a result of the third merger wave, which stretched between 1948 and 1969. In that span, many large firms were absorbed by other, usually larger, firms. The third merger wave peaked during 1964 to 1969, when **conglomerate mergers**, which join firms in different industries, accounted for four-fifths of all mergers. For example, Litton Industries combined firms that made calculators, appliances, electrical equipment, and machine tools. Merging firms were looking to diversify their product mix and perhaps achieve some *economies of scope*—meaning, to reduce average costs by producing a variety of goods. The firm resulting from a conglomerate merger no longer focused on producing a particular good efficiently. Instead, it tried to produce different goods efficiently. Many conglomerate mergers stretched management expertise and thereby lost the efficiency gains arising from specialization and comparative advantage.

The fourth merger wave began in 1982 and involved both horizontal and vertical mergers. Some large conglomerate mergers from the third wave were dissolved during the fourth wave, as core firms sold off unrelated operations. About one-third of mergers in the 1980s resulted from *hostile takeovers*, where one firm would buy control of another against the wishes of the target firm's management. Hostile takeovers dwindled to less than one-tenth of mergers during the 1990s and later.

Merger activity gained momentum during the latter half of the 1990s, with the dollar value of each new merger topping the previous record. Most mergers during this period were financed by the exchange of corporate stock and were spurred on by a booming stock market (like the mergers of the 1920s). The dissolution of the Soviet Union ended the Cold War and boosted capitalism around the world. Companies merged to achieve a stronger competitive position

in global markets. The largest mergers in history have taken place since the late 1990s, with the biggest action in banking, radio and television, insurance, telecommunications, and health services. The fourth merger wave continues: the global economic slump of 2008 and 2009 forced firms in some industries, especially banking and finance, to merge in order to survive. For example, Wachovia merged with Wells Fargo and Merrill Lynch with Bank of America. The merger wave that began in 1982 continues today. Many merging firms hope to achieve economies of scale, and some do. For example, some hospital mergers achieve cost savings right away.[7] Merged hospitals could offer patients more specialists and better technology.[8]

But not all mergers work out. For example, Daimler-Benz bought Chrysler for $36 billion in 1998. After nearly a decade of disappointing results, the merged company had to pay $650 million in 2007 to unload 80 percent of its Chrysler division (Chrysler stayed in business in 2009 only after filing for bankruptcy, then getting billions in aid from the federal government for the newly reorganized company).

In recent years, there have been fewer objections to mergers on antitrust grounds either from academics or regulatory officials. The government shifted from rules that restrict big mergers to a more flexible approach that allows big companies to merge. For example, after several months of review, the U.S. Justice Department concluded in 2005 that Whirlpool's acquisition of Maytag would not reduce competition substantially and could achieve efficiencies and cost savings. What's more, the government believed that growing competition from Asia would prevent the merged company from raising prices. That merger went through, but a recent study suggests it harmed U.S. consumers because of large price increases both for Maytag dishwashers and for Whirlpool clothes dryers.[9] On the other hand, the 2008 merger of Coors and Miller brewers was found to have no net effect on consumers; the combined brewer was more efficient and this cost advantage offset the price effects of greater market power.[10]

Antitrust officials ask, "will the merger hurt competition?" Most, apparently, do not. Regulators have in recent years ultimately challenged only about 2 percent

conglomerate merger
A merger of firms in different industries

7. Teresa Harrison, "Do Mergers Really Reduce Costs? Evidence from Hospitals," *Economic Inquiry*, 49 (October 2011): 1054–1069.

8. Kenneth Davis, "Hospital Mergers Can Lower Costs and Improve Medical Care," *Wall Street Journal*, 15 September 2014.

9. Orley Ashenfelter, Daniel Hosken, and Matthew Weinberg, "The Price Effects of a Large Merger of Manufacturers: A Case Study of Maytag-Whirlpool" American Economic Journal: Economic Policy, 5 (February 2013): 239–261.

10. Orley Ashenfelter, Daniel Hosken, and Matthew Weinberg, "Efficiencies Brewed: Pricing and Consolidation in the U.S. Beer Industry," *RAND Journal of Economics*, 46 (Summer 2015): 328–361.

Exhibit 4
Competitive Trends in the U.S. Economy: 1939 to 2000

Sources: William G. Shepherd, "Causes of Increased Competition in the U.S. Economy, 1939–1980," *Review of Economics and Statistics*, 64 (November 1982): 613–626; and William G. Shepherd and Joanna M. Shepherd, *The Economics of Industrial Organization*, 5th ed. (Waveland Press, 2004).

of all mergers proposed, though just the threat of a legal challenge has probably deterred many potentially anticompetitive mergers and acquisitions.

15-5 COMPETITIVE TRENDS IN THE U.S. ECONOMY

For years, there has been concern about the sheer size of some firms because of the real or potential power they might exercise in the economy. But size alone is not the same as market power. A very big firm, such as a large chipmaker, may face stiff competition from another large chipmaker, foreign or domestic. On the other hand, the only movie theater in an isolated community may be able to raise its price with less concern about competition.

15-5a Competition Over Time

More important than the size of the largest firms in the nation is the market structure of each industry. Various studies have examined the level of competition by

industry and changes in competition over the years. All began with some measure of market share, such as the HHI. Among the most comprehensive is the research of William G. Shepherd, who relied on a variety of sources to determine the competitiveness of each industry in the U.S. economy.[11] He sorted industries into four groups: (1) pure monopoly, in which a single firm controlled the entire market and was able to block entry; (2) dominant firm, in which a single firm had more than half the market share and no close rival; (3) tight oligopoly, in which the top four firms supplied more than 60 percent of market output, with stable market shares and evidence of cooperation; and (4) effective competition, in which firms in the industry exhibited low concentration, low entry barriers, and little or no collusion.

Exhibit 4 presents Shepherd's breakdown of U.S. industries into the four categories for 1939, 1958, and 2000. Between 1939 and 1958, the table shows a modest growth in competition, with the share of those industries

11. William G. Shepherd, "Causes of Increased Competition in the U.S. Economy, 1939–1980," *Review of Economics and Statistics*, 64 (November 1982): 613–626; and William G. Shepherd and Joanna M. Shepherd, *The Economics of Industrial Organization*, 5th ed. (Waveland Press, 2004).

rated as "effectively competitive" increasing from 52 percent to 56 percent of all industries. Between 1958 and 2000, however, the share of effectively competitive industries jumped from 56 percent to 77 percent.

According to Shepherd, the growth in competition from 1958 to 2000 can be traced to three sources: (1) *competition from imports,* (2) *deregulation,* and (3) *antitrust policy.* Foreign imports between 1958 and 2000 increased competition in more than a dozen industries, including autos, tires, and steel. The growth in imports accounted for one-sixth of the overall increase in competition during the period. Imports were attractive to consumers because of their higher quality and lower price. Finding themselves at a cost and technological disadvantage, U.S. producers initially sought protection from foreign competitors through trade barriers, such as quotas and tariffs.

Shepherd argues that deregulation accounted for one-fifth of the increase in competition. Trucking, airlines, securities trading, banking, and telecommunications were among the industries deregulated between 1958 and 2000.

Although it is difficult to attribute an increase in competition to specific antitrust cases, Shepherd credits antitrust policy with two-fifths of the growth in competition between 1958 and 2000.

15-5b Recent Competitive Trends

Shepherd's analysis of competition extended to 2000. What has been the trend since then? Growing world trade has increased competition in the U.S. economy. For example, the share of the U.S. auto market controlled by General Motors, Ford, and Chrysler fell from 80 percent in 1970 to 45 percent by 2015. And federal action to deregulate international phone service forced down the average price of international phone calls from $0.88 a minute in 1997 to more like a penny a minute by 2015. In an effort to reduce international phone rates, federal officials even subpoenaed Filipino phone executives who were attending a conference in Hawaii, alleging they colluded on phone rates to the United States.

Technological change is boosting competition in many markets. For example, Uber's entry into local transportation networks had an immediate effect on competition, as discussed earlier in this chapter. The media industry has also been shaken up by technological change. For example, the prime-time audience share of the three major

> **"Technological change is boosting competition in many markets."**

Companies like Netflix, Amazon, and Hulu now compete with traditional television and cable stations by offering original programming like "Orange is the New Black."

K.C. Bailey/©Netflix/Everett

television networks (NBC, CBS, and ABC) dropped from 90 percent in 1980 to under 30 percent today as FOX became a fourth major network, and as cable and satellite technology delivered hundreds of networks and channels. About 90 percent of U.S. households have either cable or satellite television. Now Amazon.com, Netflix, Hulu, and other streaming services are slicing into these markets.[12] And the 15,400 radio stations now available is more than double the number in 1970 (satellite radio alone has about 30 million subscribers).

Despite Microsoft's dominance in operating systems, the software market that barely existed in 1980 now flourishes in a technology-rich environment populated by more than 10,000 producers, with Microsoft scrambling to catch up with search technology, with mobile apps, and with social networking. And the Internet has opened far-ranging possibilities for greater competition in a number of industries, from online stock trading to all manner of electronic commerce and information distribution to more than a million mobile apps.

Let's not forget that competition benefits society by forcing producers to become more efficient. A study of 732 firms in the United States, France, Germany, and the United Kingdom found that firms in competitive industries are more efficient than other firms.[13]

12. Suzanne Vranica and Shalini Ramachandran, "Streaming Services Hammer Cable-TV Ratings," *Wall Street Journal,* 10 March 2015.

13. Nicholas Bloom and John Van Reenen, "Measuring and Explaining Management Practices Across Firms and Countries," *Quarterly Journal of Economics,* 122 (November 2007): 1351–1408.

15-5c Problems With Antitrust Policy

There is growing doubt about the economic value of the lengthy antitrust cases pursued in the past. A case against Exxon, for example, was in the courts for 17 years before the company was cleared of charges in 1992. Another big case began in 1969 when IBM, with nearly 70 percent of domestic sales of electronic data-processing equipment, was accused of monopolizing that market. In 1982, the government dropped the case, noting that the threat of monopoly had diminished enough that the case was "without merit." The more recent U.S. case against Microsoft began in 1998 and took nearly six years to resolve; the case dragged on in state courts five more years.

Technological Change Fosters Competition

Joseph Schumpeter argued half a century ago that competition should be viewed as a dynamic process, one of "creative destruction." Firms are continually in flux—introducing new products, phasing out old ones, trying to compete for the consumer's dollar in a variety of ways. For example, cell phones replaced landlines (and now smartphones are replacing cell phones); GPS replaced road maps; digital cameras replaced cameras using film (Kodak went bankrupt in 2012), but now smartphones are replacing digital cameras, online news has erased the monopoly advantage once held by local newspapers, online sellers are cutting into bricks-and-mortar businesses, mobile apps such as Yelp are chipping away at Google's search dominance, and Chegg, Amazon.com, and Half.com are eroding the market power once held by college bookstores. *Competition is a dynamic process fueled by technological change.* Technological change makes antitrust policy less relevant.

Competition May Not Require Many Firms

Antitrust policy should not necessarily aim at increasing the *number* of firms in each industry. In some cases, firms grow large because they are better than rivals at offering what consumers want. Accordingly, firm size should not be the primary concern. Moreover, as noted in the chapter on perfect competition, economists have shown through market experiments that most of the desirable properties of perfect competition can be achieved with relatively few firms.[14] For example, the two leading chipmakers, Intel and Advanced Micro Devices, have been locked in a price war for years, as each fights for market share. Likewise,

Boeing, the only U.S. maker of commercial jets, competes fiercely with Europe's Airbus for every new contract. The worldwide market share for Airbus increased from 18 percent in 2000 to 43 percent in 2014.[15] And U.S. airline service is dominated by just a few carriers, but they compete so fiercely that each passenger trip in 2012 yielded less than a dollar of profit on average.[16]

Antitrust Abuses

Parties that can show injury from firms that violate antitrust laws can sue the offending company and recover three times the damages sustained. These so-called *treble damage* suits increased after World War II. About 90 percent of antitrust suits in the United States are filed by individuals or firms and just about all seek treble damages. Courts have been relatively generous to those claiming to have been wronged. Even foreign firms have started suing in U.S. courts. And, in an unusual twist, foreign firms are now suing other foreign firms using U.S courts, laws, and lawyers. But studies show that such suits can be used to intimidate an aggressive competitor or to convert a contract dispute between, say, a firm and its supplier into treble damage payoffs. The result can have a chilling effect on competition. Many economists now believe that the anticompetitive costs from this abuse of treble damage suits may exceed any competitive benefits of these laws.

Growth of International Markets

Finally, a standard approach to measuring the market power of a firm is its share of the market. With greater international trade, however, the local or even national market share becomes less relevant. General Motors may still dominate U.S. auto manufacturing, accounting for 40 percent of national sales by U.S. firms in 2015.

> **"Where markets are open to foreign competition, antitrust enforcement that focuses on domestic producers makes less economic sense."**

---

14. See, for example, Vernon Smith, "Markets as Economizers of Information: Experimental Examination of the 'Hayek Hypothesis,'" *Economic Inquiry*, 20 (April 1982): 165–179; and Douglas Davis and Charles Holt, *Experimental Economics* (Princeton University Press, 1993).

15. Jon Ostrower and Robert Wall, "Boeing Weighs Options to Reprise Aging 757s," *Wall Street Journal*, 11 February 2015.

16. Peter Theil, "Competition Is for Losers," *Wall Street Journal*, 12 September 2014.

But when Japanese and European producers are included, GM's share of the U.S. auto market falls to only about 18 percent of all sales. GM's share of world production has declined steadily since the mid-1950s. After 77 years as the world's largest automaker, GM was surpassed by Toyota in 2008. GM and Chrylser's very survival came into question in 2009 as the two car makers sought and received federal aid. *Where markets are open to foreign competition, antitrust enforcement that focuses on domestic producers makes less economic sense.*

In response to the global nature of markets, antitrust policy is starting to take an international approach. The U.S. government has signed cooperative agreements with some other governments, including Japan and the European Union, to promote antitrust enforcement and reduce conflicting decisions. For example, investigators from the United States, the European Union, and Japan simultaneously raided car-parts manufacturers in a price-fixing probe.[17] Through the International Competition Network, more than 100 nations discuss antitrust procedures and policies. Such discussions have thrown light on anticompetitive regulations in place around the world. Many countries for decades have sheltered firms in some politically powerful industries. For example, until recently, regulations in India restricted entry into the hotel business. As a result, there were fewer hotel rooms in all of India, a country with 1.3 billion people, than in New York City, with less than 1 percent of India's population.

Bailing Out Troubled Industries

Finally, the collapse of housing prices in 2007 and 2008 caused mortgage defaults and led to rising unemployment. The federal government responded by aiding affected industries, especially financial institutions and two of the big three automakers. The intent was to promote financial stability and keep the economy from sinking further. But the long-term effect of such market intervention on competition remains to be seen in industries such as auto manufacturing and banking, where firms are considered so important to the economy that they cannot be allowed to fail.

15-6 FINAL WORD

Market competition in the United States has been growing in recent decades because of changing technology, greater international trade, industry deregulation, and antitrust policy. Consumers benefit as firms compete by offering lower prices, better products, and new services to keep existing customers and attract new ones. Competition also ensures that the economy's resources find their most efficient uses. Through the process of creative destruction, competition promotes the survival of the fittest. Market forces continuously pressure firms to innovate—that is, to develop new and better products, services, methods of doing business, and technologies.

STUDY TOOLS 15

READY TO STUDY? IN THE BOOK, YOU CAN:

☐ Work the Problems at the end of the chapter.

☐ Rip out the chapter review card for a handy summary of the chapter and key terms.

ONLINE AT CENGAGEBRAIN.COM YOU CAN:

☐ Collect StudyBits while you read and study the chapter.

☐ Quiz yourself on key concepts.

☐ Prepare for tests with chapter flash cards as well as flash cards that you create.

☐ Watch videos to explore economics further.

17. Jeff Bennett and Peppi Kiviniemi, "Car-Parts Makers Raided in Price-Fixing Probe," *Wall Street Journal*, 26 February 2010.

CHAPTER 15 PROBLEMS

Your instructor can access the answers to these problems online at http://cengagebrain.com.

15-1 Describe three types of government regulation of business

1. *(Government Regulations)* Describe the three types of government regulation of business. Which two are discussed at length in this chapter?
2. *(Business Behavior and Public Policy)* Define market power, and then discuss the rationale for government regulation of firms with market power.

15-2 Evaluate alternative ways government can regulate a natural monopoly

3. *(Regulating Natural Monopolies)* The following graph represents a natural monopoly.
   a. Why is this firm considered a natural monopoly?
   b. If the firm is unregulated, what price and output would maximize its profit? What would be its profit or loss?
   c. If a regulatory commission establishes a price with the goal of achieving allocative efficiency, what would be the price and output? What would be the firm's profit or loss?
   d. If a regulatory commission establishes a price with the goal of allowing the firm a normal profit, what would be the price and output? What would be the firm's profit or loss?
   e. Which one of the prices in parts (b), (c), and (d) maximizes consumer surplus? What problem, if any, occurs at this price?

15-3 Describe two alternative theories of economic regulation

4. *(Theories of Regulation)* Why do producers have more interest in government regulations than consumers do?
   a. Compare and contrast the public-interest and special-interest theories of economic regulation. What is the capture theory of regulation?

   b. Which theory of regulation explains why the massive fraud of Bernie Madoff went undetected for years?
5. *(Origins of Antitrust Policy)* Identify the type of anticompetitive behavior illustrated by each of the following:
   a. A university requires buyers of season tickets for its basketball games to buy season tickets for its football games as well.
   b. Dairies that bid on contracts to supply milk to school districts collude to increase what they charge.
   c. The same individual serves on the boards of directors of General Motors and Ford.
   d. A large retailer sells merchandise below cost in certain regions to drive competitors out of business.
   e. A producer of soft drinks sells to a retailer only if the retailer agrees not to buy from the producer's major competitor.

15-4 Summarize the driving causes behind each of the four U.S. merger waves

6. *(U.S. Merger Waves)* Identify the four U.S. merger waves and explain the driving force behind each.
7. *(Mergers and Public Policy)* Calculate the Herfindahl-Hirschman Index (HHI) for each of the following industries. Which industry is the most concentrated?
   a. An industry with five firms that have the following market shares: 50 percent, 30 percent, 10 percent, 5 percent, and 5 percent
   b. An industry with five firms that have the following market shares: 60 percent, 20 percent, 10 percent, 5 percent, and 5 percent
   c. An industry with five firms, each of which has a 20 percent market share

15-5 Evaluate whether the U.S. economy has become more competitive or less competitive since 1958, and explain why

8. *(Competitive Trends in the U.S. Economy)* William Shepherd's research of U.S. industries showed a clear trend in the competitiveness of the U.S. economy between 1958 and 2000. Is the economy growing more or less competitive, and how did Shepherd explain this trend?

16 | Public Goods and Public Choice

LEARNING OUTCOMES

After studying this chapter, you will be able to…

16-1 Differentiate four categories of goods in terms of their exclusivity and rivalry

16-2 Identify four categories of legislation based on the distribution of costs and the distribution of benefits, and provide examples of each

16-3 Explain why some people want to use government power to increase their income, while others try to avoid government

16-4 Outline the differences between government bureaus and for-profit firms

After finishing this chapter go to **PAGE 282** for **STUDY TOOLS**

Topics discussed in Chapter 16 include:

- Private versus public goods
- Representative democracy
- Rational ignorance
- Special-interest legislation
- Rent seeking
- The underground economy
- Bureaucratic behavior
- Private versus public production

The effects of government are all around us. Stitched into the clothes you put on this morning are government-required labels about washing instructions. Government subsidies and federal trade regulations affect the prices of your Cheerios and the milk and sugar you put on them. Governments regulate the motor vehicle you drive as well your speed and sobriety. Taxpayers subsidize your education in a variety of ways. Yes, government plays a major role in the economy. The federal government alone spends about $4,000,000,000,000—about $4 *trillion*. Spending by governments at all levels in the United States tops $6 trillion.

> "Why do some politicians express concern for average Americans, but vote for special interests?"

The role of government has been discussed throughout this book. For the most part, we have assumed that government makes optimal adjustments to the shortcomings of the private sector—that is, when confronted with market failure, government adopts and implements the appropriate program to address the problem. But, just as there are limits to the market's effectiveness, there are also limits to government's effectiveness.

In this chapter, we look at the pros and cons of government activity. We begin with public goods, discuss the decision-making process, and then examine the limitations of that process.

16-1 PUBLIC GOODS

Throughout most of this book, we have been talking about *private goods*, such as pizzas and haircuts ("goods" in this chapter usually means goods and services). As noted in Chapter 3, private goods have two important features. First, they are *rival* in consumption, meaning that the amount consumed by one person is unavailable for others to consume. For example, when you and friends share a pizza, each slice others eat is one less available for you (which is why you might eat a little faster when sharing—hey, you're just trying to keep up). A second key feature of private goods is that suppliers can easily *exclude* those who don't pay. Only paying customers get pizzas. Thus, private goods are said to be *rival* and *exclusive*.

16-1a Private Goods, Public Goods, and in Between

In contrast to private goods, *public goods*, such as national defense, the National Weather Service, the Centers for Disease Control, or a local mosquito-control program, are *nonrival* in consumption. One person's consumption does not diminish the amount available to others. Once produced, such goods are available to all in equal amount; the good can be supplied to an additional consumer for zero marginal cost. But once a public good is produced, suppliers cannot easily deny it to those who

With congestion or over-use, a natural monopoly good such as this toll road can become a private good as others' usage affects your utility.

the same lines, short of the point of congestion, additional people can benefit from a subway system, golf course, swimming pool, rock concert, or highway without diminishing the benefit to other users. These goods, when not congested, are nonrival. Yet producers can, with relative ease, exclude anyone who doesn't pay the subway fare, greens fee, pool admission, ticket price, or road toll. These uncongested goods are both nonrival and exclusive and are therefore natural monopolies. Once congestion sets in, however, these goods become rival—space is scarce on a stuffed subway car, on a backed-up golf course, in a crowded swimming pool, at a jam-packed concert, or on a bumper-to-bumper highway. Once congestion sets in, these natural monopolies morph into private goods—both rival *and* exclusive.

Some other goods are *rival* but *nonexclusive*. The fish in the ocean are rival in the sense that every fish caught is no longer available for others to catch; the same goes for migratory game, like geese. But ocean fish and migratory game are nonexclusive in that it would be costly if not impossible to block access to these goods. A good that is rival but nonexclusive is called an **open-access good**. Problems that arise with open-access goods will be discussed in the next chapter.

Exhibit 1 sorts out the four categories of goods. Across the top, goods are classified as either *rival* or *nonrival*, and along the left margin, goods are classified as either *exclusive* or *nonexclusive*. Private goods are usually provided by the private sector. Natural monopolies are sometimes provided by the private sector, as with a private golf course, and sometimes provided by government, as with a municipal golf course. Open-access goods are usually regulated by

don't pay. There are no vending machines for public goods. For example, if a firm sprays a neighborhood for mosquitoes, all those in the neighborhood benefit. The firm can't easily exclude those who fail to pay. Thus, mosquito spraying is *nonexclusive*—it benefits everyone in the neighborhood. Some people figure, "Since I can enjoy the benefits without paying, why bother paying?" As a consequence, for-profit firms can't profitably sell public goods. In this case of market failure, the government comes to the rescue by providing public goods and paying for them through enforced taxation. Sometimes nonprofit agencies also provide public goods, funding them through contributions and other revenue sources.

But the economy consists of more than just the polar cases of private and public goods. Some goods are *nonrival* but *exclusive*. For example, additional households can watch a TV show without affecting the reception of other viewers. It's not as if there is only so much TV signal to go around. Television signals are nonrival in consumption. Yet the program's producers, should they choose to, could charge each household for reception, as with cable TV and streaming services like Netflix, so the TV signal is nonrival but exclusive. A good that is nonrival but exclusive is called a *natural monopoly*, a term already introduced. Along

open-access good A good such as ocean fish that is rival in consumption but from which nonpayers cannot be excluded easily

Exhibit 1
Categories of Goods

	Rival	Nonrival
Exclusive	1. Private —Pizza —Crowded Subway	2. Natural Monopolies —Cable TV —Uncrowded Subway
Nonexclusive	3. Open Access —Ocean fish —Migratory birds	4. Public —National defense —Mosquito control

government, as you will see in the next chapter. And public goods are usually provided by government.

16-1b Optimal Provision of Public Goods

Because private goods are rival in consumption, the market demand for a private good at a given price is the sum of the quantities demanded by each consumer. For example, the market quantity of pizza demanded when the price is $10 is the quantity demanded by Alan plus the quantity demanded by Maria plus the quantity demanded by all other consumers in the market. The market demand curve for a private good is the *horizontal* sum of individual demand curves, an idea developed in Exhibit 7 of Chapter 6. The efficient quantity of a private good occurs where the market demand curve intersects the market supply curve.

But a public good is nonrival in consumption, so that good, once produced, is available in that amount to all consumers. For example, the market demand for a given level of mosquito control reflects the marginal benefit that Alan gets from that amount plus the marginal benefit that Maria gets plus the marginal benefit that all others in the community get from that amount of the good. Therefore, the market demand curve for a public good is the *vertical* sum of each consumer's demand for the public good. To arrive at the efficient level of the public good, we find where the market demand curve intersects the marginal cost curve—that is, where the sum of the marginal valuations equals the marginal cost.

Suppose the public good in question is mosquito control in a neighborhood, which, for simplicity, has only two households, one headed by Alan and the other by Maria. Alan spends more time in the yard than does Maria and thus values a mosquito-free environment more than she does. Their individual demand curves are shown in Exhibit 2 as D_a and D_m, reflecting the marginal benefits that Alan and Maria enjoy at each rate of output. Quantity is measured here as hours of mosquito spraying per week. By vertically summing marginal valuations at each rate of output, we derive the neighborhood demand curve, D, for mosquito spraying. For example, when the

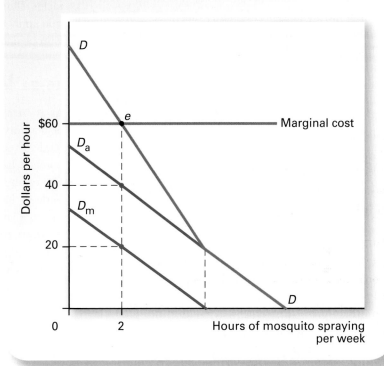

Exhibit 2
Market for Public Goods

Because public goods, once produced, are available to all in identical amounts, the demand for a public good is the vertical sum of each individual's demand. Thus, the market demand for mosquito spraying is the vertical sum of Maria's demand, D_m, and Alan's demand, D_a. The efficient level of provision is found where the marginal cost of mosquito spraying equals its marginal benefit. This occurs at point e, where the marginal cost curve intersects the market demand curve, D.

town sprays two hours a week, Maria values the second hour at $20 and Alan values it at $40. To get the market demand for the second hour of spraying, we simply add each resident's marginal benefit to get $60, as identified by point e.

How much mosquito spraying should the government provide? Suppose the marginal cost of spraying is a constant $60 an hour, as shown in Exhibit 2. The efficient level of output is found where the marginal benefit to the neighborhood equals the marginal cost, which occurs where the neighborhood demand curve intersects the marginal cost curve. In our example, these curves intersect where quantity is two hours per week.

16-1c Paying for Public Goods

Suppose the government pays for the mosquito spray through taxes. The efficient approach would be to impose a tax on each resident equal to his or her marginal valuation. Simple enough, but there are at least two problems with this. First, once people realize their taxes are based on government estimates of how much they value the good, some people tend to understate their true valuation. Why admit you really value the good if, as a result, you get socked with a higher tax bill? After all, people in the neighborhood can enjoy mosquito abatement whether or not they pay for it. So taxpayers tend to understate their true valuation of public goods. This creates the **free-rider problem**, which occurs because some people try to benefit from the public good without paying for it.

But even if the government has accurate information about everyone's marginal valuations, some households have a greater ability to pay taxes than others. In our example, Alan values mosquito control more because he spends more time in the yard than does Maria. What if Alan is around more because he can't find a job? Should his taxes be double those of Maria, who has, say, a high-paying job? *Taxing people according to their marginal valuations of the public good may be efficient, but it may not be fair if the ability to pay differs.*

> **"Public goods are more complicated than private goods in terms of what goods should be provided, in what quantities, and who should pay."**

Once the public good is produced, only that quantity is available, such as two hours of mosquito spraying per week. With private goods, each consumer can buy any quantity he or she demands and each can purchase a different amount. Thus, *"public goods are more complicated than private goods in terms of what goods should be provided, in what quantities, and who should pay."* These decisions are thrashed out through public choices, which we explore in the balance of this chapter.

free-rider problem
Because nobody can be easily excluded from consuming a public good, some people may try to reap the benefits of the good without paying for it

median-voter model
Under certain conditions, the preferences of the median, or middle, voter will dominate the preferences of all other voters

16-2 PUBLIC CHOICE IN REPRESENTATIVE DEMOCRACY

Government decisions about public goods and taxes are *public choices*. In a democracy, public choices usually require approval by a majority of voters. About 60 percent of the world's 200 independent nations are democracies. Thus, issues raised in this section about majority rule apply to most of the world, including all of Western Europe and nearly all of the Americas.

16-2a Median-Voter Model

As it turns out, we can usually explain the outcome of majority rule by focusing on the preferences of the median voter. The *median voter* is the one whose preferences lie in the middle of all voters' preferences. For example, if the issue is the size of the government budget, half the voters prefer a larger budget than the median voter and half prefer a smaller one. The **median-voter model** predicts that under certain conditions, the preference of the median, or middle, voter will dominate other choices. Here's an example. Suppose you and two roommates have just moved into an apartment, and the three of you must decide on furnishings. You agree to share common expenses equally and to make choices by majority rule. The issue at hand is whether to buy a TV and, if so, of what size. You each have a different preference. Your studious roommate considers a TV an annoying distraction and would rather go without one; otherwise, the smaller, the better. Your other roommate, an avid TV watcher, prefers a 60-inch screen but would settle for a smaller one rather than go without. A 42-inch screen is your first choice, but you would prefer the 60-inch screen rather than go without. What to do, what to do?

You all agree to make the decision by voting on two alternatives at a time, then pairing the winner against the remaining alternative until one choice dominates the others. When the 42-inch screen is paired with the no-TV option, the 42-inch screen gets both your vote and the TV fan's vote. When the 42-inch screen is then paired with the 60-inch screen, the 42-inch screen wins again, this time because your studious roommate sides with you.

Majority voting in effect delegates the public choice to the person whose preference is the median for the group. As the median voter in this example, you get your way. You have the votes for any choice between no TV and a 60-incher. Similarly, *the median voter in an electorate often determines public choices. Political candidates try to get elected by appealing to the median voter.* This is why candidates focus their rhetoric on "hard-working Americans," "middle-class America," or "American families." They are targeting median voters. This is one reason why candidates often seem so much alike. Note that under majority rule, only the median voter gets his or her way. Other voters must go along with the median choice. Thus, other voters usually end up paying for what they consider to be either too much or too little of the public good. On the contrary, in private markets each individual gets whatever amount he or she is willing and able to buy.

People vote directly on issues at New England town meetings and on the occasional referendum, but *direct democracy* is not the most common form of public choice. When you consider the thousands of choices made in the public sector—from the number of teachers to hire to what software to maintain municipal records—it becomes clear that direct democracy for all public choices through referenda would be unwieldy and impractical. Rather than make decisions by direct referenda, voters elect *representatives*, who, at least in theory, make public choices that reflect constituents' views. More than 500,000 elected officials serve in the United States. Under certain conditions, the resulting public choices reflect the preferences of the median voter. Some complications of representative democracy are explored next.

Lee Torrens/Shutterstock.com

> **❝** Because information and the time required to acquire and digest it are scarce, consumers concentrate on private choices rather than public choices. The payoff in making better private choices is usually more immediate, more direct, and more substantial. **❞**

16-2b Special Interest and Rational Ignorance

We assume that consumers maximize utility and firms maximize profit, but what about governments? As noted in Chapter 3, there is no common agreement about what, if anything, governments try to maximize or, more precisely, what elected officials try to maximize. One theory that stems from the rational self-interest assumption of economic behavior is that elected officials try to *maximize their political support.*

To maximize political support, elected officials may cater to special interests rather than serve the public interest. The possibility arises because of the asymmetry between special interest and public interest, an idea introduced in the previous chapter. Consider only one of the thousands of decisions elected representatives make: funding an obscure federal program that subsidizes U.S. wool production. Under the wool-subsidy program, the federal government guarantees that a floor price is paid to sheep farmers for each pound of wool they produce, a subsidy that has cost taxpayers over $75 million since 2000. During deliberations to renew the program, the only person to testify before Congress was a representative of the National Wool Growers Association, who claimed that the subsidy was vital to the nation's economic welfare. Why didn't a single taxpayer challenge the subsidy?

Households consume so many different public and private goods and services that they have neither the time nor the incentive to understand the effects of public choices on every product. What's more, voters realize that each of them has but a tiny possibility of influencing public choices. And even if an individual voter is somehow able to affect the outcome, the impact on that voter is likely to be small. For example, if a taxpayer could have successfully staged a grassroots campaign in 2000 to eliminate the wool subsidy, the average taxpayer would have saved a total of 50 cents in federal income taxes since then. Therefore, unless voters have a *special* interest in the legislation, they adopt a stance of **rational ignorance**, which means that they remain largely oblivious to most public choices. The cost to the typical voter of acquiring information about each public choice and acting on it usually exceeds any expected benefit. It's not easy to interest the public in the public interest. Or as Joseph Pulitzer, who funded the Pulitzer Prize, said, "What is everybody's business is nobody's business—except the journalist's."

In contrast, consumers have much more incentive to gather and act on information about private choices because they benefit directly and immediately from such information. *"Because information and the time required to acquire and digest it are scarce, consumers concentrate on private choices rather than public choices. The payoff in making better private choices is usually more immediate, more direct, and more substantial."* For example, a consumer in the market for a new car has an incentive to examine the performance records of different models, test-drive a few, and check prices at dealerships and online. That same person has less incentive to examine the performance records of candidates for public office because that single voter has virtually no chance of deciding the election. What's more, because candidates aim to please the median voter anyway, they often take positions that are similar.

Some researchers have argued that the media can partly offset rational ignorance by combining politics with entertainment. For example, media can inform passive voters about public policy issues by uncovering inappropriate links between public officials and private interests or by highlighting public corruption.[1]

16-2c Distribution of Benefits and Costs

Let's turn now to a different topic—how the benefits and costs of public choices are spread across the population.

1. Alexander Dyck, David Moss, and Luigi Zingales, "Media Versus Special Interests," *Journal of Law and Economic,* 56 (August 2013): 521–553.

rational ignorance A stance adopted by voters when they realize that the cost of understanding and voting on a particular issue exceeds the benefit expected from doing so

traditional public-goods legislation Legislation that involves widespread costs and widespread benefits—nearly everyone pays and nearly everyone benefits

special-interest legislation Legislation with concentrated benefits but widespread costs

pork-barrel spending Special-interest legislation that has narrow geographical benefits but is funded by all taxpayers

"Depending on the issue, particular legislation may benefit only a small group or much of the population." Likewise, the costs of that legislation may be imposed only on a small group or on much of the population. The combinations of benefits and costs yield four possible categories of distributions: (1) widespread benefits and widespread costs, (2) concentrated benefits and widespread costs, (3) widespread benefits and concentrated costs, and (4) concentrated costs and concentrated benefits.

> **"Depending on the issue, particular legislation may benefit only a small group or much of the population. Likewise, the costs of that legislation may be imposed only on a small group or on much of the population."**

Traditional public-goods legislation, such as for national defense, road safety, a justice system, or cancer research, involve widespread benefits and widespread costs—nearly everyone benefits and nearly everyone pays. Traditional public-goods legislation usually has a positive impact on the economy because total benefits exceed total costs.

With **special-interest legislation**, benefits are concentrated but costs widespread. For example, as you'll see shortly, price supports for dairy products have benefited a small group—dairy farmers. To benefit dairy farmers, a special interest, the program spread costs across nearly all taxpayers and consumers. Legislation that caters to special interests usually harms the economy, on net, because total costs often exceed total benefits. Special-interest legislation benefitting a narrow geographical interest is called **pork-barrel spending**. To boost their reelection prospects, members of Congress "bring home the bacon" by delivering pork-barrel programs for their constituents. For example, the federal budget in 2014 appropriated $50,000 to help process, package, and market alpaca manure ("Poop Paks") in Virginia, and $32,000 to help market goat's milk soap in Florida.[2]

Populist legislation involves widespread benefits but concentrated costs. Such legislation usually has a tough time getting approved because the widespread group that benefits typically remains rationally ignorant about the proposed legislation, so these voters provide little political support. But the concentrated group who would get whacked by the taxes object strenuously. Most economists agree that tort-reform legislation, for example, would benefit the economy as a whole by limiting product liability lawsuits, reducing insurance costs, and bringing some goods to the market that, because of liability suits, have all but disappeared, such as personal aircraft. But trial lawyers, the group that would be most harmed by such limits, have successfully blocked reforms for years. Because the small group that bears the cost is savvy about the impact of such proposals but those who would reap the benefits remain rationally ignorant, populist legislation has little chance of approval. The only way such measures get approved is if some political entrepreneur raises enough visibility about the issue to gather public attention and votes. For example, a candidate for governor may run against high electric bills. The key is to somehow get the issue on voters' radar screens.

Finally, **competing-interest legislation** involves both concentrated benefits and concentrated costs, such

as labor unions versus employers, steel makers versus steel-using industries, or sugar growers versus industries such as soft drink bottlers that buy sugar by the truckload. These are fierce political battles because both sides have a heavy stake in the outcome. Elected officials usually are not very willing to get in the middle of such disputes.

Exhibit 3 arrays the four categories of distributions. Across the top, benefits of legislation are either *widespread* or *concentrated,* and along the left margin, costs are either *widespread* or *concentrated.* Box 1 shows *traditional public-goods legislation,* such as national defense, with both widespread benefits and widespread costs. Box 2 shows *special-interest legislation,* such as farm subsidies, with concentrated benefits but widespread costs. Box 3 shows *populist legislation,* such as tort reform, with widespread benefits but concentrated costs. And Box 4 shows *competing-interest legislation,* such as labor union issues, with both concentrated benefits and concentrated costs.

The following section considers a special-interest program—farm price supports.

Farm Subsidies[3]

The Agricultural Marketing Agreement Act became law in 1937 to prevent what was viewed as "ruinous competition" among farmers. At the time, one in four Americans lived on a farm. In the years since, the government

Exhibit 3

Categories of Legislation Based on the Distribution of Costs and Benefits

		Distribution of Benefits	
		Widespread	**Concentrated**
Distribution of Costs	**Widespread**	1. Traditional Public Goods —*National defense*	2. Special Interest —*Farm subsidies*
	Concentrated	3. Populist —*Tort reform*	4. Competing Interest —*Labor union issues*

3. Kym Anderson, Gordon Rausser, and Johan Swinnen, "Political Economy of Public Policies: Insights from Distortions to Agricultural and Food Markets," *Journal of Economic Literature,* 51 (June 2013): 423–477; Barratt Kirwan, "The Incidence of U.S. Agricultural Subsidies on Farmland Rental Rates," *Journal of Political Economy,* 117 (February 2009): 138–164; Ani Katchova, "A Comparison of Economic Well-Being of Farm and Nonfarm Households," *American Journal of Agricultural Economics,* 90 (August 2008): 733–747; Jacob Bunge and David Kesmodel, "America's Move to Soy Hobbles Dairy," *Wall Street Journal,* 18 July 2014; and "Milking Taxpayers," *The Economist,* 14 February 2014.

populist legislation
Legislation with widespread benefits but concentrated costs

competing-interest legislation Legislation that confers concentrated benefits on one group by imposing concentrated costs on another group

2. These two were among hundreds of grants awarded by the U.S. Department of Agriculture in 2014. The complete list is available at http://www.rurdev.usda.gov/supportdocuments/RD_2014VAPGRecipients.pdf.

introduced a variety of policies that set floor prices for a wide range of farm products. Now, only 1 in 50 Americans lives on a farm, but this program is still with us. Subsidies in the 2008 Farm Act cost U.S. taxpayers about $20 billion a year.

Let's see how price supports worked in the dairy industry, using a simplified example. Exhibit 4 presents the market for milk. Without government intervention, suppose the market price of milk would average $1.50 per gallon for a market quantity of 100 million gallons per month. In long-run equilibrium, dairy farmers would earn a normal profit in this competitive industry. Consumer surplus is shown by the blue-shaded area. Recall that consumer surplus is the difference between the most that consumers would be willing to pay for that quantity and the amount they actually pay.

Now suppose the dairy lobby persuades Congress that milk should sell for no less than $2.50 per gallon.

The higher price encourages farmers to increase their quantity supplied to 150 million gallons. Consumers, however, reduce their quantity demanded to 75 million gallons. To make the floor price of $2.50 stick, the government every month must buy the 75 million gallons of surplus milk generated by the floor price or must somehow get dairy farmers to cut output to only 75 million gallons per month. For example, to reduce supply, the government under one federal program spends about $1 billion a year on milk products.

Consumers end up paying dearly to subsidize farmers. First, the price consumers pay increases, in this example by $1 per gallon. Second, as taxpayers, consumers must also pay for the surplus milk or otherwise pay farmers not to produce that milk. So consumers pay $2.50 for each gallon they buy on the market and pay another $2.50 in higher taxes for each surplus gallon the government must buy. Instead of paying a free-market price of just $1.50 for each gallon consumed, the typical consumer-taxpayer in effect pays $5.00 for each gallon actually consumed.

How do farmers make out? Each receives an extra $1 per gallon in revenue compared to the free-market price. As farmers increase their quantity supplied in response to the higher price, however, their marginal cost of production increases. At the margin, the higher price just offsets the higher marginal cost of production. The government subsidy also bids up the price of specialized resources, such as cows and especially pasture land. Anyone who owned these resources when the subsidy was introduced would benefit. Farmers who purchased them after that (and, hence, after resource prices increased) earn only a normal rate of return on their investment. Because farm subsidies were originally introduced more than half a century ago, most farmers today earn just a normal return on their investment, despite the billions spent annually on subsidies.

If the extra $1 per gallon that farmers receive for milk were pure profit,

Don Mason/Jupiter Images

Exhibit 4
Effects of Milk Price Supports

In the absence of government intervention in this simplified example, the market price of milk is $1.50 per gallon, and 100 million gallons are sold per month. If government establishes a floor price of $2.50 per gallon, then the quantity supplied increases and the quantity demanded decreases. To maintain the higher price, the government must buy the excess quantity supplied at $2.50 per gallon or must otherwise pay farmers to limit their quantity supplied to only 75 million gallons a month.

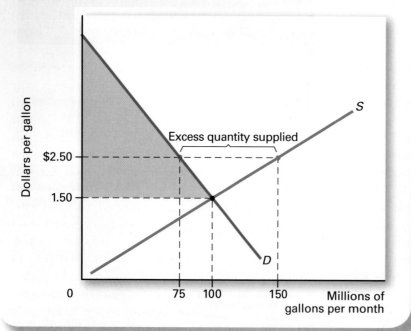

farm profit would increase by $150 million per month under the government program. But total outlays by consumer-taxpayers jumped from $150 million per month for 100 million gallons to $375 million per month for just 75 million gallons. Thus, cost to consumer-taxpayers increases by $225 million, though they consume 25 million fewer gallons. Like other special-interest legislation, farm subsidies have a negative impact on the economy, as the losses outweigh the gains. The real winners are those who owned specialized resources when the subsidy was first introduced. Young farmers must pay more to get into a position to reap the subsidies. Ironically, subsidies aimed at preserving the family farm raise the costs of entry.

16-3 EXPLOITING GOVERNMENT VERSUS AVOIDING GOVERNMENT

Some people want to use government power to increase their income. Others try to avoid government. Here we look at these two extremes.

16-3a Rent Seeking

An important feature of representative democracy is the incentive and political power it offers interest groups to increase their income, either from direct government transfers or from favorable public expenditures and regulations. Special-interest groups, such as dairy farmers, trial lawyers, government employees, and other producers, seek from government some special advantage or some outright transfer or subsidy. Such benefits are often called *rents* because they exceed what the producer would require to supply the product. Thus, rents represents earnings that exceed opportunity cost. The activity that interest groups undertake to secure these special favors from government is called *rent seeking*, a term already introduced.

The government frequently bestows some special advantage

"Resources employed to persuade government to redistribute income and wealth to special interests are unproductive because they do nothing to increase total output and usually end up reducing it."

on a producer or group of producers, and abundant resources are expended to acquire these advantages. For example, *political action committees*, known more popularly as *PACs*, contribute millions to congressional campaigns.

To the extent that special-interest groups engage in rent seeking, they shift resources from productive endeavors that create output and income to activities that focus more on transferring income to their special interests. *"Resources employed to persuade government to redistribute income and wealth to special interests are unproductive because they do nothing to increase total output and usually end up reducing it."* Often many firms compete for the same government advantage, thereby wasting still more resources in the process. If the advantage conferred by government on some special-interest group requires higher income taxes, the earnings people expect from working and investing fall, so they may work less and invest less. If this happens, productive activity declines.

As a firm's profitability relies more and more on decisions made in Washington, in state capitals, or in city halls, resources are diverted from productive activity to rent seeking, or lobbying efforts. One firm may thrive because it secured some special government advantage at a critical time; another firm may fail because its managers were more concerned with productive efficiency than with rent seeking.

Special-interest groups have little incentive to make the economy more efficient. In fact, they usually support legislation that transfers income to them even if the economy suffers. For example, suppose lawyers are able to change product liability laws in a way that boosts their aggregate annual incomes by a total of $10 billion, or about $10,000 for each of the million or so lawyers practicing in the United States. Suppose, too, that this measure drives up the insurance premiums of producers, raising the total cost of production by, say, $20 billion per year. Lawyers themselves have to bear part of this higher cost for products they buy, but because their personal consumption accounts for only about 1 percent of total spending in the economy, they bear only about 1 percent of the $20 billion in higher costs, or about $200 million. This amounts to $200 per lawyer per year. Thus, the legislation is a good deal for lawyers because their annual incomes grow about $10,000 each but their annual costs increase only about $200 each, resulting in the net average gain of $9,800 per lawyer. Much special-interest legislation leads to a net reduction in social welfare. For example, some of the nation's best minds are now occupied devising schemes to avoid taxes or divert income to favored groups at the expense of market efficiency.

An important special interest group is made up of government workers themselves. They can vote for and otherwise support the elected official who will increase their pay and benefits. Government employees are also more organized than other workers. As noted earlier, 35.7 percent of them are represented by unions, compared with just 6.6 percent of workers in the private sector. And public sector workers at all levels have more job security on average than do private sector workers.[4]

There are hundreds of special-interest groups representing farmers, physicians, lawyers, teachers, manufacturers, barbers, government workers, massage therapists, real estate agents, and so on. For example, at the urging of real estate professionals, Massachusetts adopted a continuing-education requirement for real estate agents. In seeking the legislation, the industry lobbying group argued that the measure would improve the quality of real estate service for the public. Subsequent research failed to find any improvement as measured by consumer complaints to the real estate licensing board. But the requirement did reduce the number of licensed real estate agents by about 50 percent and increased the income of remaining agents by about 14 percent.[5] Thus, the restrictions appear to be more in the special interest of realtors than in the public interest of consumers. Similarly, massage therapists working in states with licensing requirements earn significantly more than those in other states. Licensing reduces their supply.[6] And some elected officials enrich themselves while in office. For example,

research in India finds that elected officials increased their wealth significantly more during their term of office than did runner-ups during the same period.[7]

16-3b The Underground Economy

A government subsidy promotes production, as we saw in the case study on milk price supports. Conversely, a tax discourages production. Perhaps it would be more accurate to say that when government taxes productive activity, less production gets *reported*. If you ever worked as a waitress or waiter, did you faithfully report all your tip income to the Internal Revenue Service? If not, your unreported income became part of the underground economy. The **underground economy** describes all market activity that goes unreported either to evade taxes or because the activity itself is illegal. Income arising in the underground economy ranges from unreported tips to the earnings of drug dealers.

Taxing productive activity has two effects. First, resource owners may supply less of the taxed resource because the after-tax earnings decline. Second, to evade taxes, some people shift from the formal, reported economy to an underground, "off the books" economy. Thus, when the government taxes market exchange and the income it generates, less market activity and less income get reported. The underground economy is known by a variety of other names in different countries, including the shady economy, informal economy, second economy, cash economy, hidden economy, unrecorded economy, parallel economy, off-the-books economy, and black economy. The underground economy plays a larger role in less developed countries, accounting for up to half of all production in the poorest countries.[8]

We should take care to distinguish between tax *avoidance* and tax *evasion*. Tax avoidance is a *legal* attempt to arrange one's economic affairs to minimize taxes, such as buying municipal bonds because they yield interest free of federal income taxes. When the federal income tax was established in 1913, the tax code was 400 pages long. By 2014, the federal income tax code filled about 74,000 pages.[9] Complying with those laws employs armies of lawyers and tax advisers. About a million people work in the United States as

4. Jason Kopelman and Harvey Rosen, "Are Public Sector Jobs Recession Proof? Were They Ever?" *Public Finance Review* (forthcoming).

5. Benjamin Powell and Evgeny Vorotnikov, "Real Estate Education: Rent Seeking or Improvement in Service Quality?," *Eastern Economic Journal*, 38 (March 2012): 57–73.

6. Robert Thornton and Edward Timmons, "Licensing One of the World's Oldest Professions: Massage," *Journal of Law & Economics*, 56 (May 2013): 371–388.

7. Raymond Fisman, Florian Schulz, and Vikrant Vig, "The Private Returns to Public Office," *Journal of Political Economy*, 122 (August 2014): 806–862.

8. Rafael La Porta and Andrei Schleifer, "Informality and Development," *Journal of Economic Perspectives*, 28 (Summer 2014): 109–126.

9. Based on the page count in the *Commerce Clearing House Federal Tax Reporter* at http://www.cch.com/TaxLawPileUp.pdf.

underground economy
Market activity that goes unreported either because it is illegal or because those involved want to evade taxes

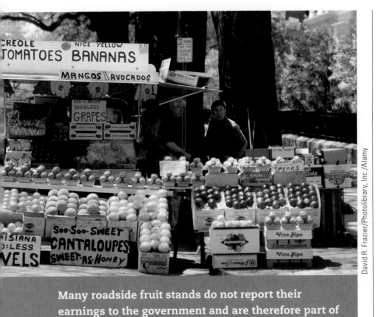

Many roadside fruit stands do not report their earnings to the government and are therefore part of the underground economy.

David R. Frazier/Photolibrary, Inc./Alamy

professional tax preparers. Tax evasion, on the other hand, is *illegal;* it takes the form of either failing to file a tax return or filing a fraudulent return by understating income or overstating deductions. Research around the world indicates that the underground economy grows more when (1) government regulations increase, (2) tax rates increase, and (3) government corruption is more widespread.[10]

An Internal Revenue Service survey estimates that only about 85 percent of taxable income gets reported on tax returns. This implies an underground economy of about $2.7 trillion in 2015.

Those who pursue rent-seeking activity and those involved in the underground economy view government from opposite sides. Rent seekers want government to become actively involved in transferring income to them, but those in the underground economy want to avoid government contact. *"Subsidies and other advantages bestowed by government draw some people closer to government; taxes and regulations drive some others underground."*

10. For a summary of these studies, see Simon Johnson, Daniel Kaufmann, and Pablo Zoido-Lobaton, "Regulatory Discretion and the Unofficial Economy," *American Economic Review,* 88 (May 1998): 387–392.

> **"Subsidies and other advantages bestowed by government draw some people closer to government; taxes and regulations drive some others underground."**

16-4 BUREAUCRACY AND REPRESENTATIVE DEMOCRACY

Elected officials approve legislation, but the task of implementing that legislation is typically left to **bureaus**, which are government agencies whose activities are financed by appropriations from legislative bodies.

16-4a Ownership and Funding of Bureaus

We can get a better feel for government bureaus by comparing them to corporations. Stockholders own a corporation and share any profit or loss. Stockholders also get to vote on important corporate matters based on the number of shares owned. Corporate shares can be bought and sold in the stock market: ownership is *transferable* to whomever buys the shares. Taxpayers are in a sense the "owners" of government bureaus. If the bureau earns a "profit," taxes may decline; if the bureau operates at a "loss," as most do, this loss must be made up by more taxes. Each taxpayer has just one vote, regardless of the taxes he or she pays. Ownership in the bureau is surrendered only if the taxpayer dies or moves out of the jurisdiction, but ownership is not transferable—it cannot be bought or sold directly.

Although corporations cover their costs if enough people buy their products, bureaus are usually financed by government appropriation, most of which comes from taxpayers. Bureaus do not have to meet a market test. Some bureaus get revenue through user charges, such as admission fees to state parks or tuition at state colleges, but even these bureaus typically rely on taxes for part of their revenue. Because of these differences in the forms of ownership and in the sources of funding, bureaus have different incentives than do for-profit firms, so they are likely to behave differently, as we'll see next.

bureaus Government agencies charged with implementing legislation and financed by appropriations from legislative bodies

16-4b Ownership and Organizational Behavior

"A central assumption of economics is that people behave rationally and respond to economic incentives." The more tightly compensation is linked to individual incentives, the more people behave in accordance with those incentives. For example, if a letter carrier's pay is based on customer satisfaction, the carrier will make a greater effort to deliver mail promptly and intact.

> **"A central assumption of economics is that people behave rationally and respond to economic incentives."**

A private firm receives a steady stream of consumer feedback. If the price is too high or too low, surpluses or shortages become obvious. Not only is consumer feedback abundant, but the firm's owners have a profit incentive to act on that information to satisfy consumer wants. The promise of profits also creates an incentive to produce output at the lowest cost per unit. Thus, the firm's owners stand to gain from any improvement in customer satisfaction for a given cost or any reduction in cost for a given level of consumer satisfaction.

Because public goods and services are not sold in markets, government bureaus receive less consumer feedback and have less incentive to act on any feedback they do receive. There are usually no prices and no obvious shortages or surpluses. For example, how would you know whether there was a shortage or a surplus of police protection in your community? Not only do bureaus receive less consumer feedback than firms do, bureaus have less incentive to act on the information available. If a corporation is run poorly, someone could buy the majority of shares, improve performance, then profit from a higher share price. But because the ownership of bureaus is not transferable, there is less incentive to eliminate waste and inefficiency.

To be sure, voters could pressure their elected representatives to make bureaus more responsive. But this discipline is rather crude. Most voters remain rationally ignorant about government performance in part because each voter has little impact on the outcome and each stands to gain so little from any gain in efficiency. For example, suppose that you are one of a million taxpayers in a city and you learn that by having a FedEx Office do all public copying, the city could save $1 million a year. If, through letters to the editor and calls to local officials, you somehow convince the city to adopt this cost-saving measure, you, as a typical taxpayer, would save yourself about a dollar a year in taxes.

Voters can leave a jurisdiction if they believe government is inefficient. This mechanism, whereby people "vote with their feet," does promote some efficiency and consumer satisfaction at the state and local levels, but it's also crude. What if you like some public programs but not others? Moreover, voters dissatisfied with the biggest spender and taxer, the federal government, cannot easily vote with their feet. If you were to move abroad, you, as a U.S. citizen, would still have to pay U.S. federal taxes on your worldwide income even if you earned not a dime from U.S. sources (nearly all other countries exempt the foreign earnings of those living abroad).

Because of differences between public and private organizations—in the owners' ability both to transfer ownership and to appropriate profits—we expect bureaus to be less concerned with satisfying consumer demand or with minimizing costs than private firms are. A variety of empirical studies compares costs for products that are provided by both public bureaus and private firms, such as garbage collection. Of those studies that show a difference, most find private firms are more efficient.

16-4c Bureaucratic Objectives

Assuming that bureaus are not simply at the beck and call of the legislature—that is, assuming that bureaucrats have some autonomy—what sort of objectives do *they* pursue? The traditional view is that bureaucrats are "public servants," who try to serve the public as best they can. No doubt some public employees do just that, but is this a realistic assumption for bureaucrats more generally? Why should we assume self-sacrificing behavior by public-sector employees when we make no such assumption about private-sector employees?

One widely discussed theory of bureaucratic behavior claims that bureaus try to *maximize their budget*, for along with a bigger budget come size, prestige, amenities, staff, and pay—all features that are valued by bureaucrats.[11] According to this view, bureaus are monopoly suppliers of their output to elected officials. Rather than charge a price per unit, bureaus offer the entire amount as a package deal in return for the requested appropriation. This theory assumes that the elected officials have only limited ability to dig into the budget and cut particular items. If elected officials do try to cut the bureau's budget, the bureau may threaten to make those cuts as painful to constituents as possible. For example, if city officials attempt to slow the growth of the school budget, school bureaucrats, rather than increase teaching loads or reduce pay, may threaten to eliminate kindergarten, abolish the high school football team, or disband the school band. If such threats force elected officials to back off, the government budget turns out to be larger than the public would prefer. *Budget maximization by bureaus results in a larger budget than that desired by the median voter.* The key to this argument is that bureaus are monopoly suppliers of public goods and elected officials have only limited ability to cut that budget. If taxpayers have alternatives in the private sector or if elected officials can dig into the budget, the monopoly power of the bureau is diminished. Some support for the budget-maximization approach comes from findings that federal bureaus spend down any remaining funds toward the end of their budget year on inefficient projects rather than return any unspent funds to the Treasury.[12]

16-4d Private Versus Public Production

Simply because some goods and services are *financed* by the government does not mean that they must be *produced* by the government. Elected officials may contract directly with private firms to produce public output. For example, city officials may contract with a private firm to collect garbage or offer bus service for the city. In some jurisdictions, for-profit firms now provide everything from fire protection to prisons. Elected officials may also use a combination of bureaus and firms to produce the desired output. For example, the Pentagon, a giant bureau, hires and trains military personnel, yet contracts with private firms to develop and produce various weapon systems. State governments typically hire private contractors to build

highways but employ state workers to maintain them. Likewise, school districts hire private contractors to build schools but staff them with government employees. The mix of firms and bureaus varies over time and across jurisdictions, but the trend is toward increased *privatization,* or production by the private sector, of public goods and services.

When governments produce public goods and services, they are using *the internal organization of government*—the bureaucracy—to supply the product. When governments contract with private firms to produce public goods and services, they are using *the market* to supply the product. While private firms have more incentives to be efficient than bureaus do, public officials sometimes prefer dealing with bureaus. Public officials may have more control over a bureau than over a private firm. Bureaus may also offer public officials more opportunities to appoint friends and political supporters to government jobs.

In situations where it would be difficult to specify a contract for the public good in question, a bureau may be more responsive to public concerns than a for-profit firm would be. Suppose the service provided by social workers is put out for bid. The firm that wins the bid may be tempted to skimp on quality, particularly if quality can be determined only by direct observation at the time the service is provided. Government officials would have difficulty monitoring the quality provided by a private contractor. The services of social workers might be better provided by a government bureau. Because profit is not its goal, a bureau may be less inclined to minimize cost by reducing quality. For example, one study found that privately operated juvenile correction facilities in Florida had lower costs but experienced higher rates of recidivism than state-operated juvenile correction facilities. The lower costs of privately operated facilities were more than offset by the increased recidivism, making state operation the better choice.[13]

16-5 FINAL WORD

Governments attempt to address market failures in the private economy. But simply turning problems of perceived market failure over to government may not always be the best solution, because government has limitations

---

11. William A. Niskanen Jr., *Bureaucracy and Representative Government* (Aldine-Atherton, 1971).

12. Jeffrey Liebman and Neale Mahoney, "Do Expiring Budgets Lead to Wasteful Year-End Spending? Evidence from Federal Procurement," *American Economic Review* (forthcoming).

13. Patrick Bayer and David Pozen, "The Effectiveness of Juvenile Correction Facilities: Public Versus Private Management," *Journal of Law and Economics,* 48 (October 2005): 549–589.

and failings of its own. Participation in markets is based on voluntary exchange. Governments, however, have the legal power to enforce public choices. We should employ at least as high a standard in judging the performance of government, where allocations have the force of law, as we do in judging the private market, where allocations are decided by voluntary exchange between consenting parties. In other words, we should scrutinize a system that is compulsory at least as much as we scrutinize a system that is voluntary. After all, nobody is forcing you to buy tofu, but if you refuse to pay taxes to fund public programs you hate, you could go to prison.

STUDY TOOLS 16

READY TO STUDY? IN THE BOOK, YOU CAN:

☐ Work the Problems at the end of the chapter.

☐ Rip out the chapter review card for a handy summary of the chapter and key terms.

ONLINE AT CENGAGEBRAIN.COM YOU CAN:

☐ Collect StudyBits while you read and study the chapter.

☐ Quiz yourself on key concepts.

☐ Prepare for tests with chapter flash cards as well as flash cards that you create.

☐ Watch videos to explore economics further.

CHAPTER 16 PROBLEMS

Your instructor can access the answers to these problems online at http://cengagebrain.com.

16-1 Differentiate four categories of goods in terms of their exclusivity and rivalry

1. *(Optimal Provision of Public Goods)* Using at least two individual consumers, show how the market demand curve is derived from individual demand curves (a) for a private good and (b) for a public good. Once you have derived the market demand curve in each case, introduce a market supply curve and then show the optimal level of production.

2. *(Private and Public Goods)* Distinguish among private goods, natural monopolies, open-access goods, and public goods. Provide examples of each.

16-2 Identify four categories of legislation based on the distribution of costs and the distribution of benefits, and provide examples of each

3. *(Types of Legislation)* Describe the four different categories of legislation based on the distribution of costs and benefits and provide examples of each.

4. *(Distribution of Costs and Benefits)* Suppose that the government decides to guarantee an above-market price for a good by buying up any surplus at that above-market price. Using a conventional supply-demand diagram, illustrate the following gains and losses from such a price support:
   a. The loss of consumer surplus
   b. The gain of producer surplus in the short run
   c. The cost of running the government program (assuming no storage costs)
   d. What is the total cost of the program to consumers?
   e. Are the costs and benefits of the support program widespread or concentrated?

5. *(Median Voter Model)* In a single-issue majority vote, such as the TV example in this chapter, does the median voter always get his or her most preferred outcome?

6. *(Representative Democracy)* Major political parties typically offer "middle of the road" platforms rather than take extreme positions. How is this consistent with the concepts of the median voter and rational ignorance discussed in this chapter?

16-3 Explain why some people want to use government power to increase their income, while others try to avoid government

7. *(Seeking vs. Avoiding Government)* Why are some people drawn to government while other people don't want to have anything to do with government?

8. *(Rent Seeking)* Explain how rent seeking can lead to a drop in production of goods and services. What role might the underground economy play in lessening the drop in productive activities?

16-4 Outline the differences between government bureaus and for-profit firms

9. *(Bureaucracy and Representative Democracy)* How do the incentives and feedback for government bureaus differ from those for profit-making firms?

10. *(Bureaucracy and Representative Democracy)* A firm is described as combining managerial coordination with market exchange in order to produce its good or service. Does similar behavior occur in government bureaus? Explain.

17 | Externalities and the Environment

LEARNING OUTCOMES

After studying this chapter, you will be able to...

 17-1 Describe the common pool problem and summarize ways to address it

 17-2 Determine the optimal level of pollution with fixed technology and with variable technology

 17-3 Summarize how the federal government has regulated air, water, and land pollution

17-4 Outline government policies designed to promote the production and consumption of goods that generate positive externalities

After finishing this chapter go to PAGE 301 for STUDY TOOLS

Topics discussed in Chapter 17 include:

- Exhaustible resources
- Renewable resources
- The common-pool problem
- Private property rights
- Optimal pollution
- Marginal social cost
- Marginal social benefit
- Coase theorem
- Markets for pollution rights
- Environmental protection

© iStockphoto.com/kshatry

The rivers in Jakarta, Indonesia, are dead—killed by acid, alcohol, and oil. Coral reefs in the South Pacific are being ripped apart by dynamite fishing. The air in New Delhi, India, is more toxic than any other city's on earth, with 15 times the pollution level considered safe by the World Health Organization. The tropical rainforest is shrinking because of slash-and-burn claims on the land's resources. The build-up of greenhouse gases threatens to warm the oceans and near-surface air. Some streams in Colorado are still considered toxic from gold mining that ended more than a century ago. These environmental problems are all negative externalities, which result from the actions of producers or consumers that affect many others. Markets can allocate resources efficiently only as long as property rights are well defined and can be easily enforced. But property rights to clean water, air, and soil, to fish in the ocean, to peace and quiet, and to scenic vistas are hard to establish and enforce. This lack of property rights to some resources results in externalities.

Externalities may be either negative, such as air and water pollution, or positive, such as the general improvement in the civic climate that results from better education. This chapter explores how public policies can reduce negative externalities and increase positive externalities.

> **"Why do people fish until the fish are all gone?"**

17-1 EXTERNALITIES AND THE COMMON-POOL PROBLEM

Let's begin by distinguishing between exhaustible resources and renewable resources. An **exhaustible resource** such as oil or coal does not renew itself and so is available in a finite amount. Technology may improve the ability to extract and utilize these resources, but each gallon of oil burned is gone forever. Sooner or later, all accessible oil and coal deposits will be gone. The world's oil and coal reserves are *exhaustible*.

17-1a Renewable Resources

A resource is renewable if, when used conservatively, it can be drawn on indefinitely. Thus, timber is a **renewable resource** if trees are cut at sustainable rates and replaced with seedlings. The atmosphere and rivers are renewable resources to the extent that they can absorb and neutralize a certain level of pollutants. More generally, biological resources like fish, game, forests, rivers, grasslands, and agricultural soil are renewable if managed appropriately.

Some renewable resources are also open-access resources, an idea introduced in the previous chapter. An open-access resource is rival in consumption, but exclusion is costly. Fish caught in the ocean, for example, are not available for others to catch, so fish are rival in consumption. Yet it would be difficult, if not impossible, for a person or a firm to "own" fish

exhaustible resource A resource in fixed supply, such as crude oil or coal

renewable resource A resource that regenerates itself and so can be used indefinitely if used conservatively, such as a well-managed forest

When harvested responsibly, timber is an indefinitely renewable resource.

still swimming in open waters and to prevent others from catching them, so ocean fish are nonexclusive. An open-access good is often subject to the **common-pool problem**, which results because people harvest a resource as long as the marginal benefit exceeds marginal cost. For example, people will fish the oceans as long as the marginal benefit of catching more fish exceeds the marginal cost. Individual fishing parties have little regard for the effects of their catch on the sustainability of fishing stocks. Practically speaking, unless otherwise checked, people will fish until the oceans become "fished out." Open-access goods are overfished, overhunted, overharvested, and overused. Because the atmosphere is an open-access resource, it's used as a dump for unwanted gases. Air pollution is a negative externality imposed on society by polluters. The problem is that people exploit any resource as long as their personal marginal benefit exceeds their personal marginal cost. As we'll see, personal marginal cost ignores the costs imposed on others.

In a market system, specific individuals usually own the rights to resources and therefore have a strong interest in using those resources efficiently. *Private property rights*, a term introduced in Chapter 2, allow individuals to use resources or to charge others for their use. Private property rights are defined and enforced by government, by informal social actions, and by ethical norms. As Robert Frost wrote, "Good fences make good neighbors."[1] Assets such as fishing rights are more valuable when they are more enforceable.[2] But because defining and enforcing property rights to open-access resources, such as the

air, are quite costly if not impossible, these resources usually are not owned as private property.

Pollution and other negative externalities arise because there are no practical, enforceable, private property rights to open-access resources, such as the air. Market prices usually fail to include the costs that negative externalities impose on society. For example, the price you pay for a gallon of gasoline does not reflect the costs imposed by the greenhouse gases, sootier air, oil spills, and greater congestion and accidents your driving creates. Electric rates do not reflect the negative externalities, or external costs, caused by fossil-fueled power plants. Note that externalities are unintended side effects of actions that are themselves useful and purposeful. Electricity producers, for example, did not go into business to pollute.

17-1b Resolving the Common-Pool Problem

Users of the atmosphere, waterways, wildlife, or other open-access resources tend to ignore the impact of their use on the resource's renewal ability. As quality and quantity diminish from overuse, the resource grows scarcer and could disappear. For example, Georges Bank, located off the New England coast, and long one of the world's most productive fishing grounds, became so depleted by overfishing that by the 1990s the catch was down 85 percent from peak years. Tuna, once abundant in the Mediterranean, now faces extinction there. The United Nations reports that at least 11 of the world's 15 primary fishing grounds are seriously depleted.

By imposing restrictions on resource use, government regulations may reduce the common-pool problem. Output restrictions or taxes could force people to use the resource at a rate that is socially optimal, a rate that supports a sustainable yield. For example, in the face of the tendency to overfish and to catch fish before they are sufficiently mature, the U.S. government has imposed a number of restrictions on the fishing industry. The laws limit the total catch, the size of fish, the length of the fishing season, the equipment used, and other aspects of the business.

More generally, when imposing and enforcing private property rights would be too costly, government regulations may improve allocative efficiency. For example, stop signs and traffic lights allocate the scarce space at intersections, minimum size restrictions control lobster fishing, hunting seasons control the stock of game, and enforced study hours may calm the din in the college dormitory.

But not all regulations are equally efficient. For example, fishing authorities sometimes limit the

1. From the poem "Mending Wall" in Robert Frost, *You Come Too* (Holt, Rinehart and Winston, 1967), p. 64.

2. Corbett Grainger and Christopher Costello, "Capitalizing Property Rights Insecurity in Natural Resource Assets," *Journal of Environmental Economics and Management*, 47 (March 2014): 224–240.

common-pool problem
Unrestricted access to a renewable resource results in overuse

total industry catch and allow all firms to fish until that limit is reached. Consequently, when the fishing season opens, there is a mad scramble to catch as much as possible before the industry limit is reached. Because time is of the essence, fishing boats make no effort to fish selectively. And the catch reaches processing plants all at once, creating congestion throughout the supply chain. Also, each firm has an incentive to expand its fishing fleet to catch more in those precious few weeks. Thus, large fleets of technologically efficient fishing vessels operate for a few weeks until the limit is reached and then sit in port for the rest of the year. Each operator is acting rationally, but the collective effect of the regulation is grossly inefficient in terms of social welfare. Consider the complicated and sometimes confounding fishing regulations in Iceland:

> *The Icelandic government realized that it would have to curb the capacity of its own fleet. But the fishermen compensated by buying more trawlers. Then the government restricted the size of the fleet and the number of days at sea; the fishermen responded by buying larger, more efficient gear. The cod stocks continued to decline. In 1984, the government introduced quotas on species per vessel per season. This was a controversial and often wasteful system. A groundfish hauled up from 50 fathoms [300 feet] is killed by the change in pressure. But if it is a cod and the cod quota has been used up, it is thrown overboard. Or if the price of cod is low that week and cod happens to come in the haddock net, the fishermen will throw them overboard because they do not want to use up their cod quota when they are not getting a good price.*[3]

Ocean fish remain a common-pool resource because firms have not yet been able to establish and enforce rights to particular schools of fish. But advances in technology may one day allow the creation of private property rights to ocean fish, migrating birds, and other open-access resources. Establishing property rights to cattle on the Great Plains once seemed impossible, but the invention

> **"The price you pay for a gallon of gasoline does not reflect the costs imposed by the greenhouse gases, sootier air, oil spills, and greater congestion and accidents your driving creates."**

of barbed wire allowed ranchers to fence the range. Patented in 1867, barbed wire was advertised as "The finest fence in the world. Light as air. Stronger than whiskey. Cheaper than dirt." In a sense, barbed wire, by reducing the cost of fencing the open range, tamed the Wild West.[4]

17-2 OPTIMAL LEVEL OF POLLUTION

Though the science is not yet fully resolved, fossil fuel used to power the likes of automobiles and electricity generators produces carbon dioxide, which mixes with other greenhouse gases that could contribute to climate change. Electricity production from fossil fuels, therefore, involves the external cost of using the atmosphere as a gas dump. This section considers a way to analyze such externalities.

17-2a External Costs with Fixed Technology

Suppose D in Exhibit 1 depicts the demand for electricity. Recall that a demand curve reflects consumers' marginal benefit of each unit. The lower horizontal line reflects the marginal private cost of generating electricity using fossil fuels. If producers base their pricing and output decisions on their marginal private costs, the equilibrium quantity per month is 50 million kilowatt-hours and the equilibrium price is $0.10 per kilowatt-hour. At that price and quantity, identified by point a, the marginal private cost of production just equals the marginal benefit enjoyed by consumers of electricity.

Electricity production involves not only the private cost of the resources employed but also the external cost of using the atmosphere as a dump for greenhouse gases. Suppose that the marginal external cost imposed on the environment by the generation of electricity is $0.04 per kilowatt-hour. If the only way to cut emissions is to reduce electricity production, then the relationship between electricity production and pollution is fixed;

3. Mark Kurlansky, *Cod: A Biography of the Fish That Changed the World* (Walker, 1997), p. 172.

4. Richard Hornbeck, "Barbed Wire: Property Rights and Agricultural Development," *Quarterly Journal of Economics,* 125 (May 2010): 767–810.

Electricity production almost always results in an external cost of some sort.

marginal benefit of electricity, identified on the demand curve at point *a*. The 50-millionth kilowatt-hour of electricity costs society $0.14 but yields only $0.10 of marginal benefit. Because the marginal social cost exceeds the marginal benefit, too much electricity is produced.

The efficient quantity of 35 million kilowatt-hours is found where the demand, or marginal benefit, curve intersects the marginal social cost curve. This intersection is identified at point *c*. How could output be restricted to the socially efficient amount? If regulators knew the demand and marginal cost curves, they could simply limit production to 35 million kilowatt-hours, the efficient quantity. Or, on each kilowatt-hour produced, they could impose a tax equal to the marginal external cost of $0.04. Such a pollution tax would lift the marginal private cost curve up to the marginal social cost curve. Thus, the tax would bring private costs in line with social costs.

With a tax of $0.04 per kilowatt-hour, the equilibrium combination of price and output moves from point *a* to point *c*. The price rises from $0.10 to $0.14 per kilowatt-hour, and output falls to 35 million kilowatt-hours. Setting the tax equal to the marginal external cost results in the efficient level of output. At point *c*, the marginal social cost of production equals the marginal

the pollution in this case occurs with **fixed-production technology**.

The vertical distance between the marginal private cost curve and the marginal social cost curve in Exhibit 1 shows the marginal external cost of $0.04 per kilowatt-hour. The **marginal social cost** includes both the marginal private cost and the marginal external cost that production imposes on society. Because the marginal external cost here is assumed to be a constant $0.04 per kilowatt-hour, the two cost curves are parallel. Notice that at the private-sector equilibrium output level of 50 million kilowatt-hours, the marginal social cost, identified at point *b*, exceeds society's

fixed-production technology Occurs when the relationship between the output rate and the generation of an externality is fixed; the only way to reduce the externality is to reduce the output

marginal social cost The sum of the marginal private cost and the marginal external cost of production or consumption

Exhibit 1

Negative Externalities: The Market for Electricity in the Midwest

If producers base their output on marginal private cost, 50 million kilowatt-hours of electricity are produced per month. The marginal external cost of electricity is the cost of pollution imposed on society. The marginal social cost curve includes both the marginal private cost and the marginal external cost. If producers base their output decisions on marginal social cost, only 35 million kilowatt-hours are produced, which is the optimal output. The total social gain from basing production on marginal social cost is reflected by the blue-shaded triangle.

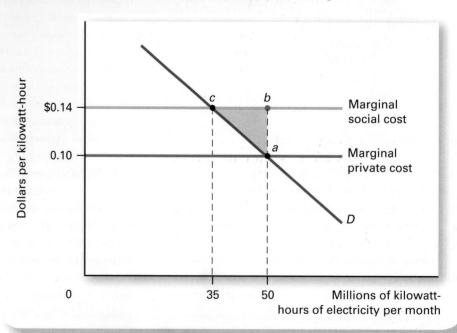

benefit. Notice that greenhouse gas emissions are not eliminated at point *c*, but the utilities no longer generate electricity for which marginal social cost exceeds marginal benefit. The social gain from reducing production to the socially optimal level is shown by the blue-shaded triangle in Exhibit 1. This triangle also measures the social cost of allowing firms to ignore the external cost of their production. Although Exhibit 1 offers a tidy solution, the external costs of greenhouse gases often cannot be easily calculated or taxed. At times, government intervention may result in more or less production than the optimal solution requires.

17-2b External Costs with Variable Technology

The previous example assumes that the only way to reduce greenhouse gases is to reduce output. But power companies, particularly in the long run, can usually change their resource mix to reduce emissions for any given rate of electricity output. If pollution can be reduced by altering the production process rather than by simply adjusting the quantity, these externalities are said to be produced under conditions of **variable technology**. For example, between 1990 and 2008 the real value of U.S. manufacturing output grew by more than one-third. But, thanks to better emission technology, pollution from U.S. factories fell by two-thirds.[5] *With variable technology, the idea is to find the most efficient level of pollution for a given rate of output.*

Let's look at Exhibit 2. The horizontal axis measures greenhouse gas emissions for a given rate of electricity production. Emissions can be reduced by adopting cleaner production technology. Yet the production of cleaner air, like the production of other goods, is subject to diminishing returns. Cutting emissions of the most offensive greenhouse gases may involve simply changing the fuel mix, but further reductions could require more sophisticated and

Exhibit 2

The Optimal Reduction in Greenhouse Gas Emissions

The optimal level of greenhouse gas emissions for a given rate of output is found at point *a*, where the marginal social benefit of reducing such emissions equals the marginal social cost. If some lower level of emissions were dictated by the government, such as A′, the marginal social cost would exceed the marginal social benefit, and social waste would result. The total social waste resulting from a lower than optimal level of emissions is shown by the pink-shaded triangle.

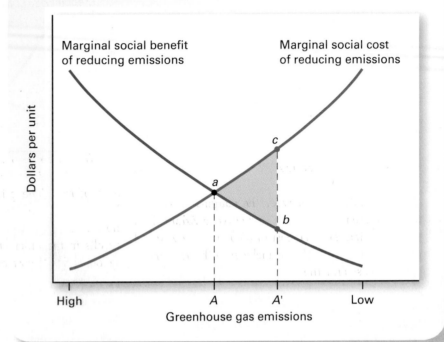

more expensive processes. Thus, the marginal social cost of reducing greenhouse gases increases, as shown by the upward-sloping marginal social cost curve in Exhibit 2.

The **marginal social benefit** curve reflects the additional benefit society derives from greenhouse gas reductions. When emissions are high, any improvement can save lives and thus is valued by society more than when emissions are low. Cleaner air, like other goods, has a declining marginal benefit to society (though the total benefit still increases). The marginal social benefit curve from cleaner air therefore slopes downward, as shown in Exhibit 2.

The optimal level of air quality for a given rate of electricity production is found at point *a*, where the marginal social benefit of cleaner air equals the marginal social cost. In this example, the optimal level of greenhouse gas emissions is A. If firms made their production decisions based

variable technology Occurs when the amount of externality generated at a given rate of output can be reduced by altering the production process

marginal social benefit The sum of the marginal private benefit and the marginal external benefit of production or consumption

5. Arik Levinson, "A Direct Estimate of the Technique Effect: Changes in Pollution Intensity of U.S. Manufacturing 1990–2008," *Journal of the Association of Environmental and Resource Economists*, 2 (June 2015): 43–56.

Exhibit 3

Effect of Changes in Costs or Benefits of Reducing Greenhouse Gas Emissions

Either a reduction in the marginal social cost of cleaner air, as shown in panel (a), or an increase in the marginal social benefit of cleaner air, as shown in panel (b), increases the optimal level of air quality.

(a) Lower cost of reducing emissions

(b) Greater benefit of reducing emissions

simply on their private cost—that is, if the emission cost is external to the firm—then firms would have little incentive to search for production methods that reduce greenhouse gas emission, so too much pollution would result.

> **"The optimal level of air quality for a given rate of electricity production is found where the marginal social benefit of cleaner air equals the marginal social cost."**

What if government regulators decree that greenhouse gas emission levels should be no greater than A'? For example, suppose a law establishes A' as the maximum acceptable level of emissions. The marginal social cost, identified as *c*, of achieving that level of air quality exceeds the marginal social benefit, identified as *b*. The total social waste associated with imposing a greater-than-optimal level of air quality is shown by the pink-shaded triangle, *abc*. This area is the total amount by which the additional social costs of cleaner air (associated with a move from A

to A') exceed the additional social benefits. Improving air quality benefits society only as long as the marginal social benefit of cleaner air exceeds its marginal social cost.

What would happen to the optimal level of emissions if either the marginal cost curve or the marginal benefit curve shifted? For example, suppose some technological breakthrough reduces the marginal cost of cutting greenhouse gas emissions. As shown in panel (a) of Exhibit 3, the marginal social cost curve of reducing emissions would shift downward to *MSC'*, leading to cleaner air as reflected by the movement from A to A'. *The simple logic is that the lower the marginal cost of reducing greenhouse gases, other things constant, the cleaner the optimal level of air quality.*

An increase in the marginal benefit of air quality has a similar effect. For example, recent research indicates that a reduction of *outside* air pollution increased the productivity of workers *inside* a factory.[6] Thus, the marginal benefit of cleaner air increases, as reflected in panel (b) of Exhibit 3 by an upward shift of the marginal social benefit curve to *MSB'*. As a result, air quality would improve, moving from A to A″ in panel (b) of Exhibit 3. *The greater the marginal benefit of reducing greenhouse gases, other things constant, the cleaner the optimal level of air quality.* As another example, recent research indicates that deaths from heart and lung disease would decrease 0.7 percent in large U.S. cities if particulates suspended in the air decrease by just 1/100,000th of a

6. Tom Chang et al., "Particulate Pollution and the Productivity of Pear Packers," NBER Working Paper No. 19944 (February 2014).

gram per cubic meter of air.[7] This finding increases the perceived benefits of cleaner air, which should increase the optimal quality of air.

17-2c The Coase Theorem

The traditional analysis of externalities assumes that market failures arise because people ignore the external effects of their actions. For example, suppose a manufacturer of heavy machinery is next door to a research laboratory that tests delicate measuring equipment. The vibrations caused by the manufacturing process throw off the delicate equipment next door. Professor Ronald Coase, who won the Nobel Prize in 1991, would argue that the negative externality in this case is not necessarily imposed by the heavy machinery—rather, it arises from the incompatible activities of the two firms. The externality is the result of both vibrations created by the factory *and* the location of the testing lab next door. Solutions might include modifying the factory, moving the factory, making the test equipment more shock resistant, or moving the testing lab.

According to Coase, the efficient solution depends on which party can avoid the externality at the lower cost. Suppose it would cost $2 million for the factory to reduce vibrations enough for the lab to function normally. On the other hand, if the factory makes no changes, the lab can't insulate its testing equipment enough to operate accurately, so the lab would have to relocate at a cost of $1 million. Based on this information, the least-cost solution would be for the testing lab to relocate at a cost of $1 million. Coase argues that, as long as transaction costs are low, the parties will reach the efficient solution if one party is assigned the property right. And here's Coase's special insight: *This efficient solution will be achieved regardless of which party gets the property right.*

Suppose the testing lab is granted the right to operate free of vibrations from next door, so the testing lab can force the factory to reduce its vibration. Rather than cut vibrations at a cost of $2 million, the factory can pay the lab to relocate. Any payment greater than $1 million but less than $2 million makes both sides better off, because the lab would receive more than its moving cost and the factory would pay less than its cost of reducing vibrations. Thus, the lab will move, which is the efficient outcome.

Alternatively, suppose the factory is granted the right to generate vibrations in its production process, regardless of the impact on the testing lab. For the factory, this means business as usual. Because the minimum payment the factory would accept to reduce vibrations is $2 million,

the lab would rather relocate at a cost of $1 million. Thus, whether property rights are granted to the lab or to the factory, the lab will move, which is the efficient, or least-cost, solution. The **Coase theorem** says that as long as bargaining costs are small, merely assigning the property right will generate an efficient solution to an externality problem regardless of which party is assigned that right. A particular assignment determines which side bears the externality costs but does not affect the efficient outcome.

Inefficient outcomes do occur, however, when the transaction costs of arriving at a solution are high. For example, an airport located in a populated area would have difficulty negotiating noise levels with all the affected residents. Or peasants contemplating clearing a portion of the tropical rainforest would be unable to negotiate with the millions, and perhaps, billions, of people ultimately affected by that decision. *When the number of parties involved in the transaction is large, Coase's solution of assigning property rights may not be enough.*

> **"If pollution can be easily monitored and polluters easily identified, the government may be able to find an efficient solution to the problem of pollution simply by assigning the right to pollute."**

17-2d Markets for Pollution Rights

According to the Coase theorem, the assignment of property rights is often sufficient to resolve the market failure typically associated with externalities. Additional government intervention is not necessary. If pollution can be easily monitored and polluters easily identified, the government may be able to find an efficient solution to the problem of pollution simply by assigning the right to pollute.

Coase theorem As long as bargaining costs are low, an efficient solution to the problem of externalities is achieved by assigning property rights to one party or the other, it doesn't matter which

7. Jonathan M. Samet et al., "Fine Particulate Air Pollution and Mortality in 20 U.S. Cities, 1987–1994," *New England Journal of Medicine*, 343 (14 December 2000): 1742–1749.

Exhibit 4

Optimal Allocation of Pollution Rights

Suppose the demand for a river as a discharge service is *D*. In the absence of any environmental controls, polluters dump 250 tons per day, where the marginal benefit of discharge drops to zero. If regulatory authorities establish 100 tons as the maximum daily level of discharge and then sell the rights, the market for these pollution rights clears at $25 per ton. If the demand for pollution rights increases to *D'*, the market-clearing price of pollution rights rises to $35 per ton.

remain clean enough for swimming and fishing? Suppose environmental engineers determine this level of water quality can be maintained as long as no more than 100 tons are discharged per day. Thus, the "supply" of the discharge service provided by the river is fixed at 100 tons per day, shown by the vertical supply curve, *S*, in Exhibit 4.

If government regulators can easily identify polluters and monitor their behavior, authorities can allocate permits to discharge a total of 100 tons per day. If polluters are simply given these permits (that is, if the price of permits is zero), there will be an excess demand for them, because the quantity supplied is 100 tons but the quantity demanded at a price of zero would be 250 tons. An alternative is to sell permits for 100 tons of pollution at the market-clearing price. The intersection of supply curve *S* and demand curve *D* yields a permit price of $25 per ton, which is the marginal value of discharging the 100th ton into the river each day. To most permit buyers, the marginal value of a permit exceeds $25 per ton.

To see how this could work, let's look at an example. Firms that dump into a river evidently value the ability to discharge waste in this way. For them, the river provides a zero cost outlet for by-products that otherwise would have to be disposed of at greater cost. The river provides a disposal service, and the demand curve for that service slopes downward, just like the demand for other resources.

The demand for the river as a discharge system is presented as *D* in Exhibit 4. The horizontal axis measures the tons of discharge dumped into the river per day, and the vertical axis measures firms' marginal benefit of disposing of each ton of waste in this way. The demand curve thus measures the marginal value to firms of using the river as a disposal service. With no restrictions on river pollution—that is, if all firms were free to dump waste into the river—dumping would continue as long as it provided firms some marginal benefit. This marginal benefit falls to zero in Exhibit 4 where 250 tons per day are discharged. At that point the marginal private cost of dumping, which is zero, equals the marginal private benefit.

The river, like the atmosphere, the soil, and the sea, can absorb and neutralize a certain amount of discharge per day without deteriorating in quality. What if voters make the public choice that the river should

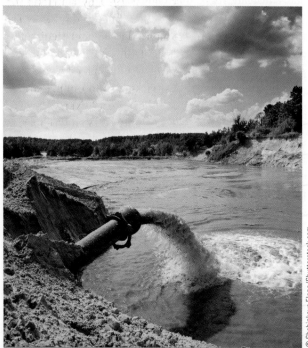

If a firm is not required to pay the social cost of dumping waste into a river, dumping will continue as long as there is a positive benefit to the firm.

The beauty of this system is that producers who value the discharge rights the most ultimately end up with them. Producers who attach a marginal value below $25 per ton apparently have cheaper ways of resolving their waste problems, including changing production techniques. And if conservation groups, such as the Sierra Club, want a cleaner river than the government's standard, such as water clean enough to drink, they can purchase pollution permits but not exercise them.

What if additional firms spring up along the river that are willing to pay more than $25 per ton for pollution rights? This greater demand is reflected in Exhibit 4 by D'. This increase of demand would bid up the market price of pollution permits to, say, $35 per ton. Some existing permit holders would sell their rights to those who value them more. Regardless of the comings and goings of would-be polluters, the total quantity of discharge rights is restricted to 100 tons per day, so the river's quality will be maintained. Thus, *the value of pollution permits, but not the total amount of pollution, may fluctuate over time.*

If the right to pollute could be granted, monitored, and enforced, then what had been a negative externality problem could be solved through market allocation. Historically, the U.S. government had relied on setting discharge standards and fining offenders. But in 1989, a pollution rights market for fluorocarbon emissions was established and was followed in 1990 by a market for sulfur dioxide. During the 1990s, sulfur dioxide emissions in the nation fell by more than half, exceeding the goals of the authorizing legislation. The "cap-and-trade" proposal by President Obama in 2009 aimed to create a market for greenhouse gas emissions. So the market for pollution rights is not simply theoretical.[8] Even China has been experimenting with this approach. Some companies and even celebrities have used a variant of pollution rights to become "carbon neutral"—that is, by estimating their carbon emissions then offsetting this impact by paying for projects such as planting trees to neutralize, or "sop up," equivalent emissions.

17-2e Pollution Rights and Public Choice

Unfortunately, legislation dealing with pollution is affected by the same problems of representative democracy that trouble other public policy questions. Big polluters have a special interest in government proposals relating to pollution, and they fight measures to reduce pollution. But members of the public remain rationally ignorant about

8. For a discussion of the market for sulfur dioxide emissions, see Richard Schmalensee and Robert Stavins, "The SO$_2$ Allowance Trading System: The Ironic History of a Grand Policy Experiment," *Journal of Economic Perspectives*, 27 (Winter 2013): 103–122.

pollution legislation. So pollution regulations may be less in accord with the public interest than with the special interests of polluters. To win their cooperation, a portion of pollution permits are often *given* to existing firms or offered at below-market prices. For example, under the sulfur dioxide program, the nation's 101 dirtiest power plants were granted credits equal to between 30 and 50 percent of the pollution they emitted before the program began. Because they received something of value, polluters were less inclined to oppose the legislation. Once permits were granted, some recipients found it profitable to sell their permits to other firms that valued them more. Thus, a market emerged that led to an efficient allocation of pollution permits. According to some analysts, the sulfur dioxide program saves up to $3 billion annually compared with the old system. More generally, a system of marketable pollution rights can reduce the cost of pollution abatement by as much as 75 percent.

> **"Pollution regulations may be less in accord with the public interest than with the special interests of polluters."**

Before 1990, **command-and-control environmental regulations** were the norm—an approach that required polluters, such as electric utilities, to introduce particular technologies to reduce emissions by specific amounts. These regulations were based on engineering standards and did not recognize unique circumstances across generating plants, such as plant design, ability to introduce scrubbers, and the ease of switching to low-sulfur fuels. But the market for pollution rights reflects an **economic efficiency approach** that offers each electric utility the flexibility to reduce emissions in the most cost-effective manner, given its unique operation. Firms with

command-and-control environmental regulations An inflexible approach that required polluters to adopt particular technologies to reduce emissions by specific amounts

economic efficiency approach An approach that offers each polluter the flexibility to reduce emissions as cost-effectively as possible, given its unique cost conditions; the market for pollution rights is an example the lowest costs of emission control have an incentive to implement the largest reduction in emissions and then sell unused pollution permits to those with greater costs of emission control. In the last two decades, for example, many U.S. electricity markets were deregulated, and this has increased production efficiency by about 10 percent. It has saved $2.5 billion a year and has cut carbon dioxide emissions by 40 million tons a year.[9]

Now that you know something about the theory of externalities, let's turn to an important application of the theory—environmental protection.

17-3 ENVIRONMENTAL PROTECTION

Federal efforts to address the common-pool problems of air, water, and ground pollution are coordinated by the Environmental Protection Agency (EPA). Four federal laws and subsequent amendments underpin U.S. efforts to protect the environment: (1) the Clean Air Act of 1970, (2) the Clean Water Act of 1972, (3) the Resource Conservation and Recovery Act of 1976 (which governs solid waste disposal), and (4) the Superfund law of 1980 (legislation focusing on toxic waste dumps). When the EPA was created in 1970, it began with about 4,000 employees and a budget of $1.3 billion (in 2015 dollars). By 2015, it had about 15,500 employees and a $7.9 billion budget.

According to EPA estimates, compliance with pollution-control regulations cost U.S. producers and consumers more than $300 billion in 2015, an amount equivalent to 2 percent of gross domestic product, the market value of all final goods and services produced in the U.S. economy. We can divide pollution control spending into three categories: for air pollution abatement, for water pollution abatement, and for solid waste disposal. About 40 percent of the pollution control expenditures in the United States goes toward cleaner air, another 40 percent goes toward cleaner water, and 20 percent goes toward disposing of solid waste. In this section, we consider, in turn, air pollution, water pollution, Superfund activities, and disposing of solid waste.

17-3a Air Pollution

Among the many harmful effects of air pollution is the impairment of fetal development as reflected later in life by lower math and language skills.[10] In the Clean Air Act of 1970 and in subsequent amendments, Congress set

While this is normally what we think of when we think of air pollution, in actuality only about 15% of air pollution results from manufacturing. Most comes from automobiles and consumer products.

national standards for the amount of pollution that could be released into the atmosphere. Congress thereby recognized the atmosphere as an economic resource, which, like other resources, has alternative uses. The air can be used as a source of life-giving oxygen, as a prism for viewing breathtaking vistas, or as a dump for carrying away unwanted soot and gases. The 1970 act gave Americans the right to breathe air of a certain quality and at the same time gave producers the right to emit certain amounts of specified pollutants. But there is no free lunch: the Clean Air Act imposes an estimated annual cost of about $25 billion. What's more, many firms respond to regulatory pressure by cutting their workforce, so some people lose jobs.[11] Still, research shows that people value clean air, and we are still discovering additional benefits. For example, there is now evidence that reductions in auto emissions reduce child mortality.[12] Throughout the world, people are willing to pay more to live where there is less pollution.[13] For example, surveys show that many people in China who become rich soon migrate to countries with cleaner air and bluer skies.[14]

Smog is the most visible form of air pollution. Automobile emissions account for 40 percent of smog. Another 40 percent comes from consumer-oriented products, such as paint thinner, fluorocarbon sprays, dry-cleaning

9. Lucas Davis and Catherine Wolfram, "Deregulation, Consolidation, and Efficiency: Evidence From U.S. Nuclear Power," *American Economic Journal: Applied Economics,* 4 (October 2012): 194–225.

10. Prashant Bharadwaj et al. "Gray Matters: Fetal Pollution Exposure and Human Capital Formation," NBER Working Paper No. 20662 (November 2014).

11. W. Reed Walker, "Environmental Regulation and Labor Reallocation: Evidence From the Clean Air Act," *American Economic Review,* 101 (May 2011), p. 442.

12. Christopher Knittel, Douglas Miller, and Nicholas Sanders, "Caution, Drivers! Children Present: Traffic, Pollution, and Infant Health," *Review of Economics and Statistics,* (forthcoming).

13. Kenneth Chay and Michael Greenstone, "Does Air Quality Matter? Evidence From the Housing Market," *Journal of Political Economy,* 113 (April 2005): 376–424.

14. Andrew Browne, "The Great China Exodus," *Wall Street Journal,* 26 September 2014.

solvents, and baker's yeast by-products. Surprisingly, only 15 percent of smog comes from manufacturing. The 1970 Clean Air Act mandated a reduction of 90 percent in auto emissions, leaving it to the auto industry to achieve this target. At the time, automakers said the target was impossible. Between 1970 and 1990, however, average emissions of lead fell 97 percent, carbon monoxide emissions fell 41 percent, and sulfur dioxide emissions fell 25 percent. In fact, an EPA study concluded that because auto emissions and industrial smoke have been reduced so much, *air pollution on average is now lower outdoors than indoors*. U.S. air quality is now considered good compared to the air quality in much of the world. For example, no U.S. city ranks among the world's worst in sulfur dioxide. Despite recent improvements in air quality, the United States is still a major source of fossil-fuel carbon dioxide emissions, a greenhouse gas. As you can see from Exhibit 5, which shows the world's 25 worst

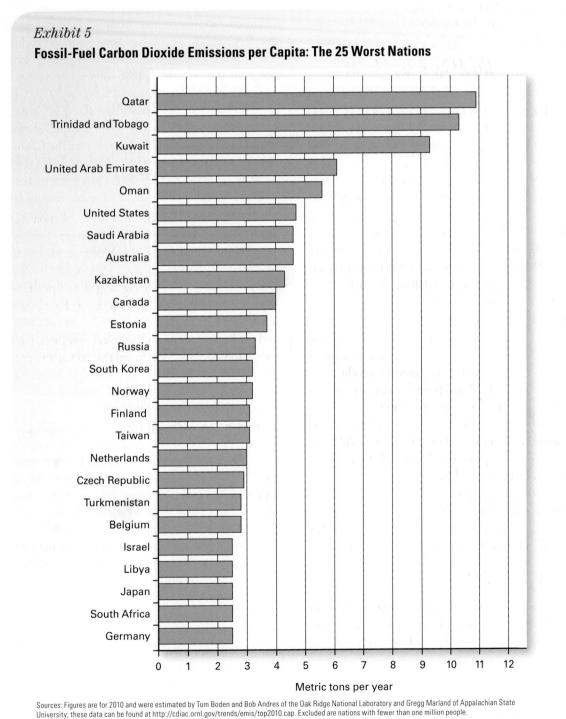

Exhibit 5

Fossil-Fuel Carbon Dioxide Emissions per Capita: The 25 Worst Nations

Metric tons per year

Sources: Figures are for 2010 and were estimated by Tom Boden and Bob Andres of the Oak Ridge National Laboratory and Gregg Marland of Appalachian State University; these data can be found at http://cdiac.ornl.gov/trends/emis/top2010.cap. Excluded are nations with fewer than one million people.

nations in annual fossil-fuel carbon dioxide emissions per capita, the United States ranks sixth worst with 4.7 tons of carbon per capita (down 14 percent from a decade earlier).

There have been efforts to address greenhouse gases on an international scale. A report by the Intergovernmental Panel on Climate Change, a group sponsored by the United Nations, was approved in 2007 by more than 120 nations.[15] The study says, to fight climate change, the world must cut emissions of carbon dioxide and other greenhouse gases by (1) sharply improving energy efficiency in buildings, vehicles, and machines; (2) shifting from fossil fuels to nuclear, wind, solar, and other renewable energy sources; (3) preserving forests as absorbers of carbon dioxide, or as "carbon sinks;" and (4) capping agricultural emissions. The United States and China, which account for more than 40 percent of the world's emissions, approved the report but offered no indication that they would reverse their opposition to mandatory emission reductions. The report said that such reforms would require lifestyle changes, increased prices for some basics including gasoline and electricity, and greater investment in research and development.

> **"Air pollution on average is now lower outdoors than indoors."**

17-3b Water Pollution

Water pollution can have serious consequences on human development. For example, polluted drinking water in New Jersey has been linked to underweight and premature births, especially among infants born to less educated mothers.[16] Three major sources of water pollution are sewage, chemicals, and oil. For decades, U.S. cities had an economic incentive to dump their sewage directly into waterways rather than clean it up first. Water current or tides would carry off the waste to become someone else's problem. Although each community found it rational, based on a narrow view of the situation, to dump into waterways, the combined effect of these local choices was massive water pollution, a negative externality imposed by one community mostly on other communities. Federal money over the years has funded thousands of sewage treatment plants, which cut water pollution substantially. Nearly all U.S. cities now have modern sewage treatment systems. Hundreds of once-polluted waterways have been cleaned up enough for swimming and fishing.

Chemicals are a second source of water pollution. Chemical pollution may conjure up an image of a pipe spewing chemicals into a river, but only about 10 percent of chemical pollution in the water comes from point pollution—pollution from factories and other industrial sites. About two-thirds come from nonpoint pollution—mostly runoff from agricultural pesticides and fertilizer. Congress has been reluctant to limit the use of pesticides, although pesticides pollute water and contaminate food. Industrial America seems an easier target than Old MacDonald's farm. In 1970, Congress shifted control of pesticides from the U.S. Department of Agriculture to the newly created EPA. But the EPA already had its hands full administering the Clean Water Act, so it turned pesticide regulation over to the states. Most states gave the job to their departments of agriculture, which usually promote the interests of farmers, not restrict what farmers can do. The EPA found that in most states pesticides fouled some groundwater.[17]

A third source of water pollution is oil. The cleanup of oil spills on land are overseen by the EPA. About 570,000 underground storage tanks for oil and chemicals pose a potential threat of contamination for groundwater, the source of drinking water for half of Americans. The cleanup of offshore oil spills is overseen by the U.S. Coast Guard. BP's oil spill in the Gulf of Mexico in 2010 was the most notable offshore spill in U.S. history.

17-3c Hazardous Waste and the Superfund

The U.S. synthetic chemical industry has flourished in the last 50 years, and over 50,000 chemicals are now in common use. But some have harmful effects on humans and other living creatures. These chemicals can pose risks at every stage of their production, use, and disposal. New Jersey manufactures more toxic chemicals than any other state and, not surprisingly, has the worst toxic waste burden. Prior to 1980, the disposal of toxic waste created get-rich-quick opportunities for anyone who could rent or buy a few acres of land to open a toxic waste dump. As an extreme example, one site in New Jersey took in 71 million gallons of hazardous chemicals during a three-year period.[18]

Before 1980, once a company paid someone to haul away its hazardous waste, that company was no

15. For panel reports, go to http://www.ipcc.ch/.

16. Janet Currie et al., "Something in the Water: Contaminated Drinking Water and Infant Health," *Canadian Journal of Economics*, 46 (August 2013): 791–810.

17. John Cushman, "E.P.A. and States Found to Be Lax on Pollution Law," *New York Times*, 7 June 1998.

18. Jason Zweig, "Real-Life Horror Story," *Forbes*, 12 December 1988.

longer responsible. The Comprehensive Environmental Response, Compensation, and Liability Act of 1980, known more popularly as the Superfund law, requires any company that generates, stores, or transports hazardous wastes to pay to clean up any wastes that are improperly disposed of. A producer or hauler who is the source of even one barrel of pollution dumped at a site can be held liable for cleaning up the entire site.

The Superfund law gave the federal government authority over sites contaminated with toxins. But to get an offending company to comply, the EPA frequently must sue. The process is slow, and nearly half the budget goes to lawyers, consultants, and administrators rather than to site cleanups. Research indicates that Superfund cleanups have little or no impact on residential property values, property rental rates, the housing supply, total population, or the types of individuals living near the sites. But more recent research suggests that Superfund cleanups have reduced birth defects by 20–25 percent among households within 2,000 meters of such sites.[19]

17-3d Solid Waste: "Paper or Plastic?"

Throughout most of human history, households tossed their trash outside as fodder for pigs and goats. New York City, like other cities, had no trash collections, so domestic waste was thrown into the street, where it mixed with mud and manure (until recently, many residents of Beijing and other parts of China did the same thing).[20] Decades of such accumulation explain why the oldest Manhattan streets are anywhere from 3 to 15 feet above their original levels. Until the last century, people also buried their trash near their homes or took it to a local dump. Most localities now forbid trash burning.

U.S. households generate about 4 pounds of garbage per resident per day—more than twice the 1960 level and the most in the world. Much of the solid waste consists of packaging. The question is: How do we dispose of the more than 200 million tons of household garbage generated in this country each year? Advanced economies produce and buy more than less developed economies, so there is more to throw away. And because of higher incomes in advanced economies, the opportunity cost of time is higher, so Americans tend to discard items rather than repair or recycle them. For example, it's cheaper to buy a new toaster for $20 than to pay someone $40 an hour to fix a broken one, assuming you can even find a repair service. (Plug "Small Appliance Repair" into a search engine and see if you can find this service in your area.)

About 70 percent of the nation's garbage is bulldozed and covered with soil in landfills. Although a well-managed landfill poses few environmental concerns, at one time, communities dumped all kinds of toxins in them—stuff that could leach into the soil, contaminating wells and aquifers. So landfills got a bad reputation. Now, the prevailing attitude with landfills is Nimby! (Not in my backyard!). We all want our garbage picked up, but nobody wants it put down anywhere nearby.

As the cost of solid waste disposal increases, some state and local governments are economizing, charging households by the pound for trash pickups, and requiring more recycling and returnable bottles. **Recycling** is the process of converting waste products into reusable materials. About half of U.S. households participate in curbside recycling programs. Still, according to the EPA, only about 15 percent of U.S. garbage gets recycled; about 15 percent is incinerated and, as noted already, the remaining 70 percent goes into landfills. Of the recycled material, three-quarters consists of corrugated boxes, newspapers, office paper, and other paper products. Some paper is shipped to Korea, Taiwan, and China, where it becomes packaging material for U.S. imports such as video and computer components. Exhibit 6 ranks the world's top 25 recyclers of paper and cardboard among major economies. Ireland heads the list, recycling 78 percent. The United States is in a five-way tie for 18th, recycling 50 percent (but more than double the rate of 1985). Poorer countries recycle much less—Mexico, for example, less than 10 percent.

Most of the 15 percent of garbage that is incinerated gets burned in trash-to-energy plants, which generate electricity using the heat from incineration. Until recently, such plants looked like the wave of the future, but less favorable tax treatment and environmental concerns over incinerator locations (Nimby strikes again!) have taken the steam out of the trash-to-energy movement. And residents have reason to be wary of plant locations. One researcher found that those living within two miles of a new power plant saw their property values drop by an average of 5 percent.[21]

To repeat, only 30 percent of U.S. garbage is recycled or incinerated, and about 70 percent goes to landfills. In contrast, the Japanese recycle or incinerate 73 percent, sending only 27 percent to landfills. Japanese households sort their trash into as many as 21 categories. Japan has only one tenth as much land per capita as does the United States. Because land is scarcer there, it is not surprising that the Japanese deposit a smaller share of their garbage in landfills.

recycling The process of converting waste products into reusable material

19. Janet Currie, Michael Greenstone, and Enrico Moretti, "Superfund Cleanups and Infant Health," *American Economic Review*, 101 (May 2011): 435–441.

20. Laurence Brahm, "Hygiene? It's a Load of Rubbish," *South China Morning Post*, 1 November 2005.

21. Lucas Davis, "The Effect of Power Plants on Local Housing Values and Rents," *Review of Economics and Statistics*, 93 (Issue 4, 2011): 1391–1402.

Exhibit 6

Paper and Cardboard Recycling: Top 25 Among Advanced Economies

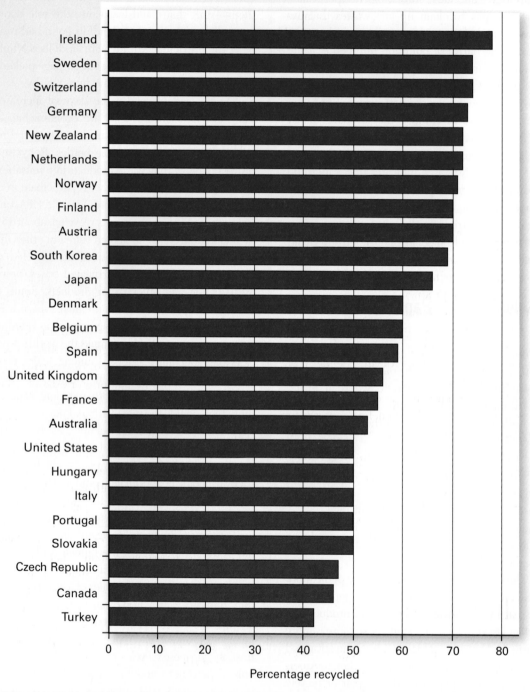

Percentage recycled

Sources: Figures, which are the latest available, are rankings among members of the Organization of Economic Cooperation and Development as reported in *OECD Environmental Data: 2006–2008*, Table 4A, p. 25. This can be found at http://www.oecd.org/dataoecd/60/59/38106368.pdf.

Some recycling is clearly economical—such as aluminum cans, which are a relatively cheap source of aluminum compared to producing raw aluminum. About two out of three aluminum cans now get recycled, though only ten states require returnable deposits on such cans. Still, returnable deposit laws increase recycling. Incentives matter. Even if you decide to discard rather than recycle your empties, chances are that someone down the line with a lower opportunity cost than you will find thexm and claim the deposits. For example, researchers found an average of 47 bottles and cans along a one-block path of city park each day prior to the enactment of a deposit law, but one year after the law was introduced, they found an average of only two bottles and cans each day along the same path.[22]

Recycling paper and cardboard is also economical and occurred long before the environmental movement. Such old standbys as paper drives, drop-off bins, and redemption centers collect more tonnage than curbside programs. Most recycling results from salvaging scrap material from business and industry, a practice that dates back decades.

Governments have tried to stimulate demand for recycled material—for example, by requiring newspapers to use a minimum percentage of recycled newsprint. Other recycled products are not in such demand. In fact, some recycled products have become worthless and must be hauled to landfills. When oil prices dropped in early 2015, the cost of producing plastic from oil also dropped. This reduced or eliminated the cost advantage of recycled plastic, driving some recyclers out of business. Recycled plastic piled up in warehouses.[23]

Recycling imposes its own environmental cost. Curbside recycling requires fleets of trucks that pollute the air. Newsprint must first be de-inked, creating a sludge that must be disposed of somehow. But greater environmental awareness has made consumers more receptive to more efficient packaging. For example, liquid laundry detergent now comes in a concentrated "ultra" form, which cuts volume in half, and Unilever's brand All Small & Mighty cuts volume by two-thirds. Fabric softener also now comes in ultra form. Labels for all kinds of products proudly identify the recycled content of the packaging.

17-4 POSITIVE EXTERNALITIES

To this point, we have considered only negative externalities. But externalities are sometimes positive, or beneficial. Positive externalities occur when consumption or production benefits other consumers or other firms. For example, people who get inoculated against a contagious disease reduce their own likelihood of contracting the disease (the personal benefit), but they also reduce

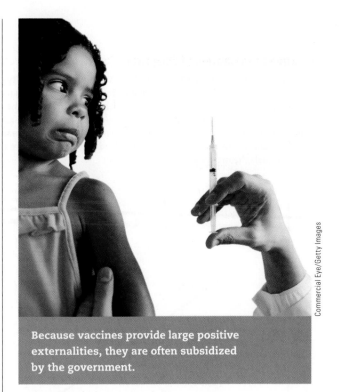

Because vaccines provide large positive externalities, they are often subsidized by the government.

the risk of transmitting the disease to others (the external benefit). Parents who don't get their children vaccinated risk triggering an epidemic, so the vaccination decision is not simply a private matter. For example, the Center for Disease Control and Prevention recently reported an outbreak of measles in 17 states because some children were not vaccinated.[24]

Another positive externality results from education. Society as a whole receives external benefits from education because those with more education become better citizens, can read road signs, are better able to support themselves and their families, and are less likely to require public assistance or to resort to violent crime for income. Researchers found that more schooling significantly reduces the probability of incarceration.[25] Also, the higher the minimum dropout age for school, the lower the arrest rate for property and violent crimes among 16-to-18-year-olds. Thus, when in school, this age group gets into less trouble, which is another external benefit of education.[26] And for the population as a whole, education reduces crime.[27] Thus, your education benefits you but it also benefits others. As the 19th century

22. J. Trinkaus, "A Bottle Law: An Informal Look," *Perceptual and Motor Skills*, 59 (December 1984), p. 806.

23. Georgi Kantchev and Serena Ng, "Recycling Becomes a Tougher Sell as Prices Drop," *Wall Street Journal*, 6 April 2015.

24. "Measles and Outbreaks from January 1 to March 13, 2015," Center for Disease Control and Prevention, at http://www.cdc.gov/measles/cases-outbreaks.html.

25. Lance Lochner and Enrico Moretti, "The Effects of Education on Crime: Evidence From Prison Inmates, Arrests, and Self-Reports," *American Economic Review*, 94 (March 2004): 155–189.

26. D. Mark Anderson, "In School and Out of Trouble? The Minimum Dropout Age and Juvenile Crime," *Review of Economics and Statistics*, 96 (May 2014): 318–331.

27. Stephen Machin, Olivier Marie, and Suncica Vujic, "The Crime-Reducing Effect of Education," *Economic Journal*, 121 (May 2011): 463–484.

Exhibit 7

Positive Externalities of Education

In the absence of government intervention, the equilibrium quantity of education is *E*, where the marginal private benefit of education equals the marginal cost as reflected by the supply curve. Education also confers a positive externality on the rest of society, so the social benefit exceeds the private benefit. At quantity *E*, the marginal social benefit, point b, exceeds the marginal cost, point e, so more education increases social welfare. In this situation, government tries to increase education to *E'*, where the marginal social benefit equals the marginal cost.

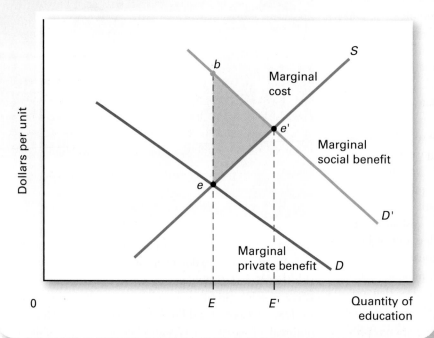

French writer Victor Hugo observed, "He who opens a school door, closes a prison."

The effect of external benefits is illustrated in Exhibit 7, which presents the demand and supply of education. The demand curve, *D*, represents the private demand for education, which reflects the marginal private benefit for those who acquire the education. More education is demanded at a lower price than at a higher price.

The benefit of education, however, spills over to others in society. If we add this positive externality, or marginal external benefit, to the marginal private benefit of education, we get the marginal social benefit of education. *The marginal social benefit includes all the benefits society derives from education, both private and external.* The marginal social benefit curve is above the private demand curve in Exhibit 7. If education were a strictly private decision, the amount purchased would be determined by the intersection of the private demand curve *D* with supply curve *S*. The supply curve reflects the marginal cost of producing each unit of education. This intersection at point *e* yields education level *E*, where the marginal private benefit of education equals its marginal

cost, as reflected by the supply curve. But at level *E*, the marginal social benefit, identified as point *b*, exceeds the marginal cost. Social welfare would increase if education expands beyond *E*. As long as the marginal social benefit exceeds the marginal cost, social welfare increases as education expands. Social welfare is maximized at point *e'* in Exhibit 7, with *E'* units of education—that is, where the marginal social benefit equals the marginal cost. The blue-shaded triangle identifies the increase in social welfare that results from increasing education from *E*, the private optimum, to *E'*, the social optimum.

Thus, society is better off if the level of education exceeds the private equilibrium. With positive externalities, decisions based on private marginal benefits result in less than the socially optimal quantity of the good. Thus, like negative externalities, positive externalities typically point to market failure, which is why government often gets into the act. When there are external benefits, public policy aims to increase quantity beyond the private optimum. For example, governments try to increase education by providing free primary and secondary education, by requiring students to stay in school until they reach a certain age, by subsidizing public higher education, and by offering tax breaks for some education expenses.

As another example, to promote so-called clean energy and discourage the use of fossil fuels, government subsidies include tax breaks for solar panels, wind power, and other alternative energy sources. But the costs of such programs sometimes exceed the benefits, as in the case of wind power subsidies.[28] Note that hefty subsidies of electric cars in Norway have cut the price of Teslas there in half. These subsidies include free electricity, free parking, and free tolls.

Another source of externalities stems from precautions people take to avoid becoming crime victims, such as LoJack, a device used to track and recover a stolen vehicle. Because the device is completely undetectable by a

28. Joseph Cullen, "Measuring the Environmental Benefits of Wind-Generated Electricity," *American Economic Journal: Economic Policy*, 5 (November 2013): 107–133.

potential thief, the more LoJacks installed, the more nervous thieves get and the fewer vehicles stolen in general. Thus, car owners without LoJack get a positive externality when other car owners install the device. Researchers estimated that a 1 percent increase in LoJack installations cuts car thefts in general by at least 20 percent.[29] On the other hand, the use of The Club, a very visible lock for the steering wheel, generates a negative externality, because it increases the likelihood that vehicles without The Club will get stolen. In terms of social welfare, there are not enough LoJacks installed and too many Clubs.

> **“When there are external benefits, public policy aims to increase quantity beyond the private optimum.”**

17-5 FINAL WORD

About 7.4 billion people live on the planet, and over 80 million are added each year. World population is projected to reach 9.4 billion by 2050, according to the U.S. Census Bureau, with most of this growth occurring in countries where many people barely eke out a living. Population pressure coupled with a lack of incentives to conserve open-access resources results in deforestation, dwindling fish stocks, and polluted air, land, and water.

Ironically, because of the tighter pollution controls in industrial countries, these countries are less polluted than developing countries, where there is more pollution from what little industry there is. Some developing countries have such profound economic problems that environmental quality is not a priority. For example, when India's Supreme Court tried to close some polluting factories in New Delhi, thousands of workers torched buses, threw

stones, and blocked major roads, demanding the factories remain open. Although New Delhi's pollution masks any trace of a blue sky, workers believe their jobs are more important. Here's one account of New Delhi's air quality:

> *In the heat of the afternoons, a yellow-white mixture hung above the city, raining acidic soot into the dust and exhaust fumes. At night the mixture condenses into a dry, choking fog that envelops the headlights of passing cars, and creeps its stink into even the tightest houses. The residents could do little to keep the poison out of their lungs or the lungs of their children, and if they were poor, they could not even try.*[30]

Market prices can direct the allocation of resources only as long as property rights are well defined. Pollution arises not so much from greed or malice of producers and consumers as from the fact that open-access resources are subject to the common-pool problem.

30. William Langewiesche, "The Shipbreakers," *Atlantic Monthly* (August 2000), p. 42.

STUDY TOOLS 17

29. Ian Ayres and Steven Levitt, "Measuring Positive Externalities for Unobservable Victim Precautions: An Empirical Analysis of Lojack," *Quarterly Journal of Economics,*" 113 (February 1998): 43–77.

CHAPTER 17 PROBLEMS

Your instructor can access the answers to these problems online at http://cengagebrain.com.

17-1 Describe the common pool problem and summarize ways to address it

1. *(Externalities)* Complete each of the following sentences:
   a. Resources for which periodic use can be continued indefinitely are known as _____ resources.
   b. Resources that are available only in a fixed amount are _____ resources.
   c. The possibility that a open-access resource is used until the net marginal value of additional use equals zero is known as the _____.

2. *(Resolving the Common-Pool Problem)* Why have authorities found it so difficult to regulate the fishing catch in the open ocean to allow for a sustainable yield?

17-2 Determine the optimal level of pollution with fixed technology and with variable technology

3. *(Negative Externalities)* Suppose you wish to reduce a negative externality by imposing a tax on the activity that creates that externality. When the amount of the externality produced per unit of output increases as output increases, the correct tax can be determined by using a demand-supply diagram; show this. Assume that the marginal private cost curve slopes upward.

Negative Externalitites: The Market for Electricity in the Midwest

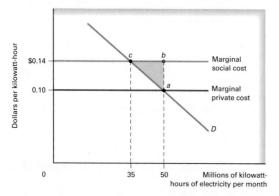

4. *(Negative Externalities)* Review the situation illustrated in the graph above. If the government sets the price of electricity at the socially optimal level, why is the net gain equal to triangle *abc*, even though consumers now pay a higher price for electricity? What would the net gain be if the government set the price above the optimal level?

5. *(External Costs)* Use the data in the table below to answer the following questions.
   a. What is the marginal external cost of production?
   b. What level is produced if there is no regulation of the externality?
   c. What level should be produced to achieve economic efficiency?
   d. Calculate the dollar value of the net gain to society from correcting the externality.

Quantity	Marginal Private Benefit (demand)	Marginal Private Cost (supply)	Marginal Social Cost
0	—	$0	$0
1	$10	2	4
2	9	3	5
3	8	4	6
4	7	5	7
5	6	6	8
6	5	7	9
7	4	8	10
8	3	9	11
9	2	10	12
10	1	11	13

6. *(External Costs with Variable Technology)* Think of an industry that pollutes the water and has access to variable technology for reducing that pollution. Graphically illustrate and explain the impact of each of the following, other things constant, on the optimal level of water quality:
   a. New evidence is discovered about a greater risk of cancer from water pollution.
   b. The cost of pollution-control equipment increases.
   c. A technological improvement reduces the cost of pollution control.

7. *(Market for Pollution Rights)* The following graph shows the market for pollution rights.
   a. If there are no restrictions on pollution, what amount is discharged?
   b. What is the quantity supplied and the quantity demanded if the government restricts the amount of discharge to Q* but gives the permits away?
   c. Where is market equilibrium if the government sells the permits at the market-clearing price? Illustrate this on the graph.

d. What happens to market equilibrium if the gvernment reduces the amount of discharge permitted to Q**? Illustrate this on the graph.

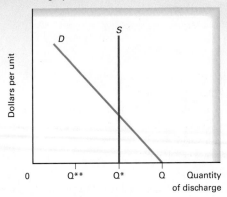

17-3 Summarize how the federal government has regulated air, water, and land pollution

8. *(Environmental Protection)* Four federal laws and subsequent amendments underpin U.S. environmental protection. Identify these laws.

17-4 Outline government policies designed to promote the production and consumption of goods that generate positive externalities

9. *(Positive Externalities)* The value of a home depends in part on how attractive other homes and yards in the neighborhood are. How do local zoning ordinances try to promote land uses that generate external benefits for neighbors?

18 | Poverty and Redistribution

AP Images/Ric Francis

LEARNING OUTCOMES

After studying this chapter, you will be able to…

18-1 Identify reasons why incomes differ across households, and why the income gap has increased

18-2 Summarize what has happened to the incidence of poverty since 1960, and determine when and why the greatest progress was made in reducing poverty

18-3 Describe a primary source of poverty among families in the United States

18-4 Outline some unintended consequences of efforts to reduce poverty

18-5 Describe how the 1996 federal welfare reforms affected the number of people on welfare

After finishing this chapter go to PAGE 322 for STUDY TOOLS

Topics discussed in Chapter 18 include:

- Distribution of income
- The value of a college education
- Marital sorting and income inequality
- The official poverty level
- Public policy and poverty
- Poverty and age
- The feminization of poverty
- Poverty and discrimination
- Unintended consequences of income assistance
- Welfare reforms

- Why are some people poor even in the largest and most productive economy on Earth?

- Who are the poor, how did they get that way, and how long do they stay poor?

- What's been the trend in U.S. poverty?

- How has changing family structure affected poverty?

- What public programs aim to reduce poverty, and how well have they worked?

- Why was someone fined more than $200,000 for driving 25 miles per hour over the limit?

Answers to these and related questions are addressed in this chapter, which discusses income distribution and poverty in America.

To establish a reference point, we first consider the distribution of income in the United States, paying special attention to trends in recent decades. We then examine the "social safety net"—government programs aimed at helping poor people. We also consider the impact of the changing family structure on poverty, focusing in particular on the increase in households headed by women.

We close by examining welfare reforms.

> "Why are some people poor even in the most productive economy on earth?"

18-1 THE DISTRIBUTION OF HOUSEHOLD INCOME

In a market economy, income depends primarily on earnings, which in turn depend on the productivity of one's resources. The problem with allocating income according to productivity is that some people have few resources to sell. People with mental or physical disabilities or a poor education, those facing discrimination, bad luck, or the demands of caring for small children, and the elderly may be less productive and therefore unable to earn a living.

18-1a Income Distribution by Quintiles

As a starting point, let's consider the distribution of income in the economy and see how it has changed over time, focusing on the household as the economic unit. After sorting U.S. households based on income into five groups of equal size, or *quintiles*, we can examine the percentage of total income received by each quintile. Such a division is presented in Exhibit 1 from 1980 to 2013. Take a moment to look over this exhibit. Notice that households in the lowest, or poorest, fifth of the population received only 4.3 percent of the income in

1980, whereas households in the highest, or richest, fifth received 43.7 percent of the income. The U.S. Census Bureau measures income after cash transfer payments are received but before taxes are paid or in-kind transfers are received (from food vouchers, Medicare, Medicaid, public housing, and employer-provided benefits).

In recent decades, the share of income going to the top fifth has increased, and the share going to the bottom fifth has declined. The richest fifth's share of income increased from 43.7 percent in 1980 to 51.0 percent in 2013. A primary contributor to the larger share of income going to the highest group has been the growth of two-earner households in that top group. Three out of four households in the top quintile have two or more people working. A primary contributor to the smaller share going to the lowest group has been the growth of single-parent households in the bottom group. Only about one in three households in the bottom quintile has anybody working, and only about one in seven has anybody working full time.

Also shown in Exhibit 1 is the share of income going to the top 5 percent of households; that share grew between 1980 and 2013, accounting for nearly all the growth of the top 20 percent of households. Because of substantial reductions in the top marginal tax rates in 1981 and 1986, high-income people had less incentive to engage in tax

Exhibit 1

Share of Aggregate Household Income by Quintile, 1980–2013

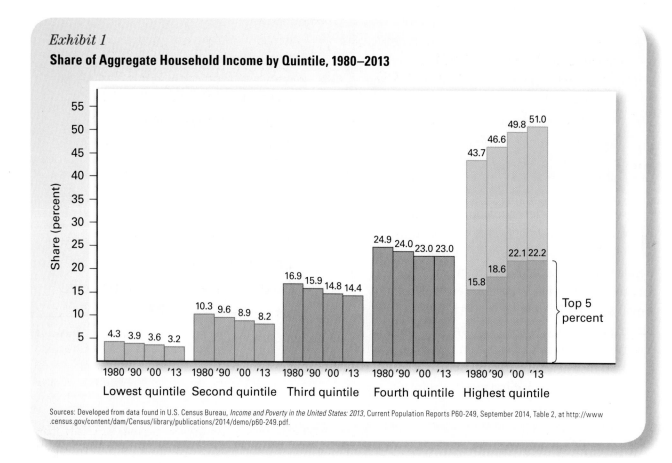

Sources: Developed from data found in U.S. Census Bureau, *Income and Poverty in the United States: 2013*, Current Population Reports P60-249, September 2014, Table 2, at http://www .census.gov/content/dam/Census/library/publications/2014/demo/p60-249.pdf.

avoidance, so their reported income increased, boosting the share of reported income going to the richest 5 percent of households. More detailed research has found that the income distribution became less equal between 1972 and 1992 but has changed little since then.[1]

18-1b The Lorenz Curve

We have just examined the distribution of income using a bar chart. Another way to picture that distribution is with a Lorenz curve. A **Lorenz curve** shows the percentage of total income received by any given percentage of households when incomes are arrayed from smallest to largest. As shown in Exhibit 2, the cumulative percentage of households is measured along the horizontal axis, and the cumulative percentage of income is measured along the vertical axis. Any given distribution of income can be compared to an equal

Lorenz curve A curve showing the percentage of total income received by a given percentage of households when incomes are arrayed from smallest to largest

1. Richard Burkhauser et al., "Estimating Trends in U.S. Income Inequality Using the Current Population Survey: The Importance of Controlling for Censoring," *Journal of Economic Inequality*, 9 (September 2011): 393–415.

distribution of income among households. If income were evenly distributed, each 20 percent of households would also receive 20 percent of the total income, and the Lorenz curve would be a straight line with a slope equal to 1.0, as shown by the "equal distribution" line in Exhibit 2.

As the distribution becomes more uneven, the Lorenz curve pulls down to the right, away from the line of equal distribution. The Lorenz curves in Exhibit 2 were calculated for 1980 and 2013 based on the data in Exhibit 1. As a reference, point *a* on the 1980 Lorenz curve indicates that in that year, the bottom 80 percent of families received 56.3 percent of the income, and the top 20 percent received 43.7 percent of the income. The Lorenz curve for 2013 is farther from the line of equal distribution than is the Lorenz curve for 1980, showing that income among households has become more unevenly distributed. Point *b* on the 2013 curve shows that the bottom 80 percent received 49.0 percent of the income and the top 20 percent received 51.0 percent of the income.

18-1c Why Incomes Differ

Income differences across households stem in part from differences in the *number* of workers in each household.

Exhibit 2

Lorenz Curves Show That Income Was Less Evenly Distributed Across U.S. Households in 2013 Than in 1980

The Lorenz curve is a convenient way of showing the percentage of total income received by any given percentage of households when incomes are arrayed from smallest to largest. For example, point a shows that in 1980, the bottom 80 percent of households received 56.3 percent of all income. Point b shows that in 2013, the share of all income going to the bottom 80 percent of households was lower than in 1980. If income were evenly distributed across households, the Lorenz curve would be a straight line.

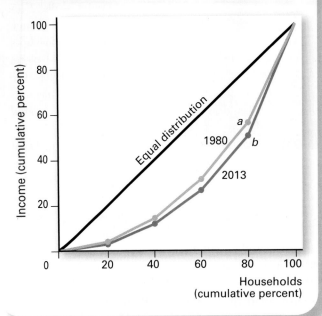

> **"A high-income household usually consists of a well-educated couple with both spouses employed. A low-income household is usually one person living alone or is a family headed by a single parent who is young, female, poorly educated, and not in the labor market."**

Thus, *one reason household incomes differ is that the number of household members who are working differs.* As noted earlier, among households in the bottom 20 percent based on income, only one in seven includes a full-time, year-round worker. Consider the link between median income and the number of workers. The **median income** of all households is the middle income when incomes are ranked from lowest to highest. In any given year, half the households are above the median income and half are below it. The median income for households with two earners is about 90 percent higher than for households with only one earner and is more than four times higher than for households with no earners.

Incomes also differ for all the reasons labor earnings differ, such as differences in education, ability, job experience, and so on. At every age, those with more education earn more, on average. As noted in Exhibit 4 of Chapter 12, those with a professional degree earn at least five times more than those without a high school diploma. Age

itself also matters. As workers mature, especially those with a good education, they acquire valuable job experience, get promoted, and earn more.

Differences in earnings based on age and education reflect a normal *life cycle* pattern of income. In fact, most income differences across households reflect the normal workings of resource markets, whereby workers are rewarded according to their productivity. Because of these lifetime patterns, it is not necessarily the same households that remain rich or poor over time. Indeed, one study of income mobility found that more than three-quarters of people in the bottom 20 percent in one particular year had moved into the top 40 percent for at least 1 year during the following 16 years.[2] What's more, researchers find that young people entering the U.S. labor market today have the same chance of moving up in the income distribution (relative to their parents) as those born in the 1970s.[3]

Despite this income mobility over time, we can still characterize rich and poor households at a point

2. W. Michael Cox and Richard Alm, "By Our Own Bootstraps," in *By Our Own Bootstraps: Economic Opportunity and the Dynamics of Income Distribution*, Federal Reserve Bank of Dallas Annual Report 1995, pp. 2–24, at http://www.dallasfed.org/assets /documents/fed/annual/1999/ar95.pdf.

3. Raj Chetty et al. "Is the United States A Land of Opportunity? Recent Trends in Intergenerational Mobility," *American Economic Review*, 104 (May 2014): 141–147.

median income The middle income when all incomes are ranked from smallest to largest in time. *A high-income household usually consists of a well-educated couple with both spouses employed. A low-income household is usually one person living alone or is a family headed by a single parent who is young, female, poorly educated, and not in the labor market.* Low incomes are a matter of public concern, especially when children are involved, as we see in the next section.

18-1d A College Education Pays More

Also contributing to the dominance of the top group is an increased pay advantage for those with college educations. In the last two decades, the median wage (adjusted for inflation) for people with only high school diplomas declined 6 percent, while the median wage for college graduates rose 12 percent. The **median wage** is the middle wage when wages are ranked from lowest to highest. Why have more-educated workers done better? First, trends such as industry deregulation, declining unionization, and freer international trade and migration have reduced the pay for workers with less education. Labor unions, for example, raised the wages of many workers who would have otherwise ended up in the bottom half of the income distribution. But the share of the workforce that is unionized declined from 26 percent in 1973 to only 11 percent in 2014. More generally, an increasing fraction of jobs in the U.S. labor market explicitly pay workers for their productivity using bonus pay, commissions, or piece-rate contracts. Research suggests that productivity pay has increased earnings inequality.[4]

Second, new computer-based information technologies have reduced the demand for low-skilled clerical workers, because their jobs became more computerized. But computers also offered more timely and accurate information to management, allowing for organizational innovations that made managers and other professionals more productive.[5] So computers reduced the demand

for workers with low skills, such as clerical staff and bank tellers, and increased the demand for those who use computers to boost labor productivity, such as managers and accountants.

Third, along the same lines, during the past three decades, U.S. manufacturers have invested heavily in computer-controlled machinery. This capital substituted for the least-skilled workers but also complemented workers with more computer skills.[6] Furthermore, technological change often made some trade-school vocational training obsolete. Such workers found that the skills so acquired became outdated as technology changed around them.[7]

Fourth, the supply of less-educated workers increased more than the supply of more-educated workers, thus increasing the rewards of education. For example, compared to average residents, recent U.S. immigrants tend to be less educated, including an estimated 11 million illegal immigrants, more than half from Mexico. The Hispanic population more than doubled between the 1980 census and 2000 census, and the percentage of foreign-born Hispanics increased. Among males age 25 and older, only 57 percent of Hispanics had at least a high school education in 2000, compared with 85 percent of whites and 79 percent of blacks. More generally, the foreign-born share of the U.S. population more than doubled from 5 percent in 1970 to over 12 percent today, the largest share since the 1930s. Thus, immigration has increased the supply of relatively poorly educated workers, which has helped depress wages of the less educated generally.

Finally, marriage trends have reinforced the income gap. For the first time in history, a growing number of women now have high-paying jobs and their spouses also have high-paying jobs.

When these couples marry and have children, their offspring benefit from the high income and any other advantages passed along from their well-educated

©Jason Stitt/Shutterstock.com

median wage The middle wage when wages of all workers are ranked from lowest to highest

4. Thomas Lemieux, W. Bentley MacCleod. and Daniel Parent, "Performance Pay and Wage Inequality," *Quarterly Journal of Economics*, 124 (February 2009): 1–49.

5. Lex Borghans and Bas ter Weel, "The Diffusion of Computers and the Distribution of Wages," *European Economic Review*, 51 (April 2007): 715–748.

6. Ethan Lewis, "Immigration, Skill Mix, and Capital Skill Complementarity," *Quarterly Journal of Economics*, 126 (May 2011): 1029–1069.

7. Eric Hanushek, Ludger Woessmann, and Lei Zhang, "General Education, Vocational Education, and Labor-Market Outcomes Over the Life Cycle," NBER Working Paper 17504 (October 2011).

parents, including better health. With this head start in life, many from that next generation, in turn, go to the best colleges, where they are likely to meet their future spouses. This marital sorting cycle thereby gets reinforced and perpetuated. College-educated couples are more likely to stay married than couples with less education. This stable marriage gives yet another advantage to the offspring.

The flip side of this is that someone with only a high school education is now less likely to marry a college graduate or marry at all than was once the case. As you will see, children born to single mothers typically face special challenges, not the least of which is a higher rate of poverty. So, a growth in power couples and in unmarried mothers anchors the top and bottom ends of the income distribution, contributing to the widening income gap observed in the U.S. economy.

Economic forces, technological change, immigration, and marriage trends have hurt those at the low end of the income distribution and have benefited those at the high end, and this helps explain the growing disparity in household income.

We end this section with a longer view of income distribution. Most countries, including the United States, experienced a sharp drop in top income shares in the first part of the twentieth century, as capital owners were hit hard by world wars and the Great Depression. Top income shares recovered only in the last 30 years in the English-speaking countries and in India and China. This increase was due in part to an unprecedented surge in top wage incomes, as we have discussed. As a result, wage incomes now make up a larger fraction of top incomes than in the past. A century ago, the rich more likely inherited their wealth. Today, they more likely earned it.[8] For example, 7 of the 15 richest Americans in 2014 derived their fortunes from the computer processor, including Bill Gates of Microsoft, Larry Ellison of Oracle, Mark Zuckerberg of Facebook, Michael Bloomberg of the financial

> **"Economic forces, technological change, immigration, and marriage trends have hurt those at the low end of the income distribution and have benefited those at the high end, and this helps explain the growing disparity in household income."**

information company Bloomberg, Larry Page and Sergey Brin of Google, and Jeff Bezos of Amazon.com.[9]

18-1e Problems with Distribution Benchmarks

One problem with assessing income distributions is that there is no objective standard for evaluating them. The usual assumption is that a more equal distribution of income is more desirable, but is an equal distribution most preferred? If not, then how uneven should it be? For example, among major league baseball players, well over half the pay goes to 20 percent of the players. Professional basketball pay skews even more, with top NBA players earning more than 40 times what the bottom players earn. Does this mean the economy, as a whole, is in some sense "fairer" than these professional sports?

A second problem is that because Exhibits 1 and 2 measure money income after cash transfers but before taxes, they neglect the effects of taxes and in-kind transfers, such as food vouchers and free medical care for poor families. The tax system as a whole is progressive, meaning that families with higher incomes pay a larger fraction of their incomes in taxes. In-kind transfers benefit the lowest income groups the most. Consequently, if Exhibit 1 incorporated the effects of taxes and in-kind transfers, the share of income going to the lower groups would increase, the share going to the higher groups would decrease, and income would become more evenly distributed.

Third, focusing on the share of income going to each income quintile overlooks the fact that household size differs across quintiles. Most households in the bottom quintile consist of one person living alone. Only one in 16 households in the top quintile consists of one person living alone.

Fourth, Exhibits 1 and 2 include only *reported* income. If people receive payment "under the table" to evade taxes, or if they earn money through illegal activities, their actual income will exceed their reported

8. Anthony Atkinson, Thomas Piketty, and Emmanuel Saez, "Top Incomes in the Long Run of History," *Journal of Economic Literature*, 39 (March 2011): 3–71.

9. "Forbes 400: The Richest People in America," *Forbes*, 29 September 2014, at http://www.forbes.com/forbes-400/.

income. The omission of unreported income distorts the data if unreported income as a percentage of total family income differs across income levels.

Fifth, broadening the definition of income to include changes in capital gains, that is, changes in net wealth from year to year, dramatically reduces the observed growth in inequality, especially since 1990.[10]

Finally, Exhibits 1 and 2 focus on the distribution of *income*, but a better measure of household welfare would be the distribution of *spending*. Available evidence indicates that *spending by quintiles is more evenly distributed than income by quintiles*.

18-2 REDISTRIBUTION PROGRAMS

Because poverty is so relative, how can we measure it objectively, and how do we ensure that the measure has equal relevance over time? The federal government has developed a method for calculating an official poverty level, which serves as a benchmark for poverty analysis in the United States.

18-2a Official Poverty Level

To derive the **U.S. official poverty level**, the U.S. Department of Agriculture in 1959 first estimated the cost of a nutritionally adequate diet. Then, based on the assumption that the poor spend about one-third of their income on food, the official poverty level was calculated by multiplying this food cost by three. The U.S. Census Bureau tracks the official poverty level from year to year, making adjustments for family size and for inflation. For example, the official poverty level of money income for a family of four was $24,250 in 2015; a family of four below that income threshold was regarded as living in poverty. Poverty levels in 2015 ranged from $11,770 for a person living alone to $45,050 for a family of nine. The poverty definition is based on pretax money income, including cash transfers, but excluding the value of noncash transfers such as food vouchers,

U.S. official poverty level Benchmark level of income computed by the federal government to track poverty over time; initially based on three times the cost of a nutritionally adequate diet

> " Poverty is a relative term. "

Medicare, Medicaid, subsidized housing, or employer-provided health insurance.

Each year since 1959, the Census Bureau has conducted a survey comparing each family's cash income to the annual poverty level applicable to that family. Results of this survey are presented in Exhibit 3, which indicates both the millions of people living below the official poverty level and the percentage of the U.S. population below that level. Periods of U.S. recession are also shown (a recession is usually defined as two or more successive quarters of declining output in the economy). Note that poverty increased during recessions.

The biggest decline in poverty occurred before 1970; *the poverty rate dropped from 22.4 percent in 1959 to 12.1 percent in 1969*. During that period, the number of poor people decreased from about 40 million to 24 million. The poverty rate has not shown huge fluctuations since that initial drop. After declining from 1994 to 2000, the poverty rate and the number of poor people drifted higher over the next five years because of the national recession in 2001. The recession of 2007–2009 increased the number of people in poverty to 46.2 million in 2010 and the poverty rate to 15.1 percent, or about one in seven U.S. residents. Since then, the poverty rate has fallen slightly (14.5% in 2013).

Poverty is a relative term. If we examined the distribution of income across countries, we would find huge gaps between rich and poor nations. The U.S. official poverty level of income is much greater than the average income for three-fourths of the world's population. The U.S. poverty level for a family of four in 2015 works out to be $16.61 per person per day. Most nations employ a much lower poverty threshold. About 40 percent of the world's population lives on $2 a day or less.[11]

18-2b Programs to Help the Poor

What should society's response to poverty be? The best predictor of poverty is whether someone has a job. Adults with full-time jobs in 2013 had a poverty rate of 2.7 percent; adults who did not work during the year had a poverty rate of 32.3 percent, or more than 10 times the rate of those with jobs. One way government can try to reduce poverty, therefore, is to promote a healthy economy, one with lots of jobs. The stronger the economy,

10. Philip Armour, Richard Burkhauser, and Jeff Larrimore, "Levels and Trends in the United States Income and Its Distribution," *Southern Economic Journal*, 81 (October 2014): 271–293.

11. As reported in Daryl Collins et al., *Portfolios of the Poor: How the World's Poor Live on $2 a Day* (Princeton University Press, 2009).

Exhibit 3

Number and Percentage of U.S. Population in Poverty Since 1959

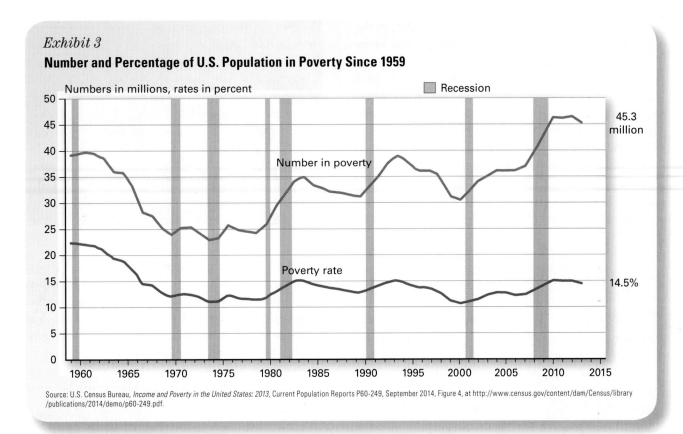

Source: U.S. Census Bureau, *Income and Poverty in the United States: 2013*, Current Population Reports P60-249, September 2014, Figure 4, at http://www.census.gov/content/dam/Census/library/publications/2014/demo/p60-249.pdf.

the greater the job opportunities, and the more likely people find work. Perhaps the best indicator of whether or not jobs are readily available is the *unemployment rate*, which shows the percentage of the labor force out of work.

The *lower* the unemployment rate, the *higher* the likelihood that someone who wants a job can find one. Thus, the lower the unemployment rate, the lower the poverty rate. Exhibit 4 shows poverty rates and unemployment rates

Exhibit 4

U.S. Poverty Rates and Unemployment Rates Are Related Over Time

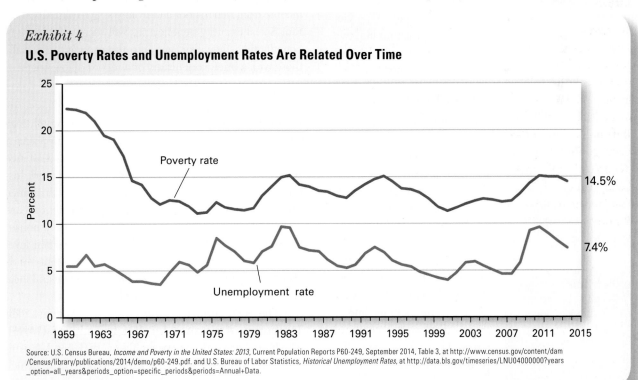

Source: U.S. Census Bureau, *Income and Poverty in the United States: 2013*, Current Population Reports P60-249, September 2014, Table 3, at http://www.census.gov/content/dam/Census/library/publications/2014/demo/p60-249.pdf. and U.S. Bureau of Labor Statistics, *Historical Unemployment Rates*, at http://data.bls.gov/timeseries/LNU04000000?years_option=all_years&periods_option=specific_periods&periods=Annual+Data.

in the United States each year since 1959. As you can see, the poverty rate, shown by the top line, tends to rise when the unemployment rate increases and to fall when the unemployment rate declines. The poverty rate fell from 22.4 percent in 1959 to 12.1 percent in 1969. During that decade, the unemployment rate not only was low by historical standards but also was falling, reaching 3.5 percent by 1969. That strong job market helped cut the poverty rate.

Thus, the government's first line of defense in fighting poverty is promoting a healthy economy. Yet even when the unemployment rate is low, some people are still poor. Although some antipoverty programs involve direct market intervention, such as minimum-wage laws, the most visible antipoverty programs redistribute income after the market has made an initial distribution. Since the mid-1960s, social welfare expenditures at all levels of government have increased sharply. We can divide these programs into two broad categories: social insurance and income assistance.

Social Insurance

Social insurance programs are designed to help make up for the lost income of people who worked but are now retired, temporarily unemployed, or unable to work because of disability or work-related injury. The major social insurance program is **Social Security**, established during the Great Depression to supplement retirement income of those with a work history and a record of contributing to the program. **Medicare**, another social insurance program, provides health insurance

Phototake Inc/Alamy

for short-term medical care, mostly to those ages 65 and older, regardless of income. There are about 50 million Social Security and Medicare beneficiaries, and together the programs cost about $1.4 trillion in 2015. Other social insurance programs include *unemployment insurance*, which supports those who have lost jobs, and *workers' compensation*, which supports workers injured on the job; both programs require that beneficiaries have a history of employment.

The social insurance system deducts "insurance premiums" from workers' pay to provide benefits to other retired, disabled, and unemployed individuals. These programs protect some families from poverty, particularly the elderly, but they are aimed more at those with a work history. Still, the social insurance system tends to redistribute income from rich to poor and from young to old. Most current Social Security beneficiaries will receive far more in benefits than they ever paid into the program, especially those with a brief work history or a record of low wages.

Income Assistance

Income assistance programs—what we usually call welfare programs—provide cash and in-kind assistance to the poor. Unlike social insurance, income assistance programs do not require recipients to have a work history or to have paid into the program. Income assistance programs are means tested. Those with sufficient means are not eligible. In a **means-tested program**, a household's income and assets must be below a certain level to qualify for benefits. The federal government funds about two-thirds of welfare spending, and state and local governments fund about one-third.

The two primary *cash transfer* programs are **Temporary Assistance for Needy Families (TANF)**, which provides cash to poor families with dependent children, and **Supplemental Security Income (SSI)**, which provides cash to the elderly poor and the disabled. SSI assists about five million adults and more than one million

social insurance
Government programs designed to help make up for lost income of people who worked but are now retired, unemployed, or unable to work because of disability or work-related injury

Social Security
Social insurance program that supplements retirement income of those with a record of contributing to the program during their working years; by far the largest government redistribution program

Medicare Social insurance program providing health insurance for short-term medical care to older Americans, regardless of income

income assistance programs Welfare programs that provide money and in-kind assistance to the poor; benefits do not depend on prior contributions

means-tested program A program in which, to be eligible, an individual's income and assets must not exceed specified levels

Temporary Assistance for Needy Families (TANF) An income assistance program funded largely by the federal government but run by the states to provide cash transfer payments to poor families with dependent children

Supplemental Security Income (SSI) An income assistance program that provides cash transfers to the elderly poor and the disabled; a uniform federal payment is supplemented by transfers that vary across states children. Cash transfers vary inversely with family income from other sources. In 1997, TANF replaced Aid for Families with Dependent Children (AFDC), which began during the Great Depression and originally supported widows with young children. Whereas AFDC was a federal *entitlement* program, meaning that anyone who met the criteria was *entitled* to benefits, TANF is under the control of each state and carries no federal entitlement. The federal government gives each state a grant to help fund TANF programs. Federal TANF grants totaled $16.5 billion in 2015 but that total has not changed since 1997.

The SSI program provides support for the elderly and disabled poor. It is the fastest-growing cash transfer program. SSI coverage has been broadened to include people addicted to drugs and alcohol, children with learning disabilities, and, in some cases, the homeless. The federal portion of this program is uniform across states, but states can supplement federal aid. For example, benefit levels in California average twice those in Alabama. Most states also offer modest *General Assistance* aid to those who are poor but do not qualify for TANF or SSI. The federal government also provides an **earned-income tax credit**, which supplements wages of the working poor. For example, a low-income family with three children would not only pay no federal income tax but would receive a cash transfer of up to $6,242 in 2015. More than 28 million tax filers received an average transfer of $2,500 in 2015, when outlays of more than $70 billion for the program were more than four times federal spending for TANF. The earned-income tax credit lifts millions of families out of poverty. Twenty-five states and the District of Columbia also offer their own earned-income tax credits on top of the federal plan.

In addition to cash transfers, a variety of *in-kind transfer* programs provide health care, food vouchers, and housing assistance to the poor. **Medicaid** pays for medical care for those with low incomes who are aged, blind, disabled, or are in families with dependent children. *Medicaid is by far the largest welfare program, costing more than all cash and other in-kind transfer programs combined.* It has grown more than any other poverty program, quadrupling in the last decade and accounting for nearly a quarter of the typical state's budget (though states receive federal grants covering half or more of their Medicaid budget). The qualifying level of income is set by each state, and some states are stricter than others. Therefore, the proportion of poor people covered by Medicaid varies across states. About 70 million U.S. residents received Medicaid benefits at a

total cost of over $500 billion in 2015 (about 10 million Medicaid beneficiaries also receive Medicare). For many elderly, Medicaid covers long-term nursing care, which can cost taxpayers up to $100,000 a year per recipient.

The Supplemental Nutrition Assistance Program, or **SNAP**, provides vouchers that the poor can redeem for food. More than 45 million people received vouchers in an average month of 2015, and the monthly benefit averaged $125 per person. SNAP outlays totaled about 82 billion in 2015. The number of people in the program nearly doubled between 2005 and 2015. Still, some of those eligible for food vouchers do not apply for them. Other in-kind transfer programs for the poor include support for housing, day care, school breakfasts and lunches, extra food for pregnant women, energy assistance, and education and training, such as Head Start. *In all, the federal government funds more than 80 means-tested programs.*

Here's an overview: Federal redistribution programs totaled about $2.1 trillion in 2015, more than three times the amount spent on national defense. Adding in state and local outlays pushes the total to $2.9 trillion.

Exhibit 5 shows the growth in federal redistribution programs from 1962 to 2015. To eliminate the effects of inflation, figures are expressed in dollars of 2015 purchasing power. Overall, redistribution outlays have grown at an annual average of 6 percent since 1962, even after netting out the effects of inflation. Since 1962, government aid as a share of personal income has more than doubled. Social Security and Medicare, programs that mostly benefit the elderly, make up the greatest share of redistribution throughout the period. Next is Medicaid, which, as noted earlier, exceeds outlays for cash transfers and other in-kind transfers combined. Health care coverage is expected to increase after the full implementation of federal health care reform.

Some countries also have far more extensive redistribution programs than does the United States, basing a variety of public policies on income. For example, in Finland, where many fines are based on the offender's income, the heir

Bluemoon Stock/Jupiter Images

earned-income tax credit A federal program that supplements the wages of the working poor

Medicaid An in-kind transfer program that provides medical care for poor people; by far the most costly welfare program

SNAP An in-kind transfer program that offers low-income households vouchers redeemable for food; benefit levels vary inversely with household income

Exhibit 5

Federal Redistribution Outlays Each Year by Category, 1962–2015

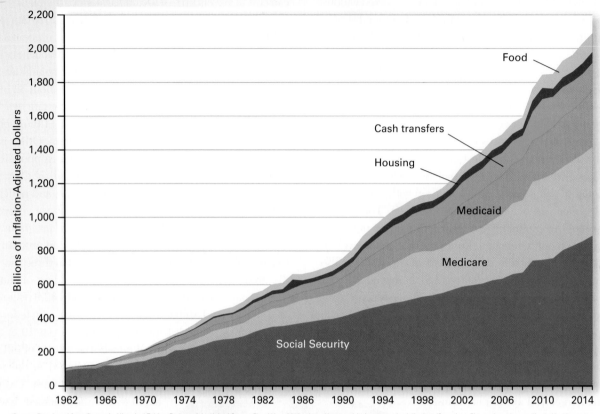

Source: Developed from figures in *Historical Tables, Budget of the United States, Fiscal Year 2015* at http://www.whitehouse.gov/omb/budget/Overview. Figures have been adjusted by the author to reflect constant purchasing power using the 2015 GDP Price Index. Data for 2015 are estimates based on the midyear budget update.

to a sausage fortune who was caught driving 50 miles per hour in a 25-miles-an-hour zone paid a $204,000 fine.[12]

18-3 WHO ARE THE POOR?

Who are the poor, and how has their composition changed over time? We will slice poverty statistics in several ways to examine the makeup of the group. Keep in mind that we are relying on official poverty estimates, which ignore the value of in-kind transfers, so, to that extent, official estimates overstate poverty.

18-3a Poverty and Age

Earlier we looked at poverty among the U.S. population. Here we focus on poverty and age. Exhibit 6 presents the

12. Joe Pinsker, "Finland, Home of the $103,000 Speeding Ticket," *The Atlantic*, 12 March 2015," at http://www.theatlantic.com/business/archive/2015/03/finland-home-of-the-103000-speeding-ticket/387484/.

poverty rates for three age groups since 1959: people less than 18 years old, those between 18 and 64, and those 65 and older. As you can see, poverty rates for each group declined between 1959 and 1968. The rate among those under 18 trended upward between the mid-1970s and the early 1980s. The rate then remained around 20 percent for a dozen years, and declined during the 1990s, and was 19.9% in 2013.

In 1959, the elderly were the poorest group, with a poverty rate of 35.2 percent. Poverty among the elderly declined to 9.5 percent by 2013, well below the rate of 13.6 percent for people 18 to 64 years of age. The decline in poverty among the elderly stems from the tremendous growth in spending for Social Security and Medicare. In real terms—that is, after adjusting for the effects of inflation—those two programs have grown more than twelvefold since 1959. (Medicare didn't even exist until 1965.) *Although not welfare programs in a strict sense, Social Security and Medicare have been hugely successful in reducing poverty among the elderly.*

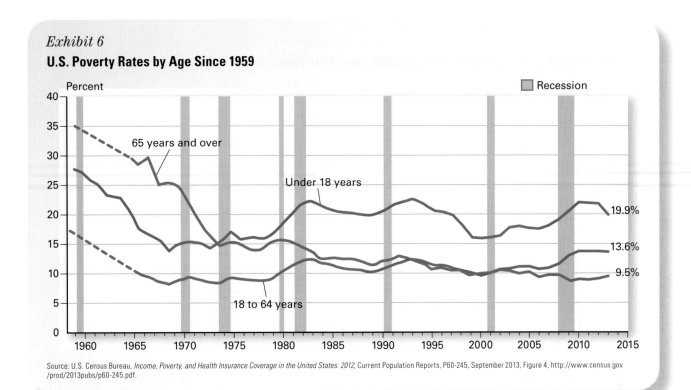

Exhibit 6

U.S. Poverty Rates by Age Since 1959

Source: U.S. Census Bureau, *Income, Poverty, and Health Insurance Coverage in the United States: 2012*, Current Population Reports, P60-245, September 2013, Figure 4, http://www.census.gov/prod/2013pubs/p60-245.pdf.

> **"Although not welfare programs in a strict sense, Social Security and Medicare have been hugely successful in reducing poverty among the elderly."**

18-3b Poverty and Public Choice

In a democracy, public policies depend very much on the political influence of the interest groups involved. In recent years, the elderly have become a powerful political force. The voter participation rate of those 65 and over is higher than that of any other age group. For example, people 65 years of age and older vote at triple the rate of those between 18 and 24 and four times that of welfare recipients. The political muscle of the elderly has been flexed whenever a question of Social Security or Medicare benefits is considered.

Unlike most interest groups, the elderly make up a group we all expect to join one day. The elderly are supported by at least five constituencies: (1) the elderly themselves; (2) people under 65 who are concerned about the current benefits of their parents or other elderly relatives; (3) people under 65 who are concerned about their own benefits in the future; (4) people who earn their living by caring for the elderly, such as doctors, nurses, and nursing-home operators; and (5) candidates for office who want to harvest the votes that seniors deliver. So the elderly have a broad constituency, and this pays off in terms of redistribution of wealth to the elderly and in the dramatic reduction of poverty among this group. The poverty rate among those 65 and over in 2013 was less than half that among those under 18.

18-3c The Feminization of Poverty

Another way to look at poverty is based on the status of the household head. Exhibit 7 compares poverty rates among families headed by females with no husband present with poverty rates for other families. Two trends are unmistakable. First, poverty rates among families headed by females are much higher than rates among other families—about four times higher. Second, poverty rates among female-headed families have trended down since the early 1990s, falling from 39.7 percent in 1991 to 33.9 percent in 2012.

The exhibit compares poverty among female householders to other families. What it doesn't show is the growth in the number of people in female-headed

Exhibit 7

Poverty Rates Are Much Higher for Families Headed by Females Than for Married-Couple Families

Source: Developed from data in U.S. Census Bureau, *Income and Poverty in the United States: 2013*, Current Population Reports P60-249, September 2014, Table 3, at http://www.census.gov/content/dam/Census/library/publications/2014/demo/p60-249.pdf.

households. The number of people in families headed by women increased 188 percent between 1965 and 2012, while the number of people in all other families grew just 26 percent. The percentage of births to unmarried mothers is five times greater today than in the 1960s. In 1960, only 1 in 200 children lived with a single parent who had never married. Today, 1 in 10 children lives with a single parent who has never married.

The United States has the highest teenage pregnancy rate in the developed world—twice the rate of Great Britain and 15 times that of Japan. Most recently, 88 percent of teen mothers in the United States were unmarried when they gave birth. Because fathers in such cases typically provide little support, children born outside marriage are likely to be poorer than other children. *The growth in the number of poor families since 1965 results overwhelmingly from a growth in the number of female householders.* The number of jobs in the U.S. economy more than doubled in the last fifty years. Families with a female householder were in the worst position to take advantage of this job growth. *Children of female householders are five times more likely to live in poverty than are other children. Young, single motherhood is a recipe for poverty.* Often the young mother drops out of school, which reduces her future earning possibilities when and if she seeks work outside the home. Even a strong economy is little help

> **"Young, single motherhood is a recipe for poverty."**

to households with nobody in the labor force. Worse yet, young, single mothers-to-be are less likely to seek adequate medical care; the result is a higher proportion of premature, underweight babies. This is one reason why the U.S. infant mortality rate exceeds that of some other industrialized countries. Compared to two-parent families, children in one-parent families are twice as likely to drop out of school, and girls from one-parent families are twice as likely to become single mothers themselves.

Because of a lack of education and limited job skills, most single mothers go on welfare. Before the 1996 welfare reform imposed lifetime limits on welfare, the average never-married mother had been on welfare for a decade, twice as long as divorced mothers on welfare. Of all teenagers who gave birth, the proportion unmarried was 13 percent in 1950, 30 percent in 1970, 67 percent in 1990, and 88 percent in 2010.[13]

13. "Births: Final Data for 2013," *National Vital Statistics Report*, 64 (Issue 1, 15 January 2015): Table 15, at http://www.cdc.gov/nchs/data/nvsr/nvsr64/nvsr64_01.pdf.

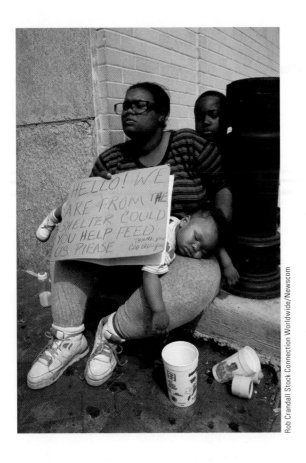

Poverty has therefore become increasingly feminized, mostly because female householders have become more common. Children from mothers who finished high school, married before having a child, and gave birth after age 20 are 10 times less likely to be poor than children from mothers who fail to do these things.[14] Worse yet, research suggests that adolescent boys engage in more delinquent behavior if there are no father figures in their lives (this does not appear to be true for adolescent girls).[15] Because the number of female householders has grown more rapidly among African Americans, the feminization of poverty has been more dramatic in those households. Seventy-two percent of all births to non-Hispanic black mothers in 2012 were to unmarried women, compared with 53 percent among women of Hispanic origin, 29 percent among non-Hispanic whites, and 17 percent among Asians and Pacific Islanders.[16] But we should be careful in drawing conclusions about the role of race or ethnicity per se, because black and Hispanic households are poorer on average than other households. Low income alone could account

for much of the difference in birth rates. In other words, a better comparison would adjust for income differences across groups, but such data are not available.

Exhibit 8 shows poverty rates for each of the 50 states in 2012. States with a deeper shade of red have higher poverty rates. States with no shading have lower rates. As you can see, poverty rates are lower along the Northeast corridor from New Hampshire to Virginia. Poverty rates are higher across the bottom half of the United States. Poverty rates tend to be higher in states where births to single mothers make up a larger percentage of all births. For example, Mississippi, Louisiana, and New Mexico have the highest rates of births to single mothers and also the highest poverty rates.

18-3d Poverty and Discrimination

To what extent has racial discrimination limited job opportunities and increased poverty among minorities? Discrimination can occur in many ways: in school funding, in housing, in employment, in career advancement. Also, discrimination in one area can affect opportunities in another. For example, housing discrimination can reduce job opportunities if a black family cannot move within commuting distance of the best jobs, or cannot take advantage of the job networking available in neighborhoods where more people are working. Researchers have found that individuals living in the same city block are more likely to have the same employer than those living in nearby blocks.[17] These neighborhood labor-market networks affect where people work, and they appear to be especially important for minorities and for those with fewer skills.[18] Job-market discrimination can take many forms. An employer may fail to hire a black job applicant because the applicant lacks training. But this lack of training can arise from discrimination in the schools, in union apprenticeship programs, or in training programs run by other employers. For example, evidence suggests that black workers receive less on-the-job training than otherwise similar white workers.

After adjusting for a variety of factors that could affect wages, such as education and work experience, research shows that white workers earn more than black workers. The gap between the two narrowed between 1940 and 1976 to the point where black workers earned only 7 percent less than white workers; then it widened

14. James Q. Wilson, "Human Remedies for Social Disorder," *National Affairs* (Spring 1998), p. 27.

15. Deborah Cobb-Clark and Erdal Tekin, "Fathers and Youth's Delinquent Behavior," *Review of Economics of the Household*, 12 (June 2014): 327–358.

16. "Births: Final Data for 2013," *National Vital Statistics Report*, 64 (Issue 1, 15 January 2015), Table 15, at http://www.cdc.gov/nchs/data/nvsr/nvsr64 /nvsr64_01.pdf.

17. Patrick Bayer, Stephen L. Ross, and Giorgio Topa, "Place of Work and Place of Residence: Informal Hiring Networks and Labor Market Outcomes," *Journal of Political Economy*, 116 (December 2008): 1150–1196.

18. Judith Hellerstein, Melissa McInerney, and David Neumark, "Neighbors and Coworkers: The Importance of Residential Labor Market Networks," *Journal of Labor Economics*, 29 (October 2011): 659–695.

Exhibit 8
Percent of Population Living in Poverty by State in 2013

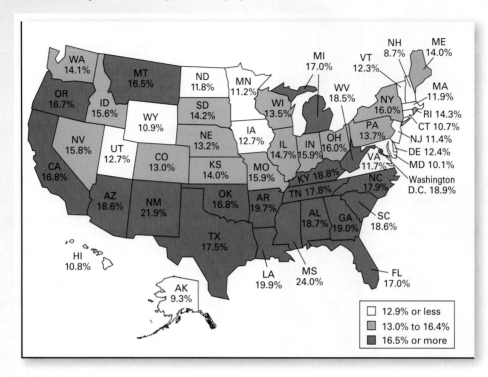

Source: U.S. Census Bureau, *Poverty: 2012 and 2013*, September, 2014 at http://www.census.gov/content/dam/Census/library/publications/2014/acs/acsbr13-01.pdf.

somewhat.[19] Since 1993, the gap has again narrowed. Could explanations besides job discrimination account for the wage gap? Though the data adjust for *years* of schooling, some research suggests that black workers received a lower *quality* of schooling than white workers. For example, black students were less likely to use computers in school. Inner-city schools often have more problems with classroom discipline, which takes time and attention away from instruction. And schools serving the poorest students experience the highest rates of teacher absences.[20] Teacher turnover from year to year also harms poor students the most (teacher turnover is 50 percent higher in poorer school districts than in more affluent ones).[21] Such differences in the quality of education could account for at least a portion of the remaining gap in standardized wages.

Evidence of discrimination comes from studies where otherwise similar white and black candidates are sent to seek jobs, rent apartments, or apply for mortgages. For example, white and black job applicants with similar qualifications and résumés applied for the same job. These studies find that employers are less likely to interview or offer a job to minority applicants. Minority applicants also tend to be treated less favorably by real estate agents and lenders. Studies conclude that one quarter to one third of the wage gap between blacks and whites was the result of discrimination.[22]

18-3e Affirmative Action

The Equal Employment Opportunity Commission, established by the Civil Rights Act of 1964, monitors cases involving unequal pay for equal work and unequal access to promotion. All companies doing business with the federal government had to set numerical hiring,

19. Michael Boozer, Alan Krueger, and Shari Wolkon, "Race and School Quality Since *Brown v. Board of Education*," *Brookings Papers on Economic Activity: Microeconomics* (1992): 269–326.

20. Charles Clotfelter, Helen Ladd, and Jacob Vigdor, "Are Teacher Absences Worth Worrying About in the United States?" *Education Finance and Policy*, 4 (Spring 2009): 115–149.

21. Matthew Ronfeldt, Susanna Loeb, and James Wyckoff, "How Teacher Turnover Harms Student Achievement," *American Educational Research Journal*, 50 (February 2013): 4–36.

22. Kerwin Kofi Charles and Jonathan Guryan, "Prejudice and Wages: An Empirical Assessment of Becker's *The Economics of Discrimination*," *Journal of Political Economy*, 116 (October 2008): 773–809; and Roland Fryer, Devah Page, and Jorg Spenkuch, "Racial Disparities in Job Finding and Offered Wages," *Journal of Law & Economics*, 56 (August 2013): 633–689.

promotion, and training goals to ensure that these firms did not discriminate in hiring on the basis of race, sex, religion, or national origin. Black employment increased in those firms required to file affirmative action plans.[23] The fraction of the black labor force employed in white-collar jobs increased from 16.5 percent in 1960 to 40.5 percent in 1981—an increase that greatly exceeded the growth of white-collar jobs in the labor force as a whole. Research also suggests that civil rights legislation played a role in narrowing the black-white earnings gap between 1960 and the mid-1970s.[24]

Attention focused on hiring practices and equality of opportunity at the state and local levels as well, as governments introduced so-called *set-aside* programs to guarantee minorities a share of contracts. But a 1995 U.S. Supreme Court decision challenged affirmative action programs, ruling that Congress must meet a rigorous legal standard to justify any contracting or hiring practice based on race, especially programs that reserve jobs for minorities and women. Programs must be shown to be in response to injustices created by past discrimination, said the Court.

In summary, evidence suggests that black workers earn less than white workers after adjustment for other factors that could affect wages, such as education and job experience. Part of this wage gap may also reflect differences in the quality of education, differences that could themselves be the result of discrimination.[25] Keep in mind that unemployment rates are higher among blacks than among whites and are higher still among black teenagers, the group most in need of job skills and job experience. *But we should also note that black families are not a homogeneous group. In fact, the distribution of income is more uneven among black families than among the population as a whole.*

On the upside, there is a growing middle class among black households. Since 1970, the number of black doctors, nurses, college professors, and newspaper reporters has more than tripled; the number of black engineers, computer programmers, accountants, managers, and administrators has quadrupled; the number of black elected officials has increased sixfold; and the number of black lawyers has increased more than sixfold. In Georgia, for example, the number of black lawyers increased from just 54 in 1970 to more than 2,000 today.

18-4 SOME UNINTENDED CONSEQUENCES OF INCOME ASSISTANCE

On the plus side, antipoverty programs increase the consumption possibilities of poor families, and that's a good thing, especially because children are the largest poverty group. And welfare payments may help reduce crime, at least temporarily.[26] But programs to assist the poor have secondary effects that limit their ability to reduce poverty over time. Here we consider some unintended consequences.

Society, through government, tries to provide families with an adequate standard of living, but society also wants to ensure that only the most needy receive benefits. As we have seen, income assistance consists of a combination of cash and in-kind transfer programs. Because these programs are designed to help the poor and only the poor, benefits decrease as income from other sources increases. With transfers declining sharply as earned income increases, welfare recipients face a high marginal tax rate on earned income. An increase in earnings may reduce benefits from TANF, Medicaid, SNAP (food vouchers), housing assistance, energy assistance, and others among the 80 means-tested programs.

With a loss in support from each program as earned income increases, working may lead to little or no increase in total income. Over certain income ranges, a welfare recipient may lose more than $1 in welfare benefits for each additional $1 in earnings. Thus, the *marginal tax rate* on earned income could exceed 100 percent! Additional benefits introduced during the Great Recession also decline as income grows, increasing the marginal tax rate between 2007 and 2009, especially among unmarried household heads.[27] For example, an $8,000 tax credit for home buyers phased out as income increased. Thus, an unintended consequence of an expanded safety net was to reduce the incentive to work and to earn.[28]

Holding even a part-time job involves some costs—for clothing, transportation, and child care, for instance—not to mention the loss of free time. Such a system of perverse incentives can frustrate people trying to work their way off welfare. *The high marginal tax rate discourages employment and self-sufficiency.* In

23. James Smith and Finis Welch, "Black Economic Progress After Myrdal," *Journal of Economic Literature*, 27 (June 1989): 519–564.

24. David Card and Alan Krueger, "Trends in Relative Black-White Earnings Revisited," *American Economic Review*, 83 (May 1993): 85–91.

25. Huoying Wu, "Can the Human Capital Approach Explain Life-Cycle Wage Differentials Between Races and Sexes?" *Economic Inquiry*, 45 (January 2007): 24–39.

26. C. Fritz Foley, "Welfare Benefits and Crime," *Review of Economics and Statistics*, 93 (March 2011): 97–112.

27. Casey Mulligan, "Recent Marginal Income Tax Rate Changes By Skill and Marital Status," in *Tax Policy and the Economy*, Jeffrey Brown, ed. (University of Chicago Press, 2013): 69–100.

28. Casey Mulligan, "The Expanding Social Safety Net," in his book *The Redistribution Recession: How Labor Market Distortions Contracted the Economy* (Oxford University Press, 2012): 41–97.

> **"The high marginal tax rate discourages employment and self-sufficiency."**

some cases, welfare benefits exceed the income resulting from full-time employment. For example, a study of just one program, housing assistance, found that among working-age, able-bodied adults, housing vouchers reduced their labor supply by 6 percent and reduced their labor-market earnings by 10 percent.[29] And a recent income-assistance program in France aimed at single adults cut the labor supply of single adults by about 8 percent.[30]

The longer people stay out of the labor force, the more their job skills deteriorate, so when they do look for work, their productivity is lower than when they were last employed. This reduces their expected wage, making work even less attractive. Some economists argue that in this way, welfare benefits can lead to long-term dependency. While welfare seems to be a rational choice for someone in the short run, it has unfavorable long-term consequences for the family, for society, and for the economy.

A serious concern is whether children on welfare are more likely to end up on welfare as adults. Is there a cycle of dependency? Why might we expect one? Children in welfare households may learn the ropes about the welfare system and may come to view welfare as a normal way of life rather than as a temporary bridge over a rough patch. Research indicates that daughters from welfare families are more likely than daughters from other families to participate in the welfare system themselves and are more likely to have premarital births.[31] It is difficult to say whether welfare "causes" the link between mother and daughter, because the same factors that contribute to a mother's welfare status could also contribute to her daughter's welfare status. Evidence of a link is weaker when it comes to sons from welfare families.

A final unintended consequence of income assistance occurs because these programs are also subject to fraud, abuse, and simple clerical errors. For example, the U.S. Treasury estimated that about one quarter of

earned-income tax credit payments were issued improperly, which in 2015 would amount to about $18 billion in improper payments.[32]

18-5 WELFARE REFORMS

There has been much dissatisfaction with the welfare system among both those who pay for the programs and direct beneficiaries. Welfare reforms introduced nearly two decades ago have been aimed at reducing long-term dependency.

18-5a 1996 Reforms

Some analysts believe that one way to reduce poverty is to provide welfare recipients with job skills and make them find jobs. Even before the 1996 federal reform of welfare, to be discussed shortly, some sort of "workfare" component for welfare recipients operated in most states. In these states, as a condition of receiving welfare, the head of the household had to participate in education and training programs, search for work, or take some paid or unpaid position. The idea was to expose people on welfare to the job market. Evidence from various states indicates that programs involving mandatory job searches, short-term unpaid work, and training could operate at low cost and could increase employment. The government saved money because those in welfare-to-work programs left welfare rolls sooner.

Reforms at the state level set the stage for federal reforms. By far the biggest reform in the welfare system in the last 75 years came with the 1996 legislation that replaced Aid to Families with Dependent Children (AFDC) with Temporary Assistance for Needy Families (TANF). Whereas the AFDC program set eligibility rules and left federal costs open ended through matching grants to the states, TANF offers a fixed grant to the states to run their welfare programs. Under the new system, states have much more control over their own welfare programs. But concerns about welfare dependency fostered some special provisions. The act imposes a five-year lifetime limit on cash transfers and requires states to move a certain percentage of people from welfare to work.

Aside from the time limits and work participation rates imposed by the federal government, states are free to set benefit levels and experiment however they choose. For example, about half the states impose time limits shorter

29. Brian Jacobs and Jens Ludwig, "The Effects of Housing Assistance on Labor Supply: Evidence From a Voucher Lottery," *American Economic Review*, 102 (January 2012): 272–304.

30. Olivier Bargain and Karina Doorley, "Caught in the Trap: Welfare's Disincentive and the Labor Supply of Single Men," *Journal of Public Economics*, 95 (October 2011): 1096–1100.

31. Robert Moffitt, "Welfare Reform: The U.S. Experience," in *From Welfare to Work*, Paper Presented at the Economic Council of Sweden Conference, 7 May 2007.

32. Treasury Inspector General for Tax Administration (TIGTA), "The Internal Revenue Service Is Not in Compliance With All Improper Payments and Recovery Act Requirements," Report No. 2012-40-028, March 2 (TIGTA, 2012).

than five years. Some observers fear that states now have an incentive to keep welfare costs down by cutting benefits. To avoid becoming destinations for poor people—that is, to avoid becoming "welfare magnets"—states may be tempted to offer relatively low benefits. The fear is that states will undercut benefits in what has been called a "race to the bottom."

18-5b Welfare Rolls Have Declined

Work requirements and time limits have resulted in substantial declines in the welfare caseload. The number of welfare recipients peaked in January 1994 at 14.2 million, mostly single women with children. By September 2014, the rolls had fallen to 3.4 million—76 percent below the peak. Exhibit 9 shows since 1960 the percentage of the U.S. population on welfare. Note the sharp decline in recent years. As a share of the U.S. population, welfare recipients fell from 5.5 percent in 1994 to only 1.1 percent in 2014, the lowest rate in the last half century. Despite the the Great Recession of 2007–2009, the worst since the Great Depression of the 1930s, welfare rolls have remained low.

A major result of welfare reform has been a substantial increase in employment among mothers who head families, especially those who have never married. About two-thirds found work during the period immediately after reform, and many more got jobs in the next year or two. This is a remarkable improvement from historical employment rates of women on welfare of about 10 percent. Their incomes went up on average, and they tended to hang onto their jobs. New York City officials reported that 85 percent of those getting off welfare did so because they had found work.

Because the welfare rolls have declined but federal grants have not, welfare spending per recipient increased significantly. Most states combined tough new eligibility rules with an expanded menu of welfare services. States have made large investments in work-related services such as job placement, transportation, and especially child care. Most of those going to work can continue to receive food vouchers, child care, and Medicaid. As noted earlier, the earned-income tax credit also helps low-income workers—boosting pay up to $6,242 in 2015. Twenty-five states have added their own earned-income tax credits.

Despite the good news, some poor people are still having a hard time, particularly after the Great Recession. Because many on welfare are poorly educated and have few job skills, wages for some remain low, and part-time work is common. Still, welfare reform has been quite successful in getting people off welfare and into jobs. And the poverty rate among families headed by women declined from 35.6 percent in 1993, before welfare reform, to 30.6 percent most recently.

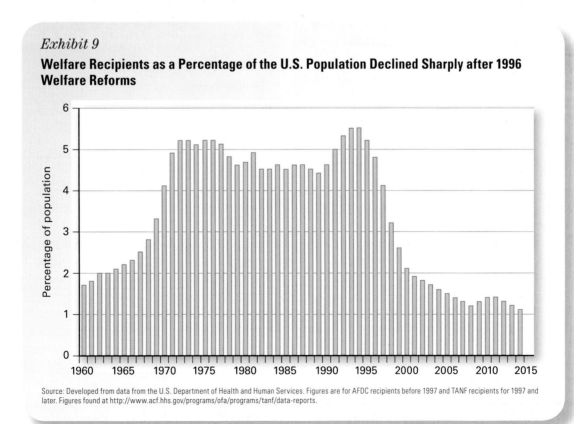

Exhibit 9

Welfare Recipients as a Percentage of the U.S. Population Declined Sharply after 1996 Welfare Reforms

Source: Developed from data from the U.S. Department of Health and Human Services. Figures are for AFDC recipients before 1997 and TANF recipients for 1997 and later. Figures found at http://www.acf.hhs.gov/programs/ofa/programs/tanf/data-reports.

family's capacity to earn income has serious consequences for dependent children. *Family structure is a primary determinant of family income.* One in five children in the United States lives in poverty. These children are the innocent victims of the changing family structure. Recent welfare reforms have succeeded in reducing welfare rolls, increasing employment among single mothers, and reducing the poverty rate among families headed by women.

18-6 FINAL WORD

Government redistribution programs have been most successful at reducing poverty among the elderly. But poverty rates among children increased because of the growth in the number of female householders. We might ask why transfer programs have reduced poverty rates more among the elderly than among female householders. Transfer programs do not encourage people to get old; that process occurs naturally and is largely independent of the level of transfers. But the level and availability of transfer programs at the margin could influence some young unmarried women as they are deciding whether or not to have a child and may, at the margin, influence a married mother's decision to get divorced.

Most transfers in the economy are not from the government but are in-kind transfers within the family, from parents to children. Thus, any change in a

STUDY TOOLS 18

READY TO STUDY? IN THE BOOK, YOU CAN:

- ☐ Work the Problems at the end of the chapter.
- ☐ Rip out the chapter review card for a handy summary of the chapter and key terms.

ONLINE AT CENGAGEBRAIN.COM YOU CAN:

- ☐ Collect StudyBits while you read and study the chapter.
- ☐ Quiz yourself on key concepts.
- ☐ Prepare for tests with chapter flash cards as well as flash cards that you create.
- ☐ Watch videos to explore economics further.

CHAPTER 18 PROBLEMS

Your instructor can access the answers to these problems online at http://cengagebrain.com.

18-1 Identify reasons why incomes differ across households, and why the income gap has increased

1. *(Distribution of Household Income)* Look at the graph below. How would you explain the shift of the U.S. income distribution in the last two decades?

Share of Aggregate Household Income by Quintile 1980–2013

2. *(Lorenz Curve)* What is a Lorenz curve? What does the Lorenz curve below illustrate?

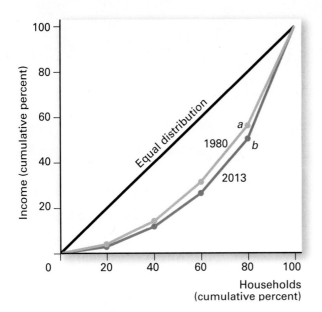

18-2 Summarize what has happened to the incidence of poverty since 1960, and determine when and why the greatest progress was made in reducing poverty

3. *(Poverty Rates Over Time)* During what period since 1960 did the U.S. poverty rate fall the most? Why? Which age group has shown the most decline in poverty rates since 1960 and why?

4. *(Official Poverty Level)* Although the poverty rate among single mothers has decreased since 1960, the number of poor children from such families has more than doubled. Explain.

5. *(Income Differences)* List some reasons why household incomes differ. Which factors are the most important?

6. *(Official Poverty Level)* How does the U.S. Department of Agriculture calculate the official poverty level? What government assistance programs does the Census Bureau consider when calculating household income? What programs are ignored?

18-3 Describe a primary source of poverty among families in the United States

7. *(Poverty and Age)* Poverty among the elderly fell dramatically between 1959 and 1974 and has continued to decline. However, poverty among those less than 18 years old is no lower today than in the 1970s. Why have the experiences of these two age groups differed?

18-4 Outline some unintended consequences of efforts to reduce poverty

8. *(Disincentives)* How does the implicit tax on earned income (in the form of lost benefits from government assistance programs as earned income increases) affect work incentives? How do some people avoid the implicit tax?

18-5 Describe how the 1996 federal welfare reforms affected the number of people on welfare

9. *(Welfare Reform)* What has happened to the percentage of the U.S. population on welfare since 1994? What explains the change over time?

19 | International Trade

LEARNING OUTCOMES

After studying this chapter, you will be able to...

19-1 Outline the gains from trade, and explain why countries might still decide to trade even if no country had a comparative advantage

19-2 Explain how trade restrictions harm an economy, and why they persist

19-3 Identify international efforts to reduce trade barriers

19-4 Summarize five arguments often used to justify trade restrictions, and describe some unintended consequences of protecting certain industries from international competition

After finishing this chapter go to **PAGE 342** for **STUDY TOOLS**

Topics discussed in Chapter 19 include:

- Gains from trade
- Absolute and comparative advantage revisited
- Tariffs and quotas
- Cost of trade restrictions
- Free trade agreements
- World Trade Organization, or WTO
- Common markets
- Arguments for trade restrictions

The world is a giant shopping mall, and Americans are big spenders. For example, the U.S. population is less than 5 percent of the world's population, but Americans buy 38 percent of the diamond jewelry sold around the world. Americans also buy Japanese cars, French wine, European vacations, Chinese products galore, and millions of other goods and services from around the globe. Foreigners buy U.S. products too—grain, aircraft, movies, software, trips to New York City, and millions of other goods and services. For example, California grows 80 percent of the world's almond supply.

In this chapter, we examine the gains from international trade and the effects of trade restrictions on the allocation of resources. The analysis is based on the familiar tools of demand and supply.

> **"Why don't we produce everything ourselves?"**

19-1 THE GAINS FROM TRADE

A Virginia family that sits down to a dinner of Kansas prime rib, Idaho potatoes, and California string beans, with Georgia peach cobbler for dessert, is benefiting from interstate trade. You already understand why the residents of one state trade with those of another. Back in Chapter 2, you learned about the gains arising from specialization and trade. You may recall how you and your roommate could maximize output when you each specialized. The law of comparative advantage says that the individual with the lowest opportunity cost of producing a particular good should specialize in that good. Just as individuals benefit from specialization and trade, so do states and, indeed, nations. To reap the gains that arise from specialization, countries engage in international trade. *Each*

> **"Each country specializes in making goods with the lowest opportunity cost."**

country specializes in making goods with the lowest opportunity cost.

19-1a A Profile of Exports and Imports

Just as some states are more involved in interstate trade than others, some nations are more involved in international trade than others. For example, exports account for about one-quarter of the gross domestic product (GDP) in Canada and the United Kingdom; about one-third of GDP in Germany, Sweden, and Switzerland; and about half of GDP in the Netherlands. Despite the perception that Japan has a huge export sector, exports make up only about one-sixth of its GDP.

U.S. Exports

U.S. exports of goods and services amounted to $2.3 trillion in 2014, or 13 percent of GDP. The left panel of Exhibit 1 shows the composition by major category in 2014.

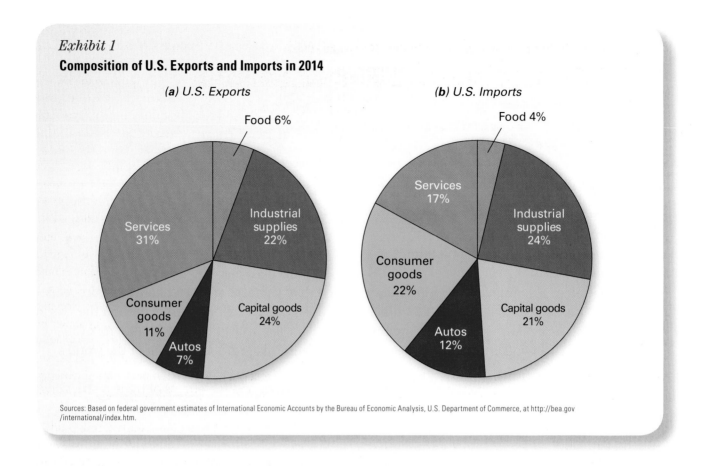

Exhibit 1

Composition of U.S. Exports and Imports in 2014

(a) U.S. Exports

- Food 6%
- Services 31%
- Industrial supplies 22%
- Consumer goods 11%
- Autos 7%
- Capital goods 24%

(b) U.S. Imports

- Food 4%
- Services 17%
- Industrial supplies 24%
- Consumer goods 22%
- Capital goods 21%
- Autos 12%

Sources: Based on federal government estimates of International Economic Accounts by the Bureau of Economic Analysis, U.S. Department of Commerce, at http://bea.gov /international/index.htm.

The largest category is services, which accounted for 31 percent of U.S. exports. U.S. service exports include transportation, insurance, banking, education, consulting, and tourism. Capital goods ranked second at 24 percent of the total, with aircraft the largest export industry (Boeing is the top U.S. exporter). The third most important are industrial supplies, at 22 percent of exports, with chemicals and plastics at the top of this list. Capital goods and industrial supplies, which help foreign producers make stuff, together accounted for nearly half of U.S. exports. Consumer goods (except food and autos, which appear separately) accounted for only 11 percent of exports (pharmaceuticals tops this group). Consumer goods also include entertainment products, such as movies and recorded music.

U.S. Imports

U.S. imports of goods and services totaled $2.8 trillion in 2014, or 16 percent relative to GDP. The right panel of Exhibit 1 shows the composition of U.S. imports. The biggest category, at 24 percent, is industrial supplies, with petroleum products accounting for most of that. Although consumer goods accounted for only 11 percent of U.S. exports, they were 22 percent of U.S. imports, with pharmaceuticals the largest item. Ranked third is

capital goods, at 21 percent, with computers the largest item. Note that services, which accounted for 31 percent of U.S. exports, were only 17 percent of U.S. imports.

Trading Partners

World trade totaled about $21 trillion in 2014, or 20 percent relative to world output of $105 trillion that year. To give you some feel for America's trading partners, here were the top 10 destinations for U.S. exports of goods and services for 2014 in order of importance: Canada, Mexico, China, the United Kingdom, Japan, Germany, Brazil, South Korea, France, and India. The top 10 sources of U.S. imports in order of importance were China, Canada, Mexico, Japan, Germany, the United Kingdom, South Korea, France, India, and Saudi Arabia.

19-1b Production Possibilities without Trade

The rationale behind most international trade is obvious. For example, the United States produces little coffee because, except for Hawaii, our climate is not suited to growing coffee beans. More revealing, however, are the gains from trade where the comparative advantage is not so obvious. Suppose

Exhibit 2

Production Possibilities Schedules for the United States and Izodia

(a) The United States						
Production Possibilities with 100 Million Workers (millions of units per day)						
	U_1	U_2	U_3	U_4	U_5	U_6
Food	600	480	360	240	120	0
Clothing	0	60	120	180	240	300

(b) Izodia						
Production Possibilities with 200 Million Workers (millions of units per day)						
	I_1	I_2	I_3	I_4	I_5	I_6
Food	200	160	120	80	40	0
Clothing	0	80	160	240	320	400

that just two goods—food and clothing—are produced and consumed and that there are only two countries in the world—the United States, with a labor force of 100 million workers, and the mythical country of Izodia, with 200 million workers. The conclusions derived from this simple model have general relevance for international trade.

Exhibit 2 presents production possibilities tables for each country, based on the size of the labor force and the productivity of workers in each country. The exhibit assumes that each country has a given technology and that labor is efficiently employed. If no trade occurs between countries, Exhibit 2 also represents each country's *consumption possibilities* table. The production numbers imply that each worker in the United States can produce either 6 units of food or 3 units of clothing per day. If all 100 million U.S. workers produce food, they make 600 million units per day, as shown in column U_1 in panel (a). If all U.S. workers make clothing, they produce 300 million units per day, as shown in column U_6. The columns in between show some workers making food and some making clothing. Because a U.S. worker can produce either 6 units of food or 3 units

of clothing, *the opportunity cost of 1 more unit of clothing is 2 units of food.*

Suppose Izodian workers are less educated, work with less capital, and farm less fertile soil than U.S. workers, so each Izodian worker can produce only 1 unit of food or 2 units of clothing per day. If all 200 million Izodian workers specialize in food, they can make 200 million units per day, as shown in column I_1 in panel (b) of Exhibit 2. If they all make clothing, total output is 400 million units per day, as shown in column I_6. Some intermediate production possibilities are also listed in the exhibit. Because an Izodian worker can produce either 1 unit of food or 2 units of clothing, *the opportunity cost of 1 more unit of clothing is ½ unit of food.*

We can convert the data in Exhibit 2 to a production possibilities frontier for each country, as shown in Exhibit 3. In each diagram, the amount of food produced is measured on the vertical axis and the amount of clothing on the horizontal axis. U.S. combinations are shown in the left panel by U_1, U_2, and so on. Izodian combinations

Exhibit 3

Production Possibilities Frontiers for the United States and Izodia Without Trade (millions of units per day)

Panel (a) shows the U.S. production possibilities frontier; its slope indicates that the opportunity cost of an additional unit of clothing is 2 units of food. Panel (b) shows production possibilities for Izodia; an additional unit of clothing costs 1/2 unit of food. Clothing has a lower opportunity cost in Izodia.

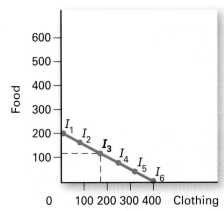

are shown in the right panel by I_1, I_2, and so on. Because we assume for simplicity that resources are perfectly adaptable to the production of either good, each production possibilities curve is a straight line. The slope of this line differs between countries because the opportunity cost of production differs between countries. The slope equals the opportunity cost of clothing—the amount of food a country must give up to produce another unit of clothing. The U.S. slope is −2, and the Izodian slope is −½. The U.S. slope is steeper because its opportunity cost of producing clothing is greater.

Exhibit 3 illustrates possible combinations of food and clothing that residents of each country can produce and consume if all resources are efficiently employed and there is no trade between the two countries. **Autarky** is the situation of national self-sufficiency, in which there is no economic interaction with foreign producers or consumers. Suppose that U.S. producers maximize profit and U.S. consumers maximize utility with the combination of 240 million units of food and 180 million units of clothing—combination U_4. This is called *autarky equilibrium.* Suppose also that Izodians are in autarky equilibrium, identified as combination I_3, with 120 million units of food and 160 million units of clothing.

19-1c Consumption Possibilities Based on Comparative Advantage

In our example, each U.S. worker can produce more clothing and more food per day than can each Izodian worker, so Americans have an *absolute advantage* in the production of both goods. Recall from Chapter 2 that having an absolute advantage means being able to produce something using fewer resources than other producers require. Should the U.S. economy remain in autarky—that is, self-sufficient in both food and clothing—or could there be gains from specialization and trade?

As long as the opportunity cost of production differs between the two countries, there are gains from specialization and trade. *According to the law of comparative advantage, each country should specialize in producing the good with the lower opportunity cost.* The opportunity cost of producing 1 more unit of clothing is 2 units of food in the United States compared with ½ unit of food in Izodia. Because the opportunity cost of producing clothing is lower in Izodia, both countries will gain if

> **"According to the law of comparative advantage, each country should specialize in producing the good with the lower opportunity cost."**

Izodia specializes in clothing and exports some to the United States, and the United States specializes in food and exports some to Izodia.

Before countries can trade, however, they must agree on how much of one good exchanges for another—that is, they must agree on the **terms of trade**. As long as Americans can get more than ½ a unit of clothing for each unit of food produced, and as long as Izodians can get more than ½ a unit of food for each unit of clothing produced, both countries will be better off specializing. After all, in autarky it costs Americans ½ unit of clothing to produce another unit of food, and it costs Izodians ½ unit of food to produce another unit of clothing, so neither country would want to trade unless they can improve on that.

Suppose that market forces shape the terms of trade so that 1 unit of clothing exchanges for 1 unit of food. To produce another unit of clothing themselves, Americans would have to sacrifice 2 units of food. Likewise, to produce another unit of food themselves, Izodians would have to sacrifice 2 units of clothing.

Exhibit 4 shows that with 1 unit of food trading for 1 unit of clothing, Americans and Izodians can consume anywhere along their blue consumption possibilities frontiers. *The consumption possibilities frontier* shows a nation's possible combinations of goods available as a result of specialization and trade. (Note that the U.S. consumption possibilities curve does not extend to the right of 400 million units of clothing, because Izodia could produce no more than that.) The amount each country actually consumes depends on the relative preferences for food and clothing. Suppose Americans select combination U in panel (a) and Izodians select point I in panel (b).

Without trade, the United States produces and consumes 240 million units of food and 180 million units of clothing. With trade, Americans specialize to

Exhibit 4

Production (and Consumption) Possibilities Frontiers With Trade (millions of units per day)

If Izodia and the United States can specialize and trade at the rate of 1 unit of clothing for 1 unit of food, both can benefit as shown by the blue lines. By trading with Izodia, the U.S. can produce only food and still consume combination *U*, which has more food and more clothing than *U₄*. Likewise, Izodia can attain preferred combination *I* by producing only clothing, then trading some clothing for U.S. food.

(a) The United States

(b) Izodia

produce 600 million units of food; they eat 400 million units and exchange the rest for 200 million units of Izodian clothing. This consumption combination is reflected by point *U*. Through exchange, Americans increase their consumption of both food and clothing.

Without trade, Izodians produce and consume 120 million units of food and 160 million units of clothing. With trade, Izodians specialize to produce 400 million units of clothing; they wear 200 million and exchange the rest for 200 million units of U.S. food. This consumption combination is shown by point *I*. Through trade, Izodians, like Americans, are able to increase their consumption of both goods. How is this possible?

Because Americans are more efficient in the production of food and Izodians more efficient in the production of clothing, total output increases when each specializes. Without specialization and trade, world production is 360 million units of food and 340 million units of clothing. With specialization and trade, food increases to 600 million units and clothing to 400 million units. Thus, both countries increase consumption with trade. *Although*

> **❝ Remember that comparative advantage, not absolute advantage, creates gains from specialization and trade. ❞**

the United States has an absolute advantage in both goods, differences in the opportunity cost of production between the two nations ensure that specialization and trade result in mutual gains. Remember that comparative advantage, not absolute advantage, creates gains from specialization and trade. The only constraint on trade is that, for each good, *world production must equal world consumption.*

We simplified trade relations in our example to highlight the gains from specialization and trade. We assumed that each country would completely specialize in producing a particular good, that resources were equally adaptable to the production of either good, that the costs of transporting goods from one country to another were inconsequential, and that there were no problems in arriving at the terms of trade. The world is not that simple. For example, we don't expect a country to produce just one good. Regardless, there is broad evidence that specialization based on the law of comparative advantage still leads to gains from trade. For example, after examining the productivity of 17 crops on 1.6 million parcels of land in 55 countries around the world, researchers found strong evidence that international trade arises from comparative advantage.[1]

19-1d Reasons for International Specialization

Countries trade with one another—or, more precisely, people, firms, and governments in one country trade with those in another—because each

1. Arnaud Costinot and David Donaldson, "Ricardo's Theory of Comparative Advantage: Old Idea, New Evidence," *American Economic Review*, 102 (May 2012): 453–458.

side expects to gain from trade. How do we know what each country should produce and what each should trade?

Differences in Resource Endowments

Differences in resource endowments often create differences in the opportunity cost of production across countries. Some countries are blessed with an abundance of fertile land and favorable growing seasons. The United States, for example, has been called the "breadbasket of the world" because of its rich farmland ideal for growing wheat and corn. Coffee grows best in the climate and elevation of Colombia, Brazil, and Vietnam. Honduras has the ideal climate for bananas. Thus, the United States exports wheat and corn and imports coffee and bananas. Seasonal differences across countries also encourage trade. For example, in the winter, Americans import fruit from Chile, and Canadians travel to Florida for sun and fun. In the summer, Americans export fruit to Chile, and Americans travel to Canada for camping and hiking.

Resources are often concentrated in particular countries: crude oil in Saudi Arabia, fertile soil in the United States, copper ore in Chile, rough diamonds in South Africa. The United States grows abundant supplies of oil seeds such as soybeans and sunflowers, but does not yet extract enough crude oil to satisfy domestic demand. Thus, the United States exports oil seeds and imports crude oil. More generally, *countries export products they can produce more cheaply in return for products that are unavailable domestically or are cheaper elsewhere.*

Exhibit 5 shows, for 12 key resources, U.S. production as a percentage of U.S. consumption. If production falls short of consumption, this means the United States imports the difference. For example, because America grows coffee only in Hawaii, U.S. production is only 1 percent of U.S. consumption, so nearly all coffee is imported. The exhibit also shows that U.S. production falls short of U.S. consumption for crude oil and natural gas, and for metals such as zinc, copper, and aluminum. If U.S. production exceeds U.S. consumption, the United States exports the difference. For example, U.S.–grown cotton amounts to 502 percent of U.S. cotton consumption, so most U.S.-grown cotton is exported. U.S. production also exceeds U.S. consumption for other crops, including wheat, oil seeds (soybeans, sunflower seeds, cottonseeds), and coarse grains (corn, barley, oats). In short, when it comes to basic resources, the United States is a net importer of crude oil, natural gas, and metals and a net exporter of coal and farm crops.

Exhibit 5

U.S. Production as a Percentage of U.S. Consumption for Various Resources

If U.S. production is less than 100 percent of U.S. consumption, then imports make up the difference. If U.S. production exceeds U.S. consumption, then the amount by which production exceeds 100 percent of consumption is exported.

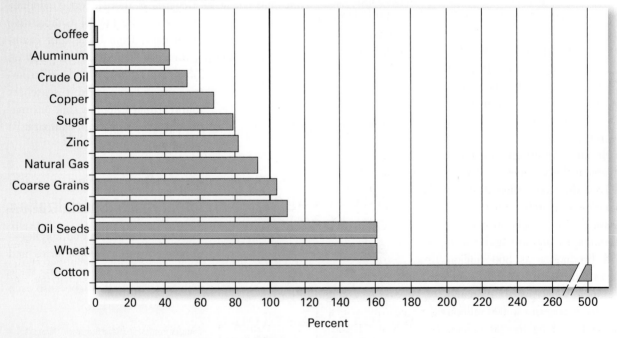

Source: Based on annual figures selected from *The Economist Pocket World in Figures: 2015 Edition* (Profile Books, 2014).

Economies of Scale

If production is subject to *economies of scale*—that is, if the long-run average cost of production falls as a firm expands its scale of operation—countries can gain from trade if each nation specializes. Such specialization allows firms in each nation to produce more of a particular good, which reduces average costs. For example, one country can make computer chips that are sold in many countries, and another country can make cars that are sold in many countries. The primary reason for establishing the single integrated market of the European Union was to offer producers there a large, open market of now more than 500 million consumers. Producers could thereby achieve economies of scale. Firms and countries producing at the lowest opportunity costs are most competitive in international markets. For example, most of the world's buttons and zippers come from the same Chinese city. Another Chinese city is the source of most of the world's socks.

Differences in Tastes

Even if all countries had identical resource endowments and combined those resources with equal efficiency, each country would still gain from trade as long as tastes differed across countries. Consumption patterns differ across countries and some of this results from differences in tastes. For example, the Czechs and Irish drink three times as much beer per capita as do the Swiss and Swedes. The French drink three times as much wine as do Australians. The Danes eat twice as much pork as do Americans. Americans eat twice as much chicken as do Hungarians. Americans like chicken, but not all of it. The United States is the world's leading exporter of chicken feet, and China is the world's leading importer (Tyson Foods alone ships

about three billion chicken feet to China each year). Residents of West Africa prefer the dark bony meat of a chicken, such as backs and necks, so chicken farmers there sell these parts locally and ship chicken breasts abroad, where they are valued more.[2] Soft drinks are four times more popular in the United States than in Europe. The English like tea; Americans, coffee. Algeria has an ideal climate for growing grapes (vineyards there date back to Roman times). But Algeria's population is 99 percent Muslim, a religion that forbids alcohol consumption. Thus, Algeria exports wine.

More Variety

Yet another reason for trade is to increase the *variety* of goods and services available. People prefer having a choice of products, and international trade helps broaden that choice.[3] International trade expands your selection of automobiles, computers, clothing, drugs, wine, cheese, ethnic foods, music, movies, and hundreds of other items.

19-2 TRADE RESTRICTIONS AND WELFARE LOSS

Despite the benefits of international trade, nearly all countries at one time or another erect trade barriers, which benefit some domestic producers but harm other domestic producers and all domestic consumers. In this section, we consider the effects of trade barriers and why they are imposed.

2. Drew Hinshaw, "As KFC Goes to Africa, It Lacks Only One Thing: Chickens," *Wall Street Journal*, 8 February 2013.

3. Marc Melitz and Daniel Trefler, "Gains from Trade When Firms Matter," *Journal of Economic Perspectives*, 26 (Spring 2012): 91–118.

Exhibit 6

Consumer Surplus and Producer Surplus

Consumer surplus, shown by the blue triangle, indicates the net benefits consumers reap from buying 60 pounds of apples at $1.00 per pound. Some consumers would have been willing to pay $3.00 or more per pound for the first few pounds. Consumer surplus measures the difference between the maximum sum of money consumers would pay for 60 pounds of apples and the actual sum they pay. Producer surplus, shown by the gold triangle, indicates the net benefits producers reap from selling 60 pounds at $1.00 per pound. Some producers would have supplied apples for %0.50 per pound or less. Producer surplus measures the difference between the actual sum of money producers receive for 60 pounds of apples and the minimum amount they would accept for this amount.

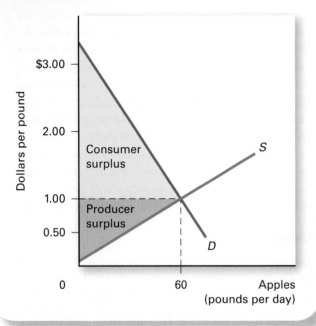

19-2a Consumer Surplus and Producer Surplus From Market Exchange

Before we explore the net effects of world trade on social welfare, let's develop a framework showing the benefits that consumers and producers get from market exchange. Consider the hypothetical market for apples shown in Exhibit 6. The height of the demand curve shows what consumers are willing and able to pay for each additional pound of apples. In effect, the height of the demand curve shows the *marginal benefit* consumers expect from each pound of apples. For example, the demand curve indicates that some consumers in this market are willing to pay $3.00 or

world price The price at which a good is traded on the world market; determined by the world demand and world supply for the good

more per pound for the first few pounds of apples. But every consumer gets to buy apples at the market-clearing price, which here is $1.00 per pound. Most consumers thus get a bonus, or a surplus, from market exchange.

The blue-shaded triangle below the demand curve and above the market price reflects the *consumer surplus* in this market, which is the difference between the most that consumers would pay for 60 pounds of apples per day and the actual amount they do pay. We all enjoy a consumer surplus from most products we buy.

Producers usually derive a similar surplus. The height of the supply curve shows what producers are willing and able to accept for each additional pound of apples. That is, the height of the supply curve shows the expected *marginal cost* from producing each additional pound. For example, the supply curve indicates that some producers face a marginal cost of $0.50 or less per pound for supplying the first few pounds. But every producer gets to sell apples for the market-clearing price of $1.00 per pound. The gold-shaded triangle above the supply curve and below the market price reflects the *producer surplus*, which is the difference between the actual amount that producers receive for 60 pounds and what they would accept to supply that amount.

The point is that market exchange usually generates a surplus, or a bonus, for both consumers and producers. In the balance of this chapter, we look at the gains from international trade and how trade restrictions affect consumer and producer surplus.

19-2b Tariffs

A *tariff,* a term first introduced in Chapter 3, is a tax on imports. (Tariffs can apply to exports, too, but we will focus on import tariffs.) A tariff can be either *specific,* such as a tariff of $5 per barrel of oil, or *ad valorem,* such as 10 percent on the import price of jeans. Consider the effects of a specific tariff on a particular good. In Exhibit 7, *D* is the U.S. demand for sugar and *S* is the supply of sugar from U.S. growers (there are about 10,000 U.S. sugarcane growers). Suppose that the world price of sugar is $0.10 per pound. The **world price** is determined by the world supply and demand for a product. It is the price at which any supplier can sell output on the world market and at which any demander can purchase output on the world market.

With free trade, any U.S. consumers could buy any amount desired at the world price of $0.10 per pound, so the quantity demanded is 70 million pounds per month, of which U.S. producers supply 20 million pounds and importers supply 50 million pounds. Because U.S. buyers can purchase sugar at the world price, U.S. producers can't charge more than that. Now suppose that a specific tariff of $0.05 is imposed on each pound of imported sugar, raising the U.S. price from $0.10 to $0.15 per pound. U.S. producers can therefore raise their own price to

$0.15 per pound without losing business to imports. At the higher price, the quantity supplied by U.S. producers increases to 30 million pounds, but the quantity demanded by U.S. consumers declines to 60 million pounds. Because quantity demanded has declined and quantity supplied by U.S. producers has increased, U.S. imports fall from 50 million to 30 million pounds per month.

Because the U.S. price is higher after the tariff, U.S. consumers are worse off. Their loss in consumer surplus is identified in Exhibit 7 by the combination of the blue- and pink-shaded areas. Because both the U.S. price and the quantity supplied by U.S. producers have increased, their total revenue increases by the areas *a* plus *b* plus *f*. But only area *a* represents an increase in producer surplus. Revenue represented by the areas *b* plus *f* merely offsets the higher marginal cost U.S. producers face in expanding sugar output from 20 million to 30 million pounds per month. Area *b* represents part of the net welfare loss to the domestic economy because those 10 million pounds could have been imported for $0.10 per pound rather than produced domestically at a higher marginal cost.

Government revenue from the tariff is identified by area *c*, which equals the tariff of $0.05 per pound multiplied by the 30 million pounds imported, for tariff revenue of $1.5 million per month. Tariff revenue is a loss to consumers, but because the tariff goes to the government, it can be used to lower taxes or to increase public services, so it's not a loss to the U.S. economy. Area *d* shows a loss in consumer surplus because less sugar is consumed at the higher price. This loss is not redistributed to anyone else, so area *d* reflects part of the net welfare loss of the tariff. Therefore, areas *b* and *d* show the domestic economy's net welfare loss of the tariff; *the two triangles measure a loss in consumer surplus that is not offset by a gain to anyone in the domestic economy.*

In summary: Of the total loss in U.S. consumer surplus (areas

Exhibit 7

Effect of a Tariff

At a world price of $0.10 per pound, U.S. consumers demand 70 million pounds of sugar per month, and U.S. producers supply 20 million pounds per month; the difference is imported. After the imposition of a $0.05 per pound tariff, the U.S. price rises to $0.15 per pound. U.S. producers supply 30 million pounds, and U.S. consumers cut back to 60 million pounds. At the higher U.S. price, consumers are worse off; their loss of consumer surplus is the sum of areas *a*, *b*, *c*, and *d*. The net welfare loss to the U.S. economy consists of areas *b* and *d*.

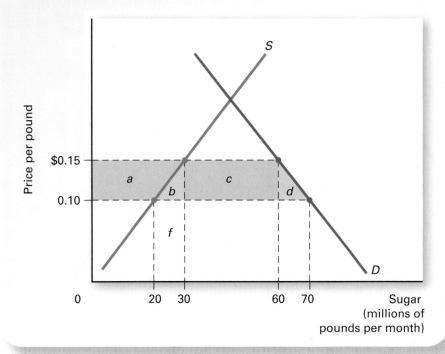

a, b, c, and *d*) resulting from the tariff, area *a* goes to U.S producers, area *c* becomes government revenue, but areas *b* and *d* are net losses in domestic social welfare.

19-2c Import Quotas

An *import quota* is a legal limit on the amount of a commodity that can be imported. Quotas usually target imports from certain countries. For example, a quota may limit furniture from China or shoes from Brazil. To have an impact on the domestic market, a quota must be less than what would be imported with free trade. Consider a quota on the U.S. market for sugar. In panel (a) of Exhibit 8, *D* is the U.S. demand curve and *S* is the supply curve of U.S. sugar producers. Suppose again that the world price of sugar is $0.10 per pound. With free trade, that price would prevail in the U.S. market as well, and a total of 70 million pounds would be demanded per month. U.S. producers would supply 20 million pounds and importers, 50 million pounds. With a quota of 50 million pounds or more per month, the U.S. price would

remain the same as the world price of $0.10 per pound, and the U.S. quantity would be 70 million pounds per month. In short, a quota of at least 50 million pounds would not raise the U.S. price above the world price because 50 million pounds were imported without a quota. A more stringent quota, however, would cut imports, which, as we'll see, would raise the U.S. price.

Suppose U.S. trade officials impose an import quota of 30 million pounds per month. As long as the U.S. price is at or above the world price of $0.10 per pound, foreign producers will supply 30 million pounds. So at prices at or above $0.10 per pound, the total supply of sugar to the U.S. market is found by adding 30 million pounds of imported sugar to the amount supplied by U.S. producers. U.S. and foreign producers would never sell in the U.S. market for less than $0.10 per pound because they can always get that price on the world market. Thus, the supply curve that sums domestic production and imports is horizontal at the world price of $0.10 per pound and remains so until the quantity supplied reaches 50 million pounds.

Exhibit 8

Effect of a Quota

In panel (a), *D* is the U.S. demand curve and *S* is the supply curve of U.S. producers. If the government establishes a sugar quota of 30 million pounds per month, the supply curve combining U.S. production and imports becomes horizontal at the world price of $0.10 per pound and remains horizontal until the quantity supplied reaches 50 million pounds. For higher prices, the new supply curve equals the horizontal sum of the U.S. supply curve, *S*, plus the quota of 30 million pounds. The new U.S. price, $0.15 per pound, is determined by the intersection of the new supply curve, *S′*, with the U.S. demand curve, *D*. Panel (b) shows the welfare effect of the quota. As a result of the higher U.S. price, consumer surplus is cut by the shaded area. The blue-shaded areas illustrate the loss in consumer surplus that is captured by domestic producers and by those who are permitted to fulfill the quota, and the pink-shaded triangles illustrate the net welfare cost of the quota on the U.S. economy.

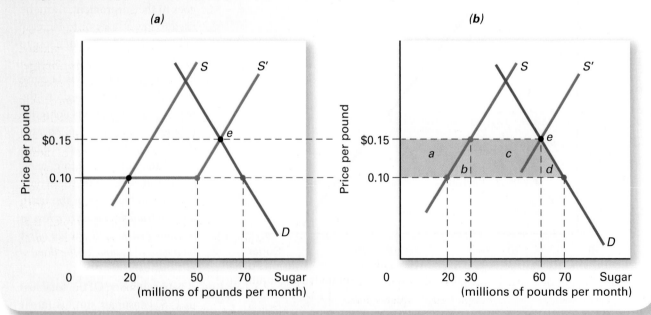

Again, for prices above $0.10 per pound, the new supply curve, S', adds horizontally the 30-million-pound quota to S, the supply curve of U.S. producers. The U.S. price is found where this new supply curve, S', intersects the domestic demand curve, which in Exhibit 8 occurs at point *e*. *By limiting imports, the quota raises the domestic price of sugar above the world price and reduces quantity below the free trade level.* (Note that to compare more easily the effects of tariffs and quotas, this quota is designed to yield the same equilibrium price and quantity as the tariff examined earlier.)

Panel (b) of Exhibit 8 shows the distribution and efficiency effects of the quota. As a result of the quota, U.S. consumer surplus declines by the combined blue and pink areas. Area *a* becomes U.S. producer surplus and thus involves no loss of U.S. welfare. Area *c* shows the increased economic profit to those permitted by the quota to sell Americans 30 million pounds for $0.15 per pound, or $0.05 above the world price. If foreign exporters rather than U.S. importers reap this profit, area *c* reflects a net loss in U.S. welfare.

Area *b* shows a welfare loss to the U.S. economy, because sugar could have been purchased abroad for $0.10 per pound, and the U.S. resources employed to increase sugar production could instead have been used more efficiently producing other goods. Area *d* is also a welfare loss because it reflects a reduction in consumer surplus with no offsetting gain to anyone. Thus, areas *b* and *d* in panel (b) of Exhibit 8 measure the minimum U.S. welfare loss from the quota. If the profit from quota rights (area *c*) accrues to foreign producers, this increases the U.S. welfare loss.

19-2d Quotas in Practice

The United States has granted quotas to specific countries. These countries, in turn, distribute these quota rights to their exporters through a variety of means. *By rewarding domestic and foreign producers with higher prices, the quota system creates two groups intent on securing and perpetuating these quotas.* Lobbyists for foreign producers work the halls of Congress, seeking the right to export to the United States. This strong support from producers, coupled with a lack of opposition from consumers (who remain rationally ignorant for the most part), has resulted in quotas that have lasted decades. For example, sugar quotas have been around more than 50 years. For the past three decades, U.S. sugar prices have ranged from 50 to 100 percent above the world price, costing American consumers billions.[4] Sugar growers, who account for only 1 percent of U.S. farm sales, accounted for 17 percent of political contributions from agriculture.[5] Sugar growers even reversed a North American Free Trade Agreement provision that would have allowed tariff-free sugar imports from Mexico.

Some economists have argued that if quotas are to be used, the United States should auction them off to foreign producers, thereby capturing at least some of the difference between the world price and the U.S. price. Auctioning off quotas would not only increase federal revenue at a time when it's desperately needed, but an auction would reduce the profitability of getting quota rights, which would reduce pressure on Washington to perpetuate them. American consumers are not the only victims of sugar quotas. Thousands of poor farmers around the world miss out on an opportunity to earn a living by growing sugar cane for export to America.

19-2e Tariffs and Quotas Compared

Consider the similarities and differences between a tariff and a quota. Because both have identical effects on the price in our example, they both lead to the same change in quantity demanded. In both cases, U.S. consumers suffer the same loss of consumer surplus, and U.S. producers reap the same gain of producer surplus. The primary difference is that the revenue from the tariff goes to the U.S. government, whereas the revenue from the quota goes to whoever secures the right to sell foreign goods in the U.S. market. *If quota rights accrue to foreigners, then the domestic economy is worse off with a quota than with a tariff.* But even if quota rights go to domestic importers, quotas, like tariffs, still increase the domestic price, restrict quantity, and thereby reduce consumer surplus and economic welfare. Quotas and tariffs can also raise production costs. For example, U.S. candy manufacturers face higher production costs

> **"Tariffs and quotas are only two of many devices used to restrict foreign trade."**

4. Burleigh Leonard, "U.S. Sugar Policy: Sweet Deal for a Few, Sour for Most," *Wall Street Journal*, 2 November 2014.

5. Michael Schroeder, "Sugar Growers Hold Up Push for Free Trade," *Wall Street Journal*, 3 February 2004.

because of sugar quotas, making them less competitive on world markets. Finally, and most importantly, *quotas and tariffs encourage foreign governments to retaliate with quotas and tariffs of their own, thus shrinking U.S. export markets, so the welfare loss is greater than shown in Exhibits 7 and 8.*

19-2f Other Trade Restrictions

Besides tariffs and quotas, a variety of other measures limit free trade. A country may provide *export subsidies* to encourage exports and *low-interest loans* to foreign buyers. Some countries impose *domestic content requirements* specifying that a certain portion of a final good must be produced domestically. Other requirements masquerading as health, safety, or technical standards often discriminate against foreign goods. For example, Nigeria protects chicken growers by banning chicken imports (which is why KFCs there added fish to the menu). To gain access to Chinese markets, foreign producers must transfer their technological know-how to a Chinese partner, so it can be made available throughout China.[6] European countries once prohibited beef from hormone-fed cattle, a measure aimed at U.S. beef. Purity laws in Germany bar many non-German beers. Until the European Community adopted uniform standards, differing technical requirements forced manufacturers to offer as many as seven different versions of the same TV for that market. Sometimes exporters will voluntarily limit exports, as when Japanese automakers agreed to cut exports to the United States. The point is that *tariffs and quotas are only two of many devices used to restrict foreign trade.*

Recent research on the cost of protectionism indicates that international trade barriers slow the introduction of new goods and better technologies. So, rather than simply raising domestic prices, trade restrictions slow economic progress.

bilateral agreement Trade agreement between two countries

multilateral agreement Trade agreement among more than two countries

General Agreement on Tariffs and Trade (GATT) An international tariff-reduction treaty adopted in 1947 that resulted in a series of negotiated "rounds" aimed at freer trade; the Uruguay Round created GATT's successor, the World Trade Organization (WTO)

dumping Selling a product abroad for less than charged in the home market or for less than the cost of production

6. Thomas J. Holmes, Ellen R. McGrattan, and Edward C. Prescott, "Quid Pro Quo: Technology Capital Transfers for Market Access in China," *Review of Economic Studies*, 82 (July 2015): 1154–1193.

19-3 EFFORTS TO REDUCE TRADE BARRIERS

Although some groups in the economy have a special interest in restricting trade, the trend has been toward freer trade. In this section, we examine international efforts to lower trade barriers. A nation sometimes negotiates a trade agreements with another nation, in what is know as a **bilateral agreement**. For example, the United States has negotiated bilateral open-skies agreements to deregulate airline competition on international routes, agreements that have generated at least $4 billion a year in gains to travelers. And travelers would gain another $4 billion a year if agreements were reached with other countries where Americans travel frequently.[7]

19-3a Freer Trade by Multilateral Agreement

Mindful of how high tariffs cut world trade during the Great Depression, the United States, after World War II, invited its trading partners to negotiate lower tariffs and other trade barriers. A **multilateral agreement** is one reached among more than two countries. The result was the **General Agreement on Tariffs and Trade (GATT)**, an international trade treaty adopted in 1947 by 23 countries, including the United States. Each GATT member agreed to (1) reduce tariffs through multinational negotiations, (2) reduce import quotas, and (3) treat all members equally with respect to trade.

Trade barriers have been reduced through trade negotiations, or "trade rounds," under the auspices of GATT. Trade rounds offer a package approach rather than an issue-by-issue approach to trade negotiations. Concessions that are necessary but otherwise difficult to defend in domestic political terms can be made more acceptable in the context of a larger package that also contains politically and economically attractive benefits. Most early GATT trade rounds were aimed at reducing tariffs. The Kennedy Round in the mid-1960s included new provisions against **dumping**, which is selling a commodity abroad for less than is charged in the home market or less than the cost of production. The Tokyo Round of the 1970s was a more sweeping attempt to extend and improve the system.

The most recently completed round was launched in Uruguay in September 1986 and ratified by 123 participating countries in 1994. The number of signing

7. Clifford Winston and Jia Yan, "Open Skies: Estimating Travelers' Benefits From Free Trade in Airline Service," *American Economic Journal: Economic Policy*, 7 (May 2015): 370–414.

countries now exceeds 150. This so-called **Uruguay Round**, the most comprehensive of the eight postwar multilateral trade negotiations, included 550 pages of tariff reductions on 85 percent of world trade. As a result of the Uruguay Round, average tariffs fell from 6 percent to 4 percent of the value of imports (when GATT began in 1947, average tariffs averaged 40 percent). The Uruguay Round also created the World Trade Organization to succeed GATT.

19-3b World Trade Organization

The **World Trade Organization (WTO)** provides the legal and institutional foundation for world trade. Although GATT was a multilateral agreement with no institutional foundation, the WTO is a permanent institution in Geneva, Switzerland. A staff of about 600 economists and lawyers helps shape policy and resolves trade disputes among member countries. Although GATT involved only merchandise trade, the WTO also covers services and trade-related aspects of intellectual property, such as books, movies, and computer programs. The WTO will eventually phase out quotas, but tariffs will remain legal.

Although GATT relied on voluntary cooperation, the WTO settles disputes in a way that is faster, more automatic, and less susceptible to blockage than the GATT system was. The WTO resolved more trade disputes in its first decade than GATT did in nearly 50 years. Since 2000, developing countries have filed 60 percent of the disputes.

19-3c Common Markets

Some countries looked to the success of the U.S. economy, which is essentially a free trade zone across 50 states, and have tried to develop free trade zones of their own. The largest and best known is the European Union, which began in 1958 with a half dozen countries and by 2015 had expanded to 28 countries and over 500 million people. The idea was to create a barrier-free European market like the United States in which goods, services, people, and capital are free to flow to their highest-valued use. As of 2015, 19 members of the European Union had also adopted a common currency, the *euro,* which replaced national currencies in 2002. The European Union is an example of a **common market**, which consists of a group of countries with few or no trade restrictions with one another.

The United States, Canada, and Mexico introduced a free trade pact in 1994 called the North American Free Trade Agreement, or NAFTA. Through NAFTA, Mexico hopes to attract more U.S. investment by guaranteeing companies that locate there duty-free access to U.S. markets, which is where over two-thirds of Mexico's exports go. Mexico's 117 million people represent an attractive export market for U.S. producers, and Mexico's oil reserves could ease U.S. energy problems. The United States would also like to support Mexico's efforts to become more market oriented, as is reflected, for example, by Mexico's privatization of its phone system and banks. Creating job opportunities in Mexico also reduces pressure for Mexicans to cross the U.S. border illegally to find work. After more than a decade of NAFTA, agricultural exports to Mexico have doubled, as has overall trade among the three nations, but Americans still buy much more from Mexicans and Canadians than the other way around.

Free trade areas are springing up around the world. The United States signed a free trade agreement with five Central American countries and the Dominican Republic, called CAFTA-DR. Ten Latin American countries form Mercosur. And in 2015, the United States was negotiating the Trans-Pacific Partnership with 11 other nations in the Pacific, including China. Together, these countries represent up to 40 percent of world output. Elsewhere in the world, the Association of Southeast Asian Nations, or ASEAN, consists of 10 member countries. And South Africa and its four neighboring countries form the Southern African Customs Union. Regional trade agreements require an exception to WTO rules because bloc members can make special deals among themselves and thus discriminate against outsiders. Under WTO's requirements, any trade concession granted to one country must usually be granted to *all other* WTO members.

Incidentally, economic initiatives such as the European Union binds nations together economically so they are less likely to go to war

> **"Free trade areas are springing up around the world."**

Uruguay Round The final multilateral trade negotiation under GATT; this 1994 agreement cut tariffs, formed the World Trade Organization (WTO), and will eventually eliminate quotas

World Trade Organization (WTO) The legal and institutional foundation of the multilateral trading system that succeeded GATT in 1995

common market Group of countries that have few of no trade restrictions with one another

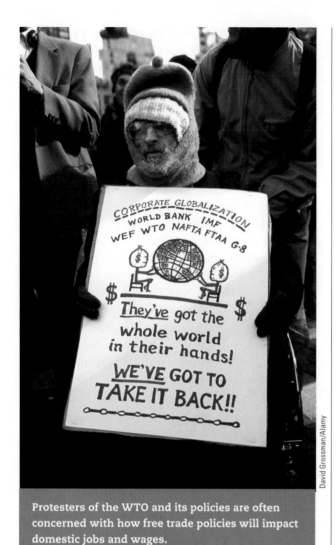

Protesters of the WTO and its policies are often concerned with how free trade policies will impact domestic jobs and wages.

against each other. War with countries that are trading partners would involve more economic loss than war with other countries. That's yet another benefit of freer trade.

Still, economic integration is not a perfect solution, as evidenced by recent financial problems in the eurozone, which arose because unsustainable government deficits in some member countries such as Greece and Spain reduced confidence in the common currency. Member countries became much more vulnerable to fiscal problems of other member countries.

19-4 ARGUMENTS FOR TRADE RESTRICTIONS

Trade restrictions are often little more than handouts for the domestic industries they protect. Given the loss in social welfare that results from these restrictions, it would be more efficient simply to transfer money from domestic consumers to domestic producers. But such a bald payoff would be politically unpopular. Arguments for trade restrictions avoid mention of transfers to domestic producers and instead cite loftier goals. As we shall now see, none of these goals makes a strong case for restrictions, but some make a little more sense than others.

> **"Trade restrictions are often little more than handouts for the domestic industries they protect."**

19-4a National Defense Argument

Some industries claim they need protection from import competition because their output is vital for national defense. Products such as strategic metals and military hardware are often insulated from foreign competition by trade restrictions. Thus, national defense considerations outweigh concerns about efficiency and equity. How valid is this argument? Trade restrictions may shelter the defense industry, but other means, such as government subsidies, might be more efficient. Or the government could stockpile basic military hardware so that maintaining an ongoing productive capacity would become less critical. Still, technological change could make certain weapons obsolete. Because most industries can play some role in national defense, instituting trade restrictions on this basis can get out of hand. For example, many decades ago U.S. wool producers secured trade protection at a time when some military uniforms were still made of wool.

The national defense argument has also been used to discourage foreign ownership of U.S. companies in some industries. For example, in 2005 a Chinese state-owned company was prevented from buying Unocal Oil. And in 2010, the Congressional Steel Caucus tried to block a Chinese attempt to buy a Mississippi steel plant, saying that such a deal "threatens American jobs and our national security."[8]

8. Yjun Zhang, "China Steel Group Accuses U.S. Lawmakers of Protectionism," *Wall Street Journal*, 5 July 2010.

19-4b Infant Industry Argument

The infant industry argument was formulated as a rationale for protecting emerging domestic industries from foreign competition. In industries where a firm's average cost of production falls as output expands, new firms may need protection from imports until these firms grow enough to become competitive. Trade restrictions let new firms achieve the economies of scale necessary to compete with mature foreign producers.

But how do we identify industries that merit protection, and when do they become old enough to look after themselves? Protection often fosters inefficiencies. The immediate cost of such restrictions is the net welfare loss from higher domestic prices. These costs may become permanent if the industry never realizes the expected economies of scale and thus never becomes competitive. As with the national defense argument, policy makers should be careful in adopting trade restrictions based on the infant industry argument. Here again, temporary production subsidies may be more efficient than import restrictions.

19-4c Antidumping Argument

As we have noted already, *dumping* is selling a product abroad for less than in the home market or less than the cost of production. Exporters may be able to sell the good for less overseas because of export subsidies, or firms may simply find it profitable to sell for less in foreign markets where consumers are more sensitive to prices. But why shouldn't U.S. consumers pay as little as possible? If dumping is *persistent,* the increase in consumer surplus would more than offset losses to domestic producers. *There is no good reason why consumers should not be allowed to buy imports for a persistently lower price.*

An alternative form of dumping, termed *predatory dumping,* is the *temporary* sale abroad at prices below cost to eliminate competitors in that target market. Once the competition is gone, so the story goes, the exporting firm can raise the price in the foreign market. The trouble with this argument is that if dumpers try to take advantage of their monopoly position by sharply increasing the price, then other firms, either domestic or foreign, could enter the market and sell for less. There are few documented cases of predatory dumping.

Sometimes dumping may be *sporadic,* as firms occasionally try to unload excess inventories. Retailers hold periodic "sales" for the same reason. Sporadic dumping can be unsettling for domestic producers, but the economic impact is not a matter of great public concern.

Regardless, all dumping is prohibited in the United States by the Trade Agreements Act of 1979, which calls for the imposition of tariffs when a good is sold for less in the United States than in its home market or less than the cost of production. In addition, WTO rules allow for offsetting tariffs when products are sold for "less than fair value" and when there is "material injury" to domestic producers. For example, U.S. producers of lumber and beer frequently accuse their Canadian counterparts of dumping.

19-4d Jobs and Income Argument

One rationale for trade restrictions that is commonly heard in the United States, and is voiced by WTO protesters, is that they protect U.S. jobs and wage levels. Using trade restrictions to protect domestic jobs is a strategy that dates back centuries. One problem with such a policy is that other countries usually retaliate by restricting *their* imports to save *their* jobs, so international trade is reduced, jobs are lost in export industries, and potential gains from trade fail to materialize. That happened big time during the Great Depression, as high tariffs choked trade and jobs.

Wages in other countries, especially developing countries, are often a fraction of wages in the United States. For example, including benefits, General Motors (GM) workers in Michigan earn about $50 per hour versus $7 for GM workers in Mexico, $4.50 in China, and $1 in India. (The minimum wage in Mexico is less than $1 per hour.) Looking simply at differences in wages, however, narrows the focus too much. Wages represent just one component of the total production cost and may not necessarily be the most important. Employers are interested in the labor cost per unit of output, which

While cheap labor in other countries may reduce the price of imports, it does not tell the whole story.

depends on both the wage and labor productivity. Wages are high in the United States partly because U.S. labor productivity remains the highest in the world. High productivity can be traced to better education and training and to the abundant computers, machines, and other physical capital that make workers more productive. U.S. workers also benefit greatly from better management and a relatively stable business climate.

But what about the lower wages in many developing countries? Low wages are often linked to workers' lack of education and training, to the meager physical capital available to each worker, and to a business climate that is less stable and hence less attractive for producers. For example, the total value of manufacturing output is about the same in the United States as in China, but Americans produce that output with only about 10 percent of the manufacturing workforce that's employed in China.[9] What's more, advances in technology are making differences in labor costs across countries less relevant. One example is, as noted earlier, that in the original iPad, manufacturing labor accounted for only $33 of its $499 retail price, and the final assembly in China accounted for just $8 of that $33.[10]

Once multinational firms build plants and provide technological know-how in developing countries, U.S. workers lose some of their competitive edge, and their relatively high wages could price some U.S. products out of the world market. This has already happened in the consumer electronics and toy industries. China makes 80 percent of the toys sold in the United States. Some U.S. toy sellers, such as the makers of Etch A Sketch, would no longer exist had they not outsourced manufacturing to China. Overall, competition from Chinese imports between 1999 and 2011 cost the U.S. economy about 2 million jobs, according to one estimate.[11]

Domestic producers do not like to compete with foreign producers whose costs are lower, so they often push for trade restrictions. Labor unions protested the Trans-Pacific Partnership on those grounds. According to one report, "Unions see the pact as one of the biggest threats to organized labor and the U.S. middle class since the North American Free Trade Agreement took effect in 1994."[12] But if restrictions negate any cost advantage a foreign producer might have, the law of comparative advantage becomes inoperative and domestic consumers are denied access to the lower-priced goods.

9. "Manufacturing and Innovation: Back to Making Stuff," *The Economist*, 21 April 2012.

10. "The Third Industrial Revolution," *The Economist*, 21 April 2012.

11. Daron Acemoglu et al. "Import Competition and the Great U.S. Employment Sag of the 2000s," NBER Working Paper No. 20395 (August 2014).

12. Melanie Trottman, "Unions Flex Muscle to Fight Pacific Trade Pace," *Wall Street Journal*, 10 June 2015.

Over time, as labor productivity in developing countries increases, wage differentials among countries will narrow, much as they narrowed between the northern and southern United States during the last century. As technology and capital spread, U.S. workers, particularly unskilled workers, cannot expect to maintain wage levels that are far above comparable workers in other countries. So far, research and development has kept U.S. producers on the cutting edge of technological developments, but staying ahead in the technological race is a constant battle. As a sign of the times about how competition could squeeze down the wage gap across countries, the Volkswagen factory in Tennessee pays workers only about half of what GM pays in Michigan, yet in 2011, many thousands of job seekers applied for the 2,000 openings at the Tennessee factory.

19-4e Declining Industries Argument

Where an established domestic industry is in jeopardy of closing because of lower-priced imports, could there be a rationale for *temporary* import restrictions? After all, domestic producers employ many industry-specific resources—both specialized labor and specialized machines. This human and physical capital is worth less in its best alternative use. If the extinction of the domestic industry is forestalled through trade restrictions, specialized workers can retire voluntarily or can gradually pursue more promising careers. Specialized machines can be allowed to wear out naturally.

Thus, in the case of declining domestic industries, trade protection can help lessen shocks to the economy and can allow for an orderly transition to a new industrial mix. But the protection offered should not be so generous as to encourage continued investment in the industry. Protection should be of specific duration and should be phased out over that period.

The clothing industry is an example of a declining U.S. industry. The 22,000 U.S. jobs saved as a result of one trade restriction paid an average of less than $30,000 per year. But a Congressional Budget Office study estimated that the higher domestic clothing prices resulting from trade restrictions meant that U.S. consumers paid two to three times more than apparel workers earned. Trade restrictions in the U.S. clothing and textile industry started phasing out in 2005 under the Uruguay Round of trade agreements.

Free trade may displace some U.S. jobs through imports, but it also creates U.S. jobs through exports. When Americans celebrate a ribbon-cutting ceremony for a new software company, nobody credits free trade for those jobs, but when a steel plant closes here, everyone talks about how those jobs went overseas. What's more, many foreign companies have built plants in the United States and employ U.S. workers. For example, a dozen foreign television manufacturers and all major Japanese automakers now operate plants in the United States.

The number employed in the United States has nearly doubled in the last four decades. To recognize this job growth is not to deny the problems facing workers displaced by imports. Some displaced workers, particularly those in steel and other unionized, blue-collar industries, are not likely to find jobs that pay nearly as well as the ones they lost. As with infant industries, however, the problems posed by declining industries need not require trade restrictions. To support the affected industry, the government could offer wage subsidies or special tax breaks that decline over time. The government has also funded programs to retrain affected workers for jobs that are in greater demand.

19-4f Problems with Trade Protection

Trade restrictions raise a number of problems in addition to those already mentioned. First, protecting one stage of production usually requires protecting downstream stages of production as well. Protecting the U.S. textile industry from foreign competition, for example, raised the cost of cloth to U.S. apparel makers, reducing *their* competitiveness. Thus, when the government protected domestic textile manufacturers, the domestic garment industry also needed protection. Second, the cost of protection includes not only the welfare loss from the higher domestic price but also the cost of the resources used by domestic producer groups to secure the favored protection. The cost of *rent seeking*—lobbying fees, propaganda, and legal actions—can sometimes equal or exceed the direct welfare loss from restrictions. The third problem with trade restrictions is the transaction costs of enforcing the myriad quotas, tariffs, and other trade restrictions. These often lead to smuggling and black markets. The fourth problem is that economies insulated from foreign competition become less innovative and less efficient. On the other hand, competing in the export market increases a firm's efficiency and productivity.[13] The final and biggest problem with imposing trade restrictions is that other countries usually retaliate, thus shrinking the gains from trade.

Retaliation can set off still greater trade restrictions, leading to an outright trade war.

19-5 FINAL WORD

International trade arises from voluntary exchange among buyers and sellers pursuing their self-interest. Since 1950 world output has risen eightfold, while world trade has increased twentyfold. World trade offers many advantages to the trading countries: access to markets around the world, lower costs through economies of scale, a wider choice of products, the opportunity to utilize abundant resources, better access to information about markets and technology, improved quality honed by competitive pressure, reduced likelihood of war, and, most importantly, lower prices for consumers. Recent research suggests that access to higher quality goods may be one of the most significant gains from international trade, especially in developing countries such as India.[14]

This kiosk is the gateway to New York City's garment district, which continues to be severely affected by low-price competition from overseas markets.

13. David Atkin, Amit K. Khandelwal, and Adam Osman, "Exporting and Firm Performance: Evidence from a Randomized Trial," NBER Working Paper No. 20690 (November 2014); and Jan De Loecker, "Detecting Learning by Exporting," American Economic Journal: Microeconomics, 5 (August 2014): 1–21.

14. Gloria Sheu, "Price, Quality, and Variety: Measuring the Gains from Trade in Differentiated Products," *American Economic Journal: Applied Economics*, 6 (October 2014): 66–89.

Comparative advantage, specialization, and trade allow people to use their scarce resources efficiently to satisfy their unlimited wants.

Despite the clear gains from free trade, restrictions on international trade date back centuries, and pressure on public officials to impose trade restrictions continues today. Domestic producers (and their resource suppliers) benefit from trade restrictions in their markets because they can charge domestic consumers more. Trade restrictions insulate domestic producers from the rigors of global competition, in the process stifling innovation and leaving protected industries vulnerable to technological change from abroad. With trade quotas, the winners also include those who have secured the right to import goods at the world prices and sell them at the domestic prices. Consumers, who must pay higher prices for protected goods, suffer from trade restrictions, as do the domestic producers who import resources. Other losers include U.S. exporters, who face higher trade barriers as their foreign counterparts retaliate with their own trade restrictions.

Producers have a laser-like focus on trade legislation, but consumers remain largely oblivious. Consumers purchase thousands of different goods and thus have no special interest in the effects of trade policy on any particular good. Congress tends to support the group that makes the most noise, so trade restrictions often persist, despite the clear and widespread gains from freer trade.

STUDY TOOLS 19

READY TO STUDY? IN THE BOOK, YOU CAN:

☐ Work the Problems at the end of the chapter.

☐ Rip out the chapter review card for a handy summary of the chapter and key terms.

ONLINE AT CENGAGEBRAIN.COM YOU CAN:

☐ Collect StudyBits while you read and study the chapter.

☐ Quiz yourself on key concepts.

☐ Prepare for tests with chapter flash cards as well as flash cards that you create.

☐ Watch videos to explore economics further.

CHAPTER 19 PROBLEMS

Your instructor can access the answers to these problems online at http://cengagebrain.com.

19-1 Outline the gains from trade, and explain why countries might still decide to trade even if no country had a comparative advantage

1. *(Trade Without Comparative Advantage)* Even if neither country had a comparative advantage, why might these countries still experience gains from trade?

2. *(Comparative Advantage)* Suppose that each U.S. worker can produce 8 units of food or 2 units of clothing daily. In Fredonia, which has the same number of workers, each worker can produce 7 units of food or 1 unit of clothing daily. Why does the United States have an absolute advantage in both goods? Which country enjoys a comparative advantage in food? Why?

3. *(Comparative Advantage)* The consumption possibilities frontiers shown by the blue lines in the following exhibit assume terms of trade of 1 unit of clothing for 1 unit of food. What would the consumption possibilities frontiers look like if the terms of trade were 1 unit of clothing for 2 units of food?

Production (and Consumption) Possibility Frontiers with Trade (millions of units per day)

4. *(Reasons for International Specialization)* What determines which goods a country should produce and export?

19-2 Explain how trade restrictions harm an economy, and why they persist

5. *(Import Quotas)* How low must a quota be to have an impact on trade? Using a demand-and-supply diagram, illustrate and explain the net welfare loss from imposing such a quota. Under what circumstances would the net welfare loss from an import quota exceed the net welfare loss from an equivalent tariff (one that results in the same price and import level as the quota)?

6. *(Trade Restrictions)* Suppose that the world price for steel is below the U.S. domestic price, but the government requires that all steel used in the United States be domestically produced.
   a. Use a diagram like the one that follows to show the gains and losses from such a policy.
   b. How could you estimate the net welfare loss (deadweight loss) from such a diagram?
   c. What response to such a policy would you expect from industries (like automobile producers) that use U.S. steel?
   d. What government revenues are generated by this policy?

Effect of a Tariff

Effect of a Quota

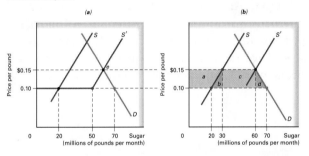

7. *(Trade Restrictions)* The previous three graphs show net losses to the economy of a country that imposes tariffs or quotas on imported sugar. What kinds of gains and losses would occur in the economies of countries that export sugar?

19-3 Identify international efforts to reduce trade barriers

8. *(The World Trade Organization)* What is the World Trade Organization (WTO) and how does it help foster multilateral trade? (Check the WTO Website at http://www.wto.org/.)

19-4 Summarize five arguments often used to justify trade restrictions, and describe some unintended consequences of protecting certain industries from international competition

9. *(Arguments for Trade Restrictions)* Explain the national defense, declining industries, and infant industry arguments for protecting a domestic industry from international competition.

10. *(Arguments for Trade Restrictions)* Firms hurt by lower priced imports typically argue that restricting trade will save U.S. jobs. What's wrong with this argument? Are there ever any reasons to support such trade restrictions?

20 | International Finance

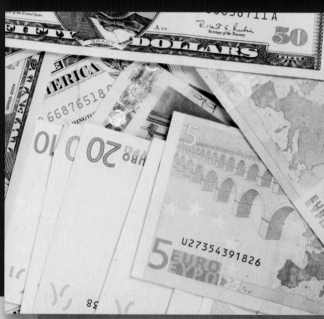

LEARNING OUTCOMES

After studying this chapter, you will be able to…

20-1 Summarize the major accounts in the balance of trade, and explain how they balance out

20-2 Describe how the foreign exchange rate is determined using demand and supply curves and explain the shapes of the curves

20-3 Describe the purchasing power parity theory

20-4 Trace the evolution of exchange rate regimes from the gold standard to the current system

After finishing this chapter go to **PAGE 357** for **STUDY TOOLS**

Topics discussed in Chapter 20 include

- Balance of payments
- Trade deficits and surpluses
- Foreign exchange markets
- Arbitrageurs and speculators
- Purchasing power parity
- Flexible exchange rates
- Fixed exchange rates
- International monetary system
- Bretton Woods agreement
- Managed float

If Starbucks wants to buy 1,000 espresso machines from the German manufacturer Krups, it will be quoted a price in euros. Suppose the machines cost a total of €1 million (euros). How much is that in dollars? The dollar cost will depend on the exchange rate. When trade takes place across international borders, two currencies are usually involved. Supporting the flows of goods and services are flows of currencies that fund international transactions. The exchange rate between currencies—the price of one in terms of the other—is how the price of a product in one country translates into the price facing a buyer in another country. Cross-border trade therefore depends on the exchange rate.

> **"Why does a nation try to influence the exchange value of its currency?"**

20-1 BALANCE OF PAYMENTS

A country's gross domestic product, or GDP, measures the economy's income and output during a given period, usually quarterly and yearly. To account for dealings abroad, countries must also keep track of international transactions. A country's *balance of payments*, as introduced in Chapter 3, summarizes all economic transactions during a given period between residents of that country and residents of other countries. *Residents* include people, firms, organizations, and governments.

20-1a International Economic Transactions

The balance of payments measures economic transactions between a country and the rest of the world, whether these transactions involve goods and services, real and financial assets, or transfer payments. The balance of payments measures a *flow* of transactions during a particular period. Some transactions do not involve actual payments. For example, if *Time* magazine ships a new printing press to its Australian subsidiary, no payment is made, yet an economic transaction involving another country has occurred. Similarly, if CARE sends food to Africa or the Pentagon provides military assistance to the Middle East, these transactions must be captured in the balance of payments. So remember, although we speak of the *balance of payments*, a more descriptive phrase would be the *balance-of-economic transactions*.

Balance-of-payments accounts are maintained according to the principles of *double-entry bookkeeping*. Some entries are called *credits*, and others are called

> **"If merchandise exports exceed merchandise imports, the trade balance is in *surplus*. If merchandise imports exceed merchandise exports, the trade balance is in *deficit*."**

debits. As you will see, the balance of payments consists of several individual accounts. An individual account may not balance, but a deficit in one or more accounts must be offset by a net surplus in the other accounts. Because total credits must equal total debits, there is a *balance* of payments—hence, the name. During a given period, such as a year, the inflow of receipts from the rest of the world, which are entered as credits, must equal the outflow of payments to the rest of the world, which are entered as debits.

The first of two major categories in the balance of payments is the current account. The current account records *current* flows of funds into and out of the country, including imports and exports of goods and services, net income earned by U.S. residents from foreign assets, and net transfer payments from abroad. These are discussed in turn.

> **"The current account records *current* flows of funds into and out of the country, including imports and exports of goods and services, net income earned by U.S. residents from foreign assets, and net transfer payments from abroad."**

20-1b The Merchandise Trade Balance

The *merchandise trade balance,* a term introduced in Chapter 3, equals the value of merchandise exports minus the value of merchandise imports. The merchandise account reflects trade in goods, or tangible products (stuff you can put in a box), like French wine or U.S. computers, and is often referred to simply as the *trade balance.* Revenue from U.S. merchandise exports is a credit in the U.S. balance-of-payments account because U.S. residents get *paid* for the exported goods. Spending

on U.S. merchandise imports is a debit in the balance-of-payments account because U.S. residents *pay* foreigners for imported goods.

If merchandise exports exceed merchandise imports, the trade balance is in *surplus.* If merchandise imports exceed merchandise exports, the trade balance is in *deficit.* The merchandise trade balance, which is reported monthly, influences foreign exchange markets, the stock market, and other financial markets. The trade balance depends on a variety of factors, including the relative strength and competitiveness of the domestic economy compared with other economies and the relative value of the domestic currency compared with other currencies. Strong economies with growing incomes tend to buy more of everything, including imports.

U.S. merchandise trade since 1960 is depicted in Exhibit 1, where exports, the blue line, and imports, the red line, are expressed as a percentage of GDP. During the 1960s, exports exceeded imports, and the resulting trade surpluses are shaded blue. Since 1976, imports have exceeded exports, and the resulting trade deficits are shaded pink. Trade deficits as a percentage of GDP increased from 1.3 percent in 1991 to a peak of 6.3 percent in 2006. The Great Recession of 2007–2009 slowed U.S. imports more than U.S. exports, so by 2009 the trade deficit relative to GDP fell to 3.6 percent, the lowest in more than a decade. Since then, merchandise imports increased more than merchandise exports, so the U.S. trade deficit rose to $735.8 billion in 2014, or 4.2 percent relative to GDP that year.

Because per capita income in the United States ranks among the highest in the world, the United States imports more goods from each of the world's major economies than it exports to them. Exhibit 2 shows the U.S. merchandise trade deficit with major economies or regions of the world in 2014. The $343 billion trade deficit with China was by far the largest, more than double that of the combined 28 countries of the European Union. The Chinese spent $125 billion on U.S. goods in 2014, but sold $468 billion to Americans, or about $3,900 per U.S. household. So China sold America nearly four times more than it bought from America. Chances are, most of the utensils in your kitchen are from China; most toys are also Chinese made. China alone accounted for nearly half the U.S. merchandise trade deficit in 2014. The United States has a trade surplus with only a few major economies.

20-1c Balance on Goods and Services

The merchandise trade balance focuses on the flow of goods, but services are also traded internationally. *Services* are intangibles, such as transportation, insurance,

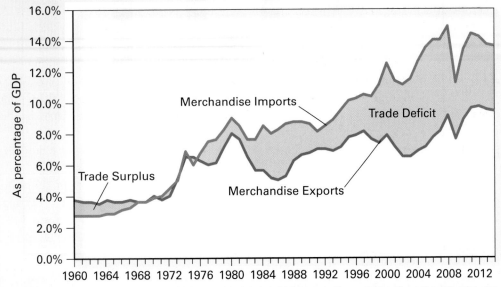

Exhibit 1

U.S. Imports Have Topped Exports Since 1976, but Both Dropped During the Great Recession

Note that since 1980, merchandise exports have remained in the range of about 5 percent to 10 percent of GDP. But merchandise imports have trended up from about 9 percent in 1980 to about 15 percent in 2008, before dropping off to 11 percent in 2009, the year following the financial crisis. Imports were back up to about 14 percent relative to GDP by 2011 and have remained there.

Source: Developed from merchandise trade data from the Bureau of Economic Analysis, U.S. Department of Commerce, at http://bea.gov/international/index.htm.

banking, education, consulting, and tourism. Services are often called "invisibles" because they are not tangible. The value of U.S. service exports, as when an Irish tourist visits New York City, is listed as a credit in the U.S. balance-of-payments account because U.S. residents get paid for these services. The value of U.S. service imports, like computer programming outsourced to India, is listed as a debit in the balance-of-payments account because U.S. residents must pay for the imported services.

Because the United States exports more services than it imports, services have been in surplus for the last three decades. In 2014, the surplus in the services account totaled $231.1 billion. The **balance on goods and services** is the export value of goods and services minus the import value of goods and services, or *net exports*, a component of GDP. Because deficits in the merchandise trade account dominated surpluses in the services account, net exports of goods and services have been in deficit for decades. That deficit in 2014 totaled $504.7 billion.

20-1d Net Investment Income

U.S. residents earn investment income, such as interest and dividends, from foreign assets. This investment

income flows to the United States and is a credit in the balance-of-payments account. On the other side, foreigners earn investment income on their U.S. assets, and this payment flows out of the United States. This outflow is a debit in the balance-of-payments account. **Net investment income from abroad** is U.S. investment earnings from foreign assets minus foreigners' earnings from their U.S. assets. This figure bounces around from year to year between a positive and a negative number. In 2014, net investment income from foreign holdings totaled $217.9 billion.

20-1e Unilateral Transfers and the Current Account Balance

Unilateral transfers consist of government transfers to foreign residents, foreign aid, money workers send to families abroad, personal gifts to friends and relatives abroad,

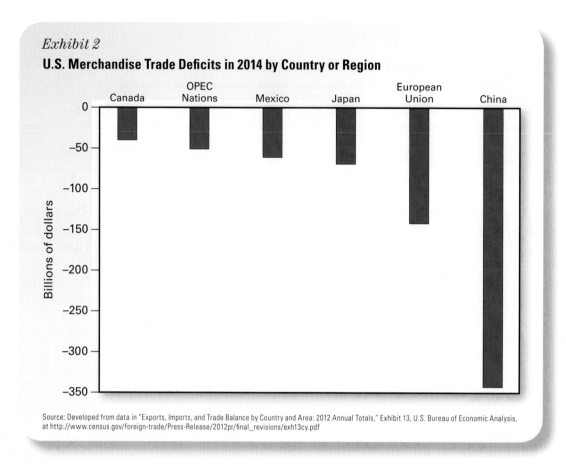

Exhibit 2

U.S. Merchandise Trade Deficits in 2014 by Country or Region

Source: Developed from data in "Exports, Imports, and Trade Balance by Country and Area: 2012 Annual Totals," Exhibit 13, U.S. Bureau of Economic Analysis, at http://www.census.gov/foreign-trade/Press-Release/2012pr/final_revisions/exh13cy.pdf

contributions of foreign charities, and the like. Money sent out of the country is a debit in the balance-of-payments account. For example, immigrants in the United States often send money to families back home. **Net unilateral transfers abroad** equal the unilateral transfers received from abroad by U.S. residents minus unilateral transfers sent abroad by U.S. residents. U.S. net unilateral transfers have been negative since World War II, except for 1991, when the U.S. government received sizable transfers from foreign governments to help pay their share of the Persian Gulf War. In 2014, net unilateral transfers were a negative $123.8 billion, with private transfers accounting for most of that (government grants and transfer payments made up the rest). Net unilateral transfers abroad averaged about $1,000 per U.S. household.

net unilateral transfers abroad The unilateral transfers (gifts and grants) received from abroad by U.S. residents minus the unilateral transfers U.S. residents send abroad

balance on current account The portion of the balance-of-payments account that measures a country's balance on goods and services, net investment income from abroad, plus net unilateral transfers abroad

financial account The record of a country's international transactions involving purchases and sales of financial and real assets

The United States places few restrictions on money sent out of the country. Other countries, particularly developing countries, strictly limit the amount that may be sent abroad. More generally, many developing countries, such as China, restrict the convertibility of their currency into other currencies.

When we add net unilateral transfers to net exports of goods and services and net income from assets owned abroad, we get the **balance on current account**, which is reported quarterly. Thus, *the current account includes all international transactions in currently produced goods and services, net income from foreign assets, and net unilateral transfers.* It can be negative, reflecting a current account deficit; positive, reflecting a current account surplus; or zero. In 2014, the current account deficit was $410.6 billion.

20-1f The Financial Account

The current account records international transactions in goods, services, asset income, and unilateral transfers. The **financial account** records international purchases of assets, including financial assets, such as stocks, bonds, and bank balances, and real assets such as land, housing, factories, and other physical assets. For example, U.S.

residents purchase foreign securities to earn a higher return and to diversify their investments. Money flows out when Americans buy foreign assets or build factories overseas. Money flows in when foreigners buy U.S. assets or build factories here. The international purchase or sale of assets is recorded in the financial account.

Between 1917 and 1982, the United States ran a financial account deficit, meaning that U.S. residents purchased more foreign assets than foreigners purchased U.S. assets. The net income from these foreign assets improved our current account balance. But in 1983, for the first time in 65 years, foreigners bought more U.S. assets than U.S. residents purchased abroad. Since 1983, foreigners have continued to buy more U.S. assets most years than the other way around, meaning there has usually been a surplus in the financial account. This is not as bad as it sounds, because foreign purchases of assets in the United States add to America's productive capacity and promote employment and labor productivity here. But any income from these assets flows to their foreign owners, not to Americans. Remember, the investment income from these assets shows up in the current account. Foreigners find America an attractive place to invest because U.S. capital markets are the deepest and most liquid in the world. In 2014, the financial account surplus was $141.6 billion.

20-1g Trade Deficits and Surpluses

Nations, like households, operate under a budget constraint. Spending cannot exceed income plus cash on hand and borrowed funds. We have distinguished between *current* transactions, which include exports, imports, asset income, and unilateral transfers, and *financial* transactions, which reflect net purchases of foreign real and financial assets. Any surplus or deficit in one account must be offset by deficits or surpluses in other balance-of-payments accounts.

Exhibit 3 presents the U.S. balance-of-payments statement for 2014. All transactions requiring payments from foreigners to U.S. residents are entered as credits, indicated by a plus sign (+), because they result in an inflow of funds from foreign residents to U.S. residents. All transactions requiring payments to foreigners from U.S. residents are entered as debits, indicated by a minus

> **"Money flows out when Americans buy foreign assets or build factories overseas. Money flows in when foreigners buy U.S. assets or build factories here."**

sign (−), because they result in an outflow of funds from U.S. residents to foreign residents. As you can see, a surplus in the financial account of $141.6 billion was more than offset by a current account deficit of $410.6 billion. A *statistical discrepancy* is required to balance the payments, and that come to $269.0 billion in 2014. Think of the statistical discrepancy as the official "fudge factor" that (1) measures the error in the balance of payments and (2) satisfies the double-entry bookkeeping requirement that total debits must equal total credits. The statistical discrepancy was large in 2014, because the global financial crisis created unusual gyrations that continued to affect international accounts.

Foreign exchange is the currency of another country needed to carry out international transactions. A country runs a deficit in its current account when the amount of foreign exchange received from exports, from foreign assets, and from unilateral transfers falls short of the

Exhibit 3

U.S. Balance of Payments for 2014 (billions of dollars)

Current Account	
1. Merchandise exports	+1,635.1
2. Merchandise imports	−2,370.9
3. Merchandise trade balance (1 + 2)	−735.8
4. Service exports	+709.4
5. Service imports	−478.3
6. Goods and services balance (3 + 4 + 5)	−504.7
7. Net investment income from abroad	+217.9
8. Net unilateral transfers	−123.8
9. Current account balance (6 + 7 + 8)	−410.6
Financial Account	
10. Change in U.S. owned assets abroad	−820.5
11. Change in foreign-owned assets in United States	+962.1
12. Financial account balance (10 + 11)	+141.6
13. Statistical discrepancy	+269.0
TOTAL (9 + 12 + 13)	**0.0**

Source: Computed from estimates by the Bureau of Economic Analysis, U.S. Department of Commerce at http://bea.gov/international/index.htm.

amount needed to pay for imports, pay foreign holders of U.S. assets, and make unilateral transfers. If the current account is in deficit, the necessary foreign exchange must come from a net inflow in the financial account. Such an inflow in the financial account could stem from borrowing from foreigners, selling domestic stocks and bonds to foreigners, selling a steel plant in Pittsburgh or a ski lodge in Aspen to foreigners, and so forth.

If a country runs a current account surplus, the foreign exchange received from exports, from foreign assets, and from unilateral transfers from abroad exceeds the amount needed to pay for imports, to pay foreign holders of U.S. assets, and to make unilateral transfers abroad. If the current account is in surplus, this excess foreign exchange results in a net outflow in the financial account through lending abroad, buying foreign stocks and bonds, buying a shoe plant in Italy or a villa on the French Riviera, and so forth.

When all transactions are considered, accounts must balance. The statistical discrepancy ensures that, in the aggregate, accounts sum to zero. A deficit in a particular account should not necessarily be viewed as a source of concern, nor should a surplus be a source of satisfaction. The deficit in the U.S. current account in recent years has usually been offset by a financial account surplus. As a result, foreigners have been acquiring more claims on U.S. assets.

20-2 FOREIGN EXCHANGE RATES AND MARKETS

Now that you have some idea about international flows, we can take a closer look at the forces that determine the underlying value of the currencies involved. Let's begin by looking at exchange rates and the market for foreign exchange.

20-2a Foreign Exchange

Foreign exchange, recall, is foreign money needed to carry out international transactions. The **exchange rate** is the cost measured in one country's currency of one unit of another country's currency. Exchange rates are determined by the interaction of the households, firms, private financial institutions, governments, and central banks that buy and sell foreign exchange. The exchange rate fluctuates to equate the quantity of foreign exchange

exchange rate The cost, measured in one country's currency, of one unit of another country's currency

demanded with the quantity supplied. Typically, foreign exchange is made up of bank deposits denominated in the foreign currency. When foreign travel is involved, foreign exchange often consists of foreign paper money.

The foreign exchange market incorporates all the arrangements used to buy and sell foreign exchange. This market is not so much a physical place as a network of telephones and computers connecting financial centers all over the world. Perhaps you have seen pictures of foreign exchange traders in New York, Frankfurt, London, or Tokyo in front of computer screens amid a tangle of phone lines. The foreign exchange market is like an all-night diner—it never closes. A trading center is always open somewhere in the world.

We will consider the market for the euro in terms of the dollar. But first, a little more about the euro. For decades the nations of Western Europe tried to increase their economic cooperation and trade. These countries believed they would be more productive and more

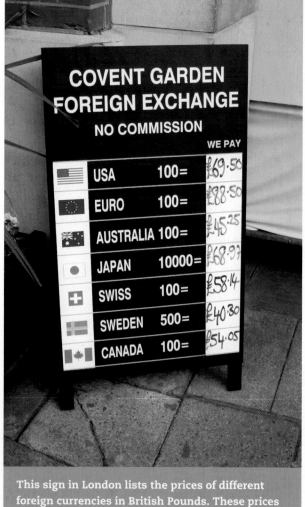

Keith Erskine/Alamy

This sign in London lists the prices of different foreign currencies in British Pounds. These prices can change daily or even several times a day!

competitive with the United States if they acted less like many separate economies and more like the 50 United States, with a single set of trade regulations and a single currency. Imagine the hassle involved if each of the 50 states had its own currency.

In 2002, euro notes and coins entered circulation in the 12 European countries adopting the common currency. The big advantage of a common currency is that Europeans no longer have to change money every time they cross a border or trade with another country in the group. Again, the inspiration for this is the United States, arguably the most successful economy in world history.

So the euro is the common currency of the *eurozone,* as the now 19-country region is usually called. The cost, or exchange rate, of the euro in terms of the dollar is the number of dollars required to purchase one euro. An increase in the number of dollars needed to purchase a euro indicates weakening, or **depreciation**, of the dollar. A decrease in the number of dollars needed to purchase a euro indicates strengthening, or **appreciation**, of the dollar. Put another way, a decrease in the number of euros needed to purchase a dollar is a depreciation of the dollar, and an increase in the number of euros needed to purchase a dollar is an appreciation of the dollar.

Because the exchange rate is usually a market price, it is determined by demand and supply: The equilibrium price is the one that equates quantity demanded with quantity supplied. To simplify the analysis, suppose that the United States and the eurozone make up the entire world, so the demand and supply for euros in international finance is the demand and supply for foreign exchange from the U.S. perspective.

20-2b The Demand for Foreign Exchange

Whenever U.S. residents need euros, they must buy them in the foreign exchange market, which could include your local bank, paying for them with dollars. Exhibit 4 depicts a market for foreign exchange—in this case, euros. The horizontal axis shows the quantity

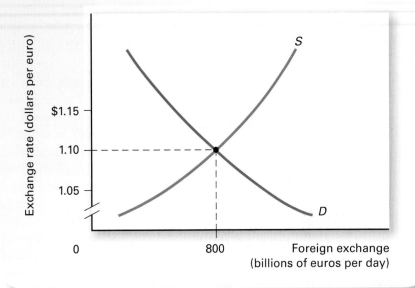

Exhibit 4
The Foreign Exchange Market

The fewer dollars needed to purchase one unit of foreign exchange, the lower the price of foreign goods and the greater the quantity of foreign goods demanded. Thus, the demand curve for foreign exchange slopes downward. An increase in the exchange rate makes U.S. products cheaper for foreigners. This implies an increase in the quantity of foreign exchange supplied. The supply curve of foreign exchange slopes upward.

of foreign exchange, measured here in billions of euros per day. The vertical axis shows the price per unit of foreign exchange, measured here in dollars per euro. The demand curve D for foreign exchange shows the inverse relationship between the dollar price of the euro and the quantity of euros demanded. Assumed constant along the demand curve are the incomes and preferences of U.S. consumers, expected inflation in the United States and in the eurozone, the euro price of goods in the eurozone, and interest rates in the United States and in the eurozone. U.S. residents have many reasons for demanding foreign exchange, but in the aggregate, the lower the dollar price of foreign exchange, other things constant, the greater the quantity of foreign exchange demanded.

A drop in the dollar price of foreign exchange, in this case the euro, means that fewer dollars are needed to purchase each euro, so the dollar prices of eurozone products (like German cars, Italian shoes, tickets to the

currency depreciation
With respect to the dollar, an increase in the number of dollars needed to purchase one unit of foreign exchange in a flexible rate system

currency appreciation
With respect to the dollar, a decrease in the number of dollars needed to purchase one unit of foreign exchange in a flexible rate system

Louvre, and eurozone securities) become cheaper. The cheaper it is to buy euros, the lower the dollar price of eurozone products to U.S. residents, so the greater the quantity of euros demanded by U.S. residents, other things remain constant. For example, a cheap enough euro might persuade you to tour Rome, climb the Austrian Alps, wander the museumsw of Paris, or crawl the pubs of Dublin.

> **"The cheaper it is to buy euros, the lower the dollar price of eurozone products to U.S. residents, so the greater the quantity of euros demanded by U.S. residents, other things remain constant."**

20-2c The Supply of Foreign Exchange

The supply of foreign exchange is generated by the desire of foreign residents to acquire dollars—that is, to exchange euros for dollars. Eurozone residents want dollars to buy U.S. goods and services, acquire U.S. assets, make loans in dollars, or send dollars to their U.S. friends and relatives. Euros are supplied in the foreign exchange market to acquire the dollars people want. An increase in the dollar-per-euro exchange rate, other things constant, makes U.S. products cheaper for eurozone residents because foreign residents need fewer euros to get the same number of dollars. For example, suppose a Dell computer sells for $1,155. If the exchange rate is $1.05 per euro, that computer costs 1,100 euros; if the exchange rate is $1.10 per euro, it costs only 1,050 euros. The number of Dell computers demanded in the eurozone increases as the dollar-per-euro exchange rate increases, other things constant, so more euros will be supplied on the foreign exchange market to buy dollars.

The positive relationship between the dollar-per-euro exchange rate and the quantity of euros supplied on the foreign exchange market is expressed in Exhibit 4 by the upward-sloping supply curve for foreign exchange

(again, euros in our example). The supply curve assumes that other things remain constant, including eurozone incomes and tastes, expectations about inflation in the eurozone and in the United States, and interest rates in the eurozone and in the United States.

20-2d The Foreign Exchange Rate

Exhibit 4 brings together the demand and supply for foreign exchange to determine the exchange rate. At a rate of $1.10 per euro, the quantity of euros demanded equals the quantity supplied—in our example, 800 billion euros per day. Once achieved, this equilibrium rate will hold until a change occurs in one of the factors that affect supply or demand. If the exchange rate is allowed to adjust freely, or to *float*, in response to market forces, the market will clear continually, as the quantities of foreign exchange demanded and supplied are equated.

What if the initial equilibrium is upset by a change in one of the underlying forces that affect demand or supply? For example, suppose higher U.S. incomes increase American demand for all normal goods, including those from the eurozone. This shifts the U.S. demand curve for foreign exchange to the right, as Americans buy more Italian marble, Dutch chocolate, German automobiles, Parisian vacations, and eurozone securities.

This increased demand for euros is shown in Exhibit 5 by a rightward shift of the demand curve for foreign exchange. The demand increase from D to D' leads to an increase in the exchange rate per euro from $1.10 to $1.12. Thus, the euro increases in value, or appreciates, while the dollar falls in value, or depreciates. An increase in U.S. income should not

> **"An increase in the dollar-per-euro exchange rate, other things constant, makes U.S. products cheaper for foreigners because foreign residents need fewer euros to get the same number of dollars."**

If the exchange rate is allowed to adjust freely, or to float, in response to market forces, the market will clear continually, as the quantities of foreign exchange demanded and supplied are equated.

Don Farrall/Getty Images

affect the euro supply curve, though it does increase the *quantity of euros supplied*. The higher exchange value of the euro prompts those in the eurozone to buy more American products and assets, which are now cheaper in terms of the euro.

TO REVIEW: Any increase in the demand for foreign exchange or any decrease in its supply, other things constant, increases the number of dollars required to purchase one unit of foreign exchange, which is a depreciation of the dollar. On the other hand, any decrease in the demand for foreign exchange or any increase in its supply, other things constant, reduces the number of dollars required to purchase one unit of foreign exchange, which is an appreciation of the dollar.

20-3 OTHER FACTORS INFLUENCING FOREIGN EXCHANGE MARKETS

So far, the market for foreign exchange has been presented just like any other market: Demand and supply come together to determine the equilibrium exchange rate, or price of foreign exchange. Simple enough, but the market for foreign exchange is complicated by the types of actors in this market and by the types of regulations and restrictions involved. In this section, we look at how these other factors shape this market.

20-3a Arbitrageurs and Speculators

Exchange rates between two currencies are nearly identical at any given time in markets around the world. For example, the dollar price of a euro is usually the same in New York, Frankfurt, Tokyo, London, Zurich, Hong Kong, Istanbul, and other financial centers. **Arbitrageurs**—dealers who take advantage of tiny differences in exchange rates across markets by buying low and selling high—ensure this equality. For example, if one euro

arbitrageur Someone who takes advantage of tiny differences in the exchange rate across markets by simultaneously purchasing currency in one market and selling it in another market

Exhibit 5

Effect on the Foreign Exchange Market of an Increased Demand for Euros

The intersection of the demand curve for foreign exchange, *D*, and the supply curve for foreign exchange, *S*, determines the exchange rate. At an exchange rate of $1.10 per euro, the quantity of euros demanded equals the quantity supplied. An increase in the demand for euros from *D* to *D'* increases the exchange rate from $1.10 to $1.12 per euro.

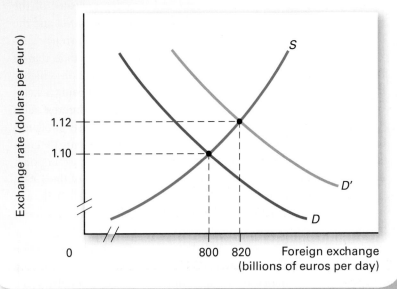

costs $1.09 in New York but $1.10 in Frankfurt, an arbitrageur could buy, say, $1,000,000 worth of euros in New York and at the same time sell them in Frankfurt for $1,009,174, thereby earning $9,174 minus the transaction costs of the trades.

Because an arbitrageur buys and sells simultaneously, little risk is involved. In our example, the arbitrageur increased the demand for euros in New York and increased the supply of euros in Frankfurt. These actions increased the dollar price of euros in New York and decreased it in Frankfurt, thereby squeezing down the difference in exchange rates. Note that arbitrage opportunities are short lived; most are available for less than a second. High speed computers act on such opportunities instantly.[1] Exchange rates may still change because of market forces, but they tend to change in all markets simultaneously.

The demand and supply of foreign exchange arises from many sources—from importers and exporters, investors in foreign assets, central banks, tourists, arbitrageurs, and speculators. **Speculators** buy or sell foreign exchange in hopes of profiting by trading the currency at a more favorable exchange rate later. By taking risks, speculators aim to profit from market fluctuations—they try to buy low and sell high. In contrast, arbitrageurs take less risk, because they *simultaneously* buy currency in one market and sell it in another.

Finally, people in countries suffering from economic and political turmoil, such as occurred in Russia, Indonesia, the Philippines, and Zimbabwe, may buy *hard* currency as a hedge against the depreciation and instability of their own currencies. The dollar has long been accepted as an international medium of exchange. It is also the currency of choice in the world markets for oil and illegal drugs. But the euro eventually may challenge that dominance, in part because the largest euro denomination, the 500-euro note, is worth more than five times the largest U.S. denomination, the $100 note. So it would be about five times easier to smuggle euro notes than U.S. notes of equal value. Still, fiscal problems in some eurozone nations such as Greece and Spain have taken some of the shine off the euro.

speculator Someone who buys or sells foreign exchange in hopes of profiting from fluctuations in the exchange rate over time

purchasing power parity theory The idea that the exchange rate between two countries will adjust in the long run to equalize the cost of a basket of internationally traded goods

1. Takatoshi Ito et al. "Free Lunch: Arbitrage Opportunities in the Foreign Exchange Markets," NBER Working Paper No. 18541 (November 2012).

20-3b Purchasing Power Parity

As long as trade across borders is unrestricted and as long as exchange rates are allowed to adjust freely, the **purchasing power parity (PPP) theory** predicts that the exchange rate between two currencies will adjust in the long run to equalize the cost across countries of an internationally traded basket of goods. *A given basket of internationally traded goods should therefore sell for about the same around the world (except for differences reflecting transportation costs and the like).* Suppose a basket of internationally traded goods that sells for $11,000 in the United States sells for €10,000 in the eurozone. According to the purchasing power parity theory, the equilibrium exchange rate should be $1.10 per euro. If this were not the case—if the exchange rate were, say, $1.05 per euro—then you could exchange $10,500 for €10,000, with which you buy the basket of commodities in the eurozone. You could then sell that basket of goods in the States for $11,000, yielding you a profit of $500 minus any transaction costs. Selling dollars and buying euros will also drive up the dollar price of euros.

> **"A given basket of internationally traded goods should sell for about the same around the world."**

The purchasing power parity theory is more of a long-run predictor than a day-to-day indicator of the relationship between changes in the price level and the exchange rate. For example, a country's currency generally appreciates when inflation is lower than that of other countries and depreciates when inflation is higher compared to other countries. Likewise, a country's currency generally appreciates when its real interest rates are higher than in other countries, because foreigners are more willing to buy and hold investments denominated in that high-interest currency. As a case in point, the dollar appreciated during the first half of the 1980s, when real U.S. interest rates were relatively high, and depreciated during 2002 to 2004, when real U.S. interest rates were relatively low.

Because of trade barriers, central bank intervention in exchange markets, and the fact that many products are not traded or are not comparable across countries, the purchasing power parity theory usually does not explain exchange rates at a particular point in time that well. For example, if you went shopping in Switzerland tomorrow, you would soon notice a dollar does not buy as much there as it does in the United States.

20-3c Flexible Exchange Rates

For the most part, we have been discussing **flexible exchange rates**, which are determined by demand and supply. Flexible, or *floating*, exchange rates adjust continually to the myriad forces that buffet foreign exchange markets. Consider how the exchange rate is linked to the balance-of-payments accounts. Debit entries in the current or financial accounts increase the demand for foreign exchange, resulting in a depreciation of the dollar. Credit entries in these accounts increase the supply of foreign exchange, resulting in an appreciation of the dollar.

20-3d Fixed Exchange Rates

When exchange rates are flexible, governments usually have little direct role in foreign exchange markets. But if governments try to set exchange rates, active and ongoing central bank intervention is often necessary to establish and maintain these **fixed exchange rates**. Suppose the European Central Bank selects what it thinks is an appropriate rate of exchange between the dollar and the euro. It attempts to *fix*, or to *peg*, the exchange rate within a narrow band around the particular value selected. If the euro threatens to climb above the maximum acceptable exchange rate, monetary authorities must sell euros and buy dollars, thereby keeping the dollar price of the euro down. Conversely, if the euro threatens to drop below the minimum acceptable exchange rate, monetary authorities must sell dollars and buy euros. This increased demand for the euro will keep its value up relative to the dollar. Through such intervention in the foreign exchange market, monetary authorities try to stabilize the exchange rate, keeping it within the specified band.

If monetary officials must keep selling foreign exchange to keep the value of their domestic currency from falling, they risk running out of foreign exchange reserves. Faced with this threat, the government has several options for eliminating the exchange rate disequilibrium. First, the pegged exchange rate can be increased, meaning that foreign currency costs more dollars. This is a **devaluation** of the dollar. (A decrease in the pegged exchange rate is called a **revaluation**.) Second, the government can reduce the domestic demand for foreign exchange directly by imposing restrictions on imports or on financial outflows. Many developing countries do

this. Third, the government can adopt policies to slow the domestic economy, increase interest rates, or reduce inflation relative to that of the country's trading partners, thereby indirectly decreasing the demand for foreign exchange and increasing the supply of foreign exchange. Several Asian economies, such as South Korea and Indonesia, pursued such policies to stabilize their currencies. Finally, the government can allow the disequilibrium to persist and ration the available foreign reserves through some form of foreign exchange control.

This concludes our introduction to the theories of international finance. Let's examine international finance in practice.

20-4 INTERNATIONAL MONETARY SYSTEM

From 1879 to 1914, the international monetary system operated under a **gold standard**, whereby the major currencies were convertible into gold at a fixed rate. For example, the U.S. dollar could be redeemed at the U.S. Treasury for one-twentieth of an ounce of gold. The British pound could be redeemed at the British Exchequer, or treasury, for one-fourth of an ounce of gold. Because each British pound could buy five times as much gold as each dollar, one British pound exchanged for $5.

The gold standard provided a predictable exchange rate, one that did not vary as long as currencies could be redeemed for gold at the official rate. But the money supply in each country was determined in part by the flow of gold among countries, so each country's monetary policy was influenced by the supply of gold. A balance-of-payments deficit resulted in a loss of gold, which theoretically caused a country's money supply to shrink. A balance-of-payments surplus resulted in an influx of gold, which theoretically caused a country's money supply to expand. The supply of money throughout the

flexible exchange rate Rate determined in foreign exchange markets by the forces of demand and supply without government intervention

fixed exchange rate Rate of exchange between currencies pegged within a narrow range and maintained by the central bank's ongoing purchases and sales of currencies

currency devaluation An increase in the official pegged price of foreign exchange in terms of the domestic currency

currency revaluation A reduction in the official pegged price of foreign exchange in terms of the domestic currency

gold standard An arrangement whereby the currencies of most countries were convertible into gold at a fixed rate world also depended on the vagaries of gold discoveries. When gold production did not keep pace with the growth in economic activity, the price level dropped. When gold production exceeded the growth in economic activity, the price level rose. For example, gold discoveries in Alaska and South Africa in the late 1890s expanded the U.S. money supply, leading to inflation.

20-4a The Bretton Woods Agreement

During World War I, many countries could no longer convert their currencies into gold, and the gold standard eventually collapsed, disrupting international trade during the 1920s and 1930s. Once an Allied victory in World War II appeared certain, the Allies met in Bretton Woods, New Hampshire, in July 1944 to formulate a new international monetary system. Because the United States had a strong economy and was not ravaged by the war, the dollar was selected as the key reserve currency in the new international monetary system. All exchange rates were fixed in terms of the dollar, and the United States, which held most of the world's gold reserves, stood ready to convert foreign holdings of dollars into gold at a rate of $35 per ounce. Even though the rate that dollars could be exchanged for gold was fixed by the Bretton Woods agreement, *other* countries could adjust *their* exchange rates relative to the U.S. dollar if they found a chronic disequilibrium in

International Monetary Fund An international organization that establishes rules for maintaining the international monetary system and makes loans to countries with temporary balance-of-payments problems

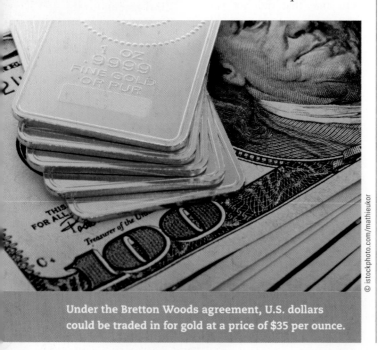

Under the Bretton Woods agreement, U.S. dollars could be traded in for gold at a price of $35 per ounce.

their balance of payments—that is, if a country faced a large and persistent deficit or surplus. In short, America's promise to redeem foreign holdings of U.S. dollars for a fixed amount of gold anchored the international monetary system.

The Bretton Woods agreement also created the **International Monetary Fund (IMF)** to set rules for maintaining the international monetary system, to standardize financial reporting for international trade, and to make loans to countries with temporary balance-of-payments problems. The IMF lends a revolving fund of about $400 billion to economies in need of reserves. Headquartered in Washington, D.C., the IMF has about 190 member countries and a staff of 2,600 drawn from around the world (half the staff are economists).

20-4b Demise of the Bretton Woods System

During the latter part of the 1960s, inflation increased in the United States more than in other countries. Because of U.S. inflation, the dollar had become *overvalued* at the official exchange rate, meaning that the gold value of the dollar exceeded the exchange value of the dollar. In 1971, U.S. merchandise imports exceeded merchandise exports for the first time since World War II. Foreigners exchanged dollars for gold. To stem this gold outflow, the United States stopped exchanging gold for dollars, but this just made the dollar less attractive. In December 1971, the world's 10 richest countries met in Washington and devalued the dollar by 8 percent. They hoped this would put the dollar on firmer footing and would save the "dollar standard." With prices rising at different rates around the world, however, an international monetary system based on fixed exchange rates was doomed.

When the U.S. trade deficit tripled in 1972, it became clear that the dollar was still overvalued. In early 1973, the dollar was devalued another 10 percent, but this did not quiet foreign exchange markets. The dollar, for three decades the anchor of the international monetary system, suddenly looked vulnerable, and speculators began betting that the dollar would fall even more, so they sold dollars. Dollars were exchanged for German marks because the mark appeared to be the most stable currency. Bundesbank, Germany's central bank, tried to defend the dollar's official exchange rate by selling marks and buying dollars. Why didn't Germany want the mark to appreciate? Appreciation would make German goods more expensive abroad and foreign goods cheaper in Germany, thereby reducing German exports and increasing German imports. So the mark's appreciation would

© istockphoto.com/mathieukor

reduce German output and employment. But after selling $10 billion worth of marks to buy dollars, the Bundesbank gave up defending the dollar. As soon as the value of the dollar was allowed to float against the mark, the Bretton Woods system, already on shaky ground, collapsed.

20-4c The Current System: Managed Float

The Bretton Woods system has been replaced by a **managed float system**, which combines features of a freely floating exchange rate with sporadic intervention by central banks as a way of moderating exchange rate fluctuations among the world's major currencies. Most small countries, particularly developing countries, still peg their currencies to one of the major currencies (such as the U.S. dollar) or to a "basket" of major currencies. What's more, in developing countries, private international borrowing and lending are severely restricted; some governments allow residents to purchase foreign exchange only for certain purposes. In some countries, different exchange rates apply to different categories of transactions.

> **"An ideal exchange rate system is one that would foster international trade, lower inflation, and promote a more stable world economy."**

Critics of flexible exchange rates argue that they are inflationary, because they free monetary authorities to pursue expansionary policies; furthermore, flexible exchange rates have often been volatile. This volatility creates uncertainty and risk for importers and exporters, increasing the transaction costs of international trade. Furthermore, exchange rate volatility can lead to wrenching changes in the competitiveness of a country's export sector. These changes cause swings in employment, resulting in louder calls for import restrictions. For example, the exchange rate between the Japanese yen and the U.S. dollar has been relatively unstable, particularly because of international speculation.

Policy makers are always on the lookout for a system that will perform better than the current managed float system, with its fluctuating currency values. *Their ideal is a system that will foster international trade, lower inflation, and promote a more stable world economy.* International finance ministers have acknowledged that the world must find an international standard and establish greater exchange rate stability.

20-5 FINAL WORD

The United States is very much a part of the world economy, not only as one of the largest exporter nations but also as the largest importer nation. Although the dollar remains the unit of transaction in many international settlements—OPEC, for example, still prices crude oil in dollars—gyrations of exchange rates have made those involved in international finance wary of putting all their eggs in one basket. The international monetary system is now going through a difficult period as it gropes for a new source of stability more than four decades after the collapse of the Bretton Woods agreement.

> **managed float system**
> An exchange rate system that combines features of freely floating rates with sporadic intervention by central banks

STUDY TOOLS 20

READY TO STUDY? IN THE BOOK, YOU CAN:

☐ Work the Problems at the end of the chapter.

☐ Rip out the chapter review card for a handy summary of the chapter and key terms.

ONLINE AT CENGAGEBRAIN.COM YOU CAN:

☐ Collect StudyBits while you read and study the chapter.

☐ Quiz yourself on key concepts.

☐ Prepare for tests with chapter flash cards as well as flash cards that you create.

☐ Watch videos to explore economics further.

CHAPTER 20 PROBLEMS

Your instructor can access the answers to these problems online at http://cengagebrain.com.

20-1 Summarize the major accounts in the balance of trade, and explain how they balance out

1. *(Balance of Payments)* The following are hypothetical data for the U.S. balance of payments. Use the data to calculate each of the following:
   a. Merchandise trade balance
   b. Balance on goods and services
   c. Balance on current account
   d. Financial account balance
   e. Statistical discrepancy

	Billions of Dollars
Merchandise exports	350.0
Merchandise imports	2,425.0
Service exports	2,145
Service imports	170
Net income and net transfers	221.5
Change in U.S.-owned assets abroad	245.0
Change in foreign-owned assets in U.S.	100.0

2. *(Balance of Payments)* Explain where in the U.S. balance of payments an entry would be recorded for each of the following:
   a. A Hong Kong financier buys some U.S. corporate stock.
   b. A U.S. tourist in Paris buys some perfume to take home.
   c. A Japanese company sells machinery to a pineapple company in Hawaii.
   d. U.S. farmers gave food to starving children in Ethiopia.
   e. The U.S. Treasury sells a bond to a Saudi Arabian prince.
   f. A U.S. tourist flies to France on Air France.
   g. A U.S. company sells insurance to a foreign firm.

20-2 Describe how the foreign exchange rate is determined using demand and supply curves and explain the shapes of the curves

3. *(Determining the Exchange Rate)* Use these data to answer the following questions about the market for British pounds:

Pound Price (in $)	Quantity Demanded (of pounds)	Quantity Supplied (of pounds)
$4.00	50	100
3.00	75	75
2.00	100	50

   a. Draw the demand and supply curves for pounds, and determine the equilibrium exchange rate (dollars per pound).
   b. Suppose that the supply of pounds doubles. Draw the new supply curve.
   c. What is the new equilibrium exchange rate?
   d. Has the dollar appreciated or depreciated?
   e. What happens to U.S. imports of British goods?

20-3 Describe the purchasing power parity theory

4. *(Purchasing Power Parity Theory)* What is the purchasing power parity theory. Is it a short-run or a long-run theory. Why may it not always work?

20-4 Trace the evolution of exchange rate regimes from the gold standard to the current system

5. *(Exchange Rate Regimes)* Briefly trace the exchange rate regimes beginning with the gold standard up to our current system.
6. *(Exchange Rates)* Discuss the differences between a flexible exchange rate and a fixed exchange rate. What measures can the government take to maintain fixed exchange rates?
7. *(The Current System: Managed Float)* What is a managed float? What are the disadvantages of freely floating exchange rates that led countries to the managed float system?

MICRO
ECON
ONLINE

REVIEW FLASHCARDS
ANYTIME, ANYWHERE!

**Create Flashcards
from Your StudyBits**

**Review Key Term
Flashcards Already
Loaded on the
StudyBoard**

21 | Economic Development

dbimages/Alamy

LEARNING OUTCOMES

After studying this chapter, you will be able to...

21-1 Besides income, identify ways that low-income economies differ from high-income economies

21-2 Describe the factors that help make workers in high-income economies more productive than workers in other economies

21-3 Explain how trade restrictions can slow economic development in poorer countries

21-4 Outline some unintended consequences of foreign aid on economic development

After finishing this chapter go to **PAGE 378** for **STUDY TOOLS**

Topics discussed in Chapter 21 include

- Developing countries
- The key to development
- Privatization
- The poorest billion
- Foreign trade and development
- Foreign aid and development
- Import substitution vs. export promotion
- Economic convergence

▸ Why are some countries so poor while others are so rich?

▸ What determines the wealth of nations?

▸ Why do families in low-income countries have more children than those in higher-income countries?

▸ And how might programs that send subsidized food and used clothing to poor countries have the unintended consequence of retarding economic development there?

People around the world face the day under quite different circumstances. Even during a national recession, most Americans rise from a comfortable bed in a nice home, select the day's clothing from a wardrobe, choose from a variety of breakfast foods, and ride to school or to work in one of the family's personal automobiles. But some of the world's 7.4 billion people have little housing, clothing, or food. They have no automobile and no formal job. Their health is poor, as is their education. Many cannot read or write. The World Health Organization (WHO) estimates that a billion people need eyeglasses but can't afford them.

> **"Why are some countries so poor while others are so rich?"**

In this chapter, we sort out rich nations from poor ones and try to explain the difference. We discuss sources of economic development, weigh the pros and cons of foreign aid, and see whether poorer countries are closing the income gap with richer ones.

21-1 WORLDS APART

Differences in economic vitality among countries are huge. Countries are classified in a variety of ways based on their economic development. The yardstick most often used to compare living standards across nations is the amount an economy produces per capita, or *output per capita*. The World Bank, an economic development institution affiliated with the United Nations (UN), classifies economies based on income per capita. The measure begins with *gross national income (GNI)*, which is the market value of all goods and services produced by resources supplied by the countries' residents and firms, regardless of the location of the resources. For example, U.S. GNI includes profit earned by an American factory in Great Britain but excludes profits earned by a Japanese factory in Kentucky.

GNI measures both the value of output produced and the income that output generates. The World Bank estimates the GNI per capita, then adjusts figures across countries based on the purchasing power of that income in each country. Using this measure, the World Bank sorts countries around the world into three major groups: *high-income economies*, *middle-income economies*, and *low-income economies*.

Data on world population and world output are summarized in Exhibit 1. High-income economies in 2014 made up only 18 percent of the world's population, but accounted for 52 percent of world output. So high-income economies, *with less than one fifth of the world's population, produced more than half of the world's output*. Middle-income economies made up 70 percent of the world's population, but accounted for 46 percent of world output. And low-income countries made up 12 percent of the world's population, but account for just 2 percent of world output.

21-1a Developing and Industrial Economies

The low- and middle-income economies are usually referred to as **developing countries**. Most high-income economies are also referred to as **industrial market countries**. So low- and middle-income economies, what are called developing countries, made up 82 percent of the world's

developing countries Low-income and middle-income economies; most are also known as emerging market economies

industrial market countries Economically advanced capitalist countries of Europe, North America, Australia, New Zealand, and Japan; also known as developed countries and high-income economies

Exhibit 1

Share of World Population and World Output From High-, Middle-, and Low-Income Economies as of 2014

(a) Share of world population from high-, middle-, and low-income economies

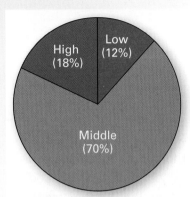

(b) Share of world output from high-, middle-, and low-income economies

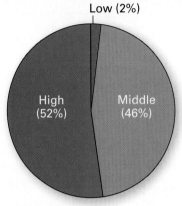

Source: Based on population and output estimated from the World Bank's *World Development Indicators: 2015*, Table 1. Find the World Bank at http://data.worldbank.org/products/wdi.

population in 2014 but produced only 48 percent of the output. Compared to industrial market countries, developing countries usually have higher rates of illiteracy, higher unemployment, faster population growth, and exports consisting mostly of agricultural products and raw materials. Most developing countries are also known as emerging market economies.

On average, nearly half of the labor force in developing countries works in agriculture versus only about 3 percent in industrial market countries. Because farming methods are sometimes primitive in developing countries, farm productivity is low and some households barely subsist. For example, over half the labor force in India works in agriculture, but that sector accounts for less than one-fifth of the nation's output.[1] Industrial market countries, or *developed countries*, are primarily the economically advanced capitalist countries of Europe, North America, Australia, New Zealand, and Japan. They were the first to experience long-term economic growth during the 19th century.

Exhibit 2 presents income per capita in 2014 for a sample of high-, middle-, and low-income economies. Because most countries in the sample have large populations, together they account for about 55 percent of the world's population. Countries are listed from top to bottom in descending order based on income per capita. Again,

figures have been adjusted to reflect the actual purchasing power of the local currency in its respective economy. The bars in the chart are color-coded, with high-income economies in blue, middle-income economies in orange, low-income economies in red, and the world average in green. Per capita income in the United States, the exhibit's top-ranked country, was more than 4 times that of China, a middle-income economy. But per capita in China, in turn, was more than 8 times that of Ethiopia and 18 times that of the Democratic Republic of the Congo, both poor African nations. Residents of China likely feel poor relative to Americans, but they appear well off compared to residents of the poorest nations. U.S per capita income was 36 times that of Ethiopia, and 78 times that of the Congo, one of the poorest nations on Earth. Thus, there is a tremendous range of per capita income around the world. World per capita income in 2014 was $16,100, as shown by the green bar.

Exhibit 2 looks at income per capita, but neither income nor population is always measured accurately, especially in the poorest countries. Some economists have looked for other ways of measuring an economy, such as how lit up a country is at night. Consumption of most goods and services at night requires light. As personal income rises, so does consumption and night lights, which can be measured by satellite from outer space. This night-light measure is useful when other data are of poor quality, as with many African economies, or when data are simply not available, as in Somalia, Liberia, and North Korea.[2]

21-1b Health and Nutrition

Different stages of development among countries are reflected in a number of ways besides per capita income. For example, many people in developing countries suffer from poor health as a result of malnutrition and disease.

1. U.S. International Trade Commission, *Effect of Tariffs and Nontariff Measures on U.S. Agricultural Exports*, Investigation No. 332-504, USITC Publication 4107 (November 2009).

2. J. Vernon Henderson, Adam Storeygard, and David Weil, "Measuring Economic Growth from Outer Space," *American Economic Review*, 102 (April 2012): 994–1028.

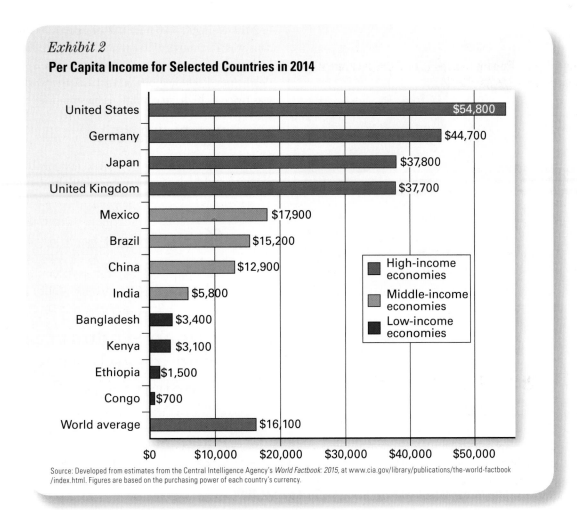

Exhibit 2

Per Capita Income for Selected Countries in 2014

Country	Income
United States	$54,800
Germany	$44,700
Japan	$37,800
United Kingdom	$37,700
Mexico	$17,900
Brazil	$15,200
China	$12,900
India	$5,800
Bangladesh	$3,400
Kenya	$3,100
Ethiopia	$1,500
Congo	$700
World average	$16,100

Legend:
- High-income economies
- Middle-income economies
- Low-income economies

Source: Developed from estimates from the Central Intelligence Agency's *World Factbook: 2015*, at www.cia.gov/library/publications/the-world-factbook/index.html. Figures are based on the purchasing power of each country's currency.

HIV/AIDS is devastating some developing countries, particularly those in sub-Saharan Africa. In 2013, about 25 percent of people ages 15 to 49 in Swaziland, Botswana, and Lesotho had HIV/AIDS, compared to less than 1 percent in the United States.[3] The 20 countries with the highest incidence of HIV/AIDS were in Africa. Another health scourge in Africa is the tsetse fly. Harmful to humans and lethal to livestock, this fly has slowed the domestication of animals and reduced the use of plows, all of which has retarded economic development in Africa.[4] In sub-Saharan Africa, life expectancy at birth averaged 53 years versus 80 years in high-income economies, 69 years in middle-income economies, and 58 years in all low-income economies. Poor health has other bad consequences for the individual and the economy. For example, research shows that a higher rate of HIV/AIDS cuts the general level of education in the country. Even those not infected are less willing to invest in their own education.[5]

3. *World Development Indicators: 2015*, World Bank, Table 3 at http://data.worldbank.org/products/wdi.

4. Marcella Alsan, "The Effects of the TseTse Fly on African Development," *American Economic Review*, 105 (January 2015): 382–410.

5. Jane Fortson, "Mortality Risk and Human Capital Investment: The Impact of HIV/AIDS in Sub-Saharan Africa," *Review of Economics and Statistics*, 93 (February 2011): 1–15.

Malnutrition

Those in the poorest countries consume only half the calories of those in high-income countries. Even if an infant survives the first year, malnutrition can turn normal childhood diseases, such as measles, into life-threatening events. The WHO cites malnutrition as the biggest single threat to the world's public health. Malnutrition is a primary or contributing factor in more than half of the deaths of children under the age of 5 in low-income countries. Diseases that are well controlled in the industrial countries—malaria, whooping cough, polio, dysentery, typhoid, and cholera—can become epidemics in poor countries. About a billion people on Earth don't have enough to eat.

Infant Mortality

Health differences among countries are reflected in mortality rates among infants less than one year old. These rates are much greater in low-income countries than in high-income countries. Rates for our representative sample of high-, medium-, and low-income economies appear in Exhibit 3. Again, high-income

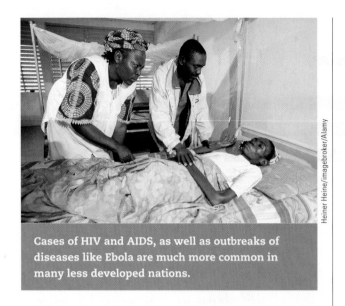

Cases of HIV and AIDS, as well as outbreaks of diseases like Ebola are much more common in many less developed nations.

Heiner Heine/imagebroker/Alamy

in 2014 averaged 53.6 infant deaths per 1,000 live births. This was 13 times greater than the 4.1 rate for the four high-income economies. The world averaged 35.6 infant deaths per 1,000 live births. In 1990, the world average was twice as high, so conditions have improved.

21-1c High Birth Rates

Developing countries are identified not only by their low incomes and high mortality rates but also by their high

economies are blue bars, middle-income are orange bars, low-income are red bars, and the world average is the green bar. Among the dozen countries shown, infant mortality was highest in the sub-Saharan African nation of the Congo. Rates for the four low-income economies

"The birth rate is one of the clearest ways of distinguishing between industrial and developing countries."

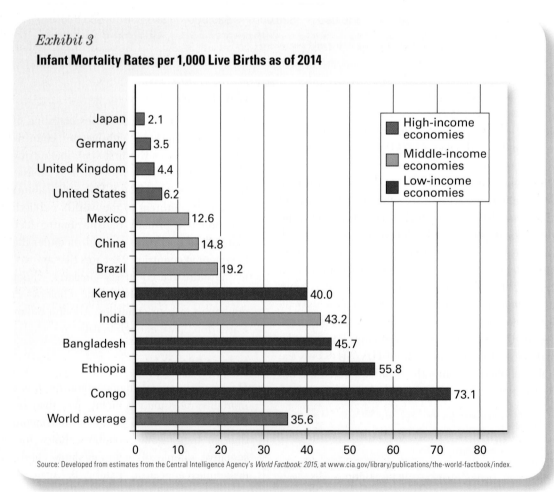

Exhibit 3

Infant Mortality Rates per 1,000 Live Births as of 2014

Country	Rate
Japan	2.1
Germany	3.5
United Kingdom	4.4
United States	6.2
Mexico	12.6
China	14.8
Brazil	19.2
Kenya	40.0
India	43.2
Bangladesh	45.7
Ethiopia	55.8
Congo	73.1
World average	35.6

Legend: High-income economies, Middle-income economies, Low-income economies

Source: Developed from estimates from the Central Intelligence Agency's *World Factbook: 2015,* at www.cia.gov/library/publications/the-world-factbook/index.

Exhibit 4

Average Number of Births During a Woman's Lifetime as of 2014

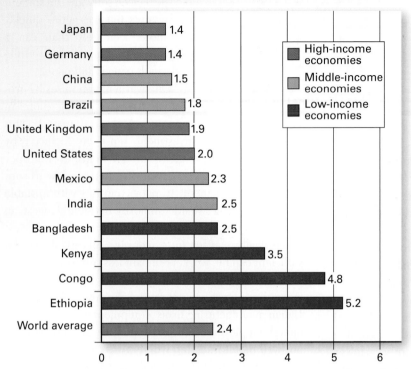

Legend:
- High-income economies
- Middle-income economies
- Low-income economies

Country	Births
Japan	1.4
Germany	1.4
China	1.5
Brazil	1.8
United Kingdom	1.9
United States	2.0
Mexico	2.3
India	2.5
Bangladesh	2.5
Kenya	3.5
Congo	4.8
Ethiopia	5.2
World average	2.4

Source: Developed from estimates from the Central Intelligence Agency's *World Factbook: 2015,* at www.cia.gov/library/publications /the-world-factbook/index.html.

birth rates. In fact, the birth rate is one of the clearest ways of distinguishing between industrial and developing countries. Few low-income economies have a fertility rate below 2.2 births on average over a woman's lifetime, but no industrial market economy has a fertility rate above that level.

Exhibit 4 presents total fertility rates per woman for selected countries as of 2014. Ethiopia and the Congo, the two poorest nations on the list, each has among the world's highest fertility rates. For example, each woman in Ethiopia on average gave birth to 5.2 children during her lifetime. Note that the four low-income economies, shown as red bars, have the highest fertility rates. Historically, families tend to be larger in poor countries because children are viewed as a source of farm labor and as economic and social security as the parents age. Most developing countries have no pension or social security system for the aged. The higher child mortality rates in poorer countries also engender higher birth rates, as parents strive to ensure a sufficiently large family.

Sub-Saharan African nations are the poorest in the world and have the fastest-growing populations. Because of high fertility rates in the poorest countries, children under 15 years old make up nearly half the population there. In high-income countries, children make up less than one-fifth of the population. Italy, a high-income economy, was the first country in history to have more people over the age of 65 than under the age of 15. Germany, Greece, Spain, Portugal, Japan, Hungary, Switzerland, and Canada have since followed. In the United States, 19.4 percent of the population in 2014 was under 15 years of age and 14.5 percent was 65 or older. An aging population poses fiscal problems for any country, because these same countries typically offer generous health and pension benefits to the elderly.

Again, fertility rates are higher in developing economies than in industrial economies. The exceptions in Exhibit 4 are China and Brazil, middle-income countries with fertility rates lower than those of the United States and the United Kingdom. Fearing overpopulation, Chinese officials limit each family to one child. Brazil's fertility rate has declined because of greater urbanization, more women in the workforce, and wider availability of birth-control information.

In some developing countries, the population growth rate has exceeded the growth rate in total production, so the standard of living as measured by per capita output has declined. Still, even in the poorest of countries, attitudes about family size are changing. According to the United Nations, the birth rate during a typical woman's lifetime in a developing country has fallen from six children in 1965 to under three children today. Evidence from developing countries more generally indicates that when women have employment opportunities outside the home, fertility rates decline. And as women become better educated, they earn more and tend to have fewer children. Incidentally, after taking child mortality into account, a fertility rate of 2.1 would keep the population constant over time. Because the world average in 2014 was 2.4 births per woman, the world population will continue to grow.

21-1d Women in Developing Countries

Throughout the world, the poverty rate is higher for women than men, particularly women who head households. The percent of households headed by women varies from country to country, but nears 50 percent in some areas of Africa and the Caribbean. Because women often must work in the home as well as in the labor market, poverty can impose a special hardship on them. In many cultures, women's responsibilities include gathering firewood and carrying water, tasks that are especially burdensome if firewood is scarce and water is far from home.

Women in developing countries tend to be less educated than men. In the countries of sub-Saharan Africa and South Asia, for example, only half as many women as men complete high school. In Ethiopia, among those ages 15 and older, 57 percent of the males could read and write in 2015, versus 41 percent of females. Women have fewer employment opportunities and earn lower wages than men do. For example, Sudan's Muslim fundamentalist government bans women from working in public places after 5:00 p.m. In Algeria, Egypt, Jordan, Libya, and Saudi Arabia, women account for only about one-quarter of the workforce. Women are often on the fringes of the labor market, working long hours in agriculture. They also have less access to other resources, such as land, capital, and technology.

> **"Women in developing countries tend to be less educated than men."**

21-2 PRODUCTIVITY: KEY TO DEVELOPMENT

We have examined some signs of poverty in developing countries, but not why poor countries are poor. At the risk of appearing simplistic, we might say that poor countries are poor because they do not produce many goods and services. In this section, we examine why some developing countries experience such low productivity.

21-2a Low Labor Productivity

Labor productivity, measured in terms of output per worker, is by definition low in low-income countries. Why? Labor productivity depends on the quality of the labor and on the amount of capital, natural resources, and other inputs that combine with labor. For example, one certified public accountant with a computer and specialized software can sort out a company's finances more quickly and more accurately than can a thousand high school–educated file clerks with pencils and paper.

One way a nation raises its productivity is by investing more in human and physical capital. This investment must be financed by either domestic savings or foreign funds. Income per capita in the poorest countries is often too low to support much investment. In poor countries with unstable governments, the wealthy minority frequently invests in more stable foreign economies. This leaves less to invest domestically in either human or physical capital; without sufficient capital, workers remain less productive.

Another reason why wages are low in poor countries is that businesses are poorly run. For example, in many Indian manufacturing firms, equipment is not well maintained, employee theft is common because inventory is not well monitored, and workers are poorly trained and managed. A recent World Bank study found that offering simple management advice to Indian factories increased productivity by 20 percent.

21-2b Technology and Education

What exactly is the contribution of education to the process of economic development? Education helps people make better use of resources. If knowledge is lacking, other resources may not be used efficiently. For example, a country may be endowed with fertile land, but farmers may lack knowledge of irrigation and fertilization techniques. Or farmers may not have learned how to rotate crops to avoid soil depletion. In low-income countries, 39 percent of those 15 and older were illiterate during the period 2005 to 2009, compared to 17 percent in middle-income countries, and only 2 percent in high-income countries. Many children in developing countries drop out of school because their families can't afford it or would rather put the child to work. Child labor in developing countries obviously limits educational opportunities.

Education also makes people more receptive to new ideas and methods. Countries with the most advanced educational systems were also the first to develop. In the 20th century, the leader in schooling and economic development was the United States. In Latin America, Argentina was the most educationally advanced nation

100 years ago, and it is one of the most developed Latin American nations today. The growth of education in Japan during the 19th century contributed to a ready acceptance of technology and thus to Japan's remarkable economic growth in the 20th century.

Education is valued more in some economies than in others. For example, many teachers in Mexico are allowed to sell their tenured positions or pass them on to their children.[6] And in India, about one-quarter of teachers in rural public schools were absent on any given day.[7]

21-2c Inefficient Use of Labor

Another feature of developing countries is that they use labor less efficiently than do industrial nations. Unemployment and underemployment reflect inefficient uses of labor. *Underemployment* occurs when skilled workers are employed in low-skill jobs or when people are working less than they would like— for example, a worker seeking full-time employment may find only a part-time job. *Unemployment* occurs when those willing and able to work can't find jobs.

Unemployment is measured primarily in urban areas, because in rural areas farm work is usually an outlet for labor even if many workers are underemployed there. The unemployment rate in developing nations on average is about 10 percent to 15 percent of the urban labor force. Unemployment among young workers—those aged 15 to 24—is typically twice that of older workers. In developing nations, about 30 percent of the combined urban and rural workforce is either unemployed or underemployed. In Zimbabwe, most people are unemployed; it's no surprise why Zimbabwe is so poor.

In some developing countries, the average farm is as small as two acres. Productivity is also low because few other inputs, such as capital and fertilizer, are used. *Although more than half the labor force in developing countries works in agriculture, only about one-third of output in these countries stems from agriculture.* In the United States, farmers account for only 2 percent of the labor force, but because of modern equipment one farmer can work hundreds or even thousands of acres (the average U.S. farm is about 500 acres). U.S. farmers, though only one-fiftieth of the labor force, grow enough to feed a nation and to lead the world in exports of grain, oil seeds, and cotton. The average value added per U.S.

Susan Liebold/Alamy

farm worker is about 75 times that of farm workers in low- and middle-income countries.

Low productivity obviously results in low income, but low income can, in turn, affect worker productivity. Low income means less saving and less saving means less investment in human and physical capital. Low income can also mean poor nutrition during the formative years, which can retard mental and physical development. These difficult beginnings may be aggravated by poor diet and insufficient health care in later life, making workers poorly suited for regular employment. Poverty can result in less saving, less education, less capital formation, a poor diet, and little health care—all of which can reduce a worker's productivity. Thus, *low income and low productivity may reinforce each other in a cycle of poverty.*

> **"Low income and low productivity may reinforce each other in a cycle of poverty."**

21-2d Natural Resources

Some countries are rich in natural resources. The difference is most striking when we compare countries with oil reserves and those without. The Middle East countries of Bahrain, Kuwait, Qatar, Saudi Arabia, and the United Arab Emirates are classified as high-income economies because they are lucky enough to be sitting atop huge oil reserves. But oil-rich countries are the exception. Many developing countries, such as Chad and Ethiopia, have

6. "Why Are Mexico's Teachers Wielding Axes?" *The Economist*, 28 April 2013.

7. Karthik Muralidharan et al. "The Fiscal Cost of Weak Governance: Evidence from Teacher Absences in India," NBER Working Paper No. 20299 (July 2014).

Penka Todorova Vitkova/Shutterstock

little in the way of natural resources. Most developing countries without oil reserves are in trouble whenever oil prices rise. Since oil must be imported, higher oil prices drain oil-poor countries of precious foreign exchange.

Oil-rich countries also show us that an abundant supply of a natural resource is not in itself enough to create a modern industrial economy. On the other hand, Japan has one of the most developed economies in the world, yet has no oil reserves and little in the way of natural resources. Connecticut is consistently the most productive of the United States as measured by per capita income, but the state has few natural resources (its main natural resource is gravel). In fact, many researchers believe that reliance on resource wealth can be something of a curse for a nation.

21-2e Financial Institutions

Another requirement for development is an adequate and trusted system of financial institutions. An important source of funds for investment is the savings of households and firms. People in some developing countries have little confidence in their currency because their governments finance a large fraction of public outlays by printing money. This practice results in high inflation and sometimes very high inflation, or hyperinflation, as has occurred recently in Zimbabwe, where annual inflation was just about incalculable. High and unpredictable inflation discourages saving and hurts development.

Developing countries have special problems because banks are often viewed with suspicion. At the first sign of trouble, many depositors withdraw their funds. Because banks cannot rely on a continuous supply of deposits, they cannot make loans for extended periods. If financial institutions fail to serve as intermediaries between savers

and borrowers, the lack of funds for investment becomes an obstacle to growth. During the global financial crisis of 2008, banks in industrial market countries also suffered from depositors' sagging confidence. One measure of banking presence is the credit provided by banks as a percent of that nation's total output. This measure is more than five times greater in high-income countries than in low-income countries.

21-2f Capital Infrastructure

Production and exchange depend on a reliable infrastructure of transportation, communication, sanitation, and electricity. Roads, bridges, airports, harbors, and other transportation facilities are vital to commercial activity. Reliable mail service, telephone communications, Internet connections, clean water, and electricity are also essential for advanced production techniques. Imagine how difficult it would be to run even a personal computer if the supply of electricity and access to the Internet were unavailable or continually interrupted, as is often the case in many developing countries.

Some developing countries have serious deficiencies in their physical infrastructures. As just one measure, Exhibit 5 shows the number of mobile telephones per 100 people in 2013 for the 12 countries examined earlier. The high-income countries averaged about twice as many mobile phones per 100 people as the low-income countries. Brazil, the top rated in this category, had 135 mobile phones per 100 people. Bottom-ranked Ethiopia had just 27 mobile phones per 100 people. The world average was 93 mobile phones per 100 people. More Indians have access to mobile phones than to toilets (only about half the population has access to toilets). Incidentally, mobile phones in poor countries create opportunities to deliver education to those without access to schools. In an experiment in the African nation of Niger, those who took lessons on mobile phones tested quite well and retained what they learned.[8]

Phone lines help knit together an economy's communications network. Countries without reliable phone service have difficulty not only communicating but also reaping the benefits of other technology advances, such as the Internet. Exhibit 6 shows Internet users as a percent of the population in 2013 for our sample of countries. There is an unmistakable digital divide between high-income and low-income economies. In the four high-income economies, an average 86 percent of the population used

8. Jenny C. Aker, Christopher Ksoll, and Travis J. Lybbert, "Can Mobile Phones Improve Learning? Evidence from a Field Experiment in Niger," *American Economic Journal: Applied Economics*, 4 (October 2012): 94–120.

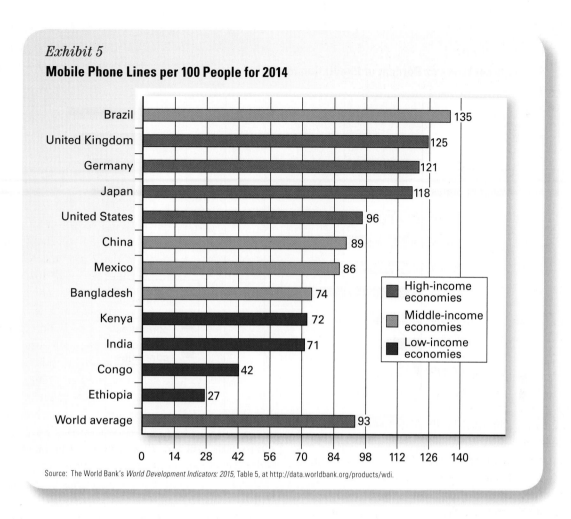

Exhibit 5

Mobile Phone Lines per 100 People for 2014

Country	Mobile Phone Lines per 100 People
Brazil	135
United Kingdom	125
Germany	121
Japan	118
United States	96
China	89
Mexico	86
Bangladesh	74
Kenya	72
India	71
Congo	42
Ethiopia	27
World average	93

Legend:
- High-income economies
- Middle-income economies
- Low-income economies

Source: The World Bank's *World Development Indicators: 2015*, Table 5, at http://data.worldbank.org/products/wdi.

the Internet. In the four low-income economies, just 12 percent used the Internet on average. Even in India, which has a reputation as computer savvy, what with all the online support centers and software companies we read about, only 15 percent of the population were Internet users. Worldwide, 38 percent of the population used the Internet in 2013.

21-2g Entrepreneurship

An economy can have abundant supplies of labor, capital, and natural resources, but without entrepreneurship, the other resources will not necessarily be combined efficiently to produce goods and services. Unless a country has entrepreneurs who are able to bring together resources and take the risk of profit or loss, development may never get off the ground. Many developing countries were once under colonial rule, a system of government that offered the local population fewer opportunities to develop entrepreneurial skills. One sign of entrepreneurship is a willingness to become self-employed. Immigrants to the United States from developing countries are less likely to become self-employed

here than are immigrants to the United States from industrial economies.[9]

One source of entrepreneurial experience for developing countries comes from McDonald's and other international franchises. For example, by providing management training, McDonald's stimulates entrepreneurship directly through its franchises and indirectly by showing competitors how a business is run. Such franchises also demonstrate to customers what they should come to expect in the way of service, cleanliness, quality, and the like.[10]

Franchise operators often face obstacles. For example, chicken farmers in Ghana were not up to KFC's standards for quality, so the franchise operators there tried to import chicken. But because Ghana's currency was weak, imported chicken was too expensive. Needless to say, KFC is having a hard time in Ghana.[11]

9. Ruth Owaifo Oyelere and Willie Belton, "Coming to America: Does Having a Developed Home Country Matter for Self-Employment in the United States?" *American Economic Review*, 102 (May 2012): 538–542.

10. Adrian Tschoegli, "McDonald's—Much Maligned, But an Engine of Economic Development," *Global Economy Journal*, 7 (October 2007): 1–18.

11. Drew Hinshaw, "As KFC Goes to Africa, It Lacks Only One Thing: Chickens," Wall Street Journal, 8 February 2013.

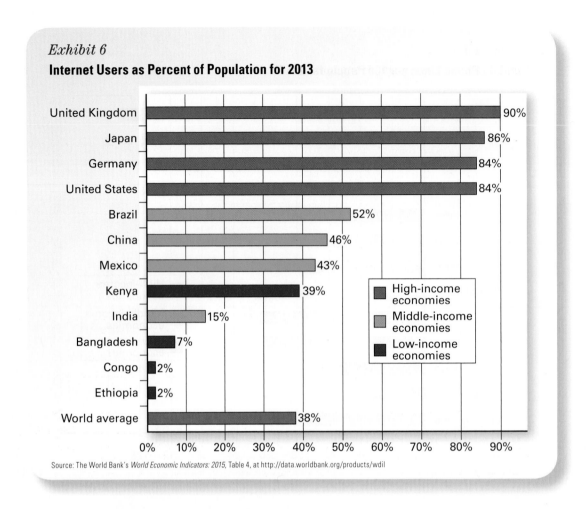

Exhibit 6

Internet Users as Percent of Population for 2013

Country	Percent
United Kingdom	90%
Japan	86%
Germany	84%
United States	84%
Brazil	52%
China	46%
Mexico	43%
Kenya	39%
India	15%
Bangladesh	7%
Congo	2%
Ethiopia	2%
World average	38%

Legend:
- High-income economies
- Middle-income economies
- Low-income economies

Source: The World Bank's *World Economic Indicators: 2015*, Table 4, at http://data.worldbank.org/products/wdil

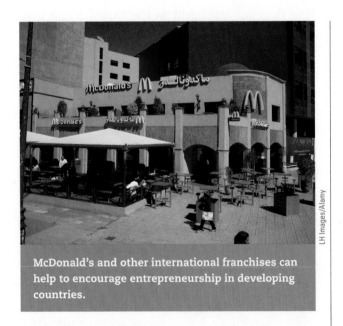

McDonald's and other international franchises can help to encourage entrepreneurship in developing countries.

LH Images/Alamy

Government officials sometimes decide that entrepreneurs are unable to generate the kind of economic growth the country needs. State enterprises are therefore created to do what government believes the free market cannot do. But state-owned enterprises may have objectives other than producing goods efficiently—objectives that could include providing jobs for friends and relatives of government officials. Also, with most state enterprises, there is little or no competition.

21-2h Rules of the Game

Finally, in addition to human capital, natural resources, financial institutions, capital infrastructure, and entrepreneurship, a successful economy needs reliable *rules of the game*. Perhaps the most elusive ingredients for development are the formal and informal institutions that promote production and exchange: the laws, customs, conventions, and other institutional elements that sustain an economy. A stable political environment with well-defined property rights is important. Little private-sector investment will occur if potential investors believe their capital might be appropriated by government, destroyed by civil unrest, blown up by terrorists, or stolen by thieves. For example, because of frequent ambushes and hijackings, many truckers have abandoned roads through Congo, South Sudan,

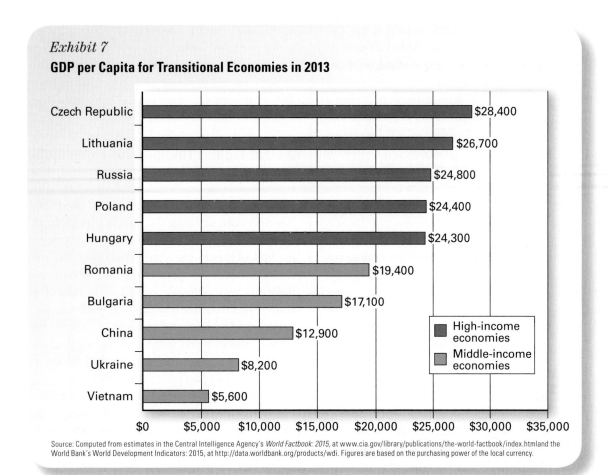

Exhibit 7

GDP per Capita for Transitional Economies in 2013

Country	GDP per Capita
Czech Republic	$28,400
Lithuania	$26,700
Russia	$24,800
Poland	$24,400
Hungary	$24,300
Romania	$19,400
Bulgaria	$17,100
China	$12,900
Ukraine	$8,200
Vietnam	$5,600

High-income economies
Middle-income economies

Source: Computed from estimates in the Central Intelligence Agency's *World Factbook: 2015*, at www.cia.gov/library/publications/the-world-factbook/index.htmland the World Bank's World Development Indicators: 2015, at http://data.worldbank.org/products/wdi. Figures are based on the purchasing power of the local currency.

and the Central African Republic, thereby reducing commercial opportunities for trade there.[12]

Under capitalism, the rules of the game include private ownership of most resources and the coordination of economic activity by the price signals generated by market forces. Market coordination answers the questions of what to produce, how to produce it, and for whom to produce it. Under socialism, the rules of the game include government ownership of most resources and the allocation of resources through central plans. For example, countries such as Cuba and North Korea carefully limit the private ownership of resources like land and capital. More generally, personal freedom is limited in centrally planned economies (e.g., in North Korea, people need a government permit just to travel outside their own town).[13]

Although there is no universally accepted theory of economic development, around the world markets have been replacing central plans in many once-socialist countries. **Privatization** is the process of turning government enterprises into private enterprises in these transitional economies. Privatization is the opposite of *nationalization* (what the U.S. government did with airport security after 9/11, taking it away from airlines and federalizing it). For example, Russian privatization began in 1992 with the sale of municipally owned shops. Exhibit 7 presents, for 10 transitional economies, the gross domestic product (GDP) per capita in 2014 based on the purchasing power of the domestic currency. Notice the differences across these economies, with GDP per capita in the Czech Republic five times that of Vietnam. The Czech Republic, Lithuania, Russia, Poland, and Hungary, identified with blue bars, have joined the ranks of high-income economies. The other five are middle-income economies, and are identified with orange bars. Some of these transitional economies still have aspects of central planning. For example, banks in Vietnam are more likely to lend to businesses that are

privatization The process of turning government enterprises into private enterprises

12. Nicholas Bariyo, "Africa's Sugar Ambitions Turn Sour," *Wall Street Journal*, 20 October 2014.

13. Peter Wonacott, "The Mystery of North Korean Fans," *Wall Street Journal*, 26 June 2010.

politically connected than to businesses that are the most profitable. Thus, the most profitable Vietnamese firms tend to avoid banks and rely instead on reinvested earnings and informal loans.[14]

But many once-communist economies are having a hard time with the transition to market economies. For example, manufacturers in Kazakhstan still have poor management practices. Such practices improve with greater privatization and more competition.[15]

21-2i Income Distribution Within Countries

Thus far the focus has been on income differences across countries, and these differences can be vast. But what about income differences within a country? Are poor countries uniformly poor or are there sizable income differences among that nation's population? One way to measure inequality across households is to look at the share of national income going to the poorest fifth of the population. As a point of reference, in the unlikely event that income in an economy were evenly distributed across all households, the poorest fifth would also receive exactly one-fifth, or 20 percent, of national income. More realistically, the poorest fifth receives less than 20 percent of the income, but how much less? Is the percent of income going to the poorest fifth higher for low-income countries than for high-income countries? In other words, is income more evenly distributed within poor countries than within rich countries? Not necessarily. Among our 12 nations, the poorest fifth of the population got an average of 7.7 percent of the income in the high-income countries, 5.8 percent in middle-income countries, and 7.2 percent in low-income countries. So, at least in this sample, income was less evenly distributed among middle-income countries than in high- or low-income countries.

21-3 INTERNATIONAL TRADE AND DEVELOPMENT

Developing countries need to trade with developed countries to acquire the capital and technology that will increase labor productivity on the farm, in the factory,

in the office, and in the home. To import capital and technology, developing countries must first acquire the funds, or foreign exchange, needed to pay for imports. Exports usually generate more than half of the annual flow of foreign exchange in developing countries. Foreign aid and private investment make up the rest.

21-3a Trade Problems for Developing Countries

Primary products, such as agricultural goods and other raw materials, make up the bulk of exports from developing countries, just as manufactured goods make up the bulk of exports from industrial countries. About half the merchandise exports from low-income countries consist of raw materials, compared to only 20 percent among high-income countries. A problem for developing countries is that the prices of primary products, such as coffee, cocoa, sugar, and rubber, fluctuate more widely than do the prices of finished goods, because crop yields fluctuate with the weather.

When developing countries experience trade deficits, they often try to restrict imports. Because imported food is critical to survival, developing countries are more likely to cut imports of capital goods—the very items needed to promote long-term growth and productivity. Thus, many developing countries cannot afford the

Ammit Jack/Shutterstock.com

14. Edmund J. Malesky and Markus Taussig, "Where Is Credit Due? Legal Institutions, Connections, and the Efficiency of Bank Lending in Vietnam," *Journal of Law, Economics, and Organization*, 25 (October 2009): 525–578.

15. Nicholas Bloom, Helena Schweiger, and John Van Reenen, "The Land That Lean Manufacturing Forgot? Management Practices in Transition Countries," *Economics of Transition*, 20 (October 2012): 593–635.

modern machinery that will help workers there become more productive. Developing countries must also confront industrial countries' trade restrictions, such as tariffs and quotas, which often discriminate against primary products. For example, the United States strictly limits sugar imports and has done so for more than half a century. Such restrictions are one reason the Doha Round of trade agreements stalled.

21-3b Migration and the Brain Drain

Migration plays an important role in the economies of developing countries. A major source of foreign exchange in some countries is the money sent home by migrants who find jobs in industrial countries. Migrant workers around the world sent home about $440 billion in 2014, and that's expected to top $500 billion by 2016, according to the World Bank. For example, migrants from Mexico send home about a third of their U.S. earnings.[16] Thus migration provides a valuable safety valve for poor countries, and remittances can account for 10 percent of all income in poor countries.[17] There is evidence that migrant remittances help family members back home get more education or even start a business. But there is a downside. Often the best and the brightest professionals, such as doctors, nurses, and engineers, migrate to developed countries. For example, every year thousands of nurses migrate from countries such as Kenya and the Philippines to the United States, where half the world's nurses are employed. The financial attraction is powerful: A nurse in the Philippines would start there at less than $8,000 a year, compared with $36,000 in the United States.

So the upside of the brain drain for the poor country is the money sent home by overseas workers. What's more, recent research suggests some benefits to the country of origin when trained professionals move abroad. For example, some Indians who have migrated to the United States to work in computer technology have helped nurture India's software industry.[18] Still, a nation is usually hurt when its best and brightest leave for opportunities elsewhere. Some African countries are demanding compensation for the cost of educating the doctors and nurses who then move to high-income economies.

16. Dean Yang, "Migrant Remittances," *Journal of Economic Perspectives*, 25 (Summer 2011): 133.

17. Julian di Giovanni, Andrei Levchenko, and Francesc Ortega, "A Global View of Cross-Border Migration," *Journal of the European Economic Association*, 13 (February 2015): 168–202.

18. Frederic Docquier and Hillel Rapoport, "Globalization, Brain Drain, and Development," *Journal of Economic Literature*, 50 (September 2012): 681–730.

21-3c Import Substitution Versus Export Promotion

An economy's progress usually involves moving up the production chain from agriculture and raw material to manufacturing then to services. If a country is fortunate, this transformation occurs gradually through natural market forces. For example, in 1850 most U.S. jobs were in agriculture. Now most U.S. jobs are in the service sector. Sometimes governments try to speed up the evolution. Many developing countries, including Argentina and India, pursued a strategy called **import substitution**, whereby domestic manufacturers made products that until then had been imported. To insulate domestic manufacturers from foreign competition, the government imposed stiff tariffs and quotas. This development strategy became popular for several reasons. First, demand already existed for these products, so the "what to produce" question was easily answered. Second, import substitution provided infant industries with a protected market. Finally, import substitution was popular with those who supplied resources to the favored domestic industries.

Like all trade protection, however, import substitution erased the gains from specialization and comparative advantage among countries. Often the developing country replaced low-cost foreign goods with high-cost domestic versions of those same goods. And domestic producers, shielded from foreign competition, often supplied inferior products and usually failed to become efficient. Worse still, other countries often retaliated with their own trade restrictions.

Critics of import substitution claim that export promotion is a surer path to economic development. **Export promotion** concentrates on producing for the export market. This development strategy begins with relatively simple products, such as textiles. As a developing country builds its technological and educational base—that is, as the developing economy learns by doing—producers can then make more complex products for export. Economists favor export promotion over import substitution because the emphasis is on comparative advantage and trade expansion rather than on trade restriction. Export promotion also forces producers to grow more efficient in order to compete on world markets. Research shows that

import substitution A development strategy that emphasizes domestic manufacturing of products that had been imported

export promotion A development strategy that concentrates on producing for the export market facing global competition boosts domestic efficiency. What's more, export promotion requires less government intervention in the market than does import substitution.

Of the two approaches, export promotion has been more successful around the world. For example, the newly industrialized countries of East Asia have successfully pursued export promotion, while Argentina, India, and Peru have failed with their import-substitution approach. In 1965, the newly industrialized economies of Hong Kong, South Korea, Singapore, and Taiwan had an average income only 20 percent that of high-income countries. Now these four are themselves high-income countries. Most Latin American nations, which for decades had favored import substitution, are now pursuing free trade agreements with each other and with the United States. Even India is dismantling trade barriers, with an emphasis on importing high-technology capital goods. One slogan of Indian trade officials is "Microchips, yes! Potato chips, no!"

21-3d Trade Liberalization and Special Interests

Although most people would benefit from freer international trade, some would be worse off. Consequently, governments in developing countries often face difficulty pursuing policies conducive to development. Often the gains from economic development are widespread, but the beneficiaries, such as consumers, do not recognize their potential gains. On the other hand, the losers tend to be concentrated, such as producers in an industry that had been sheltered from foreign competition, and they know quite well the source of their losses. So the government often lacks the political will and support to remove impediments to development, because the potential losers fight reforms that might harm their livelihood while the potential winners remain largely unaware of what's at stake. What's more, consumers have difficulty organizing even if they become aware of what's going on. A recent study by the World Bank suggests a strong link in Africa between governments that cater to special-interest groups and low rates of economic growth.

Nonetheless, many developing countries have been opening their borders to freer trade. People around the world have been exposed to information about the opportunities and products available on world markets. So consumers want the goods and firms want the technology and capital that are available abroad. Both groups want government to ease trade restrictions.

> **"Studies by the World Bank and others have underscored the successes of countries which have adopted trade liberalization policies."**

Studies by the World Bank and others have underscored the successes of countries which have adopted trade liberalization policies.

 ### 21-4 FOREIGN AID AND ECONOMIC DEVELOPMENT

We have already seen that because most poor countries do not generate enough savings to fund an adequate level of investment, these countries often rely on foreign financing. Private international borrowing and lending are heavily restricted by the governments of developing countries. Governments may allow residents to purchase foreign exchange only for certain purposes. In some developing countries, different exchange rates apply to different categories of transactions. Thus, the local currency is not easily convertible into other currencies. Some developing countries also require foreign investors to find a local partner who must be granted controlling interest. All these restrictions discourage foreign investment. In this section, we will look primarily at foreign aid and its link to economic development.

> **"Most poor countries do not generate enough savings to fund an adequate level of investment."**

21-4a Foreign Aid

Foreign aid is any international transfer made on especially favorable terms for the purposes of promoting economic development. Foreign aid includes grants, which need not be repaid, and loans extended on more favorable repayment terms than the recipient could normally secure. Such loans have lower interest rates, longer repayment periods, or grace periods during which repayments are reduced or even waived (similar to some student loans). Foreign aid can take the form of money, capital goods, technical assistance, food, and so forth.

> **"Foreign aid can take the form of money, capital goods, technical assistance, food, and so forth."**

Some foreign aid is granted by a specific country, such as the United States, to another specific country, such as the Philippines. Country-to-country aid is called

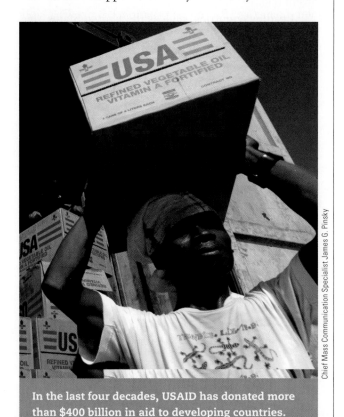

In the last four decades, USAID has donated more than $400 billion in aid to developing countries.

Chief Mass Communication Specialist James G. Pinsky

bilateral assistance. Other foreign aid goes through international bodies such as the World Bank. Assistance provided by organizations that use funds from a number of countries is called *multilateral*. For example, the World Bank provides loans and grants to support activities that are viewed as prerequisites for development, such as health and education programs or basic development projects like dams, roads, and communications networks. And the International Monetary Fund extends loans to countries that have trouble with their balance of payments.

During the last four decades, the United States has provided the developing world with over $400 billion in aid. Most U.S. aid has been coordinated by the United States Agency for International Development (USAID), which is part of the U.S. Department of State. This agency focuses on health, education, and agriculture, providing both technical assistance and loans. USAID emphasizes long-range plans to meet the basic needs of the poor and to promote self-sufficiency. Foreign aid is a controversial, though relatively small, part of the federal budget. Since 1993, official U.S. aid has been less than 0.2 percent of U.S. GDP, compared to an average of 0.3 percent from 21 other industrialized nations.

21-4b Does Foreign Aid Promote Economic Development?

In general, foreign aid provides additional purchasing power and thus the possibility of increased investment, capital imports, and consumption. But it remains unclear whether foreign aid *supplements* domestic saving, thus increasing investment, or simply *substitutes* for domestic saving, thereby increasing consumption rather than investment. What is clear is that foreign aid often becomes a source of discretionary funds that benefit not the poor but their leaders. Historically, more than 90 percent of the funds distributed by USAID have gone to governments, whose leaders assume responsibility for distributing these funds. One goal of foreign aid seems to be to keep a friendly government in power.[19]

Much bilateral funding is tied to purchases of goods and services from the donor nation, and such programs can sometimes be counterproductive—they have unintended consequences. For example, in the 1950s, the United States began the Food for Peace program,

19. Michael Faye and Paul Niehaus, "Political Aid Cycles," *American Economic Review*, 102 (December 2012): 3516–3530.

foreign aid An international transfer made on especially favorable terms for the purpose of promoting economic development

> **"It remains unclear whether foreign aid *supplements* domestic saving, thus increasing investment, or simply *substitutes* for domestic saving, thereby increasing consumption rather than investment."**

which helped supply U.S. farm products abroad, but some recipient governments turned around and sold that food to finance poorly conceived projects. Worse yet, the availability of low-priced food from abroad drove down farm prices in the developing countries, hurting poor farmers there. The same holds for clothing. Used clothing donated to thrift shops and charitable organizations in industrialized countries typically winds up for sale in Africa, where the low price discourages local production of clothing.[20] Before used clothing swamped the continent, Africa had a textile industry, but no more. Textiles are often the first rung on the ladder to developing a broader manufacturing base.

Foreign aid may have temporarily raised the standard of living in some developing countries, but it has not necessarily increased their ability to become self-supporting at that higher standard of living. Many countries that receive aid are doing less of what they had done well. Their agricultural sectors have suffered. For example, though we should be careful when drawing conclusions about causality, per capita food production in Africa has fallen since 1960. Outside aid has often insulated public officials from their own incompetence and from the fundamental troubles of their own economies. There is also evidence that food aid increases the incidence and

convergence A theory predicting that the standard of living in economies around the world will grow more similar over time, with poorer countries eventually catching up with richer ones

duration of civil conflicts in a country.[21] Most countries today that have achieved industrial status did so without foreign aid. Development success typically takes time and involves gradual movements toward freer markets.

In some cases, foreign aid has helped corrupt governments stay in power. Because of disappointment with the results of government aid, the trend is toward channeling funds through private nonprofit agencies such as CARE. More than half of foreign aid now flows through private channels. The privatization of foreign aid follows a larger trend toward privatization in transitional economies around the world.

21-4c Do Economies Converge?

If given enough time, will poor countries eventually catch up with rich ones? The **convergence** theory argues that developing countries can grow faster than advanced ones and should eventually close the gap. Here's why: It is easier to copy existing technology than to develop new technologies. Countries that are technologically backward can grow faster by adopting existing technology. But economies already using the latest technology must come up with a steady stream of breakthroughs to grow faster. For example, it's infinitely easier to buy a smartphone than to invent one.

Leading countries, such as the United States, find growth limited by the rate of creation of new knowledge and better technology. But follower countries can grow more quickly by, for example, adding computers where they previously had none. Until 1995, the United States, which made up about five percent of the world's population at the time, accounted for most of the world's computer purchases by households. But by 2000, most computers were bought by non-U.S. households.

What's the evidence on convergence? Between 1993 and 2012, growth in real GDP for developing countries averaged 5.4 percent per year, more than double the averaged for industrial countries.[22] National economies have been converging for decades, closing half the gap in the last 35 years. In 1990, 43 percent of the population in developing countries subsisted

20. Garth Frazer, "Used-Clothing Donations and Apparel Production in Africa," *Economic Journal*, 118 (October 2008): 1764–1784.

21. Nathan Nunn and Nancy Qian, "US Food Aid and Civil Conflict," *American Economic Review*, 104 (June 2014): 1630-1666; and Benjamin Crost, Joseph Felter, and Patrick Johnston, "Aid Under Fire: Development Projects and Civil Conflicts," *American Economic Review*, 104 (June 2014): 1833–1856.

22. Anusha Chari and Peter Blair Henry, "Learning from Doers: Developing Country Lessons for Advanced Economic Growth," *American Economic Review*, 104 (May 2014): 260–265.

on less than $1 a day. By 2010, after adjusting for inflation, that share had fallen to 21 percent.[23] Some formerly poor countries have become advanced economies. As noted already, the newly industrialized Asian economies of Hong Kong, Singapore, South Korea, and Taiwan, by adopting the latest technology and investing in human resources, have closed the gap with the world leaders. These *Asian Tigers* have graduated from developing economies to industrial market economies. More generally, there does appear to be convergence in manufacturing productivity across a large group of developed and developing countries.[24] Even Africa has been doing better. Living standards in Sub-Saharan Africa have been rising by an average of 3.5 percent per year over the last two decades.[25] Still as many as a billion people seem trapped in poor economies.

> **"It is easier to copy existing technology than to develop new technologies. Countries that are technologically backward can grow faster by adopting existing technology."**

One reason per capita consumption has not grown faster in the poorest economies is that birthrates there are double those in richer countries, so poor economies must produce still more just to keep up with a growing population. Another reason why convergence is slow for the poorest parts of the world is the vast difference in the quality of human capital across countries. Although technology is indeed portable, the

knowledge, skill, and training needed to take advantage of that technology are not. Common heritage seems to facilitate adoption of technology across nations. For example, some recent research finds that the closer the genetic distance between populations across nations—that is, the shorter the time since they shared common ancestors—the lower the barriers to technology adoption across nations.[26]

Countries with a high level of human capital can make up for other shortcomings. For example, much of the capital stock in Japan and Germany was destroyed during World War II. But the two countries retained enough of their well-educated and highly skilled labor force to rejoin elite industrial market economies in little more than a generation. But some countries, such as those in Africa, simply lack the human capital needed to identify and absorb new technology. As noted already, such poor economies tend to have low education levels and low literacy rates. What's more, some countries lack the stable macroeconomic environment and the established institutions needed to nurture economic growth, such as reliable banks. Many developing countries have serious deficiencies in their infrastructures, lacking, for example, the steady source of electricity to power new technologies. In Northern Nigeria, near the Sahara, most villages have no electricity. Some of the poorest nations

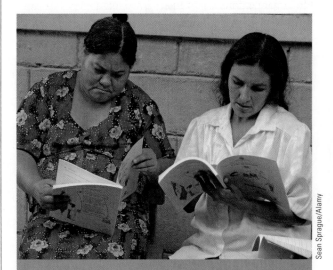

Low educational levels and literacy rates hinder economic growth in poor countries such as South Sudan, where the literacy rate is 27%. Literacy programs like this one in South Sudan are a good investments in the country's human capital.

23. Nicola Gennaioli et al. "Growth in Regions," *Journal of Economic Growth*, 19 (September 2014): 259–303.

24. See Dani Rodrik, "Unconditional Convergence," in Manufacturing, *Quarterly Journal of Economics*, 128 (February 2013): 165–204.

25. Alwyn Young, "The African Growth Miracle," *Journal of Political Economy*, 120 (August 2012): 696–739.

26. Enrico Spolaore and Romain Wacziarg, "How Deep Are the Roots of Economic Development," *Journal of Economic Literature*, 51 (June 2013): 325–369.

have been ravaged by civil war for years. And simply communicating can be challenging in some developing countries. Among Nigeria's 180 million population, for example, more than 500 languages are spoken by 250 distinct ethnic groups.

Even in the United States, with it's common language, currency, and free flow of resources across state borders, large differences in productivity across states still exist. Researchers argue that not much convergence has occurred among U.S. states since 1975.[27]

One final reason that convergence may take a long time is that the roots of economic development go back centuries. For example, researchers find that regions using the most advanced technologies in the year 1000 B.C. tended to remain the users of the most advanced technologies in 1500 A.D., and continue to do so today.[28]

27. Chi-Young Choi and Xiaojun Wang, "Discontinuity of Output Convergence Within the United States: Why Has the Course Changed," *Economic Inquiry*, 53 (January 2015): 49–71.

28. Diego Comin, William Easterly, and Efick Gong, "Was the Wealth of Nations Determined in 1000 B.C.?" *American Economic Journal: Macroeconomics,* 2 (August 2010): 65–97.

21-5 FINAL WORD

Because no single theory of economic development has become widely accepted, this chapter has been more descriptive than theoretical. We can readily identify the features that distinguish developing from industrial economies. Education is key to development, both because of its direct effect on productivity and because those who are more educated tend to be more receptive to new ideas. A physical infrastructure of transportation and communication systems and utilities is needed to link economic participants. And trusted financial institutions link savers and borrowers. A country needs entrepreneurs with the vision to move the economy forward. Finally, the most elusive ingredients are the laws, manners, customs and ways of doing business that nurture economic development. Economic history is largely a story of economies that have failed to produce a set of economic rules of the game that lead to sustained economic growth. However, some transitional economies and some newly emerging industrial countries in Asia show that economic development continues to be achievable.

STUDY TOOLS 21

READY TO STUDY? IN THE BOOK, YOU CAN:

☐ Work the Problems at the end of the chapter.

☐ Rip out the chapter review card for a handy summary of the chapter and key terms.

ONLINE AT CENGAGEBRAIN.COM YOU CAN:

☐ Collect StudyBits while you read and study the chapter.

☐ Quiz yourself on key concepts.

☐ Prepare for tests with chapter flash cards as well as flash cards that you create.

☐ Watch videos to explore economics further.

CHAPTER 21 PROBLEMS

Your instructor can access the answers to these problems online at http://cengagebrain.com.

21-1 Besides income, identify ways that low-income economies differ from high-income economies

1. *(Worlds Apart)* Per capita income most recently was about 160 times greater in the United States than in the Democratic Republic of the Congo. Suppose per capita income grows an average of 3 percent per year in the richer country and 6 percent per year in the poorer country. Assuming such growth rates continue indefinitely into the future, how many years would it take before per capita income in the Congo exceeds that of the United States? (To simplify the math, suppose at the outset per capita income is $160,000 in the richer country and $1,000 in the poorer country.)

21-2 Describe the factors that make workers in high-income economies more productive than workers in other economies

2. *(Why Incomes Differ)* What factors help workers in high-income economies become more productive than those in other economies?

3. *(Import Substitution Versus Export Promotion)* Explain why domestic producers who supply a good that competes with imports would prefer an import-substitution approach to trade policy rather than an export-promotion approach. Which policy would domestic consumers prefer and why?

21-3 Explain how trade restrictions can slow economic development in poorer countries

4. *(International Trade and Development)* From the perspective of citizens in a developing country, what are some of the benefits and drawbacks of international trade?

21-4 Outline some unintended consequences of foreign aid on economic development

5. *(Foreign Aid and Economic Development)* Foreign aid, if it is to be successful in enhancing economic development, must lead to a more productive economy. Describe some of the problems in achieving such an objective through foreign aid.

6. *(In-Kind Aid)* What has been an unintended consequences of richer countries giving food and clothing to poorer countries?

INDEX

Dominant-strategy equilibrium, 173
Double entry bookkeeping, 345
Dumping, 336
    trade restrictions and, 339
Duopoly, 173
Durable goods, 43
Duration of loans, 224

E

Earned-income tax credit, 313
Earnings, 13–15, 185–187
    See also Wages
Easily observable quality, 237–239
Economic analysis, 9–12
    faulty, 12–13
Economic efficiency approach, 293–294
Economic fluctuations, 9, 36
Economic growth, 32, 34
Economic model, defined, 10
Economic profit, 106–107, 123–124, 126
    firms, attraction of, 135, 136–137
    and natural monopolies, 256
    short run, 124–126
    zero, 132–133
Economic regulation, 254, 256–258
    See also Regulation
Economic rent, 185–187
Economics, defined, 3
Economic systems, 34–37
Economic theory, 10
Economies of scale, 114, 116–117,
        144–145, 331
    oligopolies, 167–168
Economies of scope, 239–240
    and mergers, 262
Economists, 12, 13–15
Education
    developing countries, 366–367
    effect on labor, 204
    positive effects of, 299–300
    and technology, 366–367
EEOC (Equal Employment Opportu-
        nity Commission), 318
Efficiency, 31, 34
    and perfect competition, 137–139
Efficiency wage theory, 247
Efficient boundaries, 236–238
Egyptian property taxes, 53
Elastic demand, 77, 155–156
Elastic demand curve, 79
Elasticity
    estimates of, 83
    supply, 84–85
Elasticity measures, 86–88
    See also Price elasticity of demand;
        Price elasticity of supply
Elastic supply, 84–85
Employment. *See* Labor; Labor supply
Entitlement programs, 313
Entrepreneurial ability, 4

Entrepreneurs, 4, 44, 226–229
    in developing countries, 369–370
    loans for, 221
Entry barriers. *See* Barriers to entry
Environment. *See* Externalities
Environmental protection, 294–299
Environmental Protection Agency
        (EPA), 294, 296
Equal Employment Opportunity
        Commission (EEOC), 318
Equilibrium of markets, 65–67
    changes in, 67–70
    firm supply, 130–131
    monopolistic competition, 165–166
    and perfect demand, 122
    resource demand, 190, 191
Equilibrium of utility, 97
Essential resources, 145
European Union, 337
Euros, 54, 337, 350–353
Eurozone, 351
Excess capacity, 166
Excess quantity demanded, 66
Excess quantity supplied, 66
Exchange, 28–29
Exchange rates, 54, 350–353
    arbitrageurs and speculators, 353–354
    determining, 352–353
Exclusive dealing, 259
Exclusive goods, 48, 269
Exclusive unions, 209
Exhaustible resources, 4, 285
Expected marginal benefit, 8
Expected marginal cost, 8
Expected rate of return on capital, 219
Explicit costs, 105
Export promotion, 373–374
Exports, 325–326, 372
Externalities, 49
    and the common-pool problem, 285–287
    environmental protection, 294–299
    pollution. *See* Pollution
    positive, 299–301

F

Facebook, 227
Fallacy of composition, 13
Farm subsidies, 275–277
Faulty economic analysis, 12–13
Featherbedding, 211
Federal system of government, 50
Federal Trade Commission (FTC) Act
        of 1914, 259
Financial account, international, 348–349
Financial capital, 226
Financial institutions, 368
Financial intermediaries, 222
Firms, 43–48
    and antitrust policy, 265–266
    circular-flow model and, 6

cooperatives, 46–47
corporations, 45
costs and profits, 105–107, 147–152
decision makers, 5
economies and diseconomies of scale,
        116–117
economies of scope, 239–240
efficient boundaries of, 236–238
interdependence of, 167
marginal returns of, 107–109
market equilibrium, 130–131
profits, 44, 105–107, 123–126
resource demand, 188
scope of operation, 235–240
short run supply curves, 129–130
suppliers, 239
Fiscal policy, 49
Fishing restrictions, 286–287
Fixed costs, 109, 126–127
Fixed exchange rates, 355
Fixed-production technology, 288
Fixed resources, 107
Flexible exchange rates, 355
Floating exchange rates, 352, 355
Food for Peace, 375–376
Ford, Henry, 228, 247
Foreign aid, 375–376
Foreign exchange, 54, 350–353
    and markets, 350–355
Foreign exchange markets, 54
Franklin, Benjamin, 79, 101
Free goods and services, 6, 96
Free-rider problem, 272
Free trade agreements, 337
Frost, Robert, 286
FTC (Federal Trade Commission) Act
        of 1914, 259
Full information, 241
Functional relation, 17

G

Game theory, 172–176
GDP. *See* Gross domestic product
General Agreement on Tariffs and
        Trade (GATT), 336
General Assistance aid, 313
General Electric, 239
Geographic differences in labor, 205
Gifts of nature, 4
GNI (gross national income), 361
Golden rule of profit maximization, 124
Gold standard, 355
Gompers, Samuel, 207
Goods, 4–5, 31–33, 48–49, 60, 87
    defined, 4
    durable, 43
    exclusive, 48, 270
    nonexclusive, 49, 270
    open-access, 270

Jobs
college education, 308–309
experience, 201–202
international trade, 339–340
welfare reform, 320

K

Kamen, Dean, 228
Kennedy Round, 336
Kickstarter, 232

L

Labor, 4
adverse selection, 246–247
asymmetric information, 246–247
household resource, 42
inefficient use of, 367
marginal product, 188
and marginal returns of a firm,
107–108
market supply of, 202
and unions, 209–210
Labor supply, 197–202
and unions, 207–210
and wages, 199–201, 202–206
Labor unions, 206
See also Unions
Laissez-faire, 35
Laliberte, Guy, 227
Law of comparative advantage, 27–28,
328–329
Law of demand, 57–59, 59–60
and marginal utility, 98–99
Law of diminishing marginal returns,
107–109, 113
Law of diminishing marginal utility,
94–95
Law of increasing opportunity cost, 32, 34
Law of supply, 62
Leisure, 197–198, 200
Levi's jeans, 227
Licenses, 144, 257
Life cycles, 307
Limited liability, 45
Lincoln, Abraham, 143
Linear demand curve, 77–79
Line shifts, 22
Liquidity of securities, 231
Loanable funds, 221–223
Loanable funds market, 222
Long run, 107
average cost curves, 115–116, 144,
168
costs, 114–117
demand change effects, 133–135
elasticity estimates, 83
profit maximization, 151–152
zero economic profit, 132–133,
164–165

Long-run industry supply curve, 135–137
Lorenz curves, 306
Losses, minimizing
fixed costs, 126–127
short run, 126–129, 150–151, 163–164
Low-income economies, 361–362
Low-interest loans, 336
Low labor productivity, 366
Luxuries, 87

M

Macroeconomics, 8–9
Madoff, Bernie, 258
Malnutrition, 363
Managed float system, 357
Managers, 228, 237
Marginal analysis, 19–20, 127
economic analysis, 8
Marginal benefit
expected, 8
in market exchange, 332
of search, 240–241
Marginal cost curves, 111–112
Marginal costs, 110–111
and average costs, 112–113
expected, 8
and marginal revenue, 124, 127, 148,
149, 163
in market exchange, 332
monopolies, 148, 149
and optimal output, 191
of resources, 189–190
of search, 240
supply curve, 62–63
Marginal, defined, 8
Marginal product, 101, 108
of labor, 188
Marginal product curves, 109
Marginal productivity of resources,
110–111
Marginal resource cost, 189–190
Marginal returns, 107–109
Marginal revenue, 124
and marginal costs, 127, 148, 149, 163
monopolies, 145–147
and optimal output, 191
Marginal revenue product, 188–189
Marginal social benefit, 289
Marginal social cost, 288
Marginal tax rates, 52
and income assistance programs, 319
Marginal utility, 94–95
and the law of demand, 98–99
law of diminishing, 94–95
Marginal valuation, 99
Market behavior, 240–242
Market demand, 60, 100–101
See also Demand
Market demand curves. *See* Demand
curves

Market disequilibrium, 70–72
Market efficiency, 48
Market equilibrium, changes in, 65–70,
130–131
Market exchange, 332
Market failure, 48
Market interest rate, 222–223
Market power, 253
Market prices, 50
Markets, 65–67
defined, 6
disequilibrium of, 70–72
equilibrium of, 65–70, 130–131
foreign exchange, 350–355
pollution rights, 291–293
Market structure, 121
Market supply, 63, 202
Market supply curve, 63, 64, 69–70
Market system, 35
Market work, 198
Mary Kay, Inc., 228
Maturity date, 230
Maximizing profit, 44, 123–124,
190–191
Maximizing utility, 96–98
households, 42
McDonald's, 29, 369
Means-tested program, 312
Median income, 307
Median-voter model, 272–273
Median wages, 308
Mediators, 206
Medicaid, 313, 314
Medicare, 312, 313, 314
Medium of exchange, 28
Merchandise trade balance, 53–54, 346
Mergers, 176
and public policy, 260–261
Microeconomics, 8–9
Middle-income economies, 361–362,
371
Migration, 373
Milk, price controls of, 70–71
Minimum efficient scale, 116, 237, 238
Mixed economies, 36–37
Mixed system, 36–37
Models, 10, 30
Monetary policy, 49
Money, defined, 28
Money income, 58
Money price of consumption, 101
Monopolies, 48, 143
allocative effects, 153–154
barriers to entry, 143–145
and cartels, 169–170
costs and profits, 147–152
deadweight loss of, 153–155, 157
distributive effects, 153–154
economies of scale, 144–145
of essential resources, 145
gains and losses, 146

KEY CONCEPTS

1-1 Explain the economic problem of scarce resources and unlimited wants.
The problem is that, although your wants, or desires are virtually unlimited, the resources available to satisfy these wants are scarce. Because resources are scarce, you must choose from among your many wants, and whenever you choose, you must forgo satisfying some other wants. Without scarcity, there would be no economic problem and no need for prices.

The Simple Circular-Flow Model for Households and Firms
Households earn income by supplying resources to resource markets, as shown in the lower portion of the model. Firms demand these resources to produce goods and services, which they supply to product markets, as shown in the upper portion of the model. Households spend their income to demand these goods and services. This spending flows through product markets as revenue to firms.

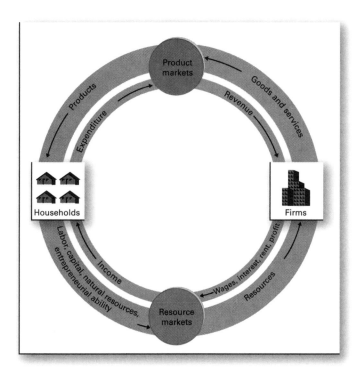

1-2 Describe the forces that shape economic choices.
An economy results from the choices that millions of individuals make in attempting to satisfy their unlimited wants. A key economic assumption is that individuals, in making choices, rationally select alternatives they perceive to be in their best interests. Economic choice is based on a comparison of the expected marginal benefit and the expected marginal cost of the action under consideration.

1-3 Explain the relationship between economic theory and economic reality.
An economic theory is a simplification of economic reality that is used to make predictions about the real world. A theory, or model, captures the important elements of the problem under study but need not spell out every detail and interrelation. You might think of economic theory as a streamlined version of economic reality.

KEY TERMS

economics The study of how people use their scarce resources to satisfy their unlimited wants

resources The inputs, or factors of production, used to produce the goods and services that people want; resources consist of labor, capital, natural resources, and entrepreneurial ability

labor The physical and mental effort used to produce goods and services

capital The buildings, equipment, and human skills used to produce goods and services

natural resources All gifts of nature used to produce goods and services; includes renewable and exhaustible resources

entrepreneurial ability The imagination required to develop a new product or process, the skill needed to organize production, and the willingness to take the risk of profit or loss

entrepreneur A profit-seeking decision maker who starts with an idea, organizes an enterprise to bring that idea to life, and assumes the risk of the operation

wages Payment to resource owners for their labor

interest Payment to resource owners for the use of their capital

rent Payment to resource owners for the use of their natural resources

profit Reward for entrepreneurial ability; sales revenue minus resource cost

good A tangible product used to satisfy human wants

service An activity, or intangible product, used to satisfy human wants

scarcity Occurs when the amount people desire exceeds the amount available at a zero price

market A set of arrangements by which buyers and sellers carry out exchange at mutually agreeable terms

product market A market in which a good or service is bought and sold

resource market A market in which a resource is bought and sold

circular-flow model A diagram that traces the flow of resources, products, income, and revenue among economic decision makers

rational self-interest Each individual tries to maximize the expected benefit achieved with a given cost or to minimize the expected cost of achieving a given benefit

marginal Incremental, additional, or extra; used to describe a change in an economic variable

microeconomics The study of the economic behavior in particular markets, such as that for computers or unskilled labor

macroeconomics The study of the economic behavior of entire economies, as measured, for example, by total production and employment

economic fluctuations The rise and fall of economic activity relative to the long-term growth trend of the economy; also called business cycles

economic theory, or economic model A simplification of reality used to make predictions about cause and effect in the real world

variable A measure, such as price or quantity, that can take on different values at different times

other-things-constant assumption The assumption, when focusing on the relation among key economic variables, that other variables remain unchanged; in Latin, *ceteris paribus*

behavioral assumption An assumption that describes the expected behavior of economic decision makers—what motivates them

hypothesis A theory about how key variables relate

positive economic statement A statement that can be proved or disproved by reference to facts

normative economic statement A statement that reflects an opinion, which cannot be proved or disproved by reference to the facts

association-is-causation fallacy The incorrect idea that if two variables are associated in time, one must necessarily cause the other

fallacy of composition The incorrect belief that what is true for the individual, or part, must necessarily be true for the group, or the whole

secondary effects Unintended consequences of economic actions that may develop slowly over time as people react to events

The Scientific Method: Step-by-Step
The steps of the scientific method are designed to develop and test hypotheses about how the world works. The objective is a theory that predicts outcomes more accurately than the best alternative theory. A hypothesis is rejected if it does not predict as accurately as the best alternative. A rejected hypothesis can be modified in light of the test results.

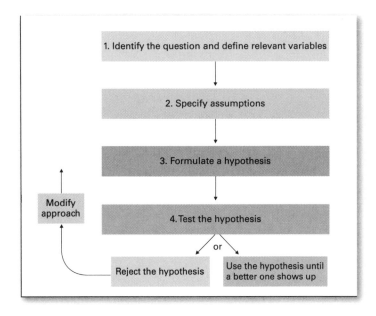

1-4 Identify some pitfalls of economic analysis. Economic analysis, like other forms of scientific inquiry, is subject to common mistakes in reasoning that can lead to faulty conclusions. Three sources of confusion are the fallacy that association is causation, the fallacy of composition, and the mistake of ignoring secondary effects.

1-5 Describe several reasons to study economics. The economics profession thrives because its models usually do a better job of making economic sense out of a confusing world than do alternative approaches. Studies show that economics majors earn more than most and they experience no pay difference based on gender.

APPENDIX TERMS

origin on a graph depicting two-dimensional space, the zero point

horizontal axis line on a graph that begins at the origin and goes to the right and left; sometimes called the *x* axis

vertical axis line on a graph that begins at the origin and goes up and down; sometimes called the *y* axis

graph a picture showing how variables relate in two-dimensional space; one variable is measured along the horizontal axis and the other along the vertical axis

dependent variable a variable whose value depends on that of the independent variable

independent variable a variable whose value determines that of the dependent variable

positive relation (direct relation) occurs when two variables increase or decrease together; the two variables move in the same direction

negative relation (inverse relation) occurs when two variables move in opposite directions; when one increases, the other decreases

slope of a line a measure of how much the vertical variable changes for a given increase in the horizontal variable; the vertical change between two points divided by the horizontal increase

tangent a straight line that touches a curve at a point but does not cut or cross the curve; used to measure the slope of a curve at a point

KEY CONCEPTS

2-1 Describe the relationship between choice and opportunity cost. Resources are scarce, but human wants are unlimited. Because you cannot satisfy all your wants, you must choose, and whenever you choose, you must forgo some option. Choice involves an opportunity cost. The opportunity cost of the selected option is the value of the best alternative forgone.

2-2 Explain how comparative advantage, specialization, and exchange affect economic outcomes (output). The law of comparative advantage says that the individual, firm, region, or country with the lowest opportunity cost of producing a particular good should specialize in that good. Specialization according to the law of comparative advantage promotes the most efficient use of resources. The specialization of labor increases efficiency by (a) taking advantage of individual preferences and natural abilities, (b) allowing each worker to develop expertise and experience at a particular task, (c) reducing the need to shift between different tasks, and (d) allowing for the introduction of more specialized machines and large-scale production techniques.

2-3 Outline how economies function as production systems. The production possibilities frontier, or PPF, shows the productive capabilities of an economy when all resources are used efficiently. The frontier's bowed-out shape reflects the law of increasing opportunity cost, which arises because some resources are not perfectly adaptable to the production of different goods. Over time, the frontier can shift in or out as a result of changes in the availability of resources, in technology, or in the rules of the game. The frontier demonstrates several economic concepts, including efficiency, scarcity, opportunity cost, the law of increasing opportunity cost, economic growth, and the need for choice.

The Economy's Production Possibilities Frontier

If the economy uses its available resources and its technology and know-how efficiently in producing consumer goods and capital goods, that economy is on its production

The Economy's Production Possibilities Frontier

KEY TERMS

opportunity cost The value of the best alternative forgone when an item or activity is chosen

sunk cost A cost that has already been incurred, cannot be recovered, and thus is irrelevant for present and future economic decisions

law of comparative advantage The individual, firm, region, or country with the lowest opportunity cost of producing a particular good should specialize in that good

absolute advantage The ability to make something using fewer resources than other producers use

comparative advantage The ability to make something at a lower opportunity cost than other producers face

barter The direct exchange of one product for another without using money

division of labor Breaking down the production of a good into separate tasks

specialization of labor Focusing work effort on a particular product or a single task

production possibilities frontier (PPF) A curve showing alternative combinations of goods that can be produced when available resources are used efficiently; a boundary line between inefficient and unattainable combinations

efficiency The condition that exists when there is no way resources can be reallocated to increase the production of one good without decreasing the production of another; getting the most from available resources

law of increasing opportunity cost To produce more of one good, a successively larger amount of the other good must be sacrificed

economic growth An increase in the economy's ability to produce goods and services; reflected by an outward shift of the economy's production possibilities frontier

economic system The set of mechanisms and institutions that resolve the what, how, and for whom questions

pure capitalism An economic system characterized by the private ownership of resources and the use of prices to coordinate economic activity in unregulated markets

private property rights An owner's right to use, rent, or sell resources or property

pure command system An economic system characterized by the public ownership of resources and centralized planning

mixed system An economic system characterized by the private ownership of some resources and the public ownership of other resources; some markets are regulated by government

possibilities frontier, *AF*. The *PPF* is bowed out to reflect the law of increasing opportunity cost: additional units of capital goods require the economy to sacrifice more and more units of consumer goods. Note that more consumer goods must be given up in moving from *E* to *F* than in moving from *A* to *B*, although in each case the gain in capital goods is 10 million units. Points inside the *PPF*, such as *I*, represent inefficient use of resources. Points outside the *PPF*, such as *U*, represent unattainable combinations.

Shifts of the Economy's Production Possibilities Frontier

When the resources available to an economy change, the *PPF* shifts. If more resources become available or if technology and know-how improve, the *PPF* shifts outward, as in panel (a), indicating that more output can be produced. A decrease in available resources causes the *PPF* to shift inward, as in panel (b). Panel (c) shows a change affecting consumer goods production. More consumer goods can now be produced at any given level of capital goods. Panel (d) shows a change affecting capital goods production.

Shifts of the Economy's Production Possibilities Frontier

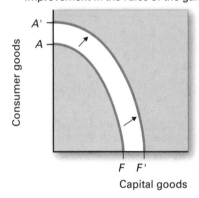

(a) Increase in available resources, better technology, more know-how, or improvement in the rules of the game

(b) Decrease in available resources or greater uncertainty in the rules of the game

(c) Change in resources, technology, know-how, or rules that benefits consumer goods

(d) Change in resources, technology, know-how, or rules that benefits capital goods

2-4 Describe different economic systems and the decision-making rules that define them. All economic systems, regardless of their decision-making processes, must answer three basic questions: What is to be produced? How is it to be produced? And for whom is it to be produced? Economies answer the questions differently, depending on who owns the resources and how economic activity is coordinated. Economies can be directed by market forces, by the central plans of government, or, in most cases, by a mix of the two.

KEY CONCEPTS

3-1 Describe the major sources of income and expenditures for households. Households play the starring role in a market economy. Their demand for goods and services determines what gets produced and their supplies of labor, capital, natural resources, and entrepreneurial ability produce that output. As demanders of goods and services and suppliers of resources, households make all kinds of choices in an attempt to maximize utility.

Where U.S. Personal Income Comes From and Where It Goes

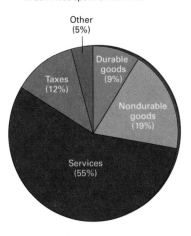

(a) More than two-thirds of personal income in 2014 was labor income

(b) More than half of U.S. personal income in 2014 was spent on services

3-2 Outline the evolution of production over the centuries from the household to the modern corporation. Household members once did everything for themselves. Over time, however, the efficiency arising from comparative advantage resulted in greater specialization. Firms are economic units formed by entrepreneurs who combine labor, capital, and natural resources to produce goods and services in an attempt to maximize profit. For-profit firms organize in one of three ways: as a sole proprietorship, as a partnership, or as a corporation. Not-for-profit organizations engage in activities that often have a social purpose, while cooperatives are groups that organize with the goal of minimizing costs.

Percent Distribution by Type of Firm Based on Number of Firms and Firm Sales

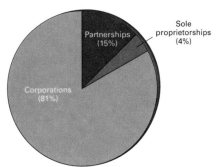

(a) Most firms are sole proprietorships

(b) Corporations account for most sales

KEY TERMS

utility The satisfaction received from consumption; sense of well-being

transfer payments Cash or in-kind benefits given to individuals by the government

Industrial Revolution Development of large-scale factory production that began in Great Britain around 1750 and spread to the rest of Europe, North America, and Australia

firms Economic units formed by profit-seeking entrepreneurs who employ resources to produce goods and services for sale

sole proprietorship A firm with a single owner who has the right to all profits but who also bears unlimited liability for the firm's losses and debts

partnership A firm with multiple owners who share the profits and bear unlimited liability for the firm's losses and debts

corporation A legal entity owned by stockholders whose liability is limited to the value of their stock ownership

cooperative An organization consisting of people who pool their resources to buy and sell more efficiently than they could individually

not-for-profit organizations Groups that do not pursue profit as a goal; they engage in charitable, educational, humanitarian, cultural, professional, or other activities, often with a social purpose

Information Revolution Technological change spawned by the microchip and the Internet that enhanced the acquisition, analysis, and transmission of information

market failure A condition that arises when the unregulated operation of markets yields socially undesirable results

antitrust laws Prohibitions against price fixing and other anticompetitive practices

monopoly A sole supplier of a product with no close substitutes

natural monopoly One firm that can supply the entire market at a lower per-unit cost than could two or more firms

private good A good, such as pizza, that is both rival in consumption and exclusive

CHAPTER REVIEW 3

public good A good that, once produced, is available for all to consume, regardless of who pays and who doesn't; such a good is nonrival and nonexclusive, such as a safer community

externality A cost or a benefit that affects neither the buyer nor seller, but instead affects people not involved in the market transaction

fiscal policy The use of government purchases, transfer payments, taxes, and borrowing to influence economy-wide variables such as inflation, employment, and economic growth

monetary policy Regulation of the money supply to influence economy-wide variables such as inflation, employment, and economic growth

ability-to-pay tax principle Those with a greater ability to pay, such as those earning higher incomes or those owning more property, should pay more taxes

benefits-received tax principle Those who get more benefits from the government program should pay more taxes

tax incidence The distribution of tax burden among taxpayers; who ultimately pays the tax

proportional taxation The tax as a percentage of income remains constant as income increases; also called a flat tax

progressive taxation The tax as a percentage of income increases as income increases

marginal tax rate The percentage of each additional dollar of income that goes to the tax

regressive taxation The tax as a percentage of income decreases as income increases

merchandise trade balance The value during a given period of a country's exported goods minus the value of its imported goods

balance of payments A record of all economic transactions during a given period between residents of one country and residents of the rest of the world

foreign exchange Foreign money needed to carry out international transactions

tariff A tax on imports

quota A legal limit on the quantity of a particular product that can be imported or exported

3-3 Summarize the seven roles of government in an economy.

Governments attempt to improve society's overall welfare by intervening in cases of market failure. Beneficial government interventions in markets include (1) establishing and enforcing the rules of the game, (2) promoting competition, (3) regulating natural monopolies, (4) providing public goods, (5) dealing with externalities, (6) more equally distributing income, and (7) pursuing full employment, price stability, and economic growth.

Redistribution Has Grown and Defense Has Declined as Share of Federal Outlays: 1960–2016

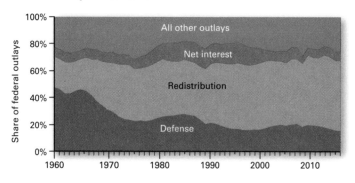

Composition of Federal Revenue Between 1960 and 2016

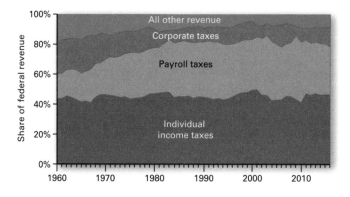

Top Marginal Rate on Federal Personal Income Tax Since 1913

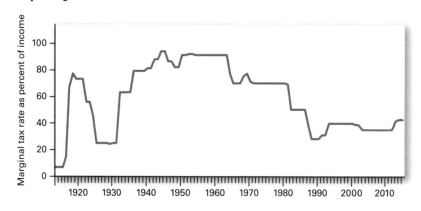

3-4 Explain why countries trade with each other and why they sometimes act to restrict that trade.

The rest of the world affects what U.S. households consume and what U.S. firms produce. U.S. households and firms are consumers and suppliers of manufactured goods and raw materials from and to foreign economies, and these transactions impact U.S. prices, wages, and profits. Although consumers gain from comparative advantage, nearly all countries impose trade restrictions to protect domestic industries from foreign competition.

KEY CONCEPTS

4-1   Explain why a demand curve slopes downward. Demand is a relationship between the price of a product and the quantity consumers are willing and able to buy per period, other things constant. According to the law of demand, quantity demanded varies negatively, or inversely, with the price. A demand curve slopes downward because a price decrease makes consumers (a) more willing to substitute this good for other goods and (b) more able to buy the good because the lower price increases real income.

4-2   Identify five things which could shift a demand curve to the right or left. A change in any of the following could shift a demand curve right or left: (1) money income, (2) prices of other goods, (3) consumer expectations, (4) the number or composition of consumers in the market, and (5) consumer tastes.

4-3   Explain why a supply curve usually slopes upward. Supply is a relationship between the price of a good and the quantity producers are willing and able to sell per period, other things constant. The supply curve slopes upward because higher prices make producers (a) more willing to supply this good rather than supply other goods that use the same resources and (b) more able to cover the higher marginal cost associated with greater output rates.

4-4   Identify five things which could shift a supply curve to the right or left. A change in any of the following could shift a supply curve right or left: (1) the state of technology and know-how, (2) the prices of resources used to produce the good, (3) the prices of other goods that could be produced with these resources, (4) supplier expectations, and (5) the number of producers in the market.

4-5   Explain why surpluses push prices down while shortages drive prices up. A surplus means there are more goods supplied at that price than demanded. Suppliers lower the price to sell these surplus goods. A shortage means there are more goods demanded than supplied. Consumers bid up the price to buy these goods.

The Market Demand Curve for Pizza

The market demand curve *D* shows the quantity of pizza demanded, at various prices, by all consumers. Price and quantity demanded are inversely related other things constant, reflecting the law of demand.

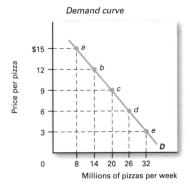

Demand curve

The Market Supply Curve for Pizza

The Market supply curve *S* shows the quantities of pizza supplied, at various prices, by all pizza makers. Price and quantity supplied are directly related.

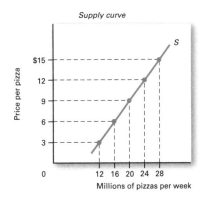

Supply curve

KEY TERMS

demand A relation between the price of a good and the quantity that consumers are willing and able to buy per period, other things constant

law of demand The quantity of a good that consumers are willing and able to buy per period relates inversely, or negatively, to the price, other things constant

substitution effect of a price change When the price of a good falls, that good becomes cheaper compared to other goods so consumers tend to substitute that good for other goods

money income The number of dollars a person receives per period, such as $400 per week

real income Income measured by the goods and services it can buy; real income changes when the price changes

income effect of a price change A fall in the price of a good increases consumers' real income, making consumers more able to purchase goods; for a normal good, the quantity demanded increases

demand curve A curve showing the relation between the price of a good and the quantity consumers are willing and able to buy per period, other things constant

quantity demanded The amount of a good consumers are willing and able to buy per period at a particular price, as reflected by a point on a demand curve

individual demand The relation between the price of a good and the quantity purchased per period by an individual consumer, other things constant

market demand The relation between the price of a good and the quantity purchased per period by all consumers in the market, other things constant; sum of the individual demands in the market

normal good A good, such as new clothes, for which demand increases, or shifts rightward, as consumer income rises

inferior good A good, such as used clothes, for which demand decreases, or shifts leftward, as consumer income rises

substitutes Goods, such as tacos and pizza, that relate in such a way that an increase in the price of one shifts the demand for the other rightward

complements Goods, such as Pepsi and pizza, that relate in such a way that an increase in the price of one shifts the demand for the other leftward

tastes Consumer preferences; likes and dislikes in consumption; assumed to remain constant along a given demand curve

movement along a demand curve A change in quantity demanded resulting from a change in the price of the good, other things constant

shift of a demand curve Movement of a demand curve right or left resulting from a change in one of the determinants of demand other than the price of the good

supply A relation between the price of a good and the quantity that producers are willing and able to sell per period, other things constant

law of supply The amount of a good that producers are willing and able to sell per period is usually directly related to its price, other things constant

supply curve A curve showing the relation between price of a good and the quantity producers are willing and able to sell per period, other things constant

quantity supplied The amount offered for sale per period at a particular price, as reflected by a point on a supply curve

individual supply The relation between the price of a good and the quantity an individual producer is willing and able to sell per period, other things constant

market supply The relation between the price of a good and the quantity all producers are willing and able to sell per period, other things constant

movement along a supply curve Change in quantity supplied resulting from a change in the price of the good, other things constant

shift of a supply curve Movement of a supply curve left or right resulting from a change in one of the determinants of supply other than the price of the good

transaction costs The costs of time and information required to carry out market exchange

surplus At a given price, the amount by which quantity supplied exceeds quantity demanded; a surplus usually forces the price down

shortage At a given price, the amount by which quantity demanded exceeds quantity supplied; a shortage usually forces the price up

equilibrium The condition that exists in a market when the plans of buyers match those of sellers, so quantity demanded equals quantity supplied and the market clears

4-6 Predict the impact of a change in demand or supply on the equilibrium price and quantity.
Market equilibrium, once established, will continue unless there is a change in a determinant that shapes demand or supply. The diagrams below demonstrate the impact of a shift of demand (upper panel) and a shift of supply (lower panel) on equilibrium price and quantity.

Effects of an Increase in Market Demand

An increase in demand is shown by a shift of the demand curve rightward from D to D'. Both price and quantity are higher following the rightward shift of the demand curve.

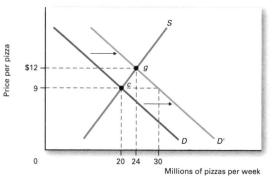

Effects of an Increase in Market Supply

An increase in supply is shown by a shift of the supply curve rightward, from S to S'. At the new equilibrium, quantity is greater and the price is lower than before the increase in supply.

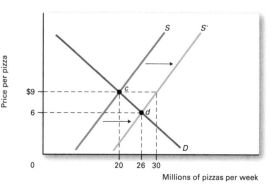

4-7 Describe the result of a government-set price floor and price ceiling on a market.
If the floor price is set above the market clearing price, quantity supplied exceeds quantity demanded, creating a surplus. If the ceiling price is set below the market clearing price, quantity demand exceeds that quantity supplied, creating a shortage.

disequilibrium The condition that exists in a market when the plans of buyers do not match those of sellers; a temporary mismatch between quantity supplied and quantity demanded as the market seeks equilibrium

price floor A minimum legal price below which a product cannot be sold; to have an impact, a price floor must be set above the equilibrium price

price ceiling A maximum legal price above which a product cannot be sold; to have an impact, a price ceiling must be set below the equilibrium price

KEY CONCEPTS

5-1 Define and graph the price elasticity of demand. The price elasticities of demand and supply show how responsive buyers and sellers are to changes in the price of a good. More elastic means more responsive. When the percentage change in quantity demanded exceeds the percentage change in price, demand is price elastic. If demand is price elastic, a price increase reduces total revenue and a price decrease increases total revenue. When the percentage change in quantity demanded is less than the percentage change in price, demand is price inelastic. If demand is price inelastic, a higher price increases total revenue and a lower price reduces total revenue. When the percentage change in quantity demanded equals the percentage change in price, demand is unit elastic; a price change does not affect total revenue.

Constant-Elasticity Demand Curves

The three panels show constant-elasticity demand curves, so named because the elasticity value does not change along the demand curve. Along the perfectly elastic, or horizontal, demand curve of panel (a), consumers will demand all that is offered for sale at price *p*, but demand zero at a price above *p*. Along the perfectly inelastic, or vertical, demand curve of panel (b), consumers demand *Q* regardless of price. Along the unit-elastic demand curve of panel (c), total revenue is the same for each price-quantity combination.

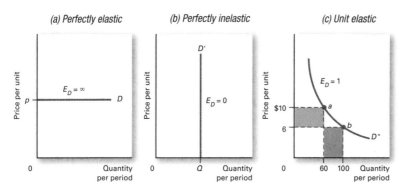

Summary of Price Elasticity of Demand: Effects of a 10 Percent Increase in Price

Absolute Value of Price Elasticity	Type of Demand	What Happens to Quantity Demanded	What Happens to Total Revenue
$E_D = 0$	Perfectly inelastic	No change	Increases by 10 percent
$0 < E_D < 1$	Inelastic	Drops by less than 10 percent	Increases by less than 10 percent
$E_D = 1$	Unit elastic	Drops by 10 percent	No change
$1 < E_D < \infty$	Elastic	Drops by more than 10 percent	Decreases
$E_D = \infty$	Perfectly elastic	Drops to 0	Drops to 0

KEY TERMS

price elasticity of demand Measures how responsive quantity demanded is to a price change; the percentage change in quantity demanded divided by the percentage change in price

price elasticity formula Percentage change in quantity demanded divided by the percentage change in price; the average quantity and the average price are used as bases for computing percentage changes in quantity and in price

inelastic demand A change in price has relatively little effect on quantity demanded; the percentage change in quantity demanded is less than the percentage change in price; the resulting price elasticity has an absolute value less than 1.0

unit-elastic demand The percentage change in quantity demanded equals the percentage change in price; the resulting price elasticity has an absolute value of 1.0

elastic demand A change in price has a relatively large effect on quantity demanded; the percentage change in quantity demanded exceeds the percentage change in price; the resulting price elasticity has an absolute value exceeding 1.0

total revenue Price multiplied by quantity demanded at that price

linear demand curve A straight-line demand curve; such a demand curve has a constant slope but usually has a varying price elasticity

perfectly elastic demand curve A horizontal line, which means that any price increase would reduce quantity demanded to zero; the elasticity has an absolute value of infinity

perfectly inelastic demand curve A vertical line, which means that any price change has no effect on the quantity demanded; the elasticity value is zero

unit-elastic demand curve Everywhere along the demand curve, the percentage change in price causes an equal but offsetting percentage change in quantity demanded, so total revenue is unchanged; the elasticity has an absolute value of 1.0

constant-elasticity demand curve The type of demand that exists when price elasticity is the same everywhere along the curve; the elasticity value is unchanged

price elasticity of supply Measures the responsiveness of quantity supplied to a price change; the percentage change in quantity supplied divided by the percentage change in price

inelastic supply A price change has relatively little effect on quantity supplied; the percentage change in quantity supplied is less than the percentage change in price; the price elasticity of supply is less than 1.0

unit-elastic supply The percentage change in quantity supplied equals the percentage change in price; the price elasticity of supply equals 1.0

elastic supply A price change has a relatively large effect on quantity supplied; the percentage change in quantity supplied exceeds the percentage change in price; the price elasticity of supply exceeds 1.0

perfectly elastic supply curve A horizontal line, which means that any price decrease drops the quantity supplied to zero; the elasticity value is infinity

perfectly inelastic supply curve A vertical line, which means that a price change has no effect on the quantity supplied; the elasticity value is zero

unit-elastic supply curve A percentage change in price causes an identical percentage change in quantity supplied; depicted by a supply curve that is a straight line from the origin; the elasticity value equals 1.0

income elasticity of demand The percentage change in demand divided by the percentage change in consumer income; the value is positive for normal goods and negative for inferior goods

cross-price elasticity of demand The percentage change in the demand of one good divided by the percentage change in the price of another good; it's positive for substitutes, negative for complements, and zero for unrelated goods

CHAPTER EQUATIONS

$$E_D = \frac{\Delta q}{(q + q')/2} \div \frac{\Delta p}{(p + p')/2}$$

$$TR = p \times q$$

$$E_S = \frac{\Delta q}{(q + q')/2} \div \frac{\Delta p}{(p + p')/2}$$

5-2 Identify the determinants of the price elasticity of demand. Demand is more elastic (a) the greater the availability of substitutes; (b) the more narrowly the good is defined; (c) the larger the share of the consumer's budget spent on the good; and (d) the longer the time period consumers have to adjust to a change in price.

Demand Becomes More Elastic Over Time

D_w is the demand curve one week after a price increase from $1.00 to $1.25. Along this curve, quantity demanded per day falls from 100 to 95. One month after the price increase, quantity demanded has fallen to 75 per day along D_m. One year after the price increase, quantity demanded has fallen to 50 per day along D_y. At any given price, D_y is more elastic than D_m, which is more elastic than D_w.

5-3 Define and graph the price elasticity of supply. The price elasticity of supply measures the responsiveness of quantity supplied to price changes. Price elasticity of supply depends on how much the marginal cost of production changes as output changes. If marginal cost rises sharply as output expands, quantity supplied is less responsive to price increases, and is thus less elastic. Also, the longer the time period producers have to adjust to price changes, the more elastic the supply.

Constant-Elasticity Supply Curves

The three panels show a constant-elasticity supply curve, so named because the elasticity value does not change along the curve. When supply is perfectly elastic, its curve S is horizontal. Along S, firms will supply any amount of output demanded at price p, but will supply none at prices below p. Supply curve S' is perfectly inelastic, or vertical. S' shows that the quantity supplied is independent of the price. In panel (c), S'', a straight line from the origin, is a unit-elastic supply curve. Any percentage change in price results in the same percentage change in quantity supplied.

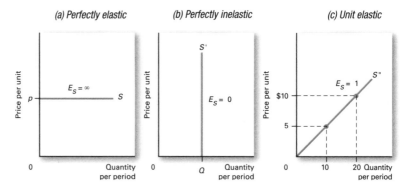

5-4 Describe other measures of elasticity. Income elasticity of demand measures the responsiveness of demand to changes in consumer income. Income elasticity is positive for normal goods and negative for inferior goods. The cross-price elasticity of demand measures the impact of a change in the price of one good on the demand for another good. Two goods are defined as substitutes, complements, or unrelated, depending on whether their cross-price elasticity of demand is positive, negative, or zero, respectively.

KEY CONCEPTS

6-1 Explain why marginal utility decreases as more of a good or service is consumed.
Utility is the sense of pleasure or satisfaction that comes from consumption. Utility is subjective. Marginal utility is the change in total utility resulting from a one-unit change in consumption. The law of diminishing marginal utility states that the more of a good you consume per period, all other things constant, the smaller the increase in your total utility from additional consumption.

6-2 Given tastes, the prices for two different goods, and a budget constraint, describe the utility-maximizing condition in your own words.
By attaching a numerical measure to utility, we can compare the total utility a particular consumer gets from different goods as well as the marginal utility that consumer gets from additional consumption. Economists assume that the purpose of consumption is to maximize your total utility. You decide how much of each good to purchase by considering your tastes, market prices, and your income. Consumers maximize utility by equalizing the marginal utility from the last dollar spent on each good.

6-3 Explain how can you get a consumer surplus from consuming a particular good if, in equilibrium, your marginal valuation of the good just equals the price you pay.
The consumer's objective is to maximize utility within

Utility Derived From Water Consumption After Running Four Miles
Total utility, shown in panel (a), increases with each of the first four glasses of water consumed but by smaller and smaller amounts. The fifth glass causes total utility to fall, implying that marginal utility is negative, as shown in panel (b).

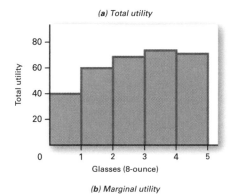

(a) Total utility

(b) Marginal utility

Your Demand Curve for Pizza Generated From Marginal Utility
At a price of $8 per pizza, the consumer is in equilibrium when consuming three pizzas per week (point a). If the price falls to $6, quantity demanded increases to four pizzas (point b). Points a and b are two points on this consumer's demand curve for pizza.

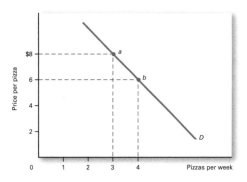

KEY TERMS

total utility The total satisfaction you derive from consumption; this could refer to either your total utility of consuming a particular good or your total utility from all consumption

marginal utility The change in your total utility from a one-unit change in your consumption of a good

law of diminishing marginal utility The more of a good a person consumes per period, the smaller the increase in total utility from consuming one more unit, other things constant

consumer equilibrium The condition in which an individual consumer's budget is exhausted and the last dollar spent on each good yields the same marginal utility; therefore, utility is maximized

marginal valuation The dollar value of the marginal utility derived from consuming each additional unit of a good

consumer surplus The difference between the most a consumer would pay for a given quantity of a good and what the consumer actually pays

CHAPTER REVIEW 6

CHAPTER EQUATION

Where x and y are any two goods.

the limits imposed by income and prices. Utility is maximized when the budget is exhausted and the marginal utility of the final unit consumed divided by that good's price is identical for each different good. Consumer surplus is the difference between the maximum amount consumers would pay for a given quantity of the good and the amount they actually pay. Consumer surplus increases as the price declines. Consumer surplus equals the value of the total utility you receive from consumption less your total spending. Although the marginal utility in equilibrium just equals the price for the final unit of the good you consume, marginal utility exceeds the price for all other units of the good you consume. This yields a consumer surplus.

Consumer Surplus from Sub Sandwiches

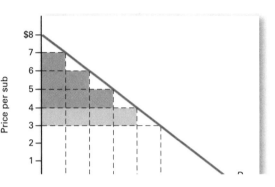

At a given quantity of sub sandwiches, the height of the demand curve shows the value of the last one purchased. The area under the demand curve for a specific quantity shows the total value a consumer attaches to that quantity. At a price of $4, the consumer purchases four subs. The first one is valued at $7, the second at $6, the third at $5, and the fourth at $4. The consumer values four at $22. Because the consumer pays $4 per sub, all four can be purchased for $16. The difference between what the consumer would have been willing to pay ($22) and what the consumer actually pays ($16) is called consumer surplus. When the price is $4, the consumer surplus is $6, as represented by the dark shaded area under the demand curve above $4. When the price of per sub falls to $3, consumer surplus increases by $4, as reflected by the lighter shaded area, to a total of $10.

Sum Individual Demand Curves Horizontally to Derive the Market Demand for Sub Sandwiches

At a price of $4 per sub, you demand 4 per month, Brittany demands 2, and Chris demands 0. Quantity demanded at a price of $4 is $4 + 2 + 0 = 6$ subs per month. At a lower price of $2, you demand 6, Brittany demands 4, and Chris demands 2. Quantity demanded at a price of $2 is 12 subs. The market demand curve D is the horizontal sum of individual demand curves d_Y, d_B, and d_C.

Market Demand and Consumer Surplus

Consumer surplus at a price of $2 is shown by the darker area. If the price falls to $1, consumer surplus increases to include the lighter area. At a zero price, consumer surplus increases to include the entire area under the demand curve.

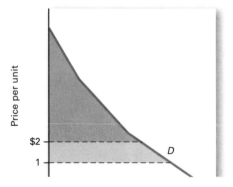

Since consumption does not occur instantly, time plays a role in demand analysis. Consumption takes time, and time has a positive value for most people. Consequently, consumption has a money price and a time price. Your willingness to pay a premium for time-saving goods and services depends on the opportunity cost of your time.

KEY CONCEPTS

7-1 Distinguish the three types of profit and explain what each reflects.
Firms try to earn a profit by transforming resources into salable products. These resources, whether explicit or implicit, have an opportunity cost that must be accounted for. Accounting profit equals total revenue minus explicit costs. Economic profit equals total revenue minus all costs, both implicit and explicit. A firm is said to earn a normal profit when total revenue just equals implicit and explicit costs.

7-2 Describe the most important feature of production in the short run and what causes it.
Output can be changed in the short run by adjusting variable resources, such as labor, but the size, or scale, of the firm is fixed in the short run. Firms experience increasing marginal returns when increasing a variable resource, but only to a certain point. Eventually, the law of diminishing marginal returns takes hold, thus restricting a firm's ability to expand in the short term. Diminishing marginal returns is the most important feature of production in the short run. As the quantity of the variable resource increases for a given amount of fixed resources, marginal product eventually declines and could turn negative.

Total and Marginal Product of Labor
When marginal product is rising, total product increases by increasing amounts. When marginal product is falling but still positive, total product increases by decreasing amounts. When marginal product equals 0, total product is at a maximum. When marginal product is negative, total product is falling.

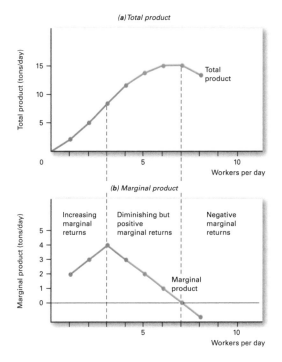

(a) Total product

(b) Marginal product

7-3 Explain why average cost is at a minimum when marginal cost equals average cost.
As long as marginal cost is below average cost, marginal cost pulls down average cost as output expands. As output continues to expand, marginal cost at some point increases because of diminishing marginal returns from the variable resource. Once marginal cost exceeds average cost, marginal cost pulls up average cost. That's why average cost is at a minimum when marginal cost equals average cost.

7-4 Explain the sources of economies of scale and diseconomies of scale.
For any given firm, the long-run average cost curve is formed by connecting the points on the various short-run average cost curves that represent the lowest per-unit cost for each rate of output. Each of the short-run average cost

KEY TERMS

explicit cost Opportunity cost of resources employed by a firm that takes the form of cash payments

implicit cost A firm's opportunity cost of using its own resources or those provided by its owners without a corresponding cash payment

accounting profit A firm's total revenue minus its explicit costs

economic profit A firm's total revenue minus its explicit and implicit costs

normal profit A firm's accounting profit when all resources earn their opportunity cost; equal to implicit cost

variable resource Any resource that can be varied in the short run to increase or decrease production

fixed resource Any resource that cannot be varied in the short run

short run A period during which at least one of a firm's resources is fixed

long run A period during which all resources under the firm's control are variable

total product A firm's total output

production function The relationship between resources employed and a firm's total product

marginal product The change in total product when a particular resource increases by one unit, all other resources constant

increasing marginal returns The marginal product of a variable resource increases as each additional unit of that resource is employed

law of diminishing marginal returns As more of a variable resource is added to a given amount of other resources, marginal product eventually declines and could become negative

fixed cost Any production cost that is independent of the firm's rate of output

variable cost Any production cost that changes as the rate of output changes

total cost The sum of fixed cost and variable cost, or $TC = FC + VC$

marginal cost The change in total cost resulting from a one-unit change in output; the change in total cost divided by the change in output, or $MC = \Delta TC/\Delta q$

average variable cost Variable cost divided by output, or $AVC = VC/q$

average total cost Total cost divided by output, or $ATC = TC/q$; the sum of average fixed cost and average variable cost, or $ATC = AFC + AVC$

economies of scale Forces that reduce a firm's average cost as the scale of operation expands in the long run

diseconomies of scale Forces that may eventually increase a firm's average cost as the scale of operation expands in the long run

long-run average cost curve A curve that indicates the lowest average cost of production at each rate of output when the size, or scale, of the firm varies; also called the planning curve

constant long-run average cost A condition that occurs if, over some range of output, long-run average cost neither increases nor decreases with changes in firm size

minimum efficient scale The lowest rate of output at which a firm takes full advantage of economies of scale

CHAPTER EQUATIONS

Total Cost
$$TC = FC + VC$$

Marginal Cost
$$MC = \Delta TC/\Delta q$$

Average Variable Cost
$$AVC = VC/q$$

Average Total Cost
$$ATC = AFC + AVC$$
$$ATC = TC/q$$

curves is tangent to the long-run average cost curve, or planning curve. These points of tangency represent the least-cost way of producing each particular rate of output.

If a firm experiences economies of scale, long-run average cost falls as output expands. A larger scale of operation allows a firm to use larger, more efficient techniques and machines and to assign workers to more specialized tasks. Diseconomies of scale may eventually take over as a firm expands its plant size, increasing long-run average cost as output expands.

Short-Run Average Total Cost Curves Form the Long-Run Average Cost Curve, or Planning Curve

Curves SS', MM', and LL' show short-run average total costs for small, medium, and large plants, respectively. For output less than q_a, average cost is lowest when the plant is small. Between q_a and q_b, average cost is lowest with a medium-size plant. If output exceeds q_b, the large plant offers the lowest average cost. The long-run average cost curve connects these low-cost segments of each curve and is identified as $SabL'$.

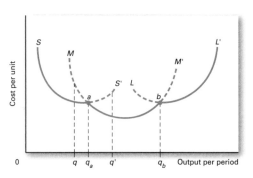

Many Short-Run Average Total Cost Curves Form a Firm's Long-Run Average Cost Curve, or Planning Curve

With many possible plant sizes, the long-run average cost curve is the envelope of portions of the short-run average cost curves. Each short-run curve is tangent to the long-run average cost curve. Each point of tangency represents the least-cost way of producing that level of output.

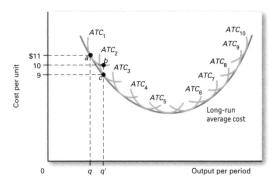

A Firm's Long-Run Average Cost Curve

Up to output level A, long-run average cost falls as the firm experiences economies of scale. Output level A is the minimum efficient scale—the lowest rate of output at which the firm takes full advantage of economies of scale. Between A and B, the average cost is constant. Beyond output level B, long-run average cost increases as the firm experiences diseconomies of scale.

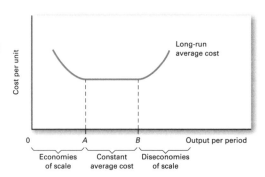

KEY CONCEPTS

8-1 Describe the market structure of perfect competition. Market structures describe important features of the economic environment in which firms operate. A firm's decisions about how much to produce or what price to charge depend on the structure of the market. Perfect competition is the most basic of market structures; if it exists, an individual buyer or seller has no control over the price. Price is determined by market demand and supply.

Market Equilibrium and a Firm's Demand Curve in Perfect Competition

In panel (a), the market price of $5 is determined by the intersection of the market demand and market supply curves. A perfectly competitive firm can sell any amount at that price. The demand curve facing the perfectly competitive firm is horizontal at the market price, as shown by demand curve *d* in panel (b).

8-2 Determine the perfectly competitive firm's profit-maximizing output in the short run. All firms try to maximize economic profit, which is any profit above normal profit, by controlling their rate of output. Subtracting total cost from total revenue is one way to find the profit-maximizing output. Another way is to focus on marginal revenue and marginal cost. On a perfectly competitive firm's demand curve, market price, marginal revenue, and average revenue are all equal. The profit maximizing rate of output is found where marginal revenue equals marginal cost.

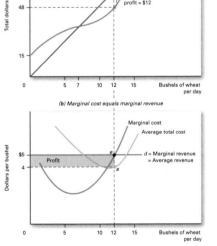

Short-Run Profit Maximization

In panel (a), the total revenue curve for a perfectly competitive firm is a straight line with a slope of 5, the market price. Total cost increases with output, first at a decreasing rate and then at an increasing rate. Economic profit is maximized where total revenue exceeds total cost by the greatest amount, which occurs at 12 bushels of wheat per day. In panel (b), marginal revenue is a horizontal line at the market price of $5. Economic profit is maximized at 12 bushels of wheat per day, where marginal revenue equals marginal cost (point *e*). That profit equals 12 bushels multiplied by the amount by which the market price of $5 exceeds the average total cost of $4. Economic profit is identified by the shaded rectangle in panel (b).

KEY TERMS

market structure Important features of a market, such as the number of firms, product uniformity across firms, firm's ease of entry and exit, and forms of competition

perfect competition A market structure with many fully informed buyers and sellers of a standardized product and with no obstacles to entry or exit of firms in the long run

commodity A standardized product; a product that does not differ across producers, such as a bushel of wheat or an ounce of gold

price taker A firm that faces a given market price and whose quantity supplied has no effect on that price; a perfectly competitive firm that decides to produce must accept, or "take," the market price

marginal revenue (MR) The firm's change in total revenue from selling an additional unit; a perfectly competitive firm's marginal revenue is also the market price

golden rule of profit maximization To maximize profit or minimize loss, a firm produces the quantity at which marginal revenue equals marginal cost; this rule holds for all market structures

average revenue (AR) Total revenue divided by quantity, or $AR = TR/q$; in all market structures, average revenue equals the market price

short-run firm supply curve A curve that shows how much a firm supplies at each price in the short run; in perfect competition, that portion of a firm's marginal cost curve that intersects and rises above the low point on its average variable cost curve

short-run industry supply curve A curve that indicates the quantity supplied by the industry at each price in the short run; in perfect competition, the horizontal sum of each firm's short-run supply curve

long-run industry supply curve A curve that shows the relationship between price and quantity supplied by the industry once firms adjust in the long run to any change in market demand

constant-cost industry An industry that can expand or contract without affecting the long-run per-unit cost of production; the long-run industry supply curve is horizontal

CHAPTER REVIEW 8

increasing-cost industry An industry that faces higher per-unit production costs as industry output expands in the long run; the long-run industry supply curve slopes upward

productive efficiency Each firm employs the least-cost combination of inputs; minimum average cost in the long run

allocative efficiency Each firm produces the output most preferred by consumers; marginal benefit equals marginal cost

producer surplus A bonus for producers in the short run; the amount by which total revenue from production exceeds variable cost

social welfare The overall well-being of people in the economy; maximized when the marginal cost of production equals the marginal benefit to consumers

CHAPTER EQUATIONS

$$Marginal\ benefit = Marginal\ cost$$
$$TR = q \times p$$
$$AR = TR/q$$
$$Economic\ Profit\ or\ Loss = TR - TC$$
$$Market\ price = Marginal\ revenue$$
$$= Average\ revenue$$

8-3 **Outline the conditions under which a firm should produce in the short run rather than shut down, even though it incurs an economic loss.** Firms that have not identified a profitable level of output can either operate at a loss or shut down. In the short run, even a firm that shuts down keeps productive capacity intact by continuing to pay fixed costs, which are sunk regardless. For a firm to produce in the short run, rather than shut down, the market price must at least cover the firm's average variable cost.

Short-Run Loss Minimization

Because total cost everywhere exceeds total revenue in panel (a), the firm suffers a loss no matter how much is produced. The loss is minimized where output is 10 bushels per day. Panel (b) shows that marginal revenue equals marginal cost at point *e*. The loss is equal to output of 10 multiplied by the difference between average total cost ($4) and price ($3). Because price exceeds average variable cost ($2.50), the firm is better off continuing to produce in the short run, since revenue covers some fixed cost.

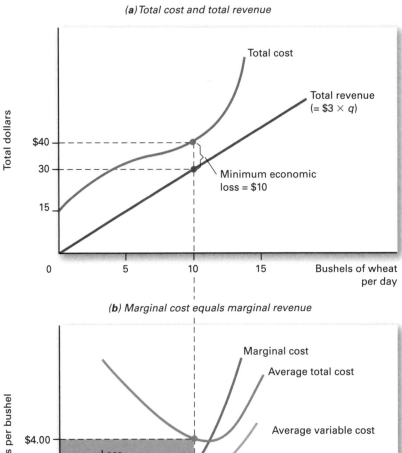

(a) Total cost and total revenue

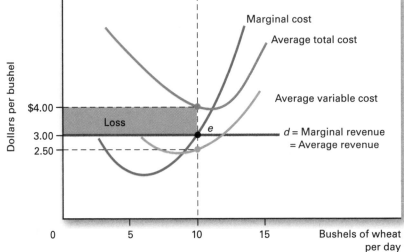

(b) Marginal cost equals marginal revenue

8-4 Describe a perfectly competitive firm's short-run supply curve. If price exceeds average variable cost, the firm produces the quantity at which marginal revenue equals marginal cost. A firm changes the rate of output if the market price changes. As long as the price covers average variable cost, the firm supplies the quantity at which the upward-sloping marginal cost curve intersects the marginal revenue, or demand, curve. A perfectly competitive firm supplies the short-run quantity that maximizes profit or minimizes loss. When confronting a loss, a firm either produces an output that minimizes that loss or shuts down temporarily. The perfectly competitive firm's short-run supply curve consists of that portion of it's marginal cost curve that's at and rising above its average variable cost curve.

8-5 Explain why in perfect competition, there are no economic profits or losses in the long run. In the long run, firms enter and leave the market, adjust the scale of operations, and experience no distinction between fixed and variable cost. Short-run economic profit attracts new entrants in the long run and may cause existing firms to expand. Market supply thereby increases, driving down the market price until economic profit disappears. When market demand decreases, firms incur short-run losses and may go out of business in the long run. This results in lower market output and reduced operational scale that increases each remaining firm's long-run average cost until economic profit disappears.

Summary of Short-Run Output Decisions

At price p_1, the firm produces nothing because p_1 is less than the firm's average variable cost. At price p_2, the firm is indifferent between shutting down or producing q_2 units of output, because in either case, the firm suffers a loss equal to its fixed cost. At p_3, it produces q_3 units and suffers a loss that is less than its fixed cost. At p_4, the firm produces q_4 and just breaks even, earning a normal profit, because p_4 equals average total cost. Finally, at p_5, the firm produces q_5 and earns an economic profit. The firm's short-run supply curve is that portion of its marginal cost curve at and rising above the minimum point of average variable cost (point 2).

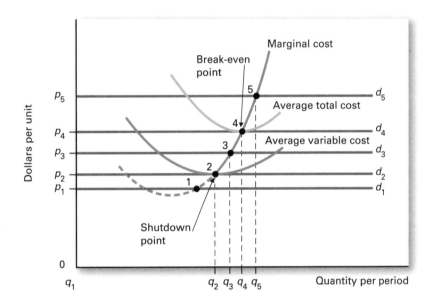

8-6 Explain why, in some perfectly competitive industries, market supply curves slope upward in the long run. The firms in some industries encounter higher average costs as industry output expands in the long run. Expanding output bids up the prices of some resources or otherwise increases per-unit production costs, and these higher costs shift up each firm's cost curves.

8-7 **Summarize how market equilibrium in perfect competition results in productive efficiency and allocative efficiency.** Perfectly competitive markets exhibit both productive efficiency (because output is produced using the most efficient combination of resources available) and allocative efficiency (because the goods produced are those most valued by consumers). In equilibrium, a perfectly competitive market allocates goods so that the marginal cost of the final unit produced equals the marginal value that consumers attach to that final unit.

Long-Run Equilibrium for a Firm and Industry

In long-run equilibrium, the firm produces q units of output per period and earns a normal profit. At point e, price, marginal cost, marginal revenue, short-run average total cost, and long-run average cost are all equal. There is no reason for new firms to enter the market or for existing firms to leave. As long as the market demand and supply curves remain unchanged, the industry will continue to produce a total of Q units of output at price p.

(a) Firm

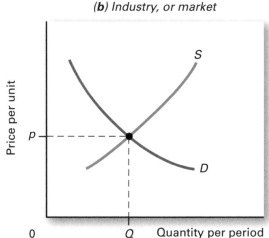

(b) Industry, or market

KEY CONCEPTS

9-1 List three barriers to entry and explain how each can help create market power.

A monopolist sells a product with no close substitutes. Short-run economic profit earned by a monopolist can persist in the long run only if the entry of new firms is blocked. Three barriers to entry are (a) legal restrictions, such as patents and operating licenses; (b) economies of scale over a broad range of output; and (c) control over a key resource.

9-2 Distinguish marginal revenue and average revenue for a monopolist, and explain why marginal revenue is less than average revenue.

Since a monopolist is the sole supplier of a product with no close substitutes, a monopolist's demand curve is also the market demand curve. Since a monopolist that does not price discriminate can sell more only by lowering the price for all units, marginal revenue is less than the price. Where demand is price elastic, marginal revenue is positive and total revenue increases as the price falls. Where demand is price inelastic, marginal revenue is negative and total revenue decreases as the price falls. A monopolist never voluntarily produces where demand is inelastic because raising the price and reducing output would increase total revenue.

Economies of Scale as a Barrier to Entry

A monopoly sometimes emerges naturally if a firm experiences economies of scale as reflected by a downward-sloping, long-run average cost curve. One firm can satisfy market demand at a lower average cost per unit than could two or more firms each operating at smaller rates of output.

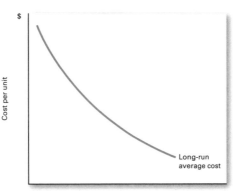

Monopoly Demand, Marginal Revenue, and Total Revenue

Where demand is price elastic, marginal revenue is positive, so total revenue increases as the price falls. Where demand is price inelastic, marginal revenue is negative, so total revenue decreases as the price falls. Where demand is unit elastic, marginal revenue is zero, so total revenue is at a maximum, neither increasing nor decreasing.

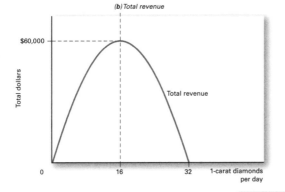

KEY TERMS

barrier to entry Any impediment that prevents new firms from entering an industry and competing on an equal basis with existing firms

patent A legal barrier to entry that grants the holder the exclusive right to sell a product for 20 years from the date the patent application is filed

innovation The process of turning an invention into a marketable product

price maker A firm with some power to set the price because the demand curve for its output slopes downward; a firm with market power

deadweight loss of monopoly Net loss to society when a firm with market power restricts output and increases the price

rent seeking Activities undertaken by individuals or firms to influence public policy in a way that increases their incomes

price discrimination Increasing profit by charging different groups of consumers different prices for the same product

perfect price discrimination Charging a different price for each unit sold

CHAPTER EQUATIONS

Total Revenue
$$TR = p \times Q$$

Marginal Revenue
$$MR = \Delta TR / \Delta Q$$

9-3 Determine the profit-maximizing or loss-minimizing production level for a monopolist. If the monopolist can at least cover variable cost, profit is maximized or loss is minimized in the short run by finding the output rate that equates marginal revenue with marginal cost. At the profit-maximizing quantity, the price is found on the demand curve.

9-4 Summarize what causes the deadweight loss of monopoly.
If costs are similar, a monopolist charges a higher price and supplies less output than does a perfectly competitive industry. Monopoly usually results in a deadweight loss when compared with perfect competition because the loss of consumer surplus exceeds the gains in monopoly profit.

9-5 Outline the factors that could cause the deadweight loss of monopoly to be lower or higher than expected. Deadweight loss can be difficult to estimate. If economies of scale are substantial enough, a monopolist might be able to produce output at a lower cost per unit than could competitive firms. The price, or at least the cost of production, could be lower under monopoly than under competition, and deadweight loss may overstate the true cost of monopoly. Alternatively, the deadweight loss of monopoly might, in fact, be greater than shown in our simple diagram. If resources must be devoted to securing and maintaining a monopoly position, monopolies may impose a greater welfare loss than simple models suggest.

9-6 Explain why a firm with market power might decide to charge different groups different prices. To increase profit through price discrimination, the monopolist must have at least two identifiable groups of customers, each with a different price elasticity of demand at a given price, and must be able to prevent customers charged the lower price from reselling to those charged the higher price. A perfect price discriminator charges a different price for each unit sold, thereby converting all consumer surplus into economic profit. Objectively, price discrimination is as efficient as perfect competition because the monopolist has no incentive to restrict output, so there is no deadweight loss.

The Monopolist Minimizes Losses in the Short Run
Marginal revenue equals marginal cost at point *e*. At quantity *Q*, price *p* (at point *b*) is less than average total cost (at point *a*), so the monopolist suffers a loss, identified by the pink rectangle. But the monopolist continues to produce rather than shut down in the short run because price exceeds average variable cost (at point *c*). Here the price covers all variable cost and a portion of fixed cost.

Perfect Competition and Monopoly Compared
A perfectly competitive industry would produce output Q_c, determined by the intersection of the market demand curve *D* and the market supply curve S_c. The price would be *pc*. A monopoly that could produce output at the same minimum average cost as a perfectly competitive industry would produce output Q_m, determined at point *b*, where the marginal cost curve intersects the monopolist's marginal revenue curve. The monopolist would charge price p_m. Thus, given the same costs, output is lower and price is higher under monopoly than under perfect competition. Consumer surplus is greater with perfect competition.

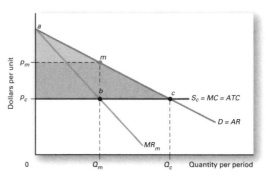

Price Discrimination with Two Groups of Consumers
A monopolist facing two groups of consumers with different demand elasticities may be able to practice price discrimination to increase profit or reduce any loss. With marginal cost the same in both markets, the firm charges a higher price to the group in panel (a), which has less elastic demand than the group in panel (b).

(a) Consumer group with less elastic demand

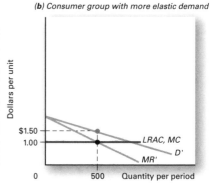

(b) Consumer group with more elastic demand

Perfect Price Discrimination
If a monopolist can charge a different price for each unit sold, it may be able to practice perfect price discrimination. By setting the price of each unit equal to the maximum amount consumers are willing to pay for that unit (shown by the height of the demand curve), the monopolist can reap an economic profit equal to the area of the shaded triangle. Consumer surplus is zero. Ironically, this outcome is efficient because the monopolist has no incentive to restrict output, so there is no deadweight loss.

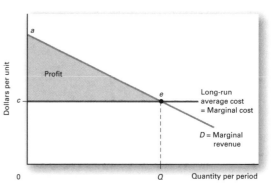

KEY CONCEPTS

10-1 Outline the monopolistic and competitive elements of monopolistic competition.
Monopolistic competition describes a market in which many producers offer products that are substitutes but are not viewed as identical by consumers. Product differentiation allows each supplier some power over the price it can charge. Because barriers to entry are low, there are enough sellers that they behave competitively and act independently.

Monopolistic competition contains elements of both monopoly and competition. Monopolistic competition is like monopoly in the sense that firms in each industry face demand curves that slope downward. Monopolistic competition is like perfect competition in the sense that easy entry and exit eliminate economic profit or economic loss in the long run.

Monopolistic Competitor in the Short Run
The monopolistically competitive firm produces the level of output at which marginal revenue equals marginal cost (point *e*) and charges the price indicated by point *b* on the downward-sloping demand curve. In panel (*a*), the firm produces *q* units, sells them at price *p*, and earns a short-run economic profit equal to $(p - c)$ multiplied by *q*, shown by the blue rectangle. In panel (*b*), the average total cost exceeds the price at the output where marginal revenue equals marginal cost. Thus, the firm suffers a short-run loss equal to $(c - p)$ multiplied by *q*, shown by the pink rectangle.

(a) Maximizing short-run profit

(b) Minimizing short-run loss

Long-Run Equilibrium in Monopolistic Competition
With monopolistic competition, if existing firms earn economic profits in the short run, new firms will enter the industry in the long run. This entry reduces the demand facing each firm. In the long run, each firm's demand curve shifts leftward until marginal revenue equals marginal cost (point *a*) and the demand curve is tangent to the average total cost curve (point *b*). Economic profit is zero at output *q*. With zero economic profit, no more firms will enter, so the industry is in long-run equilibrium. The same long-run adjustment occurs if firms suffer a short-run loss. In the long-run, firms leave until remaining firms earn just a normal profit.

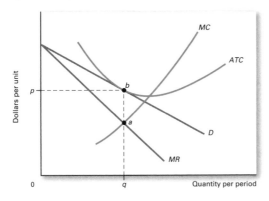

KEY TERMS

monopolistic competition A market structure with many firms selling products that are substitutes but different enough that each firm's demand curve slopes downward; firm entry is relatively easy

excess capacity The difference between a firm's profit-maximizing quantity and the quantity that minimizes average cost; firms with excess capacity could reduce average cost by increasing quantity

oligopoly A market structure characterized by so few firms that each behaves interdependently

undifferentiated oligopoly An oligopoly that sells a commodity, or a product that does not differ across suppliers, such as an ingot of steel or a barrel of oil

differentiated oligopoly An oligopoly that sells products that differ across suppliers, such as automobiles or breakfast cereal

collusion An agreement among firms to increase economic profit by dividing the market and fixing the price

cartel A group of firms that agree to coordinate their production and pricing decisions to reap monopoly profit

price leader A firm whose price is matched by other firms in the market as a form of tacit collusion

game theory An approach that analyzes oligopolistic behavior as a series of strategic moves and countermoves by rival firms

prisoner's dilemma A game that shows why players have difficulty cooperating even though they would benefit from cooperation

strategy In game theory, the operational plan pursued by a player

payoff matrix In game theory, a table listing the payoffs that each player can expect from each move based on the actions of the other player

dominant-strategy equilibrium In game theory, the outcome achieved when each player's choice does not depend on what the other player does

duopoly A market with only two suppliers; a special type of oligopoly market structure

Nash equilibrium A situation in which a firm, or a player in game theory, chooses the best strategy given the strategies chosen by others; no participant can improve his or her outcome by changing strategies even after learning of the strategies selected by other participants

tit-for-tat In game theory, a strategy in repeated games when a player in one round of the game mimics the other player's behavior in the previous round; an optimal strategy for getting the other player to cooperate

coordination game A type of game in which a Nash equilibrium occurs when each player chooses the same strategy; neither player can do better than matching the other player's strategy

Perfect Competition Versus Monopolistic Competition in Long-Run Equilibrium

Cost curves are assumed to be the same in each panel. The perfectly competitive firm of panel (a) faces a demand curve that is horizontal at market price p. Long-run equilibrium occurs at output q, where the demand curve is tangent to the average total cost curve at its lowest point. The monopolistically competitive firm of panel (b) is in long-run equilibrium at output q', where demand is tangent to the average total cost curve. Because the demand curve slopes downward in panel (b), however, the tangency does not occur at the minimum point of average total cost. Thus, the monopolistically competitive firm produces less output and charges a higher price than does a perfectly competitive firm with the same cost curves. Neither firm earns economic profit in the long run. Each earns normal profit. The firm in monopolistic competition has excess capacity, meaning that it could reduce average cost by increasing its rate of output.

10-2 Describe the sources of oligopoly and explain why some industries become oligopolies.
An oligolpoly is an industry dominated by just a few firms. Oligopolists are said to be interdependent since each one must consider the effect of its own actions on competitors' behavior. The formation of an oligopoly can often be traced to some form of barrier to entry, such as economies of scale, legal restrictions, brand names built up by years of advertising, or control over an essential resource.

Economies of Scale as a Barrier to Entry

At point b, an existing firm can produce M or more automobiles at an average cost of c_b. A new entrant able to sell only S automobiles would incur a much higher average cost of c_a at point a. If automobile prices are below c_a, a new entrant would suffer a loss. In this case, economies of scale serve as a barrier to entry, insulating firms that have achieved minimum efficient scale from new competitors.

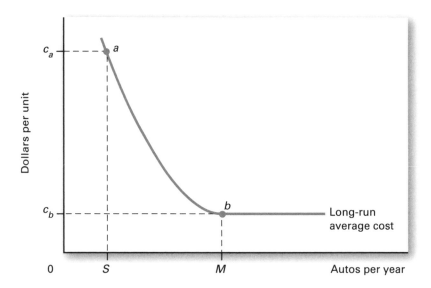

Cartel as a Monopolist

A cartel acts like a monopolist. Here, *D* is the market demand curve, *MR* the associated marginal revenue curve, and *MC* the horizontal sum of the marginal cost curves of cartel members (assuming all firms in the market join the cartel). Cartel profits are maximized when the industry produces quantity *Q* and charges price *p*.

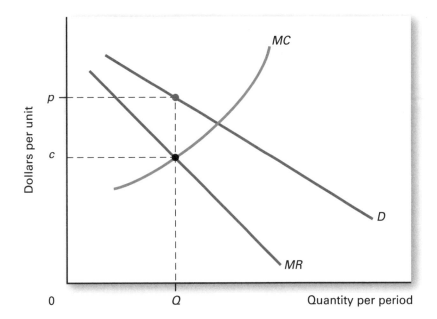

10-3 **Explain why predicting oligopoly behavior is so difficult.** There is no general theory of oligopoly but rather a set of theories, each based on the diversity of observed behavior in an interdependent market. The theories that are used to explain oligopoly behavior are: collusion, price leadership, and game theory. These models identify formal and informal efforts to collude and the strategic decision making process that firms employ when collusion does not occur.

Game theory examines oligopolistic behavior as a series of strategic moves and countermoves among rival firms. This approach analyzes the behavior of decision makers, or players, whose choices affect one another. While participation in a cartel would result in higher economic profits, game theory explains why the incentives to cheat are so great that firms often act in ways that result in lower profits.

The Prisoner's Dilemma Payoff Matrix (years in jail)

This matrix shows the years each thief can expect to spend in jail based on his actions and the actions of the other prisoner. Ben's payoff is in red and Jerry's in blue.

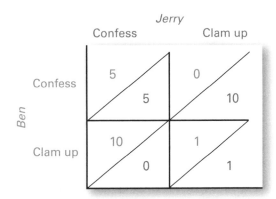

10-4 Summarize the similarities and differences between an oligopoly and perfect competition in terms of price, output, and long-run profitability. With monopolistic competition, there are so many firms in the market that each behaves independently. But with oligopoly, there are so few firms in the market that each must consider the impact its pricing, output, and marketing decisions will have on other firms. Each oligopolist behaves interdependently, and this makes oligopoly difficult to analyze. In general, price and profits are usually higher under oligopoly.

Comparison of Market Structures

	Perfect Competition	Monopoly	Monopolistic Competition	Oligopoly
Number of firms	Most	One	Many	Few
Control over price	None	Complete	Limited	Some
Product differences	None	Only one supplier	Some	None or some
Barriers to entry	None	Insurmountable	Low	Substantial
Number of buyers	Many	Many	Many	Many
Examples	Wheat	Local electricity	Convenience stores	Automobiles

KEY CONCEPTS

11-1 Determine the profit-maximizing number of workers for a firm to hire. A producer demands another unit of a resource as long as its marginal revenue exceeds its marginal cost. Profit is maximized when the marginal revenue product of a resource equals its marginal cost.

11-2 Explain why resource owners are more willing and more able to increase the quantity supplied of the resources they own as resource prices increase. People supply their resources to the highest-paying alternative, other things constant. As the price of a resource increases, each unit supplied buys more goods and services, so resource owners increase their quantity supplied.

11-3 Explain why some resource price differences are temporary while others are permanent. People supply their resources to the highest-paying alternative, other things constant. Because other things are not always constant, people must be paid more for jobs less suited to their tastes. Your utility depends on both monetary and nonmonetary aspects of the job. Sometimes the resource itself is not mobile, resulting in permanent price differences. For example, land in the city sells for more than land in rural areas.

Resource Market for Carpenters

The intersection of the upward-sloping supply curve of carpenters with the downward-sloping demand curve for carpenters determines their equilibrium wage, *W*, and their level of employment, *E*.

11-4 Clarify the distinction between a resource's opportunity cost and its economic rent. Opportunity cost is what a resource could earn in its best alternative use. Economic rent is the portion of a resource's earnings that exceeds the amount necessary to keep the resource in its present use. In other words, economic rent is earnings in excess of opportunity cost.

Opportunity Cost and Economic Rent

In panel (a), the resource supply curve is vertical, indicating that the resource has no alternative use. The price is demand-determined, and all earnings are economic rent (blue-shaded area). In panel (b), the resource supply curve is horizontal at $15 per hour, indicating that the resource can also earn that much in its best alternative use. Employment is demand-determined, and all earnings are opportunity cost (pink-shaded area). Panel (c) shows an upward-sloping resource supply curve. Earnings are partly opportunity cost and partly economic rent (blue-shaded area). Both demand and supply determine the equilibrium price and quantity.

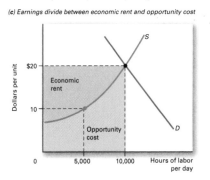

KEY TERMS

derived demand Resource demand that arises from the demand for the product the resource produces

economic rent Portion of a resource's earnings that exceeds its opportunity cost

marginal revenue product The change in total revenue when an additional unit of a resource is employed, other things constant

marginal resource cost The change in total cost when an additional unit of a resource is hired, other things constant

resource substitutes Resources that substitute in production; an increase in the price of one resource increases the demand for the other

resource complements Resources that enhance one another's productivity; a decrease in the price of one resource increases the demand for the other

11-5 Describe the economic logic of optimal resource use.

The marginal revenue product of any resource is the change in the firm's total revenue resulting from employing an additional unit of the resource, other things constant. The marginal resource cost is what an additional unit of a resource will cost the firm. The profit-maximizing level of resource employment occurs where the respective marginal revenue products equals the marginal resource costs. A resource's marginal revenue product depends on the resource's marginal product and the price at which that product is sold. Two things can change a resource's marginal product: (1) a change in the amount of other resources employed and (2) a change in technology. Only one thing can change the price of the product: a change in demand for the product.

Marginal Revenue Product When a Firm Sells in a Competitive Market

Because of diminishing marginal returns, the marginal product of labor declines as more is employed, as shown in column (3). Because this firm sells its product in a competitive market, it can sell all it wants at the market price of $20 per unit, as shown in column (4). The marginal product of labor in column (3) times the product price of $20 in column (4) yields the marginal revenue product of labor in column (6). Labor's marginal revenue product is the change in total revenue as a result of hiring another unit of labor.

(1) Workers per Day	(2) Total Product	(3) Marginal Product	(4) Product Price	(5) Total Revenue (5) = (2) × (4)	(6) Marginal Revenue Product (6) = (3) × (4)
0	0	—	$20	$ 0	—
1	10	10	20	200	$200
2	19	9	20	380	180
3	27	8	20	540	160
4	34	7	20	680	140
5	40	6	20	800	120
6	45	5	20	900	100
7	49	4	20	980	80
8	52	3	20	1040	60

The Marginal Revenue Product When a Firm Sells with Market Power

To sell more, a firm with market power must lower the price, as indicated in column (3). Total revenue in column (4) equals total product in column (2) times the product price in column (3). Labor's marginal revenue product in column (5) equals the change in total revenue from hiring another worker. The marginal revenue product declines both because of diminishing marginal returns from labor and because the product price must fall to sell more.

(1) Workers per Day	(2) Total Product	(3) Product Price	(4) Total Revenue (4) = (2) × (3)	(5) Marginal Revenue Product
0	0	—	—	—
1	10	$40	$400	$400
2	19	35	665	265
3	27	31	837	172
4	34	28	952	115
5	40	25	1000	48
6	45	23	1035	35
7	49	21	1029	−6
8	52	19	988	−41

Market Equilibrium for a Resource and the Firm's Employment Decision

Market demand and supply of a resource, in panel (a), determine that resource's market wage and quantity. In panel (b), an individual firm can employ as much as it wants at the market wage, so that wage becomes the firm's marginal resource cost curve. The marginal resource cost curve also is the supply curve of that resource to the firm. In panel (b), a resource's marginal revenue product is the firm's demand curve for that resource. The firm maximizes any profit (or minimizes any loss) by hiring a resource up to the point where the resource's marginal revenue product equals its marginal resource cost, which is six workers per day in this example.

(a) Market

(b) Firm

KEY CONCEPTS

12-1 Explain why the quantity of labor supplied increases with the wage, other things remain constant.

People allocate their time to maximize utility. There are three uses of time: market work, nonmarket work, and leisure. A person attempts to maximize utility by allocating time so that the expected marginal utility of the last unit of time spent in each activity is identical.

The higher the wage, other things constant, the more goods and services can be purchased with that wage, so a higher wage encourages people to substitute market work for other uses of their time. But a higher wage also increases income, increasing the demand for all normal goods, including leisure. The net effect of a higher wage on the quantity of labor supplied depends on both the substitution effect and the income effect.

Your Labor Supply Curve During the Summer

When the substitution effect of a wage increase outweighs the income effect, the quantity of labor you supply increases with the wage. Above some wage, shown here at $13 per hour, the income effect dominates. Above that wage, your supply curve bends backward. Further increases in the wage reduce the quantity of labor you supply.

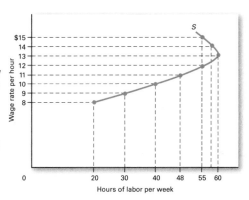

12-2 Describe why some workers earn higher wages than other workers.

The intersection of labor demand and labor supply curves determines the market wage and market employment. The supply of labor depends not only on the wage, but also on other factors, including (a) other sources of income, (b) job amenities, (c) the value of job experience, and (d) worker tastes. Market wages differ because of (a) differences in training and education; (b) differences in the skill and ability of workers; (c) risk differences, both in terms of the workers' safety and the chances of getting laid off; (d) geographic differences; and (e) racial and gender discrimination.

Deriving the Market Labor Supply Curve from Individual Labor Supply Curves

The individual labor supply curve in panel (a) bends backward. The market supply curve, however, may still slope upward over the relevant range of wages.

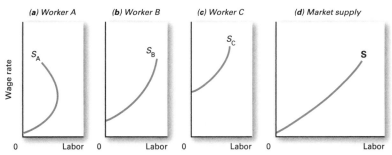

KEY TERMS

market work Time sold as labor

nonmarket work Time spent getting an education or on do-it-yourself production for personal consumption

leisure Time spent on nonwork activities

substitution effect of a wage increase A higher wage encourages more work because other activities now have a higher opportunity cost

income effect of a wage increase A higher wage raises a worker's income, increasing the demand for all normal goods, including leisure, so the quantity of labor supplied to market work decreases

backward-bending supply curve of labor As the wage rises, the quantity of labor supplied may eventually decline; the income effect of a higher wage increases the demand for leisure, which reduces the quantity of labor supplied enough to more than offset the substitution effect of a higher wage

labor union A group of workers who organize to improve their terms of employment

craft union A union whose members have a particular skill or work at a particular craft, such as plumbers or carpenters

industrial union A union consisting of both skilled and unskilled workers from a particular industry, such as all autoworkers or all steelworkers

collective bargaining The process by which union and management negotiate a labor agreement

mediator An impartial observer who helps resolve differences between union and management

binding arbitration Negotiation in which union and management must accept an impartial observer's resolution of a dispute

strike A union's attempt to withhold labor from a firm to halt production

featherbedding Union efforts to force employers to hire more workers than demanded at a particular wage

right-to-work states States where workers in unionized companies do not have to join the union or pay union dues

12-3 Summarize the objectives of labor unions and outline strategies used to achieve these objectives.

Unions can broadly be classified as either craft unions (people with a particular skill, or craft) or industrial unions (unskilled, semiskilled, and skilled workers in a particular industry). Unions and employers try to negotiate a labor contract through collective bargaining. A major source of union power has been the threat of a strike, which is an attempt to withhold labor from the firm.

12-4 Give reasons why unionization rates have declined in recent decades.

Inclusive, or industrial, unions attempt to establish a wage floor that exceeds the competitive, or market-clearing, wage. A union wage above the market-clearing level creates an excess quantity of labor supplied, so the union must somehow ration the limited jobs among its members. Exclusive, or craft, unions try to raise union wages by restricting the supply of labor. Another way to raise union wages is to increase the demand for union labor.

Union membership as a percentage of the labor force has been falling for half a century. Reasons for the decline include right-to-work laws, growing global competition, a shift in employment from goods to services, a greater willingness to hire replacements for striking workers, a greater willingness of union members and others to work during strikes, and less political support for the labor movement.

Age, Education, and Pay

For every age group, workers with more education earn more. The premium paid for years of experience also increases more for those with more education.

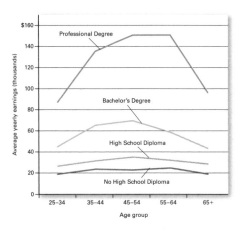

Effects of Labor Union's Wage Floor

Without a labor union, the market wage is *W* in panel (a). At that wage, each firm can hire as much labor as it wants. The individual firm in panel (b) hires more labor until the marginal revenue product equals the market wage, *W*. Each firm hires *e* units of labor, and industry employment is *E*. If a union negotiates a wage *W'*, which is above the market wage *W*, the supply curve facing the firm shifts up from s to s'. Each firm hires less labor, *e'*, so industry employment falls to *E'*. At the union wage there is now an excess quantity of labor supplied equal to *E"* – *E'*.

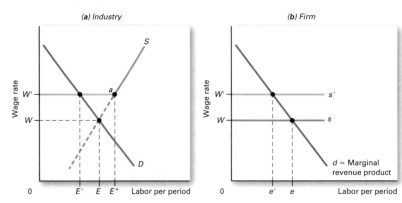

Effect of Reducing Labor Supply or Increasing Labor Demand

If a union can successfully restrict labor supply in an industry, the supply curve shifts to the left from *S* to *S'*, as in panel (a). The wage rises from *W* to *W'*, but at the cost of reducing employment from *E* to *E'*. If a union can increase the demand for union labor, as in panel (b), the demand curve shifts right from *D* to *D"*, raising both the wage and employment.

KEY CONCEPTS

13-1 Derive a firm's demand curve for investment, and determine its marginal cost of investing.
Choosing the profit-maximizing level of capital is complicated because capital purchased today usually yields a stream of benefits for years into the future. The expected rate of return on capital equals the expected annual earnings of that capital divided by that capital's purchase price. The expected rate of return on capital declines as the quantity of capital increases because of diminishing marginal returns to capital. The expected rate of return on capital is the firm's demand curve for investment. The profit-maximizing firm invests up to the point where the expected rate of return on capital equals the market rate of interest. The market interest rate is the opportunity cost and the marginal cost of investing.

Expected Rate of Return on Golf Carts and the Opportunity Cost of Funds
An individual firm invests in any project with an expected rate of return that exceeds the market interest rate. At an interest rate of 8 percent, Hacker Haven invests $15,000 in three golf carts.

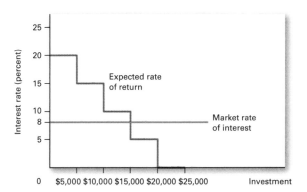

13-2 Explain what determines the interest rate for loanable funds.
The demand and supply of loanable funds determine the market interest rate as illustrated in the following exhibit.

Market for Loanable Funds
Because of the declining expected rate of return on capital, the quantity of loanable funds demanded is inversely related to the interest rate. The market rate of interest, 8 percent, is found where the demand curve for loanable funds intersects the supply curve of loanable funds. An increase in the demand for loanable funds from D to D' raises the market interest rate from 8 percent to 9 percent and increases the equilibrium quantity of loanable funds from $1.0 trillion to $1.1 trillion.

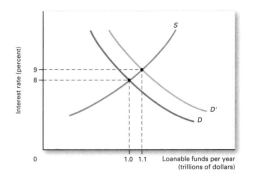

KEY TERMS

positive rate of time preference Consumers value present consumption more than future consumption

interest rate Interest per year as a percentage of the amount saved or borrowed

expected rate of return on capital The expected annual earnings divided by capital's purchase price

intellectual property An intangible asset created by human knowledge and ideas

demand for loanable funds The negative relationship between the market interest rate and the quantity of loanable funds demanded, other things constant

supply of loanable funds The positive relationship between the market interest rate and the quantity of loanable funds supplied, other things constant

loanable funds market The market in which savers (suppliers of loanable funds) and borrowers (demanders of loanable funds) come together to determine the market interest rate and the quantity of loanable funds exchanged

prime rate The interest rate lenders charge their most trustworthy business borrowers

collateral An asset pledged by the borrower that can be sold to pay off the loan in the event the borrower defaults

term structure of interest rates The relationship between the duration of a loan and the interest rate charged; typically interest rates increase with the duration of the loan, because longer loans are considered more risky

present value The value today of income to be received in the future

discounting Converting future dollar amounts into present value

annuity A given sum of money received each year for a specified number of years

initial public offering The initial sale of corporate stock to the public

corporate stock Certificate reflecting part ownership of a corporation

CHAPTER REVIEW 13

dividends After-tax corporate profit paid to stockholders rather than retained by the firm and reinvested

retained earnings After-tax corporate profit reinvested in the firm rather than paid to stockholders as dividends

bond Certificate reflecting a firm's promise to pay the lender periodic interest and to repay the borrowed sum of money on the designated maturity date

crowdfunding Raising money from many people through an online platform

CHAPTER EQUATIONS

$$\text{Present value} = \frac{M}{(1 + i)^t}$$

Present value of receiving M dollars

$$\text{each year forever} = \frac{M}{i}$$

13-3 Describe four reasons why interest rates differ across markets. At any given time, interest rates may differ across borrowers because of differences in risk, maturity, administrative costs, and tax treatment.

Interest Rates Charged for Different Types of Loans

Interest rates are higher for riskier loans. Rates for home mortgages and new cars are relatively low because these loans are backed up by the home or car as collateral. Personal loans and credit card balances face the highest rates, because these loans are riskier—that is, the likelihood borrowers fail to repay the loans is greater and the borrower offers no collateral.

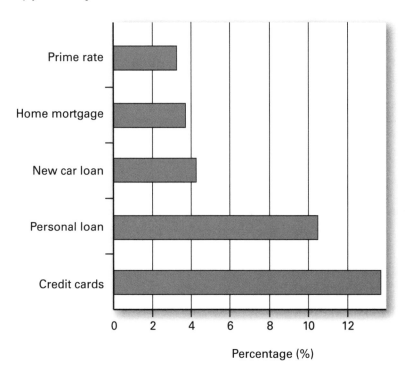

Percentage (%)

13-4 Demonstrate how to convert future dollars into their present value. The current value of future payments is the present value. The process of translating future payments into present value is called discounting. The present value of a given payment is smaller the further into the future that payment is to be received. A given sum of money received each year for a specified number of years is called an annuity. The present value of receiving a sum each year forever is the amount received each year divided by the market interest rate. The formulas for converting future dollars measured as M received in year t into present value at interest rate i are listed at left under "Chapter Equations."

13-5 Summarize how entrepreneurs drive the economy forward. An entrepreneur is a profit-seeker who comes up with an idea, tries to turn that idea into a marketable product, and accepts the risk of success or failure. The entrepreneur need not supply any resource other than entrepreneurial ability, though many manage the firm and provide some start-up funds. By developing new products, improving existing ones, employing better production methods, and finding new ways of doing business, successful entrepreneurs earn a profit and drive the economy forward.

13-6 Distinguish between stocks and bonds, and explain which involves more risk and why. Corporations fund new investment from three main sources: new stock issues, retained earnings, and borrowing (either directly from a bank or by issuing bonds). Once new stocks and bonds are issued, they can then be bought and sold on securities markets. The value of corporate stocks and bonds tends to vary directly with the firm's profit prospects. More profitable firms have more ready access to funds needed for expansion. While both stocks and bond involve risk, bonds tend to be less risky because firms are obligated to pay bond holders before stockholders get anything. And if the company goes bust, stockholders lose everything but bondholders may still recover some money.

KEY CONCEPTS

14-1 Describe the criteria a firm should apply when deciding whether to produce a component part or to purchase that part in the market.

Firms arise when production is more efficient using the hierarchy of the firm than using market transactions. Because production requires elaborate coordination of many resources, all this activity can usually be carried out more efficiently under the direction of a firm's manager than by having a consumer negotiate detailed performance contracts with many resource suppliers. One way firms establish efficient boundaries is through vertical integration. Other things constant, the firm is more likely to buy a component rather than produce it if (a) it's cheaper to buy it than make it, (b) the item is well defined and its quality easily determined, and (c) there are many suppliers of the item.

Minimum Efficient Scale and Vertical Integration

The manufacturer in panel (a) is producing at the minimum efficient scale of 1,000,000 computers per month. That output requires 1,000,000 computer chips. If the computer manufacturer produced its own chips, the cost would be much higher than if it buys them from a chipmaker operating on a much larger scale. As panel (b) shows, economies of scale in chip production are far from exhausted when 1,000,000 chips a month are produced.

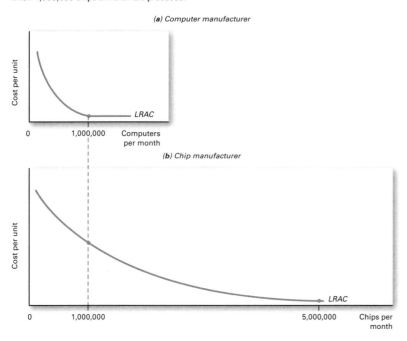

(a) Computer manufacturer

y-axis: Cost per unit
x-axis: Computers per month; 0, 1,000,000
LRAC

(b) Chip manufacturer

y-axis: Cost per unit
x-axis: Chips per month; 0, 1,000,000, 5,000,000
LRAC

14-2 Explain the optimal amount of search for information when shopping for a product.

A buyer searches for product information as long as the marginal benefit of search exceeds its marginal cost. Equilibrium, or optimal, search occurs where the marginal benefit of search equals the marginal cost of search. Because information is costly, product prices may differ across suppliers. Search costs also lead to quality differences across sellers, even for identically priced products, because consumers find the expected marginal cost of finding a higher quality product outweighs the expected marginal benefit. A new technology, such as the Internet, that reduces search costs will increase the amount of search and reduce price differences for the same good.

KEY TERMS

vertical integration The expansion of a firm into stages of production earlier or later than those in which it specializes, such as a steel maker that also mines iron ore

outsourcing A firm buys inputs from outside suppliers

core competency Area of specialty; the product or phase of production a firm supplies with greatest efficiency

bounded rationality The notion that there is a limit to the information that a firm's manager can comprehend and act on

economies of scope Average costs decline as a firm makes a range of different products rather than specializing in just one product

winner's curse The plight of the winning bidder who overestimates an asset's true value

asymmetric information One side of the market has better information about the product than does the other side

hidden characteristics One side of the market knows more than the other side about product characteristics that are important to the other side

adverse selection Those on the informed side of the market self-select in a way that harms those on the uninformed side of the market

hidden actions One side of an economic relationship can do something that the other side cannot observe

principal-agent problem The agent's objectives differ from those of the principal, and one side can pursue hidden actions

principal A person or firm who hires an agent to act on behalf of that person or firm

agent A person or firm who is supposed to act on behalf of the principal

moral hazard A situation in which one party, as a result of a contract, has an incentive to shirk responsibilities in a way that harms the other party to the contract

efficiency wage theory The idea that offering high wages attracts a more talented labor pool and encourages those hired to perform well to keep their jobs

Optimal Search with Imperfect Information

When information is not free, additional information is acquired as long as its marginal benefit exceeds its marginal cost. Equilibrium, or optimal search, occurs where marginal benefit equals marginal cost. I^* is the optimal quantity of information.

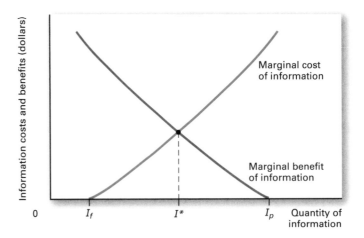

14-3 Define asymmetric information, and explain why it may pose a problem for market operations.

Asymmetric information occurs when one side of the market is better informed about a product than the other side is. The uninformed side may not know about hidden characteristics or about hidden actions. Those with more information can take advantage of those with less. Because of adverse selection, those on the uninformed side of the market may find they are dealing with exactly the wrong people. An incentive structure or an information-revealing system can be developed to reduce the problems associated with the lopsided availability of information.

14-4 Summarize how labor markets try to cope with the problem of asymmetric information.

Asymmetric information occurs in labor markets when managers cannot attribute specific outputs to particular workers. If productivity is easy to measure, workers are paid according to their efficiency, as in piece work. If marginal productivity is harder to quantify, employers pay workers by the hour. Inability to quantify productivity also affects the hiring process and the salaries employers offer. Setting above-market wages to attract top talent may result in adverse selection. Highly qualified people may not consider the wage commensurate with their abilities and do not apply, whereas less qualified applicants may find the wage attractive and apply in droves. To overcome this asymmetry, employers can screen applicants based on some signal, such as the level of education or college grades, that more-productive workers can send more easily than can less-productive workers.

14-5 Identify two types of limitations that can undermine rational decisions.

Standard economics assumes that people are rational in pursuing their self-interest. But psychologists question the ability of humans to make complex decisions and to follow through on them. Specifically, humans have only so much brainpower and so much time to solve complex production and consumption decisions. Humans also have only so much willpower to follow through on decisions they know to be in their best interests.

KEY CONCEPTS

15-1 Describe three types of government regulation of business.

Government attempts to control business behavior with (1) social regulations, such as those aimed at health and safety in the workplace: (2) economic regulations, where monopoly appears inevitable or even desirable; and (3) antitrust policy, which aims to promote market competition. This chapter examined in detail only two forms of government regulation of business: (a) economic regulation, such as the regulation of natural monopolies, and (b) antitrust policy, which promotes competition and prohibits efforts to monopolize, or cartelize, an industry.

15-2 Evaluate alternative ways government can regulate a natural monopoly.

Governments regulate natural monopolies so that output is greater and prices lower than if the monopolist was allowed to maximize profits. One problem with regulation is that the price that maximizes social welfare results in an economic loss, whereas the price that allows the firm to earn a normal profit does not maximize social welfare.

Regulating a Natural Monopoly

With a natural monopoly, the long-run average cost curve slopes downward where it intersects the market demand curve. The unregulated firm maximizes profit by producing where marginal revenue equals marginal cost, in this case, 50 million trips per month at a price of $4.00 per trip. This outcome is inefficient because price, or marginal benefit, exceeds marginal cost. To achieve the efficient output rate, regulators could set the price at $0.50 per trip. The subway would sell 105 million trips per month, which would be the efficient quantity. But at $0.50 per trip, the subway would lose money and would require a subsidy to keep going. As an alternative, regulators could set the price at $1.50 per trip. The subway would sell 90 million trips per month and would just break even (because price equals average cost).

15-3 Describe two alternative theories of economic regulation.

There are two views of economic regulation, which tries to reduce the harmful consequences of monopolistic behavior in markets where output can be most efficiently

supplied by one or two firms. The first is that economic regulation is in the public, or consumer, interest because it controls natural monopolies where production by one or just a few firms is most efficient. A second view is that regulation is more in the special interest of producers who use regulations to fix the price, block entry, and increase profits.

15-4 Summarize the driving causes behind each of the four U.S. merger waves.

See the table below, which describes the stimulus behind each merger wave. To prevent mergers from creating monopolies, the U.S. Justice Department uses the Herfindahl-Hirschman Index (HHI) to determine the sales concentration in an industry and the legality of a merger. (The higher the HHI for market, the more monopolistic it is.)

KEY TERMS

market power The ability of a firm to raise its price without losing all its customers to rival firms

social regulation Government regulation aimed at improving health and safety

economic regulation Government regulation of natural monopoly, where, because of economies of scale, average production cost is lowest when a single firm supplies the market

antitrust policy Government regulation aimed at preventing monopoly and fostering competition in markets where competition is desirable

public utilities Government-owned or government-regulated monopolies

capture theory of regulation Producers' political power and strong stake in the regulatory outcome lead them, in effect, to "capture" the regulating agency and prevail on it to serve producer interests

trust Any firm or group of firms that tries to monopolize a market

Sherman Antitrust Act of 1890 First national legislation in the world against monopolies; prohibited trusts, restraint of trade, and monopolization, but the law was vague and, by itself, ineffective

Clayton Act of 1914 Outlawed certain anticompetitive practices not prohibited by the Sherman Act, including price discrimination, tying contracts, exclusive dealing, interlocking directorates, and buying the corporate stock of a competitor

tying contract A seller of one good requires a buyer to purchase other goods as part of the deal

exclusive dealing A supplier prohibits its customers from buying from other suppliers of the product

interlocking directorate A person serves on the boards of directors of two or more competing firms

Federal Trade Commission (FTC) Act of 1914 Established a federal body to help enforce antitrust laws; run by commissioners assisted by economists and lawyers

horizontal merger A merger in which one firm combines with another that produces the same type of product

vertical merger A merger in which one firm combines with another from which it had purchased inputs or to which it had sold output

consent decree The accused party, without admitting guilt, agrees not to do whatever it was charged with if the government drops the charges

per se illegal In antitrust law, business practices deemed illegal regardless of their economic rationale or their consequences

rule of reason Before ruling on the legality of a business practice, a court examines why it was undertaken and what effect it has on competition

predatory pricing Pricing tactics employed by a dominant firm to drive competitors out of business, such as temporarily selling below marginal cost or dropping the price only in certain markets

Herfindahl-Hirschman Index, or HHI A measure of market concentration that squares each firm's percentage share of the market, then sums these squares

conglomerate merger A merger of firms in different industries

Four U.S. Merger Waves Since 1887

Wave	Years	Dominant Type of Merger	Examples	Stimulus
First	1887–1904	Horizontal	U.S. Steel, Standard Oil	Span national markets
Second	1916–1929	Vertical	Copper refiner with copper fabricator	Stock market boom
Third	1948–1969	Conglomerate	Litton Industries	Diversification
Fourth	1982–present	Horizontal and vertical	Banking, telecommunications, health services, insurance	Span national and global markets, stock market boom

Key Antitrust Legislation

Year	Act	Provision
1890	Sherman Antitrust Act	Prohibits trusts, restraint of trade, and monopolization
1914	Clayton Act	Outlaws price discrimination, tying contracts, exclusive dealing, and interlocking directorates
1914	FTC Act	Establishes agency to enforce antitrust laws
1950	Celler-Kefauver Anti-Merger Act	Gives FTC power to block horizontal and vertical mergers

Herfindahl-Hirschman Index (HHI) Based on Market Shares in Three Industries

Each of the three industries shown has 44 firms. The HHI is found by squaring each firm's market share then summing the squares. Under each industry, each firm's market share is shown in the left column and the square of the market share is shown in the right column. For ease of exposition, only the market shares of the top four firms differ across industries. The remaining 40 firms have 1 percent market share each. The HHI for Industry III is nearly triple that for each of the other two industries.

Firm	Industry I Market Share (percent)	Industry I Market Share Squared	Industry II Market Share (percent)	Industry II Market Share Squared	Industry III Market Share (percent)	Industry III Market Share Squared
A	23	529	15	225	57	3,249
B	18	324	15	225	1	1
C	13	169	15	225	1	1
D	6	36	15	225	1	1
Remaining 40 firms	1 each	40	1 each	40	1 each	40
HHI		**1,098**		**940**		**3,292**

15-5 Evaluate whether the U.S. economy has become more competitive or less competitive since 1958, and explain why.

As shown by the bar graph below, competition in U.S. industries has been increasing since 1939 and particularly since 1958. Four sources of increased competition are greater international trade, industry deregulation, antitrust policy, and technological change.

Competitive Trends in the U.S. Economy: 1939 to 2000

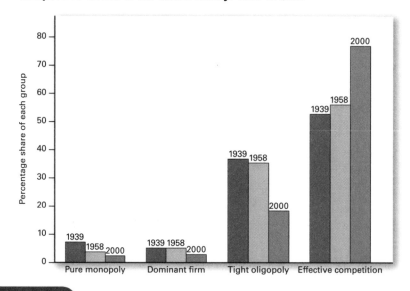

KEY CONCEPTS

16-1 Differentiate four categories of goods in terms of their exclusivity and rivalry.
Private goods are rival and exclusive, such as a pizza. Public goods are nonrival and nonexclusive, such as national defense. Goods that are in between public and private goods include natural monopolies, which are nonrival but exclusive, such as cable TV, and open-access goods, which are rival but nonexclusive, such as ocean fish. Because private-sector producers cannot easily exclude nonpayers from consuming a public good, public goods are typically provided by government, which has the power to enforce tax collections.

Categories of Goods

	Rival	Nonrival
Exclusive	1. Private —Pizza —Crowded Subway	2. Natural Monopolies —Cable TV —Uncrowded Subway
Nonexclusive	3. Open Access —Ocean fish —Migratory birds	4. Public —National defense —Mosquito control

Market for Public Goods

Because public goods, once produced, are available to all in identical amounts, the demand for a public good is the vertical sum of each individual's demand. Thus, the market demand for mosquito spraying is the vertical sum of Maria's demand, D_m, and Alan's demand, D_a. The efficient level of provision is found where the marginal cost of mosquito spraying equals its marginal benefit. This occurs at point e, where the marginal cost curve intersects the market demand curve, D.

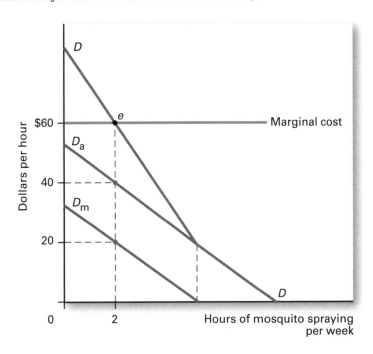

KEY TERMS

open-access good A good such as ocean fish that is rival in consumption but from which nonpayers cannot be excluded easily

free-rider problem Because nobody can be easily excluded from consuming a public good, some people may try to reap the benefits of the good without paying for it

median-voter model Under certain conditions, the preferences of the median, or middle, voter will dominate the preferences of all other voters

rational ignorance A stance adopted by voters when they realize that the cost of understanding and voting on a particular issue exceeds the benefit expected from doing so

traditional public-goods legislation Legislation that involves widespread costs and widespread benefits—nearly everyone pays and nearly everyone benefits

special-interest legislation Legislation with concentrated benefits but widespread costs

pork-barrel spending Special-interest legislation that has narrow geographical benefits but is funded by all taxpayers

populist legislation Legislation with widespread benefits but concentrated costs

competing-interest legislation Legislation that confers concentrated benefits on one group by imposing concentrated costs on another group

underground economy Market activity that goes unreported either because it is illegal or because those involved want to evade taxes

bureaus Government agencies charged with implementing legislation and financed by appropriations from legislative bodies

16-2 Identify four categories of legislation based on the distribution of costs and the distribution of benefits, and provide examples of each. Public choice based on majority rule usually reflects the preferences of the median voter. Costs and benefits of public choices are spread throughout the democracy. The combinations of benefits and costs yield four possible categories of distributions: (1) widespread benefits and widespread costs (traditional public-goods legislation), (2) concentrated benefits and widespread costs (special-interest legislation), (3) widespread benefits and concentrated costs (populist legislation), and (4) concentrated costs and concentrated benefits (competing-interest legislation). An important feature of representative democracy is the incentive and political power it offers interest groups to increase their wealth, either through direct transfers or through favorable public expenditures and regulations.

Categories of Legislation Based on the Distribution of Costs and Benefits

		Distribution of Benefits	
		Widespread	Concentrated
Distribution of Costs	**Widespread**	1. Traditional Public Goods —National defense	2. Special Interest —Farm subsidies
	Concentrated	3. Populist —Tort reform	4. Competing Interest —Labor union issues

Effects of Milk Price Supports

In the absence of government intervention, the market price of milk is $1.50 per gallon, and 100 million gallons are sold per month. If government establishes a floor price of $2.50 per gallon, then the quantity supplied increases and the quantity demanded decreases. To maintain the higher price, the government must buy the excess quantity supplied at $2.50 per gallon or must otherwise pay farmers to limit their quantity supplied to only 75 million gallons a month.

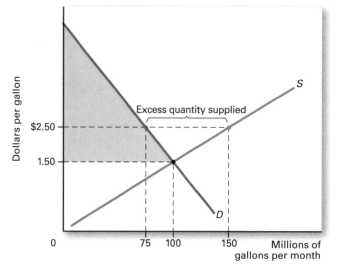

16-3 Explain why some people want to use government power to increase their income, while others try to avoid government. Producers have an abiding interest in any legislation that affects their livelihood. Consumers, however, purchase thousands of different goods and services and thus have no special interest in legislation affecting any particular product. Most consumers adopt a stance of rational ignorance because the expected costs of keeping up with special-interest issues usually outweigh the expected benefits.

The intense interest that producer groups have in relevant legislation, coupled with the rational ignorance of voters regarding most issues, leave government vulnerable to rent seeking by special interests. Elected officials trying to maximize their political support sometimes serve special interests at the expense of the public interest. Meanwhile some people resort to the underground economy to avoid government regulations and taxes.

16-4 Outline the differences between government bureaus and for-profit firms. Bureaus differ from firms in the amount of consumer feedback they receive, in their incentives to minimize costs, and in the transferability of their ownership. Because of these differences, bureaus may not be as efficient or as sensitive to consumer preferences as for-profit firms are. Just because a good or service is funded by government doesn't mean it must be produced by government. A growing number of public goods and services are the result of competitive bidding by for-profit firms.

KEY CONCEPTS

17-1 Describe the common pool problem and summarize ways to address it. An exhaustible resource is available in fixed supply, such as crude oil or coal. A renewable resource can regenerate itself if used conservatively, such as a properly managed forest. Some resources suffer from a common-pool problem because unrestricted access leads to overuse. By imposing restrictions on resource use, government regulations may be able to reduce the common pool problem. Output restrictions or taxes could force people to use the resource at a rate that is socially optimal, at a rate that supports a sustainable use of the resource.

17-2 Determine the optimal level of pollution with fixed technology and with variable technology. The optimal amount of environmental quality occurs where the marginal social benefit of an improvement equals its marginal social cost. An upward shift of the marginal benefit curve of

Negative Externalities: The Market for Electricity in the Midwest

If producers base their output on marginal private cost, 50 million kilowatt-hours of electricity are produced per month. The marginal external cost of electricity is the cost of pollution imposed on society. The marginal social cost curve includes both the marginal private cost and the marginal external cost. If producers base their output decisions on marginal social cost, only 35 million kilowatt-hours are produced, which is the optimal output. The total social gain from basing production on marginal social cost is reflected by the blue-shaded triangle.

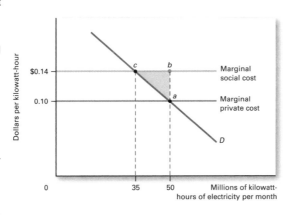

The Optimal Reduction in Greenhouse Gas Emissions

The optimal level of greenhouse gas emissions for a given rate of output is found at point *a*, where the marginal social benefit of reducing such emissions equals the marginal social cost. If some lower level of emissions were dictated by the government, such as *A'*, the marginal social cost would exceed the marginal social benefit, and social waste would result. The total social waste resulting from a lower than optimal level of emissions is shown by the pink-shaded triangle.

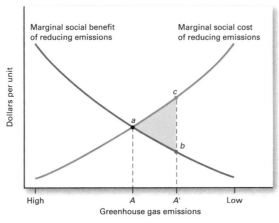

KEY TERMS

exhaustible resource A resource in fixed supply, such as crude oil or coal

renewable resource A resource that regenerates itself and so can be used indefinitely if used conservatively, such as a well-managed forest

common-pool problem Unrestricted access to a renewable resource results in overuse

fixed-production technology Occurs when the relationship between the output rate and the generation of an externality is fixed; the only way to reduce the externality is to reduce the output

marginal social cost The sum of the marginal private cost and the marginal external cost of production or consumption

variable technology Occurs when the amount of externality generated at a given rate of output can be reduced by altering the production process

marginal social benefit The sum of the marginal private benefit and the marginal external benefit of production or consumption

Coase theorem As long as bargaining costs are low, an efficient solution to the problem of externalities is achieved by assigning property rights to one party or the other, it doesn't matter which

command-and-control environmental regulations An inflexible approach that required polluters to adopt particular technologies to reduce emissions by specific amounts

economic efficiency approach An approach that offers each polluter the flexibility to reduce emissions as cost-effectively as possible, given its unique cost conditions; the market for pollution rights is an example

recycling The process of converting waste products into reusable material

Effect of Changes in Costs or Benefits of Reducing Greenhouse Gas Emissions

Either a reduction in the marginal social cost of cleaner air, as shown in panel (a), or an increase in the marginal social benefit of cleaner air, as shown in panel (b), increases the optimal level of air quality.

(a) Lower cost of reducing emissions

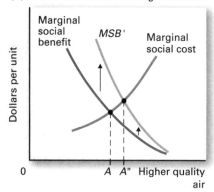

(b) Greater benefit of reducing emissions

Optimal Allocation of Pollution Rights

Suppose the demand for a river as a discharge service is D. In the absence of any environmental controls, polluters dump 250 tons per day, where the marginal benefit of discharge is zero. If regulatory authorities establish 100 tons as the maximum daily level of discharge and then sell the rights, the market for these pollution rights clears at $25 per ton. If the demand for pollution rights increases to D', the market-clearing price of pollution rights rises to $35 per ton.

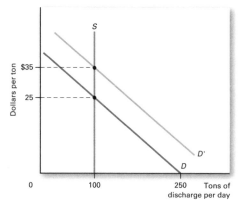

environmental quality or a downward shift of its marginal cost curve increases the optimal level of environmental quality. The Coase theorem argues that as long as bargaining costs are low, assigning property rights to one party leads to an efficient solution to the externality problem. The market for pollution permits reflects the Coase theorem in action.

17-3 Summarize how the federal government has regulated air, water, and land pollution. Federal efforts to address the common-pool problems of air, water, and soil pollution are coordinated by the Environmental Protection Agency (EPA). According to EPA estimates, compliance with pollution-control regulations cost U.S. producers and consumers about $300 billion in 2015, an amount equivalent to 2 percent of gross domestic product, the market value of all final goods and services produced in the economy. Governments have tried to stimulate demand for recycled material; however, recycling imposes its own environmental cost.

17-4 Outline government policies designed to promote the production and consumption of goods that generate positive externalities. Positive externalities occur when consumption or production benefits other consumers or other firms. When there are positive externalities, public policy aims to increase the equilibrium quantity beyond the private optimum. For example, government tries to increase education by providing free primary and secondary education, by requiring students to stay in school until they reach a certain age, by subsidizing public higher education, and by offering tax deductions for some education expenses.

Positive Externalities of Education

In the absence of government intervention, the equilibrium quantity of education is E, where the marginal private benefit of education equals the marginal cost as reflected by the supply curve. Education also confers a positive externality on the rest of society, so the social benefit exceeds the private benefit. At quantity E, the marginal social benefit, point b, exceeds the marginal cost, point e, so more education increases social welfare. In this situation, government tries to increase education to E', where the marginal social benefit equals the marginal cost.

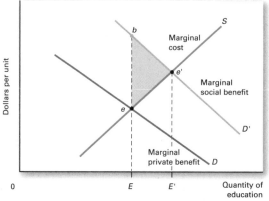

KEY CONCEPTS

18-1 Identify reasons why incomes differ across households, and why the income gap has increased. In a market economy, income depends primarily on earnings, which depend on the productivity of one's resources. The problem with allocating income according to productivity is that some people have few resources to sell. Incomes differ among households because households have different numbers of workers and because of factors such as differences in education, ability, job experience, and age. The income gap has grown because of the rise of households with just one parent, because of the growth in two-earner households, and because a decline in well-paying jobs for those with less education.

Share of Aggregate Household Income by Quintile, 1980–2013

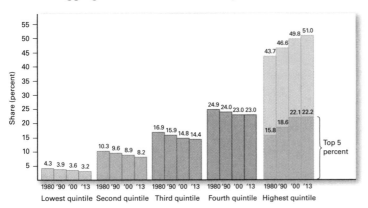

18-2 Summarize what has happened to the incidence of poverty since 1960, and determine when and why the greatest progress was made in reducing poverty. The biggest decline in the poverty rate occurred before 1970. Because of a decline in unemployment and an increase in income assistance, the U.S. poverty rate dropped from 22.4 percent in 1959 to 12.1 percent in 1969. Since that, the poverty rate has fluctuated but with no long-term trend.

Lorenz Curves Show That Income Was Less Evenly Distributed Across U.S. Households in 2013 Than in 1980

The Lorenz curve is a convenient way of showing the percentage of total income received by any given percentage of households when incomes are arrayed from smallest to largest. For example, point a shows that in 1980, the bottom 80 percent of households received 56.3 percent of all income. Point b shows that in 2013, the share of all income going to the bottom 80 percent of households was lower than in 1980. If income were evenly distributed across households, the Lorenz curve would be a straight line.

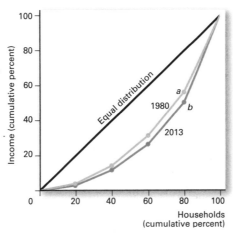

KEY TERMS

Lorenz curve A curve showing the percentage of total income received by a given percentage of households when incomes are arrayed from smallest to largest

median income The middle income when all incomes are ranked from smallest to largest

median wage The middle wage when wages of all workers are ranked from lowest to highest

U.S. official poverty level Benchmark level of income computed by the federal government to track poverty over time; initially based on three times the cost of a nutritionally adequate diet

social insurance Government programs designed to help make up for lost income of people who worked but are now retired, unemployed, or unable to work because of disability or work-related injury

Social Security Social insurance program that supplements retirement income of those with a record of contributing to the program during their working years; by far the largest government redistribution program

Medicare Social insurance program providing health insurance for short-term medical care to older Americans, regardless of income

income assistance programs Welfare programs that provide money and in-kind assistance to the poor; benefits do not depend on prior contributions

means-tested program A program in which, to be eligible, an individual's income and assets must not exceed specified levels

Temporary Assistance for Needy Families (TANF) An income assistance program funded largely by the federal government but run by the states to provide cash transfer payments to poor families with dependent children

Supplemental Security Income (SSI) An income assistance program that provides cash transfers to the elderly poor and the disabled; a uniform federal payment is supplemented by transfers that vary across states

earned-income tax credit A federal program that supplements the wages of the working poor

Medicaid An in-kind transfer program that provides medical care for poor people; by far the most costly welfare program

SNAP An in-kind transfer program that offers low-income households vouchers redeemable for food; benefit levels vary inversely with household income

18-3 Describe a primary source of poverty among families in the United States. Young, single motherhood is a recipe for poverty. Often the young mother drops out of school, which reduces her future earning possibilities when and if she seeks work outside the home. Growth in the number of female householders in the last four decades increased poverty among children, though the overall poverty rate among households headed by females has declined since peaking in 1991. More single mothers are working now. The wage gap between black and white workers narrowed between 1940 and 1976, widened until the early 1990s, and has been narrowing again since 1993. Affirmative action programs and gains in education seem to have increased employment opportunities among black workers.

Number and Percentage of U.S. Population in Poverty Since 1959

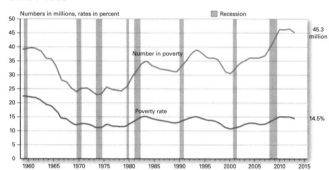

Percent of Population Living in Poverty by State in 2013

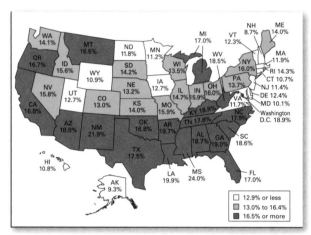

18-4 Outline some unintended consequences of efforts to reduce poverty. One unintended consequence of income assistance is a high marginal tax rate on earned income, which discourages employment and encourages welfare dependency. Worse still, welfare dependency could be passed on to the next generation.

18-5 Describe how the 1996 federal welfare reforms affected the number of people on welfare. Welfare reforms introduced by the states set the stage for federal welfare reforms aimed at breaking the cycle of poverty and promoting the transition from welfare to work. The states began experimenting with different systems to encourage more personal responsibility. As a result of state reforms, federal welfare reform, and a strengthening economy, welfare rolls as a share of the population dropped from 5.5 percent in 1994 to 1.1 percent in 2014.

Welfare Recipients as a Percentage of the U.S. Population Declined Sharply After 1996 Welfare Reforms

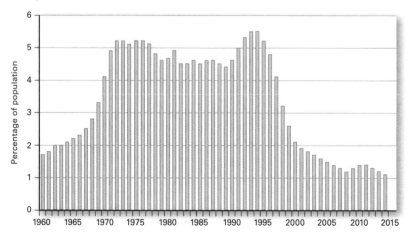

CHAPTER REVIEW 19
International Trade

KEY CONCEPTS

19-1 Outline the gains from trade, and explain why countries might still decide to trade even if no country had a comparative advantage. The law of comparative advantage says that the individual with the lowest opportunity cost of producing a particular good should specialize in that good. Just as individuals benefit from specialization and exchange, so do states and, indeed, nations. To reap the gains that arise from specialization, countries engage in international trade. Each country specializes in making goods with the lowest opportunity cost. Before countries can trade, however, they must agree on how much of one good exchanges for another (i.e., the terms of trade).

Composition of U.S. Exports and Imports in 2014

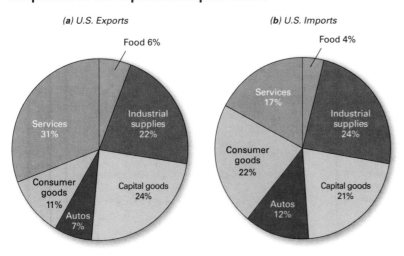

(a) U.S. Exports

Food 6%
Services 31%
Industrial supplies 22%
Consumer goods 11%
Capital goods 24%
Autos 7%

(b) U.S. Imports

Food 4%
Services 17%
Industrial supplies 24%
Consumer goods 22%
Capital goods 21%
Autos 12%

Production Possibilities Frontiers for the United States and Izodia Without Trade (millions of units per day)

Panel (a) shows the U.S. production possibilities frontier; its slope indicates that the opportunity cost of an additional unit of clothing is 2 units of food. Panel (b) shows production possibilities for Izodia; an additional unit of clothing costs 1/2 unit of food. Clothing has a lower opportunity cost in Izodia.

(a) The United States

(b) Izodia

KEY TERMS

autarky National self-sufficiency; no economic interaction with foreigners

terms of trade How much of one good exchanges for a unit of another good

world price The price at which a good is traded on the world market; determined by the world demand and world supply for the good

bilateral agreement Trade agreement between two countries

multilateral agreement Trade agreement among more than two countries

General Agreement on Tariffs and Trade (GATT) An international tariff-reduction treaty adopted in 1947 that resulted in a series of negotiated "rounds" aimed at freer trade; the Uruguay Round created GATT's successor, the World Trade Organization (WTO)

dumping Selling a product abroad for less than charged in the home market or for less than the cost of production

Uruguay Round The final multilateral trade negotiation under GATT; this 1994 agreement cut tariffs, formed the World Trade Organization (WTO), and will eventually eliminate quotas

World Trade Organization (WTO) The legal and institutional foundation of the multilateral trading system that succeeded GATT in 1995

common market Group of countries that have few of no trade restrictions with one another

Production (and Consumption) Possibilities Frontiers With Trade (millions of units per day)

If Izodia and the United States can specialize and trade at the rate of 1 unit of clothing for 1 unit of food, both can benefit as shown by the blue lines. By trading with Izodia, the U.S. can produce only food and still consume combination U, which has more food and more clothing than U_4. Likewise, Izodia can attain preferred combination I by producing only clothing, then trading some clothing for U.S. food.

(a) The United States

(b) Izodia

Countries export products they can produce more cheaply in return for products that are unavailable domestically or are cheaper elsewhere. If production is subject to economies of scale (i.e., if the long-run average cost of production falls as a firm expands its scale of operation), countries can gain from trade if each nation specializes. Consumption patterns differ across countries, and some of this results from differences in tastes, a situation that allows countries to gain from trade.

U.S. Production as a Percentage of U.S. Consumption for Various Resources

If U.S. production is less than 100 percent of U.S. consumption, then imports make up the difference. If U.S. production exceeds U.S. consumption, then the amount by which production exceeds 100 percent of consumption is exported.

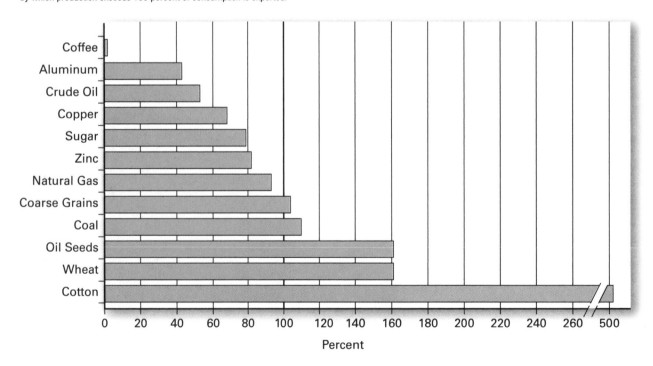

19-2 Explain how trade restrictions harm an economy, and why they persist.

Market exchange usually generates a surplus, or a bonus, for both consumers and producers. Governments try to regulate surpluses by imposing tariffs (either specific or *ad valorem*) and import quotas, granting export subsidies, or extending low-interest loans to foreign buyers. Loss in U.S. consumer surplus resulting from tariffs is divided three ways: a portion goes to domestic producers; a portion becomes government revenue; and the last portion represents net losses in domestic social welfare. Welfare loss occurs when consumers must pay a higher price for products that could have been imported and sold at a lower price.

Consumer Surplus and Producer Surplus

Consumer surplus, shown by the blue triangle, indicates the net benefits consumers reap from buying 60 pounds of apples at $1.00 per pound. Some consumers would have been willing to pay $3.00 or more per pound for the first few pounds. Consumer surplus measures the difference between the maximum sum of money consumers would pay for 60 pounds of apples and the actual sum they pay. Producer surplus, shown by the gold triangle, indicates the net benefits producers reap from selling 60 pounds at $1.00 per pound. Some producers would have supplied apples for %0.50 per pound or less. Producer surplus measures the difference between the actual sum of money producers receive for 60 pounds of apples and the minimum amount they would accept for this amount.

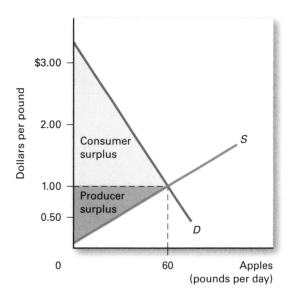

Effect of a Tariff

At a world price of $0.10 per pound, U.S. consumers demand 70 million pounds of sugar per month, and U.S. producers supply 20 million pounds per month; the difference is imported. After the imposition of a $0.05 per pound tariff, the U.S. price rises to $0.15 per pound. U.S. producers supply 30 million pounds, and U.S. consumers cut back to 60 million pounds. At the higher U.S. price, consumers are worse off; their loss of consumer surplus is the sum of areas *a*, *b*, *c*, and *d*. The net welfare loss to the U.S. economy consists of areas *b* and *d*.

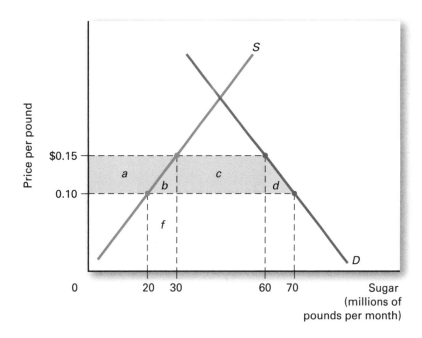

Effect of a Quota

In panel (a), *D* is the U.S. demand curve and *S* is the supply curve of U.S. producers. If the government establishes a sugar quota of 30 million pounds per month, the supply curve combining U.S. production and imports becomes horizontal at the world price of $0.10 per pound and remains horizontal until the quantity supplied reaches 50 million pounds. For higher prices, the new supply curve equals the horizontal sum of the U.S. supply curve, *S*, plus the quota of 30 million pounds. The new U.S. price, $0.15 per pound, is determined by the intersection of the new supply curve, *S'*, with the U.S. demand curve, *D*. Panel (b) shows the welfare effect of the quota. As a result of the higher U.S. price, consumer surplus is cut by the shaded area. The blue-shaded areas illustrate the loss in consumer surplus that is captured by domestic producers and by those who are permitted to fulfill the quota, and the pink-shaded triangles illustrate the net welfare cost of the quota on the U.S. economy.

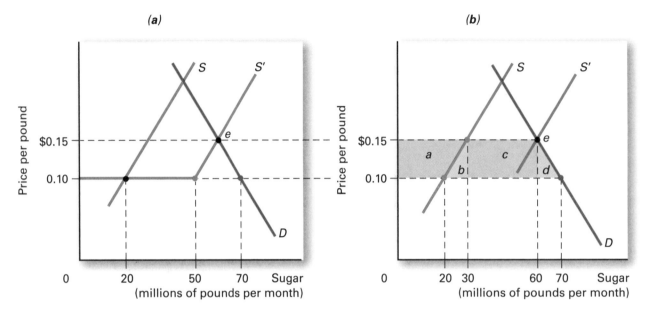

19-3 Identify international efforts to reduce trade barriers.
Trade restrictions impose a variety of strains on the economy besides the higher costs to consumers, so countries have worked to create free trade agreements and common markets to reduce or eliminate trade barriers. The General Agreement on Tariffs and Trade (GATT) was an international treaty ratified in 1947 to reduce trade barriers. Subsequent negotiations lowered tariffs and reduced trade restrictions. The Uruguay Round, ratified in 1994, lowered tariffs, phased out quotas, and created the World Trade Organization (WTO) as the successor to GATT.

19-4 Summarize five arguments often used to justify trade restrictions, and describe some unintended consequences of protecting certain industries from international competition.
Arguments used by producer groups to support trade restrictions include promoting national defense, nurturing infant industries, preventing foreign producers from dumping goods in domestic markets, protecting domestic jobs, and allowing declining industries time to wind down and exit the market.

Trade restrictions impose a variety of strains on the economy besides the higher costs to consumers. These include (1) the need to protect downstream stages of production as well, (2) expenditures made by favored domestic industries to seek and perpetuate trade protection, (3) costs incurred by the government to enforce trade restrictions, (4) the inefficiency and lack of innovation that result when an industry is insulated from foreign competition, and (5), most important, the trade restrictions imposed by other countries in retaliation.

KEY CONCEPTS

20-1 Summarize the major accounts in the balance of trade, and explain how they balance out. The balance of payments reflects all economic transactions between one country and the rest of the world. The current account measures flows from (a) goods; (b) services, including consulting and tourism; (c) income from holdings of foreign assets; and (d) unilateral transfers, or public and private transfer payments to and from foreign residents. The financial account measures international transactions in real and financial assets.

U.S. Balance of Payments for 2014 (billions of dollars)

Current Account	
1. Merchandise exports	+1,635.1
2. Merchandise imports	−2,370.9
3. Merchandise trade balance (1 + 2)	−735.8
4. Service exports	+709.4
5. Service imports	−478.3
6. Goods and services balance (3 + 4 + 5)	−504.7
7. Net investment income from abroad	+217.9
8. Net unilateral transfers	−123.8
9. Current account balance (6 + 7 + 8)	−410.6
Financial Account	
10. Change in U.S. owned assets abroad	−820.5
11. Change in foreign-owned assets in United States	+962.1
12. Financial account balance (10 + 11)	+141.6
13. Statistical discrepancy	+269.0
TOTAL (9 + 12 + 13)	**0.0**

Source: Computed from estimates by the Bureau of Economic Analysis, U.S. Department of Commerce at http://bea.gov/international/index.htm.

KEY TERMS

balance on goods and services The portion of a country's balance-of-payments account that measures the value of a country's exports of goods and services minus the value of its imports of goods and services

net investment income from abroad Investment earnings by U.S. residents from their foreign assets minus investment earnings by foreigners from their assets in the United States

net unilateral transfers abroad The unilateral transfers (gifts and grants) received from abroad by U.S. residents minus the unilateral transfers U.S. residents send abroad

balance on current account The portion of the balance-of-payments account that measures a country's balance on goods and services, net investment income from abroad, plus net unilateral transfers abroad

financial account The record of a country's international transactions involving purchases and sales of financial and real assets

exchange rate The cost, measured in one country's currency, of one unit of another country's currency

currency depreciation With respect to the dollar, an increase in the number of dollars needed to purchase one unit of foreign exchange in a flexible rate system

U.S. Imports Have Topped Exports Since 1976, but Both Dropped During the Great Recession

Note that since 1980, merchandise exports have remained in the range of about 5 percent to 10 percent of GDP. But merchandise imports have trended up from about 9 percent in 1980 to about 15 percent in 2008, before dropping off to 11 percent in 2009, the year following the financial crisis. Imports were back up to 14 percent relative to GDP by 2011 and have remained there.

Source: Developed from merchandise trade data from the Bureau of Economic Analysis, U.S. Department of Commerce, at http://bea.gov/international/index.htm.

U.S. Merchandise Trade Deficits in 2014 by Country or Region

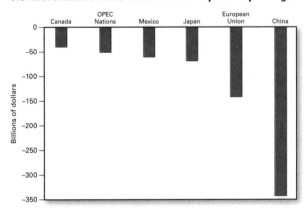

Source: Developed from data in "Exports, Imports, and Trade Balance by Country and Area: 2012 Annual Totals," Exhibit 13, U.S. Bureau of Economic Analysis, at http://www.census.gov /foreign-trade/Press-Release/2012pr/final_revisions/exh13cy.pdf

currency appreciation With respect to the dollar, a decrease in the number of dollars needed to purchase one unit of foreign exchange in a flexible rate system

arbitrageur Someone who takes advantage of tiny differences in the exchange rate across markets by simultaneously purchasing currency in one market and selling it in another market

speculator Someone who buys or sells foreign exchange in hopes of profiting from fluctuations in the exchange rate over time

purchasing power parity theory The idea that the exchange rate between two countries will adjust in the long run to equalize the cost of a basket of internationally traded goods

flexible exchange rate Rate determined in foreign exchange markets by the forces of demand and supply without government intervention

fixed exchange rate Rate of exchange between currencies pegged within a narrow range and maintained by the central bank's ongoing purchases and sales of currencies

currency devaluation An increase in the official pegged price of foreign exchange in terms of the domestic currency

currency revaluation A reduction in the official pegged price of foreign exchange in terms of the domestic currency

gold standard An arrangement whereby the currencies of most countries were convertible into gold at a fixed rate

International Monetary Fund An international organization that establishes rules for maintaining the international monetary system and makes loans to countries with temporary balance-of-payments problems

managed float system An exchange rate system that combines features of freely floating rates with sporadic intervention by central banks

20-2 Describe how the foreign exchange rate is determined using demand and supply curves and explain the shapes of the curves.

Because the exchange rate is usually a market price, it is determined by demand and supply. The equilibrium exchange rate is one that equates quantity demanded with quantity supplied (see the diagrams below).

The Foreign Exchange Market

The fewer dollars needed to purchase one unit of foreign exchange, the lower the price of foreign goods and the greater the quantity of foreign goods demanded. Thus, the demand curve for foreign exchange slopes downward. An increase in the exchange rate makes U.S. products cheaper for foreigners. This implies an increase in the quantity of foreign exchange supplied. The supply curve of foreign exchange slopes upward.

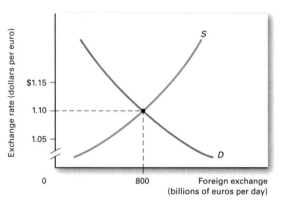

Effect on the Foreign Exchange Market of an Increased Demand for Euros

The intersection of the demand curve for foreign exchange, *D*, and the supply curve for foreign exchange, *S*, determines the exchange rate. At an exchange rate of $1.10 per euro, the quantity of euros demanded equals the quantity supplied. An increase in the demand for euros from *D* to *D'* increases the exchange rate from $1.10 to $1.12 per euro.

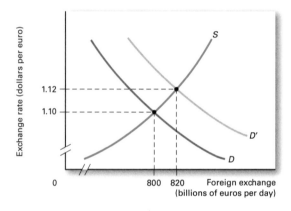

20-3 Describe the purchasing power parity theory.
According to the theory of purchasing power parity (PPP), the exchange rate between two countries will adjust in the long run to equalize the cost of a basket of internationally traded goods. A given basket of internationally traded goods should, therefore, sell for about the same around the world (except for differences reflecting transportation costs and the like).

20-4 Trace the evolution of exchange rate regimes from the gold standard to the current system.
From 1879 to 1914, the international financial system operated under a gold standard, whereby the major currencies of the world were convertible into gold at a fixed rate. During World War I, many countries could no longer convert their currencies into gold, so the gold standard eventually collapsed, disrupting international trade during the 1930s and 1940s. From 1945 to 1973 fixed exchange rates were in effect, and since 1973 a managed float has been in effect, a system that combines features of freely fluctuating rates with sporadic market intervention by central banks.

KEY CONCEPTS

21-1 Besides income, identify ways that low-income economies differ from high-income economies. The most common measure of comparison of standards of living between different countries is output per capita. Developing countries are distinguished by low output per capita, poor health and nutrition, high fertility rates, and poor education.

Share of World Population and World Output From High-, Middle-, and Low-Income Economies as of 2014

(a) Share of world population from high-, middle-, and low-income economies

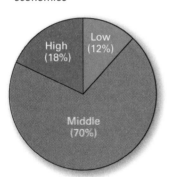

(b) Share of world output from high-, middle-, and low-income economies

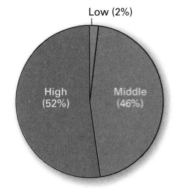

Per Capita Income for Selected Countries in 2014

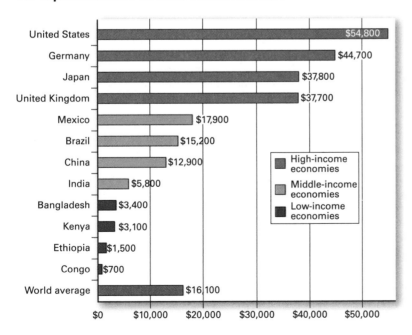

KEY TERMS

developing countries Low-income and middle-income economies; most are also known as emerging market economies

industrial market countries Economically advanced capitalist countries of Europe, North America, Australia, New Zealand, and Japan; also known as developed countries and high-income economies

privatization The process of turning government enterprises into private enterprises

import substitution A development strategy that emphasizes domestic manufacturing of products that had been imported

export promotion A development strategy that concentrates on producing for the export market

foreign aid An international transfer made on especially favorable terms for the purpose of promoting economic development

convergence A theory predicting that the standard of living in economies around the world will grow more similar over time, with poorer countries eventually catching up with richer ones

21-2 **Describe the factors that help make workers in high-income economies more productive than workers in other economies.** Labor productivity, measured in terms of output per worker, is by definition low in low-income countries, as it depends on the quality of the labor and other inputs that combine with labor, such as capital and natural resources. The key to a rising standard of living is increased productivity. To foster productivity, developing nations must stimulate investment, support education and training programs, provide sufficient infrastructure, and foster supportive rules of the game.

21-3 **Explain how trade restrictions can slow economic development in poorer countries.** Developing countries need to trade with developed countries to acquire the capital and technology that will increase labor productivity. Exports usually generate more than half of the annual flow of foreign exchange in developing countries. Foreign aid and private investment make up the rest. Developing countries often use either import substitution or export promotion strategies to improve production. With import substitution, domestic manufacturers make products that had previously been imported and the government supports them with tariffs and quotas. Export promotion concentrates on producing for the export market. Export promotion has proven generally more successful.

21-4 **Outline some unintended consequences of foreign aid on economic development.** Foreign aid has been a mixed blessing for most developing countries. In some cases, that aid has helped countries build the roads, bridges, schools, and other capital infrastructure necessary for development. In other cases, foreign aid has simply increased consumption and insulated government from painful but necessary reforms. Worse still, subsidized food from abroad has undermined domestic agriculture, hurting poor farmers. And subsidized clothing from abroad has undermined the textile industries in poor countries.

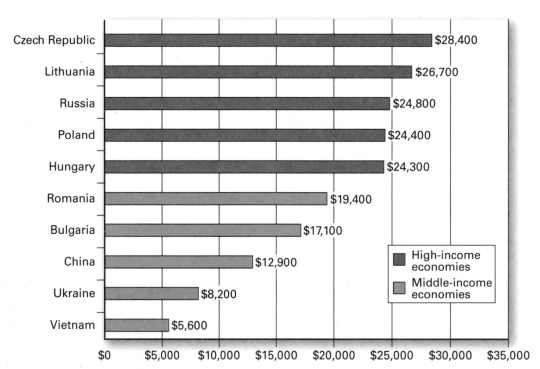

GDP per Capita for Transitional Economies in 2013